Home Inspection Business From <u>A</u> to <u>Z</u>

Just a few of the many excellent book reviews our products have received:
Top 50 book reviewers for Amazon.com have given this book the highest rating of 5 stars!

Everything you must know to inspect a home.
Amazon Top 50 Book Reviewer: Harold McFarland from Florida

Home Inspection Business from A to Z - This is a **truly eye-opening book that I would not be without** the next time I consider purchasing a new home. "The Home Inspection Business from A to Z" **provides detailed information** on what to look for and just how serious various problems might be. **Filled with copious illustrations and photographs** it is easy to see exactly the problems the author is discussing. **The coverage is extensive** enough to start you in the business of home inspections and Mr. Cozzi goes through the details of what is necessary to begin such a venture. Areas discussed include heating systems, air conditioning systems, water heaters, foundations, plumbing, septic, electrical systems, roofs, walls, decks, flooring, and just about anything else you can think of. Before reading the book I had no idea the number of potentially serious problems that can be easily discovered with a minimal inspection and some basic knowledge. **This is a highly recommended book for anyone looking to purchase a new home, considering purchasing a home for investment purposes, or looking to start a new business.**

Learn the flaws to look for in a home.
Amazon Top 50 Book Reviewer: Charles Ashbacher from Iowa

Home Inspection Business from A to Z - The primary purpose of this book is to help you become an effective inspector of homes, but the audience is much broader than that. If you own a home or are thinking about buying one, then **you should read it.** It will help you develop that critical, discerning eye concerning what to look for in spotting flaws in a house. **I spent almost eight years as a construction worker, six where I was the foreman, and have performed many repairs to my own homes. And yet, there was much in the book that I was unaware of. It was a learning experience for me, and it will be for you.** Unless you find the perfect house or are already an expert, buying this book and **reading it will be time and money that will be returned many times over.**

Knocks it out of the box!
Amazon Top 50 Book Reviewer: Mister Maxx - Amazon.com Reviewer

Home Inspection Business from A to Z - Guy Cozzi knocks it out of the box with this very informative book on what to do and look for when buying a house. **He covers everything** that must be on target when you want your house in top condition. I had the pleasure of reading this book and I was moved by the details discussed. **Everything was said in a way that anyone could relate to.** It's a very classy and well done book **with all of the details and helpful tips you must have** when buying, selling, maintaining, or renovating a home.

I would recommend this book to everyone.
Reviewer: Jennie S. Bev, Managing Editor of BookReviewClub.com

Home Inspection Business from A to Z - I didn't know the differences between a real estate appraiser and a home inspector until I read this book. **This comprehensive guidebook contains insider tips and tricks that only an experienced master could explain. This book is an eye-opener, indeed.** One doesn't need to be a home inspector or a home inspector wannabe to enjoy the inspecting techniques and examples. Just by reading it from cover to cover, readers would be able to grasp the techniques and skills needed in inspecting your own property for your own benefit. **I would recommend this book to everyone** who needs to learn more about inspecting a property for their own benefit or for business. The hard-to-find information, forms and insider tips are **more than enlightening.** They are precious!

 **Home Inspector Know-How.**
Reviewer: Author/Reviewer Denise Clark - Denise's Pieces Book Reviews Site

   Home Inspection Business from A to Z - Home inspectors are here to stay, and their services are not only needed, but are also desired in today's fluctuating economy. Home inspectors check out a home before purchase by prospective buyers to help determine the existing conditions of a home - they can also tell the prospective home buyer what repairs and upgrades might be needed. These problem spotters, and solvers, earn hundreds of dollars for their expertise, and can help save potential homebuyers thousands of dollars on repairs and upgrades. A home inspector performs a visual inspection - he identifies potential problems in a wealth of areas. he can spot trouble in septic and well water systems, and with gas and water connections, among dozens of others, including heating, air conditioning, and electrical and plumbing systems. Author Cozzi, in a **step-by-step, vastly illustrated guide** shows the reader, homeowner, or potential home inspector, exactly what to look for, both on the exterior of a home and its interior. He shows the prospective inspector how to properly fill out reports, how to handle clients, and how to maintain accurate reports and records. **Using his vast knowledge and experience,** Mr. Cozzi has the uncanny ability to take what is thought to be a convoluted process and **simplify it with his easy writing style, one which entertains as it instructs, which with most 'how-to' books, is no easy feat.** His narrative is **extremely reader-friendly and amazingly informative at the same time,** guiding the reader along on a discourse of everything that is expected of a home inspector. Mr. Cozzi has appeared in local and national newspapers, offering real estate advice. And it's easy to see why. **He's the expert. This book should be required reading for every home owner.**

 **This book is a fact-rich smart buy.**
Reviewer: Author/Reviewer Barbara Bamberger Scott
Curled Up With a Good Book - Book Review Club

   Home Inspection Business from A to Z - This book has me brooding about problems in my septic field. I now realize that despite my best hopes and my incredibly finely-honed ability to put off thinking about unpleasant problems that may cost large amounts of money, the green gooey leak in the backyard isn't going to just go away. On the other hand, looking at the stark photos in this book of other people's mistakes - ivy covered electric meters, floor separating from baseboard, holes in ceilings from long-term leaks - I guess I feel a little better. **This is a book for pros or wannabe-pro home inspectors, but it could serve as a good guide for any homeowner** trying to get a house ready for sale. Home inspection is becoming mandatory or at least highly recommended in my area and probably in yours, too, and it just makes sense to know what you're up against. Contrariwise, if you're buying, you need to know what the potential hazards are - like that pesky little fountain of sewage in my back yard - before you buy and it's too late to sue. The book is the brainchild of Guy Cozzi, who has other similar how-to volumes in print. **He knows his subject, inside and out. Full of photos illustrating the kinds of horrors you might encounter as you search for your dream home,** especially if you're hoping to save some bucks on a fixer-upper, this book is a useful manual of operations. It's clear, well-organized and not without humor (though I'm still not smiling about that septic sludge). Cozzi is a self-starter and deserves a pat on the back for making his own publishing dreams a reality, bringing him a success in at least two careers. **This book is an unabashed self-promotional organ as well as a fact-rich smart buy.**

Real Estate Press - "…the Real Estate from A to Z books and videos are the best we've ever seen."

New Home Construction Journal – "…the best selling reference books available for home builders and buyers and cover every topic from A to Z."

Seminar Progress Report - "…top-notch real estate investors, inspectors and appraisers agree the Real Estate from A to Z series is a great value."

Home-Based Business Monthly - "If you're looking to become a knowledgeable home inspector or appraiser, Real Estate from A to Z series is crucial."

Real Estate Investors Journal - "…Real Estate from A to Z series is by far the most in-depth resource for every investor, beginner to expert."

More excellent reviews and customer testimonials about our products and services

5 out of 5: "excellent book/excellent service"
Date: 11/9/2004 Rated by Buyer: davidleasparky

5 out of 5: "Excellent resource. Transaction successful"
Date: 10/17/2004 Rated by Buyer: gleach7

5 out of 5: "Quick Ship-Excellent book."
Date: 10/12/2004 Rated by Buyer: deje89

5 out of 5: "Highly recommended - superb service, fast shipment, great book! AAAAA+++!"
Date: 9/25/2004 Rated by Buyer: gemflint

5 out of 5: "fast service, great book"
Date: 9/13/2004 Rated by Buyer: mvolz92069

5 out of 5: "quick shipping honest seller great book"
Date: 9/12/2004 Rated by Buyer: patrinif

5 out of 5: "Great product, quick shipping"
Date: 08/17/2004 Rated by Buyer: bob2k

5 out of 5: "Fast shipping, great book. Thanks!"
Date: 04/24/2004 Rated by Buyer: atarikee

5 out of 5: "Great Communication! Great Book!!!"
Date: 04/11/2004 Rated by Buyer: robert a.

5 out of 5: "Very pleased! Thanks!"
Date: 02/05/2004 Rated by Buyer: hughesassociates2003

5 out of 5: "The book is the most informative I have read yet ! "
Date: 01/31/2004 Rated by Buyer: dirty123

5 out of 5: "Excellent real estate books!! They will save me thousands of dollars on my home purchase from the information I will learn in these books. "
Date: 12/27/2003 Rated by Buyer: happygoal

5 out of 5: "Fantastic product!! Great service and great products. You can't ask for more than that. Best product in it's category by far."
Date: 12/21/2003 Rated by Buyer: alberttrees

5 out of 5: "A++ Perfect transaction! I am a repeat customer since the book is the best real estate book I have ever read and I have seen a lot of books on real estate before!"
Date: 12/14/2003 Rated by Buyer: paul887

5 out of 5: "EXTREMELY happy with their book. Best books on real estate I've ever read."
Date: 12/06/2003 Rated by Buyer: aroundtee

5 out of 5: "Excellent transaction! Fast delivery and Excellent books!"
Date: 12/02/2003 Rated by Buyer: slaidl

Definitely worthwhile. Great seller!!! Buy confidently.
Buyer subroc730 (58) Oct-02-04 21:17 6304816459

Great product!!. Buy with complete confidence!!!.
Buyer subroc730 (58) Oct-02-04 21:15 6309285748

Great Book Would Buy Again AAAAA +++++
Buyer frank-rubi (491) Sep-27-04 10:29 6927595558

Great book! Thanks for the fast shipping!
Buyer flohanajo (11) Sep-23-04 11:43 6910449803

What a GREAT BOOK! Super-fast shipping and an excellent product! Recommended!
Buyer shanekw (72) Sep-16-04 10:55 6924938115

Thanks great item
Buyer hellboy714 (22) Sep-13-04 21:27 6321532616

Fast shipping great item thanks AAAA
Buyer hellboy714 (22) Sep-13-04 21:27 6321532663

Excellent transaction. product very informative. Thank you
Buyer trader1128 (24) Sep-07-04 15:16 6908719323

Great product! Very highly recommended! Thanks!
Buyer mysbyu (40) Aug-28-04 09:01 6314216042

Great book, fast delivery, was a good deal
Buyer meliheim (205) Aug-15-04 17:02 6914801318

A+ ALL THE WAY
Buyer stitz14 (12) Aug-09-04 08:45 6311529865

Quick transaction. No problems. Book is very informative.
Buyer mariadaniellek (1) Aug-02-04 14:27 6914805667

Fast shipping and the book was better than I expected... thanks!
Buyer arizona0926 (7) Jul-30-04 09:40 6912766573

GREAT
Buyer alexand7 (81) Jul-29-04 20:21 6908518676

Great A+++++
Buyer raftermanfl (105) Jul-24-04 19:55 6912772562

Great book! Thanks for the easy transaction.
Buyer mighty_sultan (27) Jul-21-04 19:21 6908518690

A++++ Thanks
Buyer 4everknight (109) Jul-20-04 19:02 4182828782

Excellent service, great purchase. This seller rates an outstanding. A+A+A+A+
Buyer gringo-rican (34) Jul-19-04 16:02 6912771572

5 out of 5: "Excellent service, great product. Thanks"
Date: 08/17/2003 Rated by Buyer: sayu8

5 out of 5: "Excellent book and quick delivery!!"
Date: 07/21/2003 Rated by Buyer: hagomes

5 out of 5: "Great service, quick delivery, excellent book"
Date: 04/24/2003 Rated by Buyer: d9910

5 out of 5: "Arrived in good condition. Great book."
Date: 03/20/2003 Rated by Buyer: oldiesdude2

Material very well done. very informative
Buyer yx981 (92) Nov-24-04 11:22 6338256963

Great quality A+++++ great seller
Buyer jotalong1000 (29) Nov-19-04 17:11 6335074277

Quick delivery - excellent book on appraisals
Buyer ziongroup (67) Nov-15-04 21:38 2495215347

Excellent book highly recommended read
Buyer juhlz (44) Nov-08-04 09:13 6927595519

Great Book Thanks!!!!!
Buyer ajok88 (109) Nov-08-04 06:58 6922358202

A+A+A+ good transaction
Buyer conestoga22 (152) Nov-03-04 12:45 6919576348

Excellent Transaction Great Book
Buyer hwkzrok (1) Oct-20-04 14:47 6922358298

AAAAAA++++++
Buyer patric55 (842) Oct-20-04 07:00 6929649552

Great book. Shipped promptly. Great Seller
Buyer tjs_914 (19) May-21-04 15:38 4205627517

Great seller. Great product. Immediate delivery. Thank you.
Buyer leontennis (442) May-19-04 17:21 4183684560

Great Book Thanks
Buyer tachmedic (93) May-17-04 20:05 4209383266

Great product, great response, many thanks
Buyer edjafe (54) Oct-15-04 15:19 6929649552

Fast delivery Great book Thanks!!
Buyer mechanician477 (5) Oct-13-04 16:11 6908719323

Great product. Would love to start a business with seller!
Buyer coreyratz (180) Oct-11-04 21:35 6929649479

Excellent!
Buyer jr333 (2992) Oct-08-04 16:15 6316419120

Great Book, good doing business with you have a great day
Buyer inspectorlake (126) Jul-12-04 18:02 6908518676

GREAT book with helpful info!...Would deal w/again!...A+++
Seller!...Thank you!
Buyer randj48 (84) Jul-08-04 15:42 4205633335

Thank You A++++++++
Buyer jims_son (144) Jul-06-04 12:59 6908518749

Super DVD lots of info
Buyer inspectorkid (115) Jun-30-04 10:48 4183683333

A++++, Thank You!!!!
Buyer mcclanesolo (1244) Jun-24-04 22:47 4191424761

Great DVD! Fast shipper and good service... Thanks
Buyer fc1sar (13) Jun-21-04 13:30 4191422938

Fast Shipping, Quality Product, Awesome deal, A ++++
Buyer info-ware (110) Jun-09-04 18:51 4193612604

Great item, fast shipping, Highly recommend
Buyer 89_mustang (141) Jun-08-04 09:13 4212285263

Very pleased with the book; its content and examples/case
studies. Excellent!
Buyer tightwadtj (36) Jun-07-04 11:40 6900685641

Great transaction! Thanks! I love the book! A+++++
Buyer cwhitby91 (40) May-15-04 14:18 4209383074

Great dvd's.......Thanks again and great doing business with you
Buyer seahawks1 (507) May-03-04 16:58 4183347687

Fast delivery-great value- thanks
Buyer jotalong1000 (29) Apr-25-04 17:53 4201591917

A++++++
Buyer florino1964 (113) Apr-22-04 20:05 3598166015

Great book. Fast service. Wonderful communication. What
more can you ask for?
Buyer maggk (66) Apr-17-04 09:34 4201591762

Great Seller! Great Product! Fast Shipping!
Buyer hooverhouse (1658) Apr-11-04 15:55 3596771099

Super smooth transaction! Excellent merchandise! A+++++
Buyer pbbuysandsells (503) Mar-26-04 15:31 3593483616

Great Product!!! Fast Delivery!!! A++++++
Buyer imtabitha (23) Mar-23-04 22:40 3593483397

Graph Pages

What's In This For You?

Home Inspectors earn **$400** or more for each inspection. Many inspectors are so busy that they do two home inspections per day!

You don't need to have any background in real estate, construction, nor engineering to become a highly paid home inspector. All you need is to obtain the right knowledge and business plan, *(which we'll give you)*. Male or female, and your current age doesn't matter either, since there is *no* manual labor or hard work involved.

Here's just a few of the
benefits you get from this book:

Earn Money in one of the fastest growing businesses in the country.

Be Your Own Boss and work part-time or full-time. <u>*You*</u> set your own hours.

Save Money when you buy, sell, or renovate your own home.

Eliminate Safety Hazards to make your home safe for you and your family.

Real Estate Related knowledge to help people with the *biggest* investment they will ever make - their own home.

What's The Income Potential?

Are you wondering about the income and growth potential of the home inspection business? Then look below because a picture is worth a thousand words. Home inspectors earn **high** incomes every year while working right out of their home. The home inspection industry has been growing by leaps and bounds every year. And remember, this growth has gone on even during some of the worst economic recessions in history! This book shows you the reasons why your home inspection business can grow even during a recession.

Growth Of Home Inspection Industry

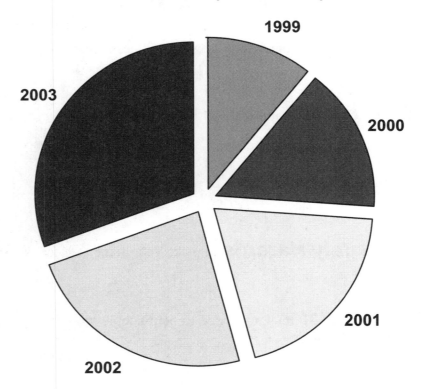

What Houses Need Inspections?

Are you wondering about the need for home inspections? Then look below because this data has been taken from evaluating thousands of homes. The graph shows the probability of finding repair problems in any house, *(including yours!)* This book shows you the reasons why <u>all</u> homes need to be inspected.
Do you really know the true condition of your house?

Average Home Repairs Needed

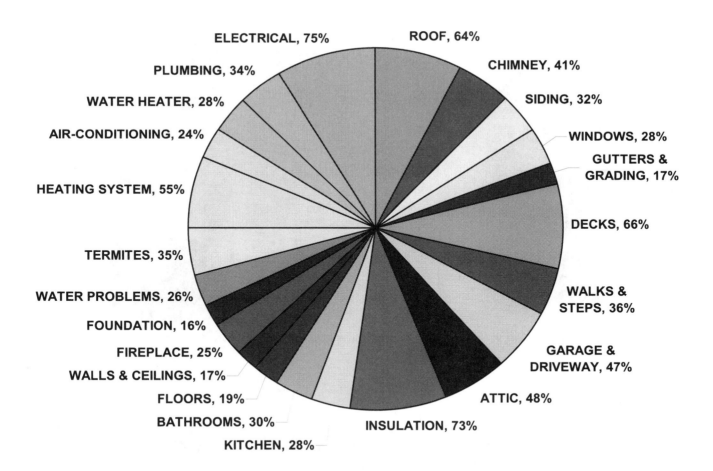

- ELECTRICAL, 75%
- ROOF, 64%
- PLUMBING, 34%
- CHIMNEY, 41%
- WATER HEATER, 28%
- SIDING, 32%
- AIR-CONDITIONING, 24%
- WINDOWS, 28%
- GUTTERS & GRADING, 17%
- HEATING SYSTEM, 55%
- DECKS, 66%
- TERMITES, 35%
- WATER PROBLEMS, 26%
- WALKS & STEPS, 36%
- FOUNDATION, 16%
- FIREPLACE, 25%
- GARAGE & DRIVEWAY, 47%
- WALLS & CEILINGS, 17%
- FLOORS, 19%
- ATTIC, 48%
- BATHROOMS, 30%
- INSULATION, 73%
- KITCHEN, 28%

What's A Buyer's Savings?

So you don't want a career change? That's fine, but would you be interested in saving thousands of dollars when you buy your own home? Then look below. This graph shows some potential repair costs found when buying your home. By identifying any problem conditions _before_ you buy, you'll be able to negotiate a lower purchase price.

Average $ Savings For Home Buyers

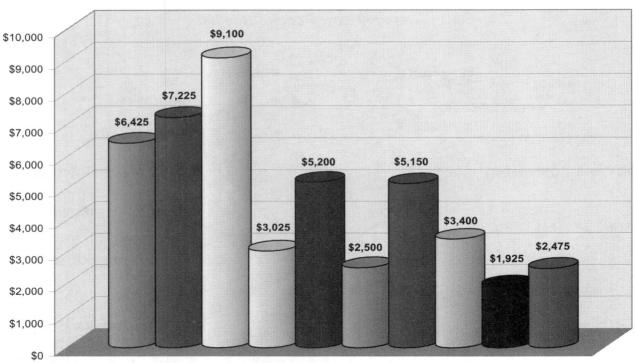

EXTERIOR ROOF INTERIOR ATTIC FOUNDATION TERMITES HEATING A/C PLUMBING ELECTRIC

Values shown on graph: $6,425 $7,225 $9,100 $3,025 $5,200 $2,500 $5,150 $3,400 $1,925 $2,475

Don't Let Your Dream House...

What's A Seller's Savings?

You're not buying a house at this time? Okay, but would you be interested in saving thousands of dollars when you renovate or sell your own home? Then look down. This graph shows your potential profit when selling your home. By eliminating these typical repairs you can earn at least an additional $1.50 for each $1.00 you invest in repair expenses.

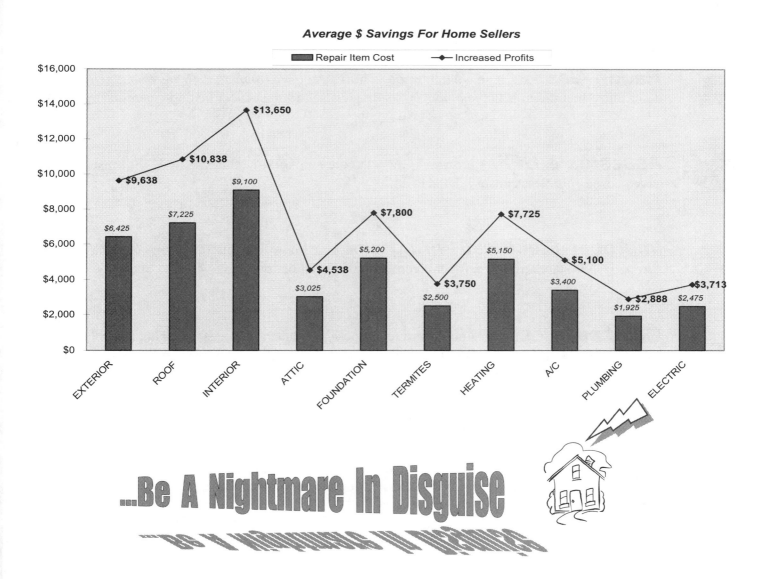

Average $ Savings For Home Sellers

Legend: Repair Item Cost ■ Increased Profits ◆

Category	Repair Item Cost	Increased Profits
EXTERIOR	$6,425	$9,638
ROOF	$7,225	$10,838
INTERIOR	$9,100	$13,650
ATTIC	$3,025	$4,538
FOUNDATION	$5,200	$7,800
TERMITES	$2,500	$3,750
HEATING	$5,150	$7,725
A/C	$3,400	$5,100
PLUMBING	$1,925	$2,888
ELECTRIC	$2,475	$3,713

...Be A Nightmare In Disguise

What Safety Hazards?

So you think there are no safety hazards around your home?
Well, think again.

 Lead In Water & Paint - Do you know how to check for lead in your home? Lead poisoning is the *number one* childhood disease in America!

 Radon Gas - Is it in your house? The EPA, *(Environmental Protection Agency)*, has determined that radon is the *number two* leading cause of lung cancer behind cigarette smoking!

 Asbestos & UFFI - Do you know what they look like? Asbestos and UFFI insulations have caused countless cancer related deaths.

 Improper Electrical Wiring - Do you know if your outlets meet the *National Electric Code* standards? Improper electrical wiring can be found in over 90% of all homes!

 Gas Leaks - Do you know how to properly evaluate your gas meter and supply lines? Natural gas is colorless and odorless before it gets to the utility company. An undetected gas leak can explode and blow up an entire building!

We're not trying to scare you, we're trying to educate you.
We just want to open your eyes to the reality of some of the
safety hazards that can be found in *any* home.

Customer Comments & Recommendations

From the Author

Thank you very much for purchasing my book. I invite you to view our web site at **www.nemmar.com** to see the other real estate products we offer that will save you thousands of dollars when you buy, sell, or renovate a home. You can sign up online to receive our **free** real estate newsletter with articles and updates that will definitely help you profit in real estate. Please email me and let me know what you think of my book after you have time to review it. Customer feedback and recommendations are greatly appreciated and help me to improve all of our products.
Thank you,

Guy Cozzi
Nemmar Real Estate Training
"Everything You Need To Know About Real Estate
From **A***sbestos to* **Z***oning"*

Nemmar Real Estate Training is ranked as the most exclusive real estate appraiser, home inspector and real estate investor training service since 1988. Our real estate books and DVDs are rated **number one** in their real estate categories nationwide! Our products have taught thousands of home buyers, sellers, and real estate professionals worldwide. You too can learn everything you need to know about Real Estate - from **A**sbestos to **Z**oning. With this knowledge you will save thousands of dollars when you buy, sell, or renovate your home. You will also learn how to eliminate safety hazards and properly maintain a home. Statistics show an average savings of at least **$4,700.00** per home for customers who have read our books.

Our home inspection, appraisal, and home improvement books have been called the "Bible" of the real estate industry. Written by Guy Cozzi who has decades of experience as a licensed appraiser, home inspector, consultant, and real estate investor. This top selling author has been quoted as a real estate expert by the *New York Times* and many other publications. He has been a guest speaker on real estate investment TV shows and has taught thousands of people how to inspect, appraise and invest in real estate and provides advice to many banks and mortgage lenders.

The real facts other books don't tell you! ***You'll learn everything that your Realtor doesn't want you to know.*** Realtors "sugar coat" the problem conditions in a house in order to close the deal and get paid their sales commission. This is unquestionably the only book of its kind that teaches you how to prevent those pitfalls. You get information that the professionals use to make you an educated consumer enabling you to negotiate a much better price on the purchase, renovation, or sale of your home.

Do you really know the true condition of your house? Don't let your **dream house** be a **nightmare** in disguise! Our *Real Estate From A to Z* books and DVDs will assist you with the biggest investment of your life - your own home! These products were originally designed to train top-notch, professional home inspectors, appraisers, investors, builders, contractors and Realtors and are now available at a price affordable to everyone.
All homes need to be inspected, appraised and updated for safety hazards,
routine maintenance, and energy efficiency.

Table of Contents

Introduction To Home Inspections

Introduction

This book is going to cover every aspect of the home inspection business from A to Z. I'm not going to paint some fairy tale, rosy picture or give you any fluff. I'm going to tell it like it is without holding anything back. **This book was originally designed to train top-notch, professional real estate home inspectors. However, this book is extremely helpful to** *anyone* **involved in real estate.** This includes a home buyer, homeowner, home seller, Realtor, appraiser, etc. See section Benefits Of Knowledge Of Home Inspections page 20 to see the reasons why **anyone** can benefit by knowing this material. A lot of the information in this educational material goes well beyond what's covered in other books. That's why I say it's "the *real facts* other books don't tell you!"

You may have purchased some of my other books and DVDs. If you have, then you will find that some of the information contained in this book is similar. This is because there are many important aspects that pertain to both the real estate appraisal and the home inspection businesses, as well as, real estate investing. I hope you don't feel that some of the information is redundant. It will only benefit you to read it several times to make sure you know the information well enough so it doesn't cost you time and money later. If you haven't purchased some of our other products, then do it now! I'm serious about that because our products are worth much more than the price we sell them for. Our customers email us all the time to tell us that.

There will be information in this book that you'll find very surprising and enlightening as to the inner workings of the real estate business. I certainly found it surprising when I got involved in real estate. The only problem was I had to find out the hard way. I'm going to tell you about it so you don't have to make the same mistakes that I made. They say a *Wise Man* learns by his mistakes, but a *Genius* learns by the mistakes of others. So I'll do the best I can to make you a genius!

I had a strong motivating factor for writing this book in the first place. I wrote it because I think there's a very important need for good, honest and thorough home inspectors. I sincerely want people to be more informed about the realities involved with the biggest investment decision they make - the purchase and sale of their own home. There is also a need to improve the integrity and professionalism of the real estate business overall. By being in the real estate business, I've seen firsthand that there are many aspects about it that need to be improved upon. These improvements would be for the benefit of everyone involved, not just inspectors. I hope this book will help increase the integrity and professionalism of the real estate business. If it does, then I will feel that this information provides a much needed service and well worth my efforts.

> *I had a strong motivating factor for writing this book in the first place. I wrote it because I think there's a very important need for good, honest and thorough home inspectors.*
> *I sincerely want people to be more informed about the realities involved with the biggest investment decision they make - the purchase and sale of their home.*

To get the most benefit, you have to read this book from cover-to-cover. So don't get lazy and cut corners; read everything! You have to read the book enough times until you've memorized enough of the information so you know what you're doing. You can't just read it once and expect to know enough to do a proper and thorough home inspection. You can't just "wing it" on a home inspection job because sometimes you'll get a client who asks a lot of questions. If you're fumbling for answers then you'll lose credibility and the client's respect.

This doesn't mean that you have to know the answer to every question the client asks. However, you need to be able to answer the vast majority of their questions. There are times that I tell clients *"I don't know"* when asked about a particular item. Because I know the answers to the vast majority of their questions, I have the client's respect for being so knowledgeable. They realize that I can't be a walking encyclopedia. I just tell them to call a contractor who specializes in that particular area or that I will research their question and get back to them with the answer.

Don't expect to make big money overnight in this business, it's not a get rich quick scheme. It takes time to build up a referral business that brings in a lot of money. But don't worry. If you learn this material well enough and keep feeding your mind with new literature and training courses, you can make big money. Your referrals will begin to come automatically, without even advertising. The whole key to making a lot of money on a steady basis is to have satisfied clients. This is the same concept in every profession and not just the home inspection business. Satisfied clients will refer their friends and neighbors to you for inspections. You'll be one of the best and busiest home inspectors in your area if you're knowledgeable and honest.

You will eventually get to the point when you're doing a lot of home inspections. When you get to this point, don't schedule more than two inspections in one day. If you try to do too many inspections, you'll be rushing to get to the next appointment or you'll be tired before the end of the day. This can cause you to miss something that could create problems later with an angry phone call from your client.

Throughout this book you will see pull quotes and icon keys that will highlight important items. The icon keys are used to highlight important safety issues and "war stories". A *war story* refers to an actual appraisal or home inspection experience that myself or someone I know has had in the real estate business. I thought you might find these stories interesting and helpful since they can help you to understand the importance of the topics discussed in this book. Sometimes when people read about safety hazards, maintenance issues, market value factors, building department permits, etc., they don't take it very seriously – unless they've actually experienced their own war story concerning that topic! When people read about actual instances of these occurrences they tend to remember the advice easier, as opposed to taking it for granted. This will assist you in learning by actual experiences of other people and not make the same mistakes they did. That will save you time, money, aggravation, and stress. Sometimes it will even save your own LIFE! I hope you find the pull quotes and icon keys to be helpful while reading this book.

  = **Important Safety Issue**

  = **War Story**

In this book, when I use the term "Third Parties" I'm talking about people involved in the transaction, not including you or your client. This could be any number of people. The list includes but isn't limited to: the seller, the Realtor or broker, the appraiser, the home inspector, the mortgage lender, the title company, the attorney, the builder or repair contractor, the mailman, the Tooth Fairy, Santa Claus, the Easter Bunny, the seller's dog or cat, and anyone else who may have an interest in the deal. Also, when I use descriptive adjectives and refer to *immoral, greedy, dishonest, ignorant, incompetent, etc.* Third Parties, it does *NOT* refer to **all** third party people, just those that match the particular adjective used. I also want to make it clear that throughout this book both males and females are being referred to whenever the pronouns *he* or *she* are used. Both males and females are also referred to when I give examples of war stories that I've

encountered in the real estate business. When the pronouns "he" or "she" are used, they are interchangeable.

Please send me an email and let me know what you think of this book and any recommendations you might have for improvements or new products. I accept positive and negative comments since both help me to improve the next version of the book. I am always looking to improve my products and services and I greatly appreciate customer feedback and suggestions.
*Also, you can sign up through our www.nemmar.com Nemmar Real Estate Training web site to receive our **free** real estate newsletter with articles and product updates that will definitely help you profit in real estate investing.*

Please send me an email and let me know what you think of this book and any recommendations you might have for improvements or new products. I accept positive and negative comments since both help me to improve the next version of the book. I am always looking to improve my products and services and I greatly appreciate customer feedback and suggestions. Also, you can sign up at our www.nemmar.com Nemmar Real Estate Training web site to receive our **free** real estate newsletter with articles and product updates that will definitely help you profit in real estate investing.

I apologize if my grammar is not perfect in some sentences of this book. However, my objective is to teach real estate in an easy-to-understand way without being too formal, technical, *or boring!* My goal is to teach you as much as possible about the topics covered in this book. All of my books and DVDs are self-edited and self-published and I do the best I can with the time I have available.

About The Author

I'll briefly walk you through my background so you'll see how I ended up in the home inspection business. My father died of cancer when I was 15, and as a result, I had to pay my own way through high school and college. I've worked many different types of service industry jobs to help pay my bills. I worked with a tree service company, a moving company, a house painting company, as a security guard, a day camp counselor, a golf caddie, in a restaurant as a dishwasher, a busboy, a waiter and a bartender, and the list goes on and on.

I studied Art History in college. When I graduated college I was working as a waiter at a local restaurant. You can see from my education and training that I had **no** experience in real estate and I knew virtually **nothing** about it. I didn't even know what a mortgage was! I knew a mortgage had something to do with real estate, but I didn't know exactly what it had to do with it. One day I saw an Infomercial TV show advertising products dealing with real estate investing. The show peaked my curiosity because it talked about buying real estate with "no money down." I ended up buying the products and I went through the material about 10 times. I memorized just about everything in that material. That's what got me started thinking about getting involved in real estate. The main problem was that I had almost no money in the bank! However, I was young and very ambitious and that can do a lot to help you get started. *(By the way, I wouldn't recommend buying the "no money down" books and products sold on TV infomercials. Statistics show that **less than 1%** of the people actually earn money who buy wealth making products, like the real estate "get rich quick" no-money down type of products. You have to be extremely ambitious, determined, plus be able to overcome major obstacles to use those products to get started in buying real estate. Moreover, many of the techniques they teach were much easier to use before the 1990's. Today they are just a pipe dream in the real world of real estate investing. The way they get customers is by preying on people's emotions. They pump you up with hyped-up customer testimonials and they make you think that with their material you'll be rich and financially independent in a few short years. It doesn't happen that way in the real world of real estate – unless you have a lot of money in the bank to start investing with).*

In the 1980's, while I was working as a waiter, my brother and I took out small personal loans to get down payment money to buy a rundown, old single-family house. This house was located in a low-income area of New York and it needed *a lot* of work. We gradually fixed this house up in our spare time, learning the ropes as we went along by trial and error. When we were finished, the house was appraised for <u>twice</u> what we paid for it. As a result, we refinanced the house. We used the money from this loan as a down payment to buy a two-family house that was in just as bad condition as the first house. We renovated the two-family house and then it was also appraised for <u>twice</u> what we paid for it. We refinanced this house and used the extra money to buy a six-family house. The six-family needed a lot of work in repairs.

So we did the same thing again, except this time when we were finished with the renovations, the house didn't appraise for twice what we paid for it. The six-family house was appraised for <u>four times</u> what we paid for it!! *(We had bought the six-family at a bargain basement price.)*

We hired the best home inspector we could find to check these houses out before we purchased them. This inspector also inspected other houses we wanted to buy, however, things came up in the inspection that made us change our minds. We were beginning to learn the ropes about real estate and construction from buying, renovating and managing our own rental properties. This inspector coincidentally offered to train us to go into the home inspection business ourselves. The only catch was that we had to pay him $10,000 to do it! We saw that this inspector was earning over $135,000 per year while working right out of his home, and so we decided to take him up on his offer. I'm glad we did, because that $10,000 investment may have seemed like a lot of money back then, but it paid for itself many times over. I trained under this home inspector and did a lot of reading, research and memorization on my own. This learning process took a long time before I really felt that I knew what I was doing.

After getting into the home inspection business, I ran into a friend of mine from high school, named Mike, who was a local real estate appraiser. Mike had become a very qualified real estate appraiser. I was curious about how Mike trained to become an appraiser and what type of income someone could make in that profession. So I asked Mike some questions and found out that many appraisers earn over $140,000 per year while working out of their homes. He told me some of the aspects about the appraisal business but I just stored it all in the back of my mind and didn't think much about it.

Shortly after that, I received a phone call from another friend of mine from college, named Phil. Phil told me he was working for a bank in their foreclosure department. Phil said that he didn't hire home inspectors as much as he did appraisers for the properties the bank would foreclose on. After a bank forecloses on a property, they have an appraisal done to determine what the present market value is. A bank needs to estimate the market value to know what to try to sell the property for. Sometimes they need to have a home inspection done as well, but not as often. Anyway, this really got me thinking about learning how to do real estate appraisals. I was making a good income with my rental properties and home inspection business. However, I'm always looking for new opportunities that peak my interest. My friend Phil at the bank said that if I learned how to do appraisals well enough, he could give me plenty of work. This **really** set the wheels turning in my head.

I called back my other friend Mike, who was an appraiser, and asked if he could train me to do appraisals for a reasonable fee. Mike agreed to train me for one-half of the fee that I would charge the bank for each appraisal. This ended up amounting to over $8,500! I called Phil at the bank and told him I could do appraisals for him. I said that I will be getting trained by a qualified appraiser who had been in the business for years. This appraiser would also review all of my appraisal reports before they were mailed to the bank. Phil then agreed to give me some appraisal work since I would have all of my appraisals reviewed by a qualified appraiser during my training.

It took about six months of working with Mike and writing up and reviewing many appraisals before I really felt that I knew what I was doing. I then went on to take the State Appraisal classes to get even more knowledge and expertise in real estate appraising. To continue building up my credentials and experience, I passed the State Appraisal examination to become a State Certified Real Estate Appraiser. With all of this training combined with my experience in the business, I have a big edge on many of the appraisers. This is because I have an extensive and diverse background in many different aspects of real estate.

In this book and educational series I'm going to tell you about all of the information and training I learned from a top-notch home inspector, a highly qualified appraiser, and the classes I have taken. Plus I'll tell you about all of the information I've learned from my own experience in real estate and in the inspection and appraisal businesses. The only part of that training I'm going to leave out is the $20,000 in up front fees and class tuition that I had to pay when I first started!! *I hope you don't mind me leaving that part out.*

Purpose Of A Home Inspection

People get very emotional and excited about purchasing a house. When they're in this highly emotional and excited state, they tend to just look at the cosmetic appeal of a house instead of the important factors. They forget that they're not buying a **_CAR,_** they're buying a **_HOUSE!!_** There's a big difference between the two. One is a normal expense everyone has to incur occasionally. The other is the biggest financial decision most people will ever make. By becoming too emotionally attached to a deal, people often pay above market value for a home. This can cost them tens of thousands of dollars in an overpriced purchase. Since a house is such a major financial decision, it's prudent for them not to take any chances. They should try to eliminate as much risk as possible. It's a great feeling to have a client thank you for helping them out with the biggest investment they'll ever make.

A house is usually the biggest investment most people will make, so it's prudent for them not to take any chances. They should try to eliminate as much risk as possible.

People shouldn't buy a house based only on its cosmetic appeal. No house is perfect, there will be repairs or upgrading needed in all homes, even brand new ones. Sometimes people think that because a house is new it doesn't need to be inspected. They don't realize that builders are businessmen trying to make a profit. Any builder who doesn't do quality construction can cut corners to save a few dollars to increase their profit. When a house is built *"up to code"* it doesn't ensure a perfect house. Local building codes are the minimum standards that a builder or contractor has to follow to obtain a building permit or a Certificate of Occupancy for the work done. There's nothing to stop a builder or a contractor from exceeding the building codes other than saving some money for themselves or their client.

A pre-purchase home inspection will inform people of the true condition of a house. This will enable them to make an educated and intelligent decision on whether or not to purchase the home. They will also know what repairs and upgrading will be needed.

Pre-sale home inspections are also recommended. Before someone puts their house up for sale they should have it inspected to find any problems that can be corrected. This will prevent any last minute holdups because of problems found during the buyer's home inspection. Any last minute problems will delay the sale or kill the deal altogether.

As an *"A to Z Home Inspector"* you will be providing a much needed and highly respected service. People are trusting you to help them with the biggest decision they will ever make!

Benefits Of Knowledge Of Home Inspections

Being an *"A to Z Home Inspector"* will enable you to be involved in a recession-proof business. Real Estate is still bought and sold during a recession in the economy. In addition to the typical home sales, there are foreclosure sales, relocations, and distressed sales. The only difference about a recession is that houses are sold for a lower price. All of these houses still need to be inspected, and as a result, your business can grow during a slow economy. Unfortunately, there are people who lose their homes due to tragic circumstances in their lives. However, you're not taking advantage of anyone or being unethical by inspecting properties that are the result of a distressed sale or a foreclosure. All of these properties have to be inspected. Therefore, someone is going to be hired to do the job. Everyone will be much better off if the client hires an *"A to Z Home Inspector"* who does top quality work.

Being an *"A to Z Home Inspector"* can make you a much better home buyer or real estate investor. Before you buy a house or a rental property you can check it from top to bottom to figure out what condition it's in. You can save up to tens of thousands of dollars by spotting a problem before it costs you money later. Many home buyers simply pay close to the asking price that the seller lists the house for. They tend to assume that the "listing price" must be close to the market value of the property. Often this is not so. The seller can ask any price they want for their property. However, the true market value could be much less than their asking price. If you have the knowledge of how to perform good, thorough home inspections then you can negotiate some price reduction or concessions. You can intelligently inform the seller if you find any problem conditions during the inspection.

Being an *"A to Z Home Inspector"* can make you a much better home seller. Before you sell your house you can bring everything up to top working condition ahead of time. An awful lot of real estate deals are killed before the real estate appraisal or inspection is done. The buyer and seller may come to an agreement on price and terms pending the home inspection or appraisal. If the home inspector is thorough, they may find problems with the house. This ends up throwing a monkey wrench into the works by lowering the sales price or killing the deal.

Being an *"A to Z Home Inspector"* can make you a much better homeowner. See the *Purpose Of A Home Inspection* section for how homeowners can benefit from this knowledge. You can make your house safe for you and your family. You'll be able to identify electrical hazards, radon, asbestos, carbon monoxide and gas leaks, etc. Prevent accidents *before* they happen! Also, eliminate building code violations or from being cheated by contractors.

Being an *"A to Z Home Inspector"* can make you a much better Realtor. If you're presently a Real Estate Agent or Broker, then you already know how a low appraisal or problems found during the home inspection can kill a deal. You can greatly increase the percentages of the deals you close. You can show the seller what problem conditions there are at the time you take the listing for the house or condo. As a Realtor, you can inform the home seller yourself without waiting for the buyer's home inspector to do it later.

I'm sure all of you that are presently Realtors are aware of possible complaints. Some people may have bought a house or condo and found out later that there was a problem. They may believe that you knew about the problem or that you should've known about it. As a Realtor, you can help to reduce your headaches and liability by knowing about any potential problems before they come back to haunt you later. You can get more listings due to your knowledge and expertise, which any home buyer or seller will respect. This will enable you to increase your business and income.

Being an *"A to Z Home Inspector"* can make you a much better real estate consultant. If you do any consulting work, you can gain much more respect and business due to your expertise and knowledge.

Being an *"A to Z Home Inspector"* can make you a much better real estate appraiser. I do appraisals as well as inspections and I can see things that the vast majority of appraisers in the business don't even know about. My appraisals are much more thorough and informative for the client. Therefore, I can charge a lot more for my work than other appraisers can.

> *So you see, I've got this baby set on automatic pilot. There's something in this material for just about anyone to benefit from.*

So you see, I've got this baby set on automatic pilot. There's something in this material for just about anyone to benefit from. There's only one type of individual that I can think of that can't benefit from this material. That's someone who has no intention of going into the real estate business in any way, shape or form. They also would need to have no intention of ever owning their own house or condominium. If that description fits you, then this book is not for you.

Description Of A Home Inspection

A home inspection is a little different depending on your regional area and the type of housing construction that's more common. However, you'll be dealing with the same general inspection process and business.

A home inspection is a visual, limited time, nondestructive inspection. There's no dismantling or using tools to take things apart. However, you will need some tools to help on the inspection. I'll tell you what tools you need a little further on in this book.

You don't turn anything on that doesn't operate by its normal controls. Meaning that you use only thermostats to test the heating or air-conditioning systems, etc. Don't test anything that has "do-it-yourself" wiring and installations. Any do-it-yourself type of setups can be dangerous to operate and you don't get paid to get injured.

You're a real estate home inspector, you're not a *repairman*. Tell the client to have something checked out by a licensed contractor if it's not operating properly, or if you have any doubts about its present condition. This means that you don't need to know how to fix everything in a house. All you need to do is to be able to identify a problem, or identify whether the operating systems are working properly. To make this point more clear, I'll use an analogy with your car. Normally, you know when your car isn't running properly or if there's a problem with it. However, you don't need to know how to fix the car. All you need to do is identify that something is wrong and that a repairman needs to check it out further. You just bring the car to an auto mechanic and let them tell you exactly what's wrong and what it will cost to repair the problem.

As a home inspector, you're not required to be the **Wizard of Oz**. You're not required to have a *magic wand* that reveals every, single problem with the house and site. You're not required to have *X-ray vision* to see things behind walls, ceilings or other finished areas. You're not required to have a *crystal ball* to foresee **all** potential problems that will arise in the future with the subject property. *(However some people expect you to have all of these qualities).*

You determine what the current condition and life expectancy is of different aspects of a house or condominium. Try to be very conservative with evaluating life expectancies of an item because you don't know what the past maintenance history was for the items you're evaluating. As a home inspector, you check all visible and accessible areas and operating systems, such as, heating, air-conditioning, electrical, plumbing, the roof, etc. Everything should be operating properly at the time of the inspection.

A home inspection is <u>not</u> a building code inspection. **Building code inspections** determine if a property adheres to all of the local building codes. The local municipality has their own building inspectors that perform these services. A home inspection and a building code inspection are two very different services. Home inspectors do not memorize the local building codes for their clients.

Professional Engineer and Registered Architect Issue

For doing home inspections there are licenses and/or certification requirements in most states. Most states generally require you to work under someone else's wing until you learn the basics of the business and get some training. It's similar to getting a State appraiser's license. Working with someone else's inspection company has many positive aspects to it. You won't be calling the shots for a while, but you won't have any overhead or liability problems either.

There are <u>no</u> Engineering or Architecture **degrees needed to do home inspections.** Let me put this issue to bed nice and early. This is a very common misconception about home inspections. The following statement was issued by the *American Society of Home Inspectors (ASHI)*. ASHI has members from all different backgrounds, including engineers and architects. This is verbatim from their statement:

> There are <u>no</u> Engineering or Architecture degrees needed to do home inspections.
> Let me put this issue to bed nice and early. This is a very common misconception about home inspections.

"It is not uncommon for buyers to be confused about who is qualified to perform home inspections. There are for example, no home inspection degrees offered or required by law. In some cases, consumers have been led to believe that a home inspection involves engineering analysis and therefore requires the use of a licensed Professional Engineer. The confusion is compounded by the inadvertent misuse of the term "engineer" and "engineering inspection."
Visual home inspections do not involve engineering analysis however even when performed by Professional Engineers. In fact, engineering is an entirely different type of investigation, which entails detailed scientific measurements, tests, calculations and/or analysis. Normally this is done on one specific component of the house (structural or electrical, for example) by, or under the direction of, an engineer trained in that area. Such a technically exhaustive analysis involves considerable time and expense, and is only appropriate on rare occasions when visual evidence exists to indicate design problems which require further, specialized investigation."

An analogy to this is, let's say you were doing an inspection on a slate roof, and there were visible signs that shingles were excessively shaling (flaking) and falling off the house. You should then instruct the client to contact an expert in that field who specializes in that one aspect of house construction. In this example the client should contact a roofer to get repair estimates. A home inspector is a generalist, in the sense that he/she knows a lot about **all** the different aspects of housing construction. A home inspector is not an expert in just **one** area of housing construction.

You have to educate potential clients when they call for price quotes and are only looking for a PE or a RA. PE and RA are the abbreviations for Professional Engineer and Registered Architect. Tell the potential clients to try to find an engineering or architecture school that teaches people how to become a home inspector. *(But don't hold your breath while you look)*. Engineering courses are a lot math and physics. Home inspectors are trained to determine the life expectancy and operating conditions of a boiler/furnace, air-conditioning, plumbing, termites, water problems in basements, roofs, septics, wells, etc.

You will come across some unethical engineers and architects that try to deceive people into believing that they're more qualified as home inspectors due to their college degree and education. There was a PE in my area who was suspended from ASHI over this issue. This dishonest PE was caught handing out flyers to Realtors and other people stating that a new law was just passed which stated you must be a Professional Engineer to be a home inspector. This PE even went a step further. He put ads in the yellow pages that misled consumers into believing only Professional Engineers were qualified to do home inspections. Inspectors in the area complained to the yellow pages and they made this PE change his ad the next year. Talk about a greedy, dishonest jerk! This guy wins the prize.

A PE can be a Nuclear Engineer, a Civil Engineer, a Chemical Engineer, an Aeronautical Engineer, a Mechanical Engineer, an Electrical Engineer, etc. which has absolutely *NOTHING* to do with a home inspection. Architects are trained to design the plans and layout for homes, not evaluate the life expectancy and condition of roofs, heating systems, plumbing, siding, insulation, water problems, termites, etc. I have friends that are architects, mechanical, electrical, and structural engineers and they know nothing about home inspections. When you come across any engineers or architects who try to tell people that they're the only ones qualified to do home inspections, then you should just ask them what they learned in college about home inspections. Ask them, what Engineering or Architecture school teaches you to become a home inspector? It's not that being a PE or a RA is bad, because it's helpful to have these qualified degrees regardless of the occupation you're in. It's just that a PE or a RA isn't any more qualified to do home inspections than a person with a good construction background or a well-trained home inspector.

You may even want to tell potential clients to call their State Board of Engineering to learn the distinction between an engineer and a home inspector. Do the same with the Board or Architects in your State. If you know what you're talking about and you're knowledgeable enough, the customer will understand the logic behind the PE and RA issue. You should even tell the potential client to question the integrity of any other home inspector that tries to convince them that only PE's or RA's are qualified to do inspections.

Starting Out And Setting Up A Business

Set up a corporation in the State that you will be doing business in. This isn't a big expense. Consult an attorney in your area to assist you. You can use your home as an office. This is the most common way to start out. There's very little overhead and you don't have to pay rent and utilities for office space. Set up a separate phone line and create a professional web site. You don't have to hire a secretary if you can't afford one. Just use an answering machine. **You** set your own hours and you can work part-time or full-time, whichever you prefer.

Have business cards, stationery and brochures made up at a local printer and drop them off and introduce yourself at the local real estate offices, law offices, banks, appraisal offices and any businesses involved in real estate. I did this for months in my beginning stages. Banks are a potential source for home inspections. They need to order inspections for some of their mortgage loans. If you get on a bank's approved inspector list you should have more than enough business to keep you busy and keep your own savings account growing.

Relocation companies are a great source of inspections. I had a friend who was doing over a million dollars a year in business with relocation companies for inspections and appraisals. Get the relocation directories for the phone numbers and addresses to contact them. When a company relocates one of their employees, they generally have two appraisals and two home inspections done. The company hires one appraiser and inspector, and the employee of the company hires the other appraiser and home inspector. The purpose of this is that they get two different opinions as to the current market value and condition of the employee's house. They then agree to a sales price and the company will reimburse their employee by buying the house from them. This enables the employee to move to the new location and buy a home. Sometimes when the first two inspectors are very different in estimating the condition, they hire a *third* inspector to settle the matter!

Some insurance companies hire inspectors before they write certain homeowner's policies. Contact some of the insurance agents in your area and see if they need inspectors. Local construction companies and the city building department may need to hire home inspectors. I did many home inspections for a construction company in my area. This construction company was hired by the city to install sewer lines in areas where the houses all have septic systems. I was paid to go out and inspect all the houses for any structural problems before the construction company started blasting to install the sewer lines.

Get email lists of real estate offices, law offices, relocation companies, etc. to email them a link to your web site. Local billboards and other ads can be inexpensive for the exposure you get.

Work with another inspection company. I worked with two local companies and one national outfit that did relocation inspections initially while I was learning the business and building up contacts. There are many benefits to doing this. You will be earning money while building up business contacts during your training. You get to learn the basics of the business and you don't have the liability and overhead costs.

Home Inspection Education

It's very important to keep educating yourself to stay up to date and knowledgeable. Join home inspection organizations and meet other inspectors. Some home inspection associations have *Errors and Omissions* insurance offered to their members. Errors and Omissions insurance is <u>not</u> to be used as a safety net. Don't think that you can do bad inspections and not have to worry about paying any losses from lawsuits because you have E and O insurance. The purpose of E and O insurance is only in the event that you accidentally miss something on an inspection. It's also used in the event that you get an unreasonable client who sues you for no-good reason. It only takes a small number of bad and dishonest inspectors that get a few really big lawsuits against them to cancel the E and O insurance program for everyone. ASHI had this problem in the past with a prior insurance company that offered E and O insurance to ASHI members. Due to some really big claims against a few inspectors, the insurance company canceled the program. So don't ruin Errors and Omissions insurance for everyone else. Do good, thorough and honest inspections.

I'll give you a perfect example of what you don't want to do concerning E and O insurance. There was some **Bozo** in my area who jumped into the home inspection business without knowing anything about it. Anyway, this new home inspector must have figured that he could learn the business overnight. He was telling potential customers, while giving them price quotes over the phone, that they should hire him because he had insurance which guaranteed they wouldn't have to pay for any problems in the house that he missed. These customers would call me and ask me if my company carried E and O insurance. I said yes but then I asked them

why. When they told me what this other inspector was telling people, I was amazed at the absurdity and ignorance of this new inspector.

Just because someone has Errors and Omissions insurance doesn't mean that their insurance company is going to send checks out to anyone who wants one! If an inspector or appraiser gets slapped with too many lawsuits, his insurance carrier will drop him like a bad habit. If that happens, then who is going to compensate all of his other clients who had totally useless home inspections or appraisals from this clown for their time and aggravation? Also, who would want to buy a house and then find out later about some major problems that should have been identified during the home inspection or appraisal? If the problems are overwhelming, then you wouldn't want to buy the house anyway, regardless of whether an insurance company was willing to compensate you for damages.

The best insurance policy and client referral potential is to do good, honest and thorough inspections. Each of your inspections should be about two to four hours long. The time will vary depending upon if it's a condo or a house and whether there's a septic and a well system on the property. I did an inspection once on a condominium, and the client told me that he was calling around for price quotes before hiring me. He told me that he actually had several inspectors tell him that their inspection would only take about **fifteen to twenty minutes!!** I could not believe it when I heard that. I couldn't even check the heating and electrical systems properly in that amount of time, let alone the entire interior and exterior! So don't be a *"Walk-Thru"* inspector by taking people's money and running. Do yourself and your clients a favor. Spend enough time to check everything out properly at the job site.

Home inspection organizations have annual national seminars. They also have classes and home inspection exams that are very good for keeping you on your toes and up to date. Your local home inspection association probably has monthly meetings with educational speakers and a newsletter that will help to keep you up to date. You can get education credits for taking home inspection classes and by going to the seminars and monthly meetings. Education credits are required for continuing membership in leading home inspection organizations to keep them professional associations of top-notch inspectors.

I highly recommend you take some of the appraisal courses needed to obtain a State appraisers license. They have a class called *The Standards Of Professional Practice* that they require appraisers to take. This class will really open your eyes to the ethical and honest conduct that's required and expected of anyone in the real estate profession. *(Unfortunately, some people who take the course are either asleep or daydreaming when they're in the classroom! This you'll see from the war stories I mention in this book).*

I became a State Certified Appraiser, as well as a full member of a leading home inspector organization. That's something you may want to consider. Being a State Certified

Appraiser gives you much more credibility in a potential client's eyes. You will have an edge over the competition when a client is calling around for price quotes and comparing the inspection company services in your area. There are very, very, few people that are good home inspectors and appraisers. I mean top-notch home inspectors and State Certified appraisers and not some guy who tells you that he does both but has no extensive training in either.

Read books and talk to local builders, contractors and building department inspectors to keep informed and educate your mind. There are constantly new technologies being applied to housing construction that you need to keep on top of.

Take some knowledgeable local contractors out to lunch occasionally. This will enable you to find out about the new trends and technologies being used in new housing construction and operating systems. You may even be able to deduct it as a business expense! You'll be *amazed* at what you can learn from a contractor who specializes in a particular field. There are times when I come across something new that I haven't seen before during an inspection. When this happens, I'll call a contractor who installs or repairs that item and ask questions about it. People love to share their expertise with someone who's interested and willing to listen.

Take continuing education classes at local colleges. You may want to take a local building inspectors licensing course or test. This isn't required but it will give you more credibility and education. BOCA, which stands for the *Building Officials and Code Administrators International*, has a monthly newsletter if you join their organization. The newsletter may provide some helpful information.

Tools That Are Helpful

◊ Road maps of your area and a car compass to find the job site.

◊ A clipboard with a notepad and pens to take your field notes.

◊ Home Inspection checklists (you can order these through our www.nemmar.com web site).

◊ Tool box to carry your tools.

◊ Reliable, powerful flashlight is a necessity.

◊ Some inspectors like to carry a camera to take pictures of the interior, exterior and the operating systems of the house to help them with writing up the inspection report.

◊ Lighted magnifying glass to view any data plates that are hard to read.

◊ Large probe and an awl to check wood for rot and termite damage.

◊ Electric screwdriver with screw bits to take off any panel covers that are meant for easy removal only.

◊ Safety glasses to wear in crawl spaces or to view the firebox in a furnace or boiler or other areas.

◊ Extendable mirror to view furnace or boiler heat exchangers.

◊ Work gloves if you work in dirty areas or have a dirty furnace or boiler.

◊ Hard hat, knee pads and a jump suit to wear in narrow crawl spaces.

◊ Voltage tester to test the electrical panel for voltage before touching it.

◊ Polarity and GFCI tester to test outlets for proper wiring and operation.

◊ Measuring tape that's 16 feet long for any measurements needed for the client.

◊ Thermometer to test the air temperature coming from forced hot air and air-conditioning vents.

◊ Extendable magnet to reach any screws or small metal parts.

◊ Calipers to measure the diameter of a pipe.

◊ Combustible gas detector is helpful to test for minor gas and carbon monoxide leaks.

◊ A marble and a six inch and a four-foot level to check walls and floors for being level.

◊ Pliers to help in necessary situations, such as lifting the corner of a rug to see the floor underneath.

◊ Binoculars to view the roof, chimney, siding and other parts of the house that you can't see clear enough from the ground.

◊ Folding ladder to look at the roof from a closer view.

◊ Radon canisters for radon gas testing. It's not so much the canister type, but the quality and sophistication of the radon lab equipment that's important for radon testing. I'll talk more about this later in the book.

◊ Septic tank dye to test septic systems.

◊ Well water bottles for water laboratory analysis.

Booking Home Inspection Jobs

To give a price quote you have to determine the amount of time and liability that's involved with the inspection. Explain to the client what a prepurchase home inspection is. Let them know it's a visual, limited time, nondestructive and nondismantling inspection. You can't be responsible for things that you can't see, such as, behind finished walls, floors and ceilings. You also can't see any underground systems like wells, septics, oil tanks, etc. Don't scare them off into thinking you won't do anything for them. Just make them realize what a home inspection is. This way everything is up front and they won't think that your inspection is a guarantee that will find all the problems, visible and nonvisible.

I'll list some items that you should find out from the client when giving a price quote for an inspection job. The following items are all listed on the appointment and price quote cards that are included in this book. These index cards will help you give price quotes and keep track of your home inspection appointments. Remember that when giving price quotes, you always have to consider the amount of time the on-site inspection and the written report will take to complete. Another factor to consider is the liability involved.

1. **Is the subject property a condominium, single family, multifamily, etc.?** Condominiums take less time than a single family house inspection. This is because the Condo Association maintains most of the exterior of the condo building. There is a monthly assessment fee charged to all of the individual condo owners to pay for this maintenance. A single family house will take less time to inspect than a multifamily house, especially if the multifamily has a separate heating and/or air-conditioning system for each unit.

2. **What's the square footage and/or the number of bedrooms and bathrooms in the house?** The larger the square footage is, then the longer the inspection will take. Sometimes the client won't know the square footage size of the house so try to find out how many bedrooms and bathrooms there are. For example, a four bedroom and three bath house will be a large home and will take some extra time to inspect.

3. **From what you know, is the house in overall good, average, fair, or poor condition?** The worse condition the house is in, then the longer the inspection will take. Also, if the house is in poor condition and needs a lot of repairs, then there's more risk for you. The client should be able to tell you what the overall appearance of the house is from what they could see. They don't have to be a home inspector to give you some idea of the general condition of the house.

4. **What's the age of the house?** Generally the older the house, the more repairs will be needed and/or there will be some outdated operating systems. This can lead to

more risk for you due to the possibility that you miss something that you should have noticed.

5. **Is there a garage?** If the house has a two car detached garage, then you'll spend a little more time evaluating this then if there was no garage.

6. **Is there a basement and/or crawl space?** Basements and crawl spaces can have serious problems in them, especially if the house is older. These areas *must* be inspected thoroughly. You have to account for all of this in your price quote. Also, ask if the basement is finished with wall, ceiling and floor coverings. If it's finished than you won't be able to see behind any inaccessible areas. Make sure your client knows this.

7. **Does the house have a central air-conditioning system?** If it does, then this must be evaluated, *(if the weather is warm enough to test it safely)*. If you include this in the inspection, then you'll spend more time at the site and in writing the report.

8. **Is the house connected to a septic system or the city sewer system?** If the house has a septic system that you're going to dye test, then you should include this in your price quote.

9. **Is the house connected to a well water system or is it supplied by the city water system?** If the house has a well water system that you're going to test, then you should also include this in your price quote.

10. **Do you want a termite and other wood destroying insect inspection?** If the client wants you to check for these insects, then you'll be more liable if you miss something that you should have noticed. So charge the client for this service.

11. **Do you want a radon gas analysis done?** If you test for radon, you want to charge for this service. All houses should be tested due to the health hazards caused by high levels of radon in a home.

12. **Do you want a laboratory water analysis done?** If you test the water, *(you should always test well water)*, for bacteria, mineral and/or radon content then you want to charge for this service also.

13. **Where is the house located?** If the subject property is farther away from your office than the normal inspection site, then you want to charge for the additional traveling time involved. This is important when you start to get busy. While you're away from your office you can't answer the phone to give price quotes. When this happens, you'll miss some jobs, unless of course you hire a secretary to answer your phone.

14. **What is the selling price of the house?** Be careful when asking this since some people don't like telling anyone the sales price when they are buying or selling their

home. If people hesitate to tell you the sales price then just explain to them the reason why you are asking that question. It's not that you're trying to be nosy, you just need to know the sales price because the liability risk and time involved to inspect a $1 million dollar home can be far greater than that involved with inspecting a $100,000 dollar home. You have to account for this in your price estimate.

> If the client asks if you're an engineer or an architect, just educate them about this common misconception. By telling the facts, you'll earn their respect for being so up-front and honest.

If the client asks if you're an engineer or an architect, just educate them about this common misconception. By telling them the facts, you'll earn their respect for being so up-front and honest.

Tell the client that it's highly recommended that they attend the inspection. This will enable them to see firsthand all of the different aspects of the house you'll be evaluating. Having the client attend the inspection also helps to eliminate questions, phone calls and problems later. Tell them that it's also recommended that they arrange the inspection at a time when the owner of the house you'll be inspecting will be home. The reason for this is that there are many questions you need to ask the owner of the house directly. As an **"A to Z Home Inspector"** you need to ask these questions to obtain some information to help you with the home inspection. I'll explain more about this later.

Sometimes you'll book jobs to inspect vacant houses. Some houses are left vacant when being sold for a number of different reasons. The homeowner could have died and it's an estate sale; the owner may have been relocated by his company for a new job position; the owner may be away for a long vacation; it could be a bank foreclosure sale, etc. If the subject property is vacant, then there are important items to be aware of. Often, vacant houses will have the utilities turned off. You should notify the client of this when booking the job. I've arrived at houses many times to do a home inspection or appraisal and the utilities were turned off. This limits what you can evaluate. For example, without electricity you can't check the outlets, switches or operating systems; without gas or oil you can't test the boiler/furnace or water heater; without the water supply turned on you can't test the plumbing pressure and drainage. There's another aspect to be aware of with vacant houses. If the property is located in cold weather areas, then the heating system must be kept on all winter or else the water pipes must be winterized. This protects the pipes from water freezing, expanding and cracking the pipes.

Pre-inspection contracts are starting to gain support among many inspection companies. The purpose of these is to have the client sign a contract before the inspection. The contract is designed so that the client will understand what the inspection involves and what the limitations of it are.

There are inspection companies that offer some of the home warranty programs that are on the market. Home warranty programs offer the home buyer a type of insurance policy. The buyer obtains the insurance so that if they buy the house and something breaks down or there's a problem, they may be reimbursed for any expenses. This is different than Errors and Omissions insurance. E and O insurance covers the home **inspector**. Home warranty insurance covers the home **buyer**. If you're going to offer a warranty policy to your clients, then make sure that you read the fine print and that you understand them **completely**. Sometimes these policies are very limited in their coverage protection, so you and your client need to know up front what your client will be getting for their money.

Many of these home warranty policies only offer the client a depreciated value reimbursement for any claims. They also do not cover certain aspects of the house and the coverage period is limited to about 12 months after the client moves in. This means that if the client buys the house and the boiler needs replacing in 14 months, then the policy will not cover this expense. Also, when a claim is paid it's usually depreciated. This is similar to auto insurance. When an insurance adjuster "totals" a used car after an accident, the insurance company only pays you the book value of that car. They don't buy you a new car! Basically it's up to you. Some people feel it's a selling point to offer their clients a warranty policy. It's pretty much a judgment call from your own perspective. So look into the warranty policies in your area and decide if there's one for you. But whatever you decide, *make sure you read the fine print* so your client doesn't think he's getting "full blanket" insurance coverage.

Some States require seller disclosure forms for home sellers to sign when they're marketing their house. You will come across some people who try to convince home buyers that they don't need to get the house inspected. They tell the home buyers that an inspection isn't needed because of a seller disclosure form and/or a warranty program.

The seller disclosure forms are **very limited** because the seller of a home knows *nothing* about home inspections. The seller can only tell the home buyer if things are working up to their standards, which may be different from the buyer's standards. For example, the seller may have no problem living in a house with low water pressure or an occasional water problem in the basement. However, your client who is the home buyer, has totally different needs and standards that they're looking for in their purchase. This can't be evaluated properly by a seller disclosure. Also, let's say the seller disclosure states that the roof has no water leaks. This could be a true statement. Maybe the roof isn't leaking now. But what if that roof is 20 years old and it's going to need replacing within a year? The seller knows **nothing** about roofs. So how can the seller tell a buyer that there's no need to worry about the roof. These are the reasons why a home inspection is still needed, even if there are a seller disclosure form and a warranty program for the house.

> *It's very important that your client understands the severe limitations of the home warranty programs and the seller disclosure forms.*
> *Your client has a right to know this information.*

⚠ It's very important that your client understands the severe limitations of the home warranty programs and the seller disclosure forms. Your client has a *right* to know this information. So don't let any Realtors, sellers or other third parties try to convince them that they don't need to get the house inspected.

House Architectural Styles

This section contains brief descriptions of various architectural styles in single family homes.

◊ **Colonial.** Cape Cod and Cape Ann styles are: generally quite small in size - minimum with good taste; symmetrical-windows balanced on both sides of front door; either one or one and one-half stories with little head room upstairs; fairly steep gable or gambrel roof covered with wood shingles; and exterior of wood siding.

◊ **New England Colonial.** A square or rectangular, box-like structure having: maximum usable space; symmetrical windows balanced on both sides of front door; either two or two and one-half stories; gable roof covered with wood shingles; exterior of wood generally painted white; and impressive front entrance usually with transom fan of glass above the door.

◊ **Dutch Colonial.** A moderate-sized home generally not more than 50 feet wide, with a symmetrical front having: an entrance at the center, balanced by the windows; low--sweeping gambrel roof; exterior generally of stone; and either one and one-half story with dormer windows or two and one-half stories with dormer windows.

◊ **Georgian and Southern Colonial.** These styles have elaborate front entrances with plain or fluted columns; are generally of brick or wood; have prominent gabled roofs, often hipped; are very symmetrical; require large plots of land; large scale, not suitable for a small house; and either two, two and one-half or three stories.

◊ **English Elizabethan.** This style has gothic refined lines with molded stone around windows and doors; generally of brick, stucco, or stone; steep pitched roof, covered with slate or shingle; usually leaded metal casement windows; and requires a large building site.

◊ **English Half-Timber.** This style has protruding timber faces with stucco between the faces; lower story of heavy masonry; steep pitched roof; generally two stories; and requires a large lot area.

◊ **Regency.** A generally symmetrical style with front entrance in center; exterior of brick or stone; shutters on each side of windows; low hipped roof; two stories in height; and octagonal window on second floor over front door.

◊ **French Provincial.** Usually a large house on a sizable plot, masonry exterior walls with very high roofs; large high windows with long shutters; and one and one-half or two and one-half stories.

◊ **French Normandy.** Generally has turrets at entry; walls of brick or stone; unsymmetrical; and steep pitched shingle roof.

◊ **True Spanish.** Enclosed patios; red mission tiled roof; wrought iron decorations; and stucco walls (usually white).

◊ **Small California Spanish.** Stucco exterior; flat composition roof with mission tile trim in the front; suitable for small lots; no patio; and one story only.

◊ **Monterey Spanish.** Two stories; stucco (generally white); red mission tiled roof; second story balconies; and decorative iron railings.

◊ **Modern and Contemporary.** Generally one story; usually flat or low pitched roof; often on concrete slab; large amount of glass; and indoor/outdoor living.

◊ **California Bungalow or Ranch House.** One story; stucco with wood trim; often on concrete slab; shingle or shake roof; low and rambling; generally attached garage; and indoor/outdoor living.

Beginning The Home Inspection

I'll go through the home inspection process. You can modify it to meet your own needs or desires. You'll be nervous for the first ten or so home inspections. This is normal. Just remember that you need to learn this material well enough, and keep up to date with all the new construction trends. If you do then you will earn the respect of the buyer and all third parties to the transaction by being so knowledgeable.

If you're young, sometimes people will get a little worried when they first meet you at the job site. I have no idea, but for some strange reason some people seem worried about a home inspector who's young. That is, until they see that you know what you're talking about. I guess some people are convinced that wisdom only comes with old age. I remember in my beginning years as a home inspector I was in my mid-late 20's. When I arrived at the site, some of my clients had a surprised look on their faces when they saw how young I was. In a way, their concern was justified since they were going to be trusting me to give them advice on the biggest financial decision they will make in their lives. However, after only about 10 minutes into the home inspection they were well aware that my youth was not a problem and did not limit my knowledge and advice that would benefit them. This is why you have to learn this material thoroughly to be a competent and knowledgeable home inspector. That's how you gain instant credibility with your clients.

When driving up to the house or condo you should take note of the condition of it, the terrain, if there are any ponds or streams, etc. Mark down the time the inspection begins and ends. Mark down the weather conditions. Any snow covered areas will not be visible for inspection. Rain may have signs, or lack of signs, of water in the lower level and any roof leaks.

Greet the owner and Realtor and just tell them you have to ask some questions about the house or condo to get some background. You need this info to help you with the report and the home inspection. There are some aspects of the house that you can't always detect or verify without some additional information from the seller or Realtor. Often you'll find that you can't get all the information you need from the questions you ask the owner or Realtor. Just get whatever information you can and keep a record of it. Make sure that you put their answers in the written report to CYA, which stands for Cover Your Assets *(or Cover Your Ass)*. This will help in the event that you find out later that someone misrepresented the house or condo. You'll be able to show proof about what was stated and represented to you and your client at the time of the inspection. This is why you want to stress to the client to arrange the inspection at a time when the owner of the house is home. It's important to tell your client this when you're booking the inspection. This way they'll have time to notify the owner to arrange the appointment. You should also get a copy of any real estate listing sheets, surveys, etc. that the third parties might have. See if there's anything important in these documents to help you or your client.

You have to be very gentle when you ask the seller of the house the following questions. Sometimes they get very upset and worried about all these questions. Just tell them that it's nothing personal or that you don't trust them, you just need this information to assist you with the inspection. There are many aspects about a house that only the owner may know about and that's what you're trying to find out. If they (the seller) were buying the house, they would want you to find out the same information from the seller as well. **Just remember that you're a guest in someone else's house! So don't be rude or get into an argument with anyone at the inspection.** You must be diplomatic and professional in this or any other business to be successful.

When you ask these preinspection questions, **make sure that you ask the owner or Realtor about information from any prior owners of the house.** Meaning that if the seller tells you, *"No, we have never made any changes to the foundation or septic system,"* then ask them if they know of any prior owners having made any changes, repairs, etc. The reason you need to specifically ask that is because if you don't, then often the third parties will never mention any details they know about it. The Realtor, seller or seller's attorney may have information about what repairs, updating, problems there are/were with the house when the prior owners lived there. For example, the seller may have found problems in the house or with town hall records concerning the subject property after they moved in that were created or occurred with the prior owners. Third parties will rarely volunteer that type of information when you inspect the home for a potential buyer. They may not be trying to hide the information from you and they may think it's not relevant anymore because the situation occurred with a prior owner in the past. However, you need to make the third parties and your client aware that "yes" it is very relevant that you know all details possible for your inspection and evaluation of the subject property.

Some of the questions to ask:

◊ Age of House/Condo
◊ How long they lived there
◊ Any damaged areas to the floors, walls, and/or ceilings that they know about. Are any damaged areas hidden by carpets, furniture, sheetrock, etc.
◊ Any insulation added or removed to the floors, walls, and/or ceilings. Any UFFI foam or asbestos insulation removed must have licensed EPA contractor certification.
◊ Any past or present problems with the water pressure and drainage.
◊ Any past or present problems with electrical overloads, outlets, switches, etc..
◊ Does the fireplace draft properly and how often do they use it *(if applicable)*.
◊ Any exterior siding added after the original construction. What's behind it.
◊ Roof age and any past or present leaks.
◊ Any decks or additions added. If yes, are all valid permits and Certificate of Occupancies, *(C of O)*, filed at town

hall.

◊ Any structural renovations done. If yes, is there a C of O for the work done.

◊ Furnace/Boiler Age. Dates and how often serviced. Are all rooms heated. Any oil tanks, used or unused, and their location. Age of any oil tanks.

◊ Age of the air-conditioning compressor. If it's too cold to test, did it operate properly last season. Dates and how often the system was serviced.

◊ Have they ever treated for termites or wood destroying insects. Date treated. Any damage from wood destroying insects, *(WDI)*. Any guarantees or documentation for any treatments performed.

◊ Any sump pumps or water problems in the house.

◊ Is house/condo connected to Municipal water & sewer systems. This is very important to get from them since there is no way to determine this at the site without checking the town hall records.

◊   Septic System:

◊ Any survey or plot plan showing the system.

◊ Any renovations or additions to the house needing septic system approvals, such as bathrooms added.

◊ Construction and size of septic tank.

◊ Is the tank original or was it upgraded.

◊ Date the tank was last pumped out and the times prior to this cleaning.

◊ Name of the septic service company for more info.

◊   Well Water System:

◊ Any survey or plot plan showing the system.

◊ Depth of the well.

◊ Is the well water pressure and volume adequate for normal use.

◊ Date the well pump was last serviced or replaced.

◊ Date the well water storage tank was last serviced and the age of the tank.

◊ Name of the well service company for more info.

◊   Swimming Pool:

◊ Age of the pool, filter, heater and liner.

◊ Do they have a Certificate of Occupancy and all valid permits.

◊ Any known leaks in the pool walls.

◊ Has it been properly winterized *(if applicable)*.

◊ Name of the pool service company for more info.

◊ Are there any outstanding building, zoning or other violations or any missing permits and/or approvals.

◊ Can I test all operating systems in the house or are there any that are being repaired or aren't functioning properly. Operating Systems refers to items such as the heating, air-conditioning, plumbing, electrical, wells, septics, etc.

Start The Inspection In The Lower Level

Some areas of the country, like Florida, don't have basements. As you move from the lower level through the interior and up to the attic, move in a clockwise direction. This will help prevent you from bouncing around from room to room which may cause you to skip a room by accident. I'll always start the home inspection in the lower level because this is usually where the operating systems are located. I usually spend at least one hour in the lower level of a house inspecting the operating systems and for structural, water and termite problems. I start the inspection with the heating system in the winter or the air-conditioning in the summer. If it's late in the afternoon, I'll start with the exterior before it gets dark. Then I can take my time on the interior.

The Operating Systems Inspection

Heating System

The average homeowner often improperly uses the term *furnace* when discussing their *boiler*. This same confusion happens with *heat pumps*. I'll explain the difference between a Furnace, Boiler and a Heat Pump:

◊ A *furnace* has a burner that heats the air and then blows it out of vents, sometimes called registers. You won't find any radiators if a furnace heats the house. Both a furnace and a heat pump use vents to discharge warm air in the house.

◊ A *boiler* heats by boiling water and making steam in a steam system. In a hot water system, a boiler heats water without reaching the boiling temperature, and circulates it through the pipes. The heated water or steam is sent through radiators to heat the house.

◊ A *heat pump* is a central air-conditioning system that works in reverse in the winter time. No matter how cold it is outside, there's always some heat in the air. The Freon in the heat pump can absorb this heat. The air is then blown over the Freon coils and the house is heated with warm air through the vents.

The basic operation of a heating system is this:

1. The temperature in the house falls below the setting on the wall *thermostat*. The thermostat then engages the *burner* or *heating coils* to turn on.

2. The air or water is then heated in an area called a *heat exchanger*. Picture the heat exchanger as a box where the burner or heating coils are located and the air or water passes around this area and the heat dissipates.

3. From the heat exchanger the water or steam in a boiler system goes through pipes to the *radiators* to heat the house. In a forced hot air system, *(FH Air)*, the air is heated as it passes over the heat exchanger. The heated air then moves through the *plenum*, which is the area just above the heat exchanger, and it goes through the *vents* to heat the house.

4. When the temperature in the house gets high enough to satisfy the thermostat setting, the thermostat tells the heating system burner or coils to shut off.

Advantages of different heating systems:

◊ *Forced Hot Air Systems:*   FH Air systems have the benefit of being used for central air-conditioning with the same ducts. If the furnace fails in the winter, there are no heating pipes to freeze. However, the house water pipes will freeze unless they've been drained. You can remove dust from the air and humidify it with a FH Air system.

◊ *Steam Systems:*   Steam systems don't have water in the pipes that can freeze or leak. It doesn't dry out the air in the house. It takes a little longer to heat the house since the water must reach boiling temperatures of 212 degrees Fahrenheit first to make steam.

◊ *Forced Hot Water Systems:*   Forced hot water systems heat faster than steam systems. You don't need to monitor the water level since the system is always filled with water.

◊ *Heat Pump Systems:*   Heat pumps are central air-conditioning systems that work in reverse. They can remove dust and humidify the air. Heat pumps can be used as an A/C system in the warmer months.

Disadvantages of different heat systems:

◊ ⚠ *Forced Hot Air Systems:*   Forced hot air systems have one main drawback. That is, if the heat exchanger leaks, there will be **lethal** carbon monoxide and products of combustion coming out of the vents in the rooms.

◊ *Steam Systems:*   Steam systems do not always have an automatic water feed on the system. When this is the case, the homeowner will have to monitor the water level in the boiler to make sure it doesn't get too high or too low.

◊   *Forced Hot Water Systems:*   Forced hot water systems heating pipes can freeze if the heating system fails in the winter. Also, the pipes can leak over time due to rust and corrosion from constantly being filled with water.

◊   *Heat Pump Systems:*   Heat pumps usually need a backup electric coil heater to assist them in very cold weather. This is because they may not be able to heat the house adequately in very cold weather. Heat pumps are mostly found in warmer climate areas and condo units.

The three most common ways to fuel a heating system are: Oil, Gas and Electric. Heating systems generally have a life expectancy of 20-25 years. Heat pump compressors last about 7-10 years. Often heating systems will last longer, especially the old cast iron boilers. However, it's like an old used car, you never know when it can die. There will be many times that you'll find a heating system that is operating past its normal life expectancy. Just tell the client to budget for a replacement in case the system dies in the near future.

Take a quick look at the heating system just to get a feel for it before turning it on for the test. Check for a service card showing the last date of maintenance service for the heating system. The ceiling over the heating system should have a covering of sheet metal or 5/8 inch fireproof sheetrock to help prevent the spread of fires in this area.

See if there's a data plate on the heating system stating how many BTU's it is. The total heating capacity of a furnace or boiler system is usually measured in BTU's *(British thermal units)* or tonnage. One BTU is the amount of heat that's required to raise the temperature of one pound of water by one degree Fahrenheit. One BTU is about the amount of heat given off by an old-fashioned wood match. An average single family house that's about 2,500 square feet in size should have at least a 125,000 BTU heating system to heat the house adequately. This number will fluctuate up and down based upon many factors. Some of the factors are: how many windows the house has, what type of insulation, if it's a condominium that has a heated condo attached to it on each side, the efficiency rating of that particular heating system, etc. The biggest factors generally are the square footage, the amount and types of windows and insulation in the house. These calculations must be carefully figured out by the heating contractor before they install the system.

There will be times when you find a house with a heating system that's too small to adequately heat in cold weather. Also, if the house has a lower level then your client may want to finish the basement to make a playroom. Another possibility is that your client may be planning to put an addition on the house. Make sure you remind your client that if they plan to heat additional areas of the house, then they need to speak to a heating contractor. Have the heating contractor figure out if the existing heating system is large enough to heat the expanded areas.

You'll also find houses with air-conditioning compressors that are too small to cool the house adequately. These types of problems are caused by an inexperienced contractor who didn't know what he was doing. It could also be caused by a homeowner who wanted to save a few dollars by installing a smaller heating or air-conditioning system.

> *The flue pipe is used to safely discharge the carbon monoxide and other products of combustion.*
> *These gases <u>must be safely discharged</u> from the house.*
> *They're <u>lethal gases!!!</u>*

⚠   Check the flue pipe on gas and oil fired heating systems. The flue pipe is usually located at the rear of the unit. This pipe is used to safely discharge the carbon monoxide and other products of combustion. All gas and oil fired burners discharge these products of combustion. These gases <u>must be safely discharged</u> from the house. They're <u>lethal gases!!!</u> It's similar to having the exhaust fumes from your car discharge inside your house. It'll kill everyone in the house! The sections of the flue pipe <u>must</u> be screwed together for safety. They must have an upward pitch and should not be within four inches of any combustible material, such as wood, to prevent fires.

Some newer heating systems have two plastic exhaust pipes. One pipe has a fan in it to remove the carbon monoxide and unburned gases from the house. These are very efficient heating systems that operate in the 90% efficiency range due to their low flue stack temperature. The temperature inside a normal flue stack is about 400 degrees Fahrenheit. With the low temperature units, the flue stack temperature is only about 100 degrees Fahrenheit. This means that there is a significant savings in the heat loss from the heating system that rises out of the flue stack. Furthermore, some of the newer systems can have a much smaller BTU capacity since they are extremely efficient units.

The drawback to these low temperature units is that they have to be installed *exactly* to the manufacturer's specifications or else there can be problems. Some problems caused are, that the heating contractor who installs the system only puts in one flue pipe. Also, the second plastic flue pipe brings cool air from the outside into the flue piping system. This cool air tends to condensate and soots up the flue pipes causing them to need frequent vacuum cleaning by a heating contractor.

Find out from the owner how many zones the heating system has. A zone is just an area of the house with a separate thermostat that can have a different setting. It's more energy efficient to have extra zones. There can be one zone or as many as you want to install. Turn up all the zone thermostats to engage the heating system for about 25 to 30 minutes to test it. Check for the installation and proper operation of the emergency shutoff switch. It's usually located on the heating system or at the top of the lower level steps. Often the switch will have a red cover plate. It's used to shut the system off during repairs and for emergencies by overriding the thermostat control. Let's say someone is working on the boiler or furnace. If the emergency shutoff switch is in the off position the burner will not turn on in the event that someone accidentally turns up the thermostat.

After the system has run during the test, remember to lower the temperature settings on the thermostats to what the owner had them set on. You don't want to get any angry phone calls from the seller after you get home complaining that you left his thermostats on 90 degrees. Make sure you check all registers and radiators before you turn down the thermostats. You need to see that they're providing heat in each room.

Oil Fired Heating Systems:

Oil fired systems must be tuned up every year by a reputable heating service contractor for efficient operation. Most oil delivery companies will provide a service contract with the owner to service and tune up the oil burner and provide emergency repairs and maintain the oil tanks. The burner flame must be adjusted every year, the oil filters changed, the flue draft regulator adjusted, and the flue pipe cleaned.

Oil is technically about 10% more efficient than natural gas for heating purposes. However, this is *only* if the oil fired system is tuned up properly, which often it isn't. A gas company in my area was sued by the oil companies. They sued because the gas company had a billboard ad that read *"Gas Heats For Less."* A court made the gas company take *"For Less"* off the sign. This is due to oil being a little more efficient than gas.

Don't discourage someone from buying a house with oil or gas heat if you prefer one to the other. Let the client decide which they like better and whether they want to switch to a different type of fuel. Just tell them the facts about the advantages and disadvantages. Oil burners are generally dirtier than natural gas, there are always fluctuating oil prices, and you have to worry about oil deliveries and spills. They're better than gas in the sense that if you have an oil leak your house won't explode as if you had a natural gas leak. Some people fear gas fuel because of the possibility of an explosion.

Oil fired burners may take a few minutes to engage after turning up the thermostats. When the oil burner engages, check for any back-smoking. If the burner doesn't turn on then press the small red button on it. This is a reset switch and should only be used when the system is not responding to the thermostat.

Be aware some Realtors and homeowners mistake the *burner* for the *boiler*. Sometimes they'll tell you that the house has a new boiler installed. When you view the boiler, you'll realize it's only a new oil burner that's been installed. This confusion happens at times with the water heater as well. A third party tells you the boiler is new and you'll find that it's the water heater that's new.

The normal pressure of the oil going into the burner is at 100 psi, *(pounds per square inch).* Some newer equipment will run at 140 psi. The oil pump creates this pressure. The oil pump is a small attachment on the side of the burner where the oil supply lines lead into. Sometimes you'll see a pressure gauge on the oil pump. This suggests that the oil service contractor may have had some trouble maintaining proper oil pressure. The gauge is installed to monitor the pressure easily. Rumbling noises from the burner or smoky fires are conditions of oil pressure that's too low.

The burner flame shouldn't be too strong or too weak. It should just barely touch the back of the firebox, which is the firebrick lining where the flame is. Check the condition of the firebox. See if there's any rust. There should also be a brick lining to prevent the burner flames from directly hitting the metal casing of the boiler/furnace. This will increase the life expectancy of the heating system since the metal will not be subjected to unnecessary heat. See if the bricks of the lining have deteriorated from high temperature.

Check the oil feed *(supply)* lines. These supply lines should be made of copper and be covered to prevent damage or a tripping hazard. They usually have a cement covering over the lines to protect them from damage. If the location of the oil tank is inside the lower level of the house, then there may only be one oil feed line. The reason for this is that gravity will be sufficient to assist the oil pump. If the oil tank is underground then it should have two feed lines. One line is for suction and one line is the return line. If there aren't two lines then the system could lose it's prime for the suction of the oil. If this happens then the homeowner will have to keep pressing the reset button on the oil burner until the oil lines are re-bled.

Check for a firematic shutoff valve within six feet of the burner. This valve is needed to safely shut off the fuel. This valve looks like a miniature water faucet handle. The purpose of this is to be able to shut off the flow of oil if it's necessary. The firematic shutoff valve is different from the emergency shutoff switch. It's different because this valve doesn't turn off the burner, it shuts off the oil supply. The firematic shutoff valve should be spring loaded with a lead center or stopper. In case of an unwanted fire in the burner area, the lead center will melt and the valve will seal itself.

> *If there's an underground oil tank, a Petro-Test by an oil contractor should be performed to find out if there are any leaks. A Petro-Test is a pressure test that an oil contractor performs.*

Check the condition of the oil filter. The location of the oil filter should be near the oil burner or the oil tank. Check the oil tank if it's located in the interior of the house and is visible. I prefer interior oil tanks more than underground tanks due to the potential expense of a leak. There have been Environmental Protection Agency court rulings about leaking oil tanks that incur stiff fines for the owner of the leaking tanks. It's also expensive to dispose of oil tanks because they're considered a contaminated waste, like asbestos and toxic chemicals.

If there's an underground oil tank, recommend that a licensed environmental contractor perform tests to find out if there are leaks. There are a number of different tests to detect a leaking oil tank. A *Petro-Test* is a pressure test that an oil contractor performs. What they do is seal off the oil tank vents and feed lines and pump air into the tank. They then monitor the pressure in the tank to determine if it drops. A drop in pressure would indicate a leak. Another test is a Water Test. If an oil tank leaks there's a good chance water will enter it. The contractor will check the tank to see if there's any water in it. Soil samples could also be taken around and under the tank to determine if oil has leaked in the ground.

There are positive and negative aspects to each test. Petro testing is not recommended by some contractors. This is because the testing pressure put on an old oil tank can create a leak. My feeling is that if the tank is so old and rusty that a Petro test creates a hole, then the tank is on its last leg anyway! If you did another type of test and it came back OK, then the home buyer would have a false sense of security. After they move-in the tank is going to leak. The buyer won't even be thinking about testing that tank again because they got the "green light" from the prepurchase tank test. The other tests don't put stress on an old tank but they won't detect a tank that's about to leak. Tell the client to ask the environmental contractor about the positive and negative aspects of each test. Also, tell the client to make sure they have the home seller's approval for any testing done at the site. I've heard of seller's suing potential home buyer's for creating a leak in their underground oil tank. Supposedly, the tank was fine until the buyer's had a petro-test done which created a leak from the pressure put on the tank.

Tell the client to determine if any Certificate of Occupancy's, permits, or surveys are needed in the local municipality with underground oil tanks. The client should also determine if there are any **unused** underground oil tanks. Occasionally you'll find an older house that has an interior oil tank that's clearly not the original tank. There are two reasons for an updated oil tank: 1) The interior oil tank rusted out and was replaced or 2) The underground oil tank was disconnected and an interior tank installed in its place.

When an underground oil tank is disconnected, it must be drained and removed from the soil. There's no getting around the fact that *all* metal tanks rust out over time. As a result, you cannot just disconnect an underground tank and leave it in the soil. When the tank gets too rusty it will collapse. This is a safety hazard if someone happens to be walking above the tank when it caves in. Moreover, if there is any oil left in the tank when it's disconnected, this will leak out and contaminate the soil. If that happens, your client will have a safety hazard

and an environmental hazard on his hands! Some town building codes allow the homeowner to leave the tank in the soil for up to one year from the time it's disconnected. But after that one year, the tank has to be pulled out of the ground. There are also some building codes that allow the tanks to be filled with sand or some other material. Just tell the client to check town hall for the local codes.

Interior and underground oil tanks made of metal will generally last about 25 to 30 years. They can last longer if they're interior tanks and they have been maintained. If there are a lot of evergreen trees around the area where an oil tank is buried, it will cut down the life expectancy of the tank. This is because evergreen trees add a lot of acid into the soil that rots the tanks quicker.

Interior oil tanks are usually a 275 gallon capacity and they're thinner than underground tanks. Fiberglass patches can be put on the tanks. Underground tanks can be up to a 1,000 gallon capacity, and can discharge an awful lot of oil if they leak. An oil contractor can patch an underground oil tank if it's needed. They cut a hole in the top of the tank that measures about two feet by two feet. The tank is emptied and sandblasted on the interior. Then a fiberglass lining is installed to coat the inside.

You have to keep interior oil tanks well painted to prevent rust. You'll find some that have been patched due to rust or leaks. You just need to find out if they're leaking now. If there's oil on the tank it doesn't necessarily mean that they're leaking now. Often the oil spills over a little when the tank is filled.

Check the draft regulator on the flue pipe. It looks like a small swinging door with a counter balance at the top or bottom. The draft regulator needs to be adjusted every year with the tune up of the system. The purpose of it is to allow cool air from the boiler room area to help the removal of carbon monoxide up the chimney. The draft regulator helps remove the carbon monoxide without letting too much heat from the boiler or furnace go up the chimney. Often this door won't swing properly or will be screwed shut. This is an improper operation and repairs will be needed to correct this. If you find the draft regulator door sealed shut, it indicates that the heating service repairman was having trouble obtaining an adequate draft in the chimney flue stack. This can also suggest that the flue stack needs to be swept clean.

Gas Fired Heating Systems:

⚠ Check for a gas shutoff valve within six feet of the burner. This is needed to safely shut off the fuel. There <u>must</u> have approved black iron gas piping for the supply lines. No copper or other materials should be used that aren't approved to carry gas fuel.

Check for the proper color of the burner flames. They should be as blue as possible with very little yellow or orange color. Too much yellow or orange color means that the fuel and air mixture needs to be adjusted. There's very little maintenance with a gas system. You just need to have the flame adjusted when it's not blue and clean out the flue pipe periodically.

There should be a thermocouple in the gas burner assembly for safety. It looks like a thin metal wire, leading to a cone shaped metal part inside the burner area, next to the pilot light. The purpose of this is to make sure that the pilot light is always lit when gas is supplied to the unit. This will help prevent gas leaking from an unlit pilot opening. When the pilot light is burning it heats up the thermocouple cone and sends an electrical current through the thermocouple to the gas burner assembly. The electrical current keeps the gas valve open. If the pilot light goes out, then the thermocouple will cool. If this happens, the electrical current will cease to the gas assembly. This should close off the gas from entering the pilot light burner jet.

Check the draft diverter hood at the base of the flue pipe. This has a very similar purpose as the oil fired draft regulator door. The draft diverter hood is used to keep downdrafts from the chimney from blowing out the pilot light. It's also designed to help keep the heat inside the boiler or furnace while the carbon monoxide is removed up the chimney. This does not need to be adjusted every year like a draft regulator door. There are no moving parts on it. It's just an opening at the base of the flue stack.

Electric Heating Systems:

Depending upon the region you're in, it may be more common to find electric baseboard radiators. It's very rare in my area due to the higher expense of electric heat. Check with the Owner or Realtor about blown fuses or tripped circuit breakers. Sometimes this can be a problem due to the additional electrical usage for electric heating systems.

You'll normally find separate thermostats in each room for electric baseboard radiators. Test all of them during a home inspection. The radiators should get warm quickly. Having a separate thermostat in each room can be a nuisance at times. The homeowner will have to raise and lower many thermostats when trying to conserve energy and adjust the house temperature.

Forced Warm Air Heating Systems:

Forced warm air heating systems have supply ducts, return ducts and vents (registers). The supply ducts and vents bring the warm air into the rooms. There should be at least one supply vent in each room providing heat. The supply vents should be located underneath a window of an exterior wall. This will provide the maximum efficiency since the warm air will mix with any cool, drafty air that comes in through the cracks of the window frames.

The return ducts and vents bring the air back into the heat exchanger where it is reheated and recirculated. If there are return vents in each room then they should be located on the opposite side of the room from the supply vents. This will allow proper circulation of the heated air before it's drawn back into the return duct. If there's a central return then there should at least an inch gap under all interior doors. This will allow the air to be properly recirculated when the interior doors are closed. You can have a return vent in each room or a central return vent on each floor of the house.

Separate heating zones are established by dampers. Dampers are small doors in the supply ducts to open and close the circulation of hot air. Damper doors can be manually or electrically operated. The electrically operated dampers are more expensive to install. During the heating system test, check for warm air discharging from all vents. If you find a weak flow from a vent it could mean that the damper door is closed. Also, the furnace fan may not be strong enough to provide an adequate flow to certain rooms.

Check the air filters for cleanliness. They need to be replaced every few months during the heating season. This is similar to changing your car air and oil filters. If you don't do it often enough, you'll create excess wear and tear on the car due to the lack of maintenance. Electronic air filters are too sophisticated to be evaluated during a home inspection. They send a static electric current through the air that attracts the dust and cleans the air. Just take a look at them for condition and cleanliness. Also, the on and off switch should be lit.

Check the air ducts for insulation. You should see external insulation or tap them to check for internal insulation. If you tap them and you hear a dull thud sound, then they probably have internal insulation. Air ducts can be vacuumed by a heating contractor if too much dirt and dust accumulates inside.

Check for a humidifier which is located in the duct near the heat exchanger plenum area. Forced hot air systems will dry out the air in a house and will lead to the occupants getting sore throats. A humidifier will help prevent this. It looks like a small box on the bottom of the air duct. They usually have a small copper line that is tapped into a plumbing water line to supply the humidifier with water. You're not able to fully test these during a home inspection due to their operation. Some of them are automatic and some have manual controls. Their life expectancy is about 5-7 years.

The furnace plenum should be separated from the heat exchanger and fan area by a canvas or flexible type of material. This will help prevent any vibrations caused by the blower fan from being transmitted through the ducts and into the livable rooms.

Open any panels on the heating system that don't require tools. You should be able to view the heat exchanger and the fan. Use an extendable mirror, if necessary, to view as much of the heat exchanger as possible. Just be careful when you do this, you don't want to get your hands burned or cut. Look for any excessive rust or any cracks. Some units are sealed systems that require tools. Tell the client that you're limited due to the sealed system.

Check the fan for any unusual noises. There may be a shutoff switch on the fan panel door. This switch will shut off the fan when the panel door is opened. It's similar to a refrigerator light switch that turns on when the door is opened and turns off when it's closed. The fan operates by a temperature control and not by the thermostat in the livable rooms. The purpose of this is to keep the fan *off* until the air is warm enough to be circulated. You don't want cold air being blown out of the vents in the winter time! The temperature control will also keep the fan *on* when the thermostat is satisfied and the burners have turned off. Warm air is still in the heat exchanger shortly after the burners turn off. For energy efficiency, the fan can continue to circulate this warm air after the burners turn off.

If you're inspecting a very old house, you may come across a **gravity** hot air heating system. It's very rare to find a gravity heating system but just be aware that some are still out there. Basically, a gravity system will have most of the same components as a forced hot air system. However, there won't be a fan to circulate the heated air through the house. Many years ago when gravity systems were designed, fans were not installed. Fans weren't used because hot air rises on its own accord. The air ducts for a gravity system had to be very wide to allow easy passage of the hot air. The problem with a gravity heating system is that it takes too long to warm the house since the air movement is so slow. Most of these systems have been updated to forced hot air heat due to the increased energy efficiency of using a fan. Also, the smaller air ducts of a forced air system take up less room in the house. If you ever find a gravity heating system, tell the client to have it updated.

> *If there are any heat exchanger or gas leaks, then notify the client, the Realtor and the seller.*
> *Insist they have the problem checked out IMMEDIATELY before using the heating system again.*

⚠️ 👮 I use a combustible gas detector to test the supply ducts and all visible gas lines for leaks. If the heat exchanger is cracked, it will leak carbon monoxide into the supply ducts where it may be detected by the combustible gas detector. I had a client who had a guest complain of headaches in the upper level bedroom of their house. I checked the supply ducts and there was a carbon monoxide leak from a cracked heat exchanger. This is a very dangerous condition and they had a baby in the house!! If there are any heat exchanger or gas leaks, then notify the client, the Realtor and the seller. Insist that they have the problem checked out *IMMEDIATELY* before using the heating system again.

Heat Pump Heating Systems:

Checking these heating systems is very similar to checking a forced hot air system. Heat pump systems are usually found in condos and warmer climate areas. Heat pumps can have an electric coil in the plenum area to assist these units in very cold weather. The electric coil is a backup heating element to warm the air in the ducts. This will help the unit to provide enough heat in very cold weather, such as, below 20 degrees Fahrenheit.

> *Do not test a heat pump in both the heating and the air-conditioning modes during an inspection. You can damage the compressor by doing this.*

Do not test a heat pump in both the heating and the air-conditioning modes during an inspection. You can damage the compressor by doing this. When it's working properly in one mode, then the most important and costly parts are operating properly.

Check the exterior compressor unit while the heating mode is on. Look at the data plate to try to learn the age of the unit. The life expectancy of the compressor is about 7-10 years since they operate all year long in the heating and A/C modes. The life expectancy also depends upon the quality of the unit and maintenance given to the system. The compressor must be sitting on a sturdy, level foundation, like concrete. Uneven installations can cause premature failure of the compressor because it will be leaning to one side while the unit is running.

See if the compressor is making any unusual noises while it's operating. Check for an exterior service disconnect switch next to the compressor for emergency and repairs shut off. Make sure there's adequate ventilation around the compressor unit for the air intake and blower fan to operate properly. You have to prune all shrubs away and there should be no obstructions overhead. Check the coils for a buildup of leaves, twigs or dirt. Ask the owner or Realtor if the unit can heat the house or condo adequately in the cold months. Sometimes they can't in very cold weather.

Forced Hot Water Heating Systems:

Forced hot water heating systems have supply and return plumbing lines to carry the heated water. They have supply lines that bring the heated water to the radiators in each room. They have return lines to bring the water back to the boiler, after it has given off its heat, to be reheated and recirculated.

There should be at least one radiator in each room. The radiators should be located underneath a window of an exterior wall. This will provide the maximum efficiency since the warm air will mix with any cool, drafty air that comes in through the cracks of the window frames. Radiators need to be *bled* about once per year. When a contractor "bleeds" a radiator, they merely open a small valve on the radiator to allow trapped air to escape. This leaves space for hot water to heat the radiator efficiently. Sometimes you'll find that only a few radiators don't get warm during your heating system test. Usually this is because the radiators need to be bled or the handle valve is turned off. Either of these conditions can be easily corrected.

Separate heating zones are established by circulator pumps or zone valves on the return pipes. The pumps or valves open and close the circulation of hot water. Circulator pumps look like a round attachment located on the return line of the boiler. When the circulator pump isn't running, the water is blocked by the pump. As a result, no water can pass through the lines to the boiler to be circulated. Zone valves are small attachments with wires leading to them on the return lines before they reach the circulator pump. When the zone valve is shut, no water can pass through that zone, even if the circulator pump is running.

One type of zone installation has a circulator pump on the return line in the back of the boiler. Then there are separate zone valves on the return lines before they reach the circulator pump. Another type of zone installation is to have a separate circulator pump for each zone return line leading back to the boiler.

Circulator pumps need just a drop of oil in the oil ports maybe once a year. Tell the client to have the service contractor check this with the tune ups. If the circulator pump is operating properly then you'll be able to see the bearings spinning in the visible areas. Also, the return line will begin to get warm.

Sometimes an aqua stat controls the circulator pump. This will keep the circulator turned off until the water gets warm enough in the boiler. The purpose of this is to prevent cold water from being sent to the radiators. After the house thermostat shuts off the burner, the circulator will usually keep running. Since there's is hot water in the boiler, the circulator still runs for energy efficiency.

If you're inspecting a very old house, you may come across a **gravity** hot water heating system. As I noted earlier, it's very rare to find a gravity heating system. A gravity hot water system will have most of the same components as a forced hot water system. However, there won't be a circulator pump to push the heated water through the house. Circulator pumps weren't used years ago because hot water rises on its own. The water pipes for a gravity system had to be much wider to allow easy passage of the hot water. Once again, the problem with a gravity heating system is that it takes too long to warm the house since the water movement is so slow. Most of these systems have been updated to forced hot water heat due to the increased energy efficiency of using a circulator. If you ever find a gravity heating system, tell the client to have it updated.

Check all heating pipe joints and the circulator for rust or leaking conditions that'll require repairs. You'll usually find some rust unless it's a new unit. Open any panels on the heating system that don't require tools. You should be able to view the heat exchanger and the firebox. Some units are sealed systems that require tools or can't be opened. Tell the client that you're limited due to the sealed system.

Check the heat exchanger for any rust or leaking conditions. Check the condition of the firebox where the burner flame is. Often the firebrick in an oil fired unit will be deteriorated from the long exposure to the heat of the burner. A new lining can usually be installed in the firebox without a major expense.

Check for a water pressure reducing valve for hot water systems. This is a small valve that looks like a miniature bell. It's located on the water line that brings water to the boiler from the plumbing system. This reduces the water pressure that's coming from the house plumbing lines. The pressure in the house plumbing lines is usually about 30 to 60 psi *(pounds per square inch)*. The water pressure reducing valve will lower the water pressure down to about 12 to 15 psi before it enters the boiler. I'll explain the reason for reducing the water pressure in a minute.

For hot water systems, there should be a backflow preventer next to the water pressure reducing valve. This prevents water that has entered the boiler from recirculating backwards into the house plumbing lines. The purpose is to prevent the unsanitary boiler water from mixing with the faucet and shower water supply for the rest of the house.

Sometimes your client will ask you, *"Do I have to add water to the boiler during the heating season?"* You don't have to add water to a forced hot water heating system because the boiler water supply valve is always open. Therefore, water enters the system on it's own whenever necessary. For safety, there should be a low water cutoff switch on the boiler in case the water level drops too low. These devices will automatically turn off the boiler when the water level gets too low for proper operation of the heating system. If someone closes the water supply valve or there is a problem with the pipes, you don't want the boiler to become empty. This can be a dangerous condition if the burner turns on because there won't be anything to transfer the heat to.

Check for an expansion tank on the boiler room ceiling for hot water systems. This is a metal tank that allows the heated water to expand. When you heat water, it expands. When water freezes it expands as well. The heated water needs a cushion to expand or else it'll burst some pipe joints. Also, heated water that doesn't have a cushion will discharge the pressure relief valve to relieve the pressure. The expansion tank has an air pocket or a rubber bag inside it. This cushions the water as it expands so the pressure in the system doesn't get too high. Expansion tanks need to be checked periodically for water logging problems. They should have a bleeder valve to put air in it if the tank becomes waterlogged. Check for a drainage valve on the bottom. These valves should be drained at least once a year to remove any rust and sediment that build up in the tank.

Check for a properly operating pressure gauge. The gauge should move while the boiler is being tested. You should tap all pressure gauges with your finger before viewing them to take a reading. Many times you'll find that the needle inside of these gauges will stick. You should also tap the gauges while checking the pressure during any testing to make sure the needle is moving properly. The proper operating pressure for a hot water heating system is 12-22 pounds per square inch. Make sure the pressure doesn't go too high and record the readings you get. There may also be a water temperature gauge in the pressure gauge. Monitor this temperature periodically during the test and record the reading.

Check for a pressure relief valve on the boiler. This is a safety device that helps prevent the heating system from becoming dangerously high in pressure. If the pressure reaches 30 psi, then the valve will discharge to relieve the system so the boiler won't explode. This is why the water pressure reducing valve has to lower the house water pressure before it enters the heating system lines. It lowers the water pressure so the pressure relief valve won't discharge right away. Let's say the water entered the boiler at the normal house water pressure of 30 to 60 psi. Then the pressure relief valve would discharge, without even turning on the heating system.

> *The pressure relief valve must be located directly on the boiler unit for proper operation. It must be piped to within eight inches of the floor to prevent scalding anyone when the valve discharges.*

⚠ The pressure relief valve must not be rusty and must be located directly on the boiler for proper operation. It *must* be piped to within eight inches of the floor to prevent scalding anyone when the valve discharges. When water or steam discharges from this valve, then there's a problem and a heating repairman has to check out the system. Sometimes you will find a hose attached to the relief valve leading into a sink or drain. This is not recommended for *any* pressure relief valves. The reason is that the homeowner must know that the valve is discharging so they can see there is a problem

condition. If the valve drains into a sink, the homeowner might not be aware of any problems that need repairs.

There should be a drain valve on the lower part of the boiler. It's usually in the rear and looks like a water faucet bib. This valve is used to drain about a half gallon of water into a bucket each month. This removes the rust and sediment that normally build up in the system. It's similar to the necessity of changing the air filters on FH Air heating systems or on air-conditioning systems. Drain a small amount of water into a bucket to determine the color and see if the system has been maintained and properly drained monthly. If the water that comes out is very dirty, then the heating system has not been maintained properly and this will cut down its life expectancy. If the water that comes out is clean, then the heating system probably has been maintained properly and this will increase its life expectancy.

Steam Heating Systems:

Testing a steam heating system is very similar to checking a hot water heating system. I'll mention some differences, but it may seem repetitive to the hot water system section. A steam system has a sight glass on the side of the boiler. This allows you to see the water level in the boiler. The sight glass should be 1/2 to 3/4 of the way full. It shouldn't be completely empty or completely full which can cause problems. The sight glass level allows you to see that there's air and water in the boiler. This is because you're making steam and you've got to have room for the heated water to boil and create steam.

> *A steam system has a sight glass on the side of the boiler. This allows you to see the water level in the boiler. The sight glass should be 1/2 to 3/4 of the way full.*

If the sight glass is completely filled with water, it could mean that the pipes are flooded because the water supply valve for the boiler was left open. This will lead to water discharging from the vents on the radiators. If the sight glass is completely empty, it could mean that the boiler has no water in it. This is a dangerous condition if the burner turns on because there won't be anything to transfer the heat to. For safety, there should be a low water cutoff switch on the boiler in case the water level drops too low. These devices will automatically turn off the boiler when the water level gets too low for proper operation of the heating system. An automatic water feed can be installed on steam heating systems. These devices are attached to the water supply pipe leading into the boiler. They automatically monitor the water level inside the boiler and add water whenever necessary.

Steam heating systems have supply and return plumbing lines to carry steam and condensation. You have supply lines that bring the steam to the radiators in each room. The return lines bring the condensation water back to the boiler after the steam has given off its heat. After the steam gives off its heat, it condenses into water and is reboiled and recirculated. There should be at least one radiator in each room.

There are no circulator pumps like on a hot water system, because steam rises on its own. As a result, steam systems have wider diameter pipes than forced hot water systems. Separate heating zones are established by zone valves on the supply pipes to open and close the circulation of steam.

Check all heating pipe joints for rust or leaking conditions that'll require repairs. You'll usually find some rust unless it's a new unit. Open any panels on the heating system that don't require tools. You should be able to view the heat exchanger and the firebox. Check the heat exchanger for rust or leaking conditions. Check the condition of the firebox where the burner flame is.

There's no water pressure reducing valve, backflow preventer or expansion tank for steam systems. This is because there's only water in 3/4 of the boiler and these items aren't needed. The supply and return lines have mostly air in them to allow for the passage of the steam.

Check for a properly operating pressure gauge. The gauge should move while the boiler is being tested. The proper operating pressure for a steam heating system is 2-5 psi. Make sure the pressure doesn't go too high and record the readings you get. There may be a water temperature gauge combined with the pressure gauge also. Monitor the water temperature during the test and record the readings.

Steam heating systems should have an upper limit switch installed directly on the boiler. The upper limit switch looks like a small electrical relay box. It's attached to the boiler by a copper pipe that's looped in the shape of a pig tail. The purpose of the pig tail is to trap water in the loop so the steam in the system doesn't rust out the upper limit switch controls. If the pressure in a steam heating system gets too high, then the upper limit switch is designed to electrically turn off the burner so that the system pressure doesn't keep rising.

⚠️ Check for a pressure relief valve on the boiler. This is a safety device that helps prevent the heating system from becoming dangerously high in pressure. If the pressure reaches 15 psi, then the valve will discharge to relieve the system so the boiler won't explode. When water or steam discharges from this valve, it indicates a problem condition. When this happens, the system _must_ be checked out immediately by a licensed heating contractor. Pressure relief valves should not be rusty and they must be located directly on the boiler for proper operation. The valve _must_ be piped to within eight inches of the floor to prevent scalding anyone if it discharges.

There should be a drain valve on the lower part of the boiler. Drain a small amount of water into a bucket to determine the color. You can get an indication of whether the system has been maintained and properly drained monthly by the color of the water.

Hydro-Therm Heating Systems:

A hydro-therm heating system is simply a combination of a forced hot water system with a forced hot air heating system. The way it's set up is, the boiler heats the water and sends it through pipes. These pipes carry the heated water through the inside of the air duct for a forced air system. The benefit of this type of system is that usually there is no need to install a humidifier on the system. A humidifier isn't needed because the warm air that's circulated isn't as dry as the air from a typical forced hot air heating system.

Hybrid and Radiant Heating Systems:

There will be times that you'll find _hybrid_ types of heating systems. This refers to a heating system that has been adapted for an individual homeowner by a heating contractor. This is a modified design installation. The most common types of hybrid systems you'll encounter are combination steam and forced hot water heaters. A steam system can have a circulator pump installed to circulate the hot water in the heat exchanger. These pipes will lead to forced hot water radiators that have been put in after the steam boiler was installed. If you ever run into a problem where you can't properly evaluate a hybrid heating system, then just tell the client to speak with the contractor who installed it. The contractor should be able to provide further information.

Radiant heat is another example of unusual heating systems you may encounter. _Radiant heat_ is a system where the heating coils or pipes are inside the floors, walls, or ceilings of a home. As the coils or pipes heat up, they will radiate the heat into the rooms. These systems can be expensive to install and operate.

Heating System photos:
P 1-P 25, P 157, P 158, P 202-P 205

Air-Conditioning System

Air-Conditioning systems are no different than any other aspect of home inspections. Due to the rapidly changing technology, you have to keep on top of the updated equipment and techniques that are being used in new construction. Find a knowledgeable contractor in your area and buy him lunch occasionally to learn about any developments in his industry.

I'll try to walk you through the basic concept of how an air-conditioning system works. If it seems too technical, don't worry. You only need to know how to decide if the A/C system is operating properly at the time of the inspection. I'm including the inner workings of an air-conditioning system because I believe it's a great help. By knowing this information, you'll earn the respect of the client and any third parties if they ever ask you how the system operates and cools the air.

1.   The basic components of an air-conditioning system are the compressor, condenser coil, receiver, expansion device and evaporator coil. Some newer units don't have an expansion device.

2.   The *evaporator coil* is what cools and removes excess moisture from the air. It looks similar to the radiator of a car. This is the part that's located inside the house in what's sometimes called the *air handler*. The air is cooled by using a "refrigerant" which cycles between the different system components.

3.   *Freon 12* and *Freon 22* are the refrigerants used in most gas compression refrigeration systems for residential use. Freon 12 has a boiling point of below -20 degrees Fahrenheit at atmospheric pressure. Freon 22 has a boiling point of below -40 degrees Fahrenheit at atmospheric pressure.

4.   The A/C cycle starts with the refrigerant *(Freon)* contained initially in the receiver. The *receiver* is usually located in the lower section of the *condenser*. While inside the condenser, the Freon is cooled by the outside air being blown over the coils. The *compressor* acts as a pump and forces the Freon under high pressure through the liquid line to the *expansion device.*

5.   The flow of Freon into the evaporator coil is regulated by the expansion device. As the high-pressure liquid Freon is forced through the expansion device, it expands into a larger volume in the evaporator. As it expands, the pressure and temperature are reduced. Due to the low boiling temperature of Freon, it boils when under this low pressure until it becomes a vapor. During this change of state, the Freon absorbs heat from the warm interior house air which is flowing across the outside of the evaporator.

6.   The Freon vapor is pumped out of the evaporator through the suction line to the compressor after it has absorbed the heat from the interior house air. The compressor then compresses the Freon vapor, increasing its temperature and pressure and forces it along to the condenser.

7.   The hot Freon vapor is cooled at the condenser unit by lower temperature air being blown over the condenser coils. This absorbs some of the heat in the Freon. As a result, the Freon temperature decreases until the Freon is cooled to its saturation condition. When the Freon reaches its saturation condition, it will cause the vapor to condense into a liquid. The liquid, still under high pressure, flows to the expansion device and completes the air-conditioning cycle.

8.   Cold is never created during the air-conditioning cycle. Instead, heat is merely transferred from one place to another. When the Freon passes through the evaporator, it absorbs heat from the room air which cools it. When the higher temperature Freon passes through the condenser, it gives up its heat to the air being blown over it.

An air-conditioning system is a closed system, and theoretically, there should never be a need for additional Freon. However, the various fittings on the connecting pipes can loosen or develop small cracks. Any loose connections or cracks can allow some Freon gas to escape. If the air-conditioning system cannot hold a Freon charge for at least one season, then the leaks in the pipes or fittings should be located and corrected.

◊   *Testing Air-Conditioning Systems:*

Don't turn on any central or window or wall air-conditioning units when the outdoor air temperature is 65 degrees Fahrenheit or lower. The interior pressure that's required to properly operate an air-conditioning system is too low when the temperature is 65 degrees or lower. If the unit is turned on, there are several ways that you could damage the compressor or other components and end up buying the owner a new A/C system.

> *Don't turn on any central or window or wall A/C units when the outdoor air temperature is 65 degrees Fahrenheit or lower. If the unit is turned on, there are a number of ways that you could damage the compressor or other components.*

There are devices that are placed on the condensing unit that can maintain the proper pressure in the system down to zero degrees Fahrenheit. Some air-conditioning units have compressor crank case heaters around the base of the compressor. Most heat pumps have these heaters and they're left on all year long. This will keep the compressor oil warm so it will start up smoother. But unless you know about these devices being installed, then I wouldn't take any chances. You're paid to inspect the house, not gamble with the sellers' property.

Don't listen to anyone that says you can test the system anyway when the outdoor temperature is too cold. Let them turn on the system so if it blows, then they have to pay for it. I've heard a few war stories about poorly trained home inspectors that turned on A/C systems in the winter time and ended up blowing the compressors. Don't let this happen to you.

I once was doing an inspection at the end of the winter time and it wasn't warm enough to test the air-conditioning system. Unfortunately, there was a *"know-it-all"* Realtor at the inspection who had been a little hostile from the time I showed up. Anyway, I told my client that I couldn't test the air-conditioning system. I told the client that they should test the system before closing on the house when the weather was warmer. This know-it-all Realtor kept insisting that I test the system that day. I just turned to them and said, *"Listen, if you know so much more than I do about home inspections and air-conditioning systems, then you turn on the air-conditioning system. And if the compressor blows, then tell the owner to send you the bill for a new one because you're the one who turned the system on."* For some strange reason this Realtor never turned on the A/C system. I also never heard a word out of that person for the rest of the inspection. Unfortunately, that's the way you have to be with some people because they think they know everything, but they just talk out of ignorance. I'll explain more about this at the end of the book.

Window and wall air-conditioning units can only by spot checked for proper operation. Remind the client to find out if they're being sold with the house. Turn the units on briefly to see if any cool air is discharging. Check the cleanliness of the air filters.

Central air-conditioning testing is very similar to the forced hot air heating system test. Review the forced hot air section for any additional information. I'll try to highlight some of the differences. Remember that if the unit is a Heat Pump, *don't* test it in both the heating and air-conditioning modes during an inspection. You can damage the unit if it's tested in both modes. If a heat pump is operating in one mode, it shows that the most important and costly parts are operating properly.

Some houses have a separate air-conditioning system for each zone. Check with the owner or Realtor about how many zones there are and the location of the air-conditioning components. You have supply and return ducts and vents *(registers)*. Check the air ducts for insulation. In expensive houses with forced hot air heat and central air-conditioning, you may find what are called *high-low* registers. Low registers are supply vents located on the floor of each room, which provide heat during the colder months. High registers are supply vents located near the ceiling of each room, which provide cool air during the warmer months. This is an energy efficient installation because heat rises upward and cold air falls downward. As a result, in the winter time the homeowner just has to close the damper doors for the high registers to get the maximum heating efficiency. In the summer time, the

homeowner just has to close the damper doors for the low registers to get the maximum air-conditioning efficiency.

Check the air filters for cleanliness. They need to be replaced every few months during the air-conditioning season. Any electronic air filters are too sophisticated to be evaluated during a home inspection. Just check the condition of them and see if the on and off switch is lit.

An air handler plenum is the section that has the blower fan and the evaporator coil in it. All air handler plenums should be separated from the air ducts by canvas or flexible materials. The location of the air handler will be in the lower level or in the attic. Sometimes the attic air handlers will be hanging from the roof rafters by strong bolts and brackets. The compressor is located on the exterior of the house.

Open any panels on the air-conditioning system that don't require tools. You should be able to view the evaporator coil and the fan. Some units are sealed systems that require tools. If this is the case, then tell the client that you're limited due to the sealed system.

Check the fan for any unusual noises. Check the evaporator coil for any rusting conditions. The evaporator coil looks like a car radiator. It's located in the air handler area of the system which is the section that contains the blower fan unit.

Freon passes through the evaporator coil while the system is running. The fan blows air over the coil and as a result, the air is cooled by the Freon. This forms condensation due to the humidity in the interior house air. The condensation drains into a pan which leads to a drainage line. Often you'll find a small plastic box that's a condensate pump that removes the condensation to a suitable location. The life expectancy of these pumps is about 5-7 years.

> *Check the supply vents with a thermometer to determine that the discharging air is cool enough. The air temperature should be about 55-58 degrees Fahrenheit.*

Check the supply vents with a thermometer to determine that the discharging air is cool enough. The air temperature should be about 55-58 degrees Fahrenheit. If the discharging air isn't cool enough, then it usually means that the system needs a recharge of Freon. This could suggest that there's a Freon leak that needs to be repaired. It's usually not a major expense to recharge an air-conditioning system with Freon.

Check the exterior compressor unit while the air-conditioning system is on. Check the data plate to try to figure out the age and size of the unit. The life expectancy of a compressor is about 10 years depending upon the amount of usage. The life expectancy also depends on the quality of the unit and the maintenance given to the system. Some homeowners will use their air-conditioning systems every day of the summer. Other homeowners will only turn on the A/C when it's an abnormally hot and humid day. Generally, the more the system is operating, then the shorter the remaining life expectancy due to the wear and tear of usage.

The size of an air-conditioning system is measured in tons. A one ton system will provide 12,000 BTU's of cooling in an hour. When an air-conditioning system is rated in BTU's per hour, it indicates the amount of heat that the unit will remove in that time. Generally, one ton is large enough to cool about a 550-700 square foot area. The square foot area will depend upon many factors, such as the type of windows, insulation, height of rooms, etc. Many times you will not find a clearly marked BTU rating on the compressor data plate. Some manufacturers use a coded numbering system on the data plate. This code will indicate an abbreviated number for the compressor's BTU rating. If the BTU's are not clearly marked, then check the data plate for a full load amperage rating, marked *FLA*. There will also be a rated load amperage rating, marked *RLA*. Since there are about 7 amps for each ton of cooling capacity, if you divide the FLA by 7, then you can estimate the tonnage of the compressor. Some of the newer units have "scroll" compressors and not the piston compressors. The scroll compressors use less electricity and the FLA divided by 7 will not be accurate for tonnage estimates. Just do the best you can and tell the client to speak to the A/C contractor for more details.

It is better for an air-conditioning system to be slightly undersized as opposed to being slightly oversized. The reason for this is that a unit that has too much cooling capacity for a house will short cycle. Meaning that the system will turn on and off too frequently because the thermostat will be satisfied quickly due to the high cooling capacity of the system. The drawback to this short cycling is that the rooms will not be adequately dehumidified since the unit will be constantly turning on and off too quickly.

The air-conditioning compressor must be sitting on a sturdy, level foundation, like concrete. Uneven installations can cause premature failure of the compressor because it will be leaning to one side while running. Check for any unusual noises while it's operating. Check for an exterior service disconnect switch that should be next to the compressor for emergency and repairs shut off. Make sure there's adequate ventilation around the compressor unit for the air intake and blower fan to operate properly. You have to prune all shrubs away and there should be no obstructions overhead. Check the coils for a buildup of leaves, twigs or dirt.

Check the high and low pressure Freon lines. These are the pipe lines that carry Freon, or the refrigerant, to the compressor and condenser unit and back to the evaporator coil unit. These lines should be made of copper. The low pressure line is the larger pipe, about 3/4 inch in diameter. This line needs to be insulated for energy efficiency since it has cold Freon in it. You'll usually find a black foam insulation over the low pressure line. The high pressure line is the thin diameter line and it doesn't need to be insulated.

Air-Conditioning System photos: P 28-P 37

Domestic Water Heater

Usually the water heaters are a separate unit but can be immersion coils inside boilers. An immersion coil system has water pipes that carry cold water inside a coil located in the side of the boiler. The coils are *immersed* in the hot boiler water, hence you get the name *immersion coils*.

The cold water in the pipes doesn't mix with the boiler water. If it did, then the dirty boiler water would be carried back to the faucets and showers. This would be a health problem. The cold water is kept inside pipes that look like a snake with many different loops inside the boiler. The purpose of the coils is to allow the cold water in the pipes to be heated by the surrounding hot boiler water. Then the heated water is carried to the faucets and showers of the house.

Some advantages are that an immersion coil system allows free hot water in the winter time. Free hot water is available because the boiler is on anyway to heat the house. Sometimes immersion coils have valves to adjust the hot and cold mixture. The disadvantages are that an immersion coil system isn't as energy efficient as using a separate water heater in the summer months. Also, an immersion coil system adds an unwanted heat load on the house in the warmer months due to the boiler being on. Since the boiler has to operate all year round, it will cut down the life expectancy of the heating system. Furthermore, immersion coils can clog over time and need occasional cleaning due to the minerals in water.

Newer types of immersion coil systems are called *indirect-fired* water heaters. At first glance, indirect-fired units look like separate water heaters. However, indirect-fired units do not have burners to heat the water at the base of the tank. As a result, they last much longer than separate water heaters because there are no burners that deteriorate the tank. The immersion coils in the boiler have a circulator pump on them. This pumps the heated water from the boiler immersion coils to the storage tank. Since you're basically dealing with an immersion coil system, you have the disadvantage of operating the boiler in the summer.

Separate water heater units can be gas, oil or electrically heated. Review the furnace or boiler section on the differences between gas, oil and electrically operated heaters and the inspection process involved.

Oil fired water heaters have a very fast recovery rate. This refers to the rate at which they can reheat the water. On oil fired units there should be a water temperature setting switch. The purpose of this is to operate like a thermostat. Water temperature switches regulate the burners to turn on and off to keep the water at a preset temperature. The factory recommended setting is usually at 125-130 degrees

Fahrenheit. If the temperature is set too high, then someone can get scalded with very hot water.

Gas fired water heaters usually have a dial type of temperature setting. You'll find the dial temperature switch located directly on the gas burner assembly near the bottom of the water heater tank.

Electrically operated water heaters have coils that are directly immersed in the water inside the tank. This is different from the oil and gas fired heaters. Oil and gas fired units heat the water holding tank and then the heat dissipates to the water inside the tank. Electric units usually aren't as energy efficient as gas or oil fired units. The reason for this is that electricity can be more expensive than the other fuels. Often you'll find electric water heaters in condos or in areas where gas service isn't available.

Electrically operated water heaters usually have two temperature setting dials inside the small cover plates on the side of the tank. Don't remove these panel covers due to the potential hazards of electricity. I once tried to remove the temperature setting cover on an electric water heater. There was a big spark as soon as I loosened the screw. The circuit breaker in the main electrical panel tripped off after this happened. When I removed the cover on the water heater, I found an exposed wire. Apparently the metal cover plate was installed too close to the temperature dial wires. This caused a small section of the wire insulation to be cut, leaving an exposed wire. We later found out that this water heater manufacturer recommends the circuit breaker be turned off *before* opening the temperature panel cover. I was certainly lucky that circuit breaker was working properly.

> *The standard size water heater for a single family house is 40 gallons. An oversized water heater isn't as energy efficient because a lot of water will be heated and then it will just sit in the tank without being used.*

The standard size water heater for a single family house is 40 gallons. Sometimes you'll find an oversized water heater in the house. An oversized water heater isn't as energy efficient because a lot of water will be heated and then it will just sit in the tank without being used.

Check for any rust or water leaking conditions on the unit. Excessive rust or leaks will indicate that a new water heater is needed. Check for a temperature/pressure relief valve on the unit. The inspection process for this valve is almost identical to what was discussed in the boiler section for the pressure relief valve. However, the difference is that the relief valve on a water heater is both temperature **and** pressure sensitive. Make sure the relief valve is piped to within eight inches of the floor for safety when discharging. The valve should have a data plate on it that's usually rated to discharge at 150 psi and 210 degrees Fahrenheit. Check the psi rating of

the relief valve, as well as the psi rating of the water heater to make sure they're properly rated. There will be times when the pounds per square inch ratings will not be marked, so do the best you can. You'll find that some contractors will install relief valves that have a higher psi rating than the maximum pressure rating capacity of the water heater tank. This is very hazardous because the pressure in the tank could exceed its maximum rating and the relief valve will not discharge for safety.

Grab the hot and cold water lines about one foot above the top of the unit to find out if they're installed properly. The hot line should be warm to the touch about a foot or so above the unit. The cold line should be cooler about a foot above the unit. Many water heaters have the hot and cold entry ports marked on the top of the unit. A reversed installation of the hot and cold lines will cut down the energy efficiency of the water heater. This is because the cold line is piped internally down near the bottom of the water tank. This brings in the cold water near the burner, where it then heats up and rises to the top where it is drawn for household use. The hot line is much shorter internally and only draws water from the top of the tank that's already been warmed.

All water heaters should be kept on the "warm" setting for maximum efficiency and life expectancy. The warm setting on the dial thermostats is usually about 125-130 degrees Fahrenheit. The life expectancy of a water heater is 10-12 years. A high temperature setting will cause the unit to constantly be heating water higher than necessary. As a result, high temperature settings can cause premature failure because the burners are constantly operating. Another factor that can really deteriorate a heater tank is the quality of the water. If the water has a high mineral content, the life expectancy of the water heater may only be about 5 years. This is due to the minerals building up inside the tank.

Check the data plate on the water heater to determine the age and gallon capacity of the unit. The date on the data plate is the date of manufacture. Often the water heater will be installed within a year or two of this date. If there is a BTU rating on the data plate, then that can help you estimate the energy efficiency of the heater. An efficient unit will have 1,000 BTU's for each gallon capacity of water it holds.

There should be a drain valve at the base of the water heater. Drain valves are needed to remove about a half gallon of water each month. This removes the rust and sediment that build up inside the tank. If the water heater isn't drained periodically, then the life expectancy of the unit will be shorter than normal.

During your interior inspection, check the water at some of the faucets and tubs. You want to make sure that adequate hot water is available.

Domestic Water Heater photos: P 39-P 46, P 206

Plumbing System

The basic operation of a plumbing system is this:

1.   The water enters the house through the *water main pipe* from the city water main in the street. If the house has an on-site well, then the water main pipe comes from the well.

2.   From this main pipe, the water is then carried to different parts of the house by the *supply* water pipes. Supply pipes branch out in different directions to bring the water to the faucets.

3.   After the water is used at a faucet or shower it goes into the drain. This dirty water is carried back by **drainage** branch lines to a *main drainage line.*

4.   The main drainage line then carries the dirty water to the municipal sewer system in the street. If the house has a septic system, the dirty water is carried to an on-site septic system for disposal.

Look at all visible plumbing lines. There will be very little to view in a finished basement or behind walls and ceilings. Check for any corrosion, leaks or for any buildup of mineral deposits. Often you'll see water stains on some of the floor joists, which are the beams that support the floor above. You'll also see water stains on the sub flooring, which is the base for the floor above. Minor water stains are normal, especially underneath kitchens and baths. You need to be concerned about extensive water damage. If any doubts exist, check the floor above the damaged or stained areas. Try bouncing on the floor above during your interior inspection to make sure that it's solid and doesn't have a spongy feel.

There are two sets of plumbing lines:

1   One type is the *Supply* lines which are the thinner lines. They're about one inch or less in diameter. Water in the supply lines is under pressure.
2   The other type is the *Drainage* and *Vent* lines, which are about 3-6 inches in diameter. Water in the drainage lines is not under pressure because it's for drainage. The water in these pipes flows by gravity instead of pressure.

The vents in a plumbing system are used to allow air from the exterior to enter the plumbing drainage system. They usually protrude through the roof top by one foot. Sometimes on older houses or commercial buildings you will see a *goose neck* vent pipe on the sidewalk in front of the property. Vent pipes keep the pressure in the drainage lines equal to the atmospheric pressure of outside air. Atmospheric pressure is the normal air pressure outside the house. The reason for this is so the plumbing lines drain properly. Improper air pressure in these lines will cause a gurgling sound in the sink and tub drains. This gurgling sound indicates that the water isn't draining properly.

The *"U"* under the sinks is designed to trap water so that the sewer gases don't follow the drainage lines back into the house. There should also be a *"U"* installed on the main drainage line. It should be near the point where the main drain line goes through the foundation wall and out into the street. Sometimes this *"U"* is not installed or not visible. If the plumbing lines don't drain properly, then the water in the *"U"* trap can be drawn out. The water is drawn out by the suction of the draining water. If this happens, there will be nothing to stop the sewer smell from entering the house through the sink drains. The *"U"* **is not** installed to catch jewelry and other objects that are dropped down the sink drain; contrary to what some people might think.

You'll also find what are called *clean out* plugs in the main drainage lines. These are metal screw-in type caps that a licensed plumber can remove to *"snake"* out the drainage lines, in case the lines get clogged. They allow convenient access to some areas that are most susceptible to clogged pipes. The clean out plugs should not be left open since the sewer lines could backup and drain into the house through the open caps.

Sometimes the homeowner will use some liquid drain clearing products that are sold in stores. These products are not recommended to be used too often. Drain clearing products have acids in them that eat away the built-up materials that are clogging the drain. However, they will also eat away the drainage lines if they're used too often. If these products are only used occasionally, it's not a problem. But if a house is susceptible to frequent drain clogging, then a plunger should be used or a licensed plumber should snake out the lines to clear them.

There are several types of plumbing line materials which include Copper, Brass, Galvanized Iron, Lead, PVC, and Cast Iron:

◊   *Copper* piping is found in newer construction and in renovated older properties. Copper has a light brown color and it'll turn green or dark as it ages. The joints of copper pipes are soldered. This makes it easier to identify when it has aged.

◊   *Brass* and *Galvanized Iron* piping are found in older construction. Brass has a yellowish or gold color. Brass is no longer used since it's too expensive and will have some lead in it. Galvanized Iron pipe has a tin or tarnished color and will attract a magnet. The joints for both of these types of pipes have threads to screw the sections together. Brass and Galvanized Iron piping tend to corrode and clog after about 30 years. It's similar to how a human artery clogs over time. If the amount of minerals in the water supply of the area is too high or too low, then these lines will clog even faster.

◊ ⚠️ *Lead* piping is very rarely found in my area. It's not used any longer because the lead content can seep into the water supply which is very hazardous. These pipes will **always** leak some amount of lead content into the house water supply. A lead main entry line will be silver in color and may have a small bubble-type bulge in the beginning of the line. This bulge is known as a "wiped" joint. The name comes from melting the lead on top of the brass pipe to connect them. Then the plumber will wipe the joint with a rag. If you find lead piping or are unsure if there is any, **highly** recommend that the client have a laboratory water analysis done. All lead pipes should be replaced with new pipes for safety.

◊ *PVC* piping, which is a plastic material, is found in newer construction drainage lines and in the drainage lines of renovated older houses. PVC has a white or black color with letter markings on the sides. The joints are slip-on sections that have an adhesive to hold them together. It's used only for drainage lines and is a noncorrosive, lightweight and easy to install piping material. Some local plumbing codes do not allow the use of PVC piping. The main drawback to PVC pipes is that a poisonous carbon monoxide gas is created if there is a fire.

◊ *Cast Iron* piping is found in older construction drainage lines. Cast Iron should be painted or it'll get rusty. The joints are slip-on sections with an adhesive and sealing material called *"Oakum."* Sometimes the Oakum is visible as a dark colored glue around the top of the pipe joints.

There shouldn't be any mixed-material pipes that are connected to each other in the supply lines. The different types of metals can cause a galvanic action when water runs through them. This accelerates the corrosion of the plumbing lines at the point where the two different metals meet. There are special plumbing tapes, joints and chemicals on the market that are used to help prevent this corrosion problem.

Check the water main line where it enters the house. The water main for a house connected to a city water system is usually located in the lower level at the base of the foundation wall facing the street. The water main for a house connected to an on-site well water system is usually located in the lower level at the base of any of the foundation walls. Ask the owner or Realtor if you can't find the main water line. Sometimes they're behind finished walls or personal items in the lower level.

> *Also, recommend that all lead piping be replaced with a new pipe for safety. The reason for this is that lead poisoning is the NUMBER ONE childhood disease in the USA.*

⚠️ Find out what type of pipe material the main water line is made of. Usually it'll be copper for a house with city water and it may be plastic for a house with well water. As I said before, if you see a lead main water line or any lead piping in the house, highly recommend that the client have a laboratory water analysis done for safety. Also, recommend that all lead piping be replaced with a new pipe for safety. The reason for this is that lead poisoning is the *NUMBER ONE* childhood disease in the USA. Lead is an element that doesn't break down when it gets in your system. The effects of lead poisoning in children are *irreversible!!* Lead poisoning can damage the kidneys, nervous system and blood, and can cause permanent brain damage. So don't take any chances with this stuff.

Lead solder can no longer be used in the plumbing pipes leading to drinking water. *Solder* is the metal used to weld the joints of metal pipes together. I don't believe that lead solder should be used on **any** pipes! Let's say a plumber is working at a house and he runs out of non-lead solder. As a result, he's only left with lead solder. What are the chances of that guy stopping what he's doing to go buy more non-lead solder? I've found many contractors don't even like to file building permits and approvals for the work they do. They don't want to do the extra work and so they never mention the need for permits to the homeowner. People like that ignore the safety concern and the law by rationalizing away the necessity for building department permits and approvals. Do you really think that they're going to care about a few lead soldered joints in contact with your drinking water?

⚠️ In older houses there will be lead in some of the soldered pipe joints. Gradually, over time the amount of lead in the solder will be reduced from leaching into the drinking water. The amount of lead that leaches into the water from the solder depends upon several factors. One is the quality of the water. Meaning, if the water has a high acid content, because of a low mineral problem, then more lead will leach into the drinking water. The other factor is how long the water sits in the pipes with the lead solder. The longer the water faucet isn't turned on, the longer the water will remain in the pipe absorbing the lead. Because of this, **ice makers are prone to very high lead levels.** The water in a freezer ice maker can sit in the pipe for days. This allows enough time for the lead to leach into the water at high levels. A lead abatement contractor told me that he's tested houses where the children had extremely high levels of lead in their bodies. **He said that after the test results came back, almost all the lead in their bodies was coming from the ice cubes!**

I hate to tell you, but it gets even worse. Brass or bronze plumbing fixtures and valves can leak lead into the water. The reason for this is that lead is used to fill the gaps in the castes when molding the fixtures. As high as 90% of all plumbing fixtures are made of brass or bronze. Because of this, all water systems have the potential to leach lead into the drinking water. This is a good reason to recommend that the client get a laboratory analysis of the water in the home.

I was doing an inspection once on a house that had a lead water main line and I told the client about it. Before I even got a chance to tell the client about the health concerns, the dishonest Realtor that was at the inspection jumped up and said, *"Oh, well so what. What's wrong with a lead pipe? Plenty of houses in this area have them."* I don't suppose his commission on the sale of the house had anything to do with that comment? Of course in his opinion it wasn't a problem for my client to buy this house with the lead water main pipe. After all, it wasn't this Realtor's children that would end up getting brain damage. I went on to tell the client about the health concerns with lead piping. The client realized the importance of getting the lead water main replaced with a new copper pipe. He contacted the water utility company to obtain an estimate to install a new water main line. You should recommend the same thing for your clients as well for health reasons.

I'm telling you ahead of time, that if you come across any lead piping in a house, some Realtors and other third parties will try to sugarcoat the problem. They're going to tell your client that *"they only need to install a water filter and it'll be fine."* Don't let your client be snowed with that line! Tell them to remove all lead piping and eliminate the problem for good.

Check to make sure that the main water line isn't loose which can cause damage at the plumbing joints and leaks. Gently check this line so you don't do any damage yourself. Tell the client to have a support bracket put on if needed. I did an inspection once that when I checked the main water line for sturdiness, it began to leak. Check the condition of the water main shutoff valve. This valve is used to turn off **all** the water entering the house in case of an emergency or if any repairs are being done. Sometimes there will be two shutoff valves at the water main entry. *Don't* test these valves by shutting them on or off. They get rusty over time and if you test them, they may "freeze" in the on or off position. There is also the possibility that they'll begin to leak and you'll have a problem on your hands.

If the shutoff valve is the older turn-knob type of handle, then you might want to recommend that a newer valve be installed. The lever-type shutoff valves are used in newer construction. The lever valves are more reliable and have less of a chance of freezing over time.

Check for the installation of a water meter reading device. Some areas don't have water meters. In these locations, the property owners are taxed a set fee for the water usage, no matter how much they use. Water meters are usually installed next to the foundation wall within a few feet of the water main entry line.

Check for a remote water meter reading device that will look like a telephone wire attached to the water meter. This wire connects to a small meter on the exterior of the house. Its purpose is to allow the water company employees to read the meter without having to enter the home.

Check for an electrical grounding wire. This is a <u>very important</u> safety item!!! It should be located by the water meter or the water main line entry.

Check for an electrical grounding wire. This is a **<u>very important</u>** safety item!!! It should be located by the water meter or the entry of the water main line. The purpose of this is to ground the house electrical system for safety. Electrical systems can also be grounded to an exterior metal rod driven 8-10 feet into the ground. The grounding wire doesn't have to be insulated like most electrical wiring because there's normally no current passing through this wire. It may be enclosed in BX cable or a conduit, which is a metal covering for protection from damage.

The grounding clamps should not be rusty or loose, but often they are. The grounding wire should be clamped on both sides of the water meter, if there is a water meter installed. If there is no water meter, then the grounding wire should be clamped on both sides of the water main shutoff valve. Often it will only be clamped to one side of the water meter or main shutoff valve. Tell the client that they need to have a *jumper cable* installed with clamps to span the water meter. This is an inexpensive item to install and it's a safety requirement of the National Electric Code. A jumper cable is merely an additional heavy gauge wire about three feet long, that's attached on both sides of the water meter. A jumper cable normally doesn't need to be an insulated wire because no electrical current should be passing through this wire unless there is a problem condition.

It's <u>very important</u> to stress to the client and all third parties about the importance of installing a proper grounding wire that spans the meter. I'll walk you through the basics of what an electrical ground does. This will give you a better understanding of its importance. Let's say, for example, that a live wire somewhere in the electrical system came loose from an outlet and rested on a plumbing pipe or another metal object. A surge in the electrical current would then follow the plumbing lines back to the grounding cable and to the water main entry line. If the grounding cable is installed properly, then the current will go literally to the earth or ground. This will cause an electrical overload and the electrical panel circuit breaker will trip off or the fuse will blow. This will then shut the power off leading to the loose electrical wire branch line. The entire electrical system will also shut off if the main disconnect is overloaded as well.

However, let's say that the electrical grounding cable did not have the proper jumper cable to span the water meter or main shutoff valve. There's a chance that the rubber washers in the water meter or shutoff valve joint connections could prevent the grounding circuit from being completed. Therefore, the unwanted electrical current from the loose wire touching the plumbing lines won't travel to the earth or ground. The circuit would be prevented from grounding because the electrical current would be blocked by the rubber washer. If this happened, then the plumbing lines would remain electrified and the first person to reach for water would get an electric shock. Another hazard would be that the metal object the loose wire was touching, would heat up from the surge in electrical current and start a fire.

Sometimes there will be a pressure reducing valve before the water meter or main shutoff valve. This is an indication that there may be strong water pressure in the water lines of the street. A water pressure reducing valve looks like a small liberty bell and is used in areas where the municipal water system has very good pressure from the street water lines. The pressure reducing valve reduces the water pressure from the street down to about 30-60 psi, *(pounds per square inch)*, before it enters the house plumbing supply lines.

During the interior inspection, check the water pressure and drainage by briefly running the faucets and tubs. In the bathrooms run the sink faucet, the tub or shower faucet and flush the toilet simultaneously. Watch the faucets to see if the pressure drops significantly. A minor pressure drop is normal but a large pressure drop can indicate either poor water pressure or possibly some clogged supply lines. Poor water pressure in some supply lines may be due to the street water pressure being too low. However, it's most likely caused by some supply pipes inside the house that have clogged over the years. Tell the client to have a licensed plumber check it out to determine if there are many clogged lines or just a small section that needs replacing.

An important point to remember is that I always try to have the client present with me when I'm testing the water pressure. This lets the client see for themselves what the water pressure level is. Your client can then decide if the pressure meets *their* standards of being acceptable. Different people have different tastes. One client might not mind low water pressure, while another client might be furious with you if you don't point that out to him and he ends up buying the house. Don't leave anything to the imagination, let the client decide for themselves if the water pressure is satisfactory or not. Don't try to make the decision for them. Remember to turn off all faucets you're testing during the inspection. You don't want to flood someone's house. Water damage can be very messy and expensive to repair.

As I mentioned earlier, there are aspects to be aware of when inspecting a vacant house. If the property is located in a cold weather area, then the heating system must be kept on all winter or else the water pipes must be winterized. This protects the pipes from water freezing, expanding and cracking the pipes. A plumber "winterizes" the plumbing system by putting an anti-freeze chemical in the drainage pipes and *"U"* trap. The supply pipes should be drained of all water. **Once the plumbing system is winterized, the water cannot be turned on in the house!** If the water is accidentally turned on then the anti-freeze chemical will be flushed out of the system and flow out of the drainage lines. This will "dewinterize" the pipes. So don't make the mistake of testing

the water pressure if the plumbing system is winterized. Plumbers usually tape notices on the water fixtures of the house to remind people that the system should not be used.

Another important aspect to note is that you should tell the client to find out how long the house has been left vacant. The client needs to get written documentation confirming when the house was vacated, if the heating system was left on, and/or when the pipes were winterized. The reason for this is that pipes that have frozen and cracked behind walls may not show water stains until **after** the home inspection. Some pipes burst when they freeze and cause extensive water damage. But some pipes only get cracks when they freeze and will not reveal water leaks for a long time.

Realtors are <u>always</u> going to say, *"Oh, the pipes were winterized before the weather got cold,"* or else they'll say, *"The heating system has been left on all winter so the pipes wouldn't freeze."* My response to that is, *"Great, just get the written documentation to my client so he can confirm that's an accurate statement."* I say this because I've learned one million times over that dishonest Realtors say ANYTHING that sounds good, whether they know if it's accurate or not!!!! I've done foreclosure appraisals on houses that were left vacant for **two** winters. The only problem was that the heating system was left on or the pipes were only winterized for **one** winter! Or, the house <u>was</u> properly winterized while the heating system was turned off – <u>but</u> later someone mistakenly turned on the water in the house to test the water pressure during a home inspection without realizing that the plumbing system was winterized. By running the water you flush-out the anti-freeze chemicals in the pipes and then the plumbing system is **no longer winterized.** Let's say this were the case in a house that you're inspecting. Your client may find cracked and leaking pipes behind the walls after he moves-in. So learn a lesson from this and tell the client to obtain written documents for: 1) the **date** the house was vacated, 2) the heating bills to prove the heat was left on during **all** vacant winters, 3) the plumber's receipt showing the **date** the pipes were winterized, 4) a written statement from the owner and Realtor that the water was **not** turned on in the house while the plumbing system was winterized.

Plumbing System photos: P 49-P 56

Well Water System

The main components of a well water system consist of a well pump, the water lines, the pressure gauge and the water storage tank. The basic operation of a well system is as follows:

1.   The *well pump* sends water up from the well through the *water lines*. The water builds up in the *water storage tank*. When the tank *pressure gauge* reaches its high setting, the pressure switch turns the well pump off. Water then sits in the water storage tank, similar to a water heater tank.

2.   When a faucet is turned on, the water is drawn from the storage tank only, and not the well. The water pressure in the storage tank begins to drop as the water continues to run from the faucet. When the pressure gauge drops a few psi, it switches on the well pump to replenish the water supply in the water storage tank. This is needed to keep the tank near full capacity or to keep up with the water being drawn from the faucets.

3.   The purpose of the water storage tank is to hold enough water so the well pump doesn't have to turn on every time someone turns on a faucet. If the storage tank is faulty or isn't large enough, then the well pump will turn on just about every time someone turns on a faucet. This is called *short cycling* and will lead to premature failure of the well pump because it's operating too often.

There are three types of well pumps: suction pumps, jet pumps, and submersible pumps. The type of well pump installed will be based upon the depth of the well.

◊   *Suction pumps* are only used for very shallow wells that are 25 feet deep or less. A suction pump is installed next to the well water storage tank. These pumps only have one water pipe in the well shaft. A vacuum must be maintained in the pipes for the pump to lift the water from the well. Suction pumps are inefficient because a <u>perfect</u> vacuum in the well pipes can only lift water about 25 feet. If there are any leaks or debris in the pipe, the vacuum pressure is reduced. As a result, the water cannot be lifted as high. Suction pumps have a life expectancy of about 15 years.

◊   *Jet pumps* can be used for wells that are 120 feet deep or less. Like a suction pump, a jet pump is installed next to the well water storage tank. These pumps have two water pipes in the well shaft. One pipe is the larger suction line. The other pipe forces water down the well to push more water back up the suction pipe. About 5 gallons of water are pumped down the well and 8 gallons of water are pushed up the larger suction pipe. This provides an overall 3 gallons of water per minute and isn't efficient. Jet pumps use much more energy because they push water down the well, while trying to lift more water out of the well shaft. Moreover, as with suction pumps, jet pumps cannot have any leaks or debris in the pipes. This would cut down the efficiency even further by fouling the vacuum needed for this system. Jet pumps are generally more expensive to repair. Jet pumps have a life expectancy of about 15 years.

◊   *Submersible pumps* can be used for the deepest wells. Unlike the other pipes, submersible pumps are installed completely inside the well shaft. As a result, you won't see any well pump parts during your inspection. Since the pump parts are not in the house, submersibles are the quietest type of pumps. Submersible pumps are the most efficient types to use. They have a life expectancy of about 10 years.

Try to get as much information as you can about the well from the owner or Realtor. Use the preinspection questions that I mentioned earlier for a guideline. And don't be afraid to ask any other questions for further information. There will be many times that the owner or Realtor won't be able to tell you very much about the well system. Unfortunately, this is often the case. Don't be surprised if the answers you get don't seem to be the truth from the results of the well test.

I did an inspection once and the seller of the house was an eye doctor who said the well was *always* running fine. This eye doctor told the client and me that he and his family had never had problems with water pressure. After testing the well for about 10 minutes, all the faucets ran dry and there was almost **no** water coming out. This *honest* eye doctor stated that he had *never* had that happen before. I told my client to call a well contractor to have the well checked out. The client found a well contractor that told him he didn't even need to go out to the house to find the problem. This contractor said that he had evaluated that well for two previous potential buyers of the home. Both other buyers didn't buy the house because the well needed to be either redrilled deeper or moved completely because it constantly ran dry. *(So much for the integrity of that eye doctor. Someone ought to tell him that you can go blind from telling too many lies).*

> You're <u>very limited</u> in what you can evaluate about a well system because some of the components are underground. You also don't have X-ray vision to see the adequacy of the underground water source.

You're <u>very limited</u> in what you can evaluate about a well system because some of the components are underground. You also don't have X-ray vision to see the adequacy of the underground water source. Some items that aren't visible are submersible well pumps, water lines and sometimes even the water storage tank. On old houses you may find the water storage tank located in a pit in the ground. To make matters worse, you have no idea of what the past maintenance history has been. These are the same limitations with evaluating septic systems, oil tanks and any underground or nonvisible item on the property. Tell the client to get documentation of the past history from the well contractor maintaining this system. They should also find out the age of the well pump and other equipment.

Most wells are over 25 feet deep, so be careful about telling your client that the system is fine. The repair costs and costs to drill deep wells are **much higher** than shallow wells. The reason for this is that the repair bills are usually based on the number of feet of water pipe used and the drilling depth.

Tell the client the limits of testing the system and the evaluations that you can make during a limited time, visual inspection. You're limited because the well is an underground system. Let them know that there aren't any other inspectors that will do a more thorough job. More importantly, most inspectors tend to be much less thorough than an **"A to Z Home Inspector."**

Before beginning your testing of the well system, turn off all of the house faucets and take a look at the well components that are above ground. You can usually find the visible well components in the lower level of the house. Look at the well system pressure gauge and record what the reading is. This is called the *static* pressure, since no water is being used and the system is idle. See if the pressure gauge has rust on it or if it's operating properly.

Look at the well water lines to determine their condition. I'll give you some background on different types of well pipe materials. You won't need to know this for most inspections, but it may come in handy. Most of the time you'll find *black polypropylene pipe*, which looks like plastic, used for well water lines. This type of pipe is good for wells up to 300 feet deep. It has a 200 psi maximum pressure rating and is installed in one, long section with no joints. *Schedule 80 PVC* pipe should be used for wells over 300 feet deep. This pipe have very thick walls to help prevent long term repair problems. Unlike the polypropylene pipe, schedule 80 PVC pipe comes in 20 foot sections. At the end of each section there are threaded grooves to attach the next pipe length. *Schedule 40 PVC* pipe is not as strong as schedule 80 pipe. The 20 foot sections of schedule 40 pipe are glued together, as opposed to having threaded ends. Schedule 40 pipe has a 400 psi maximum pressure rating. However, this pipe gets brittle after being in a well for many years. Also, the glue used to hold the sections together becomes weak over time.

Take a look at the well water storage tank. The typical life expectancy of these tanks is about 10-12 years. Check for any rust or aging signs. The water storage tank should be painted and insulated to prevent any condensation from building up on the outside. The condensation causes rust. For safety, there should always be a pressure relief valve on the tank or on the water pipe leading into the tank. This valve will discharge if the pressure in the tank gets too high. It's usually set at 75 psi depending upon the pressure rating of the storage tank. Storage tanks are designed for 75-100 pounds of working pressure.

Next to the water storage tank you'll find a small, rectangular box on the well water pipe. This box contains the pressure switch. The *pressure switch* sends an electric current to turn the well pump on and off based upon the system pressure. A pressure gauge helps the homeowner and the repair man monitor the system.

Make sure the water storage tank has an air fill valve on it. This looks like a tire air valve and is used to adjust the air-to-water ratio in the tank periodically. Don't confuse the air valve with the mounting bracket on top of some water tanks. Mounting brackets are used to hold the tank while it's being painted on the factory assembly line. They're also used to mount a suction or jet well pump if necessary.

Inside the water storage tank is an air pocket or a diaphragm bag. Over time the air becomes absorbed by the water or the bag breaks. When this happens the tank becomes waterlogged and doesn't operate properly. That's why the air-to-water ratio in the tank must be checked during routine well maintenance. The compressed air in the water tank is what gives you the water pressure at the faucets and showers. Bigger storage tanks use less well pump activity because they hold more water. This is far better for the life expectancy of the well pump electric motor. When a tank is too small for the house water usage or if the tank gets waterlogged, then you will have a *short cycling* problem. Short cycling refers to the well pump turning on and off too often. This wears out the well pump faster because it turns on every time someone opens a faucet.

The water storage tank is similar to a boiler expansion tank in that both have an air pocket inside and an air valve. This is what causes the pressure to rise in the system as water is pumped into the water storage tank. The air pocket acts as a cushion for the water filling the tank.

Most wells will have submersible pumps that aren't visible for you to inspect. The life expectancy of a well pump will be decreased if the pump is overworked or neglected. The life expectancy also depends on the type and quality of the pump installed, along with the acidity of the well water. Generally you should use the 10 year range during an inspection since you won't know much about the past pump maintenance and water quality.

The well pump is what pushes the water through the water lines. The water lines carry the well water from the pump, to the water storage tank and into the house. A pressure gauge is used to monitor the water pressure in the system. Pressure gauges often get rusty *(on all operating systems in the house)* and need to be replaced every few years. Tap these gauges with your finger to make sure they don't stick. There have been times when I was testing a well system and the pressure gauge didn't move. When I tapped the gauge, it loosened up the needle so I could get an accurate pressure reading. The water storage tank holds some of the well water until the faucets are turned on. The life expectancy of a water storage tank is about 15-20 years. It's similar to a well pump, because the life expectancy depends upon the maintenance given it and the type and quality of the tank and the acidity of the well water.

To test the well system, run the water for about 30 to 45 minutes. Run the water from the hose bib type faucet near the well water storage tank or from a laundry sink drain or an exterior hose bib. You need a wide type of faucet to get an adequate flow of water. You may need to attach a portable hose to the faucet to drain the water to a safe location. *(Unless of course you want to flood the guy's house).* You can also test the well while you're testing the septic system to save some time and "kill two birds with one stone." However, since there will be about four faucets running during the septic system test, you can cause the well storage tank pressure to drop down much lower than it would under normal usage.

During the testing, make sure that you check the faucet and sink from time to time. Do this to make sure that the sink doesn't drain too slowly, which could cause it to overflow with water. You also need to have at least one empty container that holds at least one gallon of water. During the test, measure the time the faucet takes to fill five gallons of water into the container. Obviously if you have a one gallon container, you'll have to do some simple math calculations or have extra containers.

> *The minimum acceptable flow for a well system is five gallons per minute, (GPM). Some local area codes may require a higher GPM rating, so check with your local building department.*

The average family uses 50-60 gallons of water per person each day. The minimum acceptable flow for a well system is five gallons per minute, *(GPM)*. Some local area codes may require a higher GPM rating, so check with your local building department. What you're doing with this well test, is pushing the system to see if it provides an adequate flow of water with sufficient water pressure for a sustained period. You're also trying to see if the well system can maintain the *mid-system* pressure. I'll explain this in a minute. What you need to be concerned about, is an abnormal drop in pressure. Just ask yourself and the client: Are the pressure and volume of the water flow enough to take a shower with? If the answer is no, then tell the client to have the system checked out by a licensed well service contractor.

An inadequate water flow during the test could be due a variety of factors. Some potential causes are:

◊ A water storage tank that is not operating properly. If the air-to-water ratio is improperly balanced inside the water storage tank, it'll have to be repumped with air by a licensed contractor. Possibly the water storage tank is too small for the amount of water being drawn during the test. This could create a problem for your client after they move in if they have children and take many showers or use a lot of water.

◊ Some of the plumbing lines are clogged. A small section or most of the plumbing lines could have become clogged over the years due to mineral deposits from the water.

◊ Possibly the underground well itself is insufficient. If the underground well has an inadequate water supply then a new well may have to be drilled. This can be a major expense because the property's aquifer, where the well water is drawn from, may be insufficient for normal water usage. A well contractor told me that when there's a very dry season some of the wells in the area will dry out. The only solutions to restoring the well water flow is to drill these wells deeper or drill a new well.

Either way, if there's an inadequate water flow then just tell the client to have the system checked out. They'll need to have a well contractor evaluate what repairs are needed and what costs are involved.

Keep checking the water pressure and volume from the faucet and check the pressure gauge during the well system test. Record the highs and lows on the well pressure gauge. The well pressure should remain within a 20 psi differential during and after the test. This simply means that the high and low pressure gauge reading shouldn't be over a 20 psi difference. Most well systems operate between 30-50 psi and 40-60 psi. Therefore, the mid-system pressure reading during the test should be either 40 pounds per square inch for a system that operates between 30-50 psi or 50 pounds per square inch for a system that operates between 40-60 psi. The reading will depend upon the normal operating range of that particular well system. Sometimes it's difficult to decide what the normal psi range is for a particular well system. But that's why you check the static pressure, to try to determine the range before you start the testing.

Check to see if there's an operating emergency shutoff switch for the well pump. It's usually located near the water storage tank and its operation is similar to that of a boiler or furnace shutoff switch.

Check to find out if there's a water filter installed on the system. I even recommend that the client use water filters when their house is connected to the city water system. Water filters are *highly* recommended for health reasons, especially with all of the pollutants going into the water supply these days. Check the color of the filter if there's a see-thru casing. The filters need to be replaced according to the owners manual and whenever they appear dirty. There are two kinds of water filters:

1 *Point of Entry* filters that are installed at the beginning of the house water main pipe.

2 *Point of Use* filters that are installed at the faucets, usually the kitchen faucet.

You can't evaluate water filter systems during a home inspection because of the laboratory water analysis that would be needed. I *highly* recommend to clients that they have a water sample taken and analyzed at a local laboratory whenever the house has a well or possible lead plumbing lines. Check the phone book for a licensed water analysis laboratory in your area. Water analysis can be for bacteria, mineral, metal and radon content in the water supply.

Often there are water softener systems installed with a house supplied by well water. *Water Softeners* are shaped like large scuba tanks or garbage cans. The softener equipment is usually located next to the lower level well components. They're generally made of plastic or fiberglass. They have salt, called *brine*, inside them that's used to help control the mineral content of the water. Softeners take the hardness out and raise the sodium level of the water to keep the proper chemical balance. "Hard" water has high mineral content. "Soft" water has low mineral content. Water that's too high or too low in minerals can corrode and clog the plumbing lines. If the water has too many minerals, it'll clog the interior of the pipes over time. If the water is too low in minerals it can't balance the acid that's naturally in water and this will deteriorate the pipes. Your water's acidity or alkalinity (often measured as pH) greatly affects corrosion. Temperature and mineral content also affect how corrosive it is. If you're wondering about the strength of water to deteriorate and dissolve pipes then you may not be aware that liquid water dissolves just about anything. Water is probably the best solvent in the universe according to scientists who say that *everything* is soluble in water to some degree. Even gold is somewhat soluble in seawater. *(Before you get any ideas about extracting gold from the oceans, scientists say that the value of dissolved gold in a metric ton of seawater comes to about $0.0000004).*

Water softeners should go through "backwash" cycles every few days. This rejuvenates the minerals in the softener with the brine. You can't evaluate water softener systems during a home inspection. They can't be evaluated because of the laboratory water analysis and specialized equipment and training that would be needed. Just take a look at the equipment to determine the general condition. If there's excessive rust or signs of aging, tell the client to have a well contractor evaluate the softener system.

Try to determine where the well is located on the site. Ask the owner or Realtor about this in the preinspection questions. On the exterior of the house you should see the top of the well shaft head protruding out of the ground by about one foot. If you don't see the top of the well shaft, there is a chance it's a buried well head. Buried well heads are no longer allowed to be installed in many areas. The reason for this is that buried well heads are more prone to contamination and venting problems. The pits for these well heads act like a catch basin and allow contaminants into the well shaft. This leads to unsanitary problems in the house water supply. So warn your client about buried well heads if you don't see the top of the well shaft on the site.

⚠ The local building and health codes regulate where a well can be drilled for safety. Wells should be drilled at least 25 feet from the house foundation and 50 feet away from a septic tank. The well should be at least 100 feet away from the septic fields or any underground fuel tanks. These distances are the **minimum** recommendations to help prevent well water contamination from termite chemical treatments of the house, the septic sewage, and from leaking oil tanks. Some local health and building codes don't allow termite treatments to houses that have well water systems. This leaves the homeowner in a serious predicament. They can't use the in-ground chemicals to get rid of the termites because the town doesn't want any potential well water contamination. Tell your client to talk with some local exterminators about this prior to closing.

Home owners should not have decks or patios built over a well head by the house. At the same time, well shafts inside the lower level of a home should not be installed either. The reason for this is that a well contractor has to be able to get the drill rig machinery over the well shaft to make repairs. When the well pump needs replacing, if repairs are needed, or if the well has to be dug deeper, there's no way for the contractor to do it without the well rig equipment. Sometimes a builder will have the well drilled before the construction of the house. During this time the area over the future basement or crawl space is open for the use of well drilling rigs. If the well head ends up being located in the basement or crawl space of the finished home, then the contractor can't get their rig equipment inside. The only option for a homeowner in this situation would be to have a new well drilled on the site where there is open space above the shaft.

Recommend that the client check with the local building and health departments about the well. The client needs to confirm that the well meets all local codes and they should obtain the plot plan for the well. A plot plan is a diagram of the site that should show where the well is located and how deep it is.

⚠ Sometimes you'll inspect a house that originally had a well water supply but was later hooked up to the city water pipes. Any unused wells must be professionally sealed according to the local building and health codes. A small child could fall down an open well shaft. Also, if any contaminants traveled down an open well shaft, they would get into the groundwater. This could contaminate the well water supply of the neighboring properties. The homeowner of the unused well could be held liable for the damages to the neighbors' well water.

Well Water System photos: P 57-P 64, P 230

Septic System

The main components of a septic system consist of the drainage lines, the holding tank and the leaching fields or seepage pits.

◊   The *drainage lines* are usually visible in the lower level of the house. These lines are slightly pitched downward to drain out into the septic system holding tank.

◊   The *holding tank* functions as a detention tank for the sewage solids. The tank will be buried underground and the cap, which is removable for cleaning the system out, will be about one foot below the soil.

◊   *Leaching fields* and *seepage pits* are used to drain the liquid wastes down into the earth. The leaching fields and seepage pits are connected to the holding tank by drainage lines. Leaching fields are found in newer construction or rehabilitated older septic systems. In some areas seepage pits and cesspools are no longer permitted because they are not as sanitary as leaching fields.

The life expectancy of a septic system is about 30 years. The lifespan of the system will depend upon the type of construction and the maintenance given it. The basic operation of a septic system is as follows:

1.   The drainage lines carry all of the liquid and solid wastes to the septic holding tank.

2.   The solid waste remains in the bottom of the holding tank. The liquid waste rises as the tank fills and is carried by drainage lines to the leaching fields or seepage pits.

3.   The liquid waste then runs through the drainage lines. These lines have perforated holes in the bottom when they reach the leaching field area of the lawn.

4.   The liquid waste goes through the holes in the bottom of the drainage pipes and follows the air pockets or voids in the soil as it moves downward.

You may come across septic systems that have an alarm which monitors an internal pump located inside the holding tank. The purpose of the internal pump is to carry the liquid waste *upward* to the leaching fields, to be drained away safely. A pump is required when the leaching fields are located higher in elevation than the holding tank. Therefore, the liquid waste cannot travel by gravity to be drained away. The liquid waste must be pumped to the location of the leaching fields. This is not the normal type of installation since almost all septic systems use gravity for the drainage. However, the pumps are needed on some systems due to a variety of reasons. Some reasons why a leaching field is installed higher up than the holding tank is that the property size was too small, there are excessive rocks in the soil, there are poor percolation rates in some of the soil, etc.

The alarm is installed to monitor the internal pump inside the holding tank, to make sure the pump doesn't malfunction. There is a water float in the holding tank that will trigger the alarm to go off if the water level gets too high. When the water level rises too high, then it's an indication that the pump is not operating properly and repairs are needed. You can identify the alarm by a small electrical box that's located inside the house. This box will have a red light on it and should be marked with some identification. There may be a test button on the alarm box to periodically test it for proper operation. Ask the owner if you can test the alarm during your inspection to see if it's operating properly. Don't test these alarms unless you get permission from the owner. You want to tell the client to speak to town hall and the septic installer about the septic alarm. Since they're only used for abnormal conditions, the client may find out some important information by asking questions.

Try to get as much information as you can about the septic from the owner or Realtor. Use the preinspection questions that I mentioned earlier for a guideline but don't be afraid to ask other questions for further info. Don't be surprised if they don't know very much about the septic system. Unfortunately, this is often the case.

I'll tell you another war story that ought a jar ya a little bit. I did an inspection once and the client, the Realtor, the seller, and the real estate listing **all** stated that the house was connected to the municipal sewer system. I always tell my clients that they need to confirm this with the town hall records since there is no way for me, or any inspector, <u>to see underground</u> to verify that the house is connected to the city sewers. *(I'm not Superman with X-ray vision)*. Later during the backyard inspection, the client mentioned to me that he was thinking about putting a swimming pool in the backyard after he bought the house. So, as always, I told the client to check town hall to make sure he could get the approvals to install a pool and get price estimates ***BEFORE*** closing on the house.

Well, about four months later, I got a letter from this client's attorney. The letter stated that the client went to town hall to find out about installing a pool in his backyard – ***AFTER*** he bought the house. He was awfully surprised to find out that the house had a septic system and was **not** connected to the city sewer system! As a result, the client not only couldn't put a swimming pool in his yard, but he had to deal with a septic system that hadn't been maintained for who knows how long!! If the seller of the house didn't even know he had a septic system, then obviously he didn't call any septic contractors to clean out the tank and inspect it internally every few years. So the probability of having to pay to replace a decayed and neglected septic system and leaching fields, just added insult to injury for my client! I told this client and his attorney that they were "barking up the wrong tree" if they were even thinking about complaining to me. The seller, the Realtor, and the real estate listing, and even my client, all gave me incorrect information when they told me the house was connected to the city sewer system. Moreover, the client chose on his own to **not** follow my advice to check town hall records

before he closed on the house. I also had a copy of this client's written inspection report that I had sent him. I explained to the client's attorney to read specific pages in the report which clearly stated my advice to this client **before** he closed on the house. As a result, I never heard a word from that attorney or client again about this complaint or problem. They realized the client himself was to blame and they could only consider suing the seller and Realtor – but certainly not me.

So learn a lesson from this example and don't make the same mistakes this client did. You may end up paying dearly for it later with a lot of money and aggravation. There's no way to tell for sure if a main drainage line leads to a septic system or a city sewer system because they're identical. The only hints you might have are these:

1   If the house is connected to the city sewer system then the drainage lines will usually lead through the foundation wall facing the street. This is different from many septic system installations which are located in the rear of a house, away from the street. However, there are city sewer hookups from the rear of some houses and there are septic systems hookups in the front yard of houses as well.

2   If the house is connected to the city sewer system then the main drainage line should have a "U" shaped trap near the foundation wall. This is different from septic systems which are <u>not</u> supposed to have a "U" trap. A "U" trap isn't needed because the sewer gases that build up in the septic tank should follow the drainage line up through the house and out of the plumbing vent stack in the roof. However, you will find city sewer hookups *without* the "U" trap, and you'll also find septic system hookups that have been installed *with* a "U" trap.

> The point I'm trying to make, is that there's no way to know for sure whether or not the house is connected to the municipal sewer system.
> So you want to mention to the client that the only way for him to determine this is to check with town hall.

The point I'm trying to make, is that there's no way to know for sure whether or not the house is connected to the municipal sewer system. So mention to the client that the only way for him to determine this is to check with the building or health departments at town hall. Now do you see what I mean about being thorough and Covering Your Assets. This is why you need to ask the owner the preinspection questions and be up front and honest with your client.

You're <u>very limited</u> in what you can evaluate about a septic system. You're limited because all of the components are underground and aren't visible, except the interior drainage lines. Also, you have no idea of what the past maintenance history has been. That's why you want to find out from the owner how often the system has been pumped clean. Tell the

client to get documentation of the past history from the septic contractor maintaining this system.

Often sellers will pump a septic system out just because the house is being put on the market for sale. I've seen many septic systems that haven't been pumped for over five years. However, the seller would have the system pumped just so that they could tell potential buyers it was recently cleaned. It's similar to driving a car for many years without changing the oil. The car will run on dirty oil. However, it'll cost you money in wear and tear and the car will eventually die prematurely due to the lack of proper maintenance.

Septic systems are **very** expensive to install or rebuild if they're no longer operating properly. You don't want to get stuck holding the bag to install a new septic system because you told the client the system was fine before he bought the house. If you can't get enough information about the past maintenance history or your testing shows problems with the septic system, then tell the client to have the system pumped clean and inspected **internally** by a licensed septic contractor. I *always* tell the client to have the septic system pumped clean and inspected internally. I do this regardless of whether there is evidence of problems or lack of maintenance to the system. The reason for this is the limits of evaluating an underground system that you can't even see! Also, the dye testing done during a home inspection is very limited. I'll talk more about this a little later.

Pumping the septic system clean and getting an internal inspection serves several purposes that benefit you and your client:

1   You don't have to worry about telling someone the system is OK when all of the major components are located underground and can't be seen. When the system is pumped out clean, the septic contractor can internally inspect the holding tank and the drainage lines coming into and out of the tank. This gives him a visual look at the interior of the tank and often the septic contractor will provide a written report for this service. The fee the septic contractor charges for this service is well worth the money spent. Tell the client that having the septic tank pumped and internally inspected is similar to buying an insurance policy for the system.

2   Another benefit is that if the client does buy the house, then they'll be moving in with a cleaned out septic tank. Their newly cleaned out tank shouldn't need any maintenance for quite some time.

You may also recommend that the client have a septic contractor partially dig up the leaching field area to do a more extensive evaluation. This will allow them to see if the fields or pipes are clogged.

> Septic systems MUST be pumped out clean and inspected internally every two to three years at least.

Septic systems <u>must</u> be pumped out clean and inspected internally every two to three years at least. It should be more frequent than every two years if there are many people in the house or they do a lot of entertaining. I know a septic cleaning contractor in my area who has one customer that gets their tank cleaned every 3-4 *months* because they have a very high water usage.

You will encounter some home owners who think you don't have to pump septic tanks clean. They believe in the fairy tale myth that the bacterial action inside the septic tank decomposes all the solid waste away. There are some products sold that claim to help the decomposition in septic tanks. Some home owners think you merely have to use these products instead of pumping the tank periodically. You must tell your client that this is **totally incorrect** and the client needs to have the tank pumped and internally inspected. When this occurs you'll often have a third party say, *"If it's not broken, don't fix it."* My response to that is, *"Should you wait until you're terminally ill before going to the doctor for a physical or medical check?"*

I'll explain the importance of why a septic system needs to be cleaned and inspected internally at least every 2-3 years. If a septic system is neglected, the solid waste that's in the holding tank will begin to build up. Eventually, the solid waste will rise to the top section of the holding tank where it'll be carried with the liquid waste into the drainage lines. Instead of just liquid waste entering the leaching fields, the solid waste will also begin to enter the fields.

As the solid and liquid waste moves through the perforated holes in the drainage lines, it'll move into the air pockets or voids of the soil. The solids will eventually clog the air pockets and voids of the soil until there's nowhere for the liquid waste to go but upwards. From this point on, the septic system is a *"failed"* system. It's a failed system because the liquid and solid waste will begin to rise because it can't travel down into the soil. Puddles and sewer odors will begin to develop on the lawn over the leaching fields. When a septic system has failed it may have to be moved or rebuilt. This is a **major** expense to accomplish. If you don't believe me, just call a septic contractor in your area and ask what it costs to install a new septic system.

I did a lot of home inspections for a town prior to the blasting that was required to install sewer systems in my area. The sewers were being installed in areas where there were currently septic systems in use. According to the contractor that was installing the city sewer lines, there were cases of homeowners who had failed septic systems that needed to be moved and rebuilt. The only problem with these failed systems, was that the property size was too small to move the septic system with new leaching fields. The homeowners were left with two choices: Either pay to hook up their houses to the city sewer system or have their houses condemned because of the lack of operating waste disposal systems. Could you imagine this problem happening to a house that can't hook up to any city sewer system in the street?

To test the septic system, run the water from at least four faucets and/or tubs simultaneously for about 30 minutes. Use a harmless, colored dye designed for septic system testing and put the recommended amount in a few of the toilets and flush them. I use a fluorescent green or red septic tank dye that only requires about one tablespoon to be flushed down the toilet. Flush all toilets at least four times during the test while the water is running from the faucets. Walk all around the exterior of the house and property several times during and after the septic test to check for any signs of a failed system.

This is called a *"stress"* test of the septic system. What you're doing with this test, is pushing the septic system by entering a large amount of water into the drainage lines. You're trying to see if the colored dye shows up anywhere on or near the subject property. If the septic system is operating properly, then all of the dye colored water will travel through the drainage lines, to the holding tank and then to the leaching fields. When the dye colored water reaches the leaching fields, it should percolate down into the soil. What you need to be concerned about, is if you smell any sewage odors or see the colored dye anywhere on or near the property. If there's a sewage smell or you see the dye, it means that the septic system is not operating properly. Then the system **<u>must</u>** be checked out by a licensed contractor.

Don't be surprised about some of the results you'll get from this type of septic testing. Most of the time the dye will just rise in the area over the leaching fields if the system fails the dye test. I've seen instances where the colored dye ended up rising in the driveway, the street, in a lake and pond near the rear yard, in a drainage pipe used to waterproof the lower level and many other places. I've even heard of the dye showing up several days *after* the inspection.

There have been instances where I was testing septic systems and I'd smell the sewage odor and saw the liquid waste coming out of the ground. However, I didn't see the colored dye in the waste water. This is because there's a chance that the PH content in the septic system can neutralize the colored dye so that it doesn't show up. One way to try to prevent this from happening is to put Sodium Bicarbonate into the system when you flush the colored dye down the toilets. The Sodium Bicarbonate will help to stabilize the PH content in the system so it won't neutralize the color of the septic dye.

I've also tested some septics and didn't see the liquid waste nor the dye but I could smell the sewage odor. If this happens, it's a problem condition that you have to warn the client about. When you smell the sewage odor it means that the liquid waste is too close to the surface of the soil. This could be caused by clogged leaching fields or a high groundwater table. I've done inspections where the subject property was located in an area with a high water table in the soil. This not only caused water penetration problems in the basements of this neighborhood, but it also destroyed all the septic systems!!! A high groundwater table will make a septic system fail because the tank and fields will be deteriorated by the excess water in the soil.

It's important that you notify your client about the limitations of the dye test. Don't be fooled into thinking that the dye test is infallible, because it's not. A knowledgeable septic contractor will tell you the same thing, that the dye test is very limited. I tell all my clients the limits of the septic, well and other aspects of a home inspection when I book the job over the phone. This way they know before they even get to the site what the limitations are of a home inspection. Just be honest and up front with your clients and you'll earn their respect and confidence. I'll keep repeating that in this book but I just want to make sure you don't forget it.

> *The dye test is a very limited test and many times a failed septic system, or even a system on the verge of failure, will pass the dye test.*

The dye test is a very limited test because many times a failed septic system, or even a system on the verge of failure, will pass the dye test. This is why I want to stress to you the importance of having the system, and any other aspect of a home inspection, checked out by a licensed contractor if any doubts exist. Don't get stuck holding the bag and paying for repairs that you shouldn't be responsible for.

Recommend that the client check with the local building and health departments about the septic. The client needs to confirm that the septic meets all local codes and they should obtain the plot plan for the septic. A plot plan of the site that should show where the septic tank and leaching fields are located, how big the tank is, how long the fields are, etc.

Sometimes you'll inspect a house that originally had a septic system but was later hooked up to the city sewer pipes. Any unused septics must be professionally sealed according to the local building and health codes. It's the same analogy to an unused, underground oil tank. The septic tank will collapse over time, especially if it's made of metal.

Here's a few additional points your client needs to be aware of. If there's a water softener in the house, then the brine water from the softener should **not** discharge into the septic system. The salty brine water will alter the bacterial action of the septic decomposition and change the ph in the tank. Also, the salt will corrode the interior tank parts and the distribution system. Moreover, the large quantity of water discharged by a softener system can be excessive. This can cause premature failure of the septic system. Some water softeners don't have a discharge cycle which will eliminate these problems. These systems are more expensive to install.

The same logic is used for washing machines. Dirty, soapy laundry water discharging into the septic system will also foul the bacterial action in the septic tank. A solution for the water softener and the washing machine waste water would be a grey water tank. A *grey water tank* is a small tank separate from the main septic tank. No toilet water can be discharged into a grey water tank. When the main septic tank is pumped clean, the grey water tank should be pumped as well. Some areas used to allow dry wells instead of grey water tanks. A *dry well* is merely a pit dug in the ground with gravel in it for drainage. However, due to the soil contamination problems most building codes no longer allow dry wells.

Septic System photos: P 65-P 68

Electrical System

The *National Electric Code*, or the NEC as it's also called, is the standard that most local building departments use to draw up their electrical construction codes. Most local municipalities will adapt the NEC codes to fit the needs of their local area. The NEC codes are only recommendations and the local building departments are not required to follow them. However, the local electrical codes are never far off from the NEC codes because they're very good, safe recommendations.

The basic operation of an electrical system is very similar to that of a plumbing system:

1.   Electricity is brought in through the *service entrance lines* to the house from the utility company lines in the street. It's just like a water main line.

2.   From this main line, the electricity then passes through an *electrical meter*. The electrical meter registers the amount of electricity that's used. The electricity then travels to the *main electrical panel*.

3.   From the main panel the current is then carried to different parts of the house. The current travels through the *"hot"* interior electrical wiring that branches out in different directions to all parts of the house. The hot wires are similar to the plumbing supply lines. The expression "hot" is used to describe the wires that are carrying the live electrical current to the appliance, outlet, switch, etc.

4.   After the electricity is used at an outlet or light fixture, the used electrons then go back to the main panel along the *"neutral"* wiring in the branch lines. The neutral wiring is similar to the plumbing drainage lines.

5.   Just as water in a drainage line is under extremely low gravity pressure, so the electrons flowing through the neutral wire are at close to zero volts. They've given up nearly all of their energy in operating whatever device they've passed through.

6. The neutral wiring then carries the neutral electron current back to the ground via the *grounding cable*. It's similar to a city or septic sewer system where the used water drains into.

There are three terms to describe the power of electricity: Volts, Amps and Watts.

◊ The *total* of the electrical current is called *Volts*. For example, the total potential of the electrical current in a house with three service entrance lines, is 220 volts. This is similar to the water pressure in the water main line supplying a house. Let's say you cut open that main water line that runs from the street to the house. Then the amount of water pressure rushing out of this pipe would be similar to the potential of the current in the electrical service lines. The only difference is that instead of measuring the electrical current in water pressure standards, you're measuring it in Volts.

◊ The *total* of the electrical current being used by a particular electrical branch line inside the house is called *Amps*. This is similar to the water pressure in the water supply lines inside a house. If you turn on a faucet, you don't draw <u>all</u> of the water from the water main line supplying the house. You just draw some of the water. The only difference here again is that instead of measuring the electrical current in water pressure standards, you're measuring it in Amps for that particular branch line. Amps is the abbreviation for *Amperes*. Amperes measures the rate or strength of electric flow. This is similar to the flow of water being measured in gallons per minute. *Amperage* is the actual measure of current flowing in a circuit to an appliance.

◊ The *actual* electrical power being used by a particular light bulb or appliance inside the house is called *Watts*. The only difference is that instead of measuring the electrical current in water gallons per minute standards, you're measuring it in Watts.

You're not required to do any math but if you want to use mathematical equations to impress your client, then feel free. You can use the following equations to help figure out if there are any possible overloaded electrical circuits in the house.

Watts = Volts x Amps
or
Amps = Watts / Volts

The main components of the electrical system consist of: the service entrance lines, the electrical conduit lines, the electrical meter, the main electrical panel and any sub panels, fuses or circuit breakers, the interior electrical wiring and the electrical system grounding cable.

The service entrance lines are the electrical wires carrying the electricity from the utility company wires in the street to the house. These lines are usually overhead lines and are visible from the exterior of the house. However, some installations are underground and aren't visible. Underground installations have a smaller chance of damage due to bad weather or power outages due to falling tree branches.

Check the overhead service lines to make sure that there aren't any tree branches near the wires that can cause damage. All trees should be pruned away for safety. Make sure the lines are high enough off the ground to prevent a car or truck from hitting them.

Look at the service entrance head. This is the area where the service entrance lines attach to the exterior of the house. Make sure there's no rust or corrosion. You should use binoculars for this if it's too high to view clearly. **<u>Do not use a ladder</u>** to view the service entrance head!! It could slip and touch the electrical wires. You're being paid to inspect the house, not get yourself killed.

⚠ Check for the presence of a drip loop. A *drip loop* is slack in the wiring that's in a U shape. This helps prevent rainwater from following the electrical lines down into the main panel. If the U is installed, then the rain water will drip off the loop and onto the ground before entering the electrical conduit. That's why it's called a drip loop.

> *If there are only two service entrance lines going into the house, then there's 110 volts inside. If there are three service entrance lines, then there's 220 volts.*

The service entrance head area will allow you to determine what the voltage is in the house electrical system. If there are only two service entrance lines going into the house, then there's 110 volts inside. A 110 volt electrical system will usually only have a maximum of 30-60 amps of electrical service in the main panel. If there are three service entrance lines, then there's 220 volts. A 220 volt electrical system can have up to a 200 amp electrical service in the main panel. On commercial buildings you'll find three service entrance lines that are much heavier gauge wires than those used for residential electrical systems. The commercial systems can have much more than 220 volts of power.

One of the service entrance lines leading to the house will usually be uninsulated. This wire is the grounding wire. The other line or lines carry 110 volts each. If there are three lines, then that's how you decide the house has 220 volts. Three lines prove the existence of two 110 volt service wires plus the neutral wire. Without getting into the intricacies of electrical current, each 110 line carries its current on a different phase. But for a home inspection you only need to figure out if the house has 110 or 220 volts.

Traveling from the service entrance head to the main electrical panel, the exposed service entrance lines should be enclosed in a conduit. A *conduit* is merely a covering to protect the electrical lines from the weather and damage. The conduit can consist of metal piping or a strong plastic insulator. Check the condition of the conduit to make sure there aren't any cracked or open areas and that all joints are sealed properly. The conduit will carry the service lines to the electrical meter. The location of the meter can be either inside the house or on the exterior. If the meter is on the exterior, then the utility company can take a reading without having to enter the house. In condominium buildings the meters for many of the individual units are usually located in one central area. This can be either in the lower level area or on the side of the exterior of the building.

You'll see moving parts inside the meter if any electrical appliances or outlets are being used inside the house. This is how the meter registers usage. Its operation is similar to a water or gas meter. Check to make sure that the caulking is in good condition where the electrical conduit enters the meter. This is important to prevent rust due to water entering the meter and flowing down into the main electrical panel. From the meter the conduit will carry the electrical lines to the main electrical panel. If the house has an underground service entrance line installation, then you'll see the conduit entering the main panel from the bottom, as opposed to the top. The main panel is usually located in the lower level or the garage.

 Remember that electricity can kill you!! Before touching the main panel or any sub panels check them with a voltage tester to make sure that it's not electrified. Voltage testers can be purchased very inexpensively at a local hardware or electrical supply store. There was a story in a home inspection newsletter about one inspector who noticed that the insulation on the service entrance line had worn off at the top of the main panel. This caused the main panel to be electrified. Luckily he tested the panel before touching it.

Also, don't go near any exposed wiring or any electrical panels or wiring if there's water on the floor or near the wires. Water and electricity *don't* mix! You're not paid to get electrocuted; you're paid to inspect the house. State home inspection and appraisal standards state clearly that a home inspector and/or appraiser is not required to do anything that can be hazardous to themselves or to others.

Check the main panel for any rust or corrosion. If there's excessive rust or corrosion, then recommend that a licensed electrician evaluate the system. After testing the electrical panel with a voltage tester check to make sure it's installed on the wall securely by *gently* trying to shake the panel. Be careful - you don't want to loosen the electrical panel nor any wiring, you just want to see if it's secured properly. See if there are any hazardous conditions around the panel. Some hazards to watch out for are: potential water, objects in the way, the panel being too high to reach safely, etc.

Check to see whether the system has fuses or circuit breakers. Newer houses have *circuit breakers* which are the plastic switches that can easily be turned on or off by the homeowner. Older houses have *fuses* which are the glass screw-in type. Do not turn any circuit breakers on or off and do not replace any fuses!! Sometimes a circuit will be off because the homeowner is making repairs or the circuit was overloaded. Just inform the client of this and tell them to check with the owner or a licensed electrician to figure out the cause. You aren't allowed to turn any circuits on or off or replace any fuses for safety reasons.

If a circuit breaker is overloaded, it will *"trip"* into the off position. When this happens, no more electricity will travel to the outlets or switches on that branch line until the circuit breaker is moved back to the on position. If a fuse is overloaded, it will *"blow."* When this happens, no more electricity will go to the outlets or switches on that branch line until the fuse is replaced with a new one. A blown fuse will have a burnt color and the metal connector in the middle will be cut in half.

When a circuit is overloaded, it simply means that there was too much electricity being drawn on that particular branch line wire. As a result, the circuit breaker turned off or the fuse blew, if they were operating properly. This is how circuit breakers and fuses help to prevent electrical fires.

Electrical fires are caused by the fact that when electricity passes through a wire it creates heat. Each branch wire has a particular rating in amperage. The branch wiring goes from the main electrical panel to each outlet and switch on the individual branch circuits. Let's say, for example, that a branch wire is rated for 15 amps and the electrical current on that branch wire is drawn up to over 15 amps. If this happens, then the fuse should blow or the circuit breaker should turn off. This will help to prevent the current from heating up the wire so hot that it burns off the insulation and then starts a fire in the house.

If an electrical system has had past problems with overloaded circuits, the cause could be from many different factors. Some of the more common reasons are:

◊ The electrical capacity entering the house is insufficient for the present demand due to the homeowner's electrical usage. They may be using too many window air-conditioners or electrical appliances and computers for the system to handle. If this is the case, then the system must be upgraded to provide more amps.

◊ Another common reason is that there are too many outlets and/or switches on that particular branch line. More branch circuits will need to be installed to help cure this. This problem is similar to having a plumbing supply line that's supposed to carry water to one bathroom and instead it's going to two bathrooms. The water pressure will drop due to excess water being drawn from the supply line. This water pressure analogy is the same concept used with electrical currents.

A benefit to having circuit breakers is that when a circuit is overloaded, the homeowner only has to turn the breaker switch to the on position to restore the electrical current. However, the disadvantage is that if circuit breakers aren't tested occasionally, they can *freeze* in the on or off position which can be hazardous since it won't operate properly.

⚠ With a fuse system, if the circuit is overloaded, then the fuse has to be screwed out and replaced. Often there are no spare fuses to install. Also, with a fuse system you have to be very careful that you install the right size fuse for that particular branch line. Many times homeowners will install any spare fuse that they can find lying around. If a 30 amp rated fuse is installed on a 15 amp branch wire circuit, then the circuit wiring can be overloaded and cause a fire. The electrical draw on that line might exceed 15 amps but the fuse won't blow to stop the current because it's rated at 30 amps! One way to prevent this problem is to have a licensed electrician install a *Fusestat*. A Fusestat is a screw-in part that will restrict the size of the fuse for a particular branch line. This will help prevent, for example, a 30 amp fuse being installed on a 15 amp branch line.

Check the fuses or circuit breakers to see if they're marked to show where each branch circuit leads to. This is a convenience and safety feature. For instance, if the electrical power needs to be shut off to a particular room of the house, then the markings will help to identify which circuit breaker or fuse will need to be turned off. The markings will also assist the homeowner in case of an emergency or if repairs are needed. There is **no way** for you to decide if the circuits are properly marked for the location of their corresponding branch circuits. You would have to turn off each branch circuit and see what switches and outlets were turned off to try to determine this. However, you cannot turn any branch circuits on or off during a home inspection for safety reasons.

Check to see if there are any open circuit breaker or fuse slots in the main panel or any sub panels. Open slots need to be covered with *blanks* or spare circuit breakers or fuses. This will prevent anyone from sticking their fingers or objects in the panel and getting electrocuted.

See if there's any room in the main panel for additional branch circuits. This will be noted by having blanks or unused circuits in some of the slots. Any unused circuits will allow the homeowner to expand the system by adding more branch circuits directly from the main panel without having to install sub panels.

Sub panels are small electrical panels that branch off from the main electrical panel. The purpose of sub panels is to prevent very long branch circuit runs in the house. As electricity flows through the wires it'll begin to lose some of its current potential and there will be a *"drop"* in the electrical current. It's similar to the water pressure in plumbing systems. If the branch wire is very long, then the current at the end of the circuit won't be as strong as the current at the beginning. Sub panels help to prevent some of this current drop. Sub panels are also a convenience in that they allow the homeowner to reach the circuit breaker or fuse without having to go back to the main panel.

In the main panel you'll see the main disconnect for the entire electrical system in the house. The main disconnect is similar to the water and gas main shutoff valves. Sometimes the main disconnect is located outside the house, next to the electrical meter. The main disconnect should be at least 30 inches above the ground and no more than seven feet high for safety. This will enable it to be safely turned off in case of an emergency.

Check the main disconnect for an amperage rating number. It should be written right on the circuit breaker or fuse. Fuse systems have either a *pullout* fuse box or a *cartridge* fuse for a main disconnect. A pullout fuse box is simply a cartridge fuse inside a small box that's pulled out to shut off all the electrical power to the house. A cartridge fuse is a fuse that looks like a miniature stick of dynamite that has metal blades at the top and bottom.

⚠ Do not pull out the main disconnect box or touch the cartridge fuse if you can't see their rating number!! Just tell the client that you can't determine the amperage on these disconnects due to the type of system it is. Tell them to have a licensed electrician find out the amps.

⚠ After checking the amperage rating of the main disconnect, check the main electrical panel for an amperage rating number. It should be listed on the sticker glued to the panel cover door. If it's not on the door, then the amperage rating should be listed inside the main panel cover. **Do not remove any electrical panel covers unless you are a licensed electrician!!** Just tell the client that you can't determine the amperage on the main panel due to the lack of a visible data sticker. Tell them to have a licensed electrician find out the amperage for them.

The purpose of checking these amperage ratings is so that you can learn what the maximum amperage is for the house electrical system. The house maximum amperage is the least of these three items:

◊ Number 1 is the capacity of the service entrance lines.

◊ Number 2 is the capacity of the main electrical panel.

◊ Number 3 is the capacity of the main panel disconnect switch.

⚠ Make sure the system has the proper amperage ratings for safety. For example, if the size of the service entrance lines has a capacity for only 60 amps and the main disconnect capacity is 100 amps; then the main disconnect won't provide the overload protection required for safety. It will be just like you installed a 30 amp fuse on a 15 amp branch circuit line. The wire could become overloaded and start a fire. The same is true if the main electrical panel has a capacity for only 100 amps and the main disconnect capacity is 150 amps. Here again, the main disconnect won't provide the overload protection required for safety.

The National Electric Code recommends that the minimum amperage for a house be 100 amps.

The National Electric Code recommends that the minimum amperage for a house or condo be 100 amps. This is because the older 30 and 60 amp electrical systems can't handle the extra usage more common today with air-conditioners, computers, appliances, etc. A 60 amp electrical service will generally be a nuisance for the homeowner due to blown fuses or tripped circuit breakers with the typical electrical usage.

If you recommend to the client that the electrical system be upgraded from its present amperage capacity; then tell them to get a price quote for installing a 200 amp circuit breaker system in the house. There usually isn't a big price difference between 100 amp and 200 amp electrical installations and the benefits of 200 amps far outweigh the costs. Some of the benefits are:

1   Central air-conditioning can be installed with 200 amps.

2   Additions and more branch circuits can be added to the house with 200 amps.

3   You don't have as many problems with overloaded branch circuits with 200 amp service.

4   Overall, it's much more convenient to have 200 amp service.

⚠ It's **extremely** important that the electrical system be grounded to a properly working grounding cable attached to the water main line or a grounding rod in the soil. Make sure the client understands the importance of maintaining a properly operating grounding system of the electrical service for safety. Review the plumbing section of this book which details the electrical ground cable attachment near the water meter.

As you go through the interior and exterior of the house check for any loose wiring that needs to be secured or any electrical hazards. Make sure you warn the client and the homeowner of any hazards. Remember, electricity can kill people so be very thorough and careful during the inspection.

In very old houses you might see some *Knob and Tube* wiring. This can be detected by the existence of white ceramic holders that were used many years ago to hold the electrical lines. All knob and tube wiring should be upgraded with modern electrical wiring by a licensed electrician for safety.

Check for loose switches and outlets that need to be secured. Also, check for any do-it-yourself work in the house. All electrical repairs **must** be performed by a licensed electrician. All valid permits and building department approvals must be obtained for any work done. As a safety precaution, check to make sure that the outlets and switches in the bathroom **are not** reachable from the tub or shower. Remember that water and electricity don't mix! Remind your client of this.

You should use an electrical outlet tester to spot check outlets throughout the house for proper wiring and current. These are hand held devices that plug into outlets to check for reversed wiring or improper grounding. Improper wiring can be caused by having the hot and neutral wires reversed in the back of the outlet or a false ground wire. Outlets with these conditions may still provide electrical current but they're an electrical safety hazard and must be repaired by a licensed electrician. Almost all houses you inspect will have some outlets with improper wiring. Just inform the client of the condition so it can be repaired.

Older houses will have the two pronged outlets as opposed to the modern three prong types. The third prong is used for the grounding prong in electrical cord plugs. The purpose of this grounding prong is that most appliances today have an internal ground. For example, let's say a wire came loose inside a washing machine and touched the metal parts. Well, if there was no internal ground or three pronged outlet then the metal casing of this appliance would become electrified. When someone touched the washer, they'd get an electrical shock. The purpose of the internal ground is that it would carry the current through the grounding wire to the third prong. This would then ground the circuit and the fuse should blow or the circuit breaker should trip off. This would prevent the electrical shock caused by touching the metal washing machine.

All two prong outlets should be upgraded to the modern three prong grounded outlets by a licensed electrician.

⚠ All two prong outlets should be upgraded to the modern three prong grounded outlets by a licensed electrician. If the homeowner is using plug adaptors to install a three prong appliance into a two prong outlet, then make sure that the pig tail is connected to the screw of the outlet cover plate. The pig tail is the small wire on the plug adaptor. The *pig tail* is used to help create the same effect as the use of a third grounding prong, if the two prong outlet is installed properly. However, don't use a plug adaptor and leave the pig tail wire hanging loose and don't use an adaptor that doesn't have a pig tail at all. This will defeat the whole purpose of the grounding prong on the appliance and create a false ground that is an electrical safety hazard.

In newer construction or recently renovated houses you may find *Ground Fault Circuit Interrupters* in some outlets. They're also called GFCI's for short. GFCI outlets have the two buttons in the middle that are marked *test* and *reset* A Ground Fault Circuit Interrupter is an electronic device that will trip or turn off the circuit when it senses a potentially hazardous condition. It's very sensitive and operates very quickly. The GFCI will interrupt the power in less than 1/50 of a second if it senses an imbalance in the electrical current of as little as 0.005 amps. The quick response time in interrupting the power is fast enough to prevent injury to anyone in normal health. The GFCI senses the current flow between the hot and neutral conductor in a circuit. Since the human heart begins to fibrillation (beat rapidly and irregularly) at about five milliamperes, the likelihood of electrocution is greatly reduced.

The National Electric Code recommends that Ground Fault Circuit Interrupter's be installed anywhere near water for safety. Water prone areas include basements, garages, kitchens, bathrooms and all exterior outlets.

The National Electric Code recommends that Ground Fault Circuit Interrupter's be installed anywhere near water for safety. Water prone areas include basements, garages, kitchens, bathrooms and all exterior outlets. You should recommend the installation of GFCI's to all of your clients for safety reasons. They're generally an inexpensive item to have installed and they significantly increase electrical safety in the home.

All GFCI circuit breakers, switches and receptacles should be tested to see if the fault sensing function is operating. Test them by pressing the button marked test. If the ground fault sensing device is operating properly, you'll hear a click and the reset button will pop out. This should cut off the electrical current to that outlet.

Many hand held electrical outlet testers have GFCI testing devices on them. Sometimes the hand held testers cannot trip the GFCI but the test and reset buttons on the outlet will work. If this happens, then the Ground Fault Circuit Interrupter may not be operating properly. Notify the client and the homeowner if the GFCI isn't operating properly and recommend it be repaired.

Generally, an outlet GFCI only monitors that one particular outlet it's located in. However, some GFCI's monitor more than one outlet. For example, there may be a Ground Fault Circuit Interrupter outlet in one bathroom that will monitor the outlet in another bathroom as well. This is because both outlets are on the same branch line. Also, some GFCI's are installed directly in the circuit breaker in the main electrical panel. The benefit of installing a GFCI in the circuit breaker of the main panel is that the ground fault sensing device will monitor *all* of the outlets and switches on that particular branch line. There is a drawback to this type of installation. Since GFCI's are so sensitive, often they'll go off without someone being electrocuted. If the reset button is located in a circuit breaker in the main panel the homeowner

must go to the main panel to reset the outlet. If the reset button is located in the outlet the homeowner can reset the outlet more conveniently.

If there are any Ground Fault Circuit Interrupter's in the circuit breakers of the main electrical panel, ask the homeowner if you can test them. Do not test these breakers before checking with the owner. You never know what that GFCI is supplying. It could be supplying electricity to an appliance or outlet that **must not** be shut off. So check with the owner before testing any GFCI's. When a GFCI circuit breaker is tripped off, it has to be reset properly to turn the power back on. A GFCI breaker may stay in the middle position after being tripped. The way to reset the breaker is to first push the handle so it's all the way *off*. Then push the handle back to the *on* position and electric power should be restored.

The NEC recommends that houses have an outlet for every six feet of horizontal wall space. This is because most appliances come with six foot electrical cords and if there aren't enough outlets, then the homeowner must use extension cords. Many older houses won't have enough outlets so check for any extension cords in use. Some older houses don't have outlets in the bathrooms which is an inconvenience. Extension cord wiring isn't recommended because of the possibility of someone plugging an appliance into an extension cord that has a low amperage rating. This will cause the extension cord wire to overheat and start an electrical fire. Warn your client about the use of any extension cord wiring.

If the client has children recommend that they install child proof caps for the electrical outlets. These are small plastic plugs to cover any unused outlets so a child won't stick anything into them and get electrocuted. You should also recommend that they use child guards for all cabinets to prevent children from opening cabinets that have cleansers and sharp objects inside.

Sometimes a client might ask you about aluminum wiring in the house. There have been fires in the past that were attributed to aluminum branch wiring in structures. Aluminum wiring is apparently less expensive to install than copper wiring. It was used a lot more during the 1970's when the price of copper became very expensive. The reason for these fires was aluminum wiring heats faster and hotter than copper wiring when electricity passes through it. It also cools down quicker than copper wiring when the current is shut off. When electrical wires heat up and cool down, they expand and contract, just like anything else. The problem of aluminum wiring was with branch circuits below 40 amperage ratings. These thinner gauge wires would expand and contract until the wires came loose from the electrical outlets, switches and circuit breaker screws. Once they would come loose they could touch the wooden wall studs or other combustible items and start an electrical fire.

⚠ The way to prevent this problem is to use only copper wires for any branch circuits below 40 amps. Also, all aluminum wiring, whether it is above or below 40 amps, <u>must</u> be used with aluminum rated adaptors, connections, outlets, switches, etc. The specially marked adaptors will have aluminum contacts instead of copper. This will prevent any oxidation of the nonmatching metals that could cause deterioration problems.

There are also chemicals on the market that should be put on the ends of the aluminum wires before they're attached to any connections or adaptors. These chemicals will help prevent oxidation of the wires. Some of the manufacturer name brands for these chemicals are *Penetr-Ox* and *Anti-Ox*. It's similar to using mixed material plumbing lines. Where the two different metals meet, there will be an oxidation problem that will deteriorate the lines at the point of the connection.

Electrical System photos: P 69-P 90, P 207

Operating Systems Photo Pages

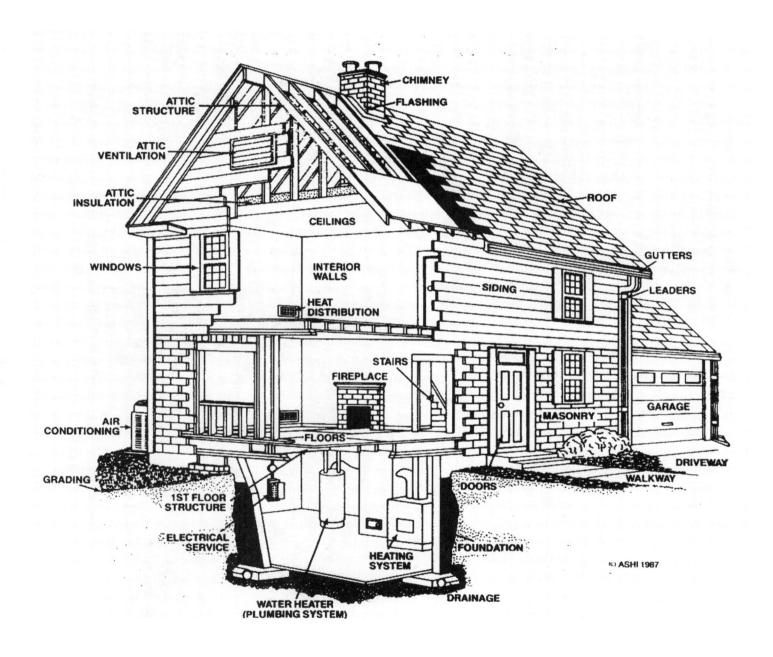

P 1. Gas fired, forced hot water heating system. Some of the components:
the flue pipe draft diverter hood,
flue pipe,
pressure relief valve,
main disconnect switch,
circulator pump,
boiler data plate with BTU rating,
heat exchanger drain valve,
gas supply shut-off valve,
thermocouple valve assembly,
the gas burners,
and the gas supply line drip trap.

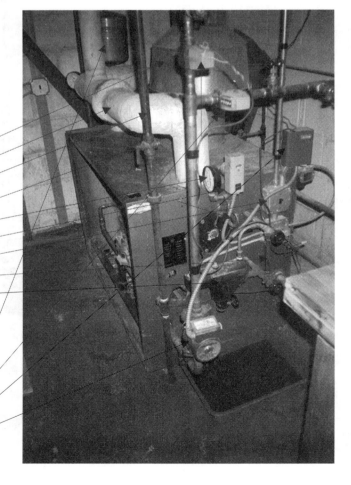

P 2. Gas fired, steam heating system. Some of the steam components are:
flue pipe and draft diverter hood,
wide diameter steam pipes,
gas supply line,
gas shutoff valve,
pressure gauge,
upper limit switch with the pig tail loop,
main disconnect switch,
water level sight glass
and low water cutoff and drain valve.

This is a "hybrid" system since it has steam plus forced hot water heat. The forced hot water components are:
the expansion tank,
heating zone valves,
relay box to turn on the zone valves,
and the circulator pump.

P 4. Oil fired, forced hot water heating system. Some of the components: expansion tank,
flue pipe,
flue pipe draft regulator door,
main disconnect switch,
a transformer for the thermostat,
pressure gauge,
circulator pump and relay box,
firematic oil shutoff valve,
oil filter,
oil burner,
and heat exchange/boiler drain valve.

P 3. Components of a forced hot water heating system:
pressure relief valve,
water pressure reducing valve,
pressure gauge,
relay control box,
main disconnect,
circulator pump,
gas supply line,
gas shut-off valve,
boiler drain valve,
and gas line drip-trap.

P 5. Gas fired, forced hot air heating system (furnace). Notice the flexible material *(dark colored area)* separating the heat exchanger fan area from the metal air ducts. This will prevent vibrations from traveling through the house.

The evaporator coil in the plenum is used for the central A/C system. The air-conditioning system uses the same air ducts and fan as the forced hot air heating system.

flue pipe,

high pressure A/C Freon pipe,

low pressure Freon pipe (insulated),

thermocouple gas valve device,

gas burners.

P 6. Oil fired, forced hot air heating system (furnace) with a close up view of the oil burner area *(below)*.

Air ducts and flue pipe,

The small, round door is an access panel to view the burner flames and the firebox area.

main disconnect switch,

The small red button on top of the relay of the oil burner is used to reset the oil burner if needed to start it.

oil burner,

firematic oil shutoff valve,

and copper oil supply line.

P 8. Two different forced hot water heating system circulator pumps:
the small one is the newer type,
the large one is the old outdated type.
There are water shot-off valves on both sides of the old circulator pump to turn off the water to simplify future replacement of this pump.
The pipes used in this system are of different metals due to repairs made over the years:
iron pipes,
and copper pipes.

oil filter,
copper oil supply line.

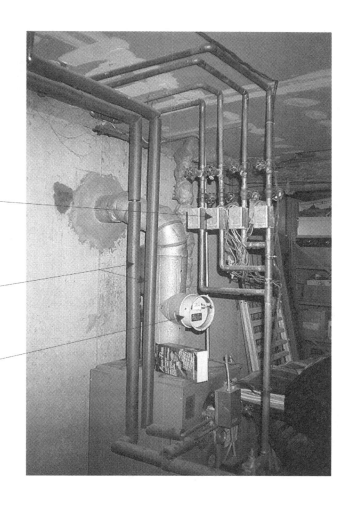

P 7. There are four zone valves to regulate the different thermostat temperature settings of four sections of this house. This is energy efficient since some zones will have lower heat needs.

The water pipes coming from the immersion coils in the boiler are insulated for energy efficiency.

Oil fired boilers and hot water heaters need the draft regulator doors in the flue pipe to help remove the carbon monoxide from the system.

P 10. The pressure relief valve to this boiler leads into a bucket. This could indicate that the valve has been discharging. The system must be evaluated for repairs when this happens. relay switch, main disconnect, asbestos insulation (must be removed), oil burner, oil filter, firematic oil shut-off valve, circulator pump.

P 9. Immersion coil pipes carrying the heated water from the coil area to the faucets and showers.

Immersion coil area of the boiler.

This immersion coil gasket has deteriorated and there is excess corrosion on this boiler.

boiler pressure gauge,
relay switch,
firebox door (to view firebox lining),
oil burner,
and the circulator pump.

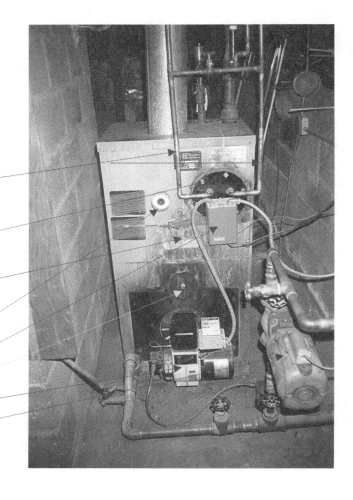

P 12. Due to old age, the metal heat exchanger in this forced hot air heating system has deteriorated.
The flue pipe and draft regulator door are very old and rusty.
The rust on the metal exterior of the furnace shows this system is on its last leg. Soon the heat exchanger will crack and lethal carbon monoxide will enter the house through the supply vents! This furnace MUST be replaced before that happens to prevent someone from getting killed!!

firebox door (to view firebox lining),
oil burner,
oil filter.

P 11. The large expansion tank over the boiler should be updated with a smaller, more modern one.

There is a fire-resistant sheetrock covering over the boiler.

The heat detector on the ceiling is recommended in areas of a house where smoke detectors can't be used.

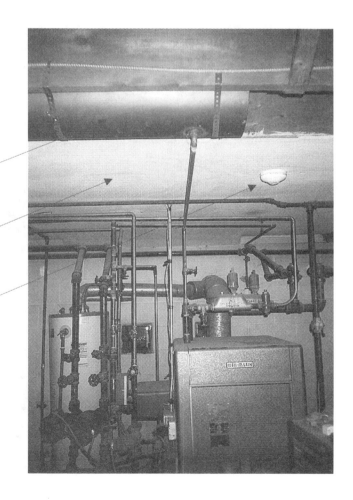

P 13. The joints where sections of the flue stack meet must be screwed together for safety to prevent them from separating and allowing carbon monoxide and unburned gases to enter the house. *These gases are LETHAL so don't take chances!!!*

A draft diverter hood is used for gas fired heating systems and water heaters. The open gap on the bottom allows entry of cool air to help carry the carbon monoxide up the flue stack and safely out of the house.

flue pipe,

pressure relief valve.

P 14. This flue pipe is touching wood which can start a fire!

Draft regulators are needed with oil fired burners. This draft regulator door is old and missing the counter balance weight which is required to allow cool air into the flue pipe to help remove the lethal carbon monoxide gases.

Screws are needed at the joint sections of the flue pipe for safety.

The open hole at the base of the flue pipe is unsafe.

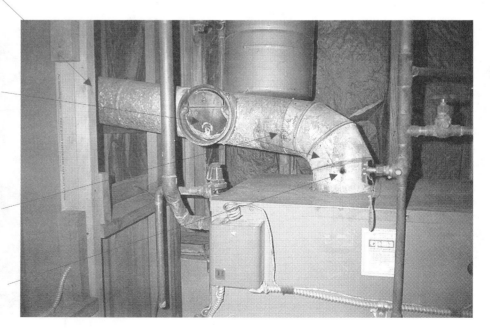

P 15. "Hybrid" heating system with an immersion coil indirect-fired water heater system. Some of the system parts are: wide steam pipes, valves to bleed out air, water level sight glass, low water cutoff, expansion tank *(there are 2 and one is old)*, circulator pump to pump the heated water, and an indirect fired water storage tank to hold the heated water that will be used for sink faucets and showers.

P 16. The sight glass allows you to see the water level in the boiler. The sight glass should be 1/2 to 3/4 of the way full. It shouldn't be completely empty or completely full which can cause problems. The sight glass level allows you to see that there's air and water in the boiler. This is because you're making steam and you've got to have room for the heated water to boil and create steam.

This is a steam heating system with an automatic water feed on it. This device adds water to the boiler automatically when the level drops too low for efficient operation.

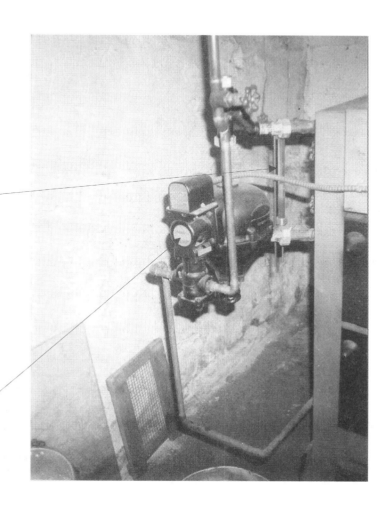

P 18. You'll find small valves, such as this one, on some heating systems. This valve is called a Spiral Vent and it's an automatic air bleeder. This valve can be used to "bleed" air out of the boiler pipes to remove any unwanted air pockets which can reduce the efficiency of the system.

P 17. A high efficiency forced hot air heating system. The fan inside the furnace panel removes carbon monoxide and unburned gases. These systems have a low flue stack temperature. A normal flue stack has a temperature of about 400 degrees Fahrenheit. With the low temperature units, the flue stack temperature is only about 100 degrees. This means that there is a significant savings in the heat loss from the heating system that rises out of the flue stack. Furthermore, some of the newer systems can have a much smaller BTU capacity since they are extremely efficient units.

P 19. All of these copper pipes embedded in the concrete floor are used for radiant heat. Radiant heat is rarely found due to the installation expense and the difficulty of making repairs. If these pipes get corroded or damaged, the concrete slab will have to be broken and removed to make repairs.

P 20. When the boiler was replaced some of the asbestos was removed to replace some of the old pipes with copper. Asbestos must only be touched by an EPA licensed asbestos contractor for safety. Notice the newer copper pipes and the old iron pipes that are still used to heat the house.

The relay box in the immersion coil area, monitors the boiler water temperature.
The pressure gauge above this has both a boiler pressure and water temperature reading on it.

The oil filter for this burner must be replaced at least one time per year.

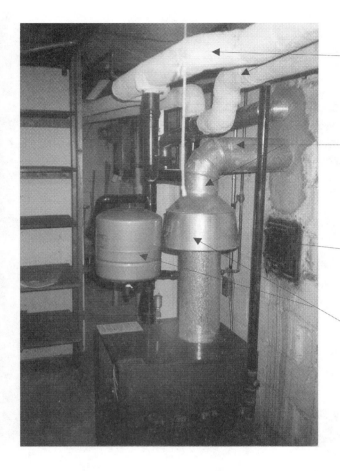

P 21. Asbestos insulation on the heating pipes that has been sealed with a protective covering to contain the asbestos fibers.

Once again, the joints where sections of the flue stack meet must be screwed together for safety to prevent carbon monoxide and unburned gases to enter the house. ***These gases are LETHAL so don't take any chances!!!***

The door at the base of the flue stack is a clean-out pit. This is used to periodically clean the flue stack and chimney areas to remove soot, sediment, and other unwanted debris.

draft diverter hood and expansion tank.

P 22. Hot water heating systems have a water pressure reducing valve on the water supply lines leading into the boiler. This valve will lower the water pressure down to about 12 to 15 psi before it enters the boiler.
There should also be a backflow preventer next to the water pressure reducing valve, like this one. This prevents water from the boiler from re-circulating back into the house plumbing lines. The purpose is to prevent the unsanitary boiler water from mixing with the faucet and shower water supply for the rest of the house.

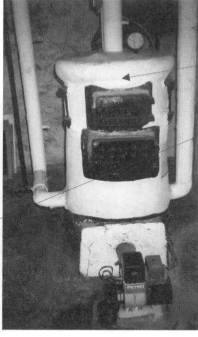

P 23. Here's some examples of dinosaur heating systems that are extinct:

Old steam boiler covered with asbestos *(updated with a new oil burner but still inefficient).*
Old expansion tank for a gravity hot water heating system.
Sheet metal used between the lower level floor joists to create a "home-made" air duct for a hot air heating system.

P 24. These open oil supply lines are a red flag that there's an underground oil tank in the yard that's no longer in use. This is an old tank gauge for an underground oil tank. The normal pressure of oil going into the burner is at 100 psi. Some newer equipment will run at 140 psi. The oil pump creates this pressure. The oil pump is a small attachment on the side of the burner where the oil supply lines lead into. Sometimes you'll see a pressure gauge on the oil pump. This suggests the oil service contractor may have had trouble maintaining proper oil pressure. Rumbling noises from the burner or smoky fires are conditions of oil pressure that's too low.

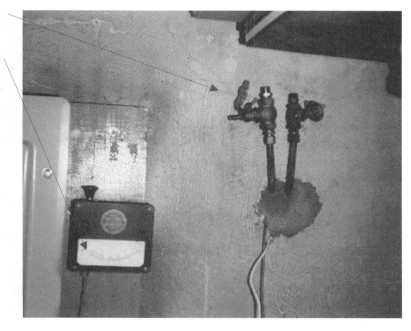

P 26. *No, that's not a submarine periscope!* It's the oil supply pipe that is used to fill this underground oil tank. The longer, iron pipe by the house, is the tank vent pipe. This allows air to escape so the tank can be filled properly. Underground oil tanks are a major expense to clean up. EPA laws have become much more strict with oil and lead problems.

P 25. There is a small fuel level gauge on the top of this interior oil tank. This interior oil tank has some signs of oil stains on the top. This can happen when the tank is overfilled.

Notice the patch on the bottom of this tank. Due to humidity, the bottom of these tanks often rust out over time. The patch is a temporary repair and replacing the tank is recommended.

The oil supply line has a firematic shut-off valve for safety.

The copper oil supply line is embedded in the concrete floor to protect it against damage.

P 28. Here is a properly installed air-conditioning compressor.

The exterior main disconnect is on the wall near the freon lines in good condition.

There are no obstructions to block the air flow around the compressor.

The concrete foundation is level and sturdy.

P 27. This is what you don't want to do to a compressor!

The shrubs around this unit are choking off the air circulation to the unit.

The freon lines are too exposed and need a conduit (tube encasing) for protection and they need to be fastened close to the house.

P 29. This large register in an interior hallway is a central return vent. This allows the air from the furnace and/or air-conditioner to be recirculated in the house. With a central return, it's not required to have a return vent in each room for the forced hot air heating or A/C systems.

P 30. The dark, flexible material between the ducts serves a purpose. This prevents the noise and vibrations from the furnace or air-conditioner fan from traveling through the ducts to the livable rooms in the house.

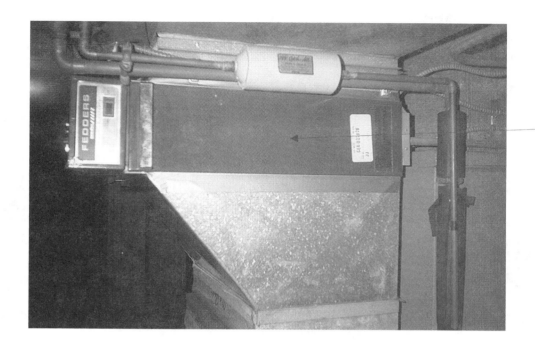

P 31. Electronic air filters can be very efficient cleaners. By using static electricity, these filters can attract dust, pollen, and other air pollutants in the home. The interior filter can be cleaned and reused.

P 32. The fan for this furnace/air-conditioning system is in very good condition.

The disposable filter above the fan, should be replaced once every month for proper efficiency of the system. These filters are relatively inexpensive to replace.

P 33. Air ducts can be zoned by using electric damper doors inside the duct. This type of control is more convenient than the manually operated levers to control the damper door of air ducts.

P 34. A condensate drip pump is used to carry water from the air-conditioning evaporator coil to a suitable drainage location. The condensation is created when the cool freon in the coil comes in contact with the warm, humid air inside the ducts.

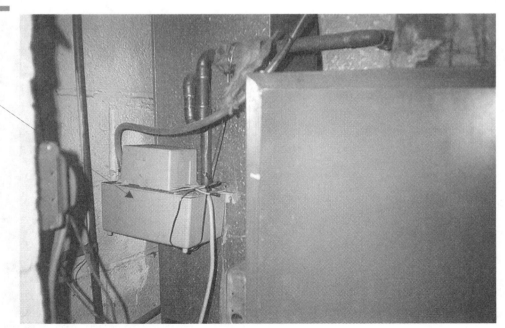

P 36. This A/C evaporator coil is "V" shaped. The small metal fins on the coil are similar to those found on the A/C compressor unit and in car radiators. The rust on this coil is due to the condensation created as the freon cools and dehumidifies the house air.

The low pressure line is the larger pipe, about 3/4 inch in diameter. This line needs to be insulated for energy efficiency since it has cold Freon in it. You'll usually find a black foam insulation over the low pressure line.

The high pressure line is the thin diameter pipe and it doesn't need to be insulated.

P 35. This is a side view of an evaporator coil for an air-conditioning system. The copper pipes carry the freon in a snake-like fashion through the coil to cool the air.

This coil has a lot of rust on it and is old.

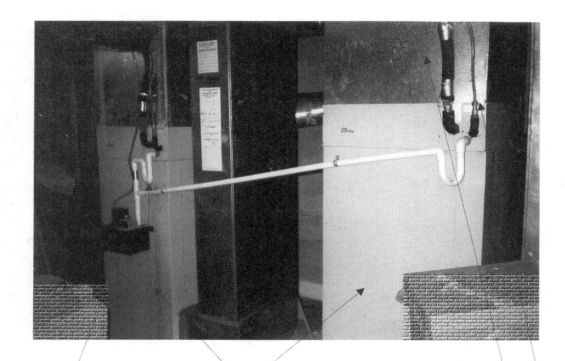

P 37. Large houses have two or more central air-conditioning units installed. You can see there are two units here.

There is one condensate drip pump for both evaporator coils. Each coil pan is connected to the pump using a plastic pipe with a "U" trap. The pipes have a downward slope since the condensation water uses gravity to get to the pump where it is then pumped to a drainage area.

The air ducts have insulation inside the duct. When you don't see external insulation, tap the air ducts to check for internal insulation. If you tap them and you hear a dull thud sound, then they probably have internal insulation.

The low pressure lines are insulated for energy efficiency. The high pressure lines don't need insulation.

P 39. This is an oil fired water heater. The relay box on the tank monitors the water temperature to turn the burner on and off when needed.

The drain valve is used to drain sediment and water from the water heater tank.

There is a small, round panel door on the right side of this unit. This allows access to view the firebox area.

The small red button on top of the relay of the oil burner is used to reset the oil burner if needed to start it.

The copper oil supply lines need to be protected to prevent leaks.

P 38. This is a gas fired water heater. There is a flue pipe and a draft diverter hood on top of the water heater.

All pressure/temperature relief valves must be piped to within 6-8 inches off the floor for safety.

The small dial on the top of the gas assembly is used to ignite the pilot light if it has turned off.

There is a temperature setting dial on the gas assembly. This will monitor the water temperature and turn the system on and off as needed.

There is a drip trap at the base of the black iron gas supply pipe.

A gas shut-off valve must be located on this supply pipe near the water heater for safety.

P 41. Electrically operated water heaters have coils inside the tank to heat the water. The two access panels on the unit, *(the lower panel is open),* allow the water temperature setting to be adjusted.

Data plates on the tank *(just above the lower panel),* indicate the gallon capacity, age, energy requirements, etc. of the water heater.

The drain valve at the base of water heaters is used to flush out any rust or sediment each month. Usually only about a half-gallon of water needs to be flushed to keep the system clean and efficient.

P 40. There is a metal conduit protecting the power supply line to this electrically operated water heater. Often you'll find the pressure relief valve installed on the top of the tank instead of on the side.
Styrofoam insulation is used on the hot water supply pipe for energy efficiency.
The cold water supply line is insulated to prevent condensation from forming. Check to make sure the hot and cold lines are installed in the proper access openings on the tank. Sometimes contractors will install them improperly. They're usually marked "hot" and "cold" for easy identification.
Bright yellow energy guides on all appliances help consumers evaluate the energy efficiency of different models.

P 42. There are wood 2 x 4 boards used to support the base of this water heater. This is a very unsafe condition. If the wood rots, then the water heater will settle unevenly. Settling will open up pipe joints and oil, gas or electric supply lines. This unit should be resting on a sturdy concrete foundation.

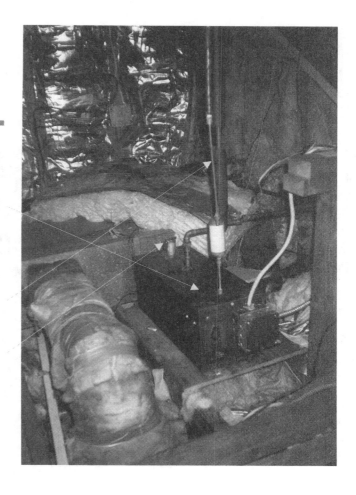

P 43. This attic has an electrically operated instant (on demand) hot water heater for a bathroom. These systems create hot water only as needed when the faucets and shower are turned on. The benefit of this type of system is that you don't heat more water than necessary, such as, the large volume inside of a standard water heater.

The hot water pipe is insulated for energy efficiency.

There is a pressure relief valve on this unit.

P 45. This indirect-fired water heater is similar to an immersion coil system of a boiler. The heated water that is inside the boiler pipes is routed through this water storage tank. Water inside the tank is heated by the warm pipes immersed inside this storage tank. It acts as a separate holding zone and gets heat from an internal coil, not from the boiler immersion coil. Circulator pumps and temperature setting dials are used on these indirect-fired water heaters. The main drawback is the same as that of a immersion coil system - the boiler will need to operate in the summer to heat the shower and sink water supply.

P 44. The large barrel shaped tank with the copper pipes coming out of the top of it is another example of an indirect-fired water heater.

P 47. Some newer, high efficiency oil and gas fired water heaters have plastic flue stack exhaust pipes. This pipe has a fan in it to remove the carbon monoxide and unburned gases from the house. These are very efficient systems due to their low flue stack temperature. The temperature inside a normal flue stack is much hotter than these newer energy efficient units. This means that there is a significant savings in the heat loss from the water heater that rises out of the flue stack. Furthermore, some of the newer systems can have a much smaller BTU capacity since they are extremely efficient units. An efficient water heater will have 1,000 BTU's for each gallon capacity of water it holds.

P 46. Due to the lack of available space, this homeowner had to install two small water heaters. This crawl space was not high enough to install one normal size water heater tank. As a result, the contractor installed two smaller sized tanks to supply adequate hot water to the house. These are electrically operated water heaters. The pressure relief valve is piped correctly to within 8 inches of the floor to prevent scalding anyone if it discharges. If this valve discharges it indicates a problem condition that needs to be evaluated.

P 49. This is a properly installed water main line. The electrical grounding cable is clamped on both sides of the meter.
The bell shaped water pressure reducing valve indicates there is strong water pressure from the street main water line.
There are shut-off valves on each side of the meter for easy replacement of the meter. The lever shut-off valve *(upper right)* is more reliable than the knob type valve.
water meter

P 48. This electrical ground cable does not span the water meter. A jumper cable is needed for safety.

A remote reading device will show the amount of water usage in this home. This wire, which looks like a telephone cord, will adjust the exterior meter reading for the utility company.

The pipe next to the water main is the gas supply line.

P 50. Due to rust, the shut-off valve and grounding clamp must be replaced for safety. The ground must span the meter.

This water main pipe is made of lead and is a serious health hazard. Lead will leach into the drinking water. When scratched, lead pipes will have a very shiny, silver color. A lead water main has a bulge or bubble known as a "wiped" joint. It can be seen next to this electrical ground clamp and is an easy indication of lead main pipes.

P 51. This is called a disaster!! This water main has so many problems that I don't know where to begin.
The water meter is very old, outdated, and probably gives inaccurate readings.
There is no electrical ground cable on the main!
The water shut-off valve is ancient and corroded.
The main water pipe is lead and must be replaced *(wiped joint noted by valve)!*
The water lines need to be properly secured to the wall. The wood board is not an acceptable support.

P 52. You can see the remote reading device wire attached to this water meter. Some water meters are installed on the water main line with oval shaped pipes. This helps to complete the grounding circuit for the electrical system grounding cable if there's a problem with the electrical system, even if the meter is removed for repairs. You still need a jumper cable to span the water meter for safety. It's better to be safe than sorry.

P 53. The round caps are clean-out plugs for these drainage lines. If the drain line gets clogged, these caps are removed and the pipes can be snaked out clean.

A "U" trap is installed on this cast iron drainage line for the plumbing system. The purpose of the "U" trap is to trap water and prevent sewer gases from entering the house through the drain pipes. Septic system drainage lines should not have a "U" trap on them.

P 55. Under this kitchen sink you see the thin copper pipe tapping into the cold water supply line. This provides water to a refrigerator ice machine or a dishwasher.

Shut-off valves are a convenience when making repairs to sink faucets, etc.

Plastic PVC pipe can be used for drain lines in most areas. The main drawback to this material is that it becomes a lethal gas during fires.

P 54. Some older homes will have small panel doors in the hallway or closet. This provides access to repair or replace the bathtub water pipes.

The discoloration on the metal parts behind this bathtub, indicate water leaks that have occured over time.

Old cast iron bathtubs are very heavy. When bathrooms are remodeled much lighter, more modern materials are used for bathtubs.

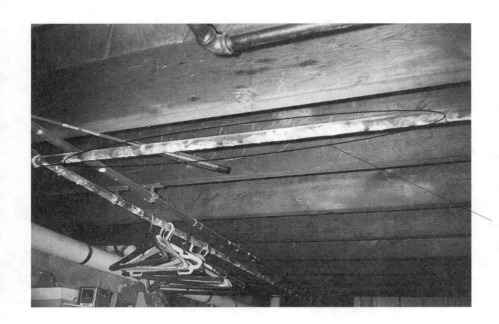

P 56. Galvanized pipes will corrode over time and should be updated with copper pipes. The interior of galvanized pipes will close as the mineral deposits from the water builds up inside the pipe. This will reduce the water pressure to the sinks, showers, and bathtubs.

The white stains on the exterior of this pipe are signs of minerals due to water leaks.

P 57. Often there are water softener systems installed with a house supplied by well water. Water Softeners are shaped like large scuba tanks or garbage cans. The softener equipment is usually located next to the lower level well components. They're generally made of plastic or fiberglass. They have salt, called brine, inside them that's used to help control the mineral content of the water. Softeners take the hardness out and raise the sodium level of the water to keep the proper chemical balance. "Hard" water has high mineral content. "Soft" water has low mineral content. Water that's too high or too low in minerals can corrode and clog the plumbing lines. If the water has too many minerals, it'll clog the interior of the pipes over time. If the water is too low in minerals it can't balance the strong acid that's naturally in water and this will deteriorate the pipes.

P 58. Water softeners should go through "backwash" cycles every few days. This rejuvenates the minerals in the softener with the brine.

Water filters are highly recommended for health reasons, especially with all of the pollutants going into the water supply these days. Check the color of the filter if there's a see-thru casing *(like in the photo below)*. The filters need to be replaced according to the owners manual and whenever they appear dirty. There are two kinds of water filters:
1) *Point of Entry* filters that are installed at the beginning of the house water main pipe.
2) *Point of Use* filters that are installed at the faucets, usually the kitchen faucet.

P 59. The well pump disonnect switch and relay boxes are located near the well water storage tank for convenience.

Insulating blankets help prevent condensation from rusting well water storage tanks.

The pressure guage on the tank should be replaced periodically.

Some corrosion is noted on the copper pipes supplying well water to the tank.

P 60. Make sure the water storage tank has an air fill valve on it. This looks like a tire air valve and is used to adjust the air-to-water ratio in the tank. Proper air-to-water ratio is needed inside the tank to maintain the operating pressure of the system. If the tank gets waterlogged over time, more air can be added to correct this problem.

Don't confuse the air valve with the mounting bracket on top of some tanks. Mounting brackets are used to hold the tank while it's being painted on the factory assembly line. They're also used to mount a suction or jet well pump if necessary.

The tank pressure gauge indicates the pressure inside the system.

P 61. The pipes coming from this well are made of plastic to prevent corrosion.

The metal Bx covering on the well relay electrical lines is rusting. This is a serious electrical safety hazard.

Excessive rust can be seen on these well pipe joints and the water storage tank, especially at the base. Leaks are beginning to develop and repairs are necessary.

Well water equipment is usually located in the lower level of a house. This promotes rust due to the humidity in these areas. An insulating blanket around the tank, along with a dehumidifier and proper ventilation will help prevent rust.

P 62. This old well equipment has part of the well pump located by the water storage tank. Due to the excessive rust and age, this pump will need to be replaced shortly. If the submersible portion of this pump is located in a deep well, the cost of replacing it increases.

The well water storage tank is insulated. These tanks should be painted and insulated to prevent condensation which will rust the tank over time.

P 63. This is an unused well shaft that is located inside the basement of a house. Unused wells should be professionally sealed for safety. Also, interior wells are not recommended. If these wells need to be drilled deeper, there is no way to bring the equipment inside the house. A new well will have to be drilled outside the house when an adequate water supply is no longer available from an interior well shaft.

P 64. Exterior well heads should be above ground, such as this one. Buried well heads are not installed in many areas due to the possibility of contamination. The small pipe on the outside of the well shaft leads to the water storage tank in the house. Wells should be at least 100 feet from the house and septic system to help prevent contamination.

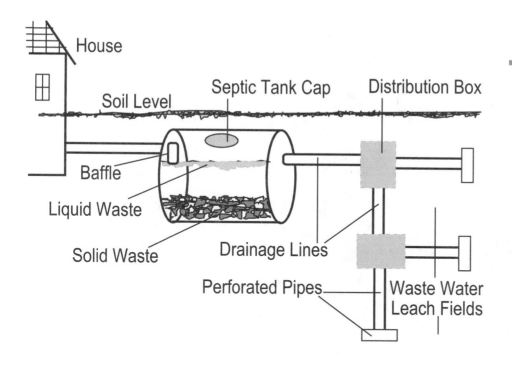

House

Soil Level

Septic Tank Cap

Distribution Box

Baffle

Liquid Waste

Solid Waste

Drainage Lines

Perforated Pipes

Waste Water Leach Fields

P 65. Sketch of a septic system for a typical residential property. The perforated pipes and leaching fields don't go down deeper vertically under the lawn, they go out horizontally underground. This sketch may give the impression that they go downward due to a lack of perspective in the art. *(I did this sketch myself and as you can see, I'm not much of an artist).*

P 66. The cap of the septic tank is located about one foot below the soil. By digging up and removing the cap, the septic tank can be pumped clean and internally inspected every 2-3 years by a septic contractor. Washing machines, water softeners, and garbage disposals should not discharge into a septic system. They can alter the natural bacterial action inside the tank.

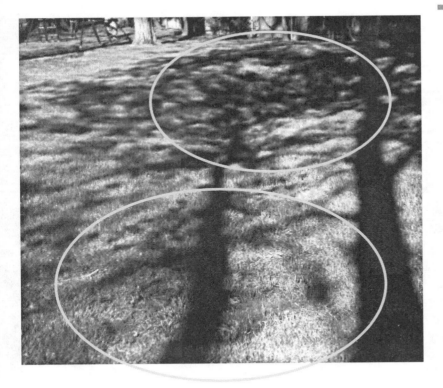

P 67. Here's a failed septic system leaching field. The sewage and excess water has started to kill the grass and has left large indentations in the yard *(indicated by the circles)*.

When you smell the sewage odor it means that the liquid waste is too close to the surface of the soil. This could be caused by clogged leaching fields or a high groundwater table. I've done inspections where the subject property was located in an area with a high water table in the soil. ***This not only caused water penetration problems in the basements of this neighborhood, but it also destroyed all the septic systems!!*** A high groundwater table will make a septic system fail because the tank and the fields will be deteriorated by the excess water in the soil.

P 68. Some septic systems have an alarm which monitors an internal pump inside the holding tank to make sure the pump doesn't malfunction. The purpose of the internal pump is to carry the liquid waste upward to the leaching fields, to be drained away safely. A pump is required when the leaching fields are located higher in elevation than the holding tank. This is **NOT** the normal type of installation since almost all septic systems use gravity for the drainage. When the water level rises too high, then it's an indication that the pump is not operating properly. You can identify the alarm by a small electrical box that's located inside the house. This box will have a red light on it. There may be a test button on the alarm box to periodically test it for proper operation. Speak to town hall and the septic installer about the septic alarm if you find one in the house since they're only used under abnormal conditions.

P 69. Electrical lines, conduits, and meters must be securely fastened to the side of the house. Tree branches need to be pruned away from the wires periodically. Three electrical lines at the service entrance head indicate 110/220 volts in this house. The "U" shape in the wires is called a drip loop. This is used to keep rainwater from entering the electrical conduit.

P 70. Caulking the joint on the top of the electrical meter and where the wires enter the house will prevent water penetration problems. Over time this exterior caulk will dry and crack and needs to be repaired.

The shingles on this house are made of asbestos/cement and are in excellent condition. EPA precautions must be taken when removing or tampering with any type of asbestos.

P 71. Here's a serious problem. This meter must be replaced and moved to a safer location on the property. This electrical meter and wires were installed next to the door of a house. This is unsafe since you don't want people to come into contact with the electrical wires.

The meter is very old and rusty.

P 72. *Is this what you call the Ivy League of electrical meters?* "Ivy" might be great to describe school universities but you certainly don't want it growing on your house electrical meters. Vines and ivy create moisture and decay problems to the sides of homes and anything else they are covering. Moisture should definitely not be in contact with electrical meters and wiring.

This condo building has five meters installed.

P 73. The messy wiring above the meter is for cable television.

Exterior main disconnect switches are not recommended. This switch panel has rust on it which is unsafe. Someone outside the home can turn off the power on the occupants. Also, if the electricity in the house needs to be turned off in case of an emergency, exterior disconnects can waste valuable time.

The small box below the electrical meter is a remote reading device for the water main line.

P 74. **Here's an example of a serious electrical hazard!** These electrical lines at the service entrance head must be securely fastened to the side of the house. This service entrance head and the electrical wires are loose and can move around in the wind. If the hot wires touch the wood siding they can start a fire.

P 75. The metal Bx cables coming out of the top of this main electrical panel protect the enlcosed branch wires. These lead to the different outlets, switches, junction boxes, etc. inside the house.

There is one plastic Romex cable on the top, left of the main panel. Romex wiring is used in parts of a home where Bx cable is not allowed, such as water prone areas.

This large 200 amp electrical panel has room to add more circuit breakers. Stickers allow the homeowner to mark where each branch circuit leads to. The main disconnect is easily accessible for safety. There is no rust on the panel and it's securely fastened to a plywood support frame.
(Just keep your main panel away from those liquor bottles. We don't want any drunk electricians around the house!)

P 76. Only a licensed electrician should remove the main panel cover or repair electrical wiring. ***Remember, electricity can kill you!!*** There are three electrical service lines at the main disconnect.

It's common to find small transformers attached to the electrical panel. The one on the bottom of this panel is used for a doorbell or thermostat.

The branch wiring inside this panel is very neatly installed. There is only one wire per circuit breaker and there is no excess slack of the wiring inside the panel. Electricians are like any other profession - some are neat, professional, and provide their customers with quality work that they can be proud of. And some are...

P 78. ...lazy and unprofessional who do electrical work that no one wants to put their name on!! Compare the inside of this electrical panel to the last one. *Tell me, which electrician do you want to work at your home?*

The wiring in this panel is all bunched up and is a mess.

The older wiring that has the canvas type of insulation should have been updated with modern electrial wires for safety reasons.

Some of the circuit breakers have two branch wires attached to them which is not recommended.

P 77. Screw-in fuses should be updated to circuit breaker electrical systems. A common problem with fuse systems is seen here. Due to lack of enough branch lines, subpanels must be installed to accomodate the increased need for outets and switches in the house. Often fuse systems will only be a 60 amp capacity, which is far too low and inconvenient for modern electrical usage. Replacing this outdated electrical equipment with a modern 200 ampere system, is highly recommended and will pay for itself over time.

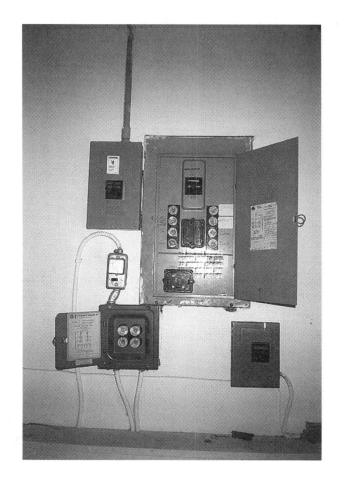

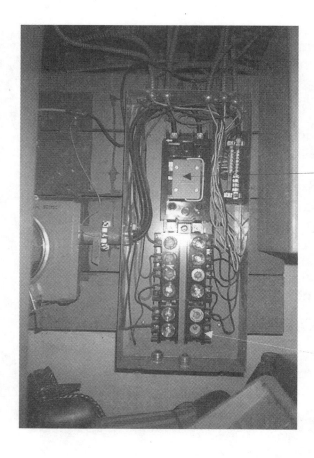

P 80. Inside this fuse panel, the wiring is neatly installed. Almost all of the old wiring has been updated with modern copper branch lines. The panel isn't cluttered or rusty. However, it still should be updated with a modern circuit breaker main panel.

The main disconnect for this panel is a pull-out cartridge fuse. This is not as safe as a circuit breaker switch because the disconnect box must be pulled-out of the electrical panel to turn off the power. This leaves exposed service entrance lines in the panel. Fusestats are recommended to prevent oversized fuses from being installed into the branch slots. Oversized fuses will cause the branch wires to overheat and start an electrical fire. Open fuse slots, such as the one on the bottom right of the panel, must be sealed for safety.

P 79. Here's a different type of cartridge fuse main disconnect. This panel has a lever on the right side to turn off all the electrical power in the house. The cartridge fuses in this panel are rated at 200 amperes. A modern circuit breaker main disconnect is more convenient and safe.

P 81. This cartridge fuse disconnect panel is for a three-phase electrical service. Each electrical line is 110 volts on a different phase. Out of the thousands of homes I've seen, this is the only three-phase electrical system I have ever encountered.

P 82. The open joints in the siding for the service entrance line and the grounding cable must be caulked shut to prevent water entry.

The National Electric Code recommends two grounding rods for an electrical system that is not grounded to a water main pipe. This is similar to the jumper cable used to span the water meter. It's safer and ensures a working electrical ground. Notice how the grounding wire from the interior electrical panel comes through the siding to the first metal rod. A second jumper cable is used to attach the first rod to the second one on the right. These metal rods must be buried at least 8 feet deep in the soil to ensure a proper ground.

P 83. In the lower level of many homes, you'll find wiring installed through the floor joists. This is acceptable as long as it meets the NEC requirements. Also, the drill holes must be in the center of the wood and less than 1/4 of the height of the beam. This will preserve the structural integrity of the wood beam.

You can see Romex and Bx cables are installed through these floor joists.

P 84. Using adapters when there is a lack of electrical outlets is a safety hazard. Too many appliances plugged into an outlet can create a fire or shock. The NEC recommends one outlet for every six feet of horizontal wall space. This will help prevent the use of unsafe extension cord wiring and plug adapters.

To make matters even worse, this gas wall heater has a flexible supply line which is unsafe.

P 86. Ground Fault Circuit Interrupter outlets, GFCI's, are recomended anywhere there is water for safety. The reason for this is that water and electricity love to get together and create fires and electrocution! Bathrooms, kitchens, basements, garages, pools and all exterior outlets should have GFCI protection. GFCI outlets and circuit breakers will turn off the electrical power very quickly if there is a malfunction or shock. Existing circuit breakers and three prong outlets can easily be replaced with GFCI's by an electrician.

(Who's that "A to Z" home inspector in the mirror taking the picture?)

P 85. The 110 volt outlet on the floor joist has a very rust coverplate and needs to be updated. Basements are prone to these types of moisture problems. The large outlet on the right is a 220 volt plug. This is used for appliances with high electrical usage, such as electric dryers, window or wall A/C units, cooking ranges, etc. Make sure your electrician follows all NEC rules when installing a 220 volt outlet.

This insulation is installed improperly between the basement floor joists. The aluminum vapor barrier always has to face the heated portion of the house.

P 87. Specially designed outlets are used for the exterior areas. This outlet has rubber gaskets and covers to help prevent water penetration. When you lift the plug doors, there should be GFCI test and reset buttons as well.

There is a heating/air-conditioning vent in front of the sliding glass door. Vents and radiators should be located by doors and windows to help prevent drafts from the exterior.

P 88. These junction boxes need covers for safety. A junction box is used to create a splice in long branch wires. They also can be used to install outlets and switches. Two wires with exposed ends are wound together. Then the plastic screw-on caps are placed over this splice to cover the ends of these wires.

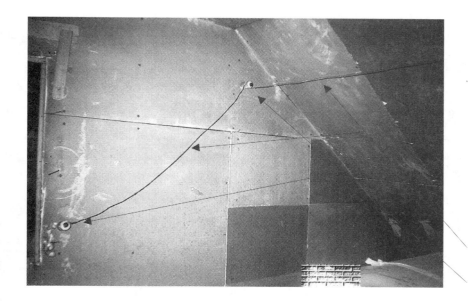

P 89. Here we have *Knob and Tube* wiring that should be removed for safety. Exposed wires run through the ceramic knobs. Many insurance companies will not provide homeowner's policies if there is knob and tube wiring in a home. In older homes you may find knob and tube wiring in the attic area or the basement. It usually has been disconnected and just has not been removed from the house yet.

exposed wiring

ceramic knobs

P 90. Apartment buildings, condominiums and some houses have underground electrical service entrance lines. This will help protect the wires from damage due to bad weather, falling tree branches, etc.

The Lower Level Inspection

Lower Level

Before a house is built, the builder and any engineers and architects will consult books that list the correct size beams and support posts needed. They will also check these books for the correct spacing needed for the beams and support posts. The sizes and spacing are based upon a particular weight factor in the construction of the building. This is why an architect has to sign off on the blueprint plans before obtaining town approvals. Anyone can use these published books but architects and engineers are more experienced at using them.

Some houses are built on a concrete slab and therefore there's no lower level to inspect. In northern climate areas, if a house has a basement or crawl space then the foundation footing must be below the frost line. The *footing* refers to the base of the foundation walls. The *frost line* is the depth of the soil where the ground moisture freezes in the winter time. When the water in the soil freezes it expands. If the footings are not installed deeper than the frost line, then the foundation walls can heave and crack when the ground freezes. How deep the frost line is will depend upon how cold it gets in the winter time.

Check the lower level steps and any exterior entrances for the lower level to make sure they're in good condition and safe. All stairs need to have handrails and evenly spaced steps for safety. This will help prevent any tripping hazards. When you're inspecting the basement area move in a clockwise or counter clockwise direction so you make sure you don't miss anything.

Some lower level areas will be finished with rugs on the floors and sheetrock on the walls and ceilings and you can't view behind these finished coverings. Finished lower level areas add more value in price to a home but they make inspections more difficult for home inspectors and appraisers. Some lower level areas will be inaccessible due to personal items of the seller put there for storage. Just tell the client that you don't have X-ray vision and you'll try to evaluate as much as possible. Any inaccessible areas can't be evaluated. So just do the best you can.

Check the construction materials used for the foundation walls. The foundation will be made of poured concrete in newer construction. Concrete block foundation walls are also common to find. Concrete block walls should be filled with concrete at the top section or have a *cap plate* at the top. This

will help prevent termites and radon gas from coming into the house. The termites and radon won't be able to travel through the voids inside the concrete blocks.

Brick construction and stone construction walls are usually found in older houses. Due to the cost of construction today, you probably won't find brick or stone foundation walls in newer houses.

The floor of the lower level should have a concrete covering. The vast majority of the time the floor will be covered with concrete. If there is a dirt floor, you should recommend that a concrete covering be installed. This will help prevent water, termite and radon entry in the house. Covering a dirt floor with concrete can be expensive, so tell the client to obtain an estimate before closing on the house.

I'll give you some background on the definitions of cement, concrete, concrete blocks, cinder blocks and mortar. You probably won't need to know this for most home inspections but it might help you in case a client asks some in-depth questions.

◊ *Cement* is in a powder form without sand and water added to it.

◊ *Concrete* is a ready-mix product that contains cement and sand so all that's needed is to add water to this mix and set it and wait for it to harden.

◊ *Concrete blocks* are used in newer construction. Concrete blocks have a gray color.

◊ *Cinder blocks* are found in older houses. They appear more porous and are usually only found on interior walls and not for foundations because they're not as strong as concrete blocks. Cinder blocks can have a blackish color to them because they've aged.

◊ *Mortar* is used as an adhesive to hold stones, bricks or blocks together. Mortar is made of cement, sand, and lime with water added. The lime is added because it acts as an adhesive. You don't need to add lime to the concrete for walls and floors. The reason for this is, you're not as interested in the adhesive qualities in these areas as you are with the rigidity of walls and floors. Lime gives the cement an adhesive quality, but at the same time it weakens the rigidity. As a result, it's not used in walls and floors.

Check for any large cracks in the walls and floors. Some concrete floors will have a gap about 1/2 inch around the perimeter of the lower level floor. This usually indicates the presence of a *floating floor* which is used to help prevent water problems in a lower level. The purpose of a floating floor is to drain away any water that enters the house through the foundation walls. The water travels through the opening around the perimeter of the wall and then down underneath the concrete slab where it can drain away.

Poured concrete foundation walls will usually have thin metal bars noticeable in some side sections of the walls. These thin metal rods are called *Form Ties* and they have no structural impact and are one of a few construction methods available to form concrete walls. The purpose of the form ties is to hold plywood boards in place to mold the concrete while it's poured during the construction of the walls. After the concrete has hardened, the plywood is removed. The metal rods should then be cut and the openings sealed to prevent any water penetration or rusting conditions. Poured concrete walls should also have thick metal reinforcing bars, often called *re-bar*, in the center sections to add support and hold the concrete together. These bars are embedded in the concrete and may only be visible from the top of the hardened wall. Re-bar is placed inside the wall to resist bending and shear loads induced on the wall and have a structural impact as to the performance of the wall.

Concrete block walls should have a metal zigzag shaped bar between every other course of blocks. This bar is called *Dura-wall* which gives strength to the block wall, similar to re-bar.

Sometimes sections of the compacted soil underneath the house will settle a little bit more than other sections. As long as the settlement cracks are less the 1/4 inch wide, then it's a normal condition.

You'll always find some minor settlement cracks in the walls and floors. These minor cracks are caused by the settling of the house and the expansion and contraction of the construction materials. When a house is built, the soil it rests on should be solid ground. The builder can compact the soil for less settlement over time. Sometimes sections of the compacted soil underneath the house will settle a little bit more than other sections. This is called differential settlement. If the foundation footings are undersized, then this too can lead to settlement cracks in the house. As long as the settlement cracks are less than 1/4 inch wide, then it's a normal condition. Just tell the client to have the cracks caulked and sealed to prevent water entry and to monitor these cracks for future movement.

⚠ All construction materials will expand and contract with the weather and temperature changes during the year. This can also create these minor cracks you'll find. However,

the cracks that you're looking for are long horizontal cracks or cracks over 1/4 inch in width. These cracks are much more serious, and if you find any, tell the client to have a licensed contractor evaluate them and give estimates for any repairs needed. Cracks over 1/4 inch wide indicate excessive differential settlement of the house and aren't normal. You'll find large cracks from time to time, so just remember to be careful and not to rush the inspection where you'll overlook them.

⚠ Long horizontal cracks are another indication of potentially serious problems with the foundation. You won't find these cracks so often, but if you do you better recommend that a licensed contractor evaluate the foundation for the client. Long horizontal cracks can indicate that the foundation wall is being pushed inward by the soil. The wall **will** collapse if this movement continues. One possible cause for this type of crack is during the original construction of the house. After the foundation walls are constructed, the soil is then pushed back up to these sides of the walls by the bulldozers. If the bulldozer exerts too much pressure on the side of the foundation wall it can cause the wall to crack and move inward. Obviously, you can't see any cracks behind finished areas or personal items in the lower level. That's why you have to notify the client of the limits of the inspection due to inaccessible areas.

Check the condition of the mortar joints and see if they need to be repointed. *Mortar joints* refers to the concrete mix that's used between the stones, bricks or concrete blocks. The purpose of mortar is to hold the construction materials in place and tie the different parts together for support. *"Repointing"* refers to the patching of any decayed areas of the mortar joints. This is a required maintenance item that needs to be done periodically.

You also want to make sure you view all visible foundation areas from the outside of the house as well. Do this during the exterior part of the inspection. On the exterior you'll be looking for the same problem conditions as those of the interior. Most of the time you'll be very limited in what you can see because the soil will cover the vast majority of the exterior foundation areas. Just do the best you can with what's visible. Often you'll find a thin concrete coating over the stone, brick and concrete block foundation walls on the exterior and sometimes even on the interior walls as well. Check to see if there are any areas of this exterior concrete coating or any settlement cracks that need to be patched to prevent water entry.

Make sure you closely view all accessible areas of the foundation, especially if the house is located on a steep hill. See if there are any areas of the foundation that have been altered from the time of the original construction of the house. If you notice any alterations, then recommend that the client check with town hall to make sure all valid permits and approvals have been obtained for the work performed. The last thing you need is to have someone buy a house and find out that the do-it-yourself work done to the original foundation doesn't pass the local codes and is unsafe.

Check the main girder beams, all support posts, the floor joists, and the sub flooring where visible and accessible. I'll describe these items and how to inspect them. The *main girder* of a house is the large beam that spans the entire width of the house. This is the beam that supports the interior portions of the house and it rests on the top of the foundation walls at the far ends. The main girder in newer construction will usually be made of a *built-up* center beam. This is usually two to three wood boards that are approximately 2 inches wide and 12 inches high that rest directly against each other. They're commonly called 2 by 12's in the construction trade. The reason for this installation is that several boards placed next to each other with a *Flitch Plate* have more strength than one large, solid beam. Built-up girders should have a Flitch Plate between each of the 2 by 12 boards. A Flitch Plate is a 1/4 inch or 3/8 inch steel plate that's added for additional support.

In older houses you'll find one large, solid wood beam. Many of these solid beams will have cracks in them. The cracks are due to settlement and from the wood drying out and expanding and contracting from the weather and temperature changes over the years. Probe all wood girders for rot or wood destroying insect damage. There shouldn't be any areas cut out from the main girder beam since this is the main support for the interior sections of the house. Check for any sagging sections of the main girder that will indicate unusual foundation settlement and sloping floors in the rooms above. Sometimes you'll find a main girder beam or another support beam, resting on a wood board that sits at the top of a concrete or metal support post. This **is not** an acceptable installation because the wood board will rot over time leaving an open area between the girder and the top of the support post. If you see this condition, recommend repairs be made by a licensed contractor.

Sometimes in some newer construction you'll find a steel *"I"* beam as the main girder of the house. This is superior construction because the steel *"I"* beams have tremendous structural support. Check any steel beams for rust that will require painting or repairs.

The *support posts* of a house are the posts that are found underneath the main girder about six feet apart. These posts support the main girder in the middle sections of the house while the ends of the main girder are supported by the foundation walls. The support posts in newer construction will usually be made up of steel columns about four inches in diameter that are filled with concrete. This is superior construction because the steel posts filled with concrete provide a lot of structural support. Check all steel posts for rust that will require painting or repairs.

In older houses you may find one large, solid wood post that's about four inches by four inches in diameter. You'll even find old tree trunks in very old houses. Many of these solid beams will have cracks in them due to settlement. Cracks are

also caused by the wood drying out and expanding and contracting due to the weather and temperature changes over the years. Probe all wood posts for rot or wood destroying insect damage.

There shouldn't be any areas cut out from the support posts. Check for any leaning or bowed sections of the support posts that will indicate the need for replacement. In older houses you often find support posts that have been installed due to sloping floors. The support posts are used to prevent the floors from sagging further. Sloping floors occur over time when the spans between the foundation beams are too wide. Building permits <u>must</u> be obtained for these changes to the original foundation. If the homeowner wants to relevel the uneven floors, this is a big expense. The house will have to be jacked up very slowly and more supports will be inserted. Only an experienced contractor should use house jacks. If you raise the house too quickly, cracks will be created in the walls and floors of the rooms.

Sometimes a house will have to be jacked up to replace the sill plate due to rot or wood destroying insect damage. The *sill plate* is the wood board at the top of the foundation wall. This is the board where the wooden wall studs are attached to. Replacing a sill plate is an expensive job that only an experienced contractor should do. Homeowners should not try to repair foundation problems themselves.

The *floor joists* are the wood boards that span the underside of the floors in the house. These are the boards that hold up the floors. The floor joists will run perpendicular to the main girder beam. The floor joists are approximately two inches wide and eight inches to twelve inches high. They rest about 16 inches apart from the center of one beam to the center of the next beam. This type of spacing is commonly referred to as *"16 inches on center"* in the construction trade. Sixteen inches on center is the typical spacing found in newer construction for all floor joists, ceiling joists, wall studs, and roof rafter beams. Sometimes for additional support, you'll find the beams to be 12 inches on center instead of 16 inches on center. Older houses will have beams that are 24 inches on center which is not as sturdy as 16 inches on center construction.

The floor joists should have diagonal bracing installed. These are small wood boards or metal straps placed diagonally in between each of the floor joists. Their purpose is to *"tie"* the floor joists together so they don't twist when the wood dries. Diagonal bracing also helps to spread the load exerted on the floor joists from the area above. This way when someone walks on the floor in the room above the weight will be spread across several floor joists, instead of just one at a time.

Probe some wood floor joists for rot or wood destroying insect damage. You don't have to probe every floor joist you see. Just spot check them and probe all areas that appear to have water stains or other potential problems. Often you'll find damage from rot due to water leaks over the years in a bathroom or kitchen above. Check for any sagging sections of the floor joists that will suggest unusual settlement and sloping floors in the rooms above.

⚠ Very often you'll find floor joists that have been cut to accommodate the installation of some heating, plumbing or electrical lines. If the cut areas are in the center of the beam and are less than 1/4 inch of the height of the beam, then they generally aren't a structural problem. For example, if a 2 x 8 inch joist has a 2 inch hole in its center, it can still be as strong as it was without the hole. However, if a 2 x 8 inch joist is notched at the top or bottom to a depth of 2 inches, then its strength will be reduced to that of a 2 x 6 inch joist. The reason for this is that when weight is being placed on top of the floor joist, the top of the beam is in a state of *compression* and the bottom of the beam is in a state of *tension*. As a result, there's no stress in the middle of the beam because that's where the compression transfers to tension. It's similar to the eye in the middle of a tornado. The two forces on each side equalize one another in the middle section. However, if there are large holes in the center, top or bottom of the beam, then they *must* be resupported. Probe these areas and tell the client that additional support posts should be installed to prevent any problems with these cut boards.

The *sub flooring* is the plywood or paneled wood boards which are located on top of the floor joists. The purpose of sub flooring is to support the finished flooring above, such as hardwood, tiles or carpeting, that rests on top of the sub flooring. Probe some wood sub flooring for rot or wood destroying insect damage. Here again you'll often find damage from rot due to water leaks over the years in a bathroom or kitchen above.

Lower Level photos: P 91-P 102, P 208

Crawl Spaces

Some houses will have crawl spaces which are small areas underneath the house that aren't high enough to stand up in. You should ask the owner if there are any crawl spaces before starting your inspection. Ask this because sometimes the entrances to the crawl space areas can be hidden by personal items or wall finishings.

You should use a jumpsuit, kneepads, a hardhat, gloves, and a flashlight to enter any crawl space areas. Do not go into any areas that are too narrow for you to safely enter. A crawl space is an area that demands attention. Crawl spaces need attention because there's a higher risk of rot and termite infestation due to these areas being dark and damp most of the time. So don't get lazy and just assume everything is OK in the crawl space. You may end up regretting it if the client calls you up six months later to complain about the termite damage

they found in the crawl space. You'll have a hard time defending yourself if you didn't check this area if it was accessible at the time of your inspection.

> *A crawl space is an area that <u>demands</u> attention. There's a higher risk of rot and termite infestation due to these areas being dark and damp.*

Crawl spaces need plenty of ventilation to help prevent rot and wood destroying insect infestation. If the crawl space has a dirt floor, you should recommend that the client get an estimate to have the floor covered with a concrete surface. Dirt floors will promote moisture from the soil and are an attraction to wood destroying insects and radon gas. If putting concrete over the dirt floor is too expensive, then a six mil plastic floor cover can be placed over the dirt areas. The plastic cover is used to help eliminate moisture problems in the crawl space. However, the plastic will not work as well as a concrete floor covering to prevent moisture problems.

Check for the condition of the foundation walls, support posts, main girder, floor joists, and sub flooring in the crawl space. Look for the same potential problems that were discussed in lower level section.

Crawl Spaces photos: P 91-P 102, P 209

Gas Service

If the house is connected to the gas utility lines in the street, check the condition of the gas meter and gas lines. If the house isn't connected to any gas service lines, recommend to the client that they check with the local utility company. They'll need to find out what the costs are to hook up or if it's even possible to get gas service in the house. Some areas don't have natural gas service and the client might not know this. Don't just assume your client is aware of the lack of gas service lines in the street. You don't want him to be confronted with any surprises after he moves into the house.

The gas meter is usually located in the lower level or just outside the house next to the foundation. If the meter is inside the house, a remote reading device should be installed. This will allow the utility company to take the meter reading when no one is at home. Make sure there's a main shutoff valve near the gas meter for safety. This will enable the gas service to be turned off for repairs or an emergency. Next to the gas meter you find a gas regulator. This looks like a small, round saucer and is installed before the meter on the high pressure gas lines. A gas regulator has a similar operation to a water pressure reducing valve. Gas from the main lines in the street may have a high pressure rating. The gas regulator parts by the meter lowers the street gas pressure before it enters the house. Gas pressure entering the house should be lowered to about 4-5 inches per water column.

⚠ All gas service lines should be approved black iron gas piping. Often you'll find copper or flexible gas pipe connectors being used to supply appliances. There should not be any copper or flexible metals used for gas feed lines. If there are, then recommend they have a licensed plumber make any necessary repairs to bring the gas lines up to the building codes. Some areas do allow copper and flexible pipe to be used to hook up appliances. However, even if the local building codes allow this, it's not as safe as using black iron pipe.

> *If you smell or detect any gas leaks IMMEDIATELY tell the client, all third parties and the homeowner to contact the local utility company to make repairs.*
> *Leaking gas will explode!!!*

If the gas lines are rusty, recommend that they be painted. You might want to purchase a hand held combustible gas detector to check the visible gas lines and the meter for any gas leaks. If you smell or detect any gas leaks ⚠ **IMMEDIATELY** tell the client, all third parties and the homeowner to contact the local utility company to make repairs. Leaking gas will explode!!! So don't take any chances. It's common to find minor gas leaks at some of the pipe joints. Gas pipe joints can come loose over time and need to be tightened and caulked periodically. Don't panic if you find a gas leak. Just call the utility company and they should send someone over immediately to make repairs. Also, if there is a strong gas odor in the house, don't use the telephones or turn on any light switches or electric appliances. Using any electrical items can create a spark and cause a serious buildup of gas to explode!

I'm not trying to scare you away from houses with gas service. The gas utility company in my area says there are a minimal number of cases of house explosions due to gas leaks. Natural gas is colorless and odorless when it comes from the earth. The gas utility companies put the odor into the gas before it reaches your house. The reason they put the odor in the gas is so that it's easier to detect a gas leak. If you couldn't see or smell a gas leak, then you wouldn't be aware of a problem until *after* an explosion occurred. The gas utility company in my areas feels that any serious gas leaks will create an easily detected odor in the house. This should allow the occupants to safely leave the home prior to an explosion.

You may find drip traps on the gas supply lines for the heating system and hot water heater. A *drip trap* is a small "dead end" section of the gas pipe installed just before the burners. The purpose of the drip trap is to catch some of the moisture and dirt before it clogs the gas burners. They were used when gas was produced at plants because this type of gas has too much moisture in it. Drip traps are not needed anymore due to the use of natural gas as opposed to man-made gas. Natural gas is dry and does not have a moisture problem.

Some houses have *Propane Gas* or *Liquid Petroleum Gas* service, also called LPG. This is similar to getting oil deliveries because the tanks are filled by a local LPG gas supplier. Propane and LPG are two different names that refer to the same thing. Check the condition of the gas tanks for any rust or corrosion. The life expectancy of propane and LPG tanks depends upon the maintenance given to them. Usually, the gas supplier owns the tanks and rents them to the homeowner. Make sure that the tank is properly leveled on a sturdy foundation. If the tank settles unevenly, it could create a leak in the gas lines. Copper pipe is allowed for LPG gas lines in some areas. Recommend that the client check with town hall to make sure all valid permits are on file for gas tanks.

⚠ Tell your client not to bring any gas tanks into the house, such as exterior barbecue tanks or automobile gas cans. Barbecue gas tanks are under extreme pressure, like scuba diving tanks. *If they ever exploded, they would cause extensive damage and probably kill someone!!*

I'll give you some interesting facts concerning the accuracy of utility company meters. You and your client might want to know this. Gas, electric and water meters have a typical life expectancy of 7-8 years. When a certain model of meters gets old, the utility company will do a random check on some of them. This is done to determine if these meters are still giving accurate readings. I see houses all the time that have utility meters that are over 25 years old! Meters that are past their life expectancy have a higher chance of being inaccurate. Water meters are supposedly the least accurate when they get old. If your client calls the local utility companies, he can find out what date the current meters were installed. From this information it's easy to conclude if the meters are old and should be replaced. In my area the utility company doesn't charge to change an old meter. However, they don't voluntarily do it unless you call to insist upon it.

Utility bill auditing has become a growing home-based business due to the inaccuracy of utility meters. Someone providing this service will generally charge a percentage of the refund money they obtain for you. As a result, if they don't get you a refund, then you don't pay any fees! Not a bad arrangement for the homeowner. If you suspect that your utility company is overcharging you, then contact a utility bill auditor or you local utility supplier. Just be aware that when you call your local utility company and question the accuracy of their meter - they're probably going to get very defensive! This has happened to me with my rental properties. I found out from the utility company that some of the meters were installed over 20 years ago. When I questioned why my bills were so high for some months, they would **insist** that they're meters are always accurate. Don't be scared off by this smoke screen. I'm convinced that utility company employees are trained to try and persuade people out of disputing their meter readings.

If a customer feels that a meter is inaccurate there are several options to take. Call your local Public Service Commission that oversees the utility company rates. Tell them you want your meters tested for accuracy. If your meters are old, then you can insist that they be replaced as well. Your PSC bureau will give you a case number for your claim. From this point, they'll contact the utility company to have your meters replaced and tested. It only takes about 10 minutes to change a utility meter. So don't be worried that you'll be without water, gas or electric while they're testing your meter. When the old meter is removed, a new one is installed in its place immediately. The old meter is then tagged and brought to the utility company testing location. You should get the results of the test in about one month.

There's another important point to this story. Remember to call the PSC to test your meter and not just the utility company. When you get a case number from the Public Service Commission, then they will have one of their employees oversee the meter tests. If you only call the utility company, then the PSC is not there to oversee the meter testing. It's a total conflict of interest if you only have the utility company employees present for the testing. What if the meter reading is high and you've been overcharged for the past 10 years? How much incentive does the utility company have to refund all your money?

Gas Service photos: P 104-P 107

Auxiliary Systems

Check for the existence of any alarm systems, fire detection systems, intercoms, burglar alarms, central vacuum systems, lawn sprinklers, etc. Often the control panels for these devices are located in the lower level. You're not required to evaluate these systems during a home inspection. Just tell the client to get any manuals from the owner and find out how to operate these systems. If you tried to evaluate these systems, you could spend a lot of extra time in the house. Feel free to go ahead and charge extra to evaluate these types of items if you want to and if you're knowledgeable enough. Just charge the client for your time and include it in your price quote when you book the job.

Tell the client to find out if any fire or alarm systems are hooked up to any monitoring services and/or the local police or fire departments. Also, have them check to see what the fees are for this service.

Auxiliary Systems photos: P 109-P 108

Water Penetration

While you're in the lower level you want to check for any signs of water problems in the house. This is something you *don't* want to forget. It certainly isn't life threatening to the occupant of the house to overlook water problems during an inspection. However, you will get phone calls from angry clients who have discovered that they get water in the lower level of their new home. Fortunately, I never got any angry phone calls but I know some inspectors who have. People get very upset if they get water in their basement.

If you're inspecting the house during the rainy season, then the groundwater table will be higher than normal. You should always tell your client to visit the house after it rains, before the closing. This way they will be able to see for themselves if there is a potential problem with water penetration. Signs of water penetration can be white mineral salts on the concrete walls and floors. This is called *efflorescence* and it's caused by water seeping through the concrete and then drying on the exterior portion. After the water dries, it leaves the white, mineral salt from the concrete as a residue. Most lower level areas will get some minor efflorescence on the lower portion of the walls and floors. This is from humidity in the lower level because these rooms are located underground. Recommend that the client use a dehumidifier to help prevent moisture.

In the corners you may see indications of water stains. Often the cause of these stains is due to the lack of gutters and downspouts on the house. Another cause is that the downspouts are draining right next to the foundation walls on the exterior. All downspouts should be piped away from the house by at least five feet so the rainwater won't drain next to the foundation and enter the lower level. Sometimes the downspouts drain into underground drain lines. These lines can become clogged due to leaves or small animals becoming stuck in them. Underground drain lines need to be checked periodically for proper operation.

The grading of the soil next to the exterior of the house can also cause minor water stains on the lower level walls and floors. All soil next to the foundation should slope away from the side of the house to help prevent rainwater from entering the lower level. We'll talk more about gutters, downspouts, and soil grading in the exterior section of the book.

> *You're looking for excessive or abnormal signs of water problems, not just normal humidity and condensation stains.*

Another way to check for water problems is to probe the wood members that are in contact with the floor, such as, workbench posts, storage items, wood shelves, etc. Check under the corner of any carpeting or floor coverings in the lower level. If there's a water problem, then these areas will have signs of it. You're looking for excessive or abnormal signs of water problems, not just normal humidity and condensation stains. Be wary of recently painted lower level walls and floors. Sometimes the homeowner will paint just before selling a house. This can hide any indications of water problems.

Check for the existence of any sump pumps. *Sump pumps* are pumps that help carry water away from the house. Sump pumps are located in small pits dug into the lower level floor. They have a drainage pipe to carry water to a more desirable location. When sump pumps are installed, it usually indicates that the lower level has a water penetration problem. Sometimes, you'll find a sump pump in a lower level that doesn't have any water problems. One reason for this is that some builders and homeowners install these pumps as a precautionary measure, even if they haven't had water penetration.

Check to see if there's any water inside the sump pit. Any water in the pit would show that the area has a high groundwater table and that there's a potential for water to enter the lower level. The sump pump should be plugged into an outlet with a Ground Fault Circuit Interrupter for safety. The sump drainage line should also have a backflow preventer. This is a check valve inside one section of the line to help prevent the drainage water from flowing backwards toward the sump pit after it's pumped out.

In most areas, the local building codes prohibit sump pump drainage lines from discharging water into the house plumbing drainage lines. This restriction is designed to prevent too much water from entering the municipal sewer system. Excess water in the city sewers will increase costs at sewage treatment plants. The sump drainage line must discharge the water at least five feet away from the exterior foundation of the house. This is required to prevent the water from flowing back into the sump pit through the foundation walls after it has already been pumped out from the lower level of the house.

Check the condition of the sump pump and the pit. If the pump is old, then recommend it be upgraded with a modern unit. If the sump pit walls are in poor condition, then recommend they be rebuilt. Often you'll find do-it-yourself installations of sump pumps.

Test the sump pump. Most sump pumps are water activated. Meaning that when the water in the pit rises to a certain height, the sump pump will automatically sense this and turn on by itself. If there's a float, then lift the float to imitate the action of water rising in the sump pit to activate it. Some sump pumps have a small plastic suction hose on the plug section. Unplug the unit and briefly suck on this hose as though it were a drinking straw. *(Of course you're not going to do this if it's dirty)*. When you remove your mouth from the hose, cover the open hose with your finger and plug the unit into a Ground Fault Circuit Interrupter electrical outlet. The sump should turn on if it's plugged in and working properly. If the sump pump doesn't turn on, then recommend it be replaced.

If you do find water in the sump pit or if there are signs of excessive water problems, tell the client to check with the local building department to find out if the subject property is located in a designated flood hazard zone. The bank appraiser is supposed to check this during the appraisal process but don't leave it up to them. They sometimes cut corners that could end up costing the client money and aggravation.

There are different types of drain systems that can be installed to eliminate water problems in a house.

◊   A *curtain drain* is installed underground on the outside of a house at the base of a swale or trench.

◊   A *footing drain* is installed on the outside of a house next to the base of the foundation footing.

◊   A *french drain* is installed underground on the inside of a house along the perimeter of the foundation walls.

A *flood hazard zone* is a designated area by the government. These areas have a certain potential of becoming flooded from time to time. Flood maps are located in every town hall and are available to the public to view for free. If a house is located in a flood hazard zone, the homeowner should obtain flood hazard insurance on top of the regular homeowner and title insurance for safety.

Water Penetration photos: P 110-P 113

Lower Level Photo Pages

P 91. Poured concrete foundation walls will usually have thin metal bars noticeable in some side sections of the walls. These thin metal rods are called Form Ties and have no structural benefit on the concrete walls. Form ties hold plywood boards in place to mold the concrete while it's poured during the construction of the walls. After the concrete has hardened, the plywood is removed. The metal rods should then be cut and the openings sealed to prevent any water penetration or rusting conditions. Poured concrete walls should also have thick metal reinforcing bars, often called re bar, in the center sections to add support and hold the concrete together. Re-bar is placed inside the wall to resist bending and shear loads induced on the wall and have a structural impact on the wall.

P 92. Steel "i beams" are a superior structural material that is used in commercial buildings and in some homes. Most houses will use wood main girders for support. Steel beams will hold a tremendous amount of weight on top of them. Also, they are rot and wood destroying insect proof. If steel beams are not kept painted, they can rust.

The air ducts in this house have external insulation for energy efficiency.

P 93. In case you were wondering what your house looked like during the construction phase:

This shows a poured concrete foundation. The soil will be moved back into place to help support the foundation walls on the outside.

P 94. Here you have the wood framing for the walls and floors of the interior of a house under construction. All of the wiring, plumbing, air ducts, etc. will be installed before these walls and floors are sealed up with the finished coverings.

You can see metal brackets for the joist hangers are used for added support and strength.

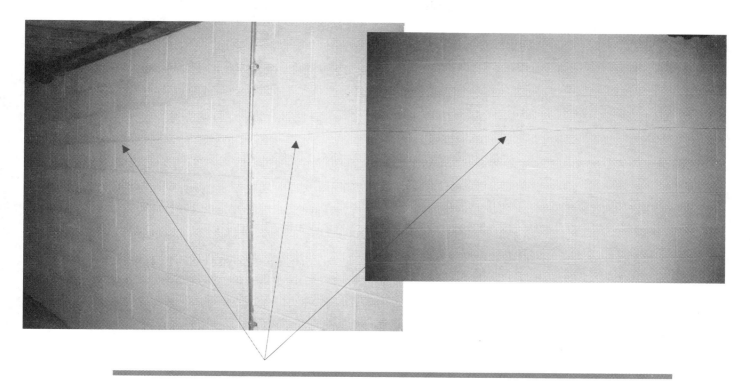

P 95. These two photos are placed side by side but they show the same very serious problem condition - *a long horizontal foundation wall crack!!* It's hard to see in these photos because the walls were recently painted *(maybe by someone who wanted to hide the cracks to sell the house).*

All construction materials will expand and contract with the weather and temperature changes during the year. This can create minor cracks.

Long horizontal cracks are an indication of potentially serious problems with the foundation. You won't find these cracks often, but if you do you better recommend that a licensed contractor evaluate the foundation. Long horizontal cracks can indicate that the foundation wall is being pushed inward by the soil. The wall will collapse if this movement continues. One possible cause for this type of crack is during the original construction of the house. After the foundation walls are constructed, the soil is then pushed back up to these sides of the walls by the bulldozers. If the bulldozer exerts too much pressure on the side of the foundation wall it can cause the wall to crack and move inward. Obviously, you can't see any cracks behind finished areas or personal items in the lower level. That's why you have to notify the client of the limits of the inspection due to inaccessible areas.

P 97. There are metal Bx cables covering the electrical lines in the house.

Notice the three 2 x 12" beams placed side-by-side. This is a stronger support than one solid, wood beam that is the same width and height.

Due to the large settlement crack in this concrete block foundation wall, more support was needed. Excessive cracks occur when the house settles unevenly over time.

An adjustable, metal lally column was placed underneath this wood main girder beam. Temporary columns should be replaced with solid, metal support posts that have a sturdy base.

P 96. Shims are used to level areas that cannot be exactly measured during the construction process. Wood shims cannot be used for structural supports. The wood boards on top of this concrete block post will eventually rot out. This will cause the main girder beam to settle unevenly. Sometimes wood shims are used to level the foundation sill plate or for interior floors. A sturdier and more permanent material must be used to level any structural areas.

Dirt floors will promote moisture from the soil and are an attraction to wood destroying insects and radon gas. If putting concrete over the dirt floor is too expensive, then a six mil plastic floor cover can be placed over the dirt areas to help eliminate moisture problems in lower level areas and crawl spaces.

P 99. Here's a quiz: *How many problem conditions do you see in this photograph?*
1. There are remnants of asbestos that was unprofessionally removed from the old steam heating pipes.
2. The heating pipes and also between the floor joists should be insulated for energy efficiency.
3. The heating system flue stack has a downward pitch after the elbow which will slow the exhaust gases from exiting.
4. There is no pipe extending the water heater pressure relief valve to within eight inches above the floor.
5. On the lower, left of the tree trunk, the flexible pipe material is unsafe for the gas supply to the water heater.
6. This tree trunk could be put to better use somewhere else. In very old homes, you may find tree trunks being used to support the main girder beam. A solid, metal support post should be used instead.

P 98. A heating contractor took the easy route while installing this steam pipe. As a result, now there is a serious structural problem with the main girder beam. One-half of this beam was cut and removed which weakens the support. This pipe should have been routed around the girder. If that was not possible, then a hole, 1/4 of the height of the beam, could have been cut in the center of this girder.

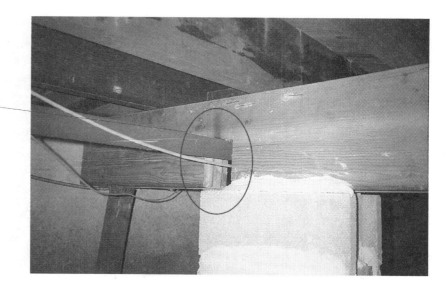

P 100. Left: This crawl space insulation is falling and it is installed upside down. The aluminum vapor barrier must always be touching the heated side of the house. For example, in attics the vapor barrier must face **downward**. In lower level areas, the vapor barrier must face **upward**. Vapor barriers block heat and moisture back towards the livable rooms.

Right: The insulation in the lower level room is installed correctly. The aluminum vapor barrier faces the heated rooms above the floor joists. The left side wall is also insulated with the vapor barrier facing the heated room on the other side.

P 101. All lower level dirt floors must have a covering to prevent moisture and wood destroying insect problems. A 6 mil plastic covering will help keep the ground moisture from creating problems in this crawl space. A poured concrete floor would be a more permanent solution to the problem. However, pouring a concrete floor in a narrow crawl space can be expensive.

P 103. Here's another quiz: *How many problems do you notice in this photo?*
1. More fiberglass insulation is needed between the floor joists.
2. The asbestos on the heating pipe should be removed by a licensed EPA contractor.
3. The water pipes need to be insulated for energy efficiency and to prevent corrosion from humidity.
4. The temporary lally column supporting the floor joists should be replaced with a solid, metal post on a sturdy base.
5. All of the debris and wood in this crawl space must be removed. Old wood will attract wood destroying insects into the house.

P 102. The floor joists should have diagonal bracing installed. These are small wood boards or metal straps placed diagonally in between each of the floor joists. Their purpose is to "tie" the floor joists together so they don't twist when the wood dries. Diagonal bracing also helps to spread the load exerted on the floor joists from the area above. This way when someone walks on the floor in the room above the weight will be spread across several floor joists, instead of just one.

P 104. Some gas utility meters are installed inside the house. Here you see the gas meter in a basement. The utility company will have to enter the house to read this meter unless a remote reading device is installed. There is no main shuf-off valve by the gas meter. This is a serious safety hazard since the gas cannot be turned off in the house for emergencies. High pressure gas parts were installed below the meter, near the bottom of the foundation wall, where the gas lines enter the house.

P 105. Only approved black iron gas piping can be safely used for gas supply lines. Often you'll find the flexible brass gas line used to hook up appliances or water heaters. Flexible pipe is easier to install. However, these flexible lines are not allowed by some building codes.

A drip trap is installed at the base of this gas pipe. Drip traps are used to help catch some of the dirt and moisture before it can clog the gas burners.

P 106. Precautions must be taken with small propane tanks for outdoor cooking grills. These tanks are under extreme pressure and can explode if mishandled or too old. Keep all propane tanks stored outside the home in case of an explosion. Due to the rust on this tank, it must be replaced immediately. Most tanks have dates stamped on them and should be not refilled by the propane supplier if the tank is over five years old.

P 107. Large propane and liquid petroleum gas tanks are usually the property of the local gas supplier. Determine what rights and responsibilities you have as the renter of these tanks. All vines and shrubbery should be pruned away from this tank. the moisture they create will rust the tank. All gas tanks must be resting on a level, sturdy foundation to keep the pipe joints from opening due to settlement. As with all other aspects of homes, local building codes will regulate the use and placement of this equipment.

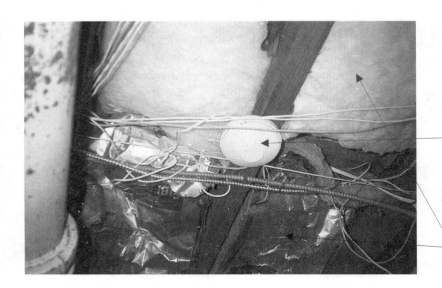

P 109. Many homes have auxiliary systems, such as burglar and fire alarms, central vacuums, in-ground lawn sprinlers, room intercoms, etc. Main control panels for auxiliary systems are usually located in the lower level or a first floor closet. Heat detectors, as seen in the photo, are used in fire prone areas that are inappropriate for smoke detector use, such as the boiler room, kitchen and attic.

Notice the vapor barrier is upside down for part of the insulation between the floor joist.

P 108. Central vacuum systems make house cleaning an easier chore. Bulky vacuums do not have to be dragged around the house while cleaning. A long, flexible hose is inserted into special vacuum outlets. These round shaped outlets are usually located in each room of the house. When the end of the hose is inserted, the central unit turns on and collects the dirt. The cap on the central unit can be opened to replace the vacuum bag when it is full.

P 110. Sump pumps in the lower level floor will help to control a high groundwater table. As the water in the soil rises, it will travel through the gravel underneath the concrete slab, to the sump pit. The pump will then send the water through a pipe to a suitable location away from the house. The sump drainage line must discharge the water at least five feet away from the exterior foundation of the house. This is required to prevent the water from flowing back into the sump pit through the foundation walls after it has already been pumped out from the lower level of the house.

All sumps should have GFCI electrical outlets and water backflow preventers for the discharge pipe.

P 111. Some sump pumps are part of a perimeter drainage system called a "floating floor". The gap around the edges of this basement floor indicates an interior drainage system was installed. Water that seeps through the foundation walls will trickle down into the gravel opening. The water then flows into the sump pump pit. These open gaps in the floor help to remove unwanted water. However, the openings also increase the chance of radon and termite problems in the house.

P 112. Left: *What a lovely bedroom this would make!* You can see that this crawl space has water penetration problems in several locations. Through the vent opening and through the crawl space floor. All of this moisture is certainly going to create rot and wood destroying insect problems. This house might be even located in a flood hazard zone so special flood insurance will be needed by the homeowner.

Right: Some lower level areas and crawl spaces have water alarms, such as this one. These will sound an alarm when they detect excess water. Signs of water penetration can be white mineral salts on the concrete walls and floors, as seen in this photo. This is called *efflorescence* and it's caused by water seeping through the concrete and then drying and leaving the white, mineral salt from the concrete as a residue.

P 113. In most areas, the local building codes prohibit sump pump drainage lines from discharging water into the house plumbing drainage lines. This restriction is designed to prevent excess water in the sewers which will unnecessarily increase costs at sewage treatment plants. Sump pumps should not discharge into septic systems due to the excess water load they create for leaching fields. If the house is connected to the city sewer system then the main drainage line should have a "U" shaped trap near the foundation wall. This is different from septic systems which are not supposed to have a "U" trap. However, you will find city sewer hookups without the "U" trap, and you'll also find septic system hookups that have been installed with a "U" trap. *So is this sump pump discharging into a city sewer or a septic system?* You need to be Superman with X-ray vision to answer that one!

More Nemmar Products

Energy Saving Home Improvements From A to Z ™

Don't let your dream house be a money pit in disguise! Our **5-star rated** book that teaches you how to **save** thousands of dollars **and** help the environment by making minor improvements to your home. You'll learn how to **lower your utility bills by 50%**, live more comfortably, and help the environment. Includes many photographs with detailed descriptions.

Home Inspection Business From A to Z ™

The REAL FACTS the other books don't tell you! Our **number one** selling home inspection book. This is **definitely** the best home inspection book on the market and has been called the "Bible" of the inspection industry. *Every* aspect of home inspections is covered with precise steps to follow. Includes many photographs with detailed descriptions.

Real Estate Appraisal From A to Z ™

The REAL FACTS the other books don't tell you! Our **number one** selling appraisal book. This is **definitely** the best real estate appraisal book on the market. *Every* aspect of real estate appraising is covered with precise steps to follow. Includes sample professional appraisal reports and many photographs with detailed descriptions.

Real Estate From A to Z ™

Don't let your dream house be a nightmare in disguise! You'll learn information the professionals use to inspect, appraise, invest, and renovate real estate. This book covers every aspect of Real Estate from A to Z and contains abbreviated versions of our three **5-star rated** books: *Home Inspection Business, Real Estate Appraisal, and Energy Saving Home Improvement From A to Z.*

DVD's - Home Inspection From A to Z ™

Our **5 star rated** DVD's have two hours of video plus you get the 80 page *HIB **DVD** Companion Guidebook!*
OPERATING SYSTEMS DVD topics including: heating systems, air-conditioning, water heaters, plumbing, well water system, septic system, electrical system, gas service, and auxiliary systems. Health Concerns topics including: asbestos insulation, radon gas, and water testing.
INTERIOR and EXTERIOR DVD topics including: roof, chimneys, siding, eaves, gutters, drainage and grading, windows, walkways, entrances and porches, driveways, walls and fences, patios and terraces, decks, swimming pools, exterior structures, wood destroying insects, garage, kitchen, bathrooms, floors and stairs, walls and ceilings, windows and doors, fireplaces, attics, ventilation, insulation, basement/lower level, and water penetration.

Home Buyer's Survival Kit ™

Don't buy, sell, or renovate your home without this! Includes: Four of our **top selling** books – *Real Estate Home Inspection Checklist From A to Z, Energy Saving Home Improvements From A to Z, Home Inspection Business From A to Z,* and *Real Estate Appraisal From A to Z.* Plus, you get both of our *Home Inspection From A to Z* – **DVD's.** As an added bonus you also get the 80 page *HIB **DVD** Companion Guidebook.*

Narrative Report Generator and On-Site Checklist

The report generator and checklist the others don't have! CD-Rom with the ***best*** Narrative Report Generator and On-Site Checklist on the market! These will enable you to *easily* do 30 page narrative, professional home inspection reports to send to your clients. These will assist you at the inspection site to be sure that you properly evaluate the subject property. Designed to walk you through the entire inspection process with very detailed instructions on how to properly evaluate the condition and status of **all** aspects of a home in a fool-proof, step-by-step system and create professional, narrative reports.

Appraiser and Home Inspector "A to Z Coach" School Training ™

Personal One-to-One Training with an "A to Z Coach" where you are the only student! Your training is personalized to meet your specific requirements and needs. Your questions are answered to make sure you learn everything you need to know about real estate - from Asbestos to Zoning. No crowded classrooms filled with students - unlike other real estate training schools. You'll learn how to become a highly paid Real Estate Appraiser or Home Inspector from top experts with many years of experience in the business!
Telephone and Email Training with an "A to Z Coach" via telephone and email. Our training school meets and exceeds the standards of all the leading home inspection and appraisal organizations. Regardless of where you live, you can enroll as a student in Nemmar Real Estate Training's "A to Z Coach" School.

Just some of our books, CD's, DVD's and much more!

Email info@nemmar.com for prices.

Visit us at www.nemmar.com

The Interior Home Inspection

Kitchen

After finishing in the lower level you're ready to begin inspecting the livable areas of the house. I usually start with the kitchen and then move from room to room in a clockwise fashion. Feel free to adapt the inspection procedure to any method you like. Check the kitchen walls and floors for any structural problems or settlement cracks. Check the condition of the kitchen floor covering. The majority of houses have vinyl linoleum or ceramic tile floor coverings. In some houses you'll find hardwood on the kitchen floors. Hardwood isn't used as a kitchen floor too often because when it gets wet the wood buckles. Be careful when inspecting older houses that have floor tiles that are 9 inches x 9 inches in size or appear to be made of a very hard type of material. These tiles are usually a Vinyl/Asbestos material so you want to notify your client about the possible asbestos problems with them.

Check the kitchen cabinets by opening and closing a few of them. Make sure the cabinets are securely fastened to the wall and floor. I know an inspector who was inspecting one home and the entire kitchen cabinet came right off the wall when he was checking it. Make sure they install child guards on the cabinets and drawers if there are any children in the house. Child guard hooks prevent children from opening drawers containing knives, cleansers or hazardous items. Check the kitchen countertop for any burned or damaged areas. Also, make sure the kitchen countertop is securely fastened and not loose.

See if there are enough electrical outlets for modern usage. All kitchen outlets should be three pronged and have ground fault circuit interrupter protection. GFCI's are important because electric countertop appliances are often used around the sink. Run the kitchen faucet hot and cold lines to make sure there's adequate hot water. Make sure there are no leaks underneath the sink. If there's a spray attachment in the sink area, check that as well. Sometimes they won't be operating properly.

Ask the client, the seller or the Realtor if the appliances are being sold with the house. Most of the time they are. If they're sold with the house, then spot check the appliances by turning them on and off briefly. For refrigerators, just open the doors to make sure they're cold inside. Tell the client you're very limited in what you can evaluate as to the life expectancy of appliances. This way the client won't think you're

guaranteeing that the appliances will work for many years to come.

Note the condition and age of the appliances and recommend that any older units be upgraded for energy efficiency and convenience. Remember to turn off any appliances that you check. You don't want to burn the house down by leaving an oven turned on!

Kitchen photos: P 114

Bathrooms

Check the bathroom walls and floors for any structural problems or settlement cracks. Check the condition of the bathroom wall and floor coverings. Most houses have ceramic tile floor coverings and part of the walls may have tile coverings. In some houses you'll find carpeting on the bathroom floors. Carpeting isn't used very often because of the possibility of the carpet getting wet. Lift up a corner of the carpet to see what's underneath. Sometimes there are cracked and damaged tiles or water stains.

Press on some tiles, especially in the bathtub and shower area to see if any are loose. Don't press or bang the tiles too hard. I once did an inspection and thought I was lightly banging the tiles. The walls were thin sheetrock without anything between the wall studs. We heard a crash in the next room and soon found I had knocked a glass ornament off the shelf!

Check to see if the tiles need to be caulked at the corners or regrouted between the joints. This is required to prevent water leaks behind the walls. *Caulk* is a flexible material used for water proofing. Caulk seals corners which are prone to movement from expansion and contraction. *Grout* is a hard material that is a thin mortar used to seal cracks between tiles. Grout will hold the tiles in place and prevent water leaks at the seams.

If there is a standup shower in the bathroom, make sure you look at the floor for any signs of prior leaks. These floors are prone to water leaks between the ceramic tiles if they're not kept caulked at all times. The reason for this is they're made of many tiles and not a one-piece unit like a bathtub. Water leaks will rot out the floor pan underneath the tiles. If the water damage goes unnoticed for a long time it will lead to extensive damage and costly repairs.

Some shower and tub areas are made of a premolded plastic and fiberglass material. Check these for any cracks and proper caulking around the edges. Check the bathroom cabinets by opening and closing them. Make sure they are securely fastened to the wall. The homeowner should install child guards on the cabinet doors if there are any children in the house.

Check the condition of the bathroom sink area for any cracks or loose sections. Make sure the drain stop mechanism in the sink is working. Often they won't be working properly and will need replacement. Test any bathroom ventilation fans for proper operation. See if there's at least one electrical outlet and that it has Ground Fault Circuit Interrupter protection. Sometimes in older houses there won't be any grounded outlets in the bathroom which is an inconvenience.

> *Check the water pressure and drainage with the client present. The reason you want the client to watch while you check the water pressure is so he can see for himself the results of your testing.*

Check the water pressure and drainage **with** the client present. The reason you want the client to watch while you check the water pressure is so he can see for himself the results of your testing. Whether or not a particular house has satisfactory water pressure is up to the individual who will be living there. What I mean is that I've seen people who wouldn't buy a house because the water pressure wasn't very strong. I've also seen people who were satisfied with water pressure that I wouldn't feel was strong enough for my usage. It's up to the individual so let *them* decide if the water pressure is strong enough.

There are usually local guidelines about what the minimum allowable water pressure should be, but generally, most houses will always meet the minimum criteria. To check the bathroom water pressure, run the bathroom faucet hot and cold lines to make sure there's adequate hot water and there are no leaks underneath the sink. While the sink faucets are running, turn on the bathtub faucet and/or the showerhead. While both of these are running simultaneously, flush the toilet and watch to see if there's a drop in the water pressure. It's normal to see a small drop in pressure. What you're looking for is a significant drop in pressure. A large drop in pressure during this test will indicate that if someone is taking a shower and the washing machine, dishwasher, other sinks, etc. are used at the same time; then the shower pressure will drop which can be a nuisance. If you like, you can purchase small water pressure reading devices. These devices can be attached to a faucet for an exact reading of the water pressure. After running the water for a few minutes check to see if the

sink and tub drain properly. Sometimes they'll drain very slowly and need to be unclogged.

If there's a Jacuzzi or hot tub in the house, you're not required to evaluate these other than the visible aspects. You don't have to fill them up with water and test the motors. *(Unless of course you decide you want to take a relaxing bath yourself while the client waits outside).*

Some houses have bathrooms in the lower level area. If the plumbing drainage lines are located higher than the drainage lines to this bathroom, then an ejector pump will be needed. *Ejector pumps* look like large sump pumps that have an enclosed cover. The purpose of these pumps is to lift the drainage water up to the main plumbing drainage line so it can be removed from the house. Just run the water in this bathroom until you hear the ejector pump turn on and drain some water away.

Bathrooms photos: P 115-P 116, P 211

Floors and Stairs

As you go through the house check the floors for any sagging or uneven areas that'll indicate structural settlement. Jump on the floor in each room to make sure they're sound. Don't jump so hard that you knock things off the walls, just do it lightly. Also, remember to look above you before you jump to test the floors. One time I forgot to do this and I hit my head on a light fixture above me in the kitchen.

Most hardwood floors today are made out of Oak wood because it is inexpensive, resilient to wear and tear, and oak can be sanded. I'll give you some basics of how wood is rated: *Select* is the best grade lumber because it has the fewest color and grain variations. The color of the wood is uniform and the character of the wood grain is evenly spaced. *Number one* is the next best with a little more variations of color and character in the wood. *Number two* is the next level and is the most common grade of flooring. Number two lumber has more knots in it and a wider range of color and grain texture. *Number three* is the next grade lower and has a lot of knots and color/grain variations.

> *Check underneath the corner of some carpeting, if you can, to find out what's underneath. It's usually hardwood or plywood underneath but check to make sure and notify the client of what you see.*

If there are hardwood floors, see if you notice any damaged areas or bowed sections. If there are carpets, check for signs of aging and worn areas that'll show the need for replacement. Check under the corner of some carpeting, if you can, to find out what's underneath. It's usually hardwood or plywood underneath but check to make sure and notify the client of what you see. The reason for this is that some people think that there's always hardwood floors underneath the carpeting. After they move into the house they may want to remove the carpets and leave the hardwood floors visible. You don't want them to be surprised about finding plywood as opposed to nice hardwood floors under the carpets.

You also have to be careful about carpets that hide damaged areas underneath. I did an inspection once, where the client bought the house from a dishonest seller. After the client moved in, they found damage under the carpeting. The seller intentionally hid the damage during the home inspection. The seller placed a couch over one section and put a large pile of toys and boxes over another section. I told the client to do a "walk-thru" inspection before the closing. This would enable them to check for any damaged areas after all furniture and personal items were removed from the house. The client did a walk-thru but they still didn't see this damage until after they removed the carpeting.

You also have to be careful to see if there are any moisture problems underneath hardwood floors. Moisture from basements, crawl spaces, water leaks, etc. will cause a hardwood floor to buckle. The reason the floor buckles, is that the wood absorbs the moisture and when it dries out, the wood will expand. If there are no gaps between the wood boards to allow for this expansion, then the boards will buckle upwards.

If the seller has any pets then recommend to your client that all carpets should be fumigated or removed prior to his taking possession of the house. I had a client who moved into a house where the seller had a dog and a cat. After my client moved in, they found out that the rugs had fleas in them.

Check all staircases for sturdiness and secure handrails. Always recommend that they install handrails on both sides of the staircases for safety. All handrails need balusters that are spaced four inches apart. *Balusters* are the guard posts under handrails that provide support. They also prevent children from falling off the sides of open stairways. There should be a light fixture and a light switch at the top and bottom of all stairways for safety.

If there's a window at the base of a staircase its sill should be at least 36 inches above the floor. This will help prevent someone from falling through the window in the event they fell down the stairs. If the sill is less than 36 inches high, a window guard should be installed as a precautionary measure.

Floors and Stairs photos: P 122, P 210

Walls and Ceilings

Check all of the walls and ceilings for any structural problems or settlement cracks. You'll usually find some minor settlement cracks but you're looking for any major problems that could be hazardous. In older houses the walls will be made of *lath and plaster* which is also called *stucco*. Lath and plaster consists of an underlying layer of metal wiring, or lath, which has a layer of concrete over it. Lath and plaster walls are very rigid and have good sound insulating and fireproofing qualities. However, since these walls are so rigid they can develop cracks from any minor settlement in the house or with temperature changes. Also, the metal lath can rust out over time and sections of the plaster can fall off which can be hazardous.

In newer houses the walls will be made of *sheetrock* which is also called *drywall*. Sheetrock consists of a gypsum material on the interior, usually about 1/2 inch thick, with exterior layers of a lightweight cardboard paper. The gypsum is a clay and plaster mixture. Sheetrock panels are sold in four feet by eight feet sections and are installed on the walls and ceilings with nails or screws. Screws are preferred to nails because they hold longer. Nails can pop loose over time which you'll see sometimes during an inspection. If you see small round areas slightly protruding from under the paint, then that's the nail head coming loose from the sheetrock. The joint sections where the different panels meet are sealed with finishing tape and spackled over to provide a smooth transition. Sheetrock is relatively inexpensive and is easy to install. Fireproof sheetrock is 5/8 inch thick and has a better fire resistance than the 1/2 inch sheetrock. However, it's also heavier and more difficult to install than 1/2 inch sheetrock.

Check for water stains on the walls or ceilings, or around skylights. If you see water stains, it indicates that there's probably damage to the areas behind the walls and ceilings that isn't visible due to the finished covering. So be very careful about telling the client anything like the water damage appears minor because the stain isn't large. Water can do an *awful* lot of damage behind the finished coverings. So if you're not sure, tell the client to have the stained area opened and evaluated further.

> *All linseed oil based paint prior to 1978 had lead in it because the lead is a good "binder" for the paint.*
> *Therefore, if a house was built before 1978, then there will be lead in some of the paint.*

See if the house needs to be painted. Sometimes the client will ask you if there's lead paint in the house. The only way to identify lead paint is to have a sample taken to a lab for analysis. You can provide this service if you like, but charge a fee for it or else you'll be running to the lab on every inspection at your own expense. All linseed oil based paint prior to 1978 had lead in it. The reason for this is lead has a good wear quality and it is a strong "binder" for the paint. Therefore, if a house was built before 1978, then there will be lead in some of the paint. Latex based paint has never had a lead content in it and all paints today are non-toxic. Latex paint peels over time as it get old. Lead based paints wear off in layers over time. This was a cosmetic benefit because when the paint layers would wear off, they would leave a renewed surface. It's similar to a snake shedding its old layer of skin. However, when lead paint wears off it creates a dust. This lead dust causes soil contamination and health problems to anyone who breathes or drinks the lead.

If the interior of the house has been painted after 1978, then the paint with the lead content will be encapsulated underneath the newer layers of non-lead paint. The main hazard of having lead in paint is if the paint is peeling and children eat small sections of it. Also, if lead paint is sanded, then the dust created will have lead in it that will be breathed-in by the occupants of the house. Each State EPA office has brochures with information about the hazards of lead in paint.

If there's wallpaper in the house, make sure it's not peeling off the walls. Tell the client that if they plan to remove the wallpaper, it is a time-consuming job that can be expensive. They should get estimates if they are not going to remove it themselves. You have to be careful removing when wallpaper from sheetrock walls because you can pull the light cardboard paper off the walls with the wallpaper.

Some ceilings have acoustic tile coverings. These are also called *drop ceilings*. Try to lift some of these tiles to view underneath. Often these ceilings are installed to cover defects in the area underneath.

> *Check for the existence and operation of any smoke detectors. Smoke detectors are required on all levels of a house or condo. Heat detectors are recommended in the garage area.*

Check for the existence and operation of any smoke detectors. Smoke detectors are **required** on all levels of a house or condominium. Heat detectors are recommended in the garage area for fire detection. If the smoke detectors are battery operated, they should have a small test button. Recommend the client replace all batteries after moving in. Some smoke detectors have a *hard wired* installation. This simply means that they're electrically operated and not battery operated. Hard wired systems can't be evaluated during a home inspection. Tell the client to get all instructions from the homeowner. I once was doing an inspection on a house and the owner had a very "unique" smoke detection system installed. He stapled fire crackers to the lower level floor joists and the attic roof rafters! He said that if there was a fire, the fire crackers would explode and wake him up. I obviously wouldn't recommend anyone using this type of a system.

Walls and Ceilings photos: P 117, P 210

Windows and Doors

Spot check the windows and doors by opening and closing all doors and at least one window in each room. Sometimes they'll be difficult to open and close due to excessive paint or settlement of the house. This is common, so just notify the client about it. It's also common to find minor settlement cracks around window and door frames. You will see thin cracks extending from the corners of the door and window frames. These areas are stress points when the house settles due to the right angles in the frames.

Check for any cracked or broken panes of glass. Make sure you move any drapes or blinds. Sometimes they're hiding broken windows. Use an awl to probe the exterior portions of the window frames for rot. If rainwater gets trapped on the window ledge, rot will develop over time. Make sure the door and window locks are operational since these are required and important security items. Sometimes you will find windows with missing locks. Recommend that the client install window locks where needed for safety. Child guards for doors and windows are a safety item needed in homes with children.

Check for any broken vacuum seals in thermal windows and doors. This can be caused by poor quality windows or from someone closing a window or door too hard and breaking the seal. A *vacuum seal* is the air pocket between the two panes of glass in thermal windows. When this seal is broken, it allows moisture to get trapped between the two window panes and leaves condensation on the glass. During the colder months, you won't see condensation between the panes of glass. In this case, check for any residue of water or dirt stains instead. Broken vacuum seals can be repaired by a glass service company but tell the client to get estimates because it can be expensive.

I heard of a home inspector who inspected a house and didn't bother to move any of the drapes or blinds. This house had all thermal windows that must have been very cheaply constructed. After the buyer moved into the home, they found that all the vacuum seals were broken! Since this home inspector was lazy during his inspection he ended up paying for all new windows in the house. So learn a lesson from his mistakes - don't cut corners on your inspections!

> *In some areas double key locks are against the local fire codes because a key is needed to exit in case of an emergency. This can cause people to get trapped inside a house during a fire.*

⚠ Check for any *double key* door locks. These are the locks that require a key to exit and enter through the door. The purpose of these locks is so that if a burglar breaks a door window, they can't just turn a bolt and open the door. They'll need a key to open the lock. However, in some areas these locks are against the local fire codes because a key is needed to exit in case of an emergency. This can cause people to get trapped inside a house during a fire. Tell the client to check with the local fire and building department for their recommendation about door locks. Recommend that the client change all of the house locks after taking possession for security reasons.

Windows and Doors photos: P 119-P 118

Fireplaces

Check all fireplaces for any structural or back-smoking problems. Make sure the mortar joints are in satisfactory condition. Back-smoking is the result of downdrafts in the chimney flue that causes the smoke to come back into the house. Signs of back-smoking are black deposits, called *creosote*, on the front of the fireplace and mantel. When you finish inspecting the fireplace, check your hands for any creosote that needs to be washed off. You don't want to get creosote on everything you touch.

If the fireplace has a sliding glass and screen cover make sure it operates smoothly. Often they're rusty and can't be opened and closed easily. The screens will help prevent ashes and sparks from flying into the room. You will find metal heat-a-lators on some fireplaces. *Heat-a-lators* are glass doors with vents at the top and bottom which make the fireplace much more energy efficient to use. The reason for this is that heat rises. As a result, about 90% of the heat from the fire goes up the chimney and out of the house. Moreover, an open firebox will allow the air from the room to feed the fire for combustion. This room air has just been heated by your boiler or furnace so the last thing you want is for it to go up in smoke!! Glass doors with vents at the bottom allow the cooler air by the floor to be drawn into the firebox to feed the flames. Vents at the top of the metal heat-a-lator will allow the warm air from the fire to go back into the room. Sometimes these heat-a-lators will have fans that circulate the air and increase the efficiency even more. Newer construction will have vents on the lower part of the exterior chimneys. This allows exterior air to feed the flames in the firebox which further increases the efficiency of the fireplace.

Check to see if the fireplace damper is operating properly. The *damper* is the metal door inside the top of the firebox area. This door is opened while a fire is burning and closed when the fireplace isn't in use. If the damper doesn't open and close properly or is very rusty, recommend it be replaced.

⚠ Most chimneys have a terra-cotta tile lining. This is a light red, tile lining inside the chimney flue stack. If you can view up the chimney flue, use a flashlight to check the mortar joints inside and see if there are thick creosote deposits. The chimney flue needs to be swept and repointed by a chimney sweep periodically. This will help prevent chimney fires. Chimney fires are similar to grease fires in a kitchen. The heavy buildup of soot becomes flammable when surrounded by hot air and it will eventually ignite in flames.

Sometimes the fireplace will have a metal firebox installed instead of brick. Check this metal firebox lining for buckled and rusting sections due to the intense heat in the firebox area. If there is damage then tell the client to get a repair estimate. Installing a new firebox lining can be expensive. You don't want to use a fireplace with a deteriorated lining. This can lead to a fire in the house because the insulating walls of the firebox are too thin.

⚠ You may find a wood burning stove. You're limited in what you can evaluate with these because there's no access to view up the chimney flue. Recommend that the client take special precautions with a wood burning stove for safety. Unlike a fireplace they are installed out of the wall and take up part of the room. This allows the heat from the iron exterior to dissipate into the house. If anyone bumps into the stove while it's hot, they're going to get **severely burned**. A guardrail must be installed around a wood burning stove if there are children in the house. These stoves can give off a tremendous amount of heat and can save a lot of money on fuel bills.

Fireplaces photos: P 120-P 123, P 205

Attic Inspection

Most houses will have an attic space that you <u>must</u> inspect if there's access to it due to the potential problems you can find. Just like crawl spaces, don't get lazy and just assume everything's OK in the attic area. Some houses won't have any accessible attic areas, so just do the best you can.

Sometimes the attic area has been finished and there are *knee wall* openings to the attic. These are small openings in the wall areas of the upper level that allow you to view a small portion of the attic and use it for storage. The access panels to most attics are located in the ceiling of the upper level hallway. Sometimes the access panel will be located in a bedroom closet. Ask the owner about this and don't assume there's no access panel because you didn't see one. It could be hidden.

Older houses sometimes have stairways leading to the attic area. Newer homes will have a pull-down stairway to provide access to the attic area. If there's no pull-down stairway, you should recommend that one be installed for convenience. Check the condition of the pull-down stairway to make sure it's sturdy and that it has handrails on the sides of the steps.

I always recommend that a handrail be installed inside the attic area surrounding the access opening. This will help prevent anyone in the attic area from falling through the access opening.

⚠ I always recommend that a handrail be installed inside the attic area surrounding the access opening. This will help prevent anyone walking in the attic area from falling through the access opening. I have no idea why, but I haven't seen any building codes that require this handrail in new construction. What will happen is somebody is going to fall through the access panel and get killed someday. After that, then the local building codes will add this safety precaution. Don't wait for that to happen, recommend they install a handrail now!

Usually you'll find most attics will have some wood board covering over the floor joists so the attic can be used to store lightweight items. If you see any very heavy objects, tell the client it's not recommended due to the excessive weight on the ceiling below. You have to be careful when you're in the attic area and not walk between any of the floor joists. If you do, then your foot will go right through the ceiling below!

Check the condition of the roof ridge beam, roof rafters and the roof sheathing while in the attic area. Use a screwdriver or an awl to probe these wood boards for sturdiness. The roof *ridge beam* is the main girder type beam at the top of the crest of the roof. The roof *rafters* are the floor joist type beams leading from the attic floor up to the roof ridge beam. The roof *sheathing* is the sub flooring type wood that the roof shingles rest upon. The sheathing is made of plywood in newer construction and smaller wood boards in older houses.

If the roof originally had a cedar wood shingle roof installed, then you'll see wooden slats, also called laths, for the roof sheathing. *Wooden slats* are one inch by two inch boards that run perpendicular to the roof rafters and are spaced about one foot apart. The purpose of the wooden slats is to allow air to get to the attic side of the shingles. This way the back of the shingles can *"breathe"* and expand and contract with the temperature and weather changes. If the house has wooden slats, then the next time it's reroofed these slats may have to be removed and plywood sheathing will need to be installed. This can be expensive so tell the client to get estimates.

In condominiums and modular homes you'll probably find roof truss construction in the attic. Roof *truss* construction refers to the wood roof framing that has metal ties to hold the boards together. This type of framing is preassembled in a factory like modular homes. The benefit of roof truss framing is that it's easier to install for simple roof designs as opposed to standard roof framing. The drawback to roof trusses is that they are hard to install for a complicated roof design since there will be too many angles to deal with. Also, roof trusses will eliminate most of the attic space due to the design of the wood framing.

Look for any water stains that are due to water leaks or abnormal humidity in the attic area. Often there are old water stains from prior roof leaks that have been repaired. Just see if they look moist or recent. Check for any bowing in the wood members of the attic. While looking at the sheathing you may be able to determine the number of layers of roof shingles. If you see many nails in the sheathing, then you can assume there are two or three layers of shingles on the roof. Sometimes you will see clear sap droplets on the roof rafters. This is caused by the greener wood drying out after the original construction of the roof.

Check for the presence of *collar beams* in the attic. Collar beams are 2 x 4 boards that are located several feet below the ridge beam. The purpose of collar beams is to *"tie"* both sides of the roof together so that all of the weight of the roof doesn't rest upon the ridge beam. It gives the roof additional support. Older houses may not have collar beams so recommend that they be installed.

Attic Inspection photos: P 125-P 137, P 212-P 214

Attic Ventilation

It's very important that the attic area be properly ventilated to prevent excessive humidity or heat in this area. Even in cold winter months humidity can cause problems in attics. As a result, ventilation to the exterior is required in the winter. In the summer months attics can reach 150 degrees Fahrenheit which adds a big heat load on the house. Check for an adequate number of attic vents. Check the condition of the screens on these vents. They need to be kept clean. Screens help to keep birds and bees out of the attic. Any bathroom fans should discharge to the exterior. Sometimes you'll find them discharging in the attic which will create moisture problems in the attic.

It's very important that the attic area be properly ventilated. In the summer months attics can reach 150 degrees Fahrenheit which adds a big heat load on the house.

Be wary of ventilation problems with finished attic areas. Often the homeowner will put insulation and sheetrock on the attic walls and ceilings. This enables them to use the attic for livable space, if allowed by the local building codes. However, many times they will not properly ventilate behind the sheetrock and insulation. This will cause the roof sheathing to become rotted from the trapped moisture. Styrofoam baffles can be used to maintain an air gap behind these finished areas. This will help prevent the roof sheathing from rotting.

Take a look at the roofing nails that protrude through the roof sheathing. If the nails are very rusty and have corrosion stains on the wood, then you know the attic ventilation needs to be improved. This corrosion is usually caused by humidity being trapped in the attic. In the winter time you may find frost on the roofing nails due to humidity in the attic. Also, check the wood roof framing for signs of mildew and moisture stains. This too will indicated inadequate ventilation in the attic.

Some houses have *soffit vents*. These are vents at the base of the roof where it overhangs the exterior siding. Soffit vents allow air to come into the base of the roof in the attic area. This air carries any unwanted heat or moisture out of the attic gable or roof vents. Make sure that the insulation isn't covering any soffit vent openings that will stop them from ventilating properly. Newer houses will have *ridge vents*. This is a vent at the very top of the roof, above the ridge beam. Ridge vents allow unwanted heat and moisture to escape from the attic through the top of the roof.

⚠ Test any attic fans or any house fans located in the attic area. Turn the fan on while you're on the floor **below** the attic. Make sure you don't go near the fan while it's running. *(They're installed to cool the house, not chop-up home inspectors).* Attic and house fans need to have adequate vents to discharge the air. If the attic vent openings aren't adequate, then the fan won't operate properly and it will break down

prematurely. If you hear the fan making funny noises or laboring while it's operating, then tell the client to have it checked out for repairs. A possible cause of the noises could be the need for additional attic vents. Also, if you put your hand over a wall electrical switch while the fan is running, you may feel a draft. If this draft is very strong it usually indicates that the attic vents need to be enlarged. The draft around the switch is caused from the air getting backed-up in the attic and coming down through the gaps behind the walls.

Some houses have *thermostatically operated power ventilators*. These are fans in the roof that operate off a thermostat. When the temperature in the attic reaches a preset level, the fan will automatically turn on to cool this area. When the temperature drops enough, the fan will automatically turn off by itself.

Attic Ventilation photos:
P 131-P 137, P 148, P 214, P 215, P 220

Attic Insulation

Check to see if there is insulation between the floor joists of the attic area. Sometimes you'll find insulation between the roof rafters in a house. The roof rafters don't need to be insulated because once heat has escaped through the upper level ceiling it's lost anyway. There's no sense trying to trap this heat in the attic. If you do, you'll only be trapping unwanted moisture in the attic by installing insulation between the roof rafters. You will also rot the roof sheathing due to the trapped moisture.

The benefit of having attic flooring is that you can use this area for storage. However, flooring prevents you from seeing if there's insulation throughout the attic area. Sometimes there's only insulation in the visible floor areas that aren't covered. The owner may have installed this insulation without bothering to remove the attic flooring that was there to insulate the entire attic.

Check to see how thick the insulation is. The insulation should be at least eight inches thick. If it isn't just recommend that the client install an additional layer of insulation for better energy efficiency. Newer construction will have about 12" of insulation in the attic. This will pay for itself due to the energy savings. If there are any air-conditioning or heating ducts in the attic make sure they're insulated. Insulation is required on the exterior or the interior for energy efficiency.

Make sure the vapor barrier is installed properly. The vapor barrier is the aluminum foil layer on one side of the insulation roll. It must always be touching the heated side of the house.

Newer construction has pink fiberglass insulation. Make sure the *vapor barrier* is installed properly. The vapor barrier is the aluminum foil layer on one side of the insulation roll. It must always be touching the **heated** side of the house. For example, if insulation is installed in an unheated basement or crawl space, the vapor barrier must face <u>upwards</u>. If insulation is installed in an attic, the vapor barrier must face <u>downwards</u>. The reason for the vapor barrier is to prevent any moisture from getting trapped in the insulation and condensing. Any condensation will decrease the energy efficiency of the insulation. The vapor barrier prevents moisture by reflecting the heated air, which has moisture in it, back toward the heated portion of the house. If you notice that the vapor barrier is installed upside down, the client has two options. He can either turn the insulation around or use a knife or razor blade to cut openings in the vapor barrier. Openings in the vapor barrier will allow the moisture to escape without getting trapped between the layers of insulation.

If you recommend that the client add an additional layer of insulation in the attic or any other areas, make sure you tell them to purchase it **without** a vapor barrier. Another option is to cut openings in the vapor barrier, if there is one, before putting the insulation on top of the existing layer. While you're in the rooms below the attic, take a look at the ceilings. On some inspections I found small, round water stains on the ceilings below the attic. When I went into the attic, I found these stains were caused by a vapor barrier that was upside down. The moisture from the warm, humid air in the house had condensed between the vapor barrier and the ceiling below. Over time, small water stains developed.

In older houses you may find *Rockwool* or *Vermiculite* insulations. This is a fibrous material and may have some asbestos in it. So warn the client about this and let them decide if they want a lab to analyze the insulation for any asbestos content. Ask the owner if he/she has installed, or knows of any prior owner's having installed, insulation in the house. You want to warn your client about any *"blown-in"* type of insulation. In the past, some houses had UFFI insulation blown-into the walls and floors. UFFI stands for *Urea Formaldehyde Foam Insulation* and the Environmental Protection Agency, *(EPA)*, has issued warnings about this type of insulation. The chemicals from this foam are a health hazard because they seep out into the air in the house. If there's UFFI or any unknown type of foam insulation in the house, recommend that an air sample be taken to see if there are any health concerns. You should also tell the client to contact the Environmental Protection Agency office to obtain more information about foam and other hazardous insulation.

Attic Insulation photos: P 134-P 136, P 185

Interior Inspection Photo Pages

P 114. When inspecting the kitchen, spot check appliances by briefly turning them on. *Just remember to turn them off when you're done - except for the refrigerator!* The countertop and cabinets should be securely fastened. All outlets by the kitchen sink must have GFCI protection. Remodeled kitchens and bathrooms are like any other changes made to a house - building department permits and final approvals are neeed from town hall.

P 115. Bathroom tiles need to be evaluated for loose sections and open gaps. Loose areas can be detected by lightly banging on the tiles. The tiles in this bathroom are buckled and uneven. Prior water leaks behind the wall has caused this problem. To solve this problem, the tiles must be removed and the area behind must be repaired. Grout is used between ceramic tiles to prevent gaps that allow water penetration. Grout is a much harder material than caulk. Caulk is more flexible and used in areas where the joints will expand and contract more often.

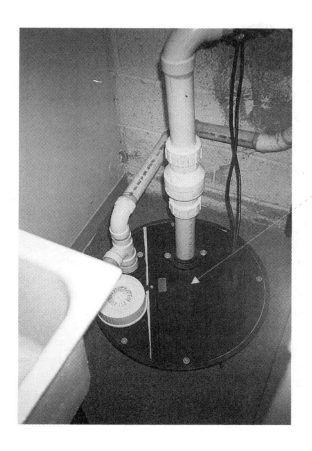

P 116. This isn't a sump pump - it's an ejector pump. Ejector pumps are used for plumbing drainage lines that are installed lower than the house main drain pipe. Ejector pumps are mostly used for bathrooms installed in the lower level of a house. The waste water flows into the pump pit. When the level rises to a certain height in the pit, the ejector pump is activated. The waste water is then pumped up to the house main drainage line. From there it will be carried by the flow of gravity to the sewer system. And yes, permits and approvals are needed for this type of plumbing work also.

P 117. This is what happens when you have water leaks behind the walls that go unnoticed or ignored for too long. This massive hole in the ceiling is due to water damage from a leaking pipe. All of the wood and sheetrock will have to be replaced, along with the leaking section of pipe. Another hazard of ignoring water leaks is the potential contact of water with the electrical wires and outlets in the house.

P 119. This window is too close to the floor level and is a safety hazard. Not only can a child fall through, but if an adult tripped, there is no window sill to stop their fall. Child guards should be installed on this window. In many areas the height of the window sill and the use of child guards are regulated by the local building and fire codes. *Don't wait for accidents to happen - take precautions ahead of time.*

While you're inspecting the interior rooms, jump on the floors to make sure they're structurally sound.

Check underneath the corner of the wall-to-wall carpeting. The only way to know what type of flooring is underneath is to check it. Don't assume there are hardwood floors under carpets just because you see hardwood in other rooms in the house.

If there are any pets in the house, you should have the carpets removed or fumigated prior to moving-in. You don't want any fleas as house guests.

P 118. A vacuum seal is the air-tight space between the panes of glass in thermal windows and doors. Broken vacuum seals are indicated by dirt and condensation stains in between the two panes of glass, such as in this sliding glass door. Over time the moisture and dust stains will increase. Since this area can't be wiped clean, the window will become white and hazy. Repairing broken vacuum seals is expensive.

P 120. Wood burning stoves can save a lot of money on heating fuel bills. These stoves can heat a large area of a home. However, safety precautions must be taken. Since these stoves radiate heat from the iron casing, they must not be touched while in use. A guardrail will help prevent accidental burns. Also, the flue stack for these stoves must be properly installed. A fireproof lining is needed and the flue should not be near any combustible materials, such as wood. Wood burning stoves, like forced hot air heating systems, will dry out the air in the house. The metal pot on this stove is used to hold water. As the pot is heated, the water boils and turns to steam. This steam will add moisture back into the air so the occupants don't get sore throats or allergy problems from the dry air.

P 121. *Creosote* is a black soot found in chimneys. Creosote is caused by the smoke from burning wood. You may find excess creosote stains on the face of a chimney and mantle, such as this one. This indicates a back-smoking problem. Back-smoking is caused by a firebox area that is too narrow and/or a flue stack that does not extend high enough above the roof to prevent downdrafts.

P 123. While you're in the lower level, this is what you'll see underneath a fireplace. The sub flooring and foundation for a fireplace needs additional support and fire protection. Typical plywood subflooring is not strong enough.

P 122. When inspecting the interior rooms make sure you look for signs of excessive structural settlement. Take a look at the floors where they meet the walls. You can see that this floor has separated from the baseboard molding due to abnormal settlement of the building over the years. It's a major expense to re-level and repair structural problems. Also, look at the window and door frames for signs of uneven and abnormal structural settlement.

P 125. Roof trusses are basically rafters and collar beams that are preassembled. The metal brackets hold the boards together at the joints. Roof truss construction has the drawback of taking up too much space in the attic area. This will eliminate room for storage. In the photo, the dark gap at the ridge beam is the ridge vent. This allows unwanted heat and moisture to vent out of the top of the roof.

P 124. Here we have another example of roof trusses. The metal brackets hold the boards together at the joints.

The dark gap at the ridge beam is the ridge vent. Ridge vents are recommended for all attic areas, in both hot and cold climates. These vents allow unwanted heat, which carries moisture, to vent out of the top of the roof.

P 126. I'm sure that I am the only home inspector and appraiser in the world that has ever seen this. You're not going to believe this, *(I didn't either when I found it in an attic and the seller told me what it was there for),* those six small tube shaped things stapled to the roof rafters are actually - firecrackers!!
Now try to guess why the homeowner put them there.
The homeowner stapled the firecrackers to the rafters in the attic so in case a fire started he would hear the bang from the firecrackers going off. Talk about an odd concept for a fire alarm system. *I wonder if he got a discount on his home insurance due to this "unique" way of detecting fires?*

P 127. Here you have an example of the most common type of roof construction. It's made of 2 x 10" boards for the roof ridge beam at the top and the roof rafters at the sides.

The 2 x 4" boards are collar beams. Collar beams give added strength by removing some of the weight off the ridge beam.

Plywood is used for the roof sheathing. This is what the exterior roof shingles rest on.

P 129. Some houses have wood shingles/shakes for the original roof. In the attic area you will see these horizontal wooden slats indicating a wood shingle/shake roof is on the house.

Plywood sheathing is not used because the wood shingles have to "breathe" on both sides. This will allow air to help prevent rot and cracking of the exterior shingles. If the roof is stripped and asphalt shingles are installed, then plywood sheathing will be needed as the base for the new shingles.

P 128. Often the chimney flashing area will have leaked over time. Here is evidence of attic water penetration around the chimney. New copper flashing is needed on the exterior to prevent the wood and mortar joints from deteriorating.

P 130. *Here we have an accident waiting to happen!* Unfortunately, I have never seen any building codes that require railings around the attic access opening. Don't wait for someone to fall down this hole and break their neck *- install a guardrail NOW!* A handrail is also needed on the steps.

If plywood flooring is installed, the attic can provide storage space for lightweight items.

P 131. This is known as a thermostatically operated power ventilator. That's just a fancy name for a fan that has a thermostat switch to turn it on and off. Attics can get to be 150 degrees farenheit in the summer. This adds a big heat load on the livable rooms below. These fans will automatically turn on when the temperature reaches a preset setting. When the attic has cooled down to a preset temperature, the fan will turn itself off. The homeowner will not have to worry about manually switching the attic fan on and off. Remember that these fans are used to cool the attic area. Don't confuse this with a whole house fan that's installed in the ceiling of the top floor hallway. Whole house fans cool the home by drawing the warm air into the attic and out of the gable and ridge vents.

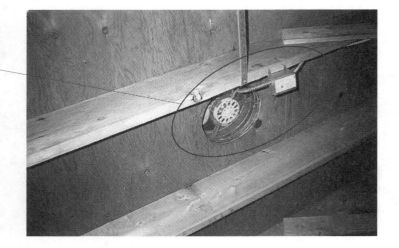

P 133. Did you ever learn about the birds and the bees? Birds, bees and wasps like to make nests in the gable vents leading to the attic area. This is why screens need to be installed on these vents. This gable vent is filled with debris and must be cleaned out. Exterior attic vents should be kept open all year round, even in cold weather climates. If these vents are sealed in the winter, then trapped heat in the attic will create moisture problems.

P 132. Bathroom vents should discharge to the exterior, unlike this vent in the photo. Any humidity carried by these vents will create moisture problems if discharged in the attic.

The white mold stains on these roof rafters has been caused by the bath fan vent discharging in the attic.
Notice the ice on the roofing nails that protrude through the plywood sheathing. This too is a sign of a moisture buildup and problem in the attic area.

P 135. Here's another example of moisture problems in an attic area. Notice the rust on the roofing nails, which hold the shingles on the exterior roof, that protrude through the plywood sheathing. This is a sign of a moisture buildup and problem in the attic area due to lack of adequate ventilation.

P 134. These Styrofoam Baffles, where the attic floor meets the base of the roof rafters, have a purpose. These baffles have a "U" shape and are designed to prevent the attic insulation from covering up the soffit vent openings in the base of the exterior roof overhang area. The "U" shape keeps a large enough gap open to allow the air to enter through the soffit vents and then carry the unwanted heat and moisture out the roof gable and ridge vents.

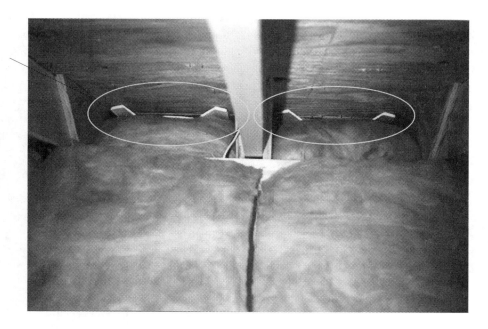

P 136. The plywood roof sheathing is in good condition with no signs of moisture problems.

These roof rafters have been bolted for a more secure hold instead of using just nails.

The Romex wiring is secured to the floor joists. Putting the wires inside a conduit pipe would be a better installation.

The insulation is installed properly with the aluminum vapor barrier facing the heated portion of the house - **downward** in the attic and **upward** in the basement.

P 137. Here's an example of an ultra-modern attic stair system! See those cinder blocks hanging from the roof rafters on pulleys? Can you guess what they're for? The cinder blocks act as counter weights to help open and close the heavy wood pull-down stairs leading into the attic area. It's clearly a very old design that must be updated with a modern attic pull-down stair system.

This attic needs a gable vent for better air circulation in the attic.

The Exterior Home Inspection

Roof

When you finish inspecting the interior, you can start on the exterior. We'll start with the roof, but as I've said before, feel free to adapt the inspection process to any way you feel comfortable with. There shouldn't be any tree branches overhanging the roof. Overhanging trees cause damage to the roof structure and shingles if branches fall. Shade created by the branches can cause mold and deteriorate the roof shingles. If you can, use a ladder to get a close look at the roof from the edge. While inside the house, you should view the roof close up from the interior windows if possible. Evaluating the roof framing from the attic area is a necessity. This will enable you to make better conclusions and evaluations when you get to the exterior. If you can't view the roof closely, you should use a pair of strong binoculars to help you.

Check for any bowing sections of the roof ridge beam, roof rafters or the roof sheathing which would suggest expensive repairs are needed. If there are any bowing sections then make sure you have take another look at these areas in the attic, if it's accessible. You should see plumbing vent stack pipes protruding through the roof by one foot. These are needed to keep the plumbing drainage lines at atmospheric pressure. Maintaining atmospheric pressure is required so the plumbing lines drain properly. If there are no plumbing vent stacks then you might hear gurgling noises from the interior sinks and drains.

Check the flashing for all roof projections and adjoining sections. *Flashing* refers to the material used around all joints to prevent water penetration into the house. Areas of the roof that need this type of water protection are: the base of chimneys and plumbing vent pipes, roof valleys, skylights, and the joint where dormers protrude through the roof. A *roof valley* refers to the area where two slopes of a roof meet to form a drainage channel. A *dormer* refers to a window or room that projects outward from the roof structure. Flashing should be made out of copper or aluminum. On higher priced homes you may find lead-lined copper flashing. Lead-lined copper has a longer lifespan and costs more.

If you find a lot of roofing tar "slopped" around the base of a chimney or over existing flashing, recommend it be repaired. Roofing tar is only a temporary fix for water leaks. It's like putting a band-aid over a cut that needs stitches. Some homeowners cut corners and have tar installed to avoid the higher cost of new flashing.

Remember that if it's raining, the roof will look newer than it actually is because of the water on it. There is one benefit to doing a home inspection on a rainy day. That is you'll have a better chance of finding any roof leaks or water problems in the lower level. If there's snow on the roof, just tell the client that you can only evaluate the visible portions.

If the house has a shingle roof it must have a high enough pitch to prevent water leaks under the shingles. A minimum pitch of 4 on 12 is recommended for shingle roofs. This means the roof pitch should rise by at least 4 inches for every 12 inches of roofing area. The slope of the roof that has a southerly or southwesterly exposure faces the sun more often. This can cause roof shingles to become brittle and show signs of aging faster. The slope of the roof that has a northerly or northeastern exposure is more likely to have mold and decay fungi on the shingles. This is caused by the lack of sunlight.

In northern climates you may find wires along the bottom edges of the roof. These wires are used to heat the show and ice so it melts off the roof without causing an ice dam. An *ice dam* refers to ice and snow that has frozen at the base of the roof above the gutters. Since the ice is trapped by the gutter, it gradually melts and the water goes underneath the roof shingles. This leads to water penetration problems in the house. Some homeowners don't like the idea of wires in their roof. If this is the case with your client, then flashing can be installed under the bottom few rows of shingles to help prevent water leaks from ice dams.

> *You have to be careful when evaluating roofs. This is another aspect of houses that can scare a buyer.*

You have to be careful when evaluating roofs. This is another aspect of houses that can really scare a buyer. Often buyers have a good reason to be scared about roof problems, but sometimes they overreact to an aging roof. In either case, you don't want to get any phone calls in the middle of the night from some guy who says his roof is leaking. Especially, if it's within twelve months after your inspection and you never warned him about it.

The life expectancy of all roofs depends upon many factors. Some factors are: the quality of the shingles, the quality of the installation of the shingles and the roofing materials, the climate and exposure to the elements, and the maintenance given to the shingles. The vast majority of houses have five types of roofing shingles:

◊   Asphalt
◊   Wood Shingles and Wood Shakes
◊   Slate
◊   Tile
◊   Flat Roofing

Check to see how many layers of shingles are currently on the roof. Most local building codes only allow up to two layers of asphalt shingles on a roof. If there are more than two layers, tell the client to find out if this is a building code violation. Three layers of shingles on a roof adds too much weight to the structure. You should only recommend that there be two layers as a maximum. Also, when shingles are placed over an existing layer, they can have a poor cosmetic appearance. The bumpy appearance of the roof is caused by the layer underneath which has cupped and curled from aging. Furthermore, placing roof shingles over an existing layer cuts down the life expectancy of the top layer of shingles.

> *If the house has two layers of shingles presently, then tell the client that they're going to have to strip these layers off during the next reroofing.*
> *This is a much more expensive repair.*

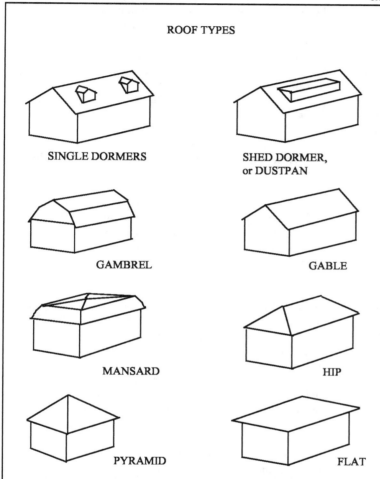

ROOF TYPES

SINGLE DORMERS

SHED DORMER, or DUSTPAN

GAMBREL

GABLE

MANSARD

HIP

PYRAMID

FLAT

If the house has two layers presently, then tell the client to budget for the next reroofing. They're going to have to strip these layers of shingles off and probably install new sheathing during the next reroofing. This is much more expensive than just having a new layer put over the existing shingles. Especially, if the roof sheathing has to be replaced as well. To determine the number of layers of shingles, look at the visible edges of the roof. If you see two or three shingles, then the roof probably only has one layer. This is because an extra layer of shingles is installed at the edges to keep rainwater from being blown underneath the shingles. Sometimes a roofing contractor will place a strip of aluminum flashing along the edge of the roof shingles. This will prevent rainwater from getting under the shingles but it also prevents you from seeing the number of layers of shingles.

To determine the age of the roof shingles you have to use some basic math and your own judgment. This is a good example of where the owner's answers to your preinspection questions come in handy. For instance, the life expectancy of average weight asphalt shingles is about 20 years. Let's say you are inspecting a house that's 30 years old and the roof doesn't show signs of aging. If you see four or more shingles at the exposed edges of the roof, you can assume the top layer is about 8-10 years old. It's just basic math: the first layer lasted about 21 years before a new roof was installed over it.

Asphalt shingles are classified by their weight. Shingles are rated by their weight per roofing square. A roofing square is a 100 square foot area of the rooftop. Lightweight shingles weigh about 215 pounds per roofing square. Heavyweight shingles weigh about 350 pounds per roofing square. Most asphalt shingles have a fiberglass mat instead of an organic type of mat. Asphalt-Fiberglass shingles have a typical life expectancy of 18 to 22 years. If a heavy weight shingle is used, then the life expectancy can be 30 years. This is because the roofing will stand up to the elements better. Quality roofers give warranties for these shingles as long as 20 to 30 years. As asphalt roofs age, they begin to cup and curl. You'll see these shingles fraying at the edges when they get old. You'll also see pitting of the granules. This is caused by the exterior of the shingle beginning to wear away. These granules are needed to protect the shingle from the sun and weather.

Be careful when evaluating roofs on houses that are about 20 to 25 years old. If there are heavyweight shingles the roof might not show clear signs of aging yet. If you don't check for the number of layers, you could incorrectly assume it's the second roof. This would cause the client to think he has another 15 years of roof life when actually there's only 5 years left. I made a mistake like this on one of my first home inspections in this business. The roof of the house had heavyweight shingles that were in excellent condition. There was no way to get close to the roof with my ladder. This house was located on a slope and my ladder couldn't reach near the roof edge. I did check the sides with binoculars and saw an extra layer of shingles along the edges. As a result, I thought the roof was relatively new since it was in excellent condition. The extra layer of shingles on the edges gave the indication that a second layer of roofing was installed within the past five years or so. Yes, I was wrong on that one. However, Lady Luck was on my side. The client had a friend who was a general contractor come by the house before the closing to give him some price estimates. The estimates were needed for some of the problem conditions I identified in other parts of the house inspection. Fortunately, the contractor had a long ladder that reached up to the roof line. He noticed that this was not a second layer of roofing shingles even though the shingles were in great condition. The client called me and told me about the mistake I made. I felt terrible that I missed this one and offered to refund his home inspection fee. However, the client was happy with the overall inspection I did and the problems I was able to identify. He said he would still recommend me to other people for home inspections.

You also have to be careful when inspecting houses that have sections of roofing that are different ages. For example, some homeowners will only replace 1/2 of a roof when a leak develops. Also, if an addition is installed to the house, this roofing will be newer. So don't just look at one side of the roof and assume that all the shingles are the same age. View all areas of the roofing shingles. On occasions you'll come across sections of a roof that were replaced at different times. This happens when a homeowner only wants to pay for part of the roof to be replaced. It's more cost efficient in the long run to reroof the entire house at the same time. However, if the homeowner cannot afford this, they'll only replace the shingles that are leaking water. Due to this possibility, you have to make sure you evaluate the roofing shingles from all sides of the house. Also, you may find "woven valleys" on some asphalt shingle roofs. A woven valley is shingles installed to overlap one another where roof sections meet. This is done for cosmetic purposes so the valley flashing is not visible.

Wood Shingle and *Wood Shake* roofs have a typical life expectancy of about 40 years. The lifespan will vary depending upon the maintenance given to them. They should be sprayed about every 4 years with a water repellant stain or sealant. This will prevent the wood from drying out and splitting. Wood shingle and wood shake roofs are more expensive to install than asphalt shingle roofs. As a result, they're usually only found on higher priced houses. Often you'll find asphalt shingles installed over a wood shingle roof. This is because the homeowner wanted to save money when reroofing. They did not want to pay the higher cost to install new wood shingles when the first layer needed replacing.

The difference between wood shingles and wood shakes is that wood shingles are sawn when they're manufactured. This gives them a smooth surface. Wood shakes are split when they're manufactured. Therefore, they're thicker and have a rougher surface. Wood shingles are spaced about 1/4 inch apart so they can expand and contract with the temperature changes. However, there shouldn't be any open gaps allowing water into the attic. Wood shingles and wood shakes are usually made from cedar or redwood. The reason for this is that these woods are more rot resistant and have less knots. Check for any signs of dry or rotted shingles that indicate a need for repairs.

Slate roofs are *very* expensive to install. Because of this, they're usually only found on older houses or very high priced newer houses. Slate roofs will only have one layer of shingles on the roof. This is due to their being very heavy and brittle. **Do not** walk on a slate roof; you'll damage the shingles. The life expectancy of a slate roof can be anywhere from 50 years to 150 years or more. The lifespan will depend upon the quality of the slate and the installation of the shingles. If the roofing nails are intact then the thicker the slate shingles, the longer they will last.

When slates are shaling (flaking) and excessively falling off the roof, it's an indication that repairs are needed. The slate shingles will have to be removed carefully so they aren't damaged. After that, new tar paper needs to be placed over the roof sheathing to provide a weather covering. Then the slate shingles will be reinstalled with copper nails. Don't take any chances with a slate roof; they're extremely expensive to reroof. If you're not sure of it's condition, tell the client to get an estimate from a roofing contractor.

You'll usually find a few fallen slate shingles. However, you're looking for an excessive amount of shingles that have fallen off the roof. This is an indication that the roofing nails are all corroding. The only way to correct this problem is to remove each slate and reinstall it with copper nails. In northern climates where there's snow, you might see snow guards along the bottom rows of slate shingles. Snow guards are small metal fins that stick up from the slates. Their purpose is to stop snow from falling off the roof so it doesn't drop to the ground with excessive force. Large amounts of falling snow could hurt someone or damage cars and other objects located below the roof line.

Tile roofs are similar to slate roofs. They're very expensive to install and are usually only found on older houses or very high priced newer houses. Tile roofs will only have one layer of shingles. This is due to their being very heavy and brittle. **Do not** walk on a tile roof; you'll damage the shingles. The life expectancy of a tile roof can be anywhere from 50 years to 100 years or more. The lifespan will depend upon the quality of the tile and the installation of the shingles.

As with slate roofs, you're looking for any shaling or an excessive number of falling tiles from the roof. Don't take any chances with a tile roof as well; they're very expensive to reroof. If you're not sure of it's condition, tell the client to get an estimate from a roofing contractor. There are concrete roofing shingles that look identical to slate and tile shingles. The purpose of these concrete shingles is to give the home an expensive roof appearance. In reality the cost can be far less than installing an actual slate or tile roof.

Flat roofs usually consist of asphalt rolled roofing material. Asphalt Rolled flat roofs generally are the least expensive type of roofing to repair or replace. Flat roofs have to be monitored by the homeowner, more often than other types of roofs, to make sure they're watertight. The reason for this is that they don't just shed water like pitched roofs do. Flat roofs have a tendency for ponding water conditions. The life expectancy for an asphalt flat roof is about 8 to 10 years. There are rubber material flat roofs that are superior to asphalt rolled roofing. These rubber roofs have a 30 year life expectancy.

As with asphalt shingle roofs, flat roofs can be installed over existing layers when a new roof is needed. You should try to determine how many current layers there are when evaluating these roofs. You won't be able to see an exposed edge like on a pitched roof. Just use some basic math and your own judgment based upon the age of the house and the owner's answers to the preinspection questions.

Check for any ponding water conditions on a flat roof. Ponding water will decrease the life expectancy of these roofs and must be repaired to help prevent leaks. If you see a flat roof bubbling in areas, it shows the roof covering is near the end of its life expectancy. As a result, the roof will need to be replaced.

Roof photos: P 138-P 144, P 215-P 217

Chimney

Use your binoculars to view the chimney. The base may be built in the middle of the house. In this situation you'll only see the portion of the stack that protrudes through the attic and roof. Some homes will have the chimney built along the side of the exterior. This type of installation will have a chimney foundation that is separate from that of the house. As with the house foundation, the footing must be below the frost line in cold climate areas. Check to make sure that the chimney isn't leaning. A leaning condition is a serious problem and it would have to be repaired.

Make sure the mortar joints are in good condition and don't need repointing. You may see the terra-cotta tile flue linings at the top of the chimney. Make sure they aren't cracked or broken. Each flue pipe in the chimney should vent out of a separate stack. When you see two flue pipes, one is for the fireplace and the other is for the heating system exhaust. The top of the chimney stack should be high enough above the roof line to prevent downdrafts. Downdrafts are caused by air currents over the roofline pushing cold air down the chimney flue pipe. This will prevent the exhaust gases from properly venting out of the house.

If there's an antenna attached to the chimney or the roof, make sure it's caulked. Caulking is needed so that there won't be any openings to allow water into the house. If there's cable TV in the house and the antenna is no longer in use, then the antenna should be removed. Antennas add stress to the roof and chimney when they move around in the wind. They can create water leaks.

There should be a weather cover about one foot above the top of the chimney stack to prevent water from entering the flue. There should be a screen over the top of the flue stack to prevent animals, such as raccoons, squirrels and birds, from entering the flue. I once did an inspection on a vacant house and when I looked up the interior of the fireplace flue, a raccoon was sitting there. This raccoon took one look at me and ran like hell out of the top of the chimney. *(I guess that doesn't say much for my looks, especially if that was a female raccoon!)* By the way, don't go near any raccoons. They're beautiful looking animals but they carry all sorts of diseases, including rabies. You also want to be careful if you're allergic to bee stings or if there are ticks that carry lime disease in your area. Sometimes while you're inspecting the exterior of a house, you'll have to move through the shrubs to get a closer view of the foundation area. By doing this, you can get stung.

Some chimneys are made of metal piping. Check these chimneys for any rust. Often on condominiums you'll find that metal chimneys are covered with a finished wood siding to match the exterior wall siding. You'll be limited in what you can see with this type of installation. Just do the best you can.

Chimney photos:
P 138, P 145, P 147, P 205, P 218, P 219

Siding

The siding on a house is used to provide weather protection. The siding doesn't support the house structurally. A load bearing wall is what provides the structural support of the house. If you find a building constructed of brick, stone or masonry, then these materials aren't considered the siding since they are load bearing walls. Check these types of structures for problems with bulging or leaning walls and deteriorated mortar joints. The are many different types of sidings used on residential homes. The types you will generally encounter during a home inspection are the following:

◊   Wood Boards *(often called Clapboard Siding)*
◊   Wood Shingles
◊   Wood Shakes
◊   Plywood Panels
◊   Aluminum Siding
◊   Vinyl Siding
◊   Asbestos-Cement Shingles
◊   Asphalt Siding
◊   Stucco
◊   Veneer Walls

Wood siding can be painted or stained. Painted wood will have a more uniform appearance but needs more maintenance. Stained wood will have spotty areas due to the wood absorbing the stain unevenly in some sections. However, staining lasts a lot longer than painting and is less maintenance.

Make sure all joints around windows and doors are caulked properly. If there any are vines growing up the side of the house, recommend that they be removed. Many people like the cosmetic look of the vines but it's terrible from a maintenance point of view. The vine roots create rot and moisture problems, as well as, deteriorating any mortar joints.

> *All siding should be at least eight inches above the soil all around the structure.*
> *This will help prevent termite and rot problems.*

All siding should be at least eight inches above the soil all around the structure. This will help prevent termite and rot problems. The moisture in the soil will rot out the siding. Also, when the siding is in contact with the ground, wood destroying insects can get behind the siding very easily. All siding should be installed with galvanized nails to prevent rust over time. If you see many parts of the siding that are loose or missing, then check the nails. You may find they're becoming too rusty and corroding away. If this is the case, then all the siding will need to be reinstalled with galvanized nails. This is a major expense so tell the client to get estimates.

Check all wood siding for rot and wood destroying insect damage. Use an awl to probe sections of the siding. Near the ground level areas you want to look for termite, carpenter ant,

and powder post beetle damage. Use binoculars to check the wood siding and trim work near the roofline areas. This is a common place to find small holes due to carpenter bee damage.

Check with the seller to see if they've replaced any siding or if there's an underlying layer of older siding on the house. You want to try to find out what's underneath the exterior layer. The exterior maintenance of condominium units is usually paid for by a monthly charge assessed to all of the condo owners in the complex. Recommend that the client check with the Condo/Owner's Association to find out what the fees and responsibilities are for each owner in the complex.

Wooden Clapboard siding can be installed vertically or horizontally. The majority of the time wooden clapboards are installed horizontally. Horizontal installations make the house appear lower and longer. Vertical installations make the house appear taller and are used more often on one-story houses. Check the condition of the wooden clapboard siding. See if it needs to be painted or stained, if there are any knots in the wood, if there are any damaged or rotted sections, etc.

Wood Shingle and *Wood Shake* sidings are usually made of cedar or redwood. This is due to the lack of knots in these types of wood. Also, these woods are rot resistant due to the oils in the wood. These sidings are very similar to wood shingle and shake installations found on roofs. Wood shingle and wood shake sidings are also expensive to install and are usually only found on higher priced homes. These sidings have a life expectancy of about 40 to 45 years or more. The lifespan will depend upon the climate and maintenance given to them over the years. Check the condition of the wood shake or wood shingle siding. See if it needs to be painted or stained, if there are any knots in the wood, if there are damaged or rotted sections, etc.

Plywood Panel siding is made of an exterior type of plywood with a waterproof glue. A common type of exterior plywood is called T1-11 siding. Plywood is an inexpensive siding material to install on homes. Check for any loose, warped, damaged or rotted sections. This siding is prone to warping over time since it is a cheaper construction material. When this happens, water will get behind the panels and cause damage.

I have seen houses that needed all new wood panel siding due to warped and curling sections. The damage was caused by the lack of gutters on the house or a proper roof overhang area. Some architects designed these houses thinking gutters were not needed. They also felt the roof overhang was unnecessary. Due to their ignorance, the rain water prematurely destroyed the siding on these homes. Rain water must be kept away from the side of the house as far as possible.

Aluminum siding is relatively maintenance free and termite proof. Aluminum won't rot like wood sidings. Often you'll find aluminum siding installed over an older siding that was originally on the house. In some areas, it's required that aluminum siding be grounded to an exterior grounding rod embedded in the soil. The reason for this is to prevent shock hazards from electrical currents contacting the aluminum. After about 15 to 20 years, this siding can begin to fade and may need to be painted. Aluminum siding is a rigid material and can dent if hit hard enough.

Vinyl siding is very similar to aluminum in that it's relatively maintenance free and termite proof. It also will not rot like wood sidings. Vinyl siding is a flexible material, unlike aluminum. Aluminum siding can dent, but vinyl siding can crack if hit with hard objects in cold weather. Often you'll find vinyl siding installed over an older siding that was originally on the house.

⚠ *Asbestos-Cement Shingles* are made by combining asbestos fibers with Portland cement under high pressure. This siding is termite proof and rot resistant. However, it's a very rigid material and you'll generally find some cracked and damaged shingles. It's not used for newer construction and is found on older houses. Often it can be found under aluminum or vinyl sidings. Some areas have requirements that Asbestos-Cement Shingles must be removed by an EPA licensed contractor. This is due to the asbestos fiber content in the shingles. If they're removed improperly, the fibers can blow around in the wind and create health hazards.

Asphalt siding is similar to asphalt shingle roofing. It can be installed in either a shingle form or a roll product. Asphalt siding is found in many different colors and styles. This siding isn't used in newer construction. Asphalt siding is usually found underneath aluminum or vinyl sidings. The life expectancy of asphalt siding is about 30 years. As it ages it becomes brittle and will cup and curl, like asphalt roofing shingles. Any open or brittle areas need to be sealed to prevent water problems.

Stucco siding is the same composition as the lath and plaster or stucco walls found on the interior of older houses. This exterior siding will have a backing paper, called sheathing, to help prevent water penetration through any open joints. Stucco siding is very rigid. You'll probably find some settlement cracks that need to be sealed periodically. Be very careful to check for any loose sections of stucco. This indicates that the metal lath underneath the concrete coating may be rusty and deteriorating. Falling stucco can be heavy and is a hazard that needs to be repaired.

Veneer Walls refers to a layer of brick, stone or textured masonry siding that's a decorative covering on the exterior of the house. These materials are used to give the appearance of a solid brick or masonry constructed house. It's a decorative type of installation and it doesn't support the walls of the house like a load bearing wall would. Veneer walls are attached to the side of the house with corrosion resistant metal ties. Make sure you check to see if the wall is leaning which

may suggest the ties are rusted and need replacing. There should be a one inch gap behind veneer walls to help prevent any water or moisture problems due to lack of ventilation. There should also be *weep holes* at the base of the wall. These are small holes that are needed to allow any water that might accumulate behind the wall to safely drain away.

Siding photos: P 146-P 158, P 220-P 222

Fascia, Soffits and Eaves

The *Fascia, Soffits* and *Eaves* are the molding areas at the bottom of the roof and the top of the siding. It's the small area where the roof overhangs the sides of the house. Check to see if the wood is rotted or if it needs to be painted or stained. Often you'll find there's an aluminum siding covering over the fascia, soffits and eaves. If you see vents at the bottom of the roof overhang area it indicates that the house may have soffit vents. *Soffit vents* allow air to enter the bottom of the attic area and help to remove heat and moisture from a house.

Fascia, Soffits and Eaves photos: P 148

Gutters, Downspouts and Leaders

Gutters are installed along the bottom edge of the roof. Their purpose is to catch the rainwater running off the roof. *Downspouts* are installed near the ends of the gutters. They're used to drain the water so the gutters don't overflow. *Leaders* are installed at the bottom of the downspouts. Leaders are used to direct the rainwater away from the side of the structure.

The vast majority of gutters, downspouts and leaders are made of aluminum because it's lightweight, inexpensive and resistant to rust and rot. Sometimes on older houses the gutters, downspouts and leaders will be made of copper. If copper gutters are painted, the only way to find out if they are copper is to look for the soldered joints or scratch the metal to see if it's a copper color. Wood gutters are not recommended since they have a short life expectancy due to rot.

There should be at least one downspout for every 30 feet of gutter to prevent excessive weight from the rainwater from damaging the gutters. All downspouts should have leaders to pipe the rainwater at least five feet away from the foundation to help prevent any water problems in the lower level.

Some downspouts drain directly into the ground. These lead to dry-wells or underground drainage lines. They need to be checked periodically for clogging due to leaves and small animals getting stuck in them. In most areas the local building codes prohibit sump pumps, gutters and downspouts from discharging water into the house plumbing drainage lines. These drainage lines must discharge into a dry-well. A *dry-well* is a small pit dug into the soil with rocks and gravel inside the hole to help drain away water accumulations. This building code restriction is designed to prevent too much water from entering the municipal sewer system.

A *built-in* gutter is one that is "enclosed" around the edge of the roof area. Built-in gutters are not recommended since they can cause water leaks in the house. When these gutters leak, the water can go undetected for a long time. This leads to extensive water damage inside the walls of the house.

Gutters, Downspouts and Leaders photos:
P 153, P 155, P 157, P 156

Windows, Screens and Storms

Check the condition of the exterior window frames for any rot or if they need to be painted or stained. Check the condition of any storms and screens. If there are no storm windows you should recommend that they be installed in northern climates where the temperature gets cold. More heat is lost in a house through the windows than through any other area. Storm or thermal windows can reduce the heat loss by as much as 50%.

> *If there are no storm windows you should recommend that they be installed in northern climates where the temperature gets cold. More heat is lost in a house through the windows than through any other area.*

If you are inspecting a brick or stone house, metal lintels should be installed above the window and door frames. A *lintel* is a metal support used to give added strength. When a lintel is not installed the weight of the masonry can cause the frame to crack over time.

Windows, Screens and Storms photos: P 151, P 162

Entrances, Steps and Porches

Check all entrances, steps and porches for structural sturdiness and any tripping hazards. Make sure there are no cracks or uneven sections in any of the steps. The landing platform is the standing area in front of a door. Make sure that there is a large enough space to safely open the exterior doors while someone is standing in front of them. You don't want anyone to be knocked down the steps when the door is opened. *(Unless of course it's an unwanted guest).*

⚠ There should be handrails and closely spaced balusters for **_all_** stairs that are more than two steps in height. The *balusters* are the railing posts that run vertically under the handrails. Make sure the handrails aren't loose or decayed. Recommend that handrails be installed when they are not noted on stairs.

All steps should have even and uniform riser heights and treads so there are no tripping hazards. The *riser* refers to the vertical section of a stair step. The *tread* refers to the horizontal section of a stair step. If there are any wood stairs, the base of the wood should be resting on concrete supports above the soil. This will help to prevent rot and termite infestation. If there's an enclosed porch, tell the client to check with town hall to see if all valid permits and approvals have been obtained. Some homeowners will enclose an open porch area without knowing that most areas require building permits for this work.

Entrances, Steps and Porches photos: P 160-P 162

Walks

Check all walks for any tripping hazards. There shouldn't be any weeds growing between the walkway sections. If there are any uneven sections, recommend that they be repaired. Sometimes the sidewalk at the street will be uneven due to tree roots. Tell the client to check with the local building department to find out whose responsibility it is to repair the sidewalk. In most areas, the homeowner is responsible for repairing and shoveling the sidewalk in front of their house.

My brother and I received a building violation once for a sidewalk that was a tripping hazard. The sidewalk in front of one of our rental properties had some cracks due to the growth of roots from a large tree planted there. We had the sidewalk repaired by a contractor and then the violation was removed. Also, we received a summons for not shoveling the snow immediately after a snowfall in front of one of our rental properties. We paid someone to shovel the snow whenever it was necessary in front of the building. However, one time he didn't do it fast enough after the snowfall stopped. As a result, we were given a ticket.

Sometimes you'll inspect a house that's located on a private street. In this situation, tell the client to determine what rights and responsibilities they have as a homeowner on that road. Often homeowners who live on private streets have to pay for the repaving and maintenance of the street.

Patios and Terraces

As with walks, check all patios and terraces for any tripping hazards. There shouldn't be any weeds growing between the joints of the sections. Any uneven sections need to be repaired. If the patio touches the side of the foundation, then it must be well caulked and sloped away to prevent water from draining toward the house. In most areas building permits and approvals are needed to build patios. Tell the client to check this at town hall.

Patios and Terraces photos: P 162, P 223

Decks

Decks *always* require building department permits because of the safety concern if they're improperly built. Check for rotted sections of wood that need replacing. Some decks will be too low to the ground to view the structural members. Just do the best you can. The deck perimeter railings should be sturdy. The balusters under the railing must be spaced so that a maximum gap of four inches exists between them. This is to help prevent small children or dogs from falling through.

> *Decks always require building department approvals because of the safety concern if they're improperly built.*

There should be lag bolts in the main beam, called the *header beam*, where the deck is attached to the side of the house. *Lag bolts* are a **far superior** way to support the deck as opposed to just using nails. Copper flashing should be installed between the header beam and the side of the house. This will prevent water from getting trapped and rotting the wood.

The floor joists of the deck should have steel support hangers. Steel support hangers give the floor joists more support then by just nailing them. All deck support posts and girders should have steel brackets at the top and the base for support. This will also keep the wood from being in contact with the soil. The base should be resting on a concrete support post.

Decks photos: P 163-P 166, P 224

Walls and Fences

Retaining walls are used to support the soil in areas, such as driveways or yards, which are dug into the earth. Some different types of retaining walls are: stone and cement walls, dry stone walls, gabion walls, concrete block walls and wood timber walls.

◊ *Stone and Cement* walls have mortar between the stones to hold them in place. Check the condition of all mortar joints.

◊ *Dry Stone* walls don't have mortar to hold the stones together. This is because they are carefully placed so that the weight of each stone supports one another. Dry stone walls are expensive and time consuming to build.

◊ *Gabion* walls are stones in a steel wire covering. The steel covering holds the stones in place.

◊ *Concrete Block* walls need to be checked for deteriorating mortar joints.

◊ *Wood Timber* walls need to be checked for rot and wood destroying insect infestation.

Retaining walls should have *weep holes* at the base to allow any water that builds up behind them to drain away. Wood timber, dry stone and gabion retaining walls don't need to have weep holes because there are spaces between the construction materials to drain the water away.

⚠ Check to see if any retaining walls are leaning. Any leaning conditions indicate that repairs **must** be made to prevent the wall from moving any further or collapsing.

All fences need to be checked for sturdiness. Tell the client to check with town hall to find out if the fence is within the subject property line. Often the homeowner, or a neighbor, will have a fence, wall, driveway, or shed installed and the contractor will just guess where the property line is. This can lead to an *encroachment* on someone else's property. Chain link fences will rust with age and wood fences will rot. So look for these signs of aging.

Walls and Fences photos: P 165-P 167, P 225-P 227

Drainage and Grading

The soil next to the foundation should slope away from the house to prevent any rainwater from building up next to the foundation. Usually the soil only needs to slope 1/2 inch for every foot away from the house to properly drain the water accumulations. All bushes, shrubs and trees should be pruned away from the side of the house. This will allow enough sunlight and air next to the foundation to help prevent rot and wood destroying insect problems.

If the house is located at the base of a hill there should be a *catch basin* to prevent water problems. These are large concrete underground drains. You also may find a large dip in the soil that looks like a long, narrow trench for water drainage. These dug-out areas are called *swales*. The purpose of a swale is to drain the water away to a suitable location before it reaches the house. It's similar to the design of highways. The paved road is set at a higher level than the side areas with the grass and trees. This will help drain the rainwater away from the roadway.

As I said earlier in the book, recommend that the client check with the local building department to figure out if the house is located in a designated flood hazard zone. If it is, then flood hazard insurance will be needed.

Drainage and Grading photos: P 157, P 170

Driveways

Check all asphalt and concrete driveways for cracked and uneven sections. Asphalt driveways need to be sealed with a driveway sealer every two or three years to prevent them from drying out and cracking. Repaving an asphalt driveway can be expensive. If the driveway needs to be repaved, tell the client to get an estimate prior to closing on the house.

If there's an underground drain at the base of the driveway look at it to see if it's clogged. Often you'll find these drains filled with leaves and dirt. Some driveways don't have a finished surface and are made of gravel and dirt. Often they have holes that are tripping hazards that need to be repaired. Unfinished driveways can lead to people tracking dirt into the house and they can't be shoveled for snow removal in northern areas.

Driveways photos: P 170-P 169

Garage

The different types of garages you'll encounter are Detached, Attached and Built-in or Tuck-under garages.

◊ *Detached* garages are separate structures from the main house.

◊ *Attached* garages are attached to the main house.

◊ *Built-in* or *Tuck-under* garages are set underneath the house and take up a section of the lower level.

⚠ A benefit of having an attached or built-in garage is that you can park the car and enter the house without worrying about the weather conditions. A detached garage is safer in the event that a car is left running by mistake, the exhaust fumes can't enter the house easily. A detached garage is also safer in the event of a fire, the flames and smoke can't spread to the house easily.

⚠ The inspection procedure for the garage is the same as with the exterior and interior aspects of the main house. Review those sections for recommendations. One of the additional aspects to evaluate with the garage is to make sure the overhead doors operate properly. Open and close the doors to see if they're difficult to operate or if they come down with excessive force. The springs will need to be adjusted or lubricated if there's a problem. Doors that come down with excessive force can crush a child if they're caught underneath.

> *Check all electric door openers to make sure they operate. Electric door openers should have an automatic reverse function that's working properly.*

⚠️ Check all electric door openers to make sure they operate. Electric door openers should have an *automatic reverse* function that's working properly. This is a setting in the opener that will reverse the direction of the doors if a person or a car gets caught underneath. To test the automatic reverse function, activate the opener to close the garage door. While it's coming down, lightly put some pressure on the bottom of the door or on the handle. If the reversing function is operating properly, the door should stop or reverse itself back to the open position. **Don't** stand underneath the door or do anything to get your hands caught while testing this device. You don't want to find out it's not working properly by getting hurt!! Remember you're not paid to do anything hazardous.

⚠️ All water pipes and heating pipes in the garage need to be insulated to prevent them from freezing and for energy efficiency. All heating ducts in the garage need to be insulated for energy efficiency. Check the floor for any oil or gas drippings that need to be cleaned to help prevent any fires. The garage walls and ceilings should be covered with fireproof sheetrock to help prevent the spread of any fires. Masonry walls and ceilings are an acceptable fireproof covering. If the garage is attached or built-in there should be a fireproof entry door leading to the house. Also, this door must have a self-closing device to prevent the door from being left open. This will help prevent **lethal** car exhaust fumes or fires from spreading into the house.

Garage photos: P 169-P 171, P 229

Other Exterior Structures

Check all garden and tool sheds on the property for rot and wood destroying insect infestation. Make sure they're sturdy and there are no hazards. If there are any other exterior structures on the property, evaluate them just as you would the house itself. If there is anything you're unsure about, then just tell the client to have the structure evaluated further by a licensed contractor.

Other Exterior Structures photos: P 172, P 228

Swimming Pools

All swimming pools require local town approvals that need to be verified by the client. All swimming pools need to have fences surrounding them to prevent any unattended children from falling into the water and drowning. Also, special homeowner's insurance is needed with swimming pools. This is due to the increased liability of having a pool on the property. There are two types of swimming pool installations: *out-of-ground* and *in-ground*. *(I guess that's pretty obvious. Unless of course you know someone who happens to have an underground pool at their house).*

> *All swimming pools require local town approvals. All pools need to have fences surrounding them to prevent any unattended children from falling into the water and drowning.*

Check the area around the pool for any tripping hazards. Check the pool walls for any leaks, cracks or bulging sections. If it's winter time and the outdoor air temperature gets below 32 degrees Fahrenheit, then the pool must be properly winterized. When water freezes it expands and as a result, this can crack the walls of a pool if proper winter maintenance has not been taken care of. If you have any doubts about the pool, just tell the client to call a swimming pool contractor for further evaluations. I don't get involved in evaluating pools and pool equipment, such as, heaters, filters and pumps. If you want to charge extra for this service, feel free to do so. But make sure you know what you're doing before you start telling clients that you're qualified to evaluate pools and pool equipment. You don't want to give anyone the wrong impression just so that you can charge more for the inspection.

Swimming Pools photos: P 174-P 175

Wood Destroying Insects

There are many different types of wood destroying insects, including 70 species of termites throughout the world. Depending upon your area of the country, the wood destroying insects that you need to be the most concerned with are:

◊   Subterranean Termites
◊   Dry Wood Termites
◊   Damp Wood Termites
◊   Powder Post Beetles
◊   Carpenter Ants
◊   Carpenter Bees

This is another concern with buying a house that really scares people. So make sure you check thoroughly for wood destroying insects. If there was any aspect of performing home inspections that you would need X-ray vision, then this one takes the prize. If *Superman* really existed, he'd make a fortune as a Termite inspector. I've heard an awful lot of war stories about inspectors getting complaints from people because they didn't notice the termites that were behind the sheetrock walls. Some people honestly believe that you should have told them that there were termites in areas that you couldn't even see. I have know idea where they get their logic from. If there are indications out in the open and you miss the signs, that's one thing. But don't expect someone to identify a problem that they can't even see!!

> *If there was any aspect of home inspections that you would need X-ray vision, then this one takes the prize. If Superman really existed, he'd make a fortune as a Termite inspector.*

This is the reason that many home inspectors don't even offer termite inspections as part of their services. They just tell the client that they'll check everything else but for termites the client needs to hire a licensed exterminator. I personally do termite inspections because it's an additional service you can provide the client. You can also earn a small extra fee while you're at the site. I've taken the courses required to get a Pesticide Control Operators license, *(PCO)*. This license is needed to fill out the FHA/VA Wood Destroying Insect form. Virtually all lenders require this form for a house before they approve a mortgage loan. You can make your own judgments as to whether or not you want to do termite inspections. Just remember it's the same as every other business: *where there's money to be made, there's risk to assume.*

Occasionally you will have to rely on Lady Luck to help you find wood destroying insect damage. One time I was inspecting a house that was built on a concrete slab foundation. This type of construction doesn't have a basement area. As a result, termites can travel through cracks in the concrete slab. The wood beams and moldings of the livable rooms become an easy meal for the termites. I was just about finished with my inspection and only had one more closet to check. When I opened the closet door, there was termite damage all through the molding. The damaged wood was recently painted over and the termite tunnels were difficult to see. Had I cut corners by not checking that one last closet, I wouldn't have found the damaged wood. There were several times when I was in the lower level and Lady Luck was on my side. While looking around I randomly probed some wood beams. The screwdriver passed right through the beams due to wood destroying insect damage. I was lucky to find these damaged areas since there were no visible indications on the exterior of the wood.

Termites eat the wood and turn it into food. They have one-celled organisms in their digestive tracts that convert the cellulose of wood back into sugar which they can digest. In forests, termites are beneficial since they help to decompose fallen trees and stumps. They help return the wood substances to the soil to be used again by other trees. Termite damaged wood will have channels in it and there won't be any sawdust around.

With *Subterranean Termites* you'll find mud in their tunnels. These termites bring mud into the wood channels since they can only survive in a warm, dark and moist environment. Probe wood with an awl or screwdriver, especially rotted or wet beams in dark areas, to check for termite infestation. You may see signs of mud on the outside sections of the wood indicating termite damage. What these termites do is they'll eat up to the very edge of the wood they are inside and leave a thin layer on the exterior. This thin layer of wood will prevent light or air from getting inside the channels and drying out the wood.

Dry Wood Termites are found in coastal warmer climate areas of the country. They have a caste system in their colonies similar to that of the Subterranean Termites. The difference is that they live and feed on sound, dry seasoned wood and they don't need to be in contact with the soil or a moisture source. As a result you won't see any mud tubes with these insects.

Damp Wood Termites are similar to subterranean termites but seldom live in the soil. They nest in damp wood and are associated with wood decay and don't construct tubing.

Powder Post Beetle larvae eat the wood and lay their eggs in it. They can't convert the cellulose in the wood to sugar. Therefore, these insects must get their nourishment from the starch and sugar that the tree has stored in the wood cells. To these insects, the cellulose in the wood has no food value and is thus ejected from their bodies as wood powder or *frass*. They derive nourishment from the starch and sugar in the wood.

Powder Post Beetles can be brought into the factory when the wood from the forest is being milled. From this point, the beetles are brought into the home during the construction of the house. Wood that has been damaged by Powder Post Beetles will crumble like sawdust when you probe it. A common indication of these insects is the existence of many tiny, black holes in the wood. You're more likely to find these holes in very old houses. I've found the main structural beams in a few 100-200 year old houses *totally* infested with beetle damage. However, you can still find Powder Post Beetle damage in newer homes as well. If only a single generation of this beetle larvae has fed within some wood, then the wood usually is still structurally sound. It's the feeding of generation after generation that reduces the interior of the wood to a mass of powder. Before the female will attach her eggs to a piece of wood, she first actually tastes the wood. The purpose of tasting the wood is to be sure it contains enough sugar and starch to nourish her offspring. If she's prevented from doing this due to any covering on the wood, such as, paint, varnish, or stain, she won't deposit her eggs in the wood. As a result, the wood won't be reinfested with another generation of Powder Post Beetle larvae. That's why there shouldn't be any untreated wood around the house.

Carpenter Ants and *Carpenter Bees* merely excavate the wood to make nests. The damage they cause will leave sawdust outside the wood channels. Exterminators use a powder type of chemical to treat for these insects. Carpenter Ants can be black, brown, or a combination of both colors. They will only infest about 4 feet of a wood beam to make a nest and they won't go further. Carpenter Bees can dig a hole in wood in about 10 minutes. They use their tail to dig a nice, smooth opening for their nest. There are only two Carpenter Bees in each nest hole, the male and female. The best time to spray for carpenter bees is in the morning hours. The reason for this is that in the morning the bees will be in the nest while it's still cool. In the afternoon it's too hot and the bees will leave the nest due to the heat.

Since subterranean termites seem to cause the most damage to homes, we'll talk about them in more detail. There are four different types of insects or *castes* in a Subterranean Termite colony:

1   The *Swarmer* termites have wings. They're about 3/8 inch long and are dark colored. Their wings are about twice as long as their bodies. **Contrary to popular belief**, not all termites have wings. Only the Swarmers of a termite colony grow wings and swarm away from the nest to start a new colony. After they land, their wings fall off and the mated female becomes the *Queen* and the male the *King*. *(Right after the coronation where they're crowned King and Queen, they order their subjects in the termite colony to attack your house! I'm just kidding.)*

2   Very large termite colonies have *Supplemental Reproductives* in them. These insects are light in color. Supplemental Reproductives are formed, as needed, to replace the Queen if she's injured. This is required to continue the production of termite eggs in the colony.

3   The termites that eat the wood are called the *Worker* termites. They're a small 1/4 inch, white colored insect with soft bodies. I've only seen the worker termites a few times inside damaged sections of wood during an inspection. **It's very rare to see the termites while they're eating the wood.** At least in my area it's rare. If you ask an exterminator in your area, they'll probably tell you the same thing.

4   The *Soldier* is another caste of insect found in large colonies. Their primary function is the defense of the termite colony. Soldiers are easily recognized by their large, brownish, well-developed heads and jaws or mandibles.

The birth of the different types of insects or castes is regulated in a termite colony by *smell*. Each different caste gives off it's own special odor. When the numbers decrease for a particular caste, the odor in the colony changes. This change in odor instinctively makes the King and Queen lay eggs to replenish them as they are needed.

During the summer months, a mated pair of winged termites can establish a new colony. However, new colonies can also be produced by a sort of *"budding-off"* process. It's a process in which a number of workers and some supplemental reproductives become physically isolated from the original colony. As a result, when termites are found in a building, there's no sure indication of whether the infestation began: as a completely new colony, an isolated fragment of another colony, or whether a colony located nearby, as for example, in a fence post, simply moved-in to take advantage of the year round warmth of the building.

> *Often when you find damaged wood due to wood destroying insects, a Realtor, seller or other third party person will ask, "Oh, is it active or inactive." I just tell them that there's no way to know.*

Often when you find damaged wood due to wood destroying insects, a Realtor, seller or other third party person will ask, *"Oh, is it active or inactive."* I just tell them that there's no way to know since it's rare to actually find the termites in the damaged wood. The termites could just have moved to a different section of the house. There's just no way to know for sure. So **don't** let any Realtors or third parties tell your client that they don't have to worry about termites because you couldn't see them actually eating the wood. A lot of times dishonest Realtors will do this to *"gloss over"* and underestimate the potential termite problem in the house.

Subterranean Termites must have a warm, high humidity environment and they must have a constant source of food. Unlike Carpenter Ants, termites **cannot** hibernate and must feed and be active throughout the winter. The single fact that subterranean termites *must* live in a warm, high relative humidity environment is what creates their need for access to the earth. Because of soil moisture, the air spaces between soil particles are almost always very humid. It's this very humid atmosphere that's so important to the termite colony. Cutting off this ground contact with soil moisture is the principle of subterranean termite control measures.

When a corrective wood destroying insect treatment is performed to a structure, it's usually done on both the interior and the exterior. This is much more thorough than just treating inside *or* outside the building. The treatment uses the *rodding* technique, which is considered the simplest approach, as opposed to the *trenching* technique.

1   The *trenching* technique involves digging a two to three foot trench all around the structure next to the foundation. The soil is then treated with insecticide.

2   With the *rodding* technique, depending on the type of soil, the Pest Control Operator will drill holes every 6-18 inches that are three or more feet deep. The holes are drilled right next to the interior and exterior foundation walls, all around the structure. Then the insecticide is injected down into the soil.

The purpose of the treatment is to create a ring of insecticide around the structure. Any worker termites that are outside the house won't cross this line and will move to another food source. Any worker termites that are trapped inside the house will die because they can't get back to the nest for the moisture they need to survive. An important fact to remember when getting a corrective treatment is to recommend that *all* of the damaged wood be removed and replaced. This will ensure that any damaged areas are resupported with good, solid lumber. Another reason for this is that there's no way to tell down the road if the wood had gotten the termite damage before or after the corrective treatment. So if the wood isn't removed, then when the client goes to sell the house many years later, the next home inspector might see the damaged wood. This home inspector could insist that his client get another treatment. It'll eliminate any future problems, if the damaged wood is removed with the corrective treatment that's done at the present time.

The damage caused by termites is sometimes over exaggerated. There are very few houses on record that had to be knocked down due to serious structural problems due to termites. A full colony of termites can only eat about three feet of a wooden 2 x 4 beam in a year. For them to do serious structural damage they would have to go unnoticed in the house for an awfully long time. I find minor termite damage in one out of every four houses that I inspect. Of these houses, I've only seen two or three of them that had very bad termite damage. But even those two or three houses could be repaired just be replacing some floor joists and treating the house with insecticide.

There are two kinds of houses: **Houses that <u>have</u> termites and Houses that <u>will have</u> termites**. That's a fact and from my experiences I've found this to be accurate. All houses will get termite damage of some sort eventually. Sometimes builders will install a termite shield along the top of the foundation wall. *Termite shields* are similar to the cap plate used at the top of concrete block walls. A termite shield is a small metal guard. However, these shields <u>do not</u> prevent termites. The only benefit from them is that they might deter termites or make it a little more difficult for them to reach the wood. There are ways to help prevent wood destroying insect and rot damage:

1.   Use pressure treated lumber when replacing or constructing anything on the site or in the house. *Pressure treated lumber* has a greenish color to it. It's rot and termite resistant for up to 40 years. The most common type of pressure treated wood is called *CCA 40*. There's also a *CCA 60* pressure treated lumber that has a higher pressurization and lifespan than CCA 40 does.

I'll tell you the basics of the process for pressure treating lumber. The manufacturer will take the lumber and place it in large vats of chemicals. This lumber will sit there until the chemicals are absorbed sufficiently into the wood. The chemicals they use are *copper, chromate* and *arsenic*. Arsenic is the chemical that deters wood destroying insects. The type of wood that's used for pressure treated lumber is *Southern Yellow Pine*. That's because it's the best lumber to use for the chemical process involved.

2.   There's another way to help prevent wood destroying insect and rot damage. That is to keep all wood siding at least eight inches above the soil. The purpose of this is to make it more difficult for termites to get to their food source. Keep all bushes and shrubs pruned and the soil and drainage leaders must slope away from the foundation. This will help prevent any dark and moist areas that are an attraction to termites.

3.   Get a *preventive* wood destroying insect treatment. Don't wait to get a *corrective* treatment after the damage is found. Preventive treatments are usually about half the cost of a corrective treatment. The reason for this is that the Pest Control Operator only has to treat around the exterior of the house.

It's important to stress to the client about getting a corrective treatment if you find damage and a preventive treatment if you don't find any damage. Since all houses do get some form of wood destroying insect damage over time, they might as well eliminate the problem now. It's less expensive and easier to eliminate the problem ahead of time, rather than waiting for it to happen later. It's also easier to sell a house with a preventive treatment as opposed to a corrective treatment done after there was damage found. Wood destroying insect damage bothers people more than it should. A preventive treatment should help to eliminate the chance of scared off buyers.

> *There are certain houses that many Pest Control Operators, (PCO), will not treat for wood destroying insects.*

⚠ There are certain houses that many Pest Control Operators, *(PCO)*, **will not** treat for wood destroying insects. Or else there will only be a few of them that will treat the houses with insecticide.

1   One case is houses with on-site well water systems. The PCO has to worry about contaminating the well water supply. If the well is less than 100 feet from the house, your chances of finding a PCO to treat will diminish even further.

2   Another case is houses that have brick foundation walls. The PCO has to worry about contaminating the house by seepage through the brick walls.

3   Another case is houses that have air ducts embedded in the lower level cement floor for the heating or air-conditioning systems. The PCO has to worry about contaminating the ducts.

4   Also, if the inspection is being conducted on a condominium, then the By-Laws or Prospectus of the Condo/Owner's Association may have limitations. There could be requirements that can restrict wood destroying insect treatments.

⚠ Here's something you might be surprised to know related to wood destroying insect treatments:

◊   A sad, but interesting fact, is that electrical shock is the biggest killer of Pest Control Operators. You would think it was the exposure to the deadly chemicals over the years, but it isn't. Although there are many deaths of Pest Control Operators due to overexposure to the chemicals. Electrical power tools are hazardous for the Pest Control Operator. This is because they're often working around moist soil or have moist hands. Under these conditions, they can come in contact with improperly grounded power equipment. Sometimes they end up drilling into a live electrical line accidentally.

⚠ At one time the Pest Control Operators in my part of the country used *Chlordane* to treat for termites. Chlordane is a very powerful termite treatment chemical and will protect the house for over 30 years. However, the State outlawed the use of Chlordane in this area. The reason for this was that a few Pest Control Operators hired workers who improperly injected Chlordane into some houses in Long Island, NY. These houses were contaminated so badly that they had to be knocked down. They've been considering reapproving Chlordane for use because it's one of the best termite treatment chemicals on the market. However, some Pest Control Operators feel there are too many problems with using this chemical for it to be reapproved by the State.

Wood Destroying Insects photos: P 176-P 184, P 231

Exterior Inspection Photo Pages

P 138. Asphalt/fiberglass shingles come in different weights. A heavier shingle has a 30 year life expectancy. Light weight shingles last about 20 years. These shingles are in good condition and there are no signs of old age or curling shingles.

With cable TV, antennas should be removed from roofs and chimneys. Antennas move in the wind and create water leaks. A cap and screen keep animals and water out of the chimney.

The small pipe in the roof is the vent stack for the plumbing drainage lines.

P 139. A ridge vent is noted by the small gap at the top of the roof. Water is shielded from entering the attic while air can escape.

The shadows of the tree branches indicate pruning is needed. Tree branches should not overhang the roof. Branches can fall and damage the house. Also, mold forms on the roof due to lack of sunlight.

P 141. This is known as a "woven valley". Instead of copper flashing in the roof valley area, the shingles overlap one another to seal this joint. This is a less expensive method of replacing a roof. However, copper flashing is superior at preventing long term problems.

P 140. A new roof will be needed on this house soon. These asphalt shingles are old and at the end of their life expectancy. When the shingles cup and curl and get frayed edges, it's a clear sign of old age. Get estimates prior to buying this house since a roof can be a major expense. If there are two layers of shingles on the roof, a third layer should not be installed on top. Three layers are too heavy for the roof. Remove the prior two layers of shingles and check the condition of the plywood sheathing before adding the new layer of roof shingles.

P 143. Flat roofs have a tendency to create ponding water conditions. Water that sits on the roof will deteriorate the roof covering and create water leaks over time. A slight pitch is needed with flat roofs to drain the rain water to a suitable location.

P 142. Slate shingle roofs are usually only found on older, expensive homes. The reason for this is that slate roofs are very expensive to install and repair. Check for missing or damaged slates. If the nails holding the shingles have rusted out, then there will be an excessive number of missing slates. Only an experienced roofer can repair or walk on a slate shingle roof since the shingles can crack.

P 145. Copper flashing should be used at the base of chimneys and in the roof valleys, as seen in this photo. Copper has a long life and will turn green over time due to oxidation. The chimney should straight and not be leaning. Also, the flue stack in the chimney has to be high enough over the roof line to prevent downdrafts from cold air from blowing the exhaust fumes back down into the house.

P 144. In cold climates there will be days when you find the roof and yard covered in snow. You can't inspect areas that you can't see! *(Even though some people expect you to have X-ray vision, a crystal ball, and a magic wand as a home inspector).* In areas where there are large amounts of snow, the roof must be properly supported to deal with the extra weight after a heavy snowfall. Before closing on the house, you should view the roof after the snow has melted to detect any problem conditions and get repair estimates.

P 147. The foundation for a chimney is separate from the house foundation. All chimneys should be straight, such as the one in the photo. There should not be large settlement cracks in the foundation, nor at the joint where the chimney meets the house. All mortar joints between bricks, concrete blocks, or stones should be repointed (patched) periodically. The vent at the base of the brick is used to allow exterior air to feed the fireplace flames. This is much more energy efficient than having the interior heated air drawn into the fireplace to feed the flames. The interior air has been heated by the heating system. As a result, you don't want it going up in smoke! The small door at the base of this chimney is for the clean-out pit. Sometimes this door is located in the interior basement area. Clean-out pits collect the fireplace ashes and debris where it can be swept out periodically by the homeowner or a chimney sweep.

P 146. Wood is priced and selected in grades. This wooden clapboard siding was a poor choice for exterior siding. It is a poor quality lumber due to the excess number of knots in the wood. Knots refers to the dark round circle areas formed inside a tree as it grows. These knots will eventually decay and fall out over time. When this happens, it will leave holes in the siding that need to be patched.

P 148. Wood shingle siding has a smooth surface. Wood shakes have a rougher appearance. Wood siding can be painted or stained. Staining lasts longer but needs more coats. This is because wood absorbs the stain. Paint merely covers the wood surface. The siding in the photo is in excellent condition with no missing or rotted shingles on the house.

There is a soffit vent on the roof overhang leading to the attic area for ventilation.

There is a dryer vent on the lower left.

P 149. Wood Shingle and Wood Shake sidings are usually made of cedar or redwood. This is due to the lack of knots in these types of wood. Also, these woods are rot resistant due to the oils in the wood. These sidings are very similar to wood shingle and shake installations found on roofs. Wood shingle and wood shake sidings are also expensive to install and are usually only found on higher priced homes. These sidings have a life expectancy of about 40 to 45 years or more. The lifespan will depend upon the climate and maintenance given to them over the years.

These wood shingles clearly need to be painted or stained so the natural oils in wood doesn't dry out. Dried wood shingles will crack and decay.

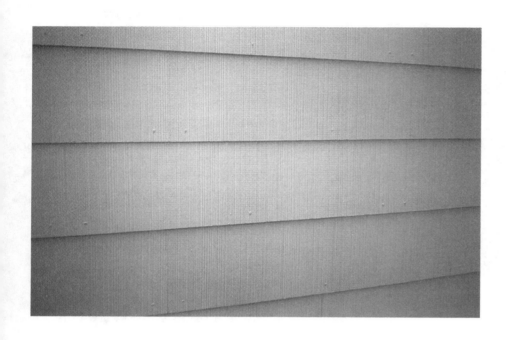

P 150. Asbestos/Cement shingles are only found on old homes. They are molded with lines on the surface to give a wood grain appearance. These shingles are rot and wood destroying insect proof. The drawbacks are asbestos/cement shingles are very hard and can crack if hit by accident. Also, due to the asbestos content, special EPA precautions must be taken when removing or repairing this siding.

P 151. Rust stains can be seen on these shingles. The rust is caused by the iron nails used to hold the shingles to the house. Over time the iron will corrode and need to be replaced. This will be an expensive repair.

Above the window there is a small aluminum flashing. This is installed to prevent water from penetrating behind the joint where the window frame attached to the siding.

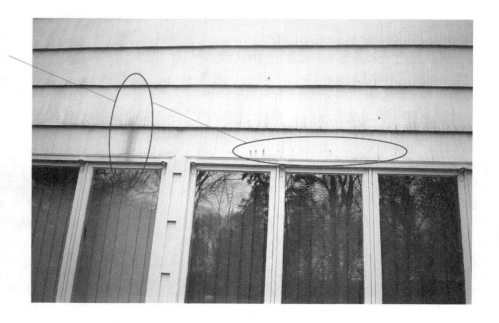

P 153. All vines, ivy, shrubbery and trees must be pruned away from the house. This ivy clearly needs to be trimmed.

A minimum of at least eight inches above the soil is needed at the base of all siding. This clearance allows air and sunlight to help prevent rot and wood destroying insect problems.

Downspouts must be cleaned periodically. Clogged downspouts and gutters will create water problems around the foundation.

P 152. *Here's an example of what can happen if you don't read my books!* The wood siding on this garage has rotted at the base. This decay was caused by the wood touching the soil. An eight inch clearance between the soil and the base of the siding would have prevented this problem.

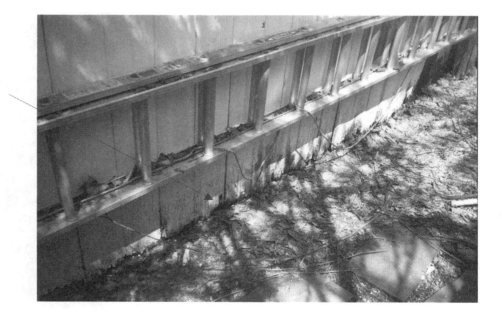

P 154. *Call for help quickly, it's the vine monster!* Vines, ivy and shrubbery attract moisture and create rot. The vine roots will even deteriorate the brick mortar joints on this house. Sometimes on older houses you'll find large sections of the exterior covered with green ivy. This may give the house a nice antique look. However, the ivy is creating damage that far outweighs the cosmetic appeal and it should be removed.

P 155. Due to the high cost to build, stone construction is only found on old homes. The mortar joints should be in good condition, such as seen in this photo. Repointing is needed periodically to patch any deteriorated mortar joints.

On older houses you may find copper downspouts which are usually round shaped like this one, instead of alumunium downspouts.

P 157. This wood clapboard siding needs a coat of paint or stain for weather protection.

Those pipes in the ground are for an underground oil tank. The grass around the pipes has died due to oil spillage when refilling the tank.

All downspouts should be piped away from the house foundation by at least five feet. Some downspouts drain into pipes buried in the soil that should lead away from the house.

The grading of the soil should slope away from the house. Usually the soil only needs to slope 1/2 inch for every foot away from the house to properly drain the water accumulations.

P 156. Here's an example of how a homeowner spent money trying to correct a problem but ended up making the problem even worse. It makes no sense to install a drainage pipe at the base of the downspout unless you're going to direct the water away from the house, not next to the foundation! This drain pipe should be turned to face away from the house to properly drain the rain water from the roof and gutters - not along the side of the home.

P 158. Windows and doors are stress points when a house settles. Often you'll find settlement cracks in the wall leading from a window or door opening.

Left: The large crack in this stucco siding must be patched to prevent water penetration.

Bottom: A reputable contractor should evaluate abnormally large cracks for structural problems.

Stucco is rot and wood destroying insect proof. However, since it's a hard material settlement cracks will form over time.

On the left side of the photo is a vent pipe for an interior oil tank.

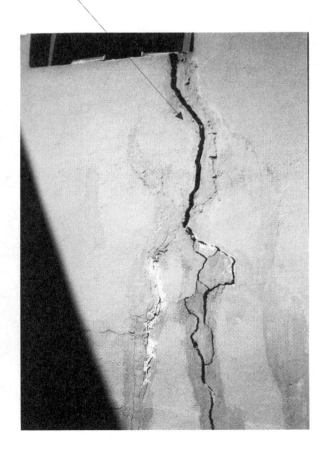

P 160. This welcome mat is resting on top of a safety hazard. Instead of "Welcome" this door mat should read: *"Stand here at your own risk!"*

A landing platforms is the standing area in front of a door. Landing platforms need to be large enough so the door can open safely. This storm door would knock someone down the steps if it was opened hastily.

The riser height is the vertical distance between each step. All risers should be evenly spaced about eight inches in height. This will help prevent tripping hazards from uneven stair heights.

P 159. Do you know what's missing in this picture? *(No, it's not a matching gargoyle that's missing).* A handrail needs to be installed on these stairs. Whenever there are more than two steps in height, a handrail is needed for safety.

All stairways should have a light to prevent tripping hazards at night.

P 161. Often you'll find exterior stairways that lead to the lower level of a house. As you can see, there is a ponding water problem at the base of these steps. A drain is needed to carry the rainwater away. In cold weather the water will freeze, then expand and crack the masonry. This creates tripping hazards and deteriorates the masonry.

A handrail is needed on this stairway.

P 162. *Who's reflection is that in the sliding glass door?* It looks like me taking a photo!

A step is needed under the full length of these sliding doors to help prevent tripping hazards.

Weeds and grass must be removed from between patio and walkway joints. This entire patio must be rebuilt due to lack of maintenance.

P 163. There are several problems with this exterior deck support post.

1) The metal bracket is not sturdy enough to support the post where it meets the deck girder beam. Proper metal brackets need to be installed.

2) The base of this post is resting on a 2 x 6" wood board. This board will eventually rot and the deck will settle unevenly. Metal brackets are also needed at the base to properly secure the deck post to the concrete foundation.

P 164. Clearly these deck support posts are unsafe! This is a high deck and if it collapses, *then someone is going to get hurt or killed!!* The posts have been installed improperly. The base of the wood is not resting evenly on the concrete foundation. The second post in the photo is off center on the concrete foundation. Metal brackets are needed to securely fasten deck supports to the concrete base.

P 166. This deck header beam has lag bolts which securely fastens the deck to the side of the house.

All deck floor joists need the metal brackets called joist hangers, as seen in this photo.

Joist hangers and lag bolts are far superior than just using nails for support.

Flashing should be installed where the header beam touches the side of the house. This prevents water from becoming trapped and rotting the wood. There is a section of copper flashing in this photo.

P 165. Gabion walls are constructed of stones held in a steel wire covering. This type of retaining wall is used for commercial purposes, such as along the side of a highway.

P 168. Dry stone retaining walls are expensive to install. More time and skill is required to build dry stone walls since no mortar is used. The stones are broken into useable pieces with a sledge hammer. Then the stones are carefully placed so that the weight of each supports one another.

P 167. The wall on top of the terraced soil uses mortar to hold the stones in place.

Due to erosion of the soil or poor craftsmanship, the dry stone retaining wall below has collapsed. Any leaning walls or fences must be repaired immediately! A falling retaining wall or fence will crush a child.

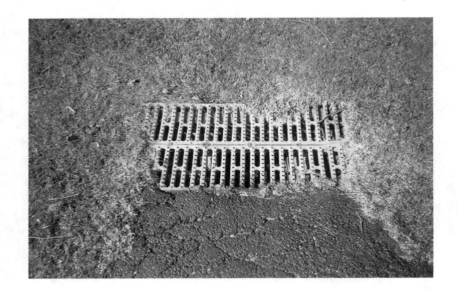

P 170. Catch basins are large underground drains that help prevent water problems. They're used in areas that are prone to excessive water accumulations. Often drains are installed in a paved driveway at the base of the garage doors. Check these drains periodically for clogging due to leaves.

P 169. The driveway at the base of this garage door has settled unevenly. Notice the right side of the overhead door has a larger gap at the base than the left side due to uneven settlement.

The large crack in the concrete can continue to grow due to water penetration and settling of the soil underneath. In cold weather water freezes and expands, creating larger cracks.

The wood touching the ground has signs of mold, rot and decay.

P 171. Special precautions must be taken with garages; especially those that are attached to the house. Any steps from an attached garage must lead downward from the house to the garage - not the other way around like in this photo. The reason for this is to help prevent car exhaust and gas fumes from entering the livable rooms of the home. The stairway in the photo is unsafe and garage fumes will easily flow into the house.

A self-closing device is needed to automatically close the door if it's left open. This will help keep any lethal garage fumes out of the house.

A fire resistant covering, such as masonry or 5/8" sheetrock, is required over the doors, walls and ceilings of a garage.

P 172. This tree has seen better days. The property owner has been trying to prolong the life of this tree. Pruning of the branches and reinforcing bars between the limbs can be seen in the photo. You don't want to cut down any trees unless it's an absolute necessity. As you probably know, trees help keep the air clean and provide oxygen. However, when a tree is clearly dying, such as this one, it becomes a safety hazard and must be removed from the site. As with any other repair work done, you should hire a licensed, reputable contractor to cut down or prune any trees. Some local town codes require permits to cut down trees. The reason for this is due to the temptation of some homeowners to wrecklessly cut down trees on their property. In a nice, suburban neighborhood the trees and plant life enhance the value of all the homes.

P 174. Are you tempted to just dive into this pool?
Well, don't because it's only a photo and you'll hit your head on the table where you're reading this book! *(Unless my book already put you to sleep).*

Check for any bulging or cracked sections of in-ground pools. The area around the pool, called the apron, should be smooth without any tripping hazards. Fences are required around all pools to prevent unattended children from entering the water. Flotation devices should be within reach in case of an emergency.

P 173. Pools need to be winterized properly to prevent the walls from cracking due to freezing water during cold months.

P 175. Out-of-ground swimming pools are less expensive to install. Check for any bulging sections in the pool walls. The inflated air bubble under the cover is used in the winter time. This prevents the water from freezing and expanding which will crack the walls. Pool equipment should be evaluated by a pool contractor. All pool outlets and switches must have GFCI protection.

P 176. On the exterior check the wood trim near the roofline. This area is prone to carpenter bee damage. The holes in this fascia board are an example of a carpenter bee nest. Carpenter bees and carpenter ants do not eat the wood for food, they merely excavate it to make a nest. Keeping a solid coat of stain or paint can reduce the chance of wood destroying insect damage.

P 178. Here we have the exposed termite damage in a lower level floor joist. This is a common area for damage since the wood is close to the soil. The termite channels can be seen when the wood is probed and opens up. The mud and termite tunnels are mostly hidden from the light under a thin, outer layer of the wood. This is because termites need a dark, warm and moist environment at all times.

P 177. Here's an example of termite damage in the floor joist of the basement. Termites eat the interior of the wood for food. They also bring mud for moisture into the tunnels they build to travel through. If you see small, round mud tunnels on any wood, like in the photo, probe these areas with a screwdriver. The screwdriver will easily penetrate termite damaged wood, such as the one in this picture.

P 179. This concrete block foundation has a cap plate at the top of the wall. Cap plates and termite shields do not guarantee a house will be termite proof. Only an exterminator treatment can eliminate a wood destroying insect infestation.

The three drill holes at the top of this wall indicate an interior termite treatment. A ring of insecticide is injected in the soil around the interior and/or exterior of the house.

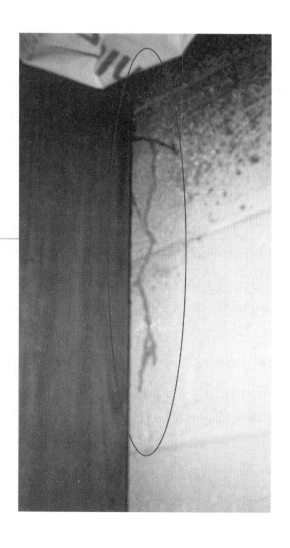

P 180. This is what a termite "mud tunnel" looks like. The termites build tunnels out of mud, like roadways for them to travel inside. That's because they need a dark, warm and moist environment at all times.

Subterranean termites seem to cause the most damage to homes. There are four different types of insects or castes in a Subterranean Termite colony:

Swarmer
Supplemental Reproductives
Worker
Soldier

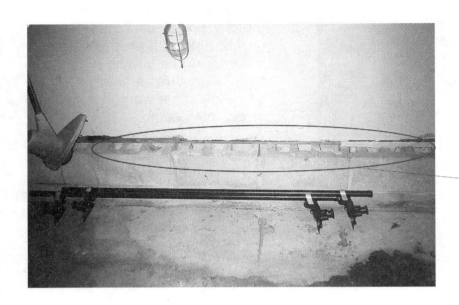

P 182. In some concrete block foundation walls there was no cap plate installed by the builder. A cap plate is a solid block on the top layer of the foundation wall. This prevents wood destroying insects from traveling through the voids in the blocks to find wood. When there is no cap plate, such as in this garage foundation, the wood sill plate at the base of the wall is easy prey to wood destroying insects.

P 181. *You don't believe me that a cap plate is important?*
This is the result if you don't take my advice!

This garage is being repaired due to excessive termite and wood destroying insect damage. The problem was mainly caused by the lack of a cap plate at the top of the concrete block foundation. A cap plate seals the holes in the concrete blocks to prevent easy access for termites and other insects.

P 184. Do not store wood inside or next to the house, such as in this photo.

Wood destroying insects can often be found in wood lying around the yard. By bringing this infested wood closer to your home, you're inviting these insects to dinner!

P 183.
Hello, my name is Mr. Ed! (Remember that TV show from the 1970's?)

Do not store wood inside your house since it will invite termites. But also don't invite any horses inside your living room, like this photo. They may leave their calling card on your floor!

Just kidding, that's only a picture of a horse on the wall. *But it does seem like he's sticking his head through a hole in the wall.*

Home Safety Topics

Why did I include the chapters about **Home Safety** and **Health Concerns**? All of my books were written to help people with the biggest investment they make – their own home! I was in the process of updating my real estate books and DVDs that I authored. Part of my research for those book updates dealt with home safety, energy efficiency, and health concerns in homes. I went through thousands of pages of documents, brochures, and studies compiled by the Home Safety Council (HSC), the U.S. Department of Energy (DOE), the U.S. Environmental Protection Agency (EPA), and all of their associated groups and laboratories. There was a tremendous amount of useful information that was extremely well researched and analyzed by the HSC, DOE, and EPA. The HSC, DOE, EPA, and their associated laboratories have spent many millions of dollars analyzing home safety, energy usage, energy saving technologies, and health concerns for residential and commercial buildings.

I read through the thousands of pages of documents from the HSC, DOE, and EPA. Then I selected, sorted, and compiled the research dealing with residential homes. The finished result are these Home Safety and Health Concerns chapters with all of the available research dealing with topics that home owners, buyers, sellers, builders, contractors, and real estate professionals would need or want to know. I cannot say enough about how impressed I am at the excellent research and data compiled by the HSC, DOE, EPA, and their associated laboratories and research affiliates. Their work on home safety, energy efficiency, and health concerns in homes and buildings is truly outstanding and the information they have gathered should be utilized by everyone involved in real estate.

Some readers of this book may not be interested in learning very in-depth information about home safety. They may only be interested in getting a general working knowledge of home safety topics. For those readers, I would recommend that you don't get too caught up in trying to memorize the in-depth details discussed in the HSC, DOE, and EPA sections. Choose the topics that you feel are most useful to you for now, and then you can learn the more in-depth topics later if needed.

Some readers of this book may not be interested in learning very in-depth information about home safety. They may only be interested in getting a general working knowledge of home safety topics. For those readers, I would recommend that you don't get too caught up in trying to memorize the in-depth details discussed in the HSC, DOE, and

EPA sections. Choose the home safety topics that you feel are most useful to you for now, and then you can learn the more in-depth topics later if needed.

⚠ I won't include the icon keys for safety items in the HSC, DOE, and EPA sections of the book. The reason I'm not including them in those sections is because they would be *filled* with safety issues and there would be icon keys for just about every paragraph!

Note: Some of the information contained in different sections of the Home Safety chapter are similar. This is because there are many important aspects that pertain to both sections discussed.

The *Home Safety Council* is a 501(c)(3) nonprofit organization dedicated to helping prevent the nearly 21 million medical visits that occur on average each year from unintentional injuries in the home. Through national programs and partners across America, the Home Safety Council works to educate and empower families to take actions that help keep them safer in and around their homes. To learn more visit the Home Safety Council site at www.homesafetycouncil.org.

Kitchen Safety

Cooking Safety
"Get a Taste" for safety when cooking. To keep unintentional injuries out of your kitchen, taking these simple steps to prevent kitchen fires and burns:

◊   Stay in the kitchen while cooking; if you must leave the kitchen briefly, turn down the heat on appliances and return to the kitchen quickly.

◊   Keep anything that can catch fire, such as dishtowels, paper or plastic bags, curtains, etc., at least three feet away from the range top.

◊   Douse cigarette and cigar butts with water before dumping them in the trash.

◊   Every kitchen should be protected by Ground-Fault Circuit Interrupters (GFCI's). If you don't have them, hire an electrician to install these devices to protect electrical receptacles in the kitchen.

◊   Avoid wearing loose-fitting clothing when cooking (such as long open sleeves) which can be ignited by hot burners. If clothes do catch fire, "Stop, Drop and Roll" by dropping immediately to the ground and rolling over and over or back and forth to put out the flames. Cool the burned area with cool water and seek medical attention for serious burns.

◊ Always turn pot handles inward to prevent small children from reaching and pulling down a hot pan.

◊ Keep hot items, such as hot beverages and trays that have just come out of the oven away from the edge of counters, so that children are not able to reach them.

◊ Hot liquid and food burns often occur when children pull hanging tablecloths or placemats. Use table cloths and decorations with care.

◊ Food cooked in a microwave can be dangerously hot. Remove the lids or other coverings from microwaved food carefully to prevent steam burns.

◊ For extra care with toddlers and infants, use travel mugs with a tight lid for coffee, tea or other hot beverages.

◊ Keep children and pets away from the range when anyone is cooking and keep a close eye on them at all times.

◊ For safer water temperatures to prevent scalds from hot tap water, keep your hot water heater set at 120 degrees Fahrenheit or below.

◊ Store knives and other sharp objects out of the reach of children and make sure children are a safe distance away when you are using knives to avoid injuries.

◊ Post emergency numbers in visible areas.

Spring Cleaning the Safe Way

Chores like re-organizing closets and tackling a thorough spring cleaning can put families at even greater risk for falls and poisoning – the two leading causes of home injury in America. Families are urged to keep safe practices at the top of their mind while cleaning up and cleaning out your home, garage and yard.

◊ When cleaning out closets or re-organizing, always keep stairs, steps, landings and all floors clear.

◊ Carry loads you can see over, and keep one hand free to hold banisters and railings.

◊ Five gallon buckets are often used while cleaning and present a serious drowning danger to young children. Never leave a bucket or any standing water unattended and store buckets empty and upside-down.

◊ Follow safety recommendations when using harsh products, such as wearing gloves and masks. Do not mix products together because their contents could react with dangerous results.

◊ Never use gasoline as a cleaning solvent and never use or store gasoline in your home, even in tiny quantities. Because its vapors can readily ignite, it is too dangerous to use gasoline for any purpose other than as a motor fuel.

◊ When cleaning out cabinets, separate dangerous products and medications and lock them up, out of reach of young children.

◊ Remember to reduce clutter and safely tuck away telephone and electrical cords out of walkways. In homes with children, make sure toys and other items are always safely put away when not in use.

◊ If you need to climb, use a stepladder or ladder. When using a ladder, stand at or below the highest safe standing level. For a stepladder, the safe standing level is the second rung from the top, and for an extension ladder, it's the fourth rung from the top. Before using, make sure the rungs are dry.

Bathroom Safety

The combination of water, medications and electrical appliances make safety precautions in and around the bathroom essential for every family member. Safe storage of supplies, constant adult supervision around water and swift cleaning of slick surfaces should be common practice to help reduce the risk of some of home injuries. Families are advised to follow these steps to help avoid slips and falls, poisoning, burns and drowning dangers:

◊ Install grab bars in bath and shower stalls. Don't use towel racks or wall-mounted soap dishes as grab bars; they can easily come loose, causing a fall.

◊ Use a non-slip mat or install adhesive safety strips or decals in bathtubs and showers.

◊ Keep the bathroom floor clean and promptly wipe up all spills.

◊ If you use a bath mat on the floor, choose one that has a non-skid bottom.

◊ Avoid using cleaning supplies that may leave a slippery residue.

◊ Use nightlights to help light hallways and bathrooms during night-time hours.

◊ Make sure that medications, including vitamins, prescription drugs and over-the-counter drugs, have child-resistant caps.

◊ Lock medicines, cosmetics and cleaning supplies in a secure cabinet.

◊ Keep medicines and cleaning products in their original containers with the original labels intact.

◊ Never leave children unattended near standing water.

◊ If you have toddlers, use toilet seat locks and keep bathroom doors closed.

◊ Always stay within touch supervision of young children – within an arm's reach -- during bath time. Never allow older children to supervise.

◊ Lower water heaters to 120 degrees Fahrenheit or less. When bathing children, use a water thermometer to ensure the temperature is safe. Turn the cold water on first, then mix in warmer water and keep the temperature at about 100F.

◊ Read and follow product use, storage instructions and safety recommendations for cosmetic, personal care and cleaning products.

◊ Never touch an electrical appliance when you are bathing.

◊ Make sure electrical appliances, cords and fixtures in your bathroom listed by an independent testing laboratory such as Underwriters Laboratories (UL).

◊ Make sure all bathrooms are protected by ground fault circuit interrupters (GFCI's). Test your GFCI monthly to determine that it is operating properly.

◊   Keep small electrical appliances such as hair dryers, curling irons, and razors away from water and unplugged and stored when not in use.

Stairway Safety

Safe Steps to Reduce Falls

Millions of Americans are only a step away from becoming victims of the leading cause of unintentional home injuries - slips and falls. According to The State of Home Safety in America™ (2004) study conducted by the Home Safety Council, falls are by far the leading cause of unintentional home injury death. Falls account for an average of 5.1 million injuries and nearly 6,000 deaths each year. The vast majority of fall deaths occur among people age 65 and older and fall death rates are higher for males. In an effort to reduce injuries among people of all ages, families are encouraged to identify and correct potential slips and falls hazards in and around the home.

Home Safety "Walk-Through"

◊   Walk through your home to identify and remedy potential slipping, tripping and falling hazards. What to look for:

◊   All stairs and steps should be protected with a secure banister or hand-rail.

◊   Make sure all porches, hallways and stairwells are well lit. Use the maximum safe wattage in light fixtures. (Maximum wattage is typically posted inside light fixtures.)

◊   Use nightlights to help light hallways and bathrooms during night-time hours.

◊   Keep stairs, steps, landings and all floors clear. Reduce clutter and safely tuck away telephone and electrical cords out of walkways.

◊   In homes with children, make sure toys and games are not left on steps or landings. When very young children are present use safety gates at the tops and bottoms of stairs.

◊   Use a non-slip mat or install adhesive safety strips or decals in bathtubs and showers. If you use a bath mat on the floor, choose one that has a non-skid bottom.

◊   Install grab bars in bath and shower stalls. Don't use towel racks or wall-mounted soap dishes as grab bars; they can easily come loose, causing a fall.

◊   Install window guards to prevent young children from falling out of upper windows. (Select guards with emergency-release devices.)

◊   Keep the floor clean. Promptly clean up grease, water and other spills.

◊   If you use throw rugs in your home place them over a rug-liner or choose rugs with non-skid backs to reduce your chance of slipping.

◊   Use a sturdy step stool with hand rails when climbing is necessary.

◊   Follow medication dosages closely. Using multiple medications and/or using medications incorrectly may cause dizziness, weakness and other side effects which can lead to a dangerous fall.

Stairway Safety

According to the Home Safety Council's national report on home injuries, the State of Home Safety in America™ (2004), falls accounted for nearly one-third of all unintentional home injury deaths each year. Falls from stairs and steps were the second leading cause of death due to falls. Follow these steps to stairway safety to make your home safer from falls:

◊   Use the handrail. (All stairways and steps, no matter how short, should have handrails on both sides.)

◊   Install bright lights and on/off switches at the top and bottom of each stairwell and over porches and entryways.

◊   Keep stairways and steps clear of all objects. Never use the stairs as temporary storage or for displaying decorative items.

◊   Check stairs for worn or loose carpeting or protruding carpet tacks. If your steps have a smooth surface, consider installing anti-slip tread to provide safer traction.

◊   Paint the bottom basement step white to make it more visible. Mistaking the lowest step for floor level can cause you to lose your balance and fall.

◊   In homes with young children, use safety gates at the tops and bottoms of stairways.

◊   Wear footwear with traction. Avoid wearing socks or smooth-soled slippers, which can slide out from under you on bare floors.

◊   Avoid carrying vision blocking loads. Carry a small enough load up and down stairs that you can see where you are stepping and can easily keep one hand free to hold onto a handrail.

◊   Avoid placing throw rugs at the top or bottom of a stairway as small scatter rugs can slide or the edges can become curled. If it is necessary to put a rug at the bottom of a stairway, make sure it has a skid-resistant backing and use carpet tape to keep the corners from curling.

◊   If you have steps outside your home, keep them free of ice and snow. To prevent a tripping hazard, periodically check steps and walkways for broken or lose bricks, cement or stone.

Stay Fit to Prevent Falls

◊   If you require eyeglasses for vision enhancement, use them. Consider keeping a spare pair of glasses near your medicine chest to ensure you can accurately read the labels on your medications before taking them.

◊   Talk with your pharmacist and physicians to ensure that all your prescription medications are being tracked and that there are no contra-indications when multiple prescriptions are taken.

◊   The risk of falling is increased by illness, fatigue, and lower extremity weakness. Researchers agree that staying healthy and fit can help prevent falls. Strengthening exercises can help. Gentle exercise programs such as Tai Chi have been shown to improve balance and strengthen muscles safely.

◊   Consult your physician before beginning any exercise program.

Be sure to check out the web site at http://www.garagesafety.info/ to learn more about how to keep your garage safe for your family.

Garage Safety

In America there are nearly 21 million medical visits as a result of unintentional home injuries. However, home safety is not limited to the immediate living area. The garage also poses formidable threat if not kept clean and organized. In order to keep your garage a safe place for the family, follow these safety tips.

1. Organize all items in designated, easy-to-reach places, so large piles don't accumulate.
2. Store shovels, rakes, lawn chairs, bikes and other sharp and large objects on the wall to prevent trips and falls.
3. Clear floors and steps of clutter, grease and spills.
4. Keep children's playthings in one area and within their reach to prevent children from exploring potentially dangerous areas.
5. Light your garage brightly with maximum safe wattage as designated by light fixtures.
6. Protect light bulbs near work areas with substantial guards to reduce risk of breakage and fire.
7. Light stairs brightly and install secure handrails or banisters on both sides that extend the entire length of the stairs.
8. Make sure poisonous products such as pesticides, automotive fluids, lighter fluid, paint thinner, antifreeze and turpentine have child-resistant caps, are clearly labeled and are stored either on a high shelf or in a locked cabinet.
9. Do not use barbeque grills and electric generators inside the garage as they emit carbon monoxide (CO) and pose a fire hazard.
10. Install a smoke alarm and CO detector in the garage.
11. Never leave cars running inside a closed or open garage to prevent CO poisoning.
12. Store gasoline in small quantities only and in a proper, tightly sealed container labeled "gasoline."
13. Do not keep gasoline in a garage with an appliance that contains a pilot light.
14. Mount a fire extinguisher and stocked first aid kit in the garage and make sure every family member knows where they are and how to use them.
15. Store pool chemicals according to the manufacturers' directions to prevent combustion and potential poisoning exposures.
16. Do not overload outlets and make sure the electrical ratings on extension cords have been checked to ensure they are carrying no more than their proper loads.
17. Lock electrical supply boxes to prevent children from opening them.
18. Clean garage of dust, webs and trash, which can interfere with the electrical system.
19. Properly secure shelving units to the wall, make sure they are not overloaded and store heavier items closest to the ground.
20. Keep a sturdy step stool within easy reach to aid in reaching items stored high up.

Electrical Safety

American homes are filled with electrical appliances and tools that enhance our lives with convenience, comfort, and entertainment. But the power that drives these important devices can be a source of pain and tragedy if it is misused. These guidelines will help you spot electrical problems which may be present in your home and take appropriate action to correct or remove dangers. For continuous safety, give your home periodic checkups to be sure that no new hazards develop.

◊ Every home should have the protection of ground fault circuit interrupters (GFCI) in bathrooms and kitchens and arc fault circuit interrupters (AFCI) in bedrooms. Contact a professional electrician to ensure your home is adequately protected.

◊ Check your GFCI monthly to determine that it is operating properly. Units can be checked by pressing the "TEST "button; the GFCI should disconnect the power to that outlet. Pressing the "RESET "button reconnects the power. If the GFCI does not disconnect the power, get assistance from a professional electrician.

◊ If young children are in your home, use child-safety caps on wall outlets.

◊ All electrical appliances, cords and fixtures in your home should be listed by an independent testing laboratory such as Underwriters Laboratories (UL).

◊ Never use worn, frayed or otherwise damaged cords or appliances.

◊ Follow the appliance manufacturer's recommendation for plugging into electrical power. Extension cords should only be used temporarily.

◊ Always use the appropriate light bulb wattage for the size of the fixture. The safe maximum wattage is posted in or on the fixture.

◊ Keep all electrically-powered appliances and equipment dry and away from places where water is used.

◊ Unplug all small kitchen appliances, hair dryers, curling irons, electric blankets and other small household appliances when not in use.

◊ Keep electrical cords out of traffic areas and away from furniture that may cause pressure. Do not place cords under rugs or carpets, which can cause overheating.

◊ Check that cords are in good condition and not knotted or coiled. Do not attach extension cords to baseboards or walls with nails or staples.

◊ Check the electrical rating on appliance cords and extension cords and make sure they are carrying no more than their proper loads.

◊ If you need to use extension cords outside, only use those specifically marked for outdoor use.

◊   Never leave the faceplates off of outlets or switches.
◊   Outdoor outlets should have waterproof covers.

Window Safety

The State of Home Safety in America™ (2002) revealed that injuries associated with windows caused more than 110,000 emergency room visits in a single year. Follow these tips to safeguard your family from preventable window injuries:

Protect Children from Window Falls
According to the U.S. Consumer Products Safety Commission (CPSC), children are more likely to die or be severely injured from window-related falls than falls associated with any other product. Additionally, most of these injuries occur during the spring and summer months. To help prevent window falls in your home, use the following precautions:
◊   Be aware that conventional window screens are not designed to prevent a child's fall from a window.
◊   Install specially designed window guards on upper windows to prevent children from falling out of windows.
◊   Purchase window guards that have a quick-release mechanism inside so that they can be easily opened by an adult in a fire emergency.
◊   Move furniture away from windows in children's rooms to prevent them from reaching windows.
◊   Never leave young children unattended near open windows.

Window Cords
CPSC reports that more than 169 strangulation deaths caused by window coverings have been tracked since 1991. Most were children three and younger, though children up to age six are considered to be at risk. While many new window treatments eliminate these hazards, older homes may still have window cord dangers that can present a risk to young children. To make sure your window cords do not present a strangulation danger, follow these tips:
◊   Inspect your window coverings for inner and outer cord loops in blinds that could pose a danger to children.
◊   If your window blinds have loops, they can easily be made safer by requesting a free repair kit from the Home Safety Council and Lowe's Home Improvement Warehouse. Call 1-800-311-7996 to request your free kits.
◊   Position cribs, playpens, beds and other furniture away from windows and out of the reach of all window covering cords, including drapery pull cords.
◊   Tie window cords up and out of a child's reach.

Window Covering Safety
The inner cords and pull cords on shades, blinds and certain draperies can pose a strangulation hazard to infants and young children. If you have young children living in or visiting your home, they may be at risk. According to the *U.S. Consumer Product Safety Commission* (CPSC), more than 169 strangulation deaths caused by window coverings have been tracked between 1991 and the present. Primarily affected were children ages three years and younger, though children up to age six are considered to be at risk.

The Hazard
The inner and outer pull cords on older window coverings are the culprit. The middle inner cord found between the slats of mini-blinds when the blind is in its fully lowered position creates a loop when pulled by a child. If the loop can be pulled and opened widely enough, the child's head can become entangled. More than 20 children have strangled in inner cord loops since 1991. The outer pull cords on blinds, shades and draperies - such as continuous loop chains and nylon cords on draperies and vertical blinds and looped pull cords on mini-blinds - can also create a strangulation hazard to children if they become entangled. At least 50 children have died in vertical/continuous loops while more than 90 died in the loops of pull cords since 1991. Children can gain access to the cords by climbing on furniture, or when cribs and playpens are placed too close to windows.

The History
New design requirements in 1994 and 2000 addressed the risk. Mini-blinds sold since 1995 no longer have looped outer pull cords; they now have individual tassels on separate cords. Vertical/continuous looped nylon and chain cords are sold with tension devices to keep the cords taut. (No deaths or injuries have occurred in taut cords.) Window coverings sold after 2000 also have special attachments near the head rail on pull cords, which reduce the size of the inner cord loop that can be formed. The national safety standard became effective August 29, 2002.

The Solution
If you are purchasing new window treatments, choose only those products that meet current safety design standards. Consider buying new cordless blinds, especially for bedrooms and family rooms where children play. If you don't know for certain that you have window coverings purchased after 2000, inspect your windows now. Look for separate cords each ending in a tassel and special attachments near the head rail on pull cords. Look for tension devices on vertical/continuous looped nylon and chain cords. Also, check draperies for tension devices.

Window coverings can be made safer
◊   Without removal
◊   Without damaging your window coverings
◊   Without affecting window covering operation

Simple instructions make the safety repair easy. Request your free window safety repair kits by calling toll-free 1-800-311-7996. The Home Safety Council is working with Lowe's Home Improvement Warehouse to raise awareness of this hidden hazard and the simple remedy. Lowe's is offering a free safety repair kit for homes with older window coverings.

A quick check-up can reveal if your window coverings need a safety repair kit. If mini-blinds contain either looped outer pull cords, or inner pull cords that when the blind is in its fully lowered position can be extended to form a loop larger than a soda can top, they need to be repaired. If continuous nylon or chain loops on vertical blinds or draperies are not taut in a tension device, request a free safety repair kit by calling toll-free 1-800-311-7996 and make all your windows safer for children.

Window Rx

Free safety repair kits are available from the Lowe's Home Improvement Warehouse to easily correct strangulation hazards on older window coverings, without having to remove them. The kit includes everything you need to bring older window coverings up to safety standards including:
◊   instructions for changing looped outer pull cords to safer individual cords with tassels
◊   special devices to place at the head rail of pull cords to prevent inner cord loops
◊   tension devices to keep continuous cords on vertical blinds and draperies taut.

Read the instructions that come with every kit.

For Added Safety

Follow these safety guidelines for all types of window coverings:
◊   Position cribs, playpens and beds away from windows and out of the reach of all window covering cords, including drapery pull cords. Remember, just because pull cords are out of reach doesn't mean that blinds are safe. Inner cords can still form loops and strangle children.
◊   Also, avoid placing furniture where children can climb to reach cords on window coverings.
◊   For additional information about window covering safety, log on to the *U.S. Consumer Product Safety Commission's* (CPSC) Website.

Exterior Safety

Lawn and Garden Safety

As the weather becomes warmer and days are longer, we spend as much time as we can outdoors enjoying our backyards. Many of us tackle do-it-yourself projects and others are happy just being outside. But, to be safe, it is important to remember the following tips when frolicking in the yard, especially if you have children:
◊   Keep children inside the house or well away from the area you are mowing.
◊   Prepare your lawn by walking over it, checking for broken sticks, stones, toys and anything else that could shoot out from under the mower or damage the blade.
◊   Before you start your lawn mower for the first time, check to make sure that all guards are in place.
◊   Don't let people stand or sit anywhere near where you are mowing. Be especially careful to keep small children away. The safest place for children while the grass is being cut in inside the home.
◊   Never reach under the mower unless it is turned off and the blade has completely stopped turning.
◊   Only refuel the mower after it has completely cooled down.
◊   Store pesticides and herbicides on high shelves or inside locked cabinets, out of the reach of children.
◊   When using a chain saw, make certain it is equipped with an anti-kickback chain that is well sharpened.
◊   Garden tools such as rakes, spades, forks, pruning clippers, files and metal plant stakes should not be left lying around when not in use.
◊   Wear proper eye protection when using any power tool.
◊   Don't wear any loose or dangling clothing that could be caught in moving parts.

Grilling Safety

According to the NFPA, gas and charcoal grills caused an average of 1,500 structure fires and 4,800 outdoor fires in or on home properties in 1999. To make sure your next barbecue doesn't go up in flames, use the following safety tips:
◊   Designate the grilling area a "No Play Zone" keeping kids and pets well away until grill equipment is completely cool.
◊   Before using, position your grill at least 3 feet away from other objects, including the house and any shrubs or bushes.
◊   Only use starter fluid made for barbecue grills when starting a fire in a charcoal grill.
◊   Before using a gas grill, check the connection between the propane tank and the fuel line to be sure it is working properly and not leaking.
◊   Never use a match to check for leaks. If you detect a leak, immediately turn off the gas and don't attempt to light the grill again until the leak is fixed.
◊   Never bring a barbecue grill indoors, or into any unventilated space. This is both a fire and carbon monoxide poisoning hazard.

Playground Safety

According to the U.S. Consumer Products Safety Commission (CPSC), there were nearly 47,000 injuries on home playgrounds to children under age 15 in the latest year studied. The report also finds that over a ten-year period, more deaths to children occurred on backyard playgrounds than on public playgrounds. Adopt the following safety guidelines with playground equipment in your home, and also use the following guidelines to inspect any equipment in your neighborhood or school before your child plays there:

◊   Cover areas under and around play equipment with soft materials such as hardwood chips, mulch, pea gravel and sand (materials should be nine to 12 inches deep and extend six feet from all sides of play equipment).

◊   Do not suspend more than two swing seats in the same section of a swing support structure.

◊   Check equipment for signs of deterioration or corrosion, including rust, chipped paint, splitting or cracked plastic components or loose splinters.

◊   Avoid putting play equipment close together. For example, stationary climbing equipment should have an uncluttered fall zone of at least six feet in all directions of equipment.

◊   Slides and platforms for climbing equipment should not exceed heights of six feet for school-age children or four feet for pre-school children.

◊   Beware of entrapment or entanglement hazards. A child's head can be trapped in openings between 3.5 and nine inches wide.

◊   Avoid elevated platforms, walkways, or ramps that lack adequate guardrails or other barriers (to help prevent children from falling).

◊   Watch for possible tripping hazards such as rocks and roots. Clear this debris from your child's play area.

◊   Always supervise children when they are using playground equipment.

Home Improvement Safety

Do-It-Yourself Safety Tips

Taking on home improvement projects can be fun and appealing. However, being handy around the home could lead to serious injury if you don't take appropriate safety precautions. The State of Home Safety in America™ report (2002) found that emergency departments reported more than 330,000 visits due to injuries with home workshop equipment in a single year. Safety practices will shield you and your loved ones from injuries related to home improvement projects:

◊   Keep a stocked first aid kit in every location that an injury may occur. First aid may make the difference between a quick recovery and permanent injury.

◊   Post emergency numbers, including the national Poison Control Hotline (1-800-222-1222) by each phone.

◊   If you decide to install a fire extinguisher in your workshop, contact your fire department to learn how to select the proper type of extinguisher and when to use it.

◊   Keep hazardous materials out of children's reach.

◊   When working with any product, check warnings and content labels to identify hazards.

◊   Follow manufacturer's instructions and heed warning labels.

◊   Use gasoline as a motor fuel only.

◊   Gasoline must never be used indoors, because its flammable vapors can be ignited by even a tiny spark. Store gasoline in an outdoor shed or garage, out of children's reach, in a vented container approved for gasoline storage.

◊   Use caution with other flammable and combustible products. Properly dispose of oily rags after use and hang them outside to dry.

◊   Falling and flying objects, especially when working in tight spaces, can pose a hazard to your head, face and eyes. Consider wearing hard hats, safety vests, protective eye wear and ear plugs while working.

◊   If you allow someone to watch you work, make sure they wear protective gear too.

◊   Wear chemical safety glasses when using hazardous solvents and cleaning products.

◊   Wear safety glasses with side shields when using power tools.

◊   Designate your work area as a "kid free zone" to keep young children out of harm's way and out of the reach of tools and equipment.

◊   Do not wear any loose or dangling clothing or jewelry that could become caught in moving parts.

◊   Keep your work area clean and free from clutter.

◊   Keep power equipment in good condition. Repair or replace damaged tools.

◊   Read and follow manufacturer's instructions and warnings on tools, power equipment and building materials.

◊   Use heavy duty extension cords for tools such as trimmers and edgers listed by Underwriters Laboratories (UL) for outdoor use.

◊   Unplug the power cord before you do any trouble-shooting on a tool that is jammed or won't start, and never walk away from a plugged-in-power tool -- even for a few minutes.

◊ Follow basic ladder safety rules whenever climbing.

Eye and Hand Protection in the Woodworking Shop

Every time you walk into a shop you potentially expose yourself to certain risks. Dust, fumes, noise and flying wood chips are sometimes waiting. But keep in mind that your shop doesn't necessarily have to be a dangerous place. Taking some basic precautions helps to prevent accidents.

Eye Protection

Back when I taught junior high, we started each quarter with a graphic film about a workshop eye injury. The scenario concluded with actual footage of unsuccessful surgery. After viewing that difficult-to-watch movie, those kids religiously wore their safety glasses.

We all need this kind of strong reminder from time to time. How many times have we heard: "I'm only making one cut...done this a million times...never had a problem"? There are always plenty of excuses for not wearing eye protection, but never good ones.

You should be sure your eyes are protected any and every time you turn on a machine. If you're in the shop with someone else running machines, you should still wear eye protection. And, remember, your prescription glasses probably don't qualify. Chances are, they lack the required impact resistance. And they also don't have side shields.

Safety glasses have come a long way from those old "frog-eyed" goggles from chemistry class. With a little shopping, you can find an attractive pair that's really quite comfortable. Be sure to look for glasses that are ANSI certified because this tells you they've been impact tested. If you wear prescription glasses and can't find safety glasses that fit over them, get a full-face shield. Here's a good final tip: To prevent your plastic safety glasses from getting covered with sawdust, wipe them with a dryer sheet. It reduces static and helps your lenses stay clear.

Gloves

Many finishes and strippers can irritate your skin, or get absorbed through your skin and end up in your bloodstream. Wear rubber gloves when handling these materials. Not only will disposable gloves protect you, they save the step of trying to wash stain off your hands. Just peel off the gloves, and your hands are clean. Some strippers are too caustic for lightweight latex disposable gloves. You may need heavy-duty rubber gloves.

It's always best to find out what specific precautions you need to take with each product you use. Yes, this means reading the instructions! It's for your own good, and not a good place to take shortcuts. Protect your hands, eyes, and lungs, and provide proper ventilation.

Safety is Smart

Unlike junior high, there's nobody in your shop to yell at you when you're not wearing the right safety gear. It's up to you to be safety smart. Get in the habit of wearing eye protection and rubber gloves when needed, and you'll be around to enjoy woodworking a lot longer.

Ladder Safety Tips

According to the Home Safety Council's State of Home Safety in America™ (2002), nearly 150,000 people were treated for home ladder injuries in U.S. emergency departments in 2000. Whether you're spring cleaning, hanging decorations or painting, the same basic ladder safety rules apply:

◊ Before using a ladder outdoors, choose a location that is well away from all power lines. Coming in contact with live wires can be fatal.

◊ Place the ladder on level ground and open it completely, making sure all locks are engaged.

◊ Use the 4-to-1 rule for extension ladders: for each 4 feet of distance between the ground and the upper point of contact (such as the wall or roof), move the base of the ladder out 1 foot.

◊ Always face the ladder when climbing and wear slip-resistant shoes, such as those with rubber soles.

◊ Keep your body centered on the ladder and gauge your safety by your belt buckle. If your buckle passes beyond the ladder rail, you are overreaching and at risk for falling.

◊ Make sure rungs are dry before using the ladder.

◊ Stand at or below the highest safe standing level on a ladder. For a stepladder, the safe standing level is the second rung from the top, and for an extension ladder, it's the fourth rung from the top.

Painting Safety Tips

Before tackling how-to painting projects, it is crucial to "brush up" on safety tips. Since painting is the most popular D-I-Y project, please read on to learn how to paint your home safely.

General Tips

You've heard it before, but please read the label on the paint can and follow manufacturer's instructions. If the paint is flammable or combustible, take these precautions:

◊ Open windows and doors to create ventilation and disperse fumes.

◊ Eliminate all sources of flame, sparks and ignition (put out pilot lights by turning off the gas and do not re-light until after room is free of fumes).

◊ While working with flammable or combustible paints, don't smoke.

◊ Don't use electrical equipment while working with paints (it may cause sparks)

◊ Make sure light bulbs are not exposed to sudden breakage.

◊ Clean up spills promptly.

◊ Keep containers closed when not in use.

Outfitting Yourself for Painting
◊   Wear long sleeve shirt and long pants when painting.
◊   Wear butyl rubber gloves. This will protect skin and make cleanup easier.
◊   Wear chemical splash goggles and paint respirator.

Health Precautions
◊   If paint is swallowed, follow the first-aid directions on the label and contact doctor or poison center immediately.
◊   While painting, if you feel dizzy or nauseous, leave work area and get fresh air. If discomfort persists, seek medical help.
◊   If solvent paint gets on your skin, wash immediately with soap and water.
◊   If solvent paint gets in your eyes, flush eyes with cold water for 15 minutes and obtain medical treatment.

Storing Paint Properly
◊   Follow label instructions for storing.
◊   Before storing, make sure containers are tightly sealed.
◊   Do not store near heat sources such as furnaces and space heaters.
◊   If you have a very small amount of solvent left, dispose of it properly; don't store it.
◊   Keep paint products out of reach of children.
◊   Do not store or re-use empty containers.

Store & Dispose of Paint Safely
Now that your paint project is over, you're probably wondering what to do with all that leftover paint.   Well, the obvious choice is to save it for touchups later. You could also donate it to local non-profit agencies, community groups or churches. But if you just want to get rid of it, you should do so in an environmentally responsible manner.

The Difference Between Oil-based and Water-based Paint
Knowing what type of paint you have is important before disposing of it. The label on a paint can should indicate whether it contains oil-based (solvent-based) or water-based (acrylic or latex) paint. If the label has been damaged, read the cleanup directions. If the directions instruct you to use turpentine or mineral spirits to clean brushes or rollers, the paint is oil-based. If you're still unsure, try mixing the paint with water. Water-based paint easily mixes with water and becomes thinner. Oil-based paint separates from water.

Storing Leftover Paint
When you are ready to store paint:
◊   Clean any dried or moist paint from the threads of the can and lid.
◊   Cover the opening of the can with plastic wrap or wax paper for oil-based paints. The wrap seals the can and makes it easier to remove the film that forms after it has been sitting around for a while.
◊   Fit the lid securely on the can and gently tap it with a hammer until it is completely sealed.
◊   Turn the paint can upside down. The paint will naturally form a skin to help seal the paint and keep it fresh.

◊   Paint is flammable. So store in a climate-controlled area away from heat sources. Cans exposed to extreme heat can expand causing the paint to leak. Also, keep water-based paint from freezing. Water-based paint can survive a couple of freeze-thaws, but the paint will degrade until it is ruined.

Disposing Of Water-Based Paint
Liquid paint should not be taken to a landfill or poured down a sink. Use the following method when disposing of water-based paints:
◊   Fill a paper bag or box with kitty litter, sand, or saw dust.
◊   Pour the remaining paint over the absorbent material.
◊   Allow to dry completely in a well-ventilated area away from children, pets, and direct heat.
◊   Dispose of the solid in the regular trash.
◊   For paint residue in the can, remove the lid and allow to dry completely. Remove the skin and dispose of it in the regular trash. Leave the label on the can and recycle if a program is available in your area.

Disposing of Oil-based Paint and Solvents
Oil-based paint and solvents, including mineral spirits, are considered hazardous waste materials. Special precautions and steps must be taken for proper disposal. Never dispose of liquid oil-based paint or solvents in the regular trash or pour them down the sink. Some communities have special hazardous waste collection programs for liquid paint. Check your local regulations to ensure proper handling. You can also visit www.paint.org for more information.

Children Safety

Crib Safety Tips
Bringing home a new baby is an exciting time for parents, and families must plan ahead and prepare the home and nursery before an infant arrives. To help ensure the safety of your youngest children, follow these guidelines to select and maintain a crib for your new baby:
◊   Find out if cribs, especially older models, have been recalled. Visit the *U.S. Consumer Product Safety Commission's* (CPSC) website at http://www.cpsc.gov/ for recent updates.
◊   Make sure crib hardware is strong and secure.
◊   Remove soft bedding, pillows, toys and stuffed animals from the crib.
◊   Use sleepers instead of blankets.
◊   Follow the product guidelines for crib toys and discontinue use at the recommended age. If toys attach to crib railings, hang these on the wall side of the crib.
◊   Make sure the crib sheet and mattress fit tightly to avoid entrapment and suffocation.
◊   Remove bumper pads to deter children from climbing out easily.
◊   Keep cribs away from windows and window blind cords.

◊ For metal or wooden cribs, make sure slats are 2 3/8 inches apart or less. Corner posts should not be over 1/16 inch high. Avoid headboards and footboards with cutouts large enough that a baby's head can become trapped.

◊ For mesh-sided cribs or playpens look for mesh less than ¼ inch in size, securely attached to the top rail and floor plate. If staples are used, make sure none are missing or exposed.

Nursery Safety Tips

The nursery should be a warm and safe environment where a baby can learn and grow. An active baby naturally climbs and crawls, rolls and rummages – and parents need to take precautions to make sure curious children avoid common home injuries. Consider the following tips to ensure that your child's haven remains safe and welcoming:

◊ Young children need close supervision, even in the nursery.

◊ Remove all plastic bags from the nursery area.

◊ Keep baby monitors and other cords a safe distance from the crib.

◊ Store diaper products and medicines up high and purchase products with child-resistant packaging.

◊ Never leave the baby unattended on the changing table and use harness straps to secure the baby from a fall injury.

◊ Purchase UL-listed nightlights and replacement bulbs.

◊ Use only safety nightlight styles that prevent children from pulling out the night light or gaining access to the bulb. Use the recommended wattage for the bulb and keep night lights at least three feet from bedding and other combustible materials.

◊ Use child safety covers for electric outlets.

◊ Repair or replace frayed cords or damaged lamps. Be sure to hide cords behind furniture.

◊ All pictures should be secured out of reach. Don't hang pictures or other heavy decorations directly over a crib.

◊ Blind cords can present a serious strangulation hazard for early walkers. If your blind cords have continuous loops, call 1-800-311-7996 to request free repair kits.

◊ Install window guards with a quick-release mechanism that can be opened easily by an adult in case of fire.

◊ Keep cribs, beds, chairs and other furniture away from windows.

◊ Anchor unstable furniture, including dressers and bookcases.

◊ Install a baby gate at the nursery door.

◊ Choose toy chests with lid supports to prevent heavy lids from falling on children's fingers and necks.

◊ Replace all door stops that have removable caps that can pose a choking hazard.

◊ Install finger pinch guards on doors or drape a towel over the hinge side to prevent painful pinching injuries.

Prevent Airway Obstruction

Research shows that suffocation/inhalation is the second leading cause of unintentional home injury related death for children under the age of 14. Follow these guidelines to reduce the risk of suffocation, choking and strangulation dangers in your home:

◊ Go to http://www.recalls.gov/ to find out if your crib model was recalled by the *U.S. Consumer Product Safety Commission* (CPSC).

◊ Place infants on their backs in cribs and make sure the sheet and mattress fit tightly to avoid entrapment and suffocation.

◊ Remove soft bedding, pillows, toys and stuffed animals from the crib.

◊ Consider buying a small parts tester to gauge whether objects present a choking hazard to young children. To approximate the test, use a cardboard toilet paper roll to measure objects and if they fit inside, keep them out of a child's reach.

◊ Always supervise children when they are playing and eating. Do not permit children under the age of 6 to consume small, round or hard foods, such as hot dogs.

◊ Keep small items including jewelry, buttons and safety pins away from children.

◊ The Home Safety Council recommends against the use of latex balloons in homes with your children, as the balloons or pieces of balloon material can become lodged in a child's throat.

◊ Make sure that rattles, squeeze toys, teething toys and pacifier shields are too large and firm to lodge in a baby's throat.

◊ Look carefully at toys and pacifiers and dispose of those with small broken parts that could be lodged in an infant's throat.

◊ Remove squeakers from squeeze toys. Babies may detach squeakers and choke.

◊ Read toy labels and other packaging information and base your selection on age recommendations.

◊ Never hang pictures, quilts or decorations containing ribbon or string on or over a crib.

◊ Window blind cords can present a serious strangulation hazard. Move cribs and playpens away from windows. Tie up window cords out of a child's reach. If your blind cords have continuous loops, call 1-800-311-7996 to request free repair kits to make them safer.

◊ Pull out drawstrings in children's outerwear and remove necklaces, purses and scarves before play.

◊ Make sure that children under 6 do not sleep on the top bunk of raised beds. Verify that spaces between the guardrail and bed frame, as well as the head and foot boards, are less than 3.5 inches.

Poison Safety

Poison Prevention Tips

Research shows that poisoning is the second leading cause of unintentional injury related death in the home. According to the American Association of Poison Control Centers (AAPCC) more than 92 percent of the 2.3 million poison exposures reported in the latest year studied occurred in the home. Yet, the Home Safety Council found that most families are not taking the appropriate precautions to reduce the risk of poison exposure.

Poison prevention is for everyone, not just children. Poisoning prevention advice can help individuals and families keep their homes safer from poisonous and toxic products, chemicals and gases, regardless of the ages of the occupants. Homes with young children need to take extra precautions. Follow these guidelines to keep your family safe from poison exposures at home:

◊   Make sure all potentially dangerous products (household cleaners, medicines, and typical garage items like antifreeze and pesticides) all have child resistant closures on them, are locked up, and are stored in high places.
◊   Homes with young children should have child locks installed on cabinets.
◊   Store food and non-food products separately. This protects consumers in the event of a leak in the product and reduces any possible confusion between items.
◊   Make sure all medicines and prescriptions have not expired. If they have expired they should be flushed down the toilet and not thrown away in the garbage.
◊   Immediately mop up puddles of anti-freeze and car oil in the garage or driveway. They are extremely harmful to children and pets.
◊   Read the use and storage directions before using products. Original labels on product containers often give important first-aid information.
◊   Wear gloves and follow manufacturer's instructions when using harsh chemicals or cleaners.
◊   Do not mix household products, because their contents could react together with dangerous results.
◊   Post the national poison control hotline (1-800-222-1222) next to every phone.
◊   To prevent carbon monoxide (CO) poisoning, have your home heating equipment inspected annually and install a UL-listed CO alarm near every sleeping area.
◊   Walk through the most common rooms where potentially harmful products are stored including the kitchen, bathrooms and garage. Learn more about room-by-room poison prevention in Home Safety Council's safety guide.

The National Poison Control Hotline and How to Use It

Poison Centers in the United States managed more than 2.3 million poison exposures in 2002, and more than half of these exposures were children under the age of six. The American Association of Poison Control Centers (AAPCC) provides a national poison control hotline, which offers the best initial line of defense for any poison emergency.

Calls to the hotline will be automatically connected to the local poison control center where specially trained nurses, pharmacists and physicians will provide immediate emergency help to callers. If necessary, the poison center will call an ambulance and will provide advice to the EMT's when they arrive.

Callers may also call the hotline any time for advice about preventing poisoning. Experts are available to answer questions about poisonous plants, poison prevention advice, and how to use pesticides safely.

The Home Safety Council recommends memorizing the national hotline number -- (800) 222-1222 -- and posting the number with other local emergency phone numbers next to every phone.

CO Poisoning

Carbon monoxide (CO) is a deadly gas that is difficult to detect because it is odorless and invisible. As a result, it is known as "the silent killer." According to the *U.S. Consumer Product Safety Commission* (CPSC), this poisonous gas kills nearly 300 people in their homes each year.

CO is produced by fuel-burning appliances and equipment in our homes. If you have heating, cooking or power equipment that uses fuels such as oil, natural gas, coal, wood, propane, gasoline, etc., then your home is at risk for potential CO poisoning. Homes with attached garages are also at risk, because vehicles left running in the garage can cause CO to seep into the home.

CO poisoning can be prevented by proper care and use of household equipment. CO alarms can provide early detection if CO leaks or accumulation occurs. Both are important for your safety.

◊   If you suspect CO poisoning in your home, call the appropriate responding agency, usually your local fire department or 9-1-1. Keep all emergency response numbers posted by every telephone.
◊   CO alarms are different from smoke alarms, and have different functions. CO alarms do not provide early warning of a fire. Smoke alarms do not provide early warning of CO exposure. Your home needs both CO and smoke alarm protection.

Symptoms of CO poisoning are similar to symptoms of the flu, and can include headache, dizziness, nausea and shortness of breath. If your CO alarm sounds check to see if it is plugged in properly, or if battery-powered, check the battery to be sure the device is operating. If you suspect that CO is leaking in your home, follow these steps:
◊   Open windows and doors to ventilate the rooms, or in severe cases of CO exposure, evacuate the home.

◊ Call to report that you suspect CO is accumulating. Usually the appropriate agency to call is the fire department or 9-1-1.

◊ Seek immediate medical treatment for anyone who has severe symptoms.

◊ Follow the advice of the responding agency before re-entering your home, and quickly obtain repairs as needed.

Preventing CO Poisoning at Home

Use the following to avoid CO poisoning in your home:

◊ Purchase CO alarms that are listed by Underwriters Laboratories (UL). Install at least one CO alarm in your home, near the sleeping areas. A hallway outside bedrooms, for example.

◊ Use appliances and equipment according to directions and only for the purposes, they are intended. For example, use a range or cook stove only for cooking, never to heat your home.

For additional safety from CO exposure:

◊ Never use a barbecue or gas grill indoors, inside a garage or in an enclosed porch.

◊ Electric generators must never be used inside the home or garage, or in any enclosed area.

◊ Back vehicles out of the garage when warming up the engine.

◊ Have a trained professional inspect, clean and tune-up your central heating system before the heating season each year.

◊ Have a professional sweep inspect your chimneys once a year and clean them if needed.

◊ If you have a wood stove, verify that it meets local fire codes. Contact your town's fire marshal if you have questions.

◊ When purchasing a new wood stove or portable space heater, choose equipment that is UL-listed.

◊ Open flues before using fireplaces.

◊ Be aware that kerosene heaters are illegal in some areas.

◊ Re-fuel kerosene heaters outdoors only, after the device has cooled.

◊ Kerosene and gas heaters should always be used with ventilation (such as an open window).

Purchasing a new home? Before you sign the contract, have the home inspected to ensure fuel-burning heating and cooking equipment is safe to use, including fireplaces, wood stoves and chimneys.

Home Heating Safety

Proper installation, use and regular maintenance of heating equipment are necessary for safe home heating. Use these guidelines to help you prevent carbon monoxide (CO) poisoning, contact burns and heating equipment fires during the winter months.

General Guidelines

◊ Purchase heating equipment listed by Underwriters Laboratories (UL); install and use it according to the manufacturer's recommendations.

◊ Furnaces and other fixed heating equipment should be installed in accordance with applicable local building and fire codes (contact your town's fire marshal for information about these).

◊ Have your furnace inspected and serviced by a professional each year.

◊ Have your woodstove and fireplace chimneys inspected each year, and cleaned as needed.

Carbon Monoxide (CO) Poisoning Prevention

If you have fuel-burning heating equipment in your home, such as kerosene heaters, woodstoves and fireplaces, and oil and natural gas furnaces, you are at risk for potential Carbon Monoxide (CO) poisoning.

◊ Proper installation, use and regular maintenance are necessary to prevent CO poisoning.

◊ In addition, every home with fuel-burning appliances should have the added protection of a UL-listed CO alarm. Install a CO alarm near sleeping areas to provide early warning if there is a serious CO leak in your home.

Burn Prevention

When you build a fire in a wood stove or fireplace, the outer surfaces get hot – hot enough to cause a burn injury if you come in contact with them. Young children are especially vulnerable to these contact burns. Portable kerosene and electric heaters can also get hot on the outside, and though newer models have grills covering the heating element, little ones' fingers may be small enough to reach through and be seriously burned.

◊ Constantly supervise children around all types of heating equipment. Keep plenty of distance between children and space heaters, woodstoves and fireplaces.

◊ For increased protection against unintentional burn injuries, install a temporary safety gate around woodstoves and hearths. Never leave a child unattended in a room with an operating fireplace, woodstove or space heater.

Fire Prevention

To reduce the risk of a heating-equipment fire in your home, follow the manufacturer's use and maintenance directions.

◊ Move anything that can burn a good distance away from heat sources – at least one yard.

◊ When buying new portable heaters look for UL-listed models with automatic shut-off technology that stops the operation if the heater tips over.

If you use a kerosene heater, be aware that this type of heater is illegal in some areas – check with your local fire department before purchasing. Kerosene is a flammable fuel which must be used with extreme caution:

◊ Use the type of kerosene recommended by the heater's manufacturer (never substitute another fuel for a heater designed to burn kerosene).

◊ Refuel outdoors only, and only after the heater has cooled completely.

◊ Clean up spills immediately.

◊   Plug a portable electric heater into a receptacle, not an extension cord, so you don't overload the circuit.
◊   Always use a screen or glass doors on working fireplaces because sparks and embers can easily pop out of the opening.

Installing and Using CO Alarms
Install at least one CO alarm in every home that has an attached garage and/or uses fuel-burning appliances or equipment.
◊   Purchase CO alarms that are listed by Underwriters Laboratories (UL)
◊   Follow the manufacturer's recommendations for installing and testing the alarm.
◊   Place one CO alarm outside each area where people sleep, such as a hallway outside bedrooms.
◊   Sound the CO alarm for all household members so everyone can identify the difference between the CO alarm signal and the smoke alarm signal.
◊   Contact your fire department to learn the appropriate local emergency telephone number to call if you suspect CO poisoning in your home.
◊   Post all emergency response numbers by every telephone.
◊   CO alarms are different from smoke alarms, and have different functions. CO alarms do not provide early warning of a fire. Smoke alarms do not provide early warning of CO exposure. Your home needs both CO and smoke alarm protection.

Protecting Children from Lead Poisoning
Lead poisoning is a hidden danger for families with young children. According to the U.S. Department of Housing and Urban Development (HUD), an estimated 38 million housing units in the United States had lead-based paint between 1998 and 2000. More than half had significant lead hazards.

Lead is toxic for all ages, but is especially harmful to young children. When they are exposed to high levels of lead, they can suffer permanent health and brain damage. According to HUD, one out of every nine American children has too much lead in their bodies. Lead-based paint hazards in older housing are a common source of lead poisoning for children.

In 1978, the U.S. Consumer Product Safety Commission (CPSC) ruled that only trace amounts of lead could be contained in paint. If your home was built before 1978, your family may be at greater risk from lead poisoning. Use the following tips to help protect against lead poisoning:
◊   Ask your doctor about testing children age six or younger for lead. Sometimes these simple blood tests are provided at no cost at local health centers and clinics. The American Academy of Pediatrics recommends lead testing of all children at the one- and two-year health supervision visits.
◊   If you rent an older home or apartment, be sure to tell the building owner if you notice peeling paint and paint chips. You can also report peeling or chipping paint to your local public health department.

◊   If your home has high levels of lead, you may need to have certain repairs made to keep your family safe.
◊   HUD offers information on testing and special renovations on its Healthy Homes Web site. Visit the web site
◊   You should not try to remove lead-based paint yourself.
◊   You cannot identify lead by looking at paint yourself. Whether you rent or own your home, consider having your home professionally tested for the presence of lead.
◊   Always supervise children closely. Do not permit them to play with, hold or chew pieces of paint that may chip or peel away from the walls.
◊   Do not permit children to play in or near buildings that are condemned or under repair or renovation. In addition to other hazards, lead can be present in the soil and dust around these sites.
◊   Wash children's hands frequently; always before they eat.

Kitchen Poison Safety
Food, drinks and household cleaners are found in kitchens across the country – yet surprisingly Home Safety Council research shows that over half of families keep cleaners and chemicals in unlocked places. The American Association of Poison Control Centers (AAPCC) reports than 92 percent of all poison exposures occur in the home every year. To help reduce the risk to your family, adopt the following safety guidelines to handle and store poisons at home:
◊   Store all products in their original containers and in accordance with the manufacturer's recommendations.
◊   Never transfer poisonous or caustic products to drinking glasses, pop bottles, or other food containers, which could be mistaken and the contents consumed.
◊   Homes with young children should have child locks installed on cabinets. Lock up all pesticides, cleaning products and other chemicals, all medications and medical supplies, and all other poisonous, toxic or caustic products.
◊   Purchase medications with child-resistant caps and make sure all dangerous products in the cabinets have child-resistant caps, including cleaning products and chemicals.
◊   Read the use and storage directions before using products. Original labels on product containers often give important first-aid information.
◊   When using harsh products follow safety recommendations, such as wearing gloves and masks. Do not mix products together because their contents could react together with dangerous results.
◊   Promptly put away products after use and wipe up spills immediately.
◊   If you purchase cleaning products or household chemicals that are packaged with labeling that includes images of food (for example citrus fruit in some cleaners), or that are packaged in containers that look similar to beverage bottles, be aware of the risk of these containers being mistaken for edible food products and ingested.
◊   Avoid purchasing cleaning products or household chemicals that are packaged with labeling that includes images of food (for example citrus fruit in some cleaners) or in containers that look similar to beverage bottles. These can easily be mistaken and the contents consumed.

◊ Store all harmful products away from food to avoid mistaken consumption.

◊ If you purchase cleaning products or household chemicals that are packaged with labeling that includes images of food (for example citrus fruit in some cleaners), or that are packaged in containers that look similar to beverage bottles, be aware of the risk of these containers being mistaken for edible food products and ingested.

◊ Post the poison control hotline (1-800-222-1222) and other emergency numbers near every phone.

Bathroom Poison Safety

All medicines, whether prescription or purchased over-the-counter, are dangerous if used improperly and potentially poisonous to people of all ages. Yet according to The State of Home Safety in America® Report, 82 percent of families report that medications are left unsecured. Household cleaners, some cosmetics and other everyday items can pose a poison risk for children. Consider the following safety advice when handling and storing medications and other potentially hazardous products:

◊ Vitamins, supplements, aspirin and other over-the-counter remedies, as well as most prescription medicines, should be purchased with child-resistant closures. Child-resistant packaging has been shown to help protect children from poisoning.

◊ Lock medicines and medical supplies, including personal syringes, in a medicine cabinet or other locking cabinet and secure the key.

◊ Do not store medicines inside purses, nightstand drawers, or other locations easily accessed by children.

◊ Capsules, tablets and liquid medications look alike and may also look similar to other dangerous products. If medications become separated from their original containers, don't assume it is safe to use them. It is too risky to consume or use unidentified medications.

◊ Flush all unidentified and out-of-date medicines down the toilet. As medicines age, the chemicals inside them can change. Rinse the container well and discard it.

◊ Store all medicines in their original containers with the original labels intact. Prescription medicines may or may not list ingredients. In an emergency, the prescription number on the label will allow rapid identification of ingredients by your pharmacist.

◊ Treat all medicines and supplements as potential poisons, especially to young children.

◊ Cosmetics and other personal care products can be highly toxic if consumed and some contain caustic ingredients that can harm skin and eyes. Read all product packaging carefully and follow use and storage instructions.

◊ Use child safety locks on all cabinets where you store medicines, cosmetics and personal care products.

◊ If you provide care for someone who uses medications, carefully dispense the medicines and keep track of doses to ensure compliance with the prescription or medical recommendation.

Poison Safety in the Garage

The garage is often a place for home improvement projects and chemical storage – and a place where some chemicals that can cause the most harm to children, such as pesticides, gasoline and automotive fluids are often stored. To help keep your family safe from one of the leading causes of home injuries, you need to keep safety at the top of mind when handling poisons and chemicals in your garage:

◊ In homes with young children, child-resistant caps should be kept on dangerous products, including those stored in the garage. Ideally, a locking cabinet should be used to store items such as pesticides, automotive fluids, charcoal lighter fluid, paint thinner, antifreeze, ice-melting products, and turpentine.

◊ Store all products in original containers and keep original labels legible.

◊ In homes with young children, it is safest to store all dangerous products out of sight and reach - or better yet, locked up.

◊ Never transfer dangerous products to glass jars, pop bottles, or other containers. Many products look alike. In addition to the risk of the products being mistakenly consumed or otherwise improperly used, the containers may leak or break and it is easy to forget what product was placed in which container.

◊ Store only a small amount of gasoline in the garage or shed, out of the reach of children, and always in an approved vented container designed and labeled for gasoline. Because of its highly volatile flammable vapors, gasoline must never be brought indoors, even in small amounts.

◊ Use a siphon hose if you must transfer gasoline; never try to siphon gasoline or other fuels by mouth.

◊ To prevent carbon monoxide (CO) poisoning, never use a barbecue or grill or keep a generator running in a garage. Always pull the car out of the garage after starting it. CO can enter the home if cars are left running in the garage, even with the garage door open.

Outdoor Chemicals & Poison Hazards

According to the State of Home Safety in America (2002, household chemicals caused more than 45,000 emergency room visits in a single year. Many families store chemicals and cleaning supplies in a garage or basement, and while those may not be high traffic areas for family members, it is important to store and handle chemicals correctly, wherever they are. Use the following guidelines when storing and handling dangerous products, including gasoline, pool chemicals and pesticides:

◊ Use child-resistant caps on dangerous products, including those stored in the garage, such as pesticides, automotive fluids, charcoal lighter, paint thinner, antifreeze, and turpentine. Ideally, hazardous products should be stored in a locking cabinet.

◊ Store all products in their original containers and in accordance with the manufacturer's recommendations.

◊ When using harsh products follow safety recommendations, such as wearing gloves and masks. Do not mix products together because their contents could react together with dangerous results.

◊   Never transfer poisonous or caustic products to drinking glasses, pop bottles, or other food containers, which could be mistaken and the contents consumed.
◊   Make sure all chemicals are stored in their original containers according to manufacturer's recommendations.
◊   Store only a small amount of gasoline, in a garage or shed, and always in an approved, vented container designed and labeled for gasoline. Because of its highly volatile flammable vapors, gasoline must never be brought indoors.
◊   Read the use and storage directions before using products. Original labels on product containers often give important first-aid information.
◊   Pesticides are extremely hazardous – consider substituting non-poisonous insecticides whenever possible.
◊   Mix insect sprays outdoors, away from areas used by your family and pets.
◊   Store and use pool chemicals according to the manufacturer's directions, always in tightly covered original containers, in a dry place. Keep these away from other chemicals and products.

Water Safety

Water Safety at Home

Standing water presents a serious hazard both inside and outside the home. Drowning is a sudden and silent danger, and young children are especially vulnerable to drowning risk areas inside the home including toilets, bathtubs and five gallon buckets. Constant adult supervision is the most effective way to keep children safe around water. Use these additional safety precautions to keep your children away from potential water hazards.
◊   Always stay within touch supervision – keeping kids within an arm's reach -- when your children are around standing water at home. This includes buckets, bathtubs, toilets and spas.
◊   Always supervise young children during bath time. Never allow older siblings to supervise children in or around standing water.
◊   Baby bath seats are not a safety device and should never substitute for adult supervision.
◊   Drain the bathtub immediately after using.
◊   Do not store electrical appliances such as blow dryers and radios near sinks and tubs. Keep these out of children's reach at all times.
◊   Set your water heater at 120 degrees Fahrenheit or below to reduce the risk of burns and scalds from hot tap water.
◊   When bathing children, turn the cold water on first and then add warm water.
◊   Keep bathroom doors closed and use door knob covers to prevent young children from accessing bathrooms.
◊   Use toilet seat locks and keep toilet lids shut.
◊   Be sure all buckets are emptied immediately after use and turned over with the opening face down.
◊   Store large buckets out of children's reach.

Scald Prevention

A scald is an injury caused by hot liquid or steam and according to Shriners Hospitals for Children, children under age 5 are at highest risk for scald injuries from hot liquids. People of all ages can be burned by liquid at 140 degrees Fahrenheit in as few as thirty seconds. It takes only five seconds for a young child to be injured by 140 degree liquid; and only one second at 160 degrees. Follow this simple advice to help reduce the risk of scald injuries at home:

◊   Lower water heaters to 120 degrees Fahrenheit or less. Ask the building owner to lower the temperature for you if you rent. If you own your home, you can often adjust your own water heater. Check with the utility company for instructions.
◊   When bathing children, use a water thermometer to ensure the temperature is safe. Turn the cold water on first, then mix in warmer water and keep the temperature at about 100 Fahrenheit.
◊   Stay within an arm's reach of young children any time they are near standing water.
◊   Use heavy oven mitts and hot pads when cooking. Avoid using a wet towel to hold a hot pan because the heat from the pan can build steam, causing a scald injury.
◊   Test heated food and bottles before feeding children.
◊   Microwaved food gets hot very fast. Heated food and steam can cause an injury. Use caution when removing food from the microwave and when taking the covers off of heated plates. Pull covers away from you, not toward you.
◊   Microwaving heats food from the inside out. Cut open heated foods and test them before feeding children.
◊   Turn pot handles toward to back of the range. When drinking hot beverages, keep the container away from the edge of tables and counters so children can't reach them.
◊   Be aware that toddlers can pull tablecloths down, spilling hot beverages and food onto them. When using tablecloths, center food and beverages in the middle of the table. Don't place hot beverages on lower tables, where children can easily reach them.
◊   Avoid drinking hot beverages when you are holding a young child. Using a "commuter mug" with a tight-fitting lid can help reduce a hot spill if the beverage tips over.

Treat a minor burn injury immediately with cool running water for 3-5 minutes. Do not apply ice, which can harm the skin. Do not apply butter or lotions, because this can keep the skin temperature hot, increasing the injury. Apply a sterile bandage to the injured area. If the scald is serious, seek medical treatment immediately.

Swimming Safety

According to The State of Home Safety in America™ report, drowning is the fifth leading cause of unintentional injury related death. Drowning is a silent and sudden event, and research found that many drowning deaths at home are related to swimming pools. Since drowning victims often do not make any noise once in distress, constant supervision around any body of water is critical. Adopt the following guidelines to help keep your pool area safe:

◊   Install four-sided fencing with self-locking and self-closing gates. Fencing should completely isolate the pool from the home and be least five feet high.

◊   Always keep gates closed and latched. Never prop a gate open or disable the lock.

◊   Always practice constant, adult supervision around any body of water, including pools and spas. Never leave your child alone or in the care of another child.

◊   When hosting a pool party, assign specific adults to keep an eye on the pool at all times.

◊   Enroll non-swimmers in swimming lessons taught by a qualified instructor.

◊   Remember that regardless of age or skill level, no one is "drown proof." Children should always be supervised by an adult while they are swimming.

◊   Never swim alone. Even adults should swim with a buddy.

◊   Learn and practice basic lifesaving techniques, including First Aid and CPR. Insist that anyone who cares for your children learn CPR.

◊   Keep poolside rescue equipment and a cordless, water resistant telephone close to the pool area.

◊   Post emergency numbers and CPR instructions near the pool area.

◊   Teach children that drains, grates and filters are not toys. Never stick fingers or toes in these openings and stay away from suction devices.

◊   Always remove toys from the pool area when not in use.

◊   Post safety rules in a highly visible location. Make sure children are familiar with the rules.

◊   Keep spas and hot tubs covered and locked when not in use.

◊   Completely remove pool and spa covers prior to swimming.

◊   Stay out of the pool during severe weather and thunderstorms, especially if lightning is forecast or present.

◊   If a child is missing, check the pool area first.

Pool Security and Maintenance

According to The State of Home Safety in America™ report drowning is the fifth leading cause of unintentional injury related death and many of these incidents involve swimming pools and spas. Use safety precautions to avoid injuries in and around a pool or spa at home:

◊   Always practice adult supervision around any body of water. Older children should not be left in charge of younger children in the pool area.

◊   Install four-sided fencing that blocks direct access to the pool from the home. Four-sided pool fencing with self-latching and self-locking gates is proven to be an effective drowning prevention intervention.

◊   Pool fencing should be at least five feet high and have self locking and self closing gates.

◊   Position gate latches out of the reach of young children.

◊   Never prop the gate open or disable the latch.

◊   Do not leave furniture near the fence that would enable a child to climb over it.

◊   Clear debris, clutter and pool toys from the pool deck and adjoining pathways to prevent slips and falls.

◊   Keep a cordless, water resistant telephone with emergency numbers posted in the pool area.

◊   Keep poolside rescue equipment close by. Equipment should include a sturdy, lightweight pole measuring at least 10-12 feet and a ring buoy with line. Do not permit children to play with these tools.

◊   Keep a life vest approved by the U.S. Coast Guard on hand. Poor and inexperienced swimmers should be required to wear a life vest while swimming.

◊   Use plastic ware instead of glassware in the pool area.

◊   As a supplemental safety precaution, consider using a pool alarm to alert you if someone falls into the pool. Recent studies show that sub surface pool alarms are most effective. These alarms are not substitutes for adult supervision of children.

◊   Keep spa and hot tub covers locked when not in use.

◊   Remove excess water from pool and spa covers.

◊   Always completely remove pool covers before swimming.

◊   Chlorine-based pool care products could be explosive and can easily combust if not handled correctly. Always follow manufacturer's instructions when using pool chemicals and store chemicals in a dry place away from heat sources.

◊   Lock all pool chemicals in a secure cabinet out of children's reach.

Fire Safety

Burn Prevention

People of all ages are at risk for painful burn injuries in the home. A burn is an injury that results from heat or flame and can lead to serious scarring, or even death in severe cases. Fortunately, these injuries are easily preventable by following appropriate safety precautions. To make your home safer for family and visitors, follow this simple advice:

◊   Electrical receptacles (outlets) in kitchens, bathrooms and other wet areas should be protected by ground fault circuit interrupters (GFCI). GFCI's help reduce electrical shock injuries. An electrician can tell you if your home's wiring needs to be updated for safety.

◊   Always stay in the kitchen when you have something cooking on the range and give it your full attention. If you must leave the range for a moment, turn down the heat first and return quickly.

◊   Teach older children who are learning to cook burn prevention tips.

◊   Roll up sleeves when cooking and avoid reaching over burners and other hot surfaces.

◊   Avoid storing items you frequently use directly over the range.

◊   Keep children well away from the cooking area and place hot pans and cookie sheets away from the edges of counters where children can reach them.

◊   Use heavy oven mitts and hot pads when cooking.

◊   Learn how to prevent and extinguish a small pan fire.

◊   Keep electrical appliances such as toasters, radios, and hairdryers, away from the sink and tub. If an appliance falls into water, un-plug it immediately. Never reach into water to retrieve it.

◊   Never touch an electrical appliance when you are bathing.

◊   Unplug these appliances when not in use.

◊   Wood stoves, fire places and other portable heaters get hot on the outside. Keep young children well away from these devices.

◊   Store matches, lighters and candles up high, ideally in a locked cabinet, so young children cannot reach them.

Treat a minor burn injury immediately with cool running water for 3-5 minutes. Do not apply ice, which can harm the skin. Do not apply butter or lotions, because this can keep the skin temperature hot, increasing the injury. Apply a sterile bandage to the injured area. If the burn is serious, seek medical treatment immediately.

If your clothing catches fire remember the phrase, "STOP, DROP and ROLL." This can save your life and limit your burn injuries. Stop where you are. Drop to the floor. Roll over and over to smother the fire. If someone else's clothing catches fire, help them by telling them to stop, drop and roll. If they attempt to run, use a heavy rug or blanket to try to stop them and use it to smother the flames if you can do so safely.

Fire Prevention Tips

According to the Home Safety Council's State of Home Safety in America™ Report, fires and burns are the third leading cause of unintentional home injury and related deaths. Fire safety and survival begin with everyone in your household being prepared. Follow these safety measures to reduce the chance of fire in your home:

◊   Keep volatile chemicals, such as fertilizers and turpentine, in their original containers in a locked storage area separate from the home.

◊   Store gasoline in a garage or shed in a container approved for gasoline storage.

◊   Never bring or use gasoline indoors; and use it as a motor fuel only.

◊   Keep things that can burn away from your fireplace and keep a glass or metal screen in front of your fireplace.

◊   Store matches and lighters in a locked cabinet.

◊   Always stay in the kitchen while cooking.

◊   Keep things that can burn, such as dishtowels, paper or plastic bags, and curtains at least three feet away from the range top.

◊   Douse cigarette and cigar butts with water before dumping them in the trash.

◊   When cooking, do not wear loose-fitting clothing ,which can be ignited by hot burners or gas flames.

◊   Never leave barbecue grills unattended while in use.

◊   Keep grills at least three feet away from other objects, including the house and any shrubs or bushes.

◊   Never leave burning candles unattended and do not allow children to keep candles or incense in their rooms.

◊   Always use stable, candle holders made of material that won't catch fire, such as metal, glass, etc.

◊   Schedule an appointment with professionals to have chimneys, fireplaces, wood and coal stoves, central furnaces and space heaters inspected once a year and cleaned as often as necessary.

◊   Keep space heaters at least three feet away from things that can burn, such as curtains or stacks of newspaper, and always turn off heaters when leaving the room or going to bed.

◊   Be careful not to overload electrical outlets, extension cords and power strips.

◊   Check all wires and cords for damage and cover all unused electrical outlets.

◊   Protect bedrooms by having arc fault circuit interrupters (AFCI's) installed. Contact a professional electrician to handle this job.

Fire Safety At Home

Safe practices at home are part of your family's fire protection plan, and it is also critical that your home and family are prepared to react quickly if a fire occurs at home. Learn more about the following essential safety practices in the Home Safety Council's Safety Guide.

◊   Develop a fire escape plan for your family that identifies two exits out of every room and an established meeting place outside. Practice makes perfect – hold a family fire drill at least twice each year.

◊   Install smoke alarms on every level of your home and test them monthly. Install additional smoke alarms inside bedrooms.
◊   Know how to extinguish a small pan fire by sliding a lid over the flames.
◊   Teach every family member to "Stop, Drop and Roll" if clothes catch fire.
◊   Consider having a home fire sprinkler system installed in your new home, or when you remodel.
◊   Learn how and when to use a fire extinguisher.

Installing and Testing Smoke Alarms
Research shows that 97 percent of American homes have at least one smoke alarm, but one may not be enough. Do you have enough smoke alarms in your home? Are they correctly installed? Early warning is essential for every fire escape plan. To ensure your family will be effectively alerted to any fire dangers, use the following guidelines when installing and testing smoke alarms:
◊   Only purchase smoke alarms that are listed by UL and carry the UL mark on packaging.
◊   Install smoke alarms on every level of your home, including the basement. Make sure there is an alarm near every sleeping area.
◊   Install additional smoke alarms inside all bedrooms.
◊   Smoke rises, so smoke alarms should be mounted high on walls or ceilings. Ceiling mounted alarms should be installed at least four inches away from the nearest wall; wall-mounted alarms should be installed four to 12 inches away from the ceiling.
◊   Choose an installation location that is well away from the path of steam from bathrooms and cooking vapors from the kitchen, which can result in false, or nuisance alarms.
◊   Don't install smoke alarms near windows, doors, or ducts where drafts might interfere with their operation.
◊   Test your smoke alarms at least once a month, following the manufacturer's instructions, which typically involves pushing the "test" button on the face of the alarm cover. Install fresh batteries at least once a year.
◊   Use hard-wired, interconnected smoke alarms with battery back-up. These alarms run on your household wiring and are tied in together so that if one alarm operates, they all signal together.
◊   Smoke alarms should be replaced at least once every 10 years.

Home Security and Fire Safety
Sometimes, families seeking to protect themselves from one hazard unknowingly put themselves at risk from others. For example, home security can protect people from intruders, but it can also be harmful if security features prevent quick escape during a fire emergency. Home security and fire safety can and should work together and you need to examine entryways, both doors and windows, to make sure home security doesn't interfere with your fire escape plan.

Security Locks
Every home entry door should be equipped with a sturdy dead-bolt lock that is properly installed and maintained in good working condition. When choosing deadbolt locks for your home, keep the following guidelines in mind.

◊   Avoid two-keyed deadbolt locks that require a key on both the inside and outside of an entry door. These keyed locks can trap people inside if there is a fire. Keys can easily be misplaced when the deadbolt is locked, making it impossible to escape.
◊   Replace any two-keyed entry locks with common deadbolt locks that only require keyed entry from the outside and have a turning or "throwing" bolt or latch inside.
◊   If your home entry doors have two-keyed deadbolt locks, protect your family in the meantime by keeping the key to your deadbolt on a hook near the door but away from any windows. Make sure all responsible family members know exactly where to find the key and how to use it quickly in an emergency.

Window Security/Burglar Bars
Security bars on doors and windows can provide a strong defense against intruders and give families greater confidence in their home's safety. However that same strength can prove deadly in a fire emergency. Bars welded over an escape route not only trap victims inside; they also prevent firefighters from being able to get them out. Families need to evaluate their fire escape route to make sure security measures do not hinder a quick escape.

Bars on doors and windows can provide a strong defense against intruders and give families greater confidence in their home's security. However that same strength can prove deadly in a fire emergency. New research shows that home fires grow so fast and spread so quickly that people may three minutes or less to survive a fire and its deadly smoke. Bars welded over an escape route not only trap victims inside; they also prevent firefighters from being able to get them out. Families are urged to make sure security measures do not slow down a quick escape:
◊   In rooms with window bars, install a quick-release mechanism on at least one exit.
◊   Purchase quick-release devices together with new bars, or have them installed on bars that are currently in your home.
◊   In an emergency you can use the release device to quickly unlock the bars from inside, usually with a lever or pedal, to make your escape path clear for immediate exit.
◊   Know that quick-release devices can only be opened from the inside of the home, and do not affect your home's security.
◊   Contact an iron contractor to have quick-release devices installed on security bars in your home.

Developing a Fire Escape Plan
Fire is a leading cause of preventable deaths in the home; but by being prepared to handle this emergency, you can help your family safely exit your home in the event of a fire. Fire safety and survival begins with everyone in your household

being prepared. In the year studied, The State of Home Safety in America™ report found that only 54 percent of families with children have discussed what to do in case of a home fire. Use the following guidelines for developing a home fire escape plan:

◊   Early warning is a key element of your fire escape plan. Every home needs working smoke alarms on each story and protecting every place that people sleep. Install additional smoke alarms inside all sleeping rooms.

◊   Sketch out a floor plan of your home, including all rooms, windows, interior and exterior doors, stairways, fire escapes and smoke alarms. Make sure that every family member is familiar with the layout.

◊   Identify and remedy anything in your home that could possibly interfere with your ability to get out quickly in an emergency, such as windows that are stuck or heavy furniture blocking an exit.

◊   You need a primary and secondary exit. If you have a multi-story home, consider if you need to purchase fire escape ladders for upstairs bedrooms. If so, they should be part of your fire drill, deployed safely from a ground-floor window for practice.

◊   Push the "test button" on a smoke alarm to ensure everyone will recognize the sound of the alarm if it goes off.

◊   Select two escape routes from each room and mark them clearly on the plan.

◊   Ensure that family members with special needs, such as someone who is ill or frail, or small children, have a buddy to help them get out safely. If anyone in the household has a hearing impairment, purchase special smoke alarms that use strobes and/or vibrations to signal a fire.

◊   Designate a place to meet outside so that everyone can be accounted and someone can be assigned to go to a neighbor's to call 911.

◊   Make copies of the escape plan sketches and post them in each room until everyone becomes familiar with them.

◊   Practice makes perfect. Every second counts during a real fire. Hold family fire drills frequently and at various times until the escape plans become second nature. Once you've mastered the escape process, hold a drill when family members are sleeping so you can test each family member's ability to waken and respond to the smoke alarm.

◊   Young children are especially susceptible to heavy sleeping and may not awaken. If any family member does not waken on his or her own during the drill, assign a buddy to help them waken and escape in future fire drills and in a real fire emergency.

Children & Smoke Alarms

Did you know that despite a piercing 70-85 decibel signal, children often sleep through the sound of a home smoke alarm? A quick response is essential in a fire emergency, so if children don't waken to the signal, parents and caregivers must wake them. Interconnected smoke alarms can make a life-saving difference. Interconnected smoke alarms are hard-wired into a home's electrical system and each alarm is connected together so that when one alarm signals, they all signal, no matter where the fire starts.

With interconnected smoke alarms, you'll have early warning of the fire wherever you are, because the smoke alarm in your room will sound at the same time as the alarm in the room with the fire. If your children or someone else in the household isn't aroused by the smoke alarm, you'll be able to waken them, hastening their safe escape.

DANGER! Even with interconnected alarms, emerging research has demonstrated that sleeping children may be able to tune out the blaring sound. Make sure your children wake and properly respond when the smoke alarms signal. Empowering children with basic fire escape skills is a very good idea - everyone should know to react immediately to the sound of the alarm and how to get outside quickly. But before assuming children will react appropriately to a late-night fire, parents must learn if their children will be roused immediately or sleep through the smoke alarm. Even those who awaken to the sound of the alarm may be groggy or move with indecision.

Learn if your children will awaken

To find out for certain, parents are urged to hold regular family fire drills. Children can participate in the drills by helping to draw the fire escape plan. Once kids have mastered fire escape skills, hold a drill when children are sleeping to learn how they will respond to the sound of the smoke alarm. Push the "test" button on the closest alarm during the drill. If children don't readily waken and demonstrate the ability to move with decision, parents must make a contingency plan for awakening them in family drills and in a fire emergency.

IMPORTANT! Children aren't the only ones who sleep through smoke alarms. Research shows that teenagers and even adults can tune out the loud sound while they sleep. Additionally, people with hearing impairments may not be able to hear conventional alarms; special smoke alarms with strobes and/or vibration are available for purchase online and through local fire equipment distributors. Make sure everyone in your family is protected by the early warning that smoke alarms provide.

Every-level fire protection

Hard-wired, interconnected smoke alarms are now required in new home construction. If you are building or remodeling your home, hire an electrician to install interconnected alarms throughout your house. Every home should have working smoke alarms on each level, and protecting each sleeping area. Install smoke alarms inside bedrooms as well. For additional protection from fire, consider installing an automatic fire sprinkler system in your new or remodeled home.

Child-Locator Window Decals

Many groups, including some safety organizations, offer adhesive "child locator" window decals to be placed on the window panes of rooms where children sleep. The decals are intended to aid firefighters in more easily locating children in a fire; however the Home Safety Council ***DOES NOT*** recommend the use of child-locator window decals. Firefighters are very systematic in their response to home fires and they thoroughly perform search and rescue operations as standard procedure.

Decals signal an area of vulnerability

Parents and caregivers should be aware of a potential safety concern about using child-locator decals. They may signal to intruders an area of vulnerability in the home, highlighting where children are asleep. That unintended possibility outweighs the questionable value the decals may have to firefighters who are trained to perform thorough searches of homes involved in serious fires, regardless of window markings.

Another concern is that window decals can be misleading. An old decal could potentially lead a firefighter on a dangerous, yet needless, prolonged search for a child who isn't there. Many fire departments do not recognize the decals as legitimate markers because they often remain affixed to windows long after a child has out-grown the room or families with children have moved away.

A proactive home fire safety program

Rather than using decals, concentrate on a home fire safety program. It is essential for everyone in the family to take a proactive role in fire safety, including children, who should be taught how to quickly and properly respond to the sound of smoke alarms and how to safely escape if fire breaks out. Firefighters agree it is counterproductive to teach children to wait to be rescued.

To survive a fire, every home needs:
◊   Working smoke alarms on each level and protecting every bedroom
◊   A carefully developed home fire escape plan
◊   Regular family fire drills so everyone can practice getting out
◊   Quick and decisive response in an emergency

For additional protection from fire, consider installing an automatic fire sprinkler system in your new or remodeled home.

Change Your Clock/Change Your Battery

Each year, the International Association of Fire Chiefs (IAFC) sponsors a campaign to help keep household smoke alarms working: Change Your Clock/Change Your Battery™.

According to research studies, 97% of American homes have at least one smoke alarm installed, but less than one in five tests the alarms at least quarterly. Safety experts recommend testing home smoke alarms monthly and replacing the batteries once a year or when they chirp, signaling low battery power.

When you change your clocks back in the fall, replace the batteries in all your smoke alarms, and then hold a family fire drill.

Home Fire Sprinkler Systems: The Ultimate in Home Fire Protection

Every home needs early warning if there is a fire. The sound of the smoke alarm provides extra time to follow your escape plan and get out safely. For additional protection from fire, it is recommended to install automatic home fire sprinkler systems. Fire sprinklers save lives and prevent injuries. They also protect your valued belongings and other property. But many home owners aren't aware that they can have sprinklers installed in their homes. In fact, only about 2% of U.S. homeowners have taken advantage of this life-saving technology.

If you are renovating your home or planning to build a new home, consider having a fire sprinkler system installed by a qualified contractor.

Fire Sprinklers: A Proven Technology

Home fire sprinklers are based on the same technology as the sprinklers you have seen at work, in high-rises and in hotels. But residential sprinklers are generally a lot less conspicuous. A network of piping installed behind the walls keeps water at the ready in case of fire. Sprinklers are located on the ceiling or wall at various junctures along the piping, protecting the rooms of your home. The sprinklers are specially designed to react only to the high temperature of a fire. When they activate, they douse the flames below with water. The sprinkler(s) closest to the fire will open; usually only one sprinkler is needed in home fires.

The sprinkler's quick response to the fire suppresses or extinguishes the blaze and limits the amount of toxic smoke that is produced by the fire. By the time the fire department arrives, the sprinkler has typically extinguished the blaze, and firefighters turn off the water supply. Automatic fire sprinkler technology is more than a century old. Today, fire sprinkler systems have been uniquely adapted to suit home environments.

Don't be taken in by sprinkler myths

There are many myths about home fire sprinkler systems. Here's the truth: Sprinklers slow a fire's dangerous growth and spread, giving you and your family the time you need to safely escape and call the fire department. Although their primary role is life safety, sprinklers also protect property.

Because they react while the fire is still small, sprinklers dramatically limit the fire and smoke damage to a home. As a result of this quick response, sprinklers also put far less water on the fire, typically only 25 gallons of water per minute. When firefighters arrive several minutes after a fire has grown and spread, they typically have to put 10 times that amount of water on the fire. The result is far greater water damage.*

Sprinklers do not activate in response to smoke; only the high temperature of a fire will trigger the sprinkler to open. Despite what you may have seen in movies, sprinklers do not all go off at once, and burned toast or cigar smoke will not trigger a sprinkler. Home fire sprinklers can be concealed under ceiling plates and painted by the manufacturer to blend in with your décor.

Residential fire sprinkler systems are affordable. According to the Home Fire Sprinkler Coalition (HFSC), sprinklers add about 1-1.5% to the overall cost of new construction for a system that can save your loved ones and irreplaceable family treasures. That's often less money than you would pay to upgrade your kitchen cabinets or carpeting. The cost of installation is higher when installing sprinklers as part of a renovation project.

Learn More: The Home Safety Council is a member of the Steering Committee of the nonprofit Home Fire Sprinkler Coalition. To learn more about this powerful fire protection technology and to watch animated clips of how home fire sprinklers work, log on to HFSC's site: http://www.homefiresprinkler.org/.

How and When to Use a Fire Extinguisher
Home Safety Council's State of Home Safety in America™ report identifies fires and burns as the third leading cause of unintentional home injury related death. While portable household fire extinguishers are not designed or intended to fight a large or spreading fire, knowing how to properly operate one may prove vital in the event of a small fire.

If fire strikes, people are advised to put their safety **first**, and belongings **second**. In many cases, the safest response is to evacuate the home and call the fire department. Under **_no circumstances_** should children be encouraged or taught to fight a home fire.

With proper training, the right portable fire extinguisher can enable you to control a containable fire until the fire department arrives, helping protect your property. Use the following guidelines if you plan to use a fire extinguisher at home:
◊   Contact your local fire department and find out where you can receive training in the proper use and selection of sizes and types of portable fire extinguishers.
◊   Select the most appropriate size and type of fire extinguisher(s) for your home
◊   Purchase UL-listed fire extinguishers and install them above the reach of children, near an exit.
◊   Read the usage and maintenance directions and keep them on hand, where you can reference them again.
◊   Before attempting to fight a fire, always report the fire by calling your local fire department emergency number.
◊   Make sure all others have evacuated the home
◊   Identify an unobstructed exit and don't ever put the fire between you and the exit.

Safety authorities use the acronym PASS to teach the preferred method of using a fire extinguisher. Position yourself near an exit to outside. Stand 6-8 feet back from the fire and don't allow the flames to come between you and the exit.
◊   **P:** Pull the pin out to unlock the operating lever
◊   **A:** Aim low: point the extinguisher nozzle (or Hose) at the base of the fire.
◊   **S:** Squeeze the lever below the handle to release the extinguishing chemical.
◊   **S:** Sweep from side to side, moving carefully toward the fire, keep the extinguisher aimed at the base of the fire and sweep back and forth until the flames appear to be out. Watch the fire area. If the fire re-ignites, repeat the process.

Be ready to abandon the effort if the fire does not extinguish or if your safety is at risk. Even if you believe you have fully extinguished the fire, have the fire department inspect the fire and check for hidden hot spots that could flare up later.

How to Handle Kitchen Fires
Research shows that most home fires begin in the kitchen. To help keep the risk of injuries low in your kitchen, keep oven mitts and pan lids easily accessible and learn the preferred method for extinguishing a pan fire. Understand how to best handle different types of fires that can occur while cooking and be aware that in many cases, evacuating the home is your best defense.

Pan Fires: Always keep a potholder, oven mitt and lid handy. If a small grease fire starts in a pan, put on an oven mitt and smother the flames by carefully sliding the lid over the pan. Sliding a lid over a burning pan is a relatively safe way to extinguish a small grease fire. Placing the lid from front to back will limit your exposure to the flames and scalding grease. With the lid covering the flames, it is easier to turn off the burner. As long as the lid stays on, the oxygen is cut off and the fire can die out naturally. This procedure is widely recommended by safety authorities and is preferred over portable fire extinguishers, which if used improperly could push burning grease and flames off the pan and spread the fire. Baking soda can also be used to extinguish a small pan fire; however the user risks greater exposure to the heat, flames and scalding grease. Do not use baking powder because it can burn and would actually add fuel to the fire.

Don't remove the lid until it is completely cool. Never pour water on a grease fire and never try to move or carry a burning pan as you can be severely burned by hot grease and can easily spread the fire.

Oven Fires: Turn off the heat and keep the door closed to prevent flames from burning you and your clothing. Call the fire department to report the incidence so that firefighters can check for possible flame spread.

Toaster Oven or Microwave Fires: Keep the door closed and unplug the appliance if you can safely reach the receptacle. Call the fire department to report the fire. Have the appliance serviced before you use it again or replace it.

Using a Portable Fire Extinguisher: If you know how to safely use a portable fire extinguisher, you may be able to put out a small, contained fire, such as a toaster oven or trash fire. Always call the fire department before fighting the fire and make sure everyone else has left the building. Never let the fire get positioned between you and the exit.

Candle Safety

Candles can provide a warm and festive atmosphere - but they can also be a fire hazard if left unattended or placed near anything flammable. Families are encouraged to enjoy the warm and inviting atmosphere of candles while always keeping fire safety in mind:

◊   Never leave burning candles unattended. Extinguish all candles before going to sleep or leaving the room.

◊   Do not permit children to keep or use candles or incense in their rooms. Candles should only be used when a sober adult is present and awake.

◊   Never use lighted candles on or near a Christmas tree or other evergreens.

◊   Keep candles at least three feet away from anything that can burn, including other decorations and wrapping paper.

◊   Always use stable, nonflammable candle holders.

◊   Place candles where they will not be knocked down or blown over and out of reach of pets and young children.

◊   Always keep burning candles up high, out of the reach of children. If you have children in your home, store candles, matches and lighters out of their sight and reach.

Home Security Safety

Home Security

Planning a vacation? Invest some time to review your home's security and to make improvements that will keep it from being vulnerable to break-ins. Walk around the perimeter of your home and objectively evaluate its vulnerability. Try to look at it the way an intruder or thief would, and make changes well before you leave town.

◊   Inspect entry doors and door frames. External doors should be hinged from the inside, not the outside where burglars can simply un-screw the hinge. If you have sliding doors, place a bar or wooden dowel in the inside track to supplement the door lock.

◊   Check to make sure all door and window locks are operable and replace or install any that are lacking or in disrepair.

◊   Purchase several light timers so you can set lights to come on in different rooms at different times during your absence.

◊   Check outside lighting and replace burned out or dim light bulbs. Re-position security lights so they shine on key areas, such as doorways, garage doors, driveways, and around windows, including the backyard. If you don't have them, consider installing motion-detection lights around the perimeter of your home.

◊   Check garage doors and windows for security and replace worn or inoperable locks. If the window is bare, install a blind or curtain over the inside so the contents cannot be viewed from outside.

◊   Do yard work before you leave. Trim limbs that could be used to access upper windows. Keep hedges neat and prune them so they can't be used by intruders for cover.

◊   Give a spare house key to a close friend or relative so they can keep an eye on the inside and outside of your home.

◊   If you plan to be gone for several days or more, arrange for someone to check your yard.

◊   To make your home even more lived in, consider asking a trusted neighbor to use your driveway to park their car while you're away.

◊   Arrange to have your newspaper delivery suspended and have mail held at the post office or picked up daily by someone you trust. Arrange for someone to take your trash out on pick-up day and return the barrels afterward.

◊   Consider purchasing a fire-proof home safe for important papers, etc. Or put valuable jewelry and paperwork in your bank safe deposit box while you're away.

◊   Avoid unwittingly inviting crime. Be careful whom you tell about your travel plans. Record a generic greeting on your answering machine rather than one indicating that you are out of town.

Before you drive away, double-check to be sure all doors and windows are locked and light timers are set. Make sure you've provided relatives or friends with your contact information so you can be reached in an emergency.

Making Your Home More Secure

If you are like most folks, your life centers on your home. It is your shelter, your gathering place and where you keep important objects and possessions relevant to your family's everyday life. You don't want anything bad to happen to it, and you don't want strangers hanging around the place. But there are times, particularly during vacations and holidays, when you just have to leave your home alone. There is no way around it unless you have someone you can really trust who is willing to housesit for you. In this How-To we look at ways to make your home more secure when you're away, as well as when you are at home.

Think Like a Burglar

According to law enforcement officials, the following facts are true:

◊   Most break-ins occur in the daytime.
◊   Most break-ins are committed by teenagers.
◊   Vacant homes are inviting targets.
◊   Burglaries are often crimes of opportunity.

You don't have to be wealthy to get robbed. People who steal for the challenge, like the cat burglars in movies and literature, are few and far between. Since there are real penalties associated with crime, people who engage in it are usually concerned with how easily they can get by with what they plan to do. Your sole possession may be your television or stereo, but if it is easy to get to it, someone may decide to make it their own. Therefore, regardless of your economic standing, the best deterrent against crime at your home involves making access difficult for potential burglars.

Have you ever had a bad day at work?--One of those days that make you want to throw up your hands and go back home to bed? As a homeowner, that is the kind of day you want any potential burglars that come sniffing around your home to have. Your goal is to install measures that will get in their hair and nip at their heels. If someone wants to get in your house bad enough, he can get in--but, you don't have to make it easy for him. There are many things that can be done to take advantage of what police consider to be the three worst enemies of a criminal: light, noise and time. Why should a burglar work himself to death and risk being caught at a well-secured house when easier prey is right down the road? Especially when there are locks at every point of entry, an alarm is blaring and the exterior of the house is lit up like a World Series game!

Shed Light on the Situation

It's funny, but people engaged in illegal activities don't care much about receiving a lot of exposure while plying their trade. It might have something to do with the threat of the criminal justice system--or of an upset homeowner with a shotgun and an attitude. When planning your home security, capitalize on this fact by refusing to cooperate with potential criminals.

Although many burglaries take place during the day, the same rule still applies: burglars want to be inconspicuous.

Most folks are at work during the day. As a bonus, the kids are at school and the neighborhood is quiet. If a burglar can look like a meter-reader, delivery person or professional mover, so much the better for his enterprise. Brazen daytime criminals may be harder to guard against, but there are a few important things you can do to help deter them from attempting to crack your house.

◊   Organize or participate in a neighborhood watch program. These programs are effective. They work to make an unfavorable atmosphere for crime.
◊   Post signs--neighborhood watch signs let potential criminals know that neighbors watch out for neighbors in your community. Also, post signs stating that you have a monitored security system in your house. It doesn't matter whether you really have one or not; potential criminals will think twice before putting it to the test.
◊   Keep bushes close to the house neatly trimmed. Large unruly shrubbery provides a hiding place for criminals who are trying to gain access to your home.

There are several things you can do to make your home less vulnerable at night. Many people are home in the evening, so burglars must rely more on being hidden from view to do their dirty work. Remember, light is one of a criminal's three main enemies. Don't give them places to hide.

◊   Motion activated flood lights are an inexpensive way to shed light on unexpected visitors. Positioned near points of entry, they automatically expose the area any time someone (or some thing) comes near.
◊   Street lights cast a pale glow over a wide area. If you don't have one, your electric company may be willing to cooperate with you and your neighbors if you express sufficient interest.
◊   Make sure your bushes are neatly trimmed, and don't position outbuildings close to points of entry to your main house. Objects that cast large shadows or otherwise obscure areas near points of entry to your house are marks in the pro column for criminals evaluating your property.
◊   Be sure to have operational porch lights. Peepholes are important for allowing you to see who is at the door before opening it. Don't rely on the little chains which are often installed on doors to prevent them from opening more than a few inches--you might get a nasty surprise!

Be Home Whether You're Gone or Not

Although some burglars are brazen enough to break in and steal from a family watching TV in the next room, most burglaries take place when the homeowners are away. So, make the house seem like it is occupied even while you are gone.

If possible, it is always good to have a trusted neighbor visit your house to open and close drapes and turn lights on and off. Have a neighbor collect your mail and newspapers, too. If this isn't possible, call and have delivery stopped while you are away. If you are to be gone for an extended period of time, arrange to have the yard maintained while you are away. You want the place to look just as it would if you were home.

Turning your lights on and off is easy, even if you don't have someone to do it for you, since programmable timers are available which can be set to do the job. The simplest timers available can turn lights on and off at the same time each day. If your house is watched over the course of several days, these timers may not be totally convincing since their performance will be predictable. More sophisticated programmable timers can vary these times by day, and new digital timers offer variable and random programming for a much more realistic touch. If you are creative with these timers you can set them to create the illusion of someone moving through the house and switching lights on and off. Also attach radios and even televisions to the timers to more fully create the illusion that someone is at home.

Lock It Up

So far we have only discussed ways to deter someone from attempting to break into your house. Suppose they decide to try; what will happen then? In two-thirds of completed burglaries, the burglar entered the home through unlocked windows or doors. Could the home-owners have made it any more simple? Time is another enemy of criminals. Make sure that getting into your house is going to take a while. Hopefully, the burglar will give up and go to greener pastures.

Garages

Garages which are attached to houses are inviting to criminals. If a burglar can gain access to the garage, he can work unseen for long periods of time to get into the main house; plus, he can often use the homeowners own tools to do it!

◊   If you have windows in your garage, keep them covered. There is a lot about your garage you don't want potential criminals to know about. For example: Are there valuable tools inside, or tools that will help with the break-in? Is the car present? Is there access to the attic from inside the garage? Is there a ladder inside which could aid in reaching upper windows even if the door going into the main house is securely dead bolted? This person is after your hard-earned stuff. Keep him guessing.

◊   Keep garage doors locked at all times with a good quality padlock when you are away. It is a good idea, although not practical for home owners with automatic garage door openers, to do this all the time--even when you are at home.

◊   Garages (or carports!) with attic access provide a convenient way to get into the house through the ceiling. At the very least, keep the attic access securely locked. Seal it completely and provide access only from inside the secured area of the house if possible.

◊   If the door separating your garage from your main house is an ordinary interior door, replace it with a solid core exterior door with a deadbolt lock. And keep it locked! Having to unlock the door each time you arrive at the house is less inconvenient than being robbed.

Patio Doors

Patio doors are another weak link in the security chain. They suffer from the combined weaknesses of windows and doors.

◊   To prevent sliding glass doors from being lifted from their frames, install shims along the top frames. These fit in the tracks between the top of the door and frame and prevent the door from being raised high enough to be removed.

◊   Patio door locks are not particularly reliable. Install locking pins which go through the doors and frames.

◊   A thick wooden dowel or piece of angle iron placed along the bottom track of a sliding door will wedge it shut and prevent it from being opened even if someone breaks the lock. You can also drill through the door frames where they overlap and insert a hollow screw which will prevent the doors from moving.

Exterior Doors

◊   Wooden exterior doors should be of solid core construction. For the best protection, doors should be metal with metal frames. Metal frames are less susceptible to tampering than wooden frames.

◊   Glass panel doors should have either safety tempered or security screen glass if breaking the glass would allow someone to reach through the door to unlock it.

◊   Standard key-in-the-knob locks provide little security. All exterior doors should include deadbolt locks with at least a one-inch throw. Deadbolt locks are available with single or double cylinders. Double cylinder locks provide additional security because they require a key for operation from both outside and inside, preventing someone from being able to open the door by breaking a glass, reaching in and flipping the bolt. Keys should be readily available to people trying to get out of the house, however, in case of an emergency.

◊   Exterior doors should not be hinged to open outward. In this case, the door can be taken down by removing the hinge pins. Remount the door with the hinges inside. If this is not possible, install hinges with non-removable pins.

◊   Don't hide your keys on or around the house, and never put your name on your key chain. An honest person might return your keys, but a dishonest person would have access to everything they were made for--and could find out where you live!

Windows

All windows should be locked or pinned. Commercial products are available to do the job, but even if you don't have the budget for commercial hardware, several simple and inexpensive solutions are available to greatly increase the security of your windows.

Drill a 3/16" hole through the inside window frame and into, but not through, the outside frame. A pin, nail or bolt can be inserted into this hole, securely locking the window closed. Taking the extra time to thread a bolt into this hole will prevent someone from being able to open the window even if they break the glass to undo the stock window latch. The bolt could be easily backed out with a screwdriver when you need to open the window.

Pay special attention to basement windows. Bushes or trees may hide these windows, providing a place for criminals to work without being seen. You may wish to reinforce the windows with security bars, wire mesh or Plexiglas.

wwwww.www.nemmar.com

Draw Attention to the Crime

Noise is another of the burglar's worst enemies, and you can generate a lot of it with the many alarm systems now available. From monitored and hard-wired systems, to battery powered local alarm components, there are many options available. Having an alarm system may certainly reduce the possibility of a burglar successfully robbing your home, and may increase the possibility that you or a neighbor will see something that may incriminate the bumbling burglar who was unfortunate enough to set it off. Alarms do not, however, reduce the need for adequate locks and other security measures.

Alarm Systems

Monitored alarm systems are the most effective, but also the most expensive. With these system, the monitoring company automatically calls your home when the alarm goes off. If there is no answer, or if the person who answers gives the wrong password, the police are dispatched to your house. Before investing in one of these systems, shop around and collect references from installers and monitoring companies.

Unmonitored alarms serve a single purpose--they are obnoxious and nerve-racking by design to draw attention to themselves and, by extension, to any criminal activities that may be taking place in their vicinity. They are deterrents only. If ignored, they will do nothing to prevent a burglary, and unmonitored alarms depend upon someone in the neighborhood to call the police. Many of these types of alarms are no longer expensive and can be purchased and installed easily by homeowners.

In Case the Burglar Succeeds

If your alarms and neighborhood watch work well, and if your local police respond quickly, your family stands a reasonable chance of losing little property in a burglary. Nothing ruins a burglar's day when she is trying to steal someone's property quite like seeing the flashing lights of police cars. Unfortunately, burglary victims seldom see their valuable property again once it has successfully been stolen. There are steps that should be taken by every homeowner, which will help when the time comes to settle with their insurance company.
◊   Maintain lists and photographs or videotapes of your possessions. This will make it easier for the insurance company to establish the value of the possessions, which have been stolen (or lost in a disaster).
◊   Keep these lists, photos and videotapes, as well as special items like small family heirlooms or small objects of high value, in a fireproof safe. These safes are readily available and are thorns in the sides of fleet-footed criminals.
◊   Mark your valuables with an engraver or ultra-violet marker. If any items are recovered, even if they are damaged, the fact that they are clearly marked as being yours may be useful evidence in the case against the person who violated your home.

Home Security and Fire Safety

Sometimes, families seeking to protect themselves from one hazard unknowingly put themselves at risk from others. For example, home security can protect people from intruders, but it can also be harmful if security features prevent quick escape during a fire emergency. Home security and fire safety can and should work together and you are encouraged to examine entryways, both doors and windows, to make sure home security doesn't interfere with your fire escape plan.

Security Locks

Every home entry door should be equipped with a sturdy dead-bolt lock that is properly installed and maintained in good working condition. When choosing deadbolt locks for your home, keep the following guidelines in mind.
Avoid two-keyed deadbolt locks that require a key on both the inside and outside of an entry door. These keyed locks can trap people inside if there is a fire. Keys can easily be misplaced when the deadbolt is locked, making it impossible to escape.
◊   Replace any two-keyed entry locks with common deadbolt locks that only require keyed entry from the outside and have a turning or "throwing" bolt or latch inside.
◊   If your home entry doors have two-keyed deadbolt locks, protect your family in the meantime by keeping the key to your deadbolt on a hook near the door but away from any windows. Make sure all responsible family members know exactly where to find the key and how to use it quickly in an emergency.

Window Security/Burglar Bars

Security bars on doors and windows can provide a strong defense against intruders and give families greater confidence in their home's safety. However that same strength can prove deadly in a fire emergency. Bars welded over an escape route not only trap victims inside; they also prevent firefighters from being able to get them out. Families need to evaluate their fire escape route to make sure security measures do not hinder a quick escape:

Bars on doors and windows can provide a strong defense against intruders and give families greater confidence in their home's security. However that same strength can prove deadly in a fire emergency. New research shows that home fires grow so fast and spread so quickly that people may three minutes or less to survive a fire and its deadly smoke. Bars welded over an escape route not only trap victims inside; they also prevent firefighters from being able to get them out. Families need to make sure security measures do not slow down a quick escape:
◊   In rooms with window bars, install a quick-release mechanism on at least one exit.
◊   Purchase quick-release devices together with new bars, or have them installed on bars that are currently in your home.
◊   In an emergency you can use the release device to quickly unlock the bars from inside, usually with a lever or pedal, to make your escape path clear for immediate exit.
◊   Know that quick-release devices can only be opened from the inside of the home, and do not affect your home's security.

◊   Contact an iron contractor to have quick-release devices installed on security bars in your home.

Winter Safety

Home Safety Tips for a Safe and Healthy Winter
Use the following tips to avoid potential dangers of home fires, carbon monoxide (CO) poisoning and power outages during the winter months:

Carbon Monoxide (CO) Poisoning Precaution: Heating Systems and Gas Appliances
◊   Install at least one CO alarm to protect sleeping areas.
◊   Have a trained professional inspect, clean and tune-up central heating system and repair leaks or other problems; fireplaces and woodstoves should also be inspected each year and cleaned or repaired as needed.
◊   Keep gas appliances properly adjusted and serviced.
◊   Never use an oven or range to heat your home.
◊   Never use a gas grill inside your home or in a closed garage.

Home Fire Precautions: Fireplaces and Wood Stoves
◊   Install at least one smoke alarm on every level of your home and near sleeping areas
◊   Burn only wood- not trash, cardboard boxes, or Christmas trees because these items increase the risk of uncontrolled fires.
◊   Have a professional chimney sweep inspect the chimneys you use regularly every year for cracks, blockages and leaks and have them cleaned and repaired as needed.
◊   Keep all persons and flammable objects, including wallpaper, bedding, clothing and pets, at least 36 inches away from fireplaces and wood stoves.
◊   Open flues before fireplaces are used.

Portable Space Heaters
◊   Purchase electric space heaters that bear the mark of an independent testing laboratory, such as UL.
◊   Turn off space heaters before leaving a room or going to sleep.
◊   Supervise children and pets at all times when a portable space heater is in use
◊   Use proper fuel in kerosene space heaters.
◊   Never use space heaters to dry flammable items such as clothing or blankets.
◊   Keep all flammable objects at least three feet from space heaters.

Power Outage Precautions: Lighting Sources and Perishable Food
◊   Stock up on batteries, flashlights, portable radios, canned foods, manual can openers, bottled water and blankets.
◊   Use flashlights instead of candles to avoid a possible fire hazard.

◊   Run water at a trickle to help prevent pipes from freezing and bursting if outside temperatures are below freezing for an extended period of time and your home has no heat.
◊   Store perishable food outside in the snow or in an unheated outside building if power goes out.

Holiday Safety

Don't Let Hazards Be an Uninvited Guest This Season
Do you have guests coming to stay this holiday season? Use this advice to help you prepare your home for friends and family of all ages:
◊   Check the lights over all stairways, hallways, porches and entries to ensure all bulbs are working and bright enough to illuminate the entire area below. Stick to the maximum safe wattage, which is printed inside the fixture.
◊   If tubs and showers don't already have non-stick strips or mats in them, install them now. Attach a sturdy grab-bar on the edge of the tub. Place nightlights inside bathrooms or in the hallways leading to them.
◊   If your guests will include toddlers, purchase safety gates and place them at the tops and bottoms of stairways.
◊   If you have an attached garage and/or fuel-burning heat or appliances, your home should have a carbon monoxide (CO) detector installed to protect sleeping areas.
◊   Post the local and national poison control hotline number, as well as other local emergency numbers, near every telephone. The National Poison Control Hotline is 1-800-222-1222.
◊   To guard against curious children, make sure all matches and lighters, medications, household cleaners, toiletries and other dangerous products are in original containers with child-proof closures and/or locked in a cabinet. Remember to keep purses, backpacks and luggage out of children's reach too.
◊   Every home must have working smoke alarms on each level and protecting all the places people will be sleeping. Before guests arrive, test every smoke alarm and replace any dead or missing batteries. Walk through your home fire escape plan with guests, pointing out primary and secondary exits and the outside meeting place.
◊   Prevent scalds by turning your hot water heater temperature to 120F or less.
◊   When toddlers are visiting, use toilet seat locks to prevent drowning. Be aware that buckets, spas, tubs and all standing water are a serious drowning risk for early walkers.
◊   Make guest rooms safe as well as welcoming. Place a nightlight inside each room and the hallway outside it. Provide each guest with a working flashlight. If possible, place a telephone in each guest room as well.

Tips for Holiday Electrical Safety
Holiday lights and electrical decorations create a warm and festive atmosphere both inside and outside the home - but they can also create fire hazards and electrical shock risks, if

they are not handled properly. Take the following precautions while decorating your home this year:

◊   Inspect holiday lights and extension cords before decorating. Replace any that are fraying or otherwise damaged. Pay special attention to lights, cords or decorations that may have been damaged from winter weather conditions.

◊   Check for red or green UL marks on all light strings and extension cords. The green holographic UL Mark means the light strings should be used only indoors. The red holographic UL Mark indicates the light strings can be used both inside and out -- and can withstand conditions related to outdoor use.

◊   Follow manufacturer's guidelines for stringing light sets together. As a general rule, Underwriters Laboratories (UL) recommends using no more than three standard-size sets of lights together.

◊   Do not overload extension cords or electrical receptacles.

◊   Unplug all holiday lights when you go to sleep or leave home.

◊   Automatic lighting timers can be used to ensure that lights are not left on. These are available for both indoor and outdoor applications.

◊   Roll up excess electrical cords and keep them away from high traffic areas. Do not run electrical cords under rugs.

◊   Never keep an extension cord plugged in when it is not in use.

◊   When replacing a light bulb, make sure that the replacement bulb is of equal or lesser wattage than that recommended by the manufacturer.

◊   If you have children in your home, use safety caps on all electrical receptacles

Trim the Tree Safely

Trimming the tree is a traditional holiday pastime; however, Christmas trees pose a serious danger to households if not properly cared for. Some tips when selecting and caring for your Christmas tree this holiday season:

◊   When purchasing live, cut trees or greens, carefully inspect the needles. If they're brown or break easily, the greenery isn't fresh and poses a greater fire risk. Test for freshness by bending a few needles in half. If they snap in two, the tree is dry - look for one on which the needles spring back to their original shape. When you take your tree home, put it in a sturdy, non-tip stand filled with water.

◊   Keep live trees supplied with water at all times; dehydrated Christmas trees can catch fire more easily.

◊   Make sure the tree is at least three feet away from any flame or heat source and try to position it near an outlet so that cords are not running long distances. Do not place the tree where it may block exits.

◊   Never decorate trees with candles.

◊   Inspect electrical lights and extension cords for wear and tear and replace any cords that are beginning to fray or have broken sockets; pay special attention to outdoor lights that have been exposed to winter weather conditions. To reduce fire hazards and extend the life of outdoor decorative lights, bring them inside after the holidays.

◊   Avoid cluttering outlets - string no more than three strands of lights together and make sure all lights bear the mark of an independent organization such as Underwriters Laboratories (UL).

◊   When decorating outdoors, use only those lights listed for outdoor use. Unplug all lights - inside and out -- before going to bed or leaving home.

◊   Safely dispose of the tree when it begins dropping needles. Dried-out trees are flammable and should not be left inside the home or garage, or placed against the house.

◊   Make sure your home is equipped with working smoke alarms and fire extinguishers. Don't forget to install, test and maintain these devices in accordance with the manufacturer's instructions.

◊   Develop and practice a fire escape plan for your household so overnight guests are familiar with your procedures.

Halloween Safety

Halloween represents a time of fun and festivity. Candy corn, costumed kids and carved pumpkins set the scene. Follow these simple tips to make sure your *Cinderella* or *Frankenstein* does not get spooked by holiday dangers:

◊   Only permit trick-or-treating at the homes of friends and neighbors you know well.

◊   When purchasing costumes and accessories, buy only those marked "flame retardant" or "flame resistant".

◊   Avoid costumes made of long, flowing material and accessories that can move or blow over open flames.

◊   Choose costumes that are light, bright and clearly visible. Apply reflective tape to the front and back of costumes to help motorists see your child.

◊   Avoid costumes that block your child's vision and increase the risk of a fall.

◊   Be sure that costume accessories, such as knives and swords, are made of soft, flexible material.

◊   To keep vision clear, consider using face paint instead of a mask.

◊   Give your child a flashlight to light the way and signal drivers of his or her presence. Never carry candles, torches or other open flames as part of a costume.

◊   Examine all treats thoroughly before allowing children to eat them.

◊   Throw away open treats, those not in their original wrapping and homemade goodies from unknown sources.

◊   Slice open fruit to check for foreign objects.

◊   Contact the Poison Control Center Hotline if you believe your child has consumed anything hazardous. The national hotline number is 1-800-222-1222. Notify local police of any suspicious candy.

◊   Young children should never help carve a pumpkin. As an alternative, decorate pumpkins with markers, paint or stickers.

When hosting trick-or-treaters at your home, keep these safety tips in mind:

◊   Do not use candles when decorating porches to prevent costumes from catching fire. Light jack-o-lanterns with small flashlights instead of candles.

◊   Provide bright walkway and porch lighting to help prevent falls.

◊   Offer treats wrapped in their original packages.

◊   If you decorate your home with candles, keep them well away from crepe paper, leaves and other flammable objects. Extinguish all candles when leaving the room.

Enjoy Fireworks Safely

According to the U.S. Consumer Product Safety Commission (CPSC), in 2003 an estimated 9,700 people were treated in hospital emergency rooms for injuries associated with fireworks. More than half the injuries were burns and most involved the hands, eyes and head and 50 percent of the victims were children under age 15.

As the July 4th holiday approaches, families are urged to enjoy fireworks the safer way, by attending locally sanctioned fireworks shows presented by professionals who adhere to safety codes.

Fireworks are not toys, they are devices designed to reach high temperatures, to burn and spark, and to explode and launch. They are unpredictable by nature and too dangerous for nonprofessional users.

Dr. Gary Smith, Director of the Center for Injury Research and Policy at Columbus Children's Research Institute in Ohio conducted a 22-year study* of fireworks injuries treated in emergency rooms. What he found may help you understand the risk. Here is a sampling:

◊   67 percent of sparkler-related injuries were among children 5 years or younger

◊   70 percent of patients treated for all fireworks injuries were male

◊   Adult supervision was present in 54 percent of the cases

◊   The eyes were injured in nearly one-third of the cases

◊   The average age of patients was eight and ½ years

Although many states permit fireworks use by consumers, only trained and experienced experts should use or transport fireworks.

Disaster Prevention Safety

<u>Emergency Planning</u>

Before an emergency occurs, consider what steps will be important to safeguard your family and loved ones. Meet with your family to discuss the plan and practice it. Keep the plan simple so all family members can remember the important points.

1. Anticipate Difficulties and Inconveniences - Create plans to anticipate situations in order to be able to make informed decisions during a crisis. Physical and emotional stresses may cloud decision-making skills.

2. Determine Your Evacuation Plan - Know the evacuation routes leading away from your community. Plan an alternative place where family members agree to meet in the event you cannot meet at home, and determine alternative modes of travel if transportation is disrupted. Remember; follow the advice of authorities about evacuation - they do not ask people to leave unless they believe lives are in danger.

3. Memorize Emergency Contacts - Be sure each family member knows whom to contact - perhaps a friend or relative out-of-state - in the event local communications are impaired. Discuss any of your family's medical needs with someone out-of-town and in the immediate neighborhood. Make a list of insurance, banking, medical and other essential telephone numbers and account information and give it to a trusted family member. Consider including a spare charge card or ATM card with the list, so that you can access money in an emergency or they can access it for you.

4. Develop a Plan at Work - Talk with co-workers to develop an internal emergency plan. Remember to include in your plan to assign specific responsibilities in the event of an emergency.

5. Plan how to Communicate in an Emergency - Keep everyone's work, home, school, and cellular numbers updated and share them with everyone in the family. Remember that often in an emergency, cellular phones may not work because the systems are over-loaded. Because communications are difficult in an emergency, it makes sense to plan a family/friend "tree", so you only need to make one or two calls, then others make designated calls on your behalf from there.

6. Keep a Battery-Operated Radio - In the event of an emergency, you will want a battery-operated radio in order to listen to what local law enforcement and emergency management authorities are telling the community.

7. Strengthen Personal Fitness - Be prepared for the physical requirements of dealing with circumstances outside your daily routine. Being healthy and alert can mean life or death.

8. Prepare Family Members, Especially Children - Reassure children that adults will take care of them in the event of a

disaster. Knowing there is a plan will minimize fear. Also consider the needs of older family members and close friends who live near you and involve them in your emergency plan and help them develop their own. Be aware of their medical needs and any immobility issues and help them craft solutions to potential problems ahead of time.

9. Plan for your Pets - Plan where you will take your pets in the event you will stay at a hotel or other public place where pets are not allowed. Store leashes and pet carriers where they can be easily retrieved. Consider placing a bottle of water inside a carrier so your pet will have a temporary water supply close at hand if you have to quickly leave.

10. Maintain a Disaster Supplies Kit - Both natural and human-made disasters can create a need to be self-sufficient for a short period until help arrives.

Family Disaster Plan
The following information is taken from publication #L-191 of the Federal Emergency Management Agency (FEMA), developed in cooperation with the American Red Cross.

Your Family Disaster Plan
Where will your family be when disaster strikes? They could be anywhere - at work, at school, or in the car. How will you find each other? Will you know if your children are safe?

Disaster can strike quickly and without warning. It can force you to evacuate your neighborhood or confine you to your home. What would you do if basic services-water, gas, electricity or telephones-were cut off? Local officials and relief workers will be on the scene after a disaster, but they cannot reach everyone right away.

Families can and do cope with disaster by preparing in advance and working together as a team. Follow the steps listed in this brochure to create your family's disaster plan. Knowing what to do in advance is your best protection and your responsibility.

4 STEPS TO SAFETY
1. Find out what could happen to you. Contact your local emergency management or civic defense office and American Red Cross chapter--be prepared to take notes:
◊   Ask what types of disasters are most likely to happen. Request information on how to prepare for each.
◊   Learn about your community's warning signals: what they sound like and what you should do when you hear them.
◊   Ask about animal care after disaster. Animals may not be allowed inside emergency shelters due to health regulations.
◊   Find out how to help elderly or disabled persons, if needed.
◊   Next, find out about the disaster plans at your workplace, your children's school or daycare center and other places where your family spends time.

2. Create a Disaster Plan - Meet with your family and discuss why you need to prepare for disaster. Explain the dangers of fire, severe weather and earthquake to children. Plan to share responsibilities and work together as a team.
◊   Discuss the types of disasters that are most likely to happen. Explain what to do in each case.
◊   Pick two places to meet:
    1.   Outside your home in case of a sudden emergency, like a fire.
    2.   Outside your neighborhood in case you can't return home. Everyone must know the address and phone number.
◊   Ask an out-of-state friend to be your "family contact." After a disaster, it's often easier to call long distance. Other family members should call this person and tell them where they are. Everyone must know your contact's phone number.
◊   Discuss what to do in an evacuation. Plan how to take care of your pets.

3. Complete This Checklist
◊   Post emergency telephone numbers by phones (fire, police, ambulance, etc.)
◊   Teach children how and when to call 911 or your local Emergency Medical Services number for emergency help.
◊   Show each family member how and when to turn off the water, gas and electricity at the main switches.
◊   Check if you have adequate insurance coverage.
◊   Make sure the adults in your home know how and when to use the fire extinguisher (ABC type), and show them where it's kept.
◊   Install smoke alarms on each level of your home especially in or near all sleeping areas.
◊   Conduct a home hazard hunt.
◊   Stock emergency supplies and assemble a Disaster Supplies Kit.
◊   Take a Red Cross first aid and CPR class.
◊   Determine the best escape routes from your home. Find two ways out (usually a door and a window) of each room.
◊   Find the safe spots in your home for each type of disaster.

4. Practice and Maintain Your Plan
◊   Quiz your kids every six months to see if they remember what to do.
◊   Conduct fire and emergency evacuation drills.
◊   Replace stored water every three months and stored food every three months.
◊   Test and recharge your fire extinguisher(s) according to manufacturer's instructions.
◊   Test your smoke alarms monthly and change the batteries at least once a year, or when the alarm "chirps" signaling that the batteries are running low.

Change batteries in _____ each year.

If Disaster Strikes:
◊   Remain calm and patient. Put your plan to action.
◊   Check for injuries
◊   Give first aid and get help for seriously injured people.

◊   Listen to your battery powered radio for news and instructions
◊   Evacuate, if advised to do so. Wear protective clothing and sturdy shoes.
◊   Check for damage in your home.
    o   Use flashlights -- do not light matches or turn on electrical switches, if you suspect damage.
    o   Check for fire hazards and other household hazards.
    o   Sniff for gas leaks, starting at the water heater. If you smell gas or suspect a leak, turn off the main gas valve, open windows, and get everyone outside quickly.
    o   Shut off any other damaged utilities.
    o   Clean up spilled medicines, bleaches, gasoline and other flammable liquids immediately.

Remember to:
◊   Confine or secure your pets.
◊   Call your family contact--do not use the telephone again unless it is a life-threatening emergency.
◊   Check on your neighbors, especially elderly or disabled persons.
◊   Make sure you have an adequate water supply in case service is cut off.
◊   Stay away from downed power lines.

The Federal Emergency Management Agency's Family Protection Program and the American Red Cross' Disaster Education Program are nationwide efforts to help citizens prepare for disasters of all types. For more information on preparing your home and family for disasters, call your local Red Cross or visit the web sites at http://www.redcross.org/ or http://www.fema.gov/.

Flood Safety
Floods are one of the most frequent and costly natural disasters - many of which fall on the heels of other disasters such as hurricanes and tornadoes. Rushing waters and debris contribute to most of the damage caused by flooding.

"Floods are among the most devastating natural disasters that many homeowners face," said Rocky Lopes, Home Safety Council board member and manager of community disaster education for the American Red Cross. "Preparedness is the key to ensure your property - and your family - stays intact."

Homeowners are urged to take the following precautions this severe weather season:
Before a Flood
◊   Develop a family disaster plan. Plan where you would go for safety if a flood required you to leave your home. Involve all family members in this planning process.
◊   Create a disaster supplies kit.
◊   Protect home heating, water and electricity systems in your home - Have your furnace, water heater and electric panel raised to higher floors or the attic by a professional if these utility systems are in a flood-prone area of the home, like the basement.
◊   Listen to the radio or television for updated emergency information - Use a National Oceanic and Atmospheric Administration (NOAA) Weather Radio or a portable, battery-powered radio to get updated flood information.
◊   Have a professional install check valves in building sewer traps - Floodwater can get backed up into the drains of your home. As a last resort, use large corks or stoppers to plug showers, tubs and basins.
◊   Fill your bathtubs, sinks and plastic bottles with clean water - Severe floods may interrupt utility services such as water. When floods threaten, it's best to keep drains corked, but be sure to fill sinks and tubs with fresh water first.

How To Prepare for Severe Storms and Hurricanes
When a hurricane threatens, your primary concern is for the safety of your family. But your house is important too, and even though you may be evacuating the area, your home requires whatever forms of protection you can provide. The key is to make plans and provisions to protect your home long before a hurricane becomes anything more than an unpleasant possibility. This way, when a storm does threaten, you can concentrate on the safety of your family and know that you've done your best to protect your home.

Before the Storm: What Can You Do To Protect Your Home?
Hurricanes pose both wind and flood damage potential, but there are things you can do to greatly reduce the impact on your home. One of your main goals is to prevent the wind from damaging the home in such a way that allows water to enter and do further damage. Make sure your doors and windows are secure. Wind inside your home will push upward against the roof and try to lift it, while winds outside create a suction pressure, almost doubling the roof's load.

Despite the best attempts at protecting your home, however, damage may still occur. Take a look at your insurance policies to make sure you're adequately covered. Keep lists or video tapes of your belongings as documentation for the insurance company.

Prepare Your Roof
◊   If you have an exterior television antenna, you may want to disconnect and remove it.
◊   Remove roof turbines and cover the holes where they were installed. Otherwise, high winds could remove them for you, leaving a gaping hole through which heavy rain could come into your home to do damage.
◊   Check for loose or damaged shingles, and seal around flashings, chimneys or vent pipes if necessary. A roof in good repair is much better able to stand the torture inflicted upon it by a storm. For more on roof repair, visit How to Repair Shingled Roofing.
◊   Check for loose and clogged gutters and downspouts. Backed-up gutters can send water flowing into your home in

the event of heavy rains. For detailed information, see How To Maintain Your Gutters.

◊   If your roof is damaged in a storm, use tarps secured with ropes and nails to cover it as soon as you can. Heavy rains usually occur during and after a hurricane, and water can cause devastating damage to the interior of your home. Any step you can take to minimize water damage will help.

Cover Those Windows

If you live in an area vulnerable to hurricanes, consider installing storm shutters. They are available in several different types, and will go a long way toward keeping the damaging wind and rain from entering through your home's windows. As a side benefit, they may reduce your home insurance premium.

Secure The Doors

Steel entry doors provide the best protection for your home. Double doors and French doors are most vulnerable to high winds. But no matter what type of door you've got, a hurricane panel is your best option to keep damage at a minimum. These galvanized steel or PVC panels are available at Lowe's. You can also nail plywood over your doors for protection and to help keep out water and debris.

If you have double doors that have no structural member in the center between them, you may need to purchase and install special hardware to more adequately secure the doors where they meet. Bolts which secure the door into the framing at both the top and bottom greatly increase the door's strength. Wedge sliding glass doors with a dowel or piece of broom handle to prevent them from jumping their tracks when the wind howls.

Provide stiffening support for garage doors. The pressure from winds increases with the door's size, and wide doors particularly need bracing for stability during high winds. Make your own vertical supports by nailing two 2x4s together and attaching them vertically to the inside of your garage door with "L" brackets. Use as many as you feel are necessary to support your door.

Button Up the Yard

Flailing tree limbs may pose a danger in high winds. Trim trees to avoid the possibility of large limbs doing damage to your house. Also, selectively thinning out the branches to allow wind to more easily pass through and will reduce the potential for damage to the tree itself. Dead or damaged branches should be removed, otherwise they could become flying missiles aimed straight for your house or that of your neighbors.

Lawn furniture, ornaments, toys, grills and exterior potted plants should be taken inside. Anything that can't be brought in should be tied down. Sheds, doghouses, playhouses, swing sets, and boat trailers should be secured with tie-downs, turnbuckles and cable or stout rope. Concrete tie-down spaces are a good home improvement in areas susceptible to hurricanes. If you don't have concrete mounted tie-downs

when the weather threatens, screw type tie-downs secured deep in the ground must suffice.

If you live in a mobile home it is particularly important that you inspect and repair your home's tie-downs.

Cars, Trucks & Boats

If you live in a low-lying area, move your car, truck or boat to higher ground, preferably to an enclosed garage or warehouse.

If you must leave a boat behind, don't leave it in the water. If the boat's left outside, anchor the trailer tongue of a trailered boat to a firm spot on the ground. Lash the boat to the trailer; let some air out of the tires. Add water for weight, but make sure you keep it below engine level. Stow all loose gear (outriggers, canvas tops, etc.) and remove electronics and other valuables to avoid damage and theft. Cover the boat to keep additional water and debris out.

Protect Your Family, Too!

The No. 1 rule: Get every member of your household involved. Set aside time for a family meeting to discuss the following:

◊   An Evacuation Package: We're talking keepsakes here - personal items you'd hate to lose, things insurance could never replace. Examples: your children's baby books and photos, an heirloom quilt. Place them in a water and fire proof container. Include important family documents, such as birth certificates and insurance policies. Make sure everyone knows where the package is kept and assign a family member responsibility for it in case you need to evacuate.

◊   Safety Kit: Put together a safety kit. Include a first aid kit and essential medications, a fire extinguisher, packaged or canned non-perishable food and a non-electric can opener, water (no more than 6 months old - mark the date) in a non-breakable container, protective clothing, rainwear and blankets. Make sure everyone in the household knows where this kit is kept.

◊   Emergency Contact: Pick someone to call (a friend or family member out of state) in case a hurricane hits or you need to evacuate. This contact can be the person who lets others know where you are and that you're safe so you won't have to spend precious time doing so.

Hurricane Safety

The Atlantic hurricane season begins in June and lasts through the end of November. There are simple steps families can take before and after a storm that will go a long way toward increased hurricane safety. By following these hurricane preparedness guidelines, you can increase your family's safety as well as the stability and security of your home.

◊   If you live in a coastal area, install hurricane shutters to protect windows and doors from powerful winds.

◊   Remove dead and diseased trees and branches. Weak trees and branches are easily broken off by hurricane winds and may damage a home.

◊   Identify items in the yard that should be brought inside in case of a hurricane. Items such as lawn furniture and trash cans may become airborne during a severe storm.

◊   If in a coastal community, elevate the home. This can help minimize the damage to property because of floods and storm surges.

◊   Hurricanes bring intense rainfall. Keep rain gutters, outside stairwells, window wells, drain lines and down sprouts clean to prevent flooding.

◊   Ask an insurance agent or local emergency management office for information about the National Flood Insurance Program. Regular homeowner policies do not cover damage from flooding that may result from a hurricane.

◊   Every family should have a disaster plan which helps avoid or lessen the impact of a natural disaster. Use Home Safety Council guidelines to develop a family emergency plan and create a disaster supply kit.

◊   During a storm, gather your family in the safest area of your home, an interior room without windows, usually on the first floor of the house or building.

◊   Always follow official instructions before, during and after a hurricane. If evacuation was necessary, do not return home until authorities say to do so.

◊   After returning home, stay away from all storm damaged areas.

Health Concerns

Some readers of this book may not be interested in learning very in-depth information about health concerns. They may only be interested in getting a general working knowledge of health concern topics. For those readers, I would recommend that you read the first two sections titled *Asbestos Insulation* and *Radon Gas*. Those are the sections I wrote completely from my own personal experience and knowledge from being involved in real estate for many years. The health concerns sections that have the DOE and EPA research get into more in-depth details about each topic. If you are only interested in learning the basics, then don't get too caught up in trying to memorize the in-depth details discussed in the DOE and EPA health concerns sections. Choose the health concern topics that you feel are most useful to you for now, and then you can learn the more in-depth topics later if needed.

Some readers of this book may not be interested in learning very in-depth information about health concerns. They may only be interested in getting a general working knowledge of health concern topics. For those readers, I would recommend that you read the first two sections titled Asbestos Insulation and Radon Gas. Those are the sections I wrote completely from my own personal experience and knowledge from being involved in real estate for many years.

Note: Some of the information contained in different sections of these Health Concerns chapters are similar. This is because there are many important aspects that pertain to both sections discussed. I hope you don't feel that the information is redundant in those sections. It will only benefit you to read it several times to make sure you know the information well enough so it doesn't cost you time and money later. Also, some of the graphics in this book are low-resolution images from the DOE and EPA web sites that do not have perfect clarity. I apologize if any of the graphics or images are a little grainy and not perfectly clear. The DOE and EPA did not have high-resolution images for some of the graphics. Since my books are all self-edited and self-published, I do the best I can with the time and resources I have available.

Asbestos Insulation

Asbestos has been used for insulation as far back in time as ancient Greece. Almost all older houses have had asbestos insulation on the heating pipes. A thin layer of asbestos can sometimes be found on old hot air ducts if there is a furnace. Old cast iron boilers had asbestos on the interior insulating walls as well. Believe it or not, years ago asbestos was **required** to be installed in all new construction. That's why so many buildings have asbestos in them. It was considered a "miracle product" when it was widely used. *(Yeah, it performs miracles with your health!)* Many floors tiles and other products found in older homes have asbestos in them.

> *Asbestos causes lung cancer when it comes loose from the pipes and the fibers get into the air.*
> *The asbestos fibers are like tiny daggers and when you breathe them in, they stick into your lungs.*

Asbestos has great insulating and fireproofing qualities, the only problem is the public wasn't made aware of the health problems with it until it was too late. This is one area you have to be careful about. Asbestos really scares potential home buyers because of the health concerns with it. Asbestos causes lung cancer when it comes loose from the pipes, floor tiles, etc. and the fibers get into the air. The asbestos fibers are like tiny daggers and when you breathe them in, they stick into your lungs and stay there. The fibers cling to dust and can be stirred up off the floor when someone walks in a room where the fibers are located. There are about five different diseases related to exposure to asbestos. There are six different types of asbestos minerals.

I did an inspection once for an attorney who handled a lawsuit filed by the relatives of residents of a small town in Australia. This attorney told me that **every** resident from that town was killed due to the *Blue Asbestos* mine that most of them worked at. Supposedly Blue Asbestos is the most dangerous type of asbestos to be exposed to. Just by getting one fiber in your lungs can be fatal!!! Just one fiber will not only create scar tissue in that section of the lung, but it will spread to cover the entire lung over time. This attorney told me that all of the workers in the mine were killed due to breathing the Blue Asbestos at work. Their families were all killed because the mine workers would bring home the fibers in their clothes which would spread in their homes. Also, the rest of the people in this town were killed due to the Blue Asbestos fibers being blown around by the wind.

An asbestos lab technician told me that Steve McQueen died of an asbestos related cancer. Supposedly Steve McQueen worked in the French Merchant Marine when he was younger and that's where he was overly exposed to asbestos. I'm not telling you these stories to try to scare you, I'm just letting you know about some potential health hazards you have to watch out for.

Asbestos pipe insulation usually has a white color and appears to have layers of ribbed cardboard in the middle sections. You'll probably see an off-white canvas covering over it. Old hot air heating ducts may have a very thin, white layer of asbestos around them. The only way to know for sure if any insulation is asbestos is to have a laboratory take a sample. You can charge an additional fee for this service if you'd like. I don't get involved in handling any asbestos myself and I don't recommend you do either.

⚠️ Don't take any chances identifying asbestos in the house. Just tell the client when you see an asbestos type of insulation, and tell them the EPA recommendations. The Environmental Protection Agency has offices in every State that will provide anyone with free brochures and information. They have information about Asbestos, Radon Gas, Oil Leaks, Lead in paint and water, and many other environmental and health concerns. Get the number for your State office and obtain their brochures for more information. There are also classes you can take that are accredited by the Environmental Protection Agency for more information about these items.

> *The EPA recommends that any asbestos insulation be professionally sealed or removed from the house by an EPA licensed asbestos contractor.*

⚠️ The Environmental Protection Agency recommends that any asbestos insulation be **professionally** sealed or removed from the house by an EPA licensed asbestos contractor. This means, the homeowner, the plumber or any other repair person should not touch any asbestos!! Often you'll see a residue from asbestos insulation on the heating pipes. Evidence of this is small white particles on sections of the pipes, usually around the joints. This indicates that a non-EPA licensed person removed the asbestos and it should immediately raise a red flag. Many times the homeowner will have a new boiler put in and some foolish contractor will just rip asbestos off the pipes not knowing what he's doing. Or worse, sometimes the contractor or the homeowner removes it intentionally just to get rid of it themselves. Big mistake on their part! When inspecting an older house you may not actually see the asbestos. If this were the case, you should assume that there was asbestos in the home at one time. It's better to be safe than sorry. Since asbestos was almost always used in older houses, it was probably unprofessionally

removed and that's why you don't see it. I've found asbestos insulation on copper water supply pipes in houses that were built as late as 1960!!!

👮 When older houses have forced hot air heating systems, then they're **really** is a problem if asbestos was used. I've found very thin layers of asbestos around forced hot air heating ducts and in the lining of furnaces. The furnace fan will circulate asbestos all over the house once it gets inside the air ducts. So not only will you have deadly fibers in the basement and behind the walls, you'll also have them in the livable rooms of the house.

👮 An often overlooked asbestos problem is the floor tiles of older homes. When these tiles get old and start to crack and wear down, the asbestos fibers come loose. I know a home inspector that was sued because his client purchased a home he inspected and this inspector never warned the client about the asbestos content in the floor tiles. The client sued this inspector for not warning him about the health risks.

⚠️ Tell your client to have a laboratory take an air sample to learn what the asbestos fiber content is in the house. There's no way for you to determine this during a home inspection. Don't take any chances with this stuff. Asbestos lawsuits are big bucks. I've only heard of one home inspector getting sued for asbestos. But I have heard of many contractors getting sued for hundreds of thousands of dollars for improperly removing asbestos.

👮 Don't let the clients be fooled by any Realtors, sellers, or other third parties telling them not to worry about the asbestos in the house. A common line that I hear Realtors and other third parties say to my clients on inspections is: *"This asbestos is just fine, the EPA says all you have to do is to wrap it in tape or plastic."* That **really** bothers me when I hear that. What gives that third party the right to sugarcoat a decision that concerns someone else's health? You can bet that if that Realtor or third party was the person buying that house, they'd insist that the asbestos be removed. They'd also make sure it was removed by a licensed EPA contractor prior to closing! Yet it's OK for them to let someone else buy the house and leave the asbestos there.

👮 I'll never forget the time that I started inspecting a house for a client before they had arrived at the site. I was in the lower level of the house with a Realtor to the transaction who was getting a commission on the sale. I mentioned that there was asbestos on the heating pipes and that some of it appeared to have been removed unprofessionally or had fallen off sections of the pipes. This Realtor got worried and asked me what type of health concern there was with breathing asbestos fibers. I told her, *"The fibers are like tiny daggers that stick in your lungs and create scar tissue."* She just turned and practically ran for the stairway and said, *"I'm getting out of this basement now, I'll be waiting upstairs."*

When my client arrived, I told him about the asbestos. He then went upstairs and told this Realtor that he wanted it removed from the pipes prior to closing on the house. I could not believe it when I went back upstairs and the Realtor said to me, *"Why are you getting the client so scared about the asbestos?"* I felt like screaming at her! Just 15 minutes earlier this Realtor **ran** out of the basement because I told her about the asbestos on the pipes. Now suddenly she was worried because I might create problems with her deal by informing my client about the same health concern that she was so concerned about herself. I guess it's different when it's somebody else's lungs and not her own. Some people have an <u>amazing</u> ability to rationalize their actions. I'll talk more about this at the end of the book.

I tell my clients that they're better off having an EPA licensed contractor remove the asbestos from the house, as opposed to just having it wrapped professionally. The reason for this is that if the asbestos is left in the house and is only sealed, then when there's a pipe leak underneath the asbestos insulation, the covering will have to be removed. The asbestos will have to be exposed so that the pipe leak can be repaired. Once it's exposed, you have the problem all over again of fibers getting into the air of the house. Also, if the client has the asbestos removed from the house, as opposed to having it wrapped, then they don't have to worry about it bothering potential buyers when they sell the house.

When an Environmental Protection Agency licensed contractor removes asbestos, they seal the entire area where it's located. They work with completely sealed suits over their bodies. They then set up a vacuum to remove all of the dust from the area. When the asbestos is totally removed from the house, they then take an air sample. The air sample is done to make sure they haven't left any fibers lying around that can be stirred up and breathed in later. Generally, any asbestos behind the walls is left alone. If there's no access to the asbestos and it can't be disturbed, there isn't much of a health concern. Just let the EPA licensed asbestos contractor tell your client what to do. You only give recommendations from a home inspector's point of view.

Asbestos Insulation photos: P 185-P 189

Radon Gas

While we're on the lovely topic of lung cancer, let's talk about radon. A radon lab technician told me the story about how radon was discovered. I thought you might find it interesting. There was a man who lived in Reading, Pennsylvania that worked for some type of nuclear laboratory. When he used to go to work, he would set off the radiation detectors at the lab. The radiation detectors are installed so that the nuclear lab can monitor their employees to see if they're being exposed to radiation inside the lab. The lab employees couldn't figure out why the detectors were setting off, so they tested his house for radiation. While studying the problem, they stumbled upon radon gas. *(Fortunately or unfortunately for mankind. I guess it's just another way to develop cancer. Like there aren't enough already!)*

Radon gas testing is really becoming a daily part of all real estate sales transactions. It's a great additional source of income and you should consider providing this service as well. Radon is a radiation gas that's released naturally by rocks and soil in the earth. The radiation gas is created by the natural breakdown or Uranium in the rocks and soil that leads to a by product called Radium. This radiation gas gradually seeps up from the ground and as long as it goes out into the open air it's not a problem. However, if the radon seeps through cracks in the foundation floor and walls it'll become trapped in the house and the levels will rise.

> *Some houses will be left vacant while they're being sold. The point is, that if a house has a high radon reading, don't let anyone tell the client that it's only because the house was sealed up.*

Some houses will be left vacant while they're being sold. Many people think this will increase the radon level reading because no windows or doors are being opened. However, radon has a half life of only 3.825 days. Because of this fact, the maximum radon level that could build up would be just under a 4 day high level. After that point, some radon will decay and then be replenished by new radon gas entering the house. The point is, that if a house has a high radon reading, ***don't let anyone tell the client that it's only because the house was sealed up!*** Realtors like to use the excuse that a house was vacant and that's the only reason why it has a high radon reading. Don't let anyone make your client think that when he moves in the radon level will be OK. If anyone says that, then tell that person to move into the house and call us in about 10 years after they have a chest X-ray.

As with asbestos and other environmental and health concerns, call your State Environmental Protection Agency office for their information, brochures and classes. The EPA considers radon to be the **number 2** leading cause of lung cancer behind smoking, so it's not something to take too lightly. Some experts feel that the Environmental Protection

Agency has over exaggerated the problem but I would let the client decide that for themselves. Don't try to make the decision for them.

The EPA uses a reading of 4 Pico Curies per liter to determine the maximum radon level in a house before mitigation is recommended. I will give you some background so you have an idea of how Pico Curies are measured. The EPA office in my area says that one Pico Curie is the average indoor radon level and this is equal to getting about 100 chest X-rays per year. Now that may seem very high, but let me put it in the proper perspective. The EPA also informed me that the amount of radiation you receive from a normal chest X-ray, usually isn't as high as most people think. For example, with a reading of one Pico Curie per liter, the Environmental Protection Agency estimates that 3-13 people out of 1,000 will die of lung cancer. This is similar to a nonsmoker's risk of dying of lung cancer.

With a reading of 4 Pico Curies per liter, it's estimated that 13-50 people out of 1,000 will die of lung cancer. This is similar to five times the nonsmoker's risk of dying of lung cancer. You still may want to inform your client about this so that *they* can decide for themselves if the radon levels found are acceptable to them or not. Don't take it upon yourself to make the decision for your client.

Mitigation is the term used for the treatment to remove the radon problem by reducing the levels in the house. When a house is mitigated, the radon contractor will seal all open cracks in the lower level walls and floors that they can find. They then drill a hole in the foundation floor which looks like a sump pump pit. Instead of installing a sump pump in this pit, the contractor will install a fan with pipes leading to the outside of the house. In some areas, the local codes require that these pipes discharge above the roof line. This will help prevent the radon from entering back into the house through an open window. The purpose of the mitigation is to vent all radon gas that builds up underneath the foundation, to the exterior of the house.

> *In some areas the radon levels tend to be higher than in other areas but all houses will get some radon gas reading!!! So don't let any Realtors, sellers, or other third parties talk your client out of getting an accurate radon test done.*

In some areas the radon levels tend to be higher than in other areas but all houses will get some radon gas reading!!! So don't let any Realtors, sellers, or other third parties talk your client out of getting an accurate radon test done. Sometimes they'll say to your client, *"Oh, you don't have to worry we don't have radon in this area."* HOGWASH!!!!! All houses will have a radon reading, even if it's minor trace element readings of 0.5 Pico Curie per liter. This is because radon is everywhere according to the EPA. There is always an average of 0.4 Pico Curie per liter reading

in the air of the atmosphere. EPA has found that the average indoor radon level is 1.5 Pico Curies per liter.

It's also important to inform your client that you might not have a high radon reading today but you might have a high reading a month from now. Or you might have a high reading and your neighbor might not and vice versa. I tested a house in the middle of August once that had a radon reading of 3.5 Pico Curies per liter. In August the readings are generally lower because the windows and doors are open more due to the warm weather, and people are going in and out of the house more often. That deal fell through and I did a radon test for another client who made an offer on that same house in January, just five months later. In January the readings are generally higher because the house is sealed up more due to the cold winter months. The lab and I couldn't figure it out, but the January reading came in at 0.9 Pico Curie per liter. The reason for this is that radon is a radiation gas that's unstable and it fluctuates. There are many factors that affect the radon level in a house, some of which include:

1   The time of the year and the climate.

2   The type of soil and rocky terrain in the area around and under the house.

3   The type of construction of the house.

4   And there are other reasons as well.

Because of these factors, the Environmental Protection Agency recommends that you retest for radon every six months. This will help to make sure that the radon levels are acceptable on a continual basis. It's also another source of income to retest all of your client's homes every six months. *Believe it or not, radon can even be found in water!* That's another reason to have a laboratory analyze well water samples. You are not misleading people or trying to milk them for money. You're simply showing them the EPA recommendations for retesting because of the unpredictability of radon.

According to the Environmental Protection Agency there currently is no evidence that there is a health problem with drinking water with radon in it. This is because radon becomes soluble (dissolves) in water. The colder the temperature of the water then the more radon will dissolve in it. The health concern of having radon in your water is that the gas is released into the air. The water releases the radon gas whenever you run the faucet or dishwasher, take a shower, flush a toilet, use the washing machine, etc. Anytime you aerate the water you'll be releasing the radon gas into the house and this is when it becomes a health concern.

The current standards that the EPA uses for the acceptable levels of radon in the water are 10,000 to 1. Meaning that for each 10,000 Pico Curies per liter of radon gas that you have in your water, you will be releasing about one Pico Curie per liter into the air in the house. For example, if you have a radon water reading of 40,000 Pico Curies per liter. Then you will have 4 Pico Curies per liter escaping into the air of the house. This is the level at which the Environmental Protection Agency recommends mitigation. Currently there is no evidence of a correlation between having a high radon reading in the air in relation to the radon reading in the water of a house. For example, let's say that you have a high radon reading in the air of your house. Well, this doesn't mean that you'll definitely have a high radon reading in the water of your house and vice versa.

Air radon gas testing is usually done with a small, round metal canister that has charcoal inside. A canister is left in the house for about 3-5 days and then it's sealed and mailed back to the radon lab for analysis. Sometimes the seller or occupant of the house will ask you if there is a health risk of being in a house while a canister is there. Radon canisters don't emit anything hazardous. The charcoal inside the canisters merely absorbs the air in the room where they're placed so the lab can analyze them. Radon canisters do not present a health risk to the occupants of the house.

You want to make sure that you purchase your radon testing canisters from a reputable lab. Don't just buy radon cans off the shelf of the local hardware store. The reason for this is that what makes a radon reading accurate **is not** the canister you use. The radon reading accuracy is determined by the sophistication of the lab's analyzing equipment. You could send the same canister to two different labs and get two totally different readings. So check the lab out and make sure they're good. That's another reason why you shouldn't let any Realtors, sellers, or other third parties talk your client out of getting an accurate radon test done. Sometimes they'll say to your client: *"Oh, you don't have to test for radon, the seller already did that when they bought the house and he's willing to give you a copy of the test results for free!"* **(That sounds like the spider talking to the fly!)** How do you know how accurate the lab's equipment was that analyzed the seller's canister? How do you know the canister wasn't tampered with? Just because the seller had a low reading when he bought the house, doesn't mean that there's a low reading in the house now. Remember, radon is always fluctuating.

Most labs recommend that you place the canister about three feet above the floor in the lowest area of the house. I always put the canister in the basement. However, some labs say you should put the canister in the lowest *livable* area of the house. This would be the floor above the basement. The EPA feels that if a basement has the potential to become a livable area in the future, then that's where the radon level should be tested due to the future potential use of the basement.

I always put the canister in the basement instead of the first livable floor. I do this because the lower level is where you're going to get the highest radon reading. Any readings on the first floor will be lower then the radon reading in the basement level. The client might not be worried about a high reading in the basement because he won't be down there that often. However, if you get the highest possible reading in the house, then it's his decision as to whether he wants to mitigate. Once again, let the client decide what he wants to do. You only provide recommendations and **objective** opinions. *(You certainly don't want a former client calling you up 10 years after you inspected his house, to complain that his doctor told him that his lungs now glow in the dark!!)*

There is another benefit of testing for radon in the lowest level. That benefit is that if you only test on the first livable floor, the reading may be below the EPA 4 Pico Curie per liter limit. However, what if the client moves in and decides he wants to finish the basement and make a playroom out of it? What if he finds that the radon level down there is above the EPA limit? Then you might have an angry client on your hands because you didn't warn him about it. If the client decides to test with two canisters; one in the basement and one on the first floor, then that's fine. Just make sure you charge him for an additional canister!

There's another point about radon that you have to stress to the client. That point concerns the potential of any *tampering* with the radon canister while it's left in the house. There's a million ways to alter a radon reading so that it comes in too low. But there's no way to make a reading come in too high. When you leave that house you have no control over anyone else tampering with the radon canister. Obviously, some actions taken by dishonest third parties will alter the radon reading. Just tell the client that you can't control what happens when you're not there. Also, recommend that the client retest after he moves in.

There are tamper resistant cages on the market that will monitor the radon canister. These cages have timers on them and if the canister is moved, the timer will be reset. A reset timer will be noticeable when you go back to pick up the canister and cage. You can charge more for providing this service. However, it must be noted that even with a tamper resistant cage, the radon reading can still be altered. A less expensive way to monitor radon canisters for tampering is to use a tamper resistant tape on the radon canisters. The tape isn't as effective as the cages to detect tampering, but it's easier and cheaper to use. These special adhesive tapes have a label and glue on one side. The tape is applied to the canister and the table that it rests upon. Windows and doors can also be taped shut so they can be monitored during the testing. If the canister is moved or the window or door is opened, then the label on the tape will come off the backing and it will be noticeable when you return to the house.

I charge more for doing radon testing with the tamper resistant cages and the tamper resistant tapes. This service provides the client with a much better chance of getting a reliable and accurate reading. It helps to reduce the chance of someone intentionally altering the radon analysis at the site. However, as I said, these devices are very helpful in preventing tampering but they're not foolproof. **I've actually** caught sellers of houses in the act of tampering with radon canisters! So don't kid yourself or your client and think that no one tampers with these canisters. You may find out the hard way that you're wrong.

As with radon canisters and well water samples, you want to make sure that you deal with a reputable laboratory for radon water analysis.
The radon reading accuracy will depend on the sophistication of the lab's analyzing equipment.

⚠ Water radon gas testing is usually done with a special water bottle. The water sample *must* be obtained without letting any aeration of the water. Any aeration would release as much as 99% of the radon in the water sample. The testing bottle has to seal the faucet so that it traps all of the radon gas as the bottle is filled with the water. Special hoses are usually included with the testing bottles. As with radon canisters and well water samples, you want to make sure that you deal with a licensed laboratory for radon water analysis. The radon reading accuracy will depend on the sophistication of the lab's analyzing equipment. So check the lab out and make sure that they know what they're doing.

If the water is found to have a high radon gas reading, then there are a number of options to take for mitigation treatments. One is to have an *activated carbon treatment* installed. This is simply a charcoal filter system installed on the water supply lines. The drawback to this type of mitigation is that the charcoal that's left over is going to be slightly radioactive. This used charcoal can be considered a hazardous and toxic waste material. This could lead to problems with disposing of it. Another method of mitigation is a system to aerate the water to release the radon gas before it enters the house.

As a home inspector I wonder sometimes what my exposure is to asbestos fibers and radon. But I guess there's risk in everything, even crossing the street, so I don't worry about it. If it bothers you, just talk to your physician or an asbestos and radon lab for their advice.

Radon Gas photos: P 188-P 191

Indoor Air Pollution

Air pollution contributes to lung disease, including respiratory tract infections, asthma, and lung cancer. Lung disease claims close to 335,000 lives in America every year and is the third leading cause of death in the United States. Over the last decade, the death rate for lung disease has risen faster than for almost any other major disease.

Poor indoor air quality can cause or contribute to the development of chronic respiratory diseases such as asthma and hypersensitivity pneumonitis. In addition, it can cause headaches, dry eyes, nasal congestion, nausea and fatigue. People who already have respiratory diseases are at greater risk.

Biological pollutants, including molds, bacteria, viruses, pollen, dust mites, and animal dander promote poor indoor air quality and may be a major cause of days lost from work and school. In office buildings, heating, cooling, and ventilation systems are frequent sources of biological substances that are inhaled, leading to breathing problems.

To help prevent growth of mold when humidity is high, make sure bathrooms, kitchens and basements have good air circulation and are cleaned often. The basement in particular may need a dehumidifier. And remember, the water in the dehumidifier must be emptied and the container cleaned often to prevent forming mildew.

An estimated one out of every 15 homes in the United States has radon levels above 4pci/L, the U. S. Environmental Protection Agency recommended action level. Radon, a naturally occurring gas, can enter the home through cracks in the foundation floor and walls, drains, and other openings. **Indoor radon exposure is estimated to be the second leading cause of lung cancer!!** A recent report by the National Research Council estimates that radon is responsible for between 15,000 and 21,000 lung cancer deaths each year in the United States.

Environmental tobacco smoke (ETS) also called "secondhand smoke," a major indoor air pollutant, contains about 4,000 chemicals, including 200 known poisons, such as formaldehyde and carbon monoxide, as well as 43 carcinogens. ETS causes an estimated 3,000 lung cancer deaths and 35,000 to 50,000 heart disease deaths in non-smokers, as well as 150,000 to 300,000 cases of lower respiratory tract infections in children under 18 months of age each year.

Formaldehyde is a common chemical, found primarily in adhesive or bonding agents for many materials found in households and offices, including carpets, upholstery, particle board, and plywood paneling. The release of formaldehyde into the air may cause health problems, such as coughing; eye, nose, and throat irritation; skin rashes, headaches, and dizziness.

Asbestos is the name given to a group of microscopic mineral fibers that are flexible and durable and will not burn. Asbestos fibers are light and small enough to remain airborne; they can be inhaled into the lungs and can cause asbestosis (scarring of the lung tissue), lung cancer and mesothelioma, a relatively uncommon cancer of the lining of the lung or abdominal cavity. Many asbestos products are found in the home, including roofing and flooring materials, wall and pipe insulation, spackling compounds, cement, coating materials, heating equipment, and acoustic insulation. These products are a potential problem indoors only if the asbestos containing material is disturbed and becomes airborne, or when it disintegrates with age.

Heating systems and other home appliances using gas, fuel, or wood, can produce several combustion products, of which the most dangerous are *carbon monoxide* (CO) and *nitrogen dioxide* (NO2). Fuel burning stoves, furnaces, fireplaces, heaters, water heaters, and dryers are all combustion appliances. Carbon monoxide is an odorless, colorless gas that interferes with the distribution of oxygen to the body. Depending on the amount inhaled, this gas can impede coordination, worsen cardiovascular conditions, and produce fatigue, headache, confusion, nausea, and dizziness. Very high levels can cause death. Nitrogen dioxide is a colorless, odorless gas that irritates the mucous membranes in the eye, nose and throat and causes shortness of breath after exposure to high concentrations. Prolonged exposure to high levels of this gas can damage respiratory tissue and may lead to chronic bronchitis.

Household cleaning agents, personal care products, pesticides, paints, hobby products, and solvents may be sources of hundreds of potentially harmful chemicals. Such components in many household and personal care products can cause dizziness, nausea, allergic reactions; eye, skin, and/or respiratory tract irritation, and cancer.

Carbon Monoxide

What You Should Know About Combustion Appliances and Indoor Air Pollution

Hazards may be associated with almost all types of appliances. The purpose of this section is to answer some common questions you may have about the potential for one specific type of hazard - indoor air pollution associated with one class of appliances - combustion appliances.

Combustion appliances are those which burn fuels for warmth, cooking, or decorative purposes. Typical fuels are gas, both natural and liquefied petroleum (LP); kerosene; oil; coal; and wood. Examples of the appliances are space heaters, ranges, ovens, stoves, furnaces, fireplaces, water heaters, and clothes dryers. These appliances are usually safe. However, under certain conditions, these appliances can produce combustion pollutants that can damage your health, or even kill you.

Possible Health Effects range from headaches, dizziness, sleepiness, and watery eyes to breathing difficulties or even death. Similar effects may also occur because of common medical problems or other indoor air pollutants. This section was written:

1. to encourage the proper use, maintenance, and installation of combustion appliances;

2. to discuss the pollutants produced by these appliances;

3. to describe how these pollutants can affect your health; and,

4. to tell you how you can reduce your exposure to them.

◊   **Should I be concerned about indoor air pollution?**
YES. Studies have shown that the air in our homes can be even more polluted than the outdoor air in big cities. Because people spend a lot of time indoors, the quality of the air indoors can affect their health. Infants, young children and the elderly are a group shown to be more susceptible to pollutants. People with chronic respiratory or cardiovascular illness or immune system diseases are also more susceptible than others to pollutants.

Many factors determine whether pollutants in your home will affect your health. They include the presence, use, and condition of pollutant sources, the level of pollutants both indoors and out, the amount of ventilation in your home, and your overall health.

Most homes have more than one source of indoor air pollution. For example, pollutants come from tobacco smoke, building materials, decorating products, home furnishings, and activities such as cooking, heating, cooling, and cleaning. Living in areas with high outdoor levels of pollutants usually results in high indoor levels. Combustion pollutants are one category of indoor air pollutants.

◊ **What are combustion pollutants?**

Combustion pollutants are gases or particles that come from burning materials. The combustion pollutants discussed in this section come from burning fuels in appliances. The common fuels burned in these appliances are natural or LP gas, fuel oil, kerosene, wood, or coal. The types and amounts of pollutants produced depend upon the type of appliance, how well the appliance is installed, maintained, and vented, and the kind of fuel it uses. Some of the common pollutants produced from burning these fuels are carbon monoxide, nitrogen dioxide, particles, and sulfur dioxide. Particles can have hazardous chemicals attached to them. Other pollutants that can be produced by some appliances are unburned hydrocarbons and aldehydes.

Combustion always produces water vapor. Water vapor is not usually considered a pollutant, but it can act as one. It can result in high humidity and wet surfaces. These conditions encourage the growth of biological pollutants such as house dust mites, molds, and bacteria.

◊ **Where do combustion pollutants come from?**

Combustion pollutants found indoors include: outdoor air, tobacco smoke, exhaust from car and lawn mower internal combustion engines, and some hobby activities such as welding, wood-burning, and soldering. Combustion pollutants can also come from vented or unvented combustion appliances. These appliances include space heaters, gas ranges and ovens, furnaces, gas water heaters, gas clothes dryers, wood or coal-burning stoves, and fireplaces. As a group these are called "combustion appliances."

◊ **What is a vented appliance? What is an unvented appliance?**

Vented appliances are appliances designed to be used with a duct, chimney, pipe, or other device that carry the combustion pollutants outside the home. These appliances can release large amounts of pollutants directly into your home, if a vent is not properly installed, or is blocked or leaking.

Unvented appliances do not vent to the outside, so they release combustion pollutants directly into the home.

Look at the table in Figure 1 page 227 for typical appliance problems that cause the release of pollutants in your home. Many of these problems are hard for a homeowner to identify. A professional is needed.

Figure 1: Combustion Appliances and Potential Problems		
Appliances	**Fuel**	**Typical Potential Problems**
Central Furnaces Room Heaters Fireplaces	Natural or Liquefied Petroleum Gas	Cracked heat exchanger; Not enough air to burn fuel properly; Defective/blocked flue; Maladjusted burner
Central Furnaces	Oil	Cracked heat exchanger; Not enough air to burn fuel properly; Defective/blocked flue; Maladjusted burner
Central Heaters Room Heaters	Wood	Cracked heat exchanger; Not enough air to burn fuel properly; Defective/blocked flue; Green or treated wood
Central Furnaces Stoves	Coal	Cracked heat exchanger; Not enough air to burn fuel properly; Defective grate
Room Heaters Central Heaters	Kerosene	Improper adjustment; Wrong fuel (not-K-1); Wrong wick or wick height; Not enough air to burn fuel properly
Water Heaters	Natural or Liquefied Petroleum Gas	Not enough air to burn fuel properly; Defective/blocked flue; Maladjusted burner

Ranges; Ovens	Natural or Liquefied Petroleum Gas	Not enough air to burn fuel properly; Maladjusted burner; Misuse as a room heater
Stoves Fireplaces	Wood Coal	Not enough air to burn fuel properly; Defective/blocked flue; Green or treated wood; Cracked heat exchanger or firebox

◊ **Can I use charcoal grills or charcoal hibachis indoors?**
No. Never use these appliances inside homes, trailers, truck-caps, or tents. Carbon monoxide from burning and smoldering charcoal can kill you if you use it indoors for cooking or heating. There are about 25 deaths each year from the use of charcoal grills and hibachis indoors.

NEVER burn charcoal inside homes, trailers, tents, or other enclosures. The carbon monoxide can kill you.

◊ **What are the health effects of combustion pollutants?**
The health effects of combustion pollutants range from headaches and breathing difficulties to death. The health effects may show up immediately after exposure or occur after being exposed to the pollutants for a long time. The effects depend upon the type and amount of pollutants and the length of time of exposure to them. They also depend upon several factors related to the exposed person. These include the age and any existing health problems. There are still some questions about the level of pollutants or the period of exposure needed to produce specific health effects. Further studies to better define the release of pollutants from combustion appliances and their health effects are needed.

The sections below discuss health problems associated with some common combustion pollutants. These pollutants include carbon monoxide, nitrogen dioxide, particles, and sulfur dioxide. Even if you are healthy, high levels of carbon monoxide can kill you within a short time. The health effects of the other pollutants are generally more subtle and are more likely to affect susceptible people. It is always a good idea to reduce exposure to combustion pollutants by using and maintaining combustion appliances properly.

▫ **Carbon Monoxide:**
Each year, according to CPSC, there are more than 200 carbon monoxide deaths related to the use of all types of combustion appliances in the home. Exposure to carbon monoxide reduces the blood's ability to carry oxygen. Often a person or an entire family may not recognize that carbon monoxide is poisoning them. The chemical is odorless and some of the symptoms are similar to common illnesses. This is particularly dangerous because carbon monoxide's deadly effects will not be recognized until it is too late to take action against them.

Carbon monoxide exposures especially affect unborn babies, infants, and people with anemia or a history of heart disease. Breathing low levels of the chemical can cause fatigue and increase chest pain in people with chronic heart disease. Breathing higher levels of carbon monoxide causes symptoms such as headaches, dizziness, and weakness in healthy people. Carbon monoxide also causes sleepiness, nausea, vomiting, confusion, and disorientation. At very high levels it causes loss of consciousness and death.

▫ **Nitrogen Dioxide:**
Breathing high levels of nitrogen dioxide causes irritation of the respiratory tract and causes shortness of breath. Compared to healthy people, children, and individuals with respiratory illnesses such as asthma, may be more susceptible to the effects of nitrogen dioxide.

Some studies have shown that children may have more colds and flu when exposed to low levels of nitrogen dioxide. When people with asthma inhale low levels of nitrogen dioxide while exercising, their lung airways can narrow and react more to inhaled materials.

▫ **Particles:**
Particles suspended in the air can cause eye, nose, throat, and lung irritation. They can increase respiratory symptoms, especially in people with chronic lung disease or heart problems. Certain chemicals attached to particles may cause lung cancer, if they are inhaled. The risk of lung cancer increases with the amount and length of exposure. The health effects from inhaling particles depend upon many factors, including the size of the particle and its chemical make-up.

▫ **Sulfur Dioxide:**
Sulfur dioxide at low levels of exposure can cause eye, nose, and respiratory tract irritation. At high exposure levels, it causes the lung airways to narrow. This causes wheezing, chest tightness, or breathing problems. People with asthma are particularly susceptible to the effects of sulfur dioxide. They may have symptoms at levels that are much lower than the rest of the population.

▫ **Other Pollutants:**
Combustion may release other pollutants. They include unburned hydrocarbons and aldehydes. Little is known about the levels of these pollutants in indoor air and the resulting health effects.

◊ **What do I do if I suspect that combustion pollutants are affecting my health?**
If you suspect you are being subjected to carbon monoxide poisoning get fresh air immediately. Open windows

and doors for more ventilation, turn off any combustion appliances, and leave the house. You could lose consciousness and die from carbon monoxide poisoning if you do nothing. It is also important to contact a doctor ***IMMEDIATELY*** for a proper diagnosis. Remember to tell your doctor that you suspect carbon monoxide poisoning is causing your problems. Prompt medical attention is important.

Remember that some symptoms from combustion pollutants - headaches, dizziness, sleepiness, coughing, and watery eyes - may also occur because of common medical problems. These medical problems include colds, the flu, or allergies. Similar symptoms may also occur because of other indoor air pollutants. Contact your doctor for a proper diagnosis.
To help your doctor make the correct diagnosis, try to have answers to the following questions:

- Do your symptoms occur only in the home? Do they disappear or decrease when you leave home, and reappear when you return?
- Is anyone else in your household complaining of similar symptoms, such as headaches, dizziness, or sleepiness? Are they complaining of nausea, watery eyes, coughing, or nose and throat irritation?
- Do you always have symptoms?
- Are your symptoms getting worse?
- Do you often catch colds or get the flu?
- Are you using any combustion appliances in your home?
- Has anyone inspected your appliances lately? Are you certain they are working properly?

Your doctor may take a blood sample to measure the level of carbon monoxide in your blood if he or she suspects carbon monoxide poisoning. This sample will help determine whether carbon monoxide is affecting your health.

Contact qualified appliance service people to have your appliances inspected and adjusted if needed. You should be able to find a qualified person by asking your appliance distributor or your fuel supplier. In some areas, the local fuel company may be able to inspect and adjust the appliance.

◊ **How can I reduce my exposure to combustion pollutants?**
Proper selection, installation, inspection and maintenance of your appliances are extremely important in reducing your exposure to these pollutants. Providing good ventilation in your home and correctly using your appliance can also reduce your exposure to these pollutants.

Additionally, there are several different residential carbon monoxide detectors for sale. The CPSC is encouraging the development of detectors that will provide maximum protection. These detectors would warn consumers of harmful carbon monoxide levels in the home. They may soon be widely available to reduce deaths from carbon monoxide poisoning.

□ **Appliance Selection**

- Choose vented appliances whenever possible.

- Only buy combustion appliances that have been tested and certified to meet current safety standards. Examples of certifying organizations are Underwriters Laboratories (UL) and the American Gas Association (AGA) Laboratories. Look for a label that clearly shows the certification.

- All currently manufactured vented gas heaters are required by industry safety standards to have a safety shut-off device. This device helps protect you from carbon monoxide poisoning by shutting off an improperly vented heater.

- Check your local and State building codes and fire ordinances to see if you can use an unvented space heater, if you consider purchasing one. They are not allowed to be used in some communities, dwellings, or certain rooms in the house.

- If you must replace an unvented gas space heater with another, make it a new one. Heaters made after 1982 have a pilot light safety system called an oxygen depletion sensor (ODS). This system shuts off the heater when there is not enough fresh air, before the heater begins producing large amounts of carbon monoxide. Look for the label that tells you that the appliance has this safety system. Older heaters will not have this protection system.

- Consider buying gas appliances that have electronic ignitions rather than pilot lights. These appliances are usually more energy efficient and eliminate the continuous low-level pollutants from pilot lights.

- Buy appliances that are the correct size for the area you want to heat. Using the wrong size heater may produce more pollutants in your home and is not an efficient use of energy.

- Talk to your dealer to determine the type and size of appliance you will need. You may wish to write to the appliance manufacturer or association for more information on the appliance.

- All new woodstoves are EPA-certified to limit the amounts of pollutants released into the outdoor air. For more information on selecting, installing, operating, and maintaining wood-burning stoves, write to the EPA Wood Heater Program. Before buying a woodstove check your local laws about the installation and use of woodstoves.

□ **Proper Installation**
You should have your appliances professionally installed. Professionals should follow the installation directions and applicable building codes. Improperly installed appliances can release dangerous pollutants in your home and may create a fire hazard. Be sure that the installer checks for back drafting

on all vented appliances. A qualified installer knows how to do this.

□   **Ventilation**

• To reduce indoor air pollution, a good supply of fresh outdoor air is needed. The movement of air into and out of your home is very important. Normally, air comes through cracks around doors and windows. This air helps reduce the level of pollutants indoors. This supply of fresh air is also important to help carry pollutants up the chimney, stovepipe, or flue to the outside.

• Keep doors open to the rest of the house from the room where you are using an unvented gas space heater or kerosene heater, and crack open a window. This allows enough air for proper combustion and reduces the level of pollutants, especially carbon monoxide.

• Use a hood fan, if you are using a range. They reduce the level of pollutants you breath, if they exhaust to the outside. Make sure that enough air is coming into the house when you use an exhaust fan. If needed, slightly open a door or window, especially if other appliances are in use. For proper operation of most combustion appliances and their venting system, the air pressure in the house should be greater than that outside. If not, the vented appliances could release combustion pollutants into the house rather than outdoors. If you suspect that you have this problem you may need the help of a qualified person to solve it.

• Make sure that your vented appliance has the vent connected and that nothing is blocking it. Make sure there are no holes or cracks in the vent. Do not vent gas clothes dryers or water heaters into the house for heating. This is unsafe.

• Open the stove's damper when adding wood. This allows more air into the stove. More air helps the wood burn properly and prevents pollutants from being drawn back into the house instead of going up the chimney. Visible smoke or a constant smoky odor inside the home when using a wood-burning stove is a sign that the stove is not working properly. Soot on furniture in the rooms where you are using the stove also tells this. Smoke and soot are signs that the stove is releasing pollutants into the indoor air.

□   **Correct Use**

• Read and follow the instructions for all appliances so you understand how they work. Keep the owner's manual in a convenient place to refer to when needed. Also, read and follow the warning labels because they tell you important safety information that you need to know. Reading and following the instructions and warning labels could save your life.

• Always use the correct fuel for the appliance.

• Only use water-clear ASTM 1-K kerosene for kerosene heaters. The use of kerosene other than 1-K could lead to

a release of more pollutants in your home. Never use gasoline in a kerosene heater because it can cause a fire or an explosion. Using even small amounts of gasoline could cause a fire.

• Use seasoned hardwoods (elm, maple, oak) instead of softwoods (cedar, fir, pine) in wood-burning stoves and fireplaces. Hardwoods are better because they burn hotter and form less creosote, an oily, black tar that sticks to chimneys and stove pipes. Do not use green or wet woods as the primary wood because they make more creosote and smoke. Never burn painted scrap wood or wood treated with preservatives, because they could release highly toxic pollutants, such as arsenic or lead. Plastics, charcoal, and colored paper such as comics, also produce pollutants. Never burn anything that the stove or fireplace manufacturer does not recommend.

• Never use a range, oven, or dryer to heat your home. When you misuse gas appliances in this way, they can produce fatal amounts of carbon monoxide. They can produce high levels of nitrogen dioxide, too.

• Never use an unvented combustion heater overnight or in a room where you are sleeping. Carbon monoxide from combustion heaters can reach dangerous levels.

• Never ignore a safety device when it shuts off an appliance. It means that something is wrong. Read your appliance instructions to find out what you should do or have a professional check out the problem.

• Never ignore the smell of fuel. This usually indicates that the appliance is not operating properly or is leaking fuel. Leaking fuel will not always be detectible by smell. If you suspect that you have a fuel leak have it fixed as soon as possible. In most cases you should shut off the appliance, extinguish any other flames or pilot lights, shut off other appliances in the area, open windows and doors, call for help, and leave the area.

□   **Inspection and Maintenance**

• Have your combustion appliance regularly inspected and maintained to reduce your exposure to pollutants. Appliances that are not working properly can release harmful and even fatal amounts of pollutants, especially carbon monoxide.

• Have chimneys and vents inspected when installing or changing vented heating appliances. Some modifications may be required. For example, if a change was made in your heating system from oil to natural gas, the flue gas produced by the gas system could be hot enough to melt accumulated oil combustion debris in the chimney or vent. This debris could block the vent forcing pollutants into the house. It is important to clean your chimney and vents especially when changing heating systems.

◊   **What are the inspection and maintenance procedures?**
The best advice is to follow the recommendations of the

manufacturer. The same combustion appliance may have different inspection and maintenance requirements, depending upon where you live. In general, check the flame in the furnace combustion chamber at the beginning of the heating season. Natural gas furnaces should have a blue flame with perhaps only a slight yellow tip. Call your appliance service representative to adjust the burner if there is a lot of yellow in the flame, or call your local utility company for this service. LP units should have a flame with a bright blue center that may have a light yellow tip. Pilot lights on gas water heaters and gas cooking appliances should also have a blue flame.

□ Have a trained service representative adjust the pilot light if it is yellow or orange.

□ Before each heating season, have flues and chimneys inspected and cleaned before each heating season for leakage and for blockage by creosote or debris. Creosote buildup or leakage could cause black stains on the outside of the chimney or flue. These stains can mean that pollutants are leaking into the house.

□ The table in Figure 2 page 231 shows how and when to take care of your appliance.

□ This section discussed the types of pollutants that may be produced by combustion appliances, described how they might affect your health, and suggested ways you could reduce your exposure to them. It also explained that proper appliance selection, installation, operation, inspection, and maintenance are very important in reducing exposure to combustion pollutants.

Figure 2: Combustion Appliance Inspection and Maintenance Schedules

Appliance	Inspection/Frequency	Maintenance/Frequency
Gas Hot Air Heating System	*Air Filters* - Clean/change filter - Monthly As needed; Look at flues for rust and soot - Yearly	Qualified person check/clean chimney, clean/adjust burners, check heat exchanger and operation - Yearly (at start of heating season)
Gas/Oil Water/Steam Heating Systems and Water Heaters	Look at flues for rust and soot - Yearly	Qualified person check/clean chimney, clean combustion chamber, adjust burners, check operation - Yearly (at start of heating season)
Kerosene Space Heaters	Look to see that mantle is properly seated - daily when in use; Look to see that fuel tank is free of water and other contaminants -- daily or before refueling	Check and replace wick -- Yearly (at start of heating season); Clean Combustion chamber -- Yearly (at start of heating season); Drain fuel tank -- Yearly (at end of heating season)
Wood/Coal Stoves	Look at flues for rust and soot - Yearly	Qualified person check/clean chimney, check seams and gaskets, check operation -- Yearly (at start of heating season)

Carbon Monoxide Concerns

◊ **What is carbon monoxide (CO) and how is it produced in the home?**

Carbon monoxide (CO) is a colorless, odorless, poisonous gas. It is produced by the incomplete burning of solid, liquid, and gaseous fuels. Appliances fueled with natural gas, liquified petroleum (LP gas), oil, kerosene, coal, or wood may produce CO. Burning charcoal produces CO. Running cars produce CO.

◊ **How many people are unintentionally poisoned by CO?**

Every year, over 200 people in the United States die from CO produced by fuel-burning appliances (boilers, furnaces, ranges, water heaters, room heaters). Others die from CO produced while burning charcoal inside a home, garage, vehicle or tent. Still others die from CO produced by cars left running in attached garages. Several thousand people go to hospital emergency rooms for treatment for CO poisoning.

◊ **What are the symptoms of CO poisoning?**

The initial symptoms of CO poisoning are similar to the flu (but without the fever). They include:

□ Headache
□ Fatigue
□ Shortness of breath
□ Nausea
□ Dizziness

Many people with CO poisoning mistake their symptoms for the flu or are misdiagnosed by physicians, which sometimes results in tragic deaths.

◊ **What should you do to prevent CO poisoning?**
Make sure appliances are installed according to manufacturer's instructions and local building codes. Most appliances should be installed by professionals. Have the heating system (including chimneys and vents) inspected and serviced annually. The inspector should also check chimneys and flues for blockages, corrosion, partial and complete disconnections, and loose connections.

▫ Install a CO detector/alarm that meets the requirements of the current UL standard 2034 or the requirements of the IAS 6-96 standard. A carbon monoxide detector/alarm can provide added protection, but is no substitute for proper use and upkeep of appliances that can produce CO. Install a CO detector/alarm in the hallway near every separate sleeping area of the home. Make sure the detector cannot be covered up by furniture or draperies.
▫ Never burn charcoal inside a home, garage, vehicle, or tent.
▫ Never use portable fuel-burning camping equipment inside a home, garage, vehicle, or tent.
▫ Never leave a car running in an attached garage, even with the garage door open.
▫ Never service fuel-burning appliances without proper knowledge, skills, and tools. Always refer to the owner's manual when performing minor adjustments or servicing fuel-burning appliances.
▫ Never use gas appliances such as ranges, ovens, or clothes dryers for heating your home.
▫ Never operate unvented fuel-burning appliances in any room with closed doors or windows or in any room where people are sleeping.
▫ Do not use gasoline-powered tools and engines indoors. If use is unavoidable, ensure that adequate ventilation is available and whenever possible place engine unit to exhaust outdoors.

◊ **What CO level is dangerous to your health?**
The health effects of CO depend on the level of CO and length of exposure, as well as each individual's health condition. The concentration of CO is measured in parts per million (ppm). Health effects from exposure to CO levels of approximately 1 to 70 ppm are uncertain, but most people will not experience any symptoms. Some heart patients might experience an increase in chest pain. As CO levels increase and remain above 70 ppm, symptoms may become more noticeable (headache, fatigue, nausea). As CO levels increase above 150 to 200 ppm, disorientation, unconsciousness, and death are possible.

◊ **What should you do if you are experiencing symptoms of CO poisoning?**
If you think you are experiencing any of the symptoms of CO poisoning, get fresh air immediately. Open windows and doors for more ventilation, turn off any combustion appliances, and leave the house. Call your fire department and

report your symptoms. You could lose consciousness and die if you do nothing. It is also important to contact a doctor immediately for a proper diagnosis. Tell your doctor that you suspect CO poisoning is causing your problems. Prompt medical attention is important if you are experiencing any symptoms of CO poisoning when you are operating fuel-burning appliances. Before turning your fuel-burning appliances back on, make sure a qualified serviceperson checks them for malfunction.

◊ **What has changed in CO detectors/alarms recently?**
CO detectors/alarms always have been and still are designed to alarm before potentially life-threatening levels of CO are reached. The UL standard 2034 (1998 revision) has stricter requirements that the detector/alarm must meet before it can sound. As a result, the possibility of nuisance alarms is decreased.

◊ **What should you do when the CO detector/alarm sounds?**
Never ignore an alarming CO detector/alarm. If the detector/alarm sounds: Operate the reset button. Call your emergency services (fire department or 911). Immediately move to fresh air -- outdoors or by an open door/window.

◊ **How should a consumer test a CO detector/alarm to make sure it is working?**
Consumers should follow the manufacturer's instructions. Using a test button, some detectors/alarms test whether the circuitry as well as the sensor which senses CO is working, while the test button on other detectors only tests whether the circuitry is working. For those units which test the circuitry only, some manufacturers sell separate test kits to help the consumer test the CO sensor inside the alarm.

◊ **What is the role of the U.S. Consumer Product Safety Commission (CPSC) in preventing CO poisoning?**
CPSC worked closely with *Underwriters Laboratories* (UL) to help develop the safety standard (UL 2034) for CO detectors/alarms. CPSC helps promote carbon monoxide safety awareness to raise awareness of CO hazards and the need for regular maintenance of fuel-burning appliances. CPSC recommends that every home have a CO detector/alarm that meets the requirements of the most recent UL standard 2034 or the IAS 6-96 standard in the hallway near every separate sleeping area. CPSC also works with industry to develop voluntary and mandatory standards for fuel-burning appliances.

◊ **Do some cities require that CO detectors/alarms be installed?**
On September 15, 1993, Chicago, Illinois became one of the first cities in the nation to adopt an ordinance requiring, effective October 1, 1994, the installation of CO detectors/alarms in all new single-family homes and in existing single-family residences that have new oil or gas furnaces. Several other cities also require CO detectors/alarms in apartment buildings and single-family dwellings.

◊ **Should CO detectors/alarms be used in motor homes and other recreational vehicles?**

CO detectors/alarms are available for boats and recreational vehicles and should be used. The *Recreation Vehicle Industry Association* requires CO detectors/alarms in motor homes and in towable recreational vehicles that have a generator or are prepped for a generator.

Protect Your Family from Carbon Monoxide Poisoning

◊ **Carbon Monoxide Can Be Deadly**

You can't see or smell carbon monoxide, but at high levels it can kill a person in minutes. Carbon monoxide (CO) is produced whenever any fuel such as gas, oil, kerosene, wood, or charcoal is burned. If appliances that burn fuel are maintained and used properly, the amount of CO produced is usually not hazardous. However, if appliances are not working properly or are used incorrectly, dangerous levels of CO can result. Hundreds of people die accidentally every year from CO poisoning caused by malfunctioning or improperly used fuel-burning appliances. Even more die from CO produced by idling cars. Fetuses, infants, elderly people, and people with anemia or with a history of heart or respiratory disease can be especially susceptible. Be safe. Practice the DO's and DON'Ts of carbon monoxide.

◊ **CO Poisoning Symptoms**

Know the symptoms of CO poisoning. At moderate levels, you or your family can get severe headaches, become dizzy, mentally confused, nauseated, or faint. You can even die if these levels persist for a long time. Low levels can cause shortness of breath, mild nausea, and mild headaches, and may have longer term effects on your health. Since many of these symptoms are similar to those of the flu, food poisoning, or other illnesses, you may not think that CO poisoning could be the cause.

◊ **Play it Safe**

If you experience symptoms that you think could be from CO poisoning:

▫ **DO *GET FRESH AIR IMMEDIATELY.*** Open doors and windows, turn off combustion appliances and *leave the house*.

▫ **DO *GO TO AN EMERGENCY ROOM*** *and tell the physician you suspect CO poisoning.* If CO poisoning has occurred, it can often be diagnosed by a blood test done soon after exposure.

▫ **DO** Be prepared to answer the following questions for the doctor:
- Do your symptoms occur only in the house?
- Do they disappear or decrease when you leave home and reappear when you return?
- Is anyone else in your household complaining of similar symptoms?

- Did everyone's symptoms appear about the same time?
- Are you using any fuel-burning appliances in the home?
- Has anyone inspected your appliances lately?
- Are you certain they are working properly?

◊ ***Prevention*** **is the Key to Avoiding Carbon Monoxide Poisoning**

▫ **DO** have your fuel-burning appliances -- including oil and gas furnaces, gas water heaters, gas ranges and ovens, gas dryers, gas or kerosene space heaters, fireplaces, and wood stoves -- inspected by a trained professional at the beginning of every heating season. Make certain that the flues and chimneys are connected, in good condition, and not blocked.

▫ **DO** choose appliances that vent their fumes to the outside whenever possible, have them properly installed, and maintain them according to manufacturers' instructions.

▫ **DO** read and follow all of the instructions that accompany any fuel-burning device. If you cannot avoid using an unvented gas or kerosene space heater, *carefully follow the cautions* that come with the device. Use the proper fuel and keep doors to the rest of the house open. Crack a window to ensure enough air for ventilation and proper fuel-burning.

▫ **DO** call EPA's *IAQ INFO Clearinghouse* (1-800-438-4318) or the *Consumer Product Safety Commission* (1-800-638-2772) for more information on how to reduce your risks from CO and other combustion gases and particles.

▫ **DON'T** idle the car in a garage -- even if the garage door to the outside is open. Fumes can build up very quickly in the garage and living area of your home.

▫ **DON'T** use a gas oven to heat your home, even for a short time.

▫ **DON'T** *ever* use a charcoal grill indoors -- even in a fireplace.

▫ **DON'T** sleep in any room with an unvented gas or kerosene space heater.

▫ **DON'T** use any gasoline-powered engines (mowers, weed trimmers, snow blowers, chain saws, small engines or generators) in enclosed spaces.

▫ **DON'T** ignore symptoms, particularly if more than one person is feeling them. You could lose consciousness and die if you do nothing.

◊ **A Few Words About CO Detectors**

Carbon Monoxide Detectors are widely available in stores and you may want to consider buying one as a back-up -- *BUT NOT AS A REPLACEMENT* for proper use and maintenance of your fuel-burning appliances. However, it is important for you to know that the technology of CO detectors is still developing, that there are several types on the market, and that they are not generally considered to be as reliable as the smoke detectors found in homes today. Some CO detectors have been laboratory-tested, and their performance varied. Some performed well, others failed to alarm even at very high CO levels, and still others alarmed even at very low levels that don't pose any immediate health risk. And unlike a smoke detector, where you can easily confirm the cause of the alarm, CO is invisible and odorless, so it's harder to tell if an alarm is false or a real emergency.

So What's a Consumer to Do? First, don't let buying a CO detector lull you into a false sense of security. Preventing CO from becoming a problem in your home is better than relying on an alarm. Follow the checklist of DOs and DON'Ts.

Second, if you shop for a CO detector, do some research on features and don't select solely on the basis of cost. Non-governmental organizations such as *Consumers Union* (publisher of *Consumer Reports*), the *American Gas Association*, and *Underwriters Laboratories* (UL) can help you make an informed decision. Look for UL certification on any detector you purchase.

Carefully follow manufacturers' instructions for its placement, use, and maintenance. If the CO detector alarm goes off:

- Make sure it is your CO detector and not your smoke detector.
- Check to see if any member of the household is experiencing symptoms of poisoning.
- If they are, get them out of the house immediately and seek medical attention. Tell the doctor that you suspect CO poisoning.
- If no one is feeling symptoms, ventilate the home with fresh air, turn off all potential sources of CO -- your oil or gas furnace, gas water heater, gas range and oven, gas dryer, gas or kerosene space heater and any vehicle or small engine.
- Have a qualified technician inspect your fuel-burning appliances and chimneys to make sure they are operating correctly and that there is nothing blocking the fumes from being vented out of the house.

Checklist to Prevent Carbon Monoxide (CO) Poisoning

Carbon monoxide is often referred to as CO, which is its chemical symbol. Unlike many gases, CO has no odor, color, or taste, and it doesn't irritate your skin. Red blood cells pick up CO quicker than they pick up oxygen. If there is a lot of CO in the air, your body may replace oxygen in your blood

with CO. This blocks oxygen from getting into your body, which can damage tissues in your body and can kill you. Knowing where CO is found and how to avoid it can protect you from serious injury or death.

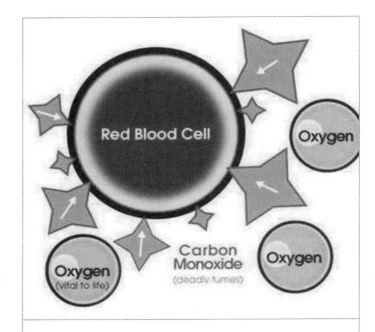

Figure 3: Red blood cells pick up CO quicker than they pick up oxygen. If there is a lot of CO in the air, your body may replace oxygen in your blood with CO. This blocks oxygen from getting into your body, which can damage tissues in your body and can kill you.

Test your Carbon Monoxide knowledge with the following interactive quizzes and review Figure 4 page 236.

◊ **The Home, Cabin, and Camper**

Most questions will apply equally to homeowners, campers, and renters. Renters should ask their landlords about maintenance and repairs.

- How often should I have my fireplace draft and the drafts of other fuel-burning appliances checked? Every year. Have all fuel-burning venting systems in your home checked by an expert every year.

- How often should my gas appliances be checked? Every year. Have all gas appliances checked every year. Your gas company may be willing to do this for you.

- Do all gas appliances need to be vented? Yes. All gas appliances must be vented so that CO will not build up in your home, cabin, or camper.

- How often should my chimney vent be checked for defects or debris? Every year. Chimneys can be blocked by debris. This can cause CO to build up inside your home or cabin. Have your chimney checked or cleaned every year.

- Is it okay to patch a vent pipe with tape, gum, or something else? No. This kind of patch can make CO build up in your home, cabin, or camper.

- Should the horizontal vent pipes to my fuel appliances be perfectly level? No. Indoor vent pipes should go up slightly as they go toward outdoors. This helps prevent CO or other gases from leaking if the joints or pipes aren't fitted tightly.

- Should I use my gas range or oven for heating? No. Using a gas range or oven for heating can cause a build up of CO inside your home, cabin, or camper.

- Is it normal for the cooling unit of my gas refrigerator give off an odor? No. An odor from the cooling unit of your gas refrigerator can mean you have a defect in the cooling unit. It could also be giving off CO. If you smell an odor from your gas refrigerator's cooling unit you should have an expert service it.

- Should I use a charcoal grill or a barbecue grill indoors? No. Using a grill indoors will cause a build up of CO inside your home, cabin, or camper unless you use it inside a vented fireplace.

- Should I burn charcoal indoors? No. Burning charcoal-- red, gray, black, or white-- gives off CO.

- Are portable flameless chemical heaters (catalytic) safe to use indoors? No. Although these heaters don't have a flame, they burn gas and can cause CO to build up inside your home, cabin, or camper.

- Should I use a portable gas camp stove indoors? No. Using a gas camp stove indoors can cause CO to build up inside your home, cabin, or camper.

◊ **Your Car or Truck**

- How often should I have a mechanic check the exhaust system of my car? Every year. A small leak in your car's exhaust system can lead to a build up of CO inside the car.

- Is it okay to run my car or truck in the garage with the garage door shut? No. CO can build up quickly while your car or truck is running an a closed garage. Never run your car in a garage unless the outside door is open to let in fresh air.

- Do I need to leave the door closed between my attached garage and my house when I run my car or truck in the garage? Yes. CO can easily go from your garage through the door that opens into your house, even if your garage door is open to let in fresh air. Keep the door connecting your garage to your house closed when your car or truck is running in your garage.

- I drive a station wagon. Should I lower the tailgate to get more air in the car? If you open the tailgate, you also need to open vents or windows to make sure air is moving through your car. If only the tailgate is open CO from the exhaust will be pulled into the car.

◊ **Appliances**

- When I choose gas equipment, how do I know what's safe? Buy only equipment carrying the seal of a national testing agency, such as the American Gas Association or the Underwriters Laboratory.

- How hard is it to convert a fuel burner from one fuel to another? It can be very hard to do this safely. You need to have an expert make the right changes and check whether the burner is venting correctly.

Here's the Safe Way to Connect Heating Equipment to the Chimney

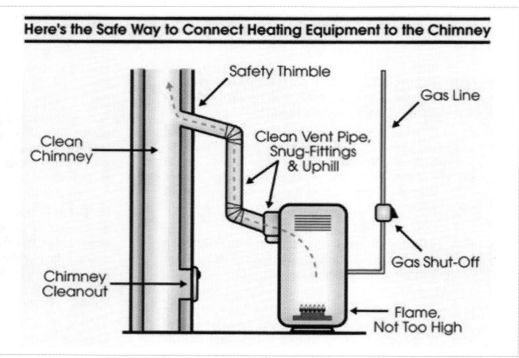

Figure 4: Carbon Monoxide is produced by fuel-burning appliances which MUST be checked every year!

Mold In Your Home

◊ **Indoor Air Molds**

Molds produce tiny spores to reproduce. Mold spores waft through the indoor and outdoor air continually. When mold spores land on a damp spot indoors, they may begin growing and digesting whatever they are growing on in order to survive. There are molds that can grow on wood, paper, carpet, and foods. When excessive moisture or water accumulates indoors, mold growth will often occur, particularly if the moisture problem remains undiscovered or un-addressed. There is no practical way to eliminate all mold and mold spores in the indoor environment; the way to control indoor mold growth is to control moisture.

The key to mold control is moisture control. It is important to dry water damaged areas and items within 24-48 hours to prevent mold growth. If mold is a problem in your home, clean up the mold and get rid of the excess water or moisture. Fix leaky plumbing or other sources of water. Wash mold off hard surfaces with detergent and water, and dry completely. Absorbent materials (such as ceiling tiles & carpet) that become moldy may have to be replaced.

◊ **Ten Things You Should Know About Mold**

Potential health effects and symptoms associated with mold exposures include allergic reactions, asthma, and other respiratory complaints. There is no practical way to eliminate all mold and mold spores in the indoor environment; the way to control indoor mold growth is to control moisture.

▫ If mold is a problem in your home or school, you must clean up the mold and eliminate sources of moisture.

▫ Fix the source of the water problem or leak to prevent mold growth.

▫ Reduce indoor humidity (to 30-60%) to decrease mold growth by: venting bathrooms, dryers, and other moisture-generating sources to the outside; using air conditioners and de-humidifiers; increasing ventilation; and using exhaust fans whenever cooking, dishwashing, and cleaning.

▫ Clean and dry any damp or wet building materials and furnishings within 24-48 hours to prevent mold growth.

▫ Clean mold off hard surfaces with water and detergent, and dry completely. Absorbent materials such as ceiling tiles, that are moldy, may need to be replaced.

▫ Prevent condensation: Reduce the potential for condensation on cold surfaces (i.e., windows, piping, exterior walls, roof, or floors) by adding insulation.

▫ In areas where there is a perpetual moisture problem, do not install carpeting (i.e., by drinking fountains, by classroom sinks, or on concrete floors with leaks or frequent condensation).

Molds can be found almost anywhere; they can grow on virtually any substance, providing moisture is present. There are molds that can grow on wood, paper, carpet, and foods.

◊ **Asthma and Mold**

Molds can trigger asthma episodes in sensitive individuals with asthma. People with asthma should avoid contact with or exposure to molds.

◊ **Floods/Flooding**

Mold growth may be a problem after flooding. Steps to take when cleaning and repairing a home after flooding. Excess moisture in the home is cause for concern about indoor air quality primarily because it provides breeding conditions for microorganisms.

◊ **Health and Mold**

Molds can trigger asthma episodes in sensitive individuals with asthma. Molds can also trigger allergies in sensitive individuals. EPA's publication, *Indoor Air Pollution: An Introduction for Health Professionals*, assists health professionals (especially the primary care physician) in diagnosis of patient symptoms that could be related to an indoor air pollution problem. It addresses the health problems that may be caused by contaminants encountered daily in the home and office. Organized according to pollutant or pollutant groups such as environmental tobacco smoke, VOCs, biological pollutants, and sick building syndrome, this booklet lists key signs and symptoms from exposure to these pollutants, provides a diagnostic checklist and quick reference summary, and includes suggestions for remedial action. Also includes references for information contained in each section. This booklet was developed by the American Lung Association, the American Medical Association, the U.S. Consumer Product Safety Commission, and the EPA. EPA Document Reference Number 402-R-94-007, 1994.

◊ **Allergic Reactions** - excerpted from *Indoor Air Pollution: An Introduction for Health Professionals* section on: *Animal Dander, Molds, Dust Mites, Other Biologicals.*

▫ "A major concern associated with exposure to biological pollutants is allergic reactions, which range from rhinitis, nasal congestion, conjunctival inflammation, and urticaria to asthma. Notable triggers for these diseases are allergens derived from house dust mites; other arthropods, including cockroaches; pets (cats, dogs, birds, rodents); molds; and protein-containing furnishings, including feathers, kapok, etc. In occupational settings, more unusual allergens (e.g., bacterial enzymes, algae) have caused asthma epidemics. Probably most proteins of non-human origin can cause asthma in a subset of any appropriately exposed population."

Consult the Centers for Disease Control (CDC) website. CDC's *National Center for Environmental Health* (NCEH) has a toll-free telephone number for information and FAXs, including a list of publications: NCEH Health Line 1-888-232-6789.

◊ **Homes and Molds**

Indoor biological pollution, health effects of biological pollutants, and how to control their growth and buildup. One third to one half of all structures have damp conditions that may encourage development of pollutants such as molds and bacteria, which can cause allergic reactions -- including asthma -- and spread infectious diseases. Moisture control is the key to mold control.

◊ **Moisture Control**
Water in your home can come from many sources. Water can enter your home by leaking or by seeping through basement floors. Showers or even cooking can add moisture to the air in your home. The amount of moisture that the air in your home can hold depends on the temperature of the air. As the temperature goes down, the air is able to hold less moisture. This is why, in cold weather, moisture condenses on cold surfaces (for example, drops of water form on the inside of a window). This moisture can encourage biological pollutants to grow. There are many ways to control moisture in your home:

▫ Fix leaks and seepage. If water is entering the house from the outside, your options range from simple landscaping to extensive excavation and waterproofing. (The ground should slope away from the house.) Water in the basement can result from the lack of gutters or a water flow toward the house. Water leaks in pipes or around tubs and sinks can provide a place for biological pollutants to grow.
▫ Put a plastic cover over dirt in crawlspaces to prevent moisture from coming in from the ground. Be sure crawlspaces are well-ventilated.
▫ Use exhaust fans in bathrooms and kitchens to remove moisture to the outside (not into the attic). Vent your clothes dryer to the outside.
▫ Turn off certain appliances (such as humidifiers or kerosene heaters) if you notice moisture on windows and other surfaces.
▫ Use dehumidifiers and air conditioners, especially in hot, humid climates, to reduce moisture in the air, but be sure that the appliances themselves don't become sources of biological pollutants.
▫ Raise the temperature of cold surfaces where moisture condenses. Use insulation or storm windows. (A storm window installed on the inside works better than one installed on the outside.) Open doors between rooms (especially doors to closets which may be colder than the rooms) to increase circulation. Circulation carries heat to the cold surfaces. Increase air circulation by using fans and by moving furniture from wall corners to promote air and heat circulation. Be sure that your house has a source of fresh air and can expel excessive moisture from the home.
▫ Pay special attention to carpet on concrete floors. Carpet can absorb moisture and serve as a place for biological pollutants to grow. Use area rugs which can be taken up and washed often. In certain climates, if carpet is to be installed over a concrete floor, it may be necessary to use a vapor barrier (plastic sheeting) over the concrete and cover that with sub-flooring (insulation covered with plywood) to prevent a moisture problem.
▫ Moisture problems and their solutions differ from one climate to another. The Northeast is cold and wet; the

Southwest is hot and dry; the South is hot and wet; and the Western Mountain states are cold and dry. All of these regions can have moisture problems. For example, evaporative coolers used in the Southwest can encourage the growth of biological pollutants. In other hot regions, the use of air conditioners which cool the air too quickly may prevent the air conditioners from running long enough to remove excess moisture from the air. The types of construction and weatherization for the different climates can lead to different problems and solutions.

◊ **Moisture On Windows**
Your humidistat is set too high if excessive moisture collects on windows and other cold surfaces. Excess humidity for a prolonged time can damage walls especially when outdoor air temperatures are very low. Excess moisture condenses on window glass because the glass is cold. Other sources of excess moisture besides overuse of a humidifier may be long showers, running water for other uses, boiling or steaming in cooking, plants, and drying clothes indoors. A tight, energy efficient house holds more moisture inside; you may need to run a kitchen or bath ventilating fan sometimes, or open a window briefly. Storm windows and caulking around windows keep the interior glass warmer and reduce condensation of moisture there.

Humidifiers are not recommended for use in buildings without proper vapor barriers because of potential damage from moisture buildup. Consult a building contractor to determine the adequacy of the vapor barrier in your house. Use a humidity indicator to measure the relative humidity in your house. The *American Society of Heating and Air Conditioning Engineers* (ASHRAE) recommends these maximum indoor humidity levels. Outdoor Recommended Indoor Temperature Relative Humidity
▫ +20 F. 35%
▫ +10 F. 30%
▫   0 F. 25%
▫ -10 F. 20%
▫ -20 F. 15%

◊ **Should You Have the Air Ducts in Your Home Cleaned?** - excerpt on duct cleaning and mold follows, please review the entire document for additional information on duct cleaning and mold. You should consider having the air ducts in your home cleaned if there is substantial visible mold growth inside hard surface (e.g., sheet metal) ducts or on other components of your heating and cooling system. There are several important points to understand concerning mold detection in heating and cooling systems:
◊
▫ Many sections of your heating and cooling system may not be accessible for a visible inspection, so ask the service provider to show you any mold they say exists.
▫ You should be aware that although a substance may look like mold, a positive determination of whether it is mold or not can be made only by an expert and may require laboratory analysis for final confirmation. For about $50, some microbiology laboratories can tell you whether a

sample sent to them on a clear strip of sticky household tape is mold or simply a substance that resembles it.

▫ If you have insulated air ducts and the insulation gets wet or moldy it cannot be effectively cleaned and should be removed and replaced.

▫ If the conditions causing the mold growth in the first place are not corrected, mold growth will recur.

Indoor Air Regulations and Mold - Standards or *Threshold Limit Values* (TLVs) for airborne concentrations of mold, or mold spores, have not been set. Currently, there are no EPA regulations or standards for airborne mold contaminants.

Large Buildings and Mold - EPA has a number of resources available, you can start with *"Building Air Quality: A Guide for Building Owners and Facility Managers"* and the *"Building Air Quality Action Plan"*. Excerpt from the *Building Air Quality: A Guide for Building Owners and Facility Managers*, Appendix C - *Moisture, Mold and Mildew*:

▫ How to Identify the Cause of a Mold and Mildew Problem. Mold and mildew are commonly found on the exterior wall surfaces of corner rooms in heating climate locations. An exposed corner room is likely to be significantly colder than adjoining rooms, so that it has a higher relative humidity (RH) than other rooms at the same water vapor pressure. If mold and mildew growth are found in a corner room, then relative humidity next to the room surfaces is above 70%. However, is the RH above 70% at the surfaces because the room is too cold or because there is too much moisture present (high water vapor pressure)?

▫ The amount of moisture in the room can be estimated by measuring both temperature and RH at the same location and at the same time. Suppose there are two cases. In the first case, assume that the RH is 30% and the temperature is 70°F in the middle of the room. The low RH at that temperature indicates that the water vapor pressure (or absolute humidity) is low. The high surface RH is probably due to room surfaces that are "too cold." Temperature is the dominating factor, and control strategies should involve increasing the temperature at cold room surfaces.

▫ In the second case, assume that the RH is 50% and the temperature is 70°F in the middle of the room. The higher RH at that temperature indicates that the water vapor pressure is high and there is a relatively large amount of moisture in the air. The high surface RH is probably due to air that is "too moist." Humidity is the dominating factor, and control strategies should involve decreasing the moisture content of the indoor air.

Guide to Mold and Moisture in Your Home

This section provides information and guidance for homeowners and renters on how to clean up residential mold problems and how to prevent mold growth. The key to mold control is moisture control.

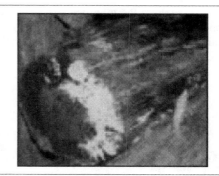

Figure 5: Mold growing outdoors on firewood. Molds come in many colors; both white and black molds are shown here.

◊ **Why is mold growing in my home?** Molds are part of the natural environment. Outdoors, molds play a part in nature by breaking down dead organic matter such as fallen leaves and dead trees, but indoors, mold growth should be avoided. Molds reproduce by means of tiny spores; the spores are invisible to the naked eye and float through outdoor and indoor air. Mold may begin growing indoors when mold spores land on surfaces that are wet. There are many types of mold, and none of them will grow without water or moisture.

◊ **Can mold cause health problems?** Molds are usually not a problem indoors, unless mold spores land on a wet or damp spot and begin growing. Molds have the potential to cause health problems. Molds produce allergens (substances that can cause allergic reactions), irritants, and in some cases, potentially toxic substances (mycotoxins).

Inhaling or touching mold or mold spores may cause allergic reactions in sensitive individuals. Allergic responses include hay fever-type symptoms, such as sneezing, runny nose, red eyes, and skin rash (dermatitis). Allergic reactions to mold are common. They can be immediate or delayed. Molds can also cause asthma attacks in people with asthma who are allergic to mold. In addition, mold exposure can irritate the eyes, skin, nose, throat, and lungs of both mold allergic and non-allergic people. Symptoms other than the allergic and irritant types are not commonly reported as a result of inhaling mold.

Research on mold and health effects is ongoing. This section provides a brief overview; it does not describe all potential health effects related to mold exposure. For more detailed information consult a health professional. You may also wish to consult your State or local health department.

◊ **How do I get rid of mold?** It is impossible to get rid of all mold and mold spores indoors; some mold spores will be found floating through the air and in house dust. The mold spores will not grow if moisture is not present. Indoor mold growth can and should be prevented or controlled by controlling moisture indoors. If there is mold growth in your home, you must clean up the mold and fix the water problem. If you clean up the mold, but don't fix the water problem, then, most likely, the mold problem will come back.

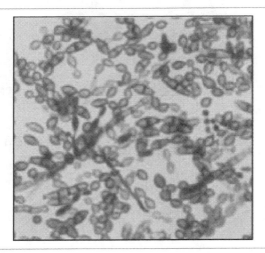

Figure 6: Magnified mold spores. Molds can gradually destroy the things they grow on. You can prevent damage to your home and furnishings, save money, and avoid potential health problems by controlling moisture and eliminating mold growth.

Mold Cleanup

If you already have a mold problem – Act Quickly! Mold damages what it grows on. The longer it grows, the more damage it can cause.

◊   **Who should do the cleanup?** Who should do the cleanup depends on a number of factors. One consideration is the size of the mold problem. If the moldy area is less than about 10 square feet (less than roughly a 3 ft. by 3 ft. patch), in most cases, you can handle the job yourself, following the guidelines below. However:

▫   If there has been a lot of water damage, and/or mold growth covers more than 10 square feet, consult the U.S. Environmental Protection Agency (EPA) guide: *Mold Remediation in Schools and Commercial Buildings*. Although focused on schools and commercial buildings, this document is applicable to other building types. It is available free by calling the EPA *Indoor Air Quality Information Clearinghouse* at (800) 438-4318, or on the Internet web site located at: www.epa.gov/iaq/molds/mold_remediation.html.

▫   If you choose to hire a contractor (or other professional service provider) to do the cleanup, make sure the contractor has experience cleaning up mold. Check references and ask the contractor to follow the recommendations in EPA's *Mold Remediation in Schools*

and Commercial Buildings, the guidelines of the *American Conference of Governmental Industrial Hygienists* (ACGIH), or other guidelines from professional or government organizations.

▫   If you suspect that the heating/ventilation/air conditioning (HVAC) system may be contaminated with mold (it is part of an identified moisture problem, for instance, or there is mold near the intake to the system), consult EPA's guide *Should You Have the Air Ducts in Your Home Cleaned?* before taking further action. Do not run the HVAC system if you know or suspect that it is contaminated with mold - it could spread mold throughout the building. Visit www.epa.gov/iaq/pubs/airduct.html, or call (800) 438-4318 for a free copy.

▫   If the water and/or mold damage was caused by sewage or other contaminated water, then call in a professional who has experience cleaning and fixing buildings damaged by contaminated water.

▫   If you have health concerns, consult a health professional before starting cleanup.

◊   **Mold Cleanup Guidelines**

Bathroom tip: Places often that or always damp can be hard to maintain completely free of mold. If there's some mold in the shower or elsewhere in the bathroom that seems to reappear, increasing the ventilation (running a fan or opening a window) and cleaning more frequently will usually prevent mold from recurring, or at least keep the mold to a minimum.

Tips and techniques: The tips and techniques presented in this section will help you clean up your mold problem. Professional cleaners or remediators may use methods not covered in this publication. Please note that mold may cause staining and cosmetic damage. It may not be possible to clean an item so that its original appearance is restored.

▫   Fix plumbing leaks and other water problems as soon as possible. Dry all items completely.

▫   Scrub mold off hard surfaces with detergent and water, and dry completely.

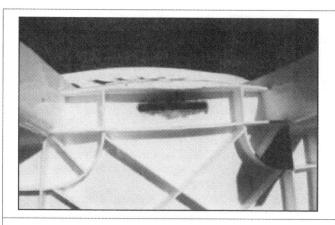

Figure 7: Mold growing on the underside of a plastic lawn chair in an area where rainwater drips through and deposits organic material.

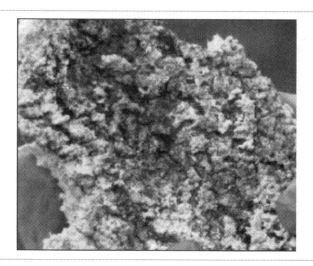

Figure 8: Mold growing on a piece of ceiling tile.

to ask for and check references. Look for specialists who are affiliated with professional organizations.

◊ **What To Wear When Cleaning Moldy Areas**
It is important to take precautions to <u>Limit Your Exposure</u> to mold and mold spores.

▫ Avoid breathing in mold or mold spores. In order to limit your exposure to airborne mold, you may want to wear an N-95 respirator, available at many hardware stores and from companies that advertise on the Internet. (They cost about $12 to $25.) Some N-95 respirators resemble a paper dust mask with a nozzle on the front, others are made primarily of plastic or rubber and have removable cartridges that trap most of the mold spores from entering. In order to be effective, the respirator or mask must fit properly, so carefully follow the instructions supplied with the respirator. Please note that the *Occupational Safety and Health Administration* (OSHA) requires that respirators fit properly (fit testing) when used in an occupational setting; consult OSHA for more information (800-321-OSHA or osha.gov/).

▫ Wear gloves. Long gloves that extend to the middle of the forearm are recommended. When working with water and a mild detergent, ordinary household rubber gloves may be used. If you are using a disinfectant, a biocide such as chlorine bleach, or a strong cleaning solution, you should select gloves made from natural rubber, neoprene, nitrile, polyurethane, or PVC (see Cleanup and Biocides section page 243). Avoid touching mold or moldy items with your bare hands.

▫ Wear goggles. Goggles that do not have ventilation holes are recommended. Avoid getting mold or mold spores in your eyes.

Figure 9: Cleaning while wearing N-95 respirator, gloves, and goggles.

▫ Absorbent or porous materials, such as ceiling tiles and carpet, may have to be thrown away if they become moldy. Mold can grow on or fill in the empty spaces and crevices of porous materials, so the mold may be difficult or impossible to remove completely.

◊ Avoid exposing yourself or others to mold (see What To Wear When Cleaning Moldy Areas section page 241.

▫ Do not paint or caulk moldy surfaces. Clean up the mold and dry the surfaces before painting. Paint applied over moldy surfaces is likely to peel.

▫ If you are unsure about how to clean an item, or if the item is expensive or of sentimental value, you may wish to consult a specialist. Specialists in furniture repair, restoration, painting, art restoration and conservation, carpet and rug cleaning, water damage, and fire or water restoration are commonly listed in phone books. Be sure

◊ **How do I know when the remediation or cleanup is finished?**

▫ You must have completely fixed the water or moisture problem before the cleanup or remediation can be considered finished.

▫ You should have completed mold removal. Visible mold and moldy odors should not be present. Please note that mold may cause staining and cosmetic damage.

▫ You should have revisited the site(s) shortly after cleanup and it should show no signs of water damage or mold growth.

▫ People should have been able to occupy or re-occupy the area without health complaints or physical symptoms.

▫ Ultimately, this is a judgment call; there is no easy answer. If you have concerns or questions call the EPA *Indoor Air Quality Information Clearinghouse* at (800) 438-4318.

◊ **Moisture and Mold Prevention and Control Tips**

Moisture control is the <u>KEY</u> to mold control. When water leaks or spills occur indoors – <u>Act Quickly</u>! If wet or damp materials or areas are dried 24-48 hours after a leak or spill happens, in most cases mold will not grow.

▫ Clean and repair roof gutters regularly.

▫ Make sure the ground slopes away from the building foundation, so that water does not enter or collect around the foundation.

▫ Keep air conditioning drip pans clean and the drain lines unobstructed and flowing properly.

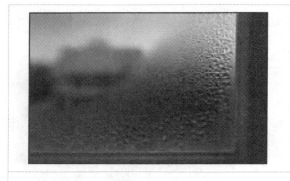

Figure 10: Condensation on the inside of a windowpane.

▫ Keep indoor humidity low. If possible, keep indoor humidity below 60 percent (ideally between 30 and 50 percent) relative humidity. Relative humidity can be measured with a moisture or humidity meter, a small, inexpensive ($10-$50) instrument available at many hardware stores.

▫ If you see condensation or moisture collecting on windows, walls or pipes - ACT QUICKLY to dry the wet surface and reduce the moisture/water source. Condensation can be a sign of high humidity.

◊ Actions that will help to reduce humidity:

▫ Vent appliances that produce moisture, such as clothes dryers, stoves, and kerosene heaters to the outside where possible. (Combustion appliances such as stoves and kerosene heaters produce water vapor and will increase the humidity unless vented to the outside.)

▫ Use air conditioners and/or de-humidifiers when needed.

▫ Run the bathroom fan or open the window when showering. Use exhaust fans or open windows whenever cooking, running the dishwasher or dishwashing, etc.

◊ Actions that will help prevent condensation:

▫ Reduce the humidity.

▫ Increase ventilation or air movement by opening doors and/or windows, when practical. Use fans as needed.

▫ Cover cold surfaces, such as cold water pipes, with insulation.

▫ Increase air temperature.

Figure 11: Mold growing on a wooden headboard in a room with high humidity.

◊ Renters: Report all plumbing leaks and moisture problems immediately to your building owner, manager, or superintendent. In cases where persistent water problems are not addressed, you may want to contact local, State, or Federal health or housing authorities.

◊ **Testing or sampling for mold**

Is sampling for mold needed? In most cases, if visible mold growth is present, sampling is unnecessary. Since no EPA or other Federal limits have been set for mold or mold spores, sampling cannot be used to check a building's compliance with Federal mold standards. Surface sampling may be useful to determine if an area has been adequately cleaned or remediated. Sampling for mold should be conducted by professionals who have specific experience in designing mold sampling protocols, sampling methods, and interpreting results. Sample analysis should follow analytical methods recommended by the *American Industrial Hygiene Association* (AIHA), the *American Conference of Governmental Industrial Hygienists* (ACGIH), or other professional organizations.

◊ **Hidden Mold**

You may suspect hidden mold if a building smells moldy, but you cannot see the source, or if you know there has been water damage and residents are reporting health problems. Mold may be hidden in places such as the back side of dry wall, wallpaper, or paneling, the top side of ceiling tiles, the underside of carpets and pads, etc. Other possible locations of hidden mold include areas inside walls around pipes (with leaking or condensing pipes), the surface of walls behind furniture (where condensation forms), inside ductwork, and in roof materials above ceiling tiles (due to roof leaks or insufficient insulation).

◊ **Investigating hidden mold problems**

Investigating hidden mold problems may be difficult and will require caution when the investigation involves disturbing potential sites of mold growth. For example, removal of wallpaper can lead to a massive release of spores if there is mold growing on the underside of the paper. If you believe that you may have a hidden mold problem, consider hiring an experienced professional.

◊ **Cleanup and Biocides**

Biocides are substances that can destroy living organisms. The use of a chemical or biocide that kills organisms such as mold (chlorine bleach, for example) is not recommended as a routine practice during mold cleanup. There may be instances, however, when professional judgment may indicate its use (for example, when immune-compromised individuals are present). In most cases, it is not possible or desirable to sterilize an area; a background level of mold spores will remain - these spores will not grow if the moisture problem has been resolved. If you choose to use disinfectants or biocides, always ventilate the area and exhaust the air to the outdoors. Never mix chlorine bleach solution with other cleaning solutions or detergents that contain ammonia because toxic fumes could be produced.

◊ *Please note:* Dead mold may still cause allergic reactions in some people, so it is not enough to simply kill the mold, it must also be removed.

◊ For more information on mold related issues including mold cleanup and moisture control/condensation/humidity issues, you can call the EPA *Indoor Air Quality Information Clearinghouse* at (800) 438-4318. Or visit: www.epa.gov/iaq/molds

Figure 12: Water stain on a basement wall — locate and fix the source of the water promptly.

Figure 13: Mold growing on fallen leaves.

Lead and Your Health

Lead in Paint, Dust, and Soil

Lead is a highly toxic metal that was used for many years in products found in and around our homes. **Lead may cause a range of health effects, from behavioral problems and learning disabilities, to seizures and death. Children 6 years old and under are most at risk, because their bodies are growing quickly.** Research suggests that the primary sources of lead exposure for most children are:

◊   Deteriorating lead-based paint
◊   Lead contaminated dust
◊   Lead contaminated residential soil

Since the 1980's, EPA and its Federal partners have phased out lead in gasoline, reduced lead in drinking water, reduced lead in industrial air pollution, and banned or limited lead used in consumer products, including residential paint. States and municipalities have set up programs to identify and treat lead poisoned children and to rehabilitate deteriorated housing. Parents, too, have greatly helped to reduce lead exposures to their children by cleaning and maintaining homes, having their children's blood lead levels checked, and promoting proper nutrition. The Agency's *Lead Awareness Program* continues to work to protect human health and the environment against the dangers of lead by developing regulations, conducting research, and designing educational outreach efforts and materials.

Basic Lead Information

Did you know the following facts about lead?
FACT: Lead exposure can harm young children and babies even before they are born.
FACT: Even children who seem healthy can have high levels of lead in their bodies.
FACT: You can get lead in your body by breathing or swallowing lead dust, or by eating soil or paint chips containing lead.
FACT: You have many options for reducing lead hazards. In most cases, lead-based paint that is in good condition is not a hazard.
FACT: Removing lead-based paint improperly can increase the danger to your family.

Health Effects of Lead

In the United States, about 900,000 children ages 1 to 5 have a blood-lead level above the level of concern. **Even children who appear healthy can have dangerous levels of lead in their bodies.** People can get lead in their body if they:
◊   Put their hands or other objects covered with lead dust in their mouths.
◊   Eat paint chips or soil that contains lead.
◊   Breathe in lead dust (especially during renovations that disturb painted surfaces).

Lead is even more dangerous to children than adults because:
◊   Babies and young children often put their hands and other objects in their mouths. These objects can have lead dust on them.
◊   Children's growing bodies absorb more lead.
◊   Children's brains and nervous systems are more sensitive to the damaging effects of lead.

If not detected early, children with high levels of lead in their bodies can suffer from:
◊   Damage to the brain and nervous system
◊   Behavior and learning problems (such as hyperactivity)
◊   Slowed growth
◊   Hearing problems
◊   Headaches

Lead is also harmful to adults. Adults can suffer from:
o   Difficulties during pregnancy
o   Other reproductive problems (in both men and women)
o   High blood pressure
o   Digestive problems
o   Nerve disorders
o   Memory and concentration problems
o   Muscle and joint pain

Where Lead is Found

In general, the older your home, the more likely it has lead-based paint.

◊   Paint. Many homes built before 1978 have lead-based paint. The Federal government banned lead-based paint from housing in 1978. Some states stopped its use even earlier. Lead can be found:
◊   In homes in the city, country, or suburbs.
◊   In apartments, single-family homes, and both private and public housing.
◊   Inside and outside of the house.
◊   In soil around a home. (Soil can pick up lead from exterior paint, or other sources, such as past use of leaded gas in cars.)
◊   Household dust. (Dust can pick up lead from deteriorating lead-based paint or from soil tracked into a home.)
◊   Drinking water. Your home might have plumbing with lead or lead solder. Call your local health department or water supplier to find out about testing your water. **You cannot see, smell, or taste lead, and boiling your water will not get rid of lead.** If you think your plumbing might have lead in it:
▫   Use only cold water for drinking and cooking.
▫   Run water for 15 to 30 seconds before drinking it, especially if you have not used your water for a few hours.

◊   The job. If you work with lead, you could bring it home on your hands or clothes. Shower and change clothes before coming home. Launder your work clothes separately from the rest of your family's clothes.
◊   Old painted toys and furniture.

◊　Food and liquids stored in lead crystal or lead-glazed pottery or porcelain.

◊　Lead smelters or other industries that release lead into the air.

◊　Hobbies that use lead, such as making pottery or stained glass, or refinishing furniture.

◊　Folk remedies that contain lead, such as "greta" and "azarcon" used to treat an upset stomach.

Where Lead is Likely to be a Hazard

Lead from paint chips, which you can see, and lead dust, which you can't always see, can be serious hazards.

◊　Peeling, chipping, chalking, or cracking lead-based paint is a hazard and needs immediate attention.

◊　Lead-based paint may also be a hazard when found on surfaces that children can chew or that get a lot of wear-and-tear. These areas include:
- Windows and window sills.
- Doors and door frames.
- Stairs, railings, and banisters.
- Porches and fences.

◊　Lead-based paint is usually not a hazard if it is in good condition, and it is not on an impact or friction surface, like a window. It is defined by the Federal government as paint with lead levels greater than or equal to 1.0 milligram per square centimeter, or more than 0.5% by weight.

◊　Lead dust can form when lead-based paint is scraped, sanded, or heated. Dust also forms when painted surfaces bump or rub together. Lead chips and dust can get on surfaces and objects that people touch. Settled lead dust can re-enter the air when people vacuum, sweep, or walk through it. The following two Federal standards have been set for lead hazards in dust:
- 40 micrograms per square foot ($\mu g/ft2$) and higher for floors, including carpeted floors.
- 250 $\mu g/ft2$ and higher for interior window sills.

◊　Lead in soil can be a hazard when children play in bare soil or when people bring soil into the house on their shoes. The following two Federal standards have been set for lead hazards in residential soil:
- 400 parts per million (ppm) and higher in play areas of bare soil.
- 1,200 ppm (average) and higher in bare soil in the remainder of the yard.
- Contact the *National Lead Information Center* (NLIC) to find out about testing soil for lead.

What You Can do to Protect Your Family

If you suspect that your house has lead hazards, you can take some immediate steps to reduce your family's risk:

◊　If you rent, notify your landlord of peeling or chipping paint.

◊　Clean up paint chips immediately.

◊　Clean floors, window frames, window sills, and other surfaces weekly. Use a mop, sponge, or paper towel with warm water and a general all-purpose cleaner or a cleaner made specifically for lead. *REMEMBER:* **NEVER Mix**

Ammonia and Bleach products together since they can form a DANGEROUS gas!!

◊　Thoroughly rinse sponges and mop heads after cleaning dirty or dusty areas.

◊　Wash children's hands often, especially before they eat and before nap time and bed time.

◊　Keep play areas clean. Wash bottles, pacifiers, toys, and stuffed animals regularly.

◊　Keep children from chewing window sills or other painted surfaces.

◊　Clean or remove shoes before entering your home to avoid tracking in lead from soil.

◊　Make sure children eat nutritious, low-fat meals high in iron and calcium, such as spinach and dairy products. Children with good diets absorb less lead.

In addition to day-to-day cleaning and good nutrition:

◊　You can temporarily reduce lead hazards by taking actions such as repairing damaged painted surfaces and planting grass to cover soil with high lead levels. These actions (called "interim controls") are not permanent solutions and will need ongoing attention.

◊　To permanently remove lead hazards, you must hire a certified lead "abatement" contractor. *Abatement* (or permanent hazard elimination) methods include removing, sealing, or enclosing lead-based paint with special materials. Just painting over the hazard with regular paint is not enough.

◊　Always hire a person with special training for correcting lead problems--someone who knows how to do this work safely and has the proper equipment to clean up thoroughly. Certified contractors will employ qualified workers and follow strict safety rules set by their State or the Federal government.

◊　Contact the *National Lead Information Center* (NLIC) for help with locating certified contractors in your area and to see if financial assistance is available.

Checking Your Family and Home for Lead

Get your children and home tested if you think your home has high levels of lead. Just knowing that a home has lead-based paint may not tell you if there is a hazard. To reduce your child's exposure to lead, get your child checked, have your home tested (especially if your home has paint in poor condition and was built before 1978), and fix any hazards you may have.

Your Family

Children's blood lead levels tend to increase rapidly from 6 to 12 months of age, and tend to peak at 18 to 24 months of age. Consult your doctor for advice on testing your children. A simple blood test can detect high levels of lead. Your doctor can explain what the test results mean and if more testing will be needed. Blood tests are important for:

◊　Children at ages 1 and 2.

◊　Children and other family members who have been exposed to high levels of lead.

◊　Children who should be tested under your State or local health screening plan.

Your Home

You can get your home checked in one of two ways, or both:

◊   A paint inspection tells you the lead content of every different type of painted surface in your home. It won't tell you whether the paint is a hazard or how you should deal with it.

◊   A risk assessment tells you if there are any sources of serious lead exposure (such as peeling paint and lead dust). It also tells you what actions to take to address these hazards.

Have qualified professionals do the work. There are standards in place for certifying lead-based paint professionals to ensure the work is done safely, reliably, and effectively. Contact the *National Lead Information Center* (NLIC) for a list of contacts in your area.

Trained professionals use a range of methods when checking your home, including:

◊   Visual inspection of paint condition and location.
◊   A portable x-ray fluorescence (XRF) machine.
◊   Lab tests of paint samples.
◊   Surface dust tests.

Note: Home test kits for lead are available, but **studies suggest that they are not always accurate.**   Consumers should not rely on these tests before doing renovations or to assure safety.

Call your State or local EPA agency for help in locating certified professionals in your area and to see if financial assistance is available.

How to find a Qualified Lead Professional

Hiring a Lead Professional - The purpose of this section is to help you find a lead professional who can test your home for lead-based paint and tell you whether the paint poses a hazard to you or your family. It also will provide you with some background on the qualifications to look for in a lead professional.

Over 80% of all housing in the U.S. built before 1978 contains some lead-based paint on the interior or exterior. If managed properly, lead-based paint that is in good condition is usually not a hazard. **If allowed to deteriorate, however, lead from the paint or lead dust can create serious health hazards.** Similarly, without proper precautions, renovations of surfaces with lead-based paint release lead dust.

If you are buying a home or renting an apartment built before 1978 you should receive a pamphlet containing general information on lead-based paint hazards. This information is being made available under a new Federal program that started in 1996. The goals of this program are to help you reduce the hazards of lead-based paint in your home and to prevent small children from being poisoned by lead from paint. If you want to find out if your house contains lead-based paint or a lead hazard, you may want to hire someone to inspect your home for lead paint and to evaluate the paint for any hazards.

What will I learn if I hire a Lead professional?

A certified lead professional offers two services: 1) an inspection, or 2) a risk assessment. Some lead professionals may be certified or licensed to conduct both. A paint inspection will tell you the lead content of every painted surface in your home. However, an inspection won't tell you whether the paint poses a hazard or how you should deal with it. **A risk assessment tells you if there are any sources of serious lead exposure** (such as peeling paint and lead dust). It also tells you what options are available for addressing these hazards.

Are Lead professionals required to be certified or licensed?

Several states have developed certification or licensing programs for individuals who identify and assess lead-based paint for hazards. Contact EPA for information on obtaining a list of state certified lead-based paint inspectors, risk assessors, and contractors. EPA also is working with States to establish a national training and certification program for lead-based paint professionals. Under this program, all lead-based paint inspectors, risk assessors and contractors must be trained and certified starting in 1999.

What if my State doesn't have a certification program?

If your State doesn't have a certification or licensing program yet, and you need to locate a lead professional, here are some suggestions:

Hire a contractor who has been certified or licensed in a State that does have a program. If you can't find a contractor who's been certified or licensed by another State, hire a contractor who has been trained to conduct lead-based paint inspections or risk assessments. Look for workers whose training was based on course work developed by EPA or approved by your State. Keep in mind that in addition to States, some cities and counties may require you to use certified or licensed contractors to conduct lead work. If you are required to use a certified or licensed professional and your State doesn't have a program, you will need to work with your county or local officials to locate a professional that meets their requirements.

Yes, there is a difference. To obtain a certification or license, most states require applicants to meet three standards. One standard requires an applicant to possess certain experience and/or skills. Second, an applicant is required to be trained to conduct specific lead-related tasks. The training an applicant receives typically must be approved by the State or an organization recognized by the State. The third and final means to ensure the competency of an applicant is a certification exam.

Individuals who have been trained, but who are **uncertified** might not possess work experience relevant to conducting lead-based paint activities. Nor have they passed an examination to test their proficiency. **For that reason, it is especially important to check the references and credentials of uncertified contractors.**

What if the Lead paint in my home poses a hazard?

You may have a range of options for addressing lead hazards in your home. A risk assessment report should contain recommendations on how to control lead-based paint hazards safely. If you have been advised to remove or control lead paint, use the advice provided by the EPA when looking for a lead abatement contractor.

Tips for Checking a Contractor's Background and Experience:

◊   Always ask to see a contractor's lead-based paint license or certificate.
◊   If they are not certified, ask to see a contractor's training certificate. EPA has developed training courses for lead-based paint professionals. Ask if the training received by a contractor was based on EPA course materials.
◊   Check the references of the last three lead inspections or risk assessments performed by the contractor.
◊   Ask what kinds of information will be included in the final inspection or risk assessment report that will be prepared for you. An *inspection* report should identify the lead content of the painted surfaces in your home. A *risk assessment* will provide you with information about the lead content of deteriorated painted surfaces, and also should tell you whether lead is present in dust and soil around your home. It should also present options for reducing the hazard.

Basic Questions about Testing Your Home For Lead In Paint, Dust, And Soil

Why Should I Test My Home For Lead? There are numerous reasons why you might want to test your home for lead, especially if built before 1978.
◊   *I. There Are (Or Will Be) Children Age Six And Younger In The Home.* Lead from paint, especially peeling or flaking paint, can get into dust and soil in and around a home. Young children may then swallow the lead during normal hand-to-mouth activity. In addition, an unborn child may be exposed to lead in the mother's womb. High levels of lead in the fetus and in children age six and younger have been linked to nervous system damage, behavior and learning problems, and slow growth. Testing can tell you whether there is lead-based paint or a lead-based paint hazard in your home.

◊   *II. You Are About To Remodel, Renovate, Or Repaint Your Home.* Any disturbance of lead-based paint can create a hazard by depositing lead chips or particles in the house dust or in the soil around the house. If you are planning on doing renovation, remodeling, or repainting, you should have testing done by a certified lead-based paint professional on any painted surfaces that will be removed, disturbed, scraped, or sanded before starting the work. If your house was built before 1978 and you hire a professional to renovate, the renovator *MUST*, before beginning renovation, give you a copy of the EPA pamphlet *Protect Your Family From Lead In Your Home.*

◊   *III. You Are Renting Or Buying A Home.* The Federal Lead-Based Paint and Lead-Based Paint Hazards Disclosure Rule requires that the landlord or seller of a residential dwelling built prior to 1978 provide the renter or buyer with:
  □   The pamphlet *Protect Your Family From Lead In Your Home* and
  □   Any available information on lead-based paint or lead-based paint hazards in the home.
  □   A buyer must be given the opportunity to conduct testing to determine whether lead-based paint or lead-based paint hazards are present. While you are not required by law to test for lead, it may be advisable if you have (or plan to have) young children in the home.

Figure 14: a homeowner is required to provide renters or buyers with any available information on lead-based paint or lead-based paint hazards in homes built before 1978.

◊   *IV. You Are A Landlord Or Selling A Home.* As discussed above, a homeowner is required to provide renters or buyers with any available information on lead-based paint or lead-based paint hazards in homes built before 1978. Testing will give you the information that may be requested by potential renters or buyers.

Why Is Testing Recommended For Houses Built Before 1978? Federal regulations placed a limit on the amount of lead in paint sold for residential use starting in 1978. That is why homes built before 1978 are subject to the Disclosure Rule. The older the home, the greater the chance of lead-based paint and lead-based paint hazards, and the more important it is to have the home tested.

What Kind Of Testing Do I Want? Three different approaches for testing lead are available: a lead-based paint inspection, a risk assessment, and a lead hazard screen. A combination inspection and risk assessment may also be done. Selection of the approach depends on why you are testing.

◊ *I. Lead-Based Paint Inspection.* A lead-based paint inspection is a surface-by-surface investigation to determine whether there is lead-based paint in the home and where it is located. An inspection may be particularly useful before renovation, repainting, or paint removal. An inspection includes:

- An inventory of all painted surfaces, including the outside as well as the inside of the home. 'Painted surfaces' include all surfaces coated with paint, shellac, varnish, stain, coating, or even paint covered by wallpaper.
- Selection and testing of each type of painted surface.
- Then you should get a report listing the painted surfaces in the home and whether each painted surface contains lead-based paint.
- An inspection does not typically test painted furniture unless it is a permanent part of the home, such as kitchen or bathroom cabinets or built-in bookshelves. Soil, dust, and water are not typically tested during an inspection.
- The presence of lead-based paint in a home does not necessarily mean there is a lead-based paint hazard to occupants. To make sure, you may want a different testing approach (either a risk assessment or hazard screen).

Figure 15: Typical Painted Surfaces Tested During Inspection	
Inside The Home	

Baseboards	Heating Units
Built-In Cabinets	Railings
Ceilings	Shelves
Chair Rails	Stairs
Doors	Walls
Fireplaces	Windows
Floors	

Outside The Home	
Chimneys	Mailboxes
Door Trim	Porches
Fascia, Soffits	Roofing
Fences	Siding
Gutters, Downspouts	Stairs
Handrails	Sheds
Lattice Work	Swing Sets

◊ *II. Risk Assessment.* A risk assessment is an on-site investigation to determine the presence, type, severity, and location of lead-based paint hazards. The presence of deteriorated lead-based paint or high levels of lead in dust or soil pose potential hazards to children who may ingest lead inside or playing outside. A risk assessment includes:

- A visual inspection of the residence to determine the location of deteriorated paint, the extent and causes of the deterioration, and other factors that may cause lead exposure to young children inside or outside the home.
- Testing deteriorated paint and paint on surfaces where there is reason to believe (from teeth marks or from reports of a parent) that a child has chewed, licked, or mouthed the paint. Painted surfaces in good condition are not tested.
- Testing household dust from floors and windows. Samples should include areas from a child's bedroom, a child's main play area, the main entrance, and other locations to be chosen by the certified Risk Assessor.
- Testing bare soil from play areas, the building foundation, and possibly other areas around the home.
- Optional water testing.
- Finally, you should get a report identifying the location of the types of lead-based paint hazards and ways to control them. Because not all paint is tested, a risk assessment cannot conclude that there is no lead-based paint in the home.

Figure 16: Test for lead in paint, especially areas where a small child could reach or chew on.

An important point is that a risk assessment identifies current lead-based paint hazards. New hazards may arise if lead-based paint is disturbed, damaged, or deteriorates.
If you want to know which painted surfaces contain lead-based paint and whether any lead-based hazards are present, you will need a combination inspection and risk assessment.

◊   *III. Lead Hazard Screen.* A lead hazard screen is a limited version of a risk assessment for houses with a low chance of lead risks. In a lead hazard screen:
   □   Any painted surfaces in a deteriorated condition are tested.
   □   Two sets of dust samples are collected in a lead hazard screen. One set represents the floors and the other set represents the windows. Typically, there is less dust sampling in a lead hazard screen than in a risk assessment.
   □   Usually soil samples are not collected in a lead hazard screen, with one exception. If there is evidence of paint chips in the soil from previous exterior repainting, then the soil should be sampled and tested.

The outcome of the lead hazard screen is either a conclusion that lead-based paint hazards are probably not present or a recommendation that a full risk assessment be conducted to determine if such hazards are present. In a lead hazard screen, only deteriorated paint is tested. Thus, a lead hazard screen cannot conclude there is no lead-based paint in the home.

A lead hazard screen is only recommended for residences that are generally in good condition, with little visible dust, and with paint in good condition (very little chipping or flaking). If not, the screen is likely to be a waste of time and money. In general, a lead hazard screen will be more useful in housing built after 1960.

As with a risk assessment, a lead hazard screen identifies current lead-based paint hazards. If there is lead-based paint in the home, new hazards may arise if that paint is disturbed, damaged, or deteriorates.

Who Can Do Lead Testing For Me? It is strongly recommended that testing be performed by a certified Inspector or certified Risk Assessor.
Certified Inspectors can perform only lead-based paint inspections.
◊   Certified Risk Assessors can perform both risk assessments and lead hazard screens.
◊   Your State may define the titles for lead-based paint professionals and the types of testing they can perform differently. You can find out by calling NLIC at 1-800-424-LEAD.

What Will The Testing Report Tell Me? That will depend on which approach has been used: inspection, risk assessment, or lead hazard screen. Request a sample report before the testing is done so that you may see what information will be provided and how it will be presented. You should also request that actual lead values (not just 'positive' or 'negative' classifications) be provided in the report as evidence that the testing was actually done.

◊   *I. Inspection Report.* If you have an inspection done, you should receive a report that tells you which painted surfaces were tested and the test results for each surface. An inspection report will not tell you the condition of the lead-based paint or whether lead-based paint hazards exist.

◊   *II. Risk Assessment Report.* If you have a risk assessment done, you will receive a report that tells you whether there are any lead-based paint hazards and recommends ways to reduce or control any hazards present.

The certified Risk Assessor will take into account the test results and the results of the visual inspection to decide if there are any lead-based paint hazards and how to control them. Lead-based paint hazards identified include lead-based paint in deteriorated condition or on surfaces mouthed by a child. In addition, house dust or bare soil with hazardous lead levels will be identified.

The certified Risk Assessor will provide a list of options for controlling each hazard. Options may include both interim controls and abatement. There is no EPA requirement for you to do anything to any lead-based paint or lead-based paint hazards found when testing your home. However, if your home was built before 1978, you will be required to provide the test results to any renter or buyer when you lease or sell the home. For more information on the responsibilities of sellers, landlords and their agents, contact NLIC at 1-800-424-LEAD or visit www.epa.gov/lead.

- **Interim Controls** – These are short-term or temporary actions. Examples include recommendations to repair deteriorated surfaces that contain lead-based paint, to clean house dust more frequently, or to plant grass or shrubs in areas with bare soil.
- **Abatement** – These are long-term or permanent actions. Examples include replacing old windows, building a new wall over an existing one, or removing soil.

The certified Risk Assessor will also identify the probable source of the paint deterioration and determine whether other repairs are warranted. For example, a water leak may need to be repaired to prevent further damage to the paint.

◊   *III. Hazard Screen Report.* If you have a lead hazard screen done, the report tells you either that there are probably no lead-based paint hazards in the house or that full-scale risk assessment is needed.

Do I Have To Do Anything After The Testing Is Completed? Be aware that there may be State or other requirements for action based on the test results. You can call NLIC at 1-800-424-LEAD for information about what is required in your locality before you start testing.

May I Abate Lead-Based Paint Hazards In My Own Home? If you decide to abate lead-based paint hazards in your own home, it is not recommended that you do the work yourself. Abatement activities must be done following careful procedures to prevent contamination of the home with lead dust. To be safe, hire a certified lead-based paint contractor (a certified professional who can do lead-based paint related abatement). Dust samples should be collected to check the thoroughness of the work.

Be aware that you must be certified yourself or you must hire a certified lead-based paint professional in the following cases: 1) if a child with a blood-lead level of 20 µg/dL (Pronounced micrograms of lead per deciliter of blood) or higher for a single venous test (or 15–19 µg/dL in two consecutive tests taken 3 to 4 months apart) lives in the house or 2) you own the house and rent it to someone else.

If you hire a firm to do testing for lead-based paint hazards, note that you are not under any obligation to hire the same firm to do the abatement. In fact, it would be better to have one firm conduct all testing and another firm conduct the abatement work. *That will prevent a conflict of interest.*

Be sure to maintain a record of the work to help during any future sale or rental of the home.

Specific Questions about Testing Paint, Dust, and Soil for Lead

Are All Painted Surfaces In the Home Tested? Not every single painted surface in the home will be tested in an inspection, but all types of painted surfaces are tested. For example, a room may have three windows, all painted the same color and all made out of wood. The certified Inspector may not test all three windows, because they appear to be the same.

In a similar fashion, the certified Inspector will go through every room and test the different types of painted surfaces in the rooms. Painted surfaces on the outside of the home, detached structures (such as garages), and items like painted fences and swing sets should also be tested.

Inspections differ from risk assessments and lead hazard screens. In a risk assessment, only deteriorated paint and paint that has been mouthed or chewed by a child will be tested. In a lead hazard screen, only deteriorated paint is tested.

How Are Painted Surfaces Tested? There are currently two methods recognized by EPA for testing paint: Portable X-Ray Fluorescence (XRF) analyzers and paint chip sampling followed by analysis by a laboratory recognized by EPA's *National Lead Laboratory Accreditation Program* (NLLAP).

◊   *I. Portable X-Ray Fluorescence Analyzers (XRFs).* A portable XRF measures lead in paint, generally without damaging the paint. However, readings from some XRFs are affected by the base material (known as the "substrate") underneath the paint, such as wood, plaster, or metal. For these cases, the certified Inspector removes paint from a few surfaces of each type and takes a measurement on the unpainted surface. These measurements provide a baseline to adjust the lead in paint value. This procedure may do some paint damage. Also, for curved surfaces or very deteriorated paint, XRF analyzers may not read accurately and a paint chip sample may be required.

When a certified lead-based paint professional follows good testing practices, XRF analyzers provide a fast and reliable method for classifying many painted surfaces. However, some XRF test results may be inconclusive (neither positive nor negative). Then laboratory testing of a paint chip sample may be necessary. Because the XRF analyzer uses a radiation source to detect lead, occupants in the household should be asked to stay out of rooms behind the surfaces being tested.

◊   *II. Paint Chip Sampling And Laboratory Analysis.* Paint chip samples are collected for laboratory analysis by removing one to four square inches of paint from the surface. All layers of paint in the sampled area are included in the sample. Usually samples will contain some of the material beneath the paint, such as wood, plaster, or concrete particles. The amount of this material will be kept to a minimum.

Tools such as chisels and scrapers are used to remove the paint. Sometimes a heat gun is used to soften the paint and make the removal easier. If so, a respirator should be worn by the person operating the heat gun for protection from lead and other fumes. In addition, the room or area should be well ventilated to protect occupants. After collecting the paint chip sample, the certified lead-based paint professional will repair the scraped area so that adjacent paint will not peel or flake off. Any paint chips or dust from the sampling should be cleaned up by the certified lead-based paint professional to ensure no lead dust is left behind.

Paint chip samples should be analyzed for lead by a laboratory recognized by EPA's NLLAP as proficient for testing lead in paint. EPA has established the NLLAP to ensure that laboratory analyses are done accurately. A laboratory on the list is recognized as proficient for testing for lead in whichever of the three sample types (paint, dust, or soil) the laboratory has qualified. The certified Inspector and certified Risk Assessor must ensure that any paint chip samples from your home are analyzed by a laboratory on the NLLAP list for paint. Your State may have its own lead program and different regulations. For more information, contact NLIC at 1-800-424-LEAD or visit www.epa.gov/lead.

While paint chip sampling followed by laboratory analysis is generally more accurate than XRF testing, sampling and analysis take longer to complete and paint chips must be scraped from many surfaces in the home. In some cases, a surface may be curved or so deteriorated that an XRF cannot be used properly and sampling may be the only way to test the paint.

What Do The Results Of Paint Testing Mean? A certified lead-based paint professional will use guidance specific for each type of XRF analyzer to determine whether a measurement indicates that:
- Lead-based paint is present,
- Lead-based paint is not present, or
- The measurement is inconclusive and a laboratory test is necessary.

The guidance ensures the XRF measurement classifies paint as lead-based when there is 1.0 milligram of lead per square centimeter of painted surface or greater (1.0 mg/cm2). An XRF analyzer typically reads in mg/cm2, meaning milligrams per square centimeter.

Figure 17: Federal Definition Of Lead-Based Paint Depends On How Test Results Are Reported

How Test Results Are Reported	Federal Definition Of Lead-Based Paint
If results are reported as percent (or equivalent)	Then, in order for it to be considered lead-based paint, the paint must have greater than or equal to 0.5% (which is the same as 5,000 µg/g or 5,000 mg/kg or 5,000 ppm) lead
If results are reported as milligrams per square centimeter	Then, in order for it to be considered lead-based paint, the paint must have greater than or equal to 1 mg/cm2 lead

When the paint chip sampling followed by laboratory analysis method is used, the Federal definition of lead-based paint is dependent on how the results are reported:
- If the laboratory report is expressed as weight of lead per weight of paint chip, the Federal definition of lead-based paint is 0.5 percent lead (0.5%). This is mathematically the same as 5,000 milligrams of lead per kilogram of paint chip (5,000 mg/kg), or 5,000 micrograms of lead per gram of paint chip (5,000 µg/g), or 5,000 parts per million lead (5,000 ppm).
- If the laboratory report is expressed as a weight of lead per unit area of painted surface, the Federal definition of lead-based paint is 1.0 mg/cm2 (the same as for XRF analysis).

It is possible to report laboratory results in both types of units, but this is rarely done because of the additional time and work required. Unfortunately, there is no universal definition of lead-based paint. Some State and local governments have definitions of lead-based paint which differ from those in Federal law. It is recommended that when there is a conflict between the Federal definition and a State or local definition, the more stringent standard (that is, the lower number) be used to define lead-based paint. A certified lead-based paint professional (certified Inspector or certified Risk Assessor) should be aware of and should follow the appropriate standard.

What If No Lead-Based Paint Is Found In My Home? Lead can still be present in paint which is not classified as "lead-based." This would occur when the paint has a lower amount of lead than the Federal government regulates. If lead is present in the paint, lead dust can be released when the paint deteriorates, or is disturbed during remodeling, renovation, sanding, or some maintenance work that breaks the surface of the paint. This is especially important in homes built before 1978. Since the amount of lead in paint was limited by Federal regulation in 1978, lead exposure during remodeling and renovation is not as much a concern in newer homes. So you should be careful when there is work that involves extensive breaking of painted surfaces in a home built before 1978. Make sure any dust and debris created by breaking painted surfaces are thoroughly cleaned up, painted surfaces are repaired and left intact when the work is done, and children stay away from the work areas until all repairs and clean-up are completed.

Figure 19: Test for lead in the soil and exterior painted surfaces where a small child could reach or chew on.

Figure 18: Test for lead in your water also.

How Are Dust Samples Collected And Analyzed?
The most common method for dust collection is a surface wipe sample. Most certified Risk Assessors will use baby wipes or wet wipes to collect dust. If dust is collected from a floor, an area of one square foot is usually sampled. The area is wiped several times in different directions to pick up all the dust. After sampling, the wipe is placed in a container and sent to a laboratory for analysis. The certified Risk Assessor will also collect wipe samples from windows and measure the surface area wiped. In some situations, special types of vacuum samplers may be used for dust collection. These are different from home vacuum cleaners, although some may look the same.

The certified lead based paint professional must send dust samples to a laboratory recognized by EPA's NLLAP that is proficient for dust analysis. Your State may have its own lead program and different regulations. For more information, contact NLIC at 1-800424-LEAD or visit www.epa.gov/lead.

What Do The Results Of Dust Sampling Mean?
Dust sample results are usually expressed as a weight of lead per unit area of surface. The units will usually be micrograms of lead per square foot. For example, a floor wipe sample may be expressed as 50 micrograms of lead per square foot. This is written as 50 $\mu g/ft2$. The certified lead-based paint professional will provide guidance in interpreting the results of the dust testing.

How Are Soil Samples Collected And Analyzed?
Soil samples are collected from bare soil areas (soil with no grass or other covering) near your home where children play and from bare soil areas near the house foundation or drip line. Optional sampling areas are gardens, pathways, and pet sleeping areas. Samples are collected by coring or scooping methods that take the top half-inch of soil. Samples of non-bare soil may sometimes be collected. Soil samples must be sent to a laboratory recognized by EPA's NLLAP that is proficient in soil analysis. Your State may have its own lead program and different regulations. For more information, contact NLIC at 1-800-424-LEAD or visit www.epa.gov/lead.

What Do The Results Of Soil Testing Mean?
Results of soil samples are expressed as a weight of lead per unit weight of soil, usually in parts per million. For example, a soil sample result may be 300 parts per million. This is written 300 ppm. The certified lead-based paint professional will help you interpret the results of the soil testing.

What Are Composite Samples? Composite samples are combinations of individual samples analyzed together in a laboratory to obtain a single average result. Both dust and soil samples may be composited. For example, a floor dust sample may be collected in each of three rooms and combined to obtain one composite dust sample to be analyzed by the laboratory. Or four soil samples taken in a play area may be combined to obtain one composite soil sample. Paint samples may also be composited, but this is not as common as compositing dust and soil samples.

Composite samples may often be used in risk assessments and lead hazard screens to reduce the cost of laboratory analysis or to increase the representativeness of a single sample. The disadvantage of composite samples is that information is not available for each room (or location) from which samples were collected. The certified Risk Assessor will interpret composite sample results, if any. The advantage of composite samples is that information is obtained at reduced cost or more samples are collected for the same cost.

Other Frequently Asked Questions about Lead Testing

What Are Home Test Kits? Home test kits are used in the home to detect lead in paint, soil, and dust (and, in some cases, water, dishware, glasses, and ceramics). A reaction occurs causing a color change when chemicals in the kit are exposed to lead.

Does EPA Recommend Test Kits For Paint, Dust, Or Soil Testing? No. EPA does not currently recommend home test kits to detect lead in paint, dust, or soil. Studies show that these kits are not reliable enough to tell the difference between high and low levels of lead. At this time, the kits are not recommended for testing performed by either homeowners or certified lead-based paint professionals.

May I Collect Paint, Dust, And Soil Samples Myself And Send Them To A Laboratory? You may do this, although your samples may not be of the same quality as those collected by a certified lead-based paint professional. If you want to collect samples yourself, it is recommended that you send paint, dust, or soil samples to a laboratory recognized by EPA's NLLAP. A list of NLLAP laboratories is available from NLIC by calling 1-800-424-LEAD. If the samples contain high levels of lead, you should have a certified lead-based paint professional do a risk assessment of your home.

What About Testing For Lead In Water? Lead pipes and lead solder were once used in plumbing and lead leaked into drinking water. Water testing is not routinely conducted by certified lead-based paint testing professionals, but you may ask for it as an optional service. If you would like information about testing for lead in water, call the EPA *Drinking Water Hotline* at 1-800-426-4791.

What About Testing For Lead In Furniture, Dishware, and Mini-Blinds? Lead may be present in the paint on furniture. If the furniture is old or the paint is damaged, you may want to have it tested. A certified Inspector or certified Risk Assessor may do this testing for you. Lead may also be present in some glassware (for example, lead crystal) and in glazes found on ceramic ware. The lead may be absorbed into the drink and food stored in these items. Contact NLIC at 1-800-424-LEAD or the *Food and Drug Administration* (FDA) *Food Information Line* at 1-800-FDA-4010 for information on testing glassware and ceramics or visit http://vm.cfsan.fda.gov/~dms/lead.html#advice.

The *Consumer Product Safety Commission* (CPSC) has issued a warning that some mini-blinds may contain lead. For further information, contact the CPSC hotline at 1-800-6382772 or access the CPSC webpage at www.cpsc.gov/cpscpub/prerel/prhtml96/96150.html.

Figure 20: If you are buying, renting, or renovating an older home, then test for lead for your family's safety!

Are You Buying or Renting a Home built before 1978?

Many houses and apartments built before 1978 have paint that contains lead. Lead from paint, chips, and dust can pose serious health hazards if not taken care of properly. Federal law requires that **individuals receive** certain information before renting or buying a pre-1978 housing:

Residential Lead-Based Paint Disclosure Program

◊   **Landlords** have to disclose known information on lead-based paint and lead-based paint hazards before leases take effect. Leases must include a disclosure form about lead-based paint.

◊   **Sellers** have to disclose known information on lead-based paint and lead-based paint hazards before selling a house. Sales contracts must include a disclosure form about lead-based paint. Buyers have up to 10 days to check for lead hazards.

Remodel or Renovate a Home with Lead-Based Paint

If not conducted properly, certain types of renovations can release lead from paint and dust into the air. Federal law requires that **contractors provide** lead information to residents before renovating a pre-1978 housing. Take precautions before your contractor or you begin remodeling or renovations that disturb painted surfaces (such as scraping off paint or tearing out walls):

◊   Have the area tested for lead-based paint.

◊   Do not use a belt-sander, propane torch, heat gun, dry scraper, or dry sandpaper to remove lead-based paint. These actions create large amounts of lead dust and fumes.

◊   Lead dust can remain in your home long after the work is done.

◊   Temporarily move your family (especially children and pregnant women) out of the apartment or house until the work is done and the area is properly cleaned. If you can't move your family, at least completely seal off the work area.

If you have already completed renovations or remodeling that could have released lead-based paint or dust, get your young children tested and follow the steps outlined to protect your family.

Reducing Lead Hazards when Remodeling your Home

The US EPA is concerned about homeowners and building professionals who may be exposed to lead as a result of remodeling or renovation projects. The purpose of this section is to help reduce lead exposure when conducting home renovation and remodeling activities.

◊   **Who Should Read This Section?**
This section is for anyone involved in a home improvement project - whether you are actually doing the work yourself or overseeing the work of renovation and remodeling professionals. Using the described practices will help keep lead dust levels lower during the project and protect homeowners and children. They also will reduce the amount of lead dust inhaled and show how to clean up lead dust once the project is completed.

This section can help homeowners and contractors do remodeling or renovation work safely. It will alert you to the hazards involved in handling lead-based painted surfaces and will provide useful methods you can use to reduce or eliminate exposures to lead. If you are uncertain how to properly perform any of these methods or where to be properly fitted for a respirator, you may want to call on a trained contractor or call your State lead program.

This section is **not intended** for use as a guide for lead-based paint abatement procedures. Unlike remodeling and renovation activities, "abatement" is a process used only to address lead-based paint hazards. EPA has promulgated regulations for certification and training of professionals engaged in lead abatement. You should check with your State lead program for further information on these regulations.

EPA has proposed a rule requiring renovation and remodeling contractors to provide the EPA pamphlet, *Protect Your Family From Lead in Your Home*, to homeowners and occupants of most pre-1978 homes before they begin work. You should call the *National Lead Information Clearinghouse* (800-424-LEAD) to get further information on the availability of the pamphlet.

◊   **Lead Hazards**
Is my family okay? Renovation and remodeling activities can make a lot of dust that contains lead in and around your home. If you are concerned that your family has been exposed to lead-based paint, call your doctor or local health department to arrange for a blood test.

Lead-based paint is poisonous. The smallest lead dust particles cannot be seen but they can get into the body. The dust and chips from lead-based paint are dangerous when swallowed or inhaled, especially to small children and pregnant women. Lead can affect children's developing nervous systems, causing reduced IQ and learning disabilities. In adults, high lead levels can cause high blood pressure, headaches, digestive problems, memory and concentration problems, kidney damage, mood changes, nerve disorders, sleep disturbances, and muscle or joint pain. **A single, very high exposure to lead can cause lead poisoning.** Lead can also affect the ability of both women and men to have healthy children.

A home built in or after 1978 should not contain lead-based paint since lead-based paint was banned for use in residences in 1978; however, a home built before 1978 is likely to have surfaces painted with lead-based paint. If you work on these painted surfaces, you can be exposed to lead. Even if the lead-based paint has been covered with new paint or another covering, cracked or chipped painted surfaces can expose the lead-based paint, possibly creating a lead hazard. Dry-sanding, scraping, brushing, or blasting lead-based paint can produce dust and paint chips. **Burning lead-based paint with open flame torches to make it easier to strip is especially dangerous.** The fumes from the hot paint contain lead and volatile chemicals that are poisonous when inhaled.

Figure 21: Be concerned if your home was built before 1978. It may have lead-based hazards.

◊   **Will the job create lead hazards?**

Can I do the work? It is <u>extremely important</u> that you properly use all the methods in this section in order to protect you and your family from lead dust, both during and after the project. Unless you can follow all of the work practices and safety precautions in this section, you should hire professionals to do your renovation or remodeling work. If you decide to hire remodeling professionals, make sure they have training and experience in dealing with the hazards of remodeling or renovating homes with lead-based paint.

To be sure that you're not dealing with lead -based paint you must have the paint tested by a qualified professional. Use a trained inspector to test your home. A trained inspector will test the surfaces of your home by using a portable X-ray fluorescence (XRF) machine which measures the amount of lead in the paint or by sending paint samples to a laboratory equipped to measure lead in paint. The results of using chemical testing kits are not recommended. To find an inspector, contact your State agency or call 1-(888) LEADLIST to obtain a list of trained inspectors.

If you are removing paint or breaking through painted surfaces, you should be concerned about lead-based paint hazards. If your job involves removing paint, sanding, patching, scraping, or tearing down walls, you should be concerned about exposure to lead-based paint hazards. If you are doing other work, such as removing or replacing windows, baseboards, doors, plumbing fixtures, heating and ventilation duct work, or electrical systems, you should be concerned about lead-based paint hazards, since you may be breaking through painted surfaces to do these jobs.

If you are working on any painted surface, you should be concerned about lead-based paint hazards. You may find lead-based paint on any surface in your home including walls, interior trim, window sashes and frames, floors, radiators, doors, stairways, railings, porches, and exterior siding.

◊   **Useful Equipment and Where to Get it**

Getting the right equipment and knowing how to use it are essential steps in protecting yourself during remodeling or renovating.

-   A *high-efficiency particulate air* (HEPA) filter equipped vacuum cleaner is a special type of vacuum cleaner that can remove very small particles from floors, window sills, and carpets and keeps them inside the vacuum cleaner. Regular household or shop vacuum cleaners are not completely effective in removing lead dust. They may blow the lead dust out through their exhausts and spread the dust throughout the home. HEPA vacuum cleaners are available through laboratory safety and supply catalogs and vendors. They can sometimes be rented at stores that carry remodeling tools.

-   You need to use a *National Institute for Occupational Safety and Health* (NIOSH) certified respirator that is properly fitted and equipped with HEPA filters to remove lead dust particles out of the air you breathe. Make sure you buy specific HEPA filters - they are always purple. Dust filters and dust masks are not effective in preventing you from breathing in lead particles. Follow the directions that come with the respirator to make sure it fits. A respirator that does not fit right will not work. Respirators are available through laboratory safety and supply catalogs and vendors, and are sometimes carried by paint and hardware stores.

-   Protective clothes, such as coveralls, shoe covers, hats, goggles, face shields, and gloves should be used to help keep lead dust from being tracked into areas outside of the work site. These items are available through laboratory safety equipment supply catalogs and vendors. Inexpensive disposable suits can sometimes be purchased at paint stores.

-   Heavy-duty polyethylene plastic sheeting for covering areas exposed to lead dust can be purchased at hardware stores or lumber yards. The label should say that the plastic is made of polyethylene and is 6 mils thick.

-   Duct tape to hold the plastic in place, and completely seal the work areas, can be purchased at hardware stores and lumber yards.

-   Wet-sanding equipment, wet/dry abrasive paper, and wet-sanding sponges for "wet methods" can be purchased at hardware stores.

-   Spray bottles for wetting surfaces to keep dust from spreading can be purchased at general retail and garden supply stores.

-   Cleaning products to use include: either a general all-purpose cleaner or a cleaner made specially for lead to clean the dust from renovation or remodeling activities. All-purpose cleaners can be found in grocery stores. Lead-specific cleaning products can be purchased from some paint and hardware stores.

▫ Buckets with wringers, debris containers, disposable heavy-duty plastic bags, rags, rakes, shovels, sponges, and string mops for ongoing, daily, and final cleaning can be purchased at hardware and retail stores.

Figure 22: Use a HEPA filter-equipped vacuum cleaner. Standard household and shop vacuum cleaners are not effective at removing lead dust.

◊ **Safe Work Practices**

You must protect yourself and your family from breathing lead dust created by renovation and remodeling projects.

▫ Keep all non-workers, especially children, pregnant women, and pets outside of the work area while doing remodeling or renovation work until cleanup is completed.
▫ Break large projects into several small projects so that you can control the amount of lead dust made.
▫ Clean up after each phase of the project.
▫ Wear a properly fitted respirator equipped with HEPA filters.
▫ Wear protective clothing such as coveralls, shoe covers, goggles, and gloves to keep dust off your skin. Launder these items separately.
▫ Change your clothes and shoes before leaving the work area to avoid carrying lead dust throughout the house.
▫ Machine wash your work clothes separately from other family laundry.
▫ Shower and wash hair right after finishing work to reduce dust contamination.
▫ Do not eat, smoke, or drink in the work area to avoid accidentally swallowing lead dust. Wash your hands and face before eating, smoking, or drinking.
▫ Dispose of used wash water down a toilet. (Check with your State lead program to make sure there are no regulations in your State that prohibit this).
▫ Never pour wash water on soil.

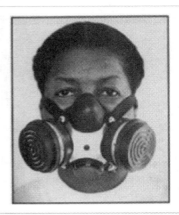

Figure 23: DO wear a respirator so you don't breathe in lead.

Figure 24: DON'T wear dust masks - they won't protect you from lead.

◊ **Setting Up To Work Inside**

Dust contaminated with lead can cling to your clothes and skin, to walls and floors, and to furniture and floor coverings. Forced-air heating and air conditioning systems also can spread dust throughout your home. To keep dust from spreading throughout your home, take the following safeguards:

▫ Remove furniture, area rugs, curtains, food, clothing, and other household items until cleanup is complete.
▫ A layer of polyethylene plastic sheeting, at least 6mils thick, should be placed on the floor and on the furnishings and exposed surfaces that cannot be removed, such as countertops and shelves. Cover openings, such as gaps around pipes, with a single sheet of plastic. All plastic should be secured with duct tape.
▫ Turn off forced-air heating and air conditioning systems during renovation and remodeling. Cover vents with plastic sheeting and tape the sheeting in place with duct tape. Windows should be kept closed unless volatile chemicals will be used.
▫ An airlock should be constructed at the entry to the work area. The airlock consists of two sheets of plastic. One sheet is completely taped along all four edges. The tape must extend all the way around the

top, two sides, and the floor. This plastic sheet is then cut down the middle. The second sheet is only taped along the top and acts as a flap covering the slit in the first sheet of plastic. If two entryways exist, one should be completely sealed in plastic. As an alternative, the doorway can be taped closed on all sides.

Figure 25: Close off entryways with an airlock.

◊ **Setting Up To Work Outside**

Exterior work often produces dust, paint chips, larger pieces of material, and liquids that contain lead. It is easy to track dust containing lead inside your home, where it can pose a hazard. Trash that contains lead also can contaminate the soil surrounding the house if you don't handle it correctly. To avoid contaminating the areas surrounding your house, take the following precautions:

▫ If using a ladder, anchor it securely to the ground, not to the plastic which can be punctured.
▫ If wind speeds exceed 20 mph, or if it begins to rain, stop and complete cleanup.
▫ One lead-safe entryway should be made available to residents at all times. Do not treat front and rear entrances simultaneously if there is not a third doorway.
▫ Cover the ground and any plants or flowers with 6mil polyethylene plastic sheeting to catch dust and trash. A single sheet of polyethylene plastic sheeting, at least 6 mils thick, should extend at least 5 feet from the base of the dwelling and an additional 3 feet for each additional story.
▫ All windows, including windows in adjacent dwellings, within 20 feet of the work area should be kept closed.
▫ Playground equipment, sandboxes, and toys should be moved at least 20 feet away from the work area. If

items cannot be moved from the area, then they should be sealed with plastic sheeting.
▫ Remove personal belongings from the area before starting work.

◊ **Carpet Removal**

If you plan to remove or replace your carpet as part of a remodeling job, take the following steps to avoid spreading lead dust:

▫ Mist the entire surface of the carpet with water to keep dust down.
▫ Roll the carpet inward to avoid spreading dust to other areas.
▫ Wrap carpet and pad in 6 mil polyethylene plastic sheeting. Tape seams closed with duct tape.
▫ Vacuum floor with a HEPA filter-equipped vacuum cleaner after the carpet is wrapped but before you remove it.
▫ HEPA vacuum the floor again after you remove the carpet.

Figure 26: Mist carpet surfaces with water to reduce spread of dust.

◊ **HVAC Ductwork**

Heating, ventilation, and air conditioning system ducts can accumulate dust for many years. If you suspect that the dust contains lead, follow these steps when replacing or cleaning the ducts:

▫ Cover the floor under the ducts with 6mil polyethylene plastic sheeting to catch dry falling dust.
▫ Use a HEPA filter-equipped vacuum cleaner to remove dust from the inside of the ducts before beginning work.

- Rinse the duct pieces in an area well away from the house before reinstalling them. If you are disposing of old duct pieces, first wrap them in plastic and seal with duct tape.

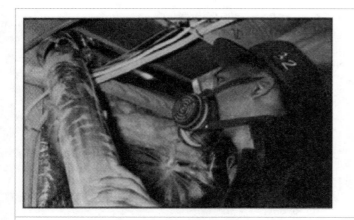

Figure 27: Heating and air conditioning ducts can accumulate dust that contains lead.

◊ **Minor Repairs**

If you plan to conduct minor repairs on painted surfaces, such as repairing or replacing a door lock, repairing a door, drilling holes to install shelves, or sawing into painted wood or plaster, then wet methods and simple cleaning can reduce hazards of lead dust:

- Cover the floor under the work area with 6 mil polyethylene plastic sheeting to catch any sludge or dust.
- Spray the work area surface with water to reduce the amount of dust generated during the minor repair.
- To eliminate friction points on a door, first mist the door, then remove the door to plane it. Keep door surfaces being planed wet during repair. Replace the door when the work is complete.
- Vacuum the floor under the work area and all surfaces within 5 feet of the work area with a HEPA filter-equipped vacuum cleaner.

◊ **Plumbing Work**

If you are working on older pipes that contain lead solder, you should be concerned about lead hazards in plumbing. Disturbing lead-soldered pipes can dislodge pieces of lead solder that can get into your drinking water or come to rest in aerators or the bottom of pipes or joints. Follow these precautions to reduce lead hazards in plumbing:

- Follow the practices outlined in the Minor repairs section when you break through walls or floors to reach pipes.
- Use adequate ventilation to avoid inhaling dangerous fumes from soldering.

- Promptly dispose of solder pieces in heavy-duty plastic bags when you finish plumbing work.
- Use lead-free solder when working on drinking water plumbing.

After work is completed:

- Remove faucet aerators and clean out any debris before re-installing them. Look carefully for grit or pieces of solder and remove them.
- Flush the supply pipes you have been working on by letting them run for several minutes with the aerators removed. The water flowing through the pipes removes small pieces of loose solder.

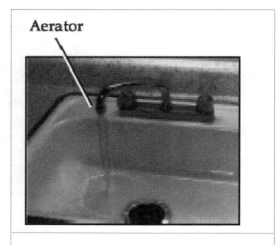

Figure 28: Remove faucet aerators and clean out any debris periodically.

◊ **Paint Removal and Floor Refinishing**

Paint removal usually creates extensive amounts of lead and lead dust when using processes such as heat, chemicals, and sharp tools. It can be performed safely and effectively by following the precautions below.

- The painted surface should be misted with water first. The paint may be removed by wet scraping or wet sanding with a HEPA vacuum attachment, or using a wet-sanding sponge. Wipe the area you are sanding often and rinse the sponge in a bucket of water.
- Chemical strippers may be used to remove paint, but those containing methylene chloride are not recommended. Exercise caution when using paint strippers since they contain toxic chemicals.
- Heat guns may be used to remove paint. However, do not use a heat gun operating above 1,100°F or open flame torches to loosen lead-based paint. Heating and burning lead based paint makes dangerous fumes and vapors.
- For mechanical removal methods (such as HEPA vacuum blasting, machine sanding or grinding), use tools equipped with HEPA exhaust capability.

- After removing the paint, wash the surface with a recommended cleaning product, rinse, and let dry before re-treating.

◊ **Preparing Surfaces for New Paint or Wallpaper**

Preparing walls and other surfaces for painting, staining, or wallpapering can create lead exposure risks. With good work practices, you can reduce the risk of exposure to lead.

- Cover the floor and furniture with 6 mil polyethylene plastic sheeting.
- Avoid sanding lead-based painted surfaces whenever possible. If you must sand, use a sander with a vacuum attachment connected to a HEPA filter equipped vacuum cleaner, or use a wet-sanding sponge.
- Wipe the area you are sanding often and rinse the sponge in a bucket of water. Strain out any chips of paint and dispose of them in heavy-duty plastic bags. Dispose of the used wash water down the toilet (check with your State lead program to make sure there are no regulations in your State that prohibit this). Wash the walls with a recommended cleaning product, rinse, and let dry before painting or wallpapering. Be careful while wet sanding because wet plastic can be very slippery.
- Exercise caution when using paint strippers since they contain toxic chemicals. Chemical strippers containing methylene chloride are not recommended.
- If you intend to feather or scrape the lead -based painted surface, spray the work area surface with water to reduce the amount of dust. For scraping, use a wet-scraper with a HEPA filter-equipped exhaust.
- Do not blast or power wash lead-based painted surfaces. Blasting and power washing create large amounts of dust and waste water that contain lead and can contaminate large areas.

◊ **Removal of Large Structures**

When you demolish and remove large structures painted with lead-based paint, such as walls, door frames, floor coverings, and ceilings, you are likely to be left with large amounts of dust and trash that contain lead. To reduce exposure to large amounts of lead dust:

- Seal off the work area by covering entryways with 6 mil polyethylene plastic sheeting.
- Cover nearby windows with 6 mil polyethylene plastic sheeting.
- Turn off forced-air heating and air conditioning systems. Then cover heating and air conditioning vents with a layer of 6 mil polyethylene plastic sheeting.
- Remove rugs and furniture from the work area, if possible.
- Cover the floors and the furniture in the work area and adjoining areas with 6 mil polyethylene plastic sheeting.

- Wet the surface and debris as you demolish it to keep dust levels down.
- Remove and dispose of trash properly. Allowing debris to accumulate in the work area increases the risk of spreading dust through the house.

Figure 29: Wear protective clothing and a respirator when removing walls that may contain lead.

◊ **Window Work**

Window sills and window frames on homes built before 1978 can have high amounts of lead-based paint. Since these items are seldom replaced, paint tends to build up on them. Follow these basic safety precautions for working on these types of windows:

- For window pane/glass replacement, cover the floor inside under the window with 6 mil polyethylene plastic sheeting to catch any dust fall. Spray the work area surface with water to reduce the amount of dust generated when replacing the window pane/glass. Score the window pane/glass with a razor knife to facilitate its removal. Collect all dust and paint chips and dispose in a sealed plastic bag.
- For window repair, cover the floor inside under the window with plastic sheeting to catch any dust fall. Spray the work area surface with water to reduce the amount of dust generated when repairing the window. Wet scrape deteriorated paint. Collect all dust and paint chips and dispose in a sealed plastic bag.
- For window replacement, cover the entire inside window opening with plastic sheeting. Cover the floor inside under the window and the ground outside the window with 6 mil polyethylene plastic sheeting to catch any dust fall. Spray the window sill and frame with water to reduce the dust. Remove the window unit from the outside, if possible. Collect all dust and paint chips and dispose of them in a sealed plastic bag.

◊ **Cleaning Up Lead Waste**

Cleaning includes not only the removal of visible debris but also the removal of leaded dust particles which are too small to be seen by the naked eye. Pay special attention to cleanup activities to prevent contaminating other areas or exposing people to lead. Everyone working on your job should take the precautions given here to help prevent lead contamination.

Personal cleanup:

▫ Vacuum dust from clothing using a HEPA filter equipped vacuum cleaner.
▫ Wash your hands and face before you leave the work site.
▫ Change your clothes and shoes before leaving the work site to prevent contaminating areas outside the work site. After removing your clothes, machine wash them separately from other family laundry.
▫ Do not take off your respirator until after you have removed your outer protective clothing.
▫ Shower and wash your hair right after finishing work to prevent spreading lead dust.

Figure 30: Vacuum dust from clothing.

◊ **Daily Site Cleanup**
Dispose of construction trash in a heavy-duty plastic bag (check with your State lead program to make sure there are no regulations in your State that prohibit this). Carefully remove the dust and trash from the plastic sheeting to avoid contaminating other areas. If possible, pass the trash out a window to avoid carrying it through the house.

▫ Strain out paint chips from liquid waste and dispose of them in a heavy-duty plastic bag. Dispose of the remaining water down a toilet (check with your State lead program to make sure there are no regulations in your State that prohibit this).

▫ Mop the floors with a recommended cleaning product using a disposable mop and water in areas where there is little dust, or vacuum with a HEPA filter-equipped vacuum cleaner. Change wash water frequently. Rinse with clean water. Dispose of used water down a toilet (check with your State lead program to make sure there are no regulations in your State that prohibit this).
▫ Vacuum the plastic sheeting covering wall-to-wall carpeting with a HEPA filter-equipped vacuum cleaner.
▫ Mist outside areas using a garden hose before sweeping these areas with a broom. Avoid dry sweeping since it spreads lead dust. Shovel, rake, or vacuum (HEPA filter-equipped) trash into heavy duty plastic bags (check with your State lead program to make sure there are no regulations in your State that prohibit this) placed in cardboard boxes for support.
▫ Clean your vacuums and tools with a recommended cleaning product and water.
▫ Seal off the entryways with 6 mil polyethylene plastic if you have to leave a work site unattended.

◊ **Final Cleanup**
Start your cleanup work from the dirtiest part of the work area and work toward the clean area of the house.

▫ Work from the top of the room toward the bottom, cleaning ceilings first, then walls, counters, and floors.
▫ Carefully remove any plastic sheeting used to protect surfaces by rolling or folding inward.
▫ Wash floors and walls with a recommended cleaning product. Dispose of used wash water down a toilet.
▫ Vacuum walls, floors, and wall-to-wall carpeting with a HEPA filter-equipped vacuum cleaner.
▫ Vacuum chair rails, window sills, casings, shelves, countertops, and baseboards again, once they are dry.

Am I done? Consider hiring a professional to test areas for lead dust contamination after your final cleanup. Call your local health department or the National Lead Information Center Clearinghouse at (800) 424-LEAD for a referral to a lead-testing professional.

◊ **Smart Remodeling Checklist**
Before the work begins:
▫ Have your paint tested for lead by a qualified professional.
▫ Cover interior and exterior exposed areas with plastic sheeting.
▫ Turn off forced-air heating and air conditioning systems.

During work:
▫ Keep all non-workers outside of the work area.
▫ Wear protective clothing and shoes while doing the work.
▫ Use a properly fitted respirator equipped with HEPA filters.
▫ Exercise caution when using paint strippers since they contain toxic chemicals.
▫ Do not eat, drink, or smoke in the work area.

- Do not dry-sand, blast, or power-wash to remove lead-based paint.
- Do not use high-temperature heat guns or open flames on lead-based paint.

After work is completed:
- Remove plastic sheeting by rolling or folding inward.
- Wrap construction debris with plastic.
- Vacuum exposed areas with a HEPA filter-equipped vacuum cleaner.
- Wash exposed areas with a general all-purpose cleaner or lead-specific cleaning product.
- Change clothes and shoes before leaving the work area. Machine wash separately.
- Shower and wash your hair right after finishing work.
- Test areas for lead dust contamination after final cleanup.

◊ **Helpful Contacts**

You may need additional information on how to protect yourself while remodeling or renovating. For more information:

- Call your State lead-poisoning prevention contact and your *State Department of Environmental Protection* to find out what assistance is available.
- Call your local building code officials to find out what regulations apply to the renovation and remodeling work that you are planning.
- Call your local health department to find out what other information is available about lead hazards and what assistance is available to you.
- Call the *National Lead Information Center* at (800)424-LEAD to get a list of laboratories that can analyze paint and dust samples for lead, and to obtain other important lead hazard information, such as the pamphlets *Lead Poisoning and Your Children* and *Protect Your Family From Lead in Your Home*. In the future, renovation and remodeling contractors may be required to provide a copy of this pamphlet to homeowners and occupants before they begin work.
- Call the *Housing and Urban Development* (HUD) *Office of Lead Hazard Control* at (888) LEADLIST to obtain a list of trained inspectors.
- Call the *Occupational Safety and Health Administration* (OSHA), *Department of Job Safety and Health* at (202) 219-8151 to get information on respirators and protective clothing.
- Call the *National Conference of State Legislatures* at (303) 830-2200 to get information about the current State regulations for disposing of lead waste in your area.

Asbestos and Your Health

What Is Asbestos?

Asbestos is the name given to a number of naturally occurring fibrous silicate minerals that have been mined for their useful properties, such as thermal insulation, chemical and thermal stability, and high tensile strength. In the past, asbestos was added to a variety of products to strengthen them and to provide heat insulation and fire resistance. The three most common types of asbestos are: a) *chrysotile*, b) *amosite*, and c) *crocidolite*. Chrysotile, also known as "white asbestos" and a member of the Serpentine mineral group is the most common. Asbestos can **only** be identified under a microscope. *(So don't let any Realtors tell you there's no asbestos in an older house you want to buy– unless they can prove they have microscopic vision!)*

Asbestos differs from other minerals in its crystal development. The crystal formation of asbestos is in the form of long thin fibers. Asbestos is divided into two mineral groups - *Serpentine* and *Amphibole*. The division between the two types of asbestos is based upon the crystalline structure. Serpentines have a sheet or layered structure where amphiboles have a chain-like structure. As the only member of the serpentine group, *Chrysotile* (A, B) is the most common type of asbestos found in buildings. Chrysotile makes up approximately 90%-95% of all asbestos contained in buildings in the United States.

In the amphibole group, there are five types of asbestos. As an acronym for the Asbestos Mines of South Africa, *Amosite* is the second most prevalent type of asbestos found in building materials. Amosite is also known as "brown asbestos." Next, there is *Crocidolite* or "blue asbestos," which is an asbestos found in specialized high temperature applications. The other three types, *Anthophyllite*, *Tremolite*, and *Actinolite*, are rare and found mainly as contaminants in other minerals. Asbestos deposits can be found throughout the world and are still mined in Australia, Canada, South Africa, and the former Soviet Union.

Why is asbestos a hazard?

Asbestos is made up of microscopic bundles of fibers that may become airborne when distributed. These fibers get into the air and may become inhaled into the lungs, where they may cause significant health problems. Researchers still have not determined a "safe level" of exposure but we know the greater and the longer the exposure, the greater the risk of contracting an asbestos related disease. Some of these health problems include:

◊ **Asbestosis** - a lung disease first found in naval shipyard workers. As asbestos fibers are inhaled, they may become trapped in the lung tissue. The body tries to dissolve the fibers by producing an acid. This acid, due to the chemical resistance of the fiber, does little to damage the fiber, but may scar the surrounding tissue. Eventually, this scarring may become so severe that the lungs cannot function. The latency period (meaning the time it takes for the disease to become developed) is often 25-40 years.

◊ **Mesothelioma** - a cancer of the pleura (the outer lining of the lung and chest cavity) and/or the peritoneum (the lining of the abdominal wall). This form of cancer is peculiar because the only known cause is from asbestos exposure. The latency period for mesothelioma is often 15-30 years.

◊ **Lung Cancer** - caused by asbestos. The effects of lung cancer are often greatly increased by cigarette smoking *(by about 50%)!* Cancer of the gastrointestinal tract can also be caused by asbestos. The latency period for cancer is often 15-30 years.

Despite the common misconception, asbestos does not cause head-aches, sore muscles or other immediate symptoms. As mentioned above, the effects often go unnoticed for 15-40 years.

Although most studies deal with occupational exposures, a growing number of studies have linked disease to environmental asbestos exposures. For instance, there are reports of markedly elevated mesothelioma rates in populations living in areas in Greece, Turkey and New Caledonia with substantial quantities of tremolite asbestos in the soil, particularly among individuals who used tremolite asbestos to whitewash their homes. In Libby, Montana, asbestos related diseases have occurred not only in miners, but among their family members and other non-workers exposed through environmental sources of asbestos. Asbestos deposits, including both chrysotile and amphibole asbestos, are located in many parts of the United States and are commonly associated with serpentine, talc or vermiculite. Environmental exposures can occur when these formations are disturbed, thus releasing fibers into the air.

When is asbestos a hazard?

Asbestos is not always an immediate hazard. In fact, if asbestos can be maintained in good condition, it is recommended that it be left alone and periodic surveillance performed to monitor its condition. It is only when asbestos containing materials *(ACM)* are disturbed or the materials become damaged that it becomes a hazard. When the materials become damaged, the fibers separate and may then become airborne. In the asbestos industry, the term "*friable*" is used to describe asbestos that can be reduced to dust by hand pressure. "*Non-friable*" means asbestos that is too hard to be reduced to dust by hand. Non-friable materials, such as transite siding and floor tiles, are not regulated provided it does not become friable. Machine grinding, sanding and dry-buffing are ways of causing non-friable materials to become friable.

Where Can Asbestos Be Found?

Asbestos is commonly used as an acoustic insulator, thermal insulation, fire proofing and in other building materials. Asbestos fibers are **incredibly strong** and have properties that make them resistant to heat. There are products still in use today that contain asbestos. Most of these are materials used in heat and acoustic insulation, fire proofing, and roofing and flooring.

Figure 31: Some of the more common products that may contain Asbestos	
Acoustical Plaster Adhesives Asphalt Floor Tile Base Flashing Blown-in Insulation Boiler Insulation Breaching Insulation Caulking/Putties Ceiling Tiles and Lay-in Panels Cement Pipes Cement Siding Cement Wallboard Chalkboards Construction Mastics (floor tile, carpet, ceiling tile, etc.) Cooling Towers Decorative Plaster Ductwork Flexible Fabric Connections Electric Wiring Insulation Electrical Cloth Electrical Panel Partitions Elevator Brake Shoes Elevator Equipment Panels	Fire Blankets Fire Curtains Fire Doors Fireproofing Materials Flooring Backing Heating and Electrical Ducts High Temperature Gaskets HVAC Duct Insulation Joint Compounds Laboratory Gloves Laboratory Hoods/Table Tops Packing Materials (for wall/floor penetrations) Pipe Insulation (corrugated air-cell, block, etc.) Roofing Felt Roofing Shingles Spackling Compounds Spray-Applied Insulation Taping Compounds (thermal) Textured Paints/Coatings Thermal Paper Products Vinyl Floor Tile Vinyl Sheet Flooring Vinyl Wall Coverings Wallboard

Those products made today which still contain asbestos that could be inhaled are required to be labeled as such. However, until the 1970s, many types of building products and insulation materials used in homes contained asbestos. Here's some more detail about common products that might have contained asbestos in the past, and conditions which may release fibers, include:

◊ **Steam Pipes**, **Boilers**, and **Furnace Ducts** insulated with an asbestos blanket or asbestos paper tape. These materials may release asbestos fibers if damaged, repaired, or removed improperly.

◊　**Resilient Floor Tiles** (vinyl asbestos, asphalt, and rubber), the backing on **Vinyl Sheet Flooring** and **Adhesives** used for installing floor tile. Sanding tiles can release fibers. So may scraping or sanding the backing of sheet flooring during removal.

◊　**Cement Sheet**, **Millboard**, and **Paper** used as insulation around furnaces and wood burning stoves. Repairing or removing appliances may release asbestos fibers. So may cutting, tearing, sanding, drilling, or sawing insulation.

◊　**Door Gaskets** in furnaces, wood stoves, and coal stoves. Worn seals can release asbestos fibers during use.

◊　**Soundproofing** or **Decorative Material** sprayed on walls and ceilings. Loose, crumbly, or water-damaged material may release fibers. So will sanding, drilling, or scraping the material.

◊　**Patching and Joint Compounds** for walls and ceilings, and **Textured Paints**. Sanding, scraping, or drilling these surfaces may release asbestos.

◊　**Asbestos Cement Roofing**, **Shingles**, and **Siding**. These products are not likely to release asbestos fibers unless sawed, dilled, or cut.

◊　**Artificial Ashes and Embers** sold for use in gas-fired fireplaces. Also, other older household products such as **Fireproof Gloves**, **Stove-Top Pads**, **Ironing Board Covers**, and certain **Hairdryers**.

◊　**Automobile Brake Pads and Linings**, **Clutch Facings**, and **Gaskets**.

What Should Be Done About Asbestos In The Home?

If you think asbestos may be in your home, don't panic! Usually the best thing is to leave asbestos material that is in good condition alone. Generally, material in good condition will not release asbestos fibers. There is no danger *UNLESS* fibers are released and inhaled into the lungs. Check material regularly if you suspect it may contain asbestos. Don't touch it, but look for signs of wear or damage such as tears, abrasions, or water damage. Damaged material may release asbestos fibers. This is particularly true if you often disturb it by hitting, rubbing, or handling it, or if it is exposed to extreme vibration or air flow. Sometimes, the best way to deal with slightly damaged material is to limit access to the area and not touch or disturb it. Discard damaged or worn asbestos gloves, stove-top pads, or ironing board covers. Check with local health, environmental, or other appropriate officials to find out proper handling and disposal procedures. **If asbestos material is more than slightly damaged, or if you are going to make changes in your home that might disturb it, repair or**

removal by a professional is needed. Before you have your house remodeled, find out whether asbestos materials are present.

How To Identify Materials That Contain Asbestos

You can't tell whether a material contains asbestos simply by looking at it, unless it is labeled. *(So don't let any Realtors tell you, "Oh, don't worry Mr. & Mrs. Buyer, I've been a real estate agent for many years and I know what asbestos looks like and there's definitely none in this house. Take my word for it!")* If in doubt, treat the material as if it contains asbestos or have it sampled and analyzed by a qualified professional. **A professional should take samples for analysis,** since a professional knows what to look for, and because there may be an increased health risk if fibers are released. **In fact, if done incorrectly, sampling can be more hazardous than leaving the material alone. Taking samples yourself is not recommended.** If you nevertheless choose to take the samples yourself, take care not to release asbestos fibers into the air or onto yourself. Material that is in good condition and will not be disturbed (by remodeling, for example) should be left alone. Only material that is damaged or will be disturbed should be sampled. Anyone who samples asbestos-containing materials should have as much information as possible on the handling of asbestos before sampling, and at a minimum, should observe the following procedures:

◊　Make sure no one else is in the room when sampling is done.

◊　Wear disposable gloves or wash hands after sampling.

◊　Shut down any heating or cooling systems to minimize the spread of any released fibers.

◊　Do not disturb the material any more than is needed to take a small sample.

◊　Place a plastic sheet on the floor below the area to be sampled.

◊　Wet the material using a fine mist of water containing a few drops of detergent before taking the sample. The water/detergent mist will reduce the release of asbestos fibers.

◊　Carefully cut a piece from the entire depth of the material using, for example, a small knife, corer, or other sharp object. Place the small piece into a clean container (for example, a 35 mm film canister, small glass or plastic vial, or high quality re-sealable plastic bag).

◊　Tightly seal the container after the sample is in it.

◊　Carefully dispose of the plastic sheet. Use a damp paper towel to clean up any material on the outside of the container or around the area sampled. Dispose of asbestos materials according to State and local procedures.

◊　Label the container with an identification number and clearly State when and where the sample was taken.

◊　Patch the sampled area with the smallest possible piece of duct tape to prevent fiber release.

◊　Send the sample to an asbestos analysis laboratory accredited by the *National Voluntary Laboratory Accreditation Program* (NVLAP) at the *National Institute of Standards and Technology* (NIST). A directory of NVLAP accredited laboratories is available on the NVLAP web site at http://ts.nist.gov/ts/htdocs/210/214/214.htm. Your State or local health department may also be able to help.

Asbestos Do's And Don'ts For The Homeowner

◊   Do keep activities to a minimum in any areas having damaged material that may contain asbestos.

◊   Do take every precaution to avoid damaging asbestos material.

◊   **Do have removal and major repair done by people trained and qualified in handling asbestos. It is highly recommended that sampling and minor repair also be done by asbestos professionals.**

◊   Don't dust, sweep, or vacuum debris that may contain asbestos.

◊   Don't saw, sand, scrape, or drill holes in asbestos materials.

◊   Don't use abrasive pads or brushes on power strippers to strip wax from asbestos flooring. Never use a power stripper on a dry floor.

◊   Don't sand or try to level asbestos flooring or its backing. When asbestos flooring needs replacing, install new floor covering over it, if possible.

◊   Don't track material that could contain asbestos through the house. If you cannot avoid walking through the area, have it cleaned with a wet mop. If the material is from a damaged area, or if a large area must be cleaned, **call an asbestos professional.**

How To Manage An Asbestos Problem

If the asbestos material is in good shape and will not be disturbed, do nothing! If it is a problem, there are two types of corrections: repair and removal. **Repair** usually involves either sealing or covering asbestos material. Sealing (encapsulation) involves treating the material with a sealant that either binds the asbestos fibers together or coats the material so fibers are not released. Pipe, furnace, and boiler insulation can sometimes be repaired this way. **This should be done only by a professional trained to handle asbestos safely!**

Covering (enclosure) involves placing something over or around the material that contains asbestos to prevent release of fibers. Exposed insulated piping may be covered with a protective wrap or jacket. With any type of repair, the asbestos remains in place. Repair is usually cheaper than removal, but it may make later removal of asbestos, if necessary, more difficult and costly.

Repairs can either be major or minor. Major repairs must be done only by a professional trained in methods for safely handling asbestos. Minor repairs should also be done by professionals since there is always a risk of exposure to fibers when asbestos is disturbed. Doing minor repairs yourself is **not recommended** since improper handling of asbestos materials can create a hazard where none existed. If you nevertheless choose to do minor repairs, you should have as much information as possible on the handling of asbestos before doing anything. Contact your State or local health department or regional EPA office for information about asbestos training programs in your area. Your local school district may also have information about asbestos professionals and training programs for school buildings. *Even if you have completed a training program, do not try anything more than minor repairs.* Before undertaking minor repairs, carefully examine the area around the damage to make sure it is stable. **As a general matter, any damaged area which is bigger than the size of your hand is not a minor repair.**

Before undertaking minor repairs, be sure to follow all the precautions described earlier for sampling asbestos material. Always wet the asbestos material using a fine mist of water containing a few drops of detergent. Commercial products designed to fill holes and seal damaged areas are available. Small areas of material such as pipe insulation can be covered by wrapping a special fabric, such as re-wettable glass cloth, around it. These products are available from stores *(listed in the telephone directory under "Safety Equipment and Clothing")* which specialize in asbestos materials and safety items.

Removal is usually the most expensive method and, unless required by State or local regulations, should be the last option considered in most situations. This is because removal poses the greatest risk of fiber release. However, removal may be required when remodeling or making major changes to your home that will disturb asbestos material. Also, removal may be called for if asbestos material is damaged extensively and cannot be otherwise repaired. **Removal is complex and must be done only by a contractor with special training. Improper removal may actually increase the health risks to you and your family.**

Asbestos Professionals: Who Are They And What Can They Do?

Asbestos professionals are trained in handling asbestos material. The type of professional will depend on the type of product and what needs to be done to correct the problem. You may hire a general asbestos contractor or, in some cases, a professional trained to handle specific products containing asbestos. Asbestos professionals can conduct asbestos home inspections, take samples of suspected material, assess its condition, and advise about what corrections are needed and who is qualified to make these corrections. Once again, material in good condition need not be sampled unless it is likely to be disturbed.

Professional correction or abatement contractors repair or remove asbestos materials. Some firms offer combinations of testing, assessment, and correction. A professional hired to assess the need for corrective action should not be connected with an asbestos-correction firm. It is better to use two different firms so there is *no conflict of interest.* Services vary from one area to another around the country.

The Federal government has training courses for asbestos professionals around the country. Some State and local governments also have or require training or certification courses. Ask asbestos professionals to **document their completion of Federal or State approved training. Each person performing work in your home should provide proof of training and licensing in asbestos work, such as completion of EPA approved training.** State and local health departments or EPA regional offices may have listings of licensed professionals in your area.

If you have a problem that requires the services of asbestos professionals, check their credentials carefully. Hire professionals who are trained, experienced, reputable, and accredited - especially if accreditation is required by State or local laws. Before hiring a professional, ask for references from previous clients. Find out if they were satisfied. Ask whether the professional has handled similar situations. Get cost estimates from several professionals, as the charges for these services can vary.

Though private homes are usually not covered by the asbestos regulations that apply to schools and public buildings, professionals should still use procedures described during Federal or State approved training. Homeowners should be alert to the chance of misleading claims by asbestos consultants and contractors. There have been reports of firms incorrectly claiming that asbestos materials in homes must be replaced. In other cases, firms have encouraged unnecessary removals or performed them improperly. Unnecessary removals are a waste of money. Improper removals may actually increase the health risks to you and your family. To guard against this, know what services are available and what procedures and precautions are needed to do the job properly.

In addition to general asbestos contractors, you may select a roofing, flooring, or plumbing contractor trained to handle asbestos when it is necessary to remove and replace roofing, flooring, siding, or Asbestos-Cement pipe that is part of a water system. Normally, roofing and flooring contractors are exempt from State and local licensing requirements because they do not perform any other asbestos-correction work. Call 1-800-USA-ROOF for names of qualified roofing contractors in your area. (Illinois residents call 708-318-6722.) For information on asbestos in floors, read *"Recommended Work Procedures for Resilient Floor Covers."* You can write for a copy from the Resilient Floor Covering Institute, 966 Hungerford Drive, Suite 12-B, Rockville, MD 20850. Enclose a stamped, business-size, self-addressed envelope.

Asbestos containing automobile brake pads and linings, clutch facings, and gaskets should be repaired and replaced only by a professional using special protective equipment. Many of these products are now available without asbestos. For more information, read *"Guidance for Preventing Asbestos Disease Among Auto Mechanics,"* available from regional EPA offices.

If You Hire A Professional Asbestos Inspector

Make sure that the inspection will include a complete visual examination and the careful collection and lab analysis of samples. If asbestos is present, the inspector should provide a written evaluation describing its location and extent of damage, and give recommendations for correction or prevention. Make sure an inspecting firm makes frequent site visits if it is hired to assure that a contractor follows proper procedures and requirements. The inspector may recommend and perform checks after the correction to assure the area has been properly cleaned.

If You Hire A Corrective-Action Contractor

◊ Check with your local air pollution control board, the local agency responsible for worker safety, and the Better Business Bureau. Ask if the firm has had any safety violations. Find out if there are legal actions filed against it.

◊ Insist that the contractor use the proper equipment to do the job. The workers must wear approved respirators, gloves, and other protective clothing.

◊ Before work begins, get a written contract specifying the work plan, cleanup, and the **applicable Federal, State, and local regulations which the contractor must follow** (such as notification requirements and asbestos disposal procedures). Contact your State and local health departments, EPA's regional office, and the Occupational Safety and Health Administration's regional office to find out what the regulations are.

◊ Be sure the contractor follows local asbestos removal and disposal laws. At the end of the job, get written assurance from the contractor that all procedures have been followed.

◊ Assure that the contractor avoids spreading or tracking asbestos dust into other areas of your home. They should seal the work area from the rest of the house using plastic sheeting and duct tape, and also turn off the heating and air conditioning system. For some repairs, such as pipe insulation removal, plastic glove bags may be adequate. They must be sealed with tape and properly disposed of when the job is complete.

◊ Make sure the work site is clearly marked as a hazard area. Do not allow household members and pets into the area until work is completed.

◊ Insist that the contractor apply a wetting agent to the asbestos material with a hand sprayer that creates a fine mist before removal. Wet fibers do not float in the air as easily as dry fibers and will be easier to clean up.

◊ Make sure the contractor does not break removed material into small pieces. This could release asbestos fibers into the air. Pipe insulation was usually installed in preformed blocks and should be removed in complete pieces.

◊ Upon completion, assure that the contractor cleans the area well with wet mops, wet rags, sponges, or *HEPA* (High Efficiency Particulate Air) vacuum cleaners. **A regular vacuum cleaner must never be used.**

◊ Wetting helps reduce the chance of spreading asbestos fibers in the air. All asbestos materials and disposable equipment and clothing used in the job must be placed in sealed, leak proof, and labeled plastic bags. The work site should be visually free of dust and debris. Air monitoring (to make sure there is no increase of asbestos fibers in the air) may be necessary to assure that the contractor's job is done properly. ***This should be done by someone not connected with the contractor.***

CAUTION!
◊   Do not dust, sweep, or vacuum debris that may contain asbestos. These steps will disturb tiny asbestos fibers and may release them into the air. Remove dust by wet mopping or with a special HEPA vacuum cleaner used by trained asbestos contractors.

Vermiculite Attic Insulation

The U.S. Environmental Protection Agency *(EPA)* offices have received a large number of phone calls from citizens concerned about vermiculite insulation in their home that might be contaminated with asbestos. EPA is gathering more information about *Vermiculite Insulation* and other products containing vermiculite. If you suspect vermiculite insulation is in your home, the safest thing is to leave the material alone. **If you decide to remove or must otherwise disturb the material due to a renovation project, consult with an experienced asbestos contractor.** The following information provides a common-sense approach to help you find out what kind of insulation is in your home and decide what to do if you have vermiculite insulation.

What is vermiculite insulation?

Vermiculite is a naturally occurring mineral that has the unusual property of expanding into worm-like accordion shaped pieces when heated. The expanded vermiculite is a light-weight, fire-resistant, absorbent, and odorless material. These properties allow vermiculite to be used to make numerous products, including attic insulation.

Do I have vermiculite insulation?

Vermiculite can be purchased in various forms for various uses. Sizes of vermiculite products range from very fine particles to large (coarse) pieces nearly an inch long. Vermiculite attic insulation is a pebble-like, pour-in product and is usually light-brown or gold in color. The photos in Figure 32, Figure 33, and Figure 34 on page 266 show several samples of vermiculite attic insulation.

Figure 32: Different Grades of Vermiculite

Figure 33: Vermiculite Insulation in an Attic

Figure 34: Attic Containing Vermiculite Insulation

Is vermiculite insulation a problem?

Prior to its close in 1990, much of the world's supply of vermiculite came from a mine near Libby, Montana. This mine had a natural deposit of asbestos which resulted in the vermiculite being contaminated with asbestos. Attic insulation produced using vermiculite ore, particularly ore that originated from the Libby mine, may contain asbestos fibers. Today, vermiculite is mined at three U.S. facilities and in other countries which have low levels of contamination in the finished material.

What should I do if I have vermiculite attic insulation in my home?

Do NOT Disturb It!! Any disturbance has the potential to release asbestos fibers into the air. Limiting the number of trips you make to your attic and shortening the length of those trips can help limit your potential exposure. EPA and the *Agency for Toxic Substances and Disease Registry* (ATSDR) strongly recommend that:
◊   Vermiculite insulation be left undisturbed in your attic. Due to the uncertainties with existing testing techniques, it is best to assume that the material may contain asbestos.
◊   You should not store boxes or other items in your attic if retrieving the material will disturb the insulation.
◊   **Children should not be allowed** to play in an attic with open areas of vermiculite insulation.
◊   If you plan to remodel or conduct renovations that would disturb the vermiculite, **hire professionals trained and certified to handle asbestos to safely remove the material.**
◊   You should never attempt to remove the insulation yourself. Hire professionals trained and certified to safely remove the material.

What if I occasionally have to go into my attic?

EPA and ATSDR *strongly recommend* that homeowners make every effort not to disturb vermiculite insulation in their attics. If you occasionally have to go into your attic, current best practices state that you should:
1. Make every effort to stay on the floored part of your attic and to not disturb the insulation.
2. If you must perform activities that may disturb the attic insulation such as moving boxes (or other materials), do so as gently as possible to minimize the disturbance.
3. Leave the attic immediately after the disturbance.
4. If you need work done in your attic, such as the installation of cable or utility lines, *hire trained and certified professionals who can safely do the work.*
5. It is possible that vermiculite attic insulation can sift through cracks in the ceiling, around light fixtures, or around ceiling fans. You can prevent this by sealing the cracks and holes that insulation could pass through.
6. **Common dust masks are not effective against asbestos fibers.** For information on the requirements for wearing a respirator mask, visit the following *Occupational Safety and Health Administration* (OSHA) website: www.osha.gov/

What are the next steps?

The guidance provided in this section reflects the current testing technology and knowledge of precautions one may take regarding vermiculite attic insulation. EPA is initiating further studies on vermiculite attic insulation and pursuing other asbestos related issues. Additional information will be provided to the public via the EPA www.epa.gov/asbestos/ and ATSDR www.atsdr.cdc.gov/ web sites and through additional outreach materials as it becomes available.

Is my health at risk from previous exposures to the asbestos in the insulation?

If you removed or disturbed the insulation, it is possible that you inhaled some asbestos fibers. Also the disturbance may have resulted in the fibers being deposited into other areas of the home. Exposure to asbestos increases your risk of developing lung disease. That risk is made worse by smoking. In general, the greater the exposure to asbestos, the greater the chance of developing harmful health effects. **Disease symptoms may take several years to develop following exposure.** If you are concerned about possible exposure, consult a physician who specializes in lung diseases - *Pulmonologist.*

Where can I get info on insulation testing or removal?

EPA and ATSDR strongly recommend using a trained and certified professional to conduct removal work. ***Removing the insulation yourself could potentially spread asbestos fibers throughout your home, putting you and your family at risk of inhaling these fibers.*** For certified asbestos removal professionals in your area, refer to your local Yellow Pages. Your State Environmental Agency can confirm that the company's credentials are current. Find your State Agency at: www.epa.gov/epahome/whereyoulive.htm

Currently, there are specific technical issues involving vermiculite sampling that can complicate testing for the presence of asbestos fibers and interpreting the risk from exposure. EPA and ATSDR are not recommending at this time that homeowners have vermiculite attic insulation tested for asbestos. As testing techniques are refined, EPA and ATSDR will provide information to the public on the benefits of testing that produce more definitive and accurate test results.

What about work-related exposure to vermiculite?

Workers who have had significant past exposure, or have significant ongoing exposure to asbestos, to vermiculite from Libby, or to other asbestos contaminated materials should consider getting a medical exam from a physician who knows about diseases caused by asbestos. For more information and to obtain a fact sheet concerning occupational exposure to vermiculite, contact the *National Institute for Occupational Safety and Health* (NIOSH) at: 1-800-35-NIOSH, or www.cdc.gov/niosh/homepage.html

Radon Gas In Your Home

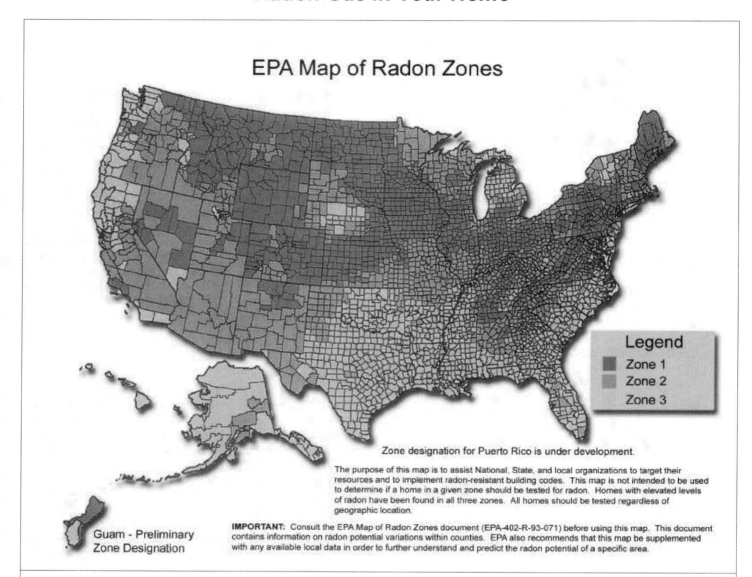

Figure 35: EPA Map of Radon Zones

The Map was developed using five factors to determine radon potential: indoor radon measurements; geology; aerial radioactivity; soil permeability; and, foundation type. Radon potential assessment is based on geologic provinces. Radon Index Matrix is the quantitative assessment of radon potential. Confidence Index Matrix shows the quantity and quality of the data used to assess radon potential. Geologic Provinces were adapted to county boundaries for the Map of Radon Zones.

Sections 307 and 309 of the Indoor Radon Abatement Act of 1988 (IRAA) directed EPA to list and identify areas of the U.S. with the potential for elevated indoor radon levels. EPA's Map of Radon Zones assigns each of the 3,141 counties in the U.S. to one of three zones based on radon potential:

◊   **Zone 1 counties** have a predicted average indoor radon screening level greater than 4 pCi/L (picoCuries per liter)
◊   **Zone 2 counties** have a predicted average indoor radon screening level between 2 and 4 pCi/L
◊   **Zone 3 counties** have a predicted average indoor radon screening level less than 2 pCi/L

Individual US State Radon Maps are available at http://www.epa.gov/iaq/radon/zonemap.html

Guide to Protecting Your Family From Radon

◊ **EPA Recommends:**

□ Test your home for radon -- it's easy and inexpensive.

□ Fix your home if your radon level is 4 picoCuries per liter (pCi/L) or higher.

□ Radon levels less than 4 pCi/L still pose a risk, and in many cases may be reduced.

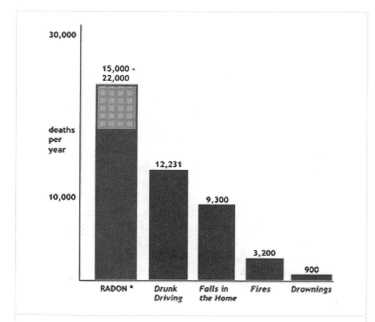

Figure 36: Radon is estimated to cause thousands of cancer deaths in the U.S. each year.

* Radon is estimated to cause between 15,000 and 22,000 lung cancer deaths per year according to the National Academy of Sciences 1998 data. The numbers of deaths from other causes are taken from 2001 National Safety Council reports.

◊ **Radon is a cancer-causing, radioactive gas.** You can't see radon. And you can't smell it or taste it. But it may be a problem in your home. Radon is estimated to cause many thousands of deaths each year. That's because when you breathe air containing radon, you can get lung cancer. In fact, the Surgeon General has warned that radon is the second leading cause of lung cancer in the United States today. Only smoking causes more lung cancer deaths. **If you smoke and your home has high radon levels, your risk of lung cancer is especially high.**

◊ **Radon can be found all over the U.S.** Radon comes from the natural (radioactive) breakdown of uranium in soil, rock and water and gets into the air you breathe. Radon can be found all over the U.S. It can get into any type of building -

homes, offices, and schools - and result in a high indoor radon level. But you and your family are most likely to get your greatest exposure at home. That's where you spend most of your time.

◊ **You should test for radon.** Testing is the only way to know if you and your family are at risk from radon. EPA and the Surgeon General recommend testing all homes below the third floor for radon. EPA also recommends testing in schools. Testing is inexpensive and easy - it should only take a few minutes of your time. Millions of Americans have already tested their homes for radon (see How to Test Your Home section page 270).

◊ **You can fix a radon problem.** There are simple ways to fix a radon problem that aren't too costly. Even very high levels can be reduced to acceptable levels.

◊ **New homes can be built with radon-resistant features.** Radon-resistant construction techniques can be effective in preventing radon entry. When installed properly and completely, these simple and inexpensive techniques can help reduce indoor radon levels in homes. In addition, installing them at the time of construction makes it easier and less expensive to reduce radon levels further if these passive techniques don't reduce radon levels to below 4 pCi/L. Every new home should be tested after occupancy, even if it was built radon-resistant.

◊ **How Does Radon Get Into Your Home?** Radon is a radioactive gas. It comes from the natural decay of uranium that is found in nearly all soils. It typically moves up through the ground to the air above and into your home through cracks and other holes in the foundation. Your home traps radon inside, where it can build up. Any home may have a radon problem. This means new and old homes, well-sealed and drafty homes, and homes with or without basements. Radon from soil gas is the main cause of radon problems. Sometimes radon enters the home through well water (see Radon **in Water** section page 271). In a small number of homes, the building materials can give off radon, too. However, building materials rarely cause radon problems by themselves.

Nearly 1 out of every 15 homes in the U.S. is estimated to have elevated radon levels. Elevated levels of radon gas have been found in homes in your State. Contact your State radon office for general information about radon in your area. While radon problems may be more common in some areas, any home may have a problem. The only way to know about your home is to test. Radon can be a problem in schools and workplaces, too. Ask your State radon office about radon problems in schools, daycare and childcare facilities, and workplaces in your area.

Figure 37: How Radon Gets Into Homes

1. Cracks in solid floors
2. Construction joints
3. Cracks in walls
4. Gaps in suspended floors
5. Gaps around service pipes
6. Cavities inside walls
7. The water supply

◊ **How to Test Your Home**

You can't see radon, but it's not hard to find out if you have a radon problem in your home. All you need to do is test for radon. Testing is easy and should only take a few minutes of your time. The amount of radon in the air is measured in "picoCuries per liter of air," or "pCi/L." Sometimes test results are expressed in Working Levels (WL) rather than picoCuries per liter (pCi/L). There are many kinds of low-cost "do-it-yourself" radon test kits you can get through the mail and in hardware stores and other retail outlets. If you prefer, or if you are buying or selling a home, you can hire a qualified tester to do the testing for you. You should contact your State radon office about obtaining a list of qualified testers. You can also contact a private radon proficiency program for lists of privately certified radon professionals serving your area. For links and information, visit www.epa.gov/radon/proficiency.html.

◊ **There are Two General Ways to Test for Radon**

▫ *SHORT-TERM TESTING:* The quickest way to test is with short-term tests. Short-term tests remain in your home for two days to 90 days, depending on the device. "Charcoal canisters," "alpha track," "electret ion chamber," "continuous monitors," and "charcoal liquid

scintillation" detectors are most commonly used for short-term testing. Because radon levels tend to vary from day to day and season to season, a short-term test is less likely than a long-term test to tell you your year-round average radon level. If you need results quickly, however, a short-term test followed by a second short-term test may be used to decide whether to fix your home.

▫ *LONG-TERM TESTING:* Long-term tests remain in your home for more than 90 days. "Alpha track" and "electret" detectors are commonly used for this type of testing. A long-term test will give you a reading that is more likely to tell you your home's year-round average radon level than a short-term test.

◊ **How To Use a Test Kit**

Follow the instructions that come with your test kit. If you are doing a short-term test, close your windows and outside doors and keep them closed as much as possible during the test. Heating and air-conditioning system fans that re-circulate air may be operated. Do not operate fans or other machines which bring in air from outside. Fans that are part of a radon-reduction system or small exhaust fans operating only for short periods of time may run during the test. If you are doing a short-term test lasting just 2 or 3 days, be sure to close your windows and outside doors at least 12 hours before beginning the test, too. You should not conduct short-term tests lasting just 2 or 3 days during unusually severe storms or periods of unusually high winds. The test kit should be placed in the lowest lived-in level of the home (for example, the basement if it is frequently used, otherwise the first floor). It should be put in a room that is used regularly (like a living room, playroom, den or bedroom) but not your kitchen or bathroom. Place the kit at least 20 inches above the floor in a location where it won't be disturbed - away from drafts, high heat, high humidity, and exterior walls. Leave the kit in place for as long as the package says. Once you've finished the test, reseal the package and send it to the lab specified on the package right away for analysis. You should receive your test results within a few weeks.

◊ **EPA Recommends the Following Testing Steps**

▫ Step 1. Take a short-term test. If your result is 4 pCi/L or higher (0.02 Working Levels [WL] or higher) take a follow-up test (Step 2) to be sure.

▫ Step 2. Follow up with either a long-term test or a second short-term test:
   ▪ For a better understanding of your year-round average radon level, take a long-term test.
   ▪ If you need results quickly, take a second short-term test.

The higher your initial short-term test result, the more certain you can be that you should take a short-term rather than a long-term follow up test. If your first short-term test result is more than twice EPA's 4 pCi/L action level, you should take a second short-term test immediately.

▫ Step 3. If you followed up with a long-term test: Fix your home if your long-term test result is 4 pCi/L or more (0.02 Working Levels [WL] or higher). If you followed up with a second short-term test: The higher your short-term results, the more certain you can be that you should fix your home. Consider fixing your home if the average of your first and second test is 4 pCi/L or higher (0.02 Working Levels [WL] or higher).

◊ **What Your Test Results Mean**

The average indoor radon level is estimated to be about 1.3 pCi/L, and about 0.4 pCi/L of radon is normally found in the outside air. The U.S. Congress has set a long-term goal that indoor radon levels be no more than outdoor levels. While this goal is not yet technologically achievable in all cases, most homes today *can* be reduced to 2 pCi/L or below.

Sometimes short-term tests are less definitive about whether or not your home is above 4 pCi/L. This can happen when your results are close to 4 pCi/L. For example, if the average of your two short-term test results is 4.1 pCi/L, there is about a 50% chance that your year-round average is somewhat below 4 pCi/L. However, EPA believes that any radon exposure carries some risk - no level of radon is safe. Even radon levels below 4 pCi/L pose some risk, and you can reduce your risk of lung cancer by lowering your radon level.

If your living patterns change and you begin occupying a lower level of your home (such as a basement) you should retest your home on that level. Even if your test result is below 4 pCi/L, you may want to test again sometime in the future.

◊ **Radon and Home Sales**

More and more, home buyers and renters are asking about radon levels before they buy or rent a home. Because real estate sales happen quickly, there is often little time to deal with radon and other issues. The best thing to do is to test for radon NOW and save the results in case the buyer is interested in them. Fix a problem if it exists so it won't complicate your home sale. If you are planning to move you can also use the results of two short-term tests done side-by-side (four inches apart) to decide whether to fix your home.

During home sales:
- Buyers often ask if a home has been tested, and if elevated levels were reduced.
- Buyers frequently want tests made by someone who is not involved in the home sale. Your State radon office can assist you in identifying a qualified tester.
- Buyers might want to know the radon levels in areas of the home (like a basement they plan to finish) that the seller might not otherwise test.

Today many homes are built to prevent radon from coming in. Your State or local area may require these radon-resistant construction features. Radon-resistant construction features usually keep radon levels in new homes below 2 pCi/L. If you are buying or renting a new home, ask the owner or builder if it has radon-resistant features. The EPA recommends building new homes with radon-resistant features in high radon potential (Zone 1) areas. For more information, refer to EPA's *Map of Radon Zones* Figure 35 page 268 and other useful EPA documents on radon-resistant new construction, or visit www.epa.gov/radon/index.html. Even if built radon-resistant, every new home should be tested for radon after occupancy. If you have a test result of 4 pCi/L or more, you can have a qualified mitigator easily add a vent fan to an existing passive system for about $300 and further reduce the radon level in your home.

◊ **Radon in Water**

The radon in your home's indoor air can come from two sources, the soil or your water supply. Compared to radon entering the home through water, radon entering your home through the soil is usually a much larger risk.

The radon in your water supply poses an inhalation risk and an ingestion risk. Research has shown that your risk of lung cancer from breathing radon in air is much larger than your risk of stomach cancer from swallowing water with radon in it. Most of your risk from radon in water comes from radon released into the air when water is used for showering and other household purposes.

Radon in your home's water is not usually a problem when its source is surface water. A radon in water problem is more likely when its source is ground water, e.g. a private well or a public water supply system that uses ground water. Some public water systems treat their water to reduce radon levels before it is delivered to your home. If you are concerned that radon may be entering your home through the water and your water comes from a public water supply, contact your water supplier.

If you've tested your private well and have a radon in water problem, it can be easily fixed. Your home's water supply can be treated in two ways. Point-of-entry treatment can effectively remove radon from the water before it enters your home. Point-of-use treatment devices remove radon from your water at the tap, but only treat a small portion of the water you use and are not effective in reducing the risk from breathing radon released into the air from all water used in the home.

For more information, call EPA's *Drinking Water Hotline* at (800) 426-4791 or visit www.epa.gov/safewater/radon.html. If your water comes from a private well, you can also contact your State radon office.

◊ **How to Lower the Radon Level in Your Home**

Since there is no known safe level of radon, there can always be some risk. But the risk can be reduced by lowering the radon level in your home. A variety of methods are used to reduce radon in your home. In some cases, sealing cracks in floors and walls may help to reduce radon. In other cases, simple systems using pipes and fans may be used to reduce radon. Such systems, known as soil suction, do not require major changes to your home. These systems remove radon gas from below the concrete floor and the foundation before it can enter the home. Similar systems can also be installed in houses with crawl spaces. Radon contractors use other methods that may also work in your home. The right system depends on the design of your home and other factors.

The cost of making repairs to reduce radon depends on how your home was built and the extent of the radon problem. Most homes can be fixed for about the same cost as other common home repairs like painting or having a new hot water heater installed. The average house costs about $1,200 for a contractor to fix, although this can range from about $800 to about $2,500. The cost is much less if a passive system was installed during construction.

◊   **Radon and Home Renovations**
If you are planning any major structural renovation, such as converting an unfinished basement area into living space, it is especially important to test the area for radon before you begin the renovation. If your test results indicate a radon problem radon-resistant techniques can be inexpensively included as part of the renovation. Because major renovations can change the level of radon in any home, always test again after work is completed to be sure that radon levels have been reduced. Most soil suction radon reduction systems include a monitor that will indicate whether the system is operating properly. In addition, it's a good idea to retest your home every two years to be sure radon levels remain low.

Lowering high radon levels requires technical knowledge and special skills. You should use a contractor who is trained to fix radon problems. A qualified contractor can study the radon problem in your home and help you pick the right treatment method. Check with your State radon office for names of qualified or State certified radon contractors in your area. You can also contact private radon proficiency programs for lists of privately certified radon professionals in your area. For more information on private radon proficiency programs, visit www.epa.gov/radon/proficiency.html. Picking someone to fix your radon problem is much like choosing a contractor for other home repairs - you may want to get references and more than one estimate. If you are considering fixing your home's radon problem yourself, you should first contact your State radon office for guidance and assistance.

◊   **The Risk of Living With Radon**
Radon gas decays into radioactive particles that can get trapped in your lungs when you breathe. As they break down further, these particles release small bursts of energy. This can damage lung tissue and lead to lung cancer over the course of your lifetime. Not everyone exposed to elevated levels of radon will develop lung cancer. And the amount of time between exposure and the onset of the disease may be many years.

Like other environmental pollutants, there is some uncertainty about the magnitude of radon health risks. However, we know more about radon risks than risks from most other cancer-causing substances. This is because estimates of radon risks are based on studies of cancer in humans (underground miners).

Smoking combined with radon is an especially serious health risk. Stop smoking and lower your radon level to reduce your lung cancer risk.

Children have been reported to have greater risk than adults of certain types of cancer from radiation, but there are currently no conclusive data on whether children are at greater risk than adults from radon.

Your chances of getting lung cancer from radon depend mostly on:
- How much radon is in your home
- The amount of time you spend in your home
- Whether you are a smoker or have ever smoked

◊   **Some Common Myths About Radon**
MYTH: Scientists are not sure that radon really is a problem.
FACT: Although some scientists dispute the precise number of deaths due to radon, all the major health organizations (like the Centers for Disease Control and Prevention, the American Lung Association and the American Medical Association) agree with estimates that radon causes thousands of preventable lung cancer deaths every year. This is especially true among smokers, since the risk to smokers is much greater than to non-smokers.

MYTH: Radon testing is difficult, time-consuming and expensive.
FACT: Radon testing is inexpensive and easy -- it should take only a little of your time.

MYTH: Radon testing devices are not reliable and are difficult to find.
FACT: Reliable testing devices are available through the mail, in hardware stores and other retail outlets. Call your State radon office for a list of radon device companies or visit our radon proficiency program web site for information on two privately run national radon proficiency programs.

MYTH: Homes with radon problems can't be fixed.
FACT: There are solutions to radon problems in homes. Thousands of homeowners have already fixed radon problems in their homes. Radon levels can be readily lowered for $500 to $2,500. Call your State radon office or visit our radon proficiency program web site for information on how to acquire the services of a qualified professional.

MYTH: Radon affects only certain kinds of homes.
FACT: House construction can affect radon levels. However, radon can be a problem in homes of all types: old homes, new homes, drafty homes, insulated homes, homes with basements and homes without basements.

MYTH: Radon is only a problem in certain parts of the country.

FACT: *High radon levels have been found in every State. Radon problems do vary from area to area, but the only way to know the home's radon level is to test.*

MYTH: A neighbor's test result is a good indication of whether your home has a problem.
FACT: *It's not. Radon levels vary from home to home. The only way to know if your home has a radon problem is to test it.*

Figure 38: A neighbor's test result is NOT a good indication of whether your home has a problem!! Radon levels vary from home to home. (So don't let any Realtors or sellers tell you anything different!)

MYTH: Everyone should test their water for radon.
FACT: *While radon gets into some homes through the water, it is important to first test the air in the home for radon. If you find high levels and your water comes from a well, call the Safe Drinking Water Hotline at 1 800-426-4791, or your State radon office for more information.*

MYTH: It is difficult to sell homes where radon problems have been discovered.
FACT: *Where radon problems have been fixed, home sales have not been blocked or frustrated. The added protection is some times a good selling point.*

MYTH: I've lived in my home for so long, it doesn't make sense to take action now.
FACT: *You will reduce your risk of lung cancer when you reduce radon levels, even if you've lived with a radon problem for a long time.*

MYTH: Short-term tests cannot be used for making a decision about whether to fix your home.
FACT: *A short-term test, followed by a second short-term test may be used to decide whether to fix your home. However, the closer the average of your two short-term tests is to 4 pCi/L, the less certain you can be about whether your year-round average is above or below that level. Keep in mind that radon levels below 4 pCi/L still pose some risk. Radon levels can be reduced in some homes to 2 pCi/L or below.*

◊   **State and Regional Radon and Indoor Air Quality Contacts**

- www.epa.gov/iaq/whereyoulive.html

- National Radon Hotline: 1-800-SOS-RADON

- For some other Indoor Air Hotlines to contact: www.epa.gov/iaq/iaqxline.html

- For more information on how to reduce your radon health risk, call your State radon office.

- If you plan to make repairs yourself, be sure to contact your State radon office.

◊   **SURGEON GENERAL HEALTH ADVISORY**
"Indoor radon gas is a national health problem. Radon causes thousands of deaths each year. Millions of homes have elevated radon levels. Homes should be tested for radon. When elevated levels are confirmed, the problem should be corrected."

Buying a New Home? How to Protect Your Family from Radon

◊   **What is Radon?**
Radon causes an estimated 14,000 lung cancer deaths each year. It is the earth's only naturally produced radioactive gas and comes from the breakdown of uranium in soil, rock, and water. You cannot see or smell radon, but it can become a health hazard when it accumulates indoors. It can enter your home through cracks and openings in the foundation floor and walls. When radon decays and is inhaled into the lungs, it releases energy that can damage the DNA in sensitive lung tissue and cause cancer.

Radon is a naturally-occurring radioactive gas that may cause cancer, and may be found in drinking water and indoor air. Some people who are exposed to radon in drinking water may have increased risk of getting cancer over the course of their lifetime, especially lung cancer. Radon in soil under homes is the biggest source of radon in indoor air, and presents a greater risk of lung cancer than radon in drinking water. As required by the *Safe Drinking Water Act*, EPA has developed a proposed regulation to reduce radon in drinking water that has a multimedia mitigation option to reduce radon in indoor air.

Radon (chemical symbol Rn) has numerous different isotopes, but radon-220, and -222 are the most common. Radon causes lung cancer, and is a threat to health because it tends to collect in homes, sometimes to very high concentrations. As a result, radon is the largest source of exposure to naturally occurring radiation.

◊   **Why Buy a Radon-Resistant Home?**
- The Techniques Work - Simple and inexpensive techniques reduce radon levels on average by 50%.

The techniques may also lower levels of other soil gases and decrease moisture problems.

- ❑ It's Cost Effective - Building in the features is much cheaper than fixing a radon problem later.
- ❑ Save Energy - Radon-reduction techniques are consistent with state-of-the-art energy-efficient construction. When using these techniques, follow the Model Energy Code (or other applicable energy codes) for weatherization, which will result in energy savings and lower utility bills.
- ❑ Upgrading is Easy - If high levels of radon are found, a fan can easily be installed as part of the system for further radon reduction.

◊ **How Do Costs Compare?**
- ❑ Average cost to install radon-resistant features in an existing home: **$800 - $2,500**
- ❑ Average cost to install radon-resistant features during new home construction: **$350 - $500**

◊ **What are Radon-Resistant Features?**
The techniques may vary for different foundations and site requirements, but the basic elements are shown in Figure 39 page 274.

Figure 39: Some Radon-Resistant Features For Homes

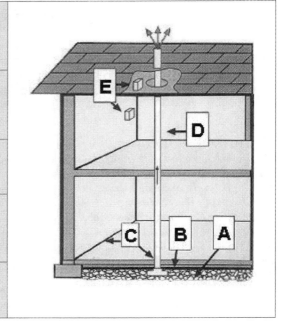

A. Gas Permeable Layer
This layer is placed beneath the slab or flooring system to allow the soil gas to move freely underneath the house. In many cases, the material used is a 4-inch layer of clean gravel.

B. Plastic Sheeting
Plastic sheeting is placed on top of the gas permeable layer and under the slab to help prevent the soil gas from entering the home. In crawlspaces, the sheeting is placed over the crawlspace floor.

C. Sealing and Caulking
All openings in the concrete foundation floor are sealed to reduce soil gas entry into the home.

D. Vent Pipe
A 3- or 4-inch gas-tight or PVC pipe (commonly used for plumbing) runs from the gas permeable layer through the house to the roof to safely vent radon and other soil gases above the house.

E. Junction Box
An electrical junction box is installed in case an electric venting fan is needed later.

◊ **Did You Know?**
- ❑ Radon is the second leading cause of lung cancer after smoking.
- ❑ High radon levels have been found in every State.
- ❑ Levels can vary widely, even from home to home in the same neighborhood.
- ❑ Radon levels can be lowered, and homes can be built radon-resistant.

◊ **What Can You Do?**
Simple, inexpensive techniques can be used to lower radon levels and increase energy efficiency in your new home. Here are basic steps to follow when buying a new home.

1. Check Your Area's Radon Potential - Find out if you are buying a home in a high radon area. The Environmental Protection Agency's map of radon zones Figure 35: EPA Map of Radon Zones page 268 shows which areas have the greatest potential for elevated indoor radon readings. Homes in places with high radon potential, called Zone 1 areas, should be built with radon-resistant features.

2. Install a Radon Reduction System - Talk to your builder about installing a radon reduction system. You can obtain free copies of the EPA's *Model Standards* and architectural drawings and use them to explain the techniques to your builder. Let your builder know that the radon resistant features can be easily installed with common building practices and materials.

3. Remember: Test Your Home - Every new home should be tested for radon after occupancy. Test your home even if it has the radon resistant features. Test kits are inexpensive and may be purchased at your local hardware store. Or simply call the *National Safety Council Radon Hotline* at (800) SOS-RADON to order a test kit.

4. If Radon Levels Are Still High, Activate - If your home tests at 4.0 picoCuries per liter (pCi/L) or above, activate the system by installing an in-line fan. Call a local radon mitigator about installing the fan. *Call your State radon office for a list of radon device companies that have met State requirements.*

Consumer's Guide to Radon Reduction

◊ **Reduce Radon Levels In Your Home**
Radon is the second leading cause of lung cancer. The Surgeon General and the EPA recommend testing for radon and reducing radon in homes that have high levels. Fix your home if your radon level is confirmed to be 4 picoCuries per liter (pCi/L) or higher. Radon levels less than 4 pCi/L still pose a risk, and in many cases may be reduced. If you smoke and your home has high radon levels, your risk of lung cancer is especially high.

◊ **Select A State Certified and/or Qualified Radon Mitigation Contractor**
Choose a qualified radon mitigation contractor to fix your home. Start by checking with your State radon office. Many states require radon professionals to be licensed, certified, or registered. You can also contact private radon proficiency programs for lists of privately certified radon professionals in your area.

◊ **Radon Reduction Techniques Work**
Radon reduction systems work. Some radon reduction systems can reduce radon levels in your home by up to 99%. The cost of fixing a home generally ranges from $800 to $2,500 (with an average cost of $1,200). Your costs may vary depending on the size and design of your home and which radon reduction methods are needed. Hundreds of thousands of people have reduced radon levels in their homes.

◊ **Maintain Your Radon Reduction System**
Maintaining a radon reduction system takes little effort and keeps the system working properly and radon levels low.

Figure 40: Make sure you read and understand your Radon testing results.

◊ **Introduction**
You have tested your home for radon, but now what? This section is for people who have tested their home for radon and confirmed that they have elevated radon levels -- 4 picoCuries per liter (pCi/L) or higher. This section can help you:
- Select a qualified radon mitigation contractor to reduce the radon levels in your home.
- Determine an appropriate radon reduction method.
- Maintain your radon reduction system.

If you want information on how to test your home for radon, call your State radon.

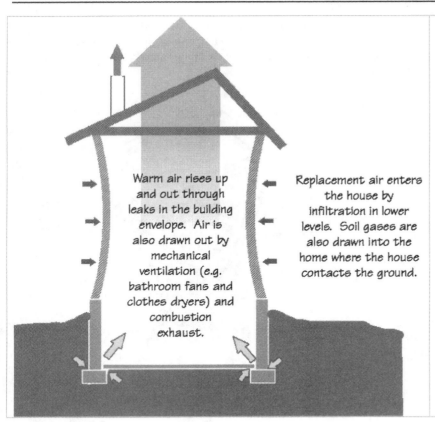

Figure 41: Air movement inside and outside effects the Radon levels in your home.

◊   **How Radon Enters Your House**
    Radon is a naturally occurring radioactive gas produced by the breakdown of uranium in soil, rock, and water. Air pressure inside your home is usually lower than pressure in the soil around your home's foundation. Because of this difference in pressure, your house acts like a vacuum, drawing radon in through foundation cracks and other openings. Radon may also be present in well water and can be released into the air in your home when water is used for showering and other household uses. In most cases, radon entering the home through water is a small risk compared with radon entering your home from the soil. In a small number of homes, the building materials (e.g., granite and certain concrete products) can give off radon, although building materials rarely cause radon problems by themselves. In the United States, radon gas in soils is the principal source of elevated radon levels in homes.

Figure 42: Air pressure inside your home is usually lower than pressure in the soil around your home's foundation. Because of this difference in pressure, your house acts like a vacuum, drawing radon in through foundation cracks and other openings.

◊   **Radon is a Cancer-causing, Radioactive Gas**

Radon is estimated to cause many thousands of lung cancer deaths each year. **In fact, the Surgeon General has warned that radon is the second leading cause of lung cancer in the United States.** Only smoking causes more lung cancer deaths. If you smoke and your home has high radon levels, your risk of lung cancer is especially high.

◊   **What Do Your Radon Test Results Mean?**

Any radon exposure has some risk of causing lung cancer. The lower the radon level in your home, the lower your family's risk of lung cancer. The amount of radon in the air is measured in "picoCuries of radon per liter of air," or "pCi/L." Sometimes test results are expressed in Working Levels, "WL," rather than picoCuries per liter of air. A level of 0.02 WL is usually equal to about 4 pCi/L in a typical home.

The U.S. Congress has set a long-term goal that indoor radon levels be no more than outdoor levels; about 0.4 pCi/L of radon is normally found in the outside air. EPA recommends fixing your home if the results one *long-term* test or the average of two *short-term* tests show radon levels of 4 pCi/L (or 0.02 WL) or higher. With today's technology, radon levels in most homes can be reduced to 2 pCi/L or below. You may also want to consider fixing if the level is between 2 and 4 pCi/L.

A short-term test remains in your home for 2 days to 90 days, whereas a long-term test remains in your home for more than 90 days. All radon tests should be taken for a minimum of 48 hours. A short-term test will yield faster results, but a long-term test will give a better understanding of your home's year-round average radon level.

The EPA recommends two categories of radon testing. One category is for concerned homeowners or occupants whose house is not for sale. The second category is for real estate transactions.

◊   **Why Hire a Contractor?**

EPA recommends that you have a qualified radon mitigation contractor fix your home because lowering high radon levels requires specific technical knowledge and special skills. Without the proper equipment or technical knowledge, you could actually increase your radon level or create other potential hazards and additional costs. However, if you decide to do the work yourself, get information on appropriate training courses and copies of EPA's technical guidance documents from the EPA web site and your State radon office.

◊   **Will Any Contractor Do?**

EPA recommends that you use a State certified and/or qualified radon mitigation contractor trained to fix radon problems. You can determine a service provider's qualifications to perform radon measurements or to mitigate your home in several ways. First, check with your State radon office. Many states require radon professionals to be licensed, certified, or registered, and to install radon mitigation systems that meet State requirements. Most states can provide you with a list of knowledgeable radon service providers doing business in the State. In states that don't regulate radon services, ask the contractor if they hold a professional proficiency or certification credential, and if they follow industry consensus standards such as the American Society for Testing and Materials (ASTM) Standard Practice for Installing Radon Mitigation Systems in Existing Low-Rise Residential Buildings, E2121 (March 2001), or the U.S. EPA's *Radon Mitigation Standards* (EPA 402-R-93-078, revised April 1994). You can contact private proficiency programs for lists of privately-certified professionals in your area. Such programs usually provide members with a photo-ID, which indicates their qualification(s) and the ID-card's expiration date. For more information on private proficiency programs, visit www.epa.gov/radon/proficiency.html, or contact your State radon office.

◊   **Selecting a Radon Test Kit**

Since you cannon see or smell radon, special equipment is needed to detect it. When you're ready to test your home, contact your State radon office (or visit www.epa.gov/radon/proficiency.html) for information on locating qualified test kits or qualified radon testers. You can also order test kits and obtain information from a radon hotline. There are two types of radon testing devices. Passive radon testing devices do not need power to function. These include charcoal canisters, alpha-track detectors, charcoal liquid scintillation devices, and electret ion chamber detectors. Both short- and long-term passive devices are generally inexpensive. Active radon testing devices require power to function and usually provide hourly readings and an average result for the test period. These include continuous radon monitors and continuous working level monitors, and these test may cost more. A State or local official can explain the differences between devices and recommend ones which are more appropriate for your needs and expected testing conditions. Make sure to use a radon testing devices from a qualified laboratory.

How To Select A Contractor

◊   **Get Estimates**

Choose a contractor to fix a radon problem just as you would choose someone to do other home repairs. It is wise to get more than one estimate, to ask for references, and to contact some of those references to ask if they are satisfied with the contractors' work. Also, ask your State radon office or your county/State consumer protection office for information about the contractors. Use this check-list when evaluating and comparing contractors and ask the following questions:

▫   Will the contractor provide references or photographs, as well as test results of 'before' and 'after' radon levels of past radon reduction work?

▫   Can the contractor explain what the work will involve, how long it will take to complete, and exactly how the radon reduction system will work?

▫   Does the contractor charge a fee for any diagnostic tests? Although many contractors give free estimates, they may charge for diagnostic tests. These tests help determine what type of radon reduction system

should be used and in some cases are necessary, especially if the contractor is unfamiliar with the type of house structure or the anticipated degree of difficulty. See "Radon Reduction Techniques" for more on diagnostic tests.
Did the contractor inspect your home's structure before giving you an estimate?

- Did the contractor review the quality of your radon measurement results and determine if appropriate testing procedures were followed?

Compare the contractors' proposed costs and consider what you will get for your money, taking into account: (1) a less expensive system may cost more to operate and maintain; (2) a less expensive system may have less aesthetic appeal; (3) a more expensive system may be best for your house; and, (4) the quality of the building material will affect how long the system lasts.

Do the contractors' proposals and estimates include:

- Proof of State certification and/or professional proficiency or certification credentials?
- Proof of liability insurance and being bonded, and having all necessary licenses to satisfy local requirements?
- Diagnostic testing prior to design and installation of a radon reduction system?
- Installation of a warning device to caution you if the radon reduction system is not working correctly?
- Testing after installation to make sure the radon reduction system works well?
- A guarantee to reduce radon levels to 4 pCi/L or below, and if so, for how long?

◊ **The Contract**
Ask the contractor to prepare a contract before any work starts. Carefully read the contract before you sign it. Make sure everything in the contract matches the original proposal. The contract should describe exactly what work will be done prior to and during the installation of the system, what the system consists of, and how the system will operate. Many contractors provide a guarantee that they will adjust or modify the system to reach a negotiated radon level. Carefully read the conditions of the contract describing the guarantee. Carefully consider optional additions to your contract which may add to the initial cost of the system, but may be worth the extra expense. Typical options might include an extended warranty, a service plan, and/or improved aesthetics.
Important information that should appear in the contract includes:

- The total cost of the job, including all taxes and permit fees; how much, if any, is required for a deposit; and when payment is due in full.
- The time needed to complete the work.
- An agreement by the contractor to obtain necessary permits and follow required building codes.

- A statement that the contractor carries liability insurance and is bonded and insured to protect you in case of injury to persons, or damage to property, while the work is done.

Figure 43: Carefully read ALL contracts before you sign them!

- A guarantee that the contractor will be responsible for damage and clean-up after the job.
- Details of any guarantee to reduce radon below a negotiated level.
- Details of warranties or other optional features associated with the hardware components of the mitigation system.
- A declaration stating whether any warranties or guarantees are transferable if you sell your home.
- A description of what the contractor expects the homeowner to do (e.g., make the work area accessible) before work begins.

◊ **What to Look for in a Radon Reduction System**
In selecting a radon reduction method for your home, you and your contractor should consider several things, including: how high your initial radon level is, the costs of installation and system operation, your house size and your foundation type.

- Installation and Operating Costs - The cost of a contractor fixing a home generally ranges from $800 to $2,500, depending on the characteristics of the house and choice of radon reduction methods. The average cost of a radon reduction system is about $1,200.
- Most types of radon reduction systems cause some loss of heated or air conditioned air, which could increase your utility bills. How much your utility bills will increase will depend on the climate you live in, what kind of reduction system you select, and how your house is built. Systems that use fans are more effective in reducing radon levels; however, they will slightly increase your electric bill. The EPA *Installation and Operating Cost Table* Figure 49 on page 283 lists the installation and average operating costs

for different radon reduction systems and describes the best use of each method.

Figure 44: Consider all factors when selecting a radon reduction method for your home.

◊ **Radon Reduction Techniques**

There are several methods that a contractor can use to lower radon levels in your home. Some techniques prevent radon from entering your home while others reduce radon levels after it has entered. EPA generally recommends methods which prevent the entry of radon. **Soil suction**, for example, prevents radon from entering your home by drawing the radon from below the house and venting it through a pipe, or pipes, to the air above the house where it is quickly diluted.

Any information that you may have about the construction of your house could help your contractor choose the best system. Your contractor will perform a visual inspection of your house and design a system that considers specific features of your house. If this inspection fails to provide enough information, the contractor will need to perform **diagnostic tests** during the initial phase of the installation to help develop the best radon reduction system for your home. For instance, your contractor can use chemical smoke to find the source and direction of air movement. A contractor can learn air flow sources and directions by watching a small amount of smoke that he or she shot into holes, drains, sumps, or along cracks. The sources of air flow show possible radon routes. A contractor may have concerns about back drafting of combustion appliances when considering radon mitigation options, and may recommend that the homeowner have the appliance(s) checked by a qualified inspector.

Another type of diagnostic test is a "soil communication test." This test uses a vacuum cleaner and chemical smoke to determine how easily air can move from one point to another under the foundation. By inserting a vacuum cleaner hose in one small hole and using chemical smoke in a second small hole, a contractor can see if the smoke is pulled down into the second hole by the force of the vacuum cleaner's suction. Watching the smoke during a soil communication test helps a

contractor decide if certain radon reduction systems would work well in your house.

Whether diagnostic tests are needed is decided by details specific to your house, such as the foundation design, what kind of material is under your house, and by the contractor's experience with similar houses and similar radon test results.

Figure 45: There are several methods that a contractor can use to lower radon levels in your home.

◊ **House Foundation Types**

Your house type will affect the kind of radon reduction system that will work best. Houses are generally categorized according to their foundation design. For example: **basement, slab-on-grade** (concrete poured at ground level), or **crawlspace** (a shallow unfinished space under the first floor). Some houses have more than one foundation design feature. For instance, it is common to have a basement under part of the house and to have a slab-on-grade or crawlspace under the rest of the house. In these situations a combination of radon reduction techniques may be needed to reduce radon levels to below 4 pCi/L.

Figure 46: Your house type will affect the kind of radon reduction system that works best. Houses are generally categorized according to their foundation design.

Radon reduction systems can be grouped by house foundation design. Determine your type of foundation design and read about which radon reduction systems may be best for your house.

□   Basement and Slab-on-Grade Houses

In houses that have a basement or a slab-on-grade foundation, radon is usually reduced by one of four types of soil suction: **subslab suction, drain tile suction, sump hole suction, or block wall suction.**

Figure 47: Active Subslab suction (also called subslab depressurization) is the most common and usually the most reliable radon reduction method.

Active Subslab suction (also called **subslab depressurization**) is the most common and usually the most reliable radon reduction method. One or more suction pipes are inserted through the floor slab into the crushed rock or soil underneath. They also may be inserted below the concrete slab from outside the house. The number and location of suction pipes that are needed depends on how easily air can move in the crushed rock or soil under the slab, and on the strength of the radon source. Often, only a single suction point is needed. A contractor usually gets this information from visual inspection, from diagnostic tests, and/or from experience. A radon vent fan connected to the suction pipe(s) draws the radon gas from below the house and releases it into the outdoor air while simultaneously creating a negative pressure (vacuum) beneath the slab. Common fan locations include unconditioned house and garage spaces, including attics, and the exterior of the house.

Passive subslab suction is the same as active subslab suction except it relies on natural pressure differentials and air currents instead of a fan to draw radon up from below the house. Passive subslab suction is usually associated with radon-resistant features installed in newly constructed homes.

Passive subslab is generally not as effective in reducing high radon levels as active subslab suction.

Some houses have **drain tiles or perforated pipe** to direct water away from the foundation of the house. Suction on these tiles or pipes is often effective in reducing radon levels.

One variation of subslab and drain tile suction is **sump hole suction**. Often, when a house with a basement has a sump pump to remove unwanted water, the sump can be capped so that it can continue to drain water and serve as the location for a radon suction pipe.

Block wall suction can be used in basement houses with hollow block foundation walls. This method removes radon and depressurizes the block wall, similar to subslab suction. This method is often used in combination with subslab suction.

□   Crawlspace Houses

An effective method to reduce radon levels in crawlspace houses involves covering the earth floor with a high-density plastic sheet. A vent pipe and fan are used to draw the radon from under the sheet and vent it to the outdoors. This form of soil suction is called **sub membrane suction, and when properly applied is the most effective way to reduce radon levels in crawlspace houses.** Another less-favorable option is active crawlspace depressurization which involves drawing air directly from the crawlspace using a fan. This technique generally does not work as well as sub membrane suction and requires special attention to combustion appliance back drafting and sealing the crawlspace from other portions of the house, and may also result in increased energy costs due to loss of conditioned air from the house.

In some cases, radon levels can be lowered by ventilating the crawlspace passively (without the use of a fan) or actively (with the use of a fan). Crawlspace ventilation may lower indoor radon levels both by reducing the home's suction on the soil and by diluting the radon beneath the house. Passive ventilation in a crawlspace is achieved by opening vents, or installing additional vents. Active ventilation uses a fan to blow air through the crawlspace instead of relying on natural air circulation. In colder climates, for either passive or active crawlspace ventilation, water pipes, sewer lines and appliances in the crawlspace may need to be insulated against the cold. These ventilation options could result in increased energy costs for the house.

□   Other Types of Radon Reduction Methods

Other radon reduction techniques that can be used in any type of house include: sealing, house/room pressurization, heat recovery ventilation, and natural ventilation.

Sealing cracks and other openings in the foundation is a basic part of most approaches to radon reduction. Sealing the cracks limits the flow of radon into your home thereby making other radon reduction techniques more effective and cost-efficient. It also reduces the loss of conditioned air. *EPA does not recommend the use of sealing alone to reduce radon because, by itself, sealing has not been shown to lower radon* *levels significantly or consistently.* It is difficult to identify and permanently seal the places where radon is entering. Normal settling of your house opens new entry routes and reopens old ones.

House/room pressurization uses a fan to blow air into the basement or living area from either upstairs or outdoors. It attempts to create enough pressure at the lowest level indoors (in a basement for example) to prevent radon from entering into the house. The effectiveness of this technique is limited by house construction, climate, other appliances in the house, and occupant lifestyle. In order to maintain enough pressure to keep radon out, the doors and windows at the lowest level must not be left opened, except for normal entry and exit. This approach generally results in more outdoor air being introduced into the home, which can cause moisture intrusion and energy penalties. *Consequently, this technique should only be considered after the other, more-common techniques have not sufficiently reduced radon.*

A **heat recovery ventilator (HRV)**, also called an **air-to-air heat exchanger**, can be installed to increase ventilation which will help reduce the radon levels in your home. An HRV will increase ventilation by introducing outdoor air while using the heated or cooled air being exhausted to warm or cool the incoming air. HRVs can be designed to ventilate all or part of your home, although they are more effective in reducing radon levels when used to ventilate only the basement. If properly balanced and maintained, they ensure a constant degree of ventilation throughout the year. HRVs also can improve air quality in houses that have other indoor pollutants. There could be *significant* increase in the heating and cooling costs with an HRV, but not as great as ventilation without heat recovery (see the EPA *Installation and Operating Cost Table* Figure 49 page 283).

Some **natural ventilation** occurs in all houses. By opening windows, doors, and vents on the lower floors you increase the ventilation in your house. This increase in ventilation mixes outdoor air with the indoor air containing radon, and can result in reduced radon levels. However, once windows, doors and vents are closed, radon concentrations most often return to previous values within about 12 hours. *Natural ventilation in any type of house should normally be regarded as only a temporary radon reduction approach because of the following disadvantages: loss of conditioned air and related discomfort, greatly increased costs of conditioning additional outside air, and security concerns.*

◊ **Checking Your Contractor's Work**
Below is a list of basic installation requirements that your contractor should meet when installing a radon reduction system in your home. It is important to verify with your contractor that the radon mitigation standards are properly met to ensure that your radon reduction system will be effective. You can also check with your State radon office to see if there are State requirements that your contractor must meet.

□ Radon reduction systems **must** be clearly labeled. This will avoid accidental changes to the system which could disrupt its function.

□ The exhaust pipe(s) of soil suction systems **must** vent above the surface of the roof and 10 feet or more above the ground, and at least 10 feet away from windows, doors, or other openings that could allow the radon to reenter the house, if the exhaust pipe(s) do not vent at least 2 feet above these openings.

□ The exhaust fan **must** not be located in or below a livable area. For instance, it should be in an unoccupied attic of the house or outside - not in a basement!

□ If installing an exhaust fan outside, the contractor **must** install a fan that meets local building codes for exterior use.

□ Electrical connections of all active radon reduction systems **must** be installed according to local electrical codes.

□ A warning device **must** be installed to alert you if an active system stops working properly. Examples of system failure warning devices are: a liquid gauge, a sound alarm, a light indicator, and a dial (needle display) gauge. The warning device **must** be placed where it can be seen or heard easily. Your contractor should check that the warning device works. Later on, if your monitor shows that the system is not working properly, call a contractor to have it checked.

□ A post-mitigation radon test should be done within 30 days of system installation, but no sooner than 24 hours after your system is in operation with the fan on, if it has one. The contractor may perform a post-mitigation test to check his work and the initial effectiveness of the system; however, it is recommended that you also get an independent follow-up radon measurement. Having an independent tester perform the test, or conducting the measurement yourself, will eliminate any potential conflict of interest. To test the system's effectiveness, a 2-7 day measurement is recommended. Test conditions: windows and doors must be closed 12 hours before and during the test, except for normal entry/exit.

□ Make sure your contractor completely explains your radon reduction system, demonstrates how it operates, and explains how to maintain it. Ask for written operating and maintenance instructions and copies of any warranties.

Living in a House with a Radon Reduction System

◊ **Maintaining Your Radon Reduction System**
Similar to a furnace or chimney, radon reduction systems need some occasional maintenance. You should look at your warning device on a regular basis to make sure the system is working correctly. Fans may last for five years or more (manufacturer warranties tend not to exceed five years) and may then need to be repaired or replaced. Replacing a fan will cost around $200 - $350 including parts and labor. It is a good

idea to retest your home at least every two years to be sure radon levels remain low.

Remember, the fan should <u>NEVER</u> be turned off; it must run continuously for the system to work correctly.
The filter in an HRV requires periodic cleaning and should be changed twice a year. Replacement filters for an HRV are easily changed and are priced between $10 and $25. Ask your contractor where filters can be purchased. Also, the vent that brings fresh air in from the outside needs to be inspected for leaves and debris. The ventilator should be checked annually by a heating, ventilating, and air-conditioning professional to make sure the air flow remains properly balanced. HRVs used for radon control should run all the time.

◊   **Remodeling Your Home After Radon Levels Have Been Lowered**
If you decide to make major structural changes to your home after you have had a radon reduction system installed (such as converting an unfinished basement area into living space), ask your radon contractor whether these changes could void any warranties. If you are planning to add a new foundation for an addition to your house, ask your radon contractor about what measures should be taken to ensure reduced radon levels throughout the home. After you remodel, retest in the lowest lived-in area to make sure the construction did not reduce the effectiveness of the radon reduction system.

◊   **Buying or Selling a Home?**
If you are selling a home that has a radon reduction system, inform potential buyers and supply them with information about your system's operation and maintenance. If you are building a new house, consider that it is almost always less expensive to build radon-resistant features into new construction than it is to fix an existing house that has high radon levels. Ask your builder if he or she uses radon-resistant construction features. Your builder can refer to EPA's document *Building Radon Out: A Step-by-Step Guide On How to Build Radon-Resistant Homes*, or your builder can work with a qualified contractor to design and install the proper radon reduction system. To obtain EPA's technical documents or to find a qualified contractor contact your State radon office or see the radon proficiency page at www.epa.gov/radon/proficiency.html.

All homes should be tested for radon and elevated radon levels should be reduced. **Even new homes built with radon-resistant features should be tested after occupancy to ensure that radon levels are below 4 pCi/L.** If you have a test result of 4 pCi/L or more, you can have a qualified mitigator easily add a vent to an existing passive system for about $300 and further reduce the radon level in your home.

Figure 48: If you are selling a home that has a radon reduction system, inform potential buyers and supply them with information about your system's operation and maintenance.

◊   **Radon in Water**
Most often, the radon in your home's indoor air can come from two sources, the soil or your water supply. Compared to radon entering your home through water, radon entering your home through soil is usually a much larger risk. If you are concerned about radon and you have a private well, consider testing for radon in both air and water. By testing for radon in both air and water, the results could enable you to more completely assess the radon mitigation option(s) best suited to your situation. The devices and procedures for testing your home's water supply are different from those used for measuring radon in air.

The radon in your water supply poses an inhalation risk and a small ingestion risk. Most of your risk from radon in water comes from radon released into the air when water is used for showering and other household purposes. Research has shown that your risk of lung cancer from breathing radon in air is much larger than your risk of stomach cancer from swallowing water with radon on it.

Radon in your home's water is not usually a problem when its source is surface water. A radon in water problem is more likely when its source is ground water, e.g., a private well or a public water supply system that uses ground water. Some public water systems treat their water to reduce radon levels before it is delivered to your home. If you are concerned that radon may be entering your home through the water and your water comes from a public water supply, contact your water supplier.

If you've tested your private well and have a radon in water problem, it can be easily fixed. Your home's water supply can be treated in one of two ways. Point-of-entry treatment for the whole house can effectively remove radon from the water before it enters your home's water distribution system. Point-of-entry treatment usually employs either granular activated carbon (GAC) filters or aeration systems. While GAC filters usually cost less than aeration systems, filters can collect radioactivity and may require a special method of disposal. Both GAC filters and aeration systems have advantages and disadvantages that should be discussed with your State radon office or a water treatment professional. Point-of-use treatment devices remove radon from your water at the tap, but only treat a small portion of the water you use, e.g., the water you drink. Point-of-use devices are not effective in reducing the risk from breathing radon released into the air from all water used in the home.

For information on radon in water, testing and treatment, and radon in drinking water standards, or for general help, call your State radon office or EPA's Drinking Water Hotline at (800) 426-4791 or visit www.epa.gov/safewater/radon.html. Your State radon office can assist you in obtaining radon-in-water test kits and interpreting test results.

Figure 49: Radon System Installation and Operating Cost Table				
Technique	**Typical Radon Reduction**	**Typical Range of Installation Costs (Contractor)**	**Typical Operating Cost Range for Fan Electricity & Heated/ Cooled Air Loss (Annual)**	**Comments**
Subslab Suction (Subslab Depressurization)	50 - 99%	$800 - $2,500	$50 - $200	Works best if air can move easily in material under slab.
Passive Subslab Suction	30 - 70%	$550 - $2,250	There may be some energy penalties	May be more effective in cold climates; not as effective as active subslab suction.
Drain tile Suction	50 - 99%	$800 - $1,700	$50 - $200	Can work with either partial or complete drain tile loops.
Block wall Suction	50 - 99%	$1,500 - $3,000	$100 - $400	Only in houses with hollow block walls; requires sealing of major openings.
Sump Hole Suction	50 - 99%	$800 - $2,500	$50 - $250	Works best if air moves easily to the sump under the slab.
Sub membrane Depressurization in a Crawlspace	50 - 99%	$1,000 - $2,500	$50 - $250	Less heat loss than natural ventilation in cold winter climates.
Natural Ventilation in a Crawlspace	0 - 50%	none $200 - $500 if additional vents installed	There may be some energy penalties.	Costs variable
Sealing of Radon Entry Routes	See Comments	$100 - $2,000	None	Normally only used with other techniques; proper materials & installation required
House (Basement) **Pressurization**	50 - 99%	$500 - $1,500	$150 - $500	Works best with tight basement isolated from outdoors & upper floors.
Natural Ventilation	Variable/ Temporary	None $200 - $500 if additional vents installed	$100 - $700	Significant heated/cooled air loss; operating costs depend on utility rates & amount of ventilation.

Heat Recovery Ventilation (HRV)	Variable/ See Comments	$1,200 - $2,500	$75 - $500 for continuous operation	Limited use; effectiveness limited by radon concentration and the amount of ventilation air available for dilution by the HRV. Best applied to limited-space areas like basements.
<u>Private Well Water Systems:</u> **Aeration**	95 - 99%	$3,000 - $4,500	$50 - $150	Generally more efficient than GAC; requires annual cleaning to maintain effectiveness and to prevent contamination; requires venting radon to outdoors.
<u>Private Well Water Systems:</u> **Granular Activated Carbon (GAC)**	85 - 99%	$1,000 - $3,000	None	Less efficient for higher levels than aeration; use for moderate levels (around 5,000 pCi/L or less in water); radioactive radon by-products can build on carbon; may need radiation shield around tank & care in disposal.

<u>NOTES:</u> 1. The fan electricity and house heating/cooling loss cost range is based on certain assumptions regarding climate, your house size, and the cost of electricity and fuel. Your costs may vary.
2. Costs for cosmetic treatments to the house may increase the typical installation costs shown above.

Figure 50: Passive and Active Radon Mitigation Systems

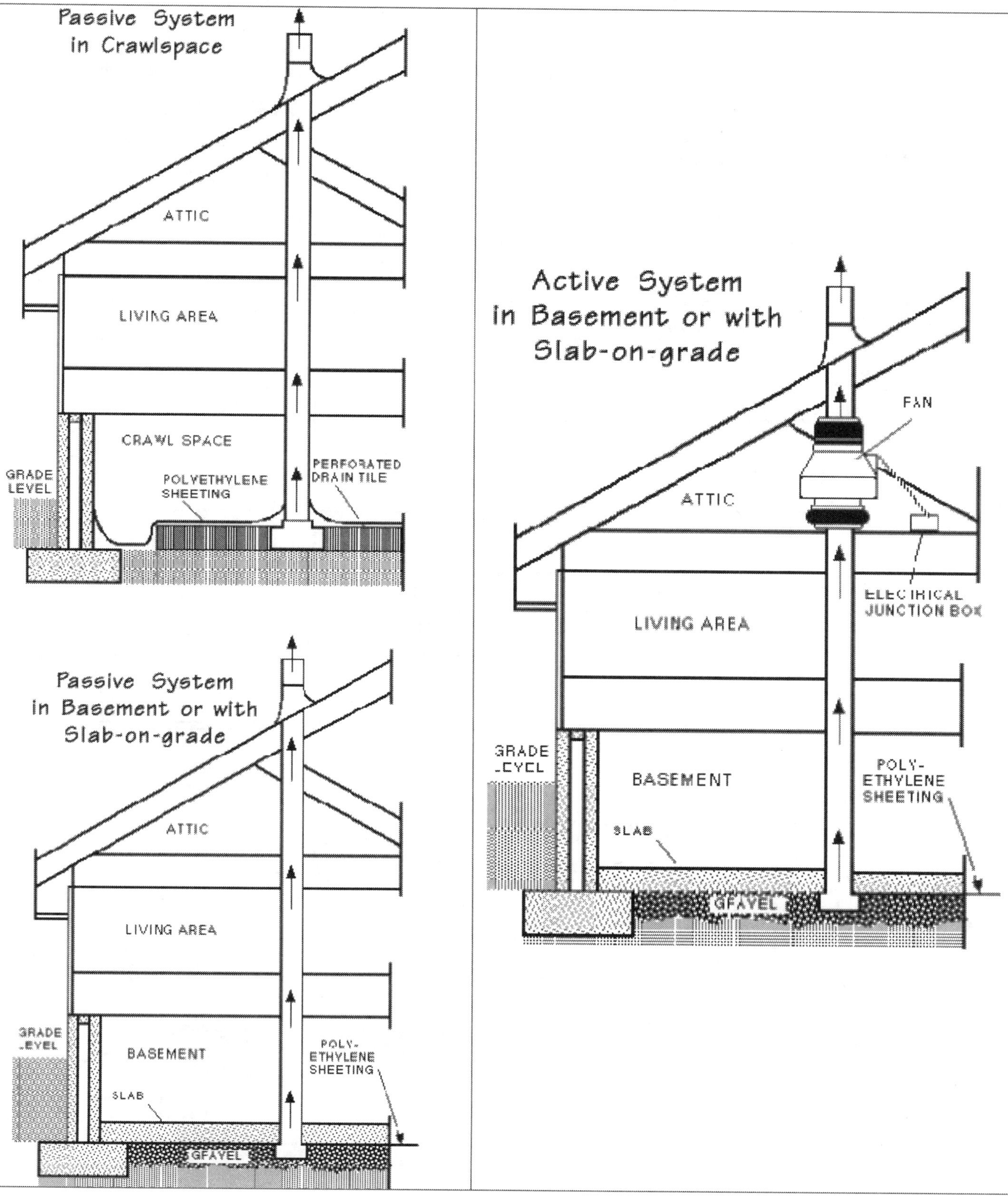

Passive System in Crawlspace

ATTIC

LIVING AREA

CRAWL SPACE

GRADE LEVEL

POLYETHYLENE SHEETING

PERFORATED DRAIN TILE

Passive System in Basement or with Slab-on-grade

ATTIC

LIVING AREA

GRADE LEVEL

BASEMENT

SLAB

POLY-ETHYLENE SHEETING

GRAVEL

Active System in Basement or with Slab-on-grade

FAN

ATTIC

LIVING AREA

ELECTRICAL JUNCTION BOX

GRADE LEVEL

BASEMENT

SLAB

POLY-ETHYLENE SHEETING

GRAVEL

Figure 51: Passive Sub-Slab Depressurization Radon Control System

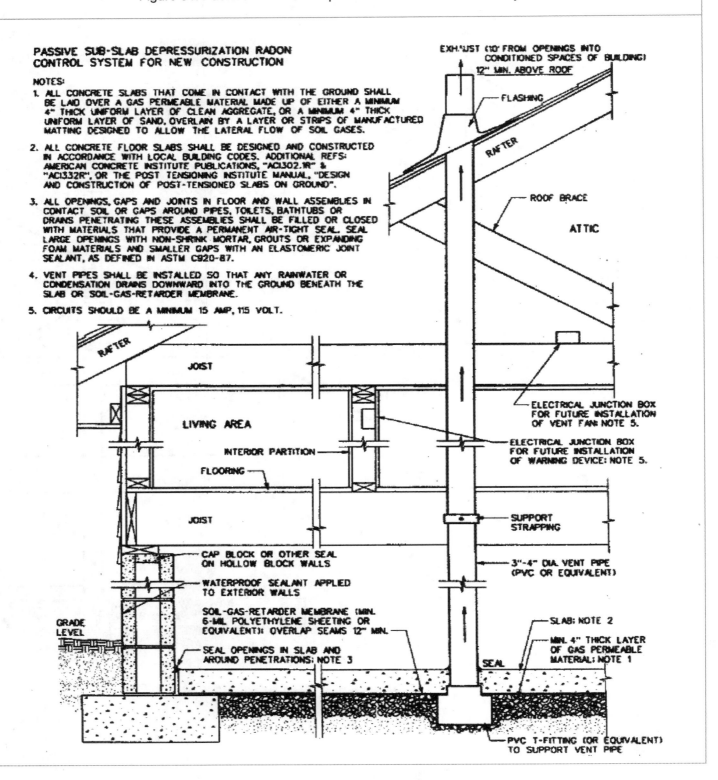

Figure 52: Additional Components For Passive Sub-Slab Depressurization Radon Control System

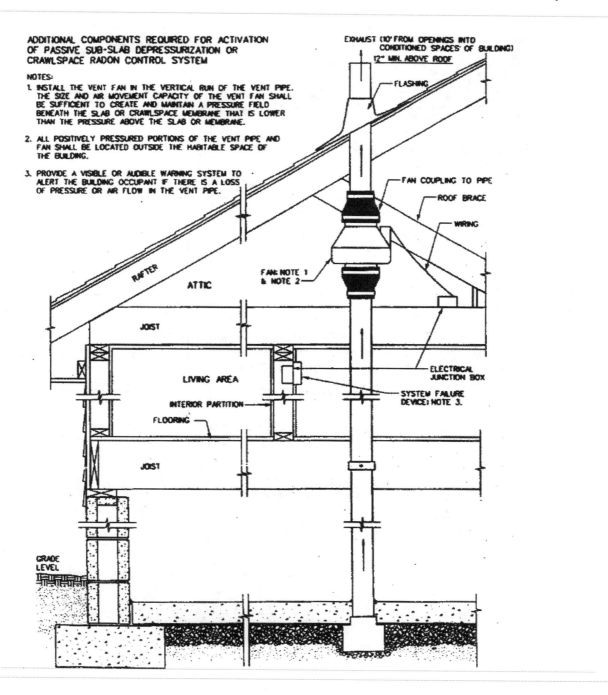

Figure 53: Passive Radon Control System In Crawl Space

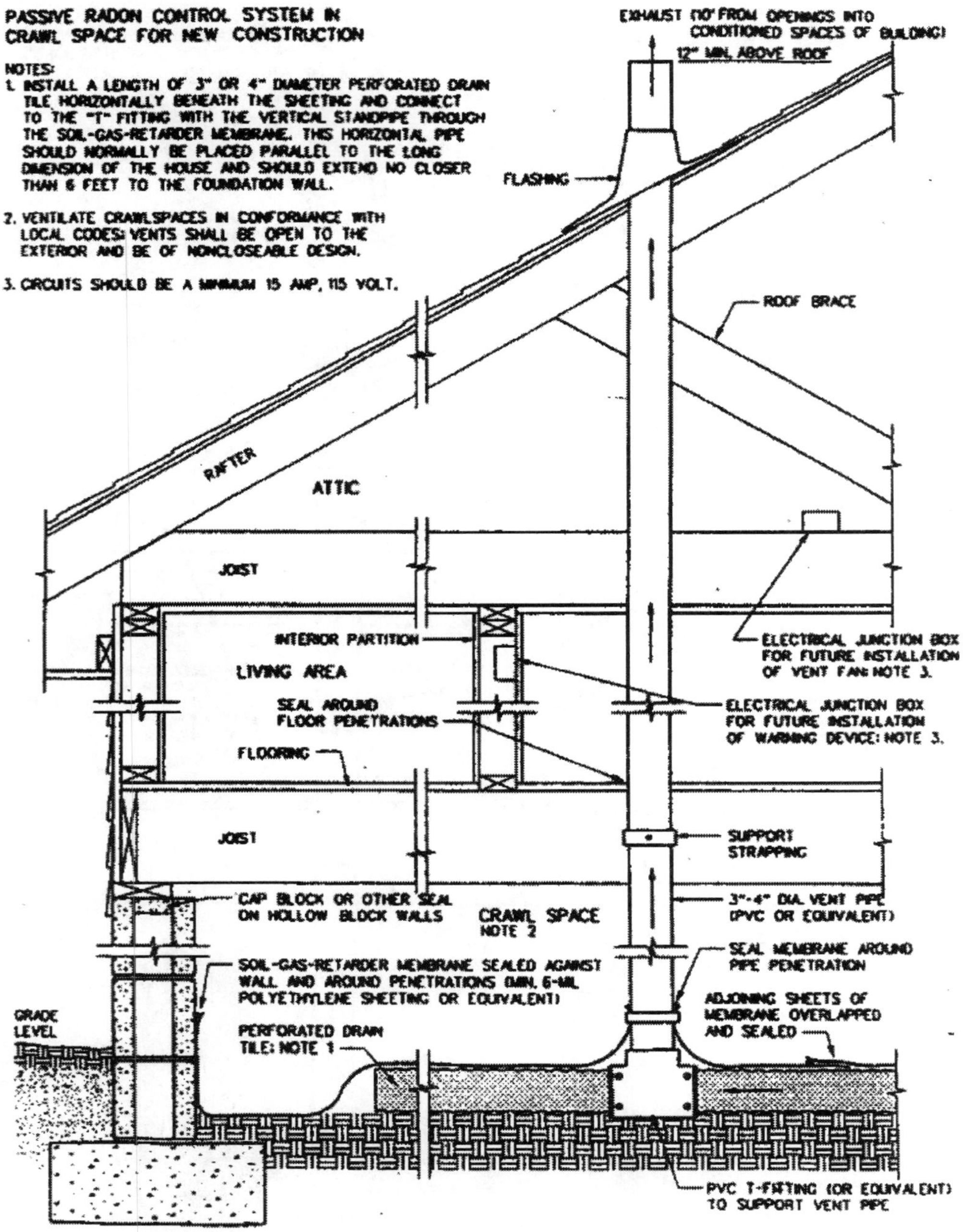

Assessment of Risks from Radon in Homes

The Agency has updated the estimates of lung cancer risks from indoor radon based on the National Academy of Sciences' (NAS) latest report on radon, the Biological Effects of Ionizing Radiation (BEIR) VI Report (1999). EPA worked closely with the Science Advisory Board (SAB), an independent panel of scientific experts, to determine how best to apply the risk models developed by the BEIR VI committee. The SAB's advice and recommendations were incorporated modifying and extending the methods and approaches used in BEIR VI to construct a single model yielding results midway between the results obtained using the two models preferred by the BEIR VI committee. The Agency's updated calculation of a best estimate of annual lung cancer deaths from radon is about 21,000 (with an uncertainty range of 8,000 to 45,000), which is consistent with the estimates of the BEIR VI Report. A single risk model also permitted the Agency to calculate a numerical estimate of the risk per unit exposure [lung cancer deaths per working level month (WLM)] which will be used to update estimated lung cancer risks from radon in various publications.

The following is an updated chart of the lifetime risk of lung cancer death per person from radon exposure in homes (excerpted from the updated radon risk assessment).

Figure 54: UPDATED chart of lifetime risk of lung cancer death per person from home radon exposure.

Radon Level (a)	Lifetime Risk of Lung Cancer Death (per person) from Radon Exposure in Homes (b)		
pCi/L	**Never Smokers**	**Current Smokers** (c)	**General Population**
20 pCi/L	36 out of 1,000	26 out of 100	11 out of 100
10 pCi/L	18 out of 1,000	15 out of 100	56 out of 1,000
8 pCi/L	15 out of 1,000	12 out of 100	45 out of 1,000
4 pCi/L	73 out of 10,000	62 out of 1,000	23 out of 1,000
2 pCi/L	37 out of 10,000	32 out of 1,000	12 out of 1,000
1.25 pCi/L	23 out of 10,000	20 out of 1,000	73 out of 10,000
0.4 pCi/L	73 out of 100,000	64 out of 10,000	23 out of 10,000

(a) - Assumes constant lifetime exposure in homes at these levels.
(b) - Estimates are subject to uncertainties as discussed in Chapter VIII of the risk assessment.
(c) - Note: BEIR VI did not specify excess relative risks for current smokers.

How Was Radon Discovered?

◊ **Who discovered radon?**
The German chemist Friedrich E. Dorn discovered radon-222 in 1900, and called it radium emanation. However, a scarcer isotope, radon-220, was actually observed first, in 1899, by British scientists R.B. Owens and Ernest Rutherford. The medical community nationwide became aware of radon in 1984 That year a nuclear plant worker in Pennsylvania discovered radioactivity on his clothing while exiting his place of work through the radiation detectors. The source of the radiation was determined to be radon decay products on his clothing originating from his home.

◊ **Where does radon come from?**
Radon-222 is the decay product of radium-226. Radon-222 and its parent, radium-226, are part of the long decay chain for uranium-238. Since uranium is essentially ubiquitous in the earth's crust, radium-226 and radon-222 are present in almost all rock, soil, and water.

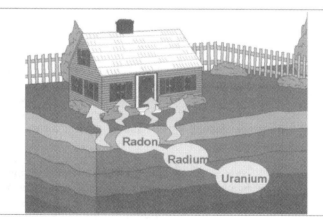

Figure 55: Radon is a radioactive gas. It comes from the natural decay of uranium that is found in nearly all soils. It typically moves up through the ground to the air above and into your home through cracks and other holes in the foundation.

◊   **What are the properties of radon?**

Radon is a noble gas, which means it is essentially inert, and does not combine with other chemicals. Radon is a heavy gas, which accounts for its tendency to collect in basements. It has no color, odor, or taste. Radon-222 is produced by the decay of radium, has a half-life of 3.8 days, and emits an alpha particle as it decays to polonium-218, and eventually to stable lead. Radon-220, is the decay product of thorium – it is sometimes called thoron, has a half-life of 54.5 seconds and emits an alpha particle in its decay to polonium-216.

◊   **Does radon have any practical uses?**

Radon has little practical use. Some medical treatments have employed radon in small sealed glass tubes, called seeds, that are specially manufactured to contain the exact amount of radioactivity needed for the application.

Exposure to Radon

◊   **How does radon get into the environment?**

Radon-222 is the radioactive decay product of radium-226, which is found at low concentrations in almost all rock and soil. Radon is generated in rock and soil, and it creeps up to the outside air. Although outdoor concentrations of radon are typically low, about 0.4 picoCuries per liter (pCi/l) of air, it can seep into buildings through foundation cracks or openings and build up to much higher concentrations indoors.

The average indoor radon concentration is about 1.3 pCi/l of air. It is not uncommon, though, for indoor radon levels to be found in the range of 5 - 50 pCi/l, and they have been found as high as 2,000 pCi/l. The concentration of radon measured in a house depends on many factors, including the design of the house, local geology and soil conditions, and the weather. Radon's decay products are all metallic solids, and when radon decay occurs in air, the decay products can cling to aerosols and dust, which makes them available for inhalation into the lungs.

Radon easily dissolves in water. In areas of the country that have high radium content in soils and rocks, local ground water may contain high concentrations of radon. For example, underlying rock such as granite, or phosphate rock, typically have increased uranium and radium, and therefore radon. While radon easily dissolves into water, it also easily escapes from water when exposed to the atmosphere, especially if it is stirred or agitated. Consequently, radon concentrations are very low in rivers and lakes, but could still be high in water pumped from the ground. Some natural springs, such as those at Hot Springs, Arkansas, contain radon, and were once considered healthful.

◊   **How does radon change in the environment?**

Because radon is a chemically inert (unreactive) gas, it can move easily through rock and soil and arrive at the surface. The half-life of radon-222 is 3.8 days. As it undergoes radioactive decay, radon-222 releases alpha radiation and changes to polonium-218, a short-lived radioactive solid. After several more decay transformations, the series ends at lead-206, which is stable.

Radon dissolves in water, and easily leaves water that is exposed to the atmosphere, especially if the water is agitated. Consequently, radon levels are very low in rivers and lakes, but water drawn from underground can have elevated radon concentrations. Radon that decays in water, leaves only solid decay products which will remain in the water as they decay to stable lead.

◊   **How are people exposed to radon?**

Most of the public's exposure to natural radiation comes from radon which can accumulate in homes, schools, and office buildings. EPA estimates that the national average indoor radon level in homes is about 1.3 pCi/l of air. We also estimate that about 1 in 15 homes nationwide have levels at or above the level of 4 pCi/l, the level at which EPA recommends taking action to reduce concentrations. Levels greater than 2,000 pCi/l of air have been measured in some homes.

Radon is also found in the water in homes, in particular, homes that have their own well rather than municipal water. When the water is agitated, as when showering or washing dishes, radon escapes into the air. However, radon from domestic water generally contributes only a small proportion (less than 1%) of the total radon in indoor air. Municipal water systems hold and treat water, which helps to release radon, so that levels are very low by the time the water reaches our homes. But, people who have private wells, particularly in areas of high radium soil content, may be exposed to higher levels of radon.

◊   **How does radon get into the body?**

People may ingest trace amounts of radon with food and water, However, inhalation is the main route of entry into the body for radon and its decay products. Radon decay products may attach to particulates and aerosols in the air we breathe (for example, cooking oil vapors). When they are inhaled, some of these particles are retained in the lungs. Radon decay products also cling to tobacco leaves, which are sticky, during the growing season, and enter the lungs when tobacco is smoked. Smoke in indoor environments also is very effective at picking up radon decay products from the air and making them available for inhalation. It is likely that radon decay products contribute significantly to the risk of lung cancer from cigarette smoke.

◊   **What does radon do once it gets into the body?**

Most of the radon gas that you inhale is also exhaled. However, some of radon's decay products attach to dusts and aerosols in the air and are then readily deposited in the lungs. Some of these are cleared by the lung's natural defense system, and swallowed or coughed out. Those particles that are retained long enough release radiation damaging surrounding lung tissues. A small amount of radon decay products in the lung are absorbed into the blood.

Most of the radon ingested in water is excreted through the urine over several days. There is some risk from drinking water with elevated radon, because radioactive decay can occur within the body where tissues, such as the stomach lining, would be exposed. However, alpha particles emitted by radon and its decay product in water prior to drinking quickly lose their energy and are taken up by other compounds in water, and do not themselves pose a health concern.

Health Effects of Radon

◊ **How can radon affect people's health?**

Almost all risk from radon comes from breathing air with radon and its decay products. Radon decay products cause lung cancer. The health risk of ingesting radon, in water for example, is dwarfed by the risk of inhaling radon and its decay products. They occur in indoor air or with tobacco smoke. Alpha radiation directly causes damage to sensitive lung tissue. Most of the radiation dose is not actually from radon itself, though, which is mostly exhaled. It comes from radon's chain of short-lived solid decay products that are inhaled and lodge in the airways of the lungs. These radionuclides decay quickly, producing other radionuclides that continue damaging the lung tissue.

There is no safe level of radon--any exposure poses some risk of cancer. In two 1999 reports, the *National Academy of Sciences* (NAS) concluded after an exhaustive review that radon in indoor air is the second leading cause of lung cancer in the U.S. after cigarette smoking. The NAS estimated that 15,000-22,000 Americans die every year from radon-related lung cancer. Cigarette smoke makes radon much more dangerous. When people who smoke are exposed to radon as well, the risk of developing lung cancer is significantly higher than the risk of smoking alone. People who don't smoke, but are exposed to second hand smoke, also have higher risk of lung cancer from radon indoors.

The NAS also estimated that radon in drinking water causes an additional 180 cancer deaths annually. However almost 90% of those projected deaths were from lung cancer from the inhalation of radon released to the indoor air from water, and only about 10% were from cancers of internal organs, mostly stomach cancers, from ingestion of radon in water.

◊ **Is there a medical test to determine exposure to radon?**

Several decay products can be detected in urine, blood, and lung and bone tissue. However, these tests are not generally available through typical medical facilities. Also, they cannot be used to determine accurate exposure levels, since most radon decay products deliver their dose and decay within a few hours. Finally, these tests cannot be used to predict whether a person's exposure will cause harmful health effects, since everyone's response to exposure is different. The best way to assess exposure to radon is by measuring concentrations of radon (or radon decay products) in the air you breathe at home.

Protecting People from Radon

◊ **How do I know if there is radon in my home?**

You cannot see, feel, smell, or taste radon. Testing your home is the only way to know if you and your family are at risk from radon. EPA and the Surgeon General recommend testing for radon in all rooms below the third floor. EPA also recommends testing in schools.

EPA recommends reducing levels of radon in homes where radon concentrations exceed the EPA radon action level of 4 picoCuries per liter.

Radon testing is inexpensive and easy--it should only take a few minutes of your time. Millions of Americans have already tested their homes for radon. Various low-cost, do-it-yourself test kits are available through the mail and in hardware stores and other retail outlets. You can also hire a trained contractor to do the testing for you.

◊ **What can I do to protect myself and my family from radon?**

The first step is to test your home for radon, and have it fixed if it is at or above EPA's Action Level of 4 picoCuries per liter. You may want to take action if the levels are in the range of 2-4 picoCuries per liter. Generally, levels can be brought below 2 pCi/l fairly simply.

The best method for reducing radon in your home will depend on how radon enters your home and the design of your home. For example, sealing cracks in floors and walls may help to reduce radon. There are also systems that remove radon from the crawl space or from beneath the concrete floor or basement slab that are effective at keeping radon from entering your home. These systems are simple and don't require major changes to your home. Other methods may be necessary.

People who have private wells should test their well water to ensure that radon levels meet EPA's newly proposed standard. Call the *National Radon Hotline* at (800) 767-7236 for more information.

◊ **What recommendations has the Federal government made to protect human health from radon?**

In 1988, EPA and the *U.S. Surgeon General* issued a Health Advisory recommending that all homes be tested below the third floor for radon. They also recommended fixing homes with radon levels at or above 4 picoCuries per liter (pCi/L), EPA's *National Voluntary Action Level*. EPA and the Surgeon General also recommend that schools nationwide be tested for radon.

◊ **What is EPA doing about radon?**

EPA has established a voluntary program to promote radon awareness, testing, and reduction. The program sets an 'Action Level' of 4 picoCuries per liter (pCi/l) of air for indoor radon. The action level is not the maximum safe level for radon in the home. Instead it is the point at which the cost to the homeowner for fixing the problem (taking action) is warranted by the risk from the radon. However, the lower the level of radon, the better. Generally, levels can be brought below 2 pCi/l fairly simply. In addition to working with homeowners, EPA is working with home builders and building code organizations. The goals are to help newly constructed homes be more radon resistant and to encourage radon testing when existing homes are sold.

The 1988 *Indoor Radon Abatement Act* authorizes EPA to provide grants to states to support testing and reducing radon in homes. With various non-governmental and public health organizations, EPA promotes awareness and reduction of indoor radon. Partners include the *American Lung Association*, the *National Environmental Health Association*, the *American Society of Home Inspectors*, and the *National Safety Council*. EPA has also proposed a standard for the maximum amount of radon that may be found in drinking from community water systems using ground water.

◊ **How to Find a Qualified Radon Service Professional in Your Area**
If you are interested in finding a qualified radon service professional to test or mitigate your home, or you need to purchase a radon measurement device, you should:

▫ Contact your State Radon Contact to determine what are, or whether there are, requirements associated with providing radon measurement and or radon mitigations/reductions in your State. Some States maintain lists of contractors available in their State or they have proficiency programs or requirements of their own.
▫ Contact one or both of the two privately-run *National Radon Proficiency Programs* who are offering proficiency listing, accreditation, and/or certification in radon testing and mitigation.
▫ *Please Note:* EPA-issued Radon Measurement (RMP) and Mitigation (RCP) photo-identification cards, listing letters and identification numbers have not been valid since EPA closed its proficiency program in October 1998. Consequently, persons and companies should not represent themselves, their products or their services as "EPA Listed" or "EPA Approved", or otherwise imply an EPA sanction. Consumers are encouraged to contact their State radon office www.epa.gov/iaq/whereyoulive.html for additional information or if you have a complaint/question.

Radon – Frequently Asked Questions

◊ **Definitions of Radon**
Radon is a gaseous radioactive element having the symbol Rn, the atomic number 86, an atomic weight of 222, a melting point of -71°C, a boiling point of -62°C, and (depending on the source, there are between 20 and 25 isotopes of radon - 20 cited in the chemical summary, 25 listed in the table of isotopes); it is an extremely toxic, colorless gas; it can be condensed to a transparent liquid and to an opaque, glowing solid; it is derived from the radioactive decay of radium and is used in cancer treatment, as a tracer in leak detection, and in radiography. (From the word radium, the substance from which it is derived.)   Sources: Condensed Chemical Dictionary, and Handbook of Chemistry and Physics, 69th ed., CRC Press, Boca Raton, FL, 1988. EPA's *Integrated Risk Information System* profile on Radon 222 [CASRN 14859-67-7] is located at: www.epa.gov/iris/subst/0275.htm

◊ **Sources of Radon**
Earth and rock beneath home; well water; building materials.

◊ **What are the Health Effects From Exposure to Radon**
No immediate symptoms. Based on an updated *Assessment of Risk for Radon in Homes* (see Figure 54 page 289) radon in indoor air is estimated to cause about 21,000 lung cancer deaths each year in the United States. Smokers are at higher risk of developing Radon-induced lung cancer. Lung cancer is the only health effect which has been definitively linked with radon exposure. Lung cancer would usually occur years (5-25) after exposure. There is no evidence that other respiratory diseases, such as asthma, are caused by radon exposure and there is no evidence that children are at any greater risk of radon induced lung cancer than adults.

◊ **What is the Average Level of Radon Found in a Home?**
Based on a national residential radon survey completed in 1991, the average indoor radon level is 1.3 picoCuries per liter (pCi/L) in the United States. The average outdoor level is about 0.4 pCi/L.

◊ **What's the Debate on Radon?**
There is no debate about radon being a lung carcinogen in humans. All major national and international organizations that have examined the health risks of radon agree that it is a lung carcinogen. The scientific community continues to conduct research to refine our understanding of the precise number of deaths attributable to radon. The *National Academy of Sciences* BEIR VI Report has estimated that radon causes about 15,000 to 22,000 lung cancer deaths annually based on their two-preferred models.

A few scientists have questioned whether low radon levels, such as those found in residences, increase the risk of lung cancer because some small studies of radon and lung cancer in residences have produced varied results. Some have shown a relationship between radon and lung cancer, some have not. However, the national and international scientific communities are in agreement that all of these residential studies have been too small to provide conclusive information about radon health risks. Major scientific organizations continue to believe that approximately 12% of lung cancers annually in the United States are attributable to radon.

◊ **How do we know radon is a carcinogen?**
The *World Health Organization* (WHO), the *National Academy of Sciences*, the *US Department of Health and Human Services*, as well as EPA, have classified radon as a

known human carcinogen, because of the wealth of biological and epidemiological evidence and data showing the connection between exposure to radon and lung cancer in humans.

There have been many studies conducted by many different organizations in many nations around the world to examine the relationship of radon exposure and human lung cancer. The largest and most recent of these was an international study, led by the National Cancer Institute (NCI), which examined the data on 68,000 underground miners who were exposed to a wide range of radon levels. The studies of miners are very useful because the subjects are humans, not rats, as in many cancer research studies. These miners are dying of lung cancer at 5 times the rate expected for the general population. Over many years scientists around the world have conducted exhaustive research to verify the cause-effect relationship between radon exposure and the observed increased lung cancer deaths in these miners and to eliminate other possible causes.

In addition, there is an overlap between radon exposures received by miners who got lung cancer and the exposures people would receive over their lifetime in a home at EPA's action level of 4 pCi/L, i.e., there are no large extrapolations involved in estimating radon risks in homes.

◊ **Does the Auvinen Finnish Study Prove that Residential Radon Does Not Cause Lung Cancer?**
No, the Finnish study by itself is too small with only 1055 subjects to provide any definitive proof. Scientists from the *U.S. Public Health Service Agencies* recently reviewed the radon risk assessment and the proliferation of small residential epidemiological studies like the Finnish study. They concluded that residential epidemiology studies would need a minimum of 10,000 to 30,000 lung cancer cases plus twice a many controls to adequately address this issue.

Clarification: The residential epidemiology study recently reported out of Finland, examined homes with low radon levels; the median indoor radon level was 1.8 picoCuries per liter (pCi/L) of air.

Dr. Jonathan Samet, chairman of the *National Academy of Sciences* BEIR VI Committee, responded to the Finnish study stating, "...by itself, the study is too small in size and consequently without sufficient statistical power to characterize precisely the risk of lung cancer associated with indoor radon. Consequently, the conclusions of the article are overstated and the authors' judgment as to the implications of their findings, "Indoor radon exposure does not appear to be an important cause of lung cancer,"" is not supported by the evidence presented."

◊ **Why does it take so many cases to make residential radon epidemiology studies meaningful?**
To have a reasonable certainty in the conclusions, many thousands of cases are required to detect the increased risk of lung cancer due to radon. This is because the more things that cause a disease the harder it is to separate one cause from

another, thus it takes many cases to pinpoint the risk from each separate cause. The *U.S. Public Health Service* radon experts estimate that 10,000 to 30,000 cases, and twice as many controls would be needed to conduct a definitive epidemiologic study of residential radon lung cancer risk. The residential studies conducted to date have all included between 50 and 1500 cases and thus have been too small to provide conclusive information.

Some years ago this same process was used to detect an increased risk of lung cancer due to cigarette smoking. It took many years of study to make the positive link between the cause and effect of smoking and lung cancer. Most of the increased lung cancer risk is attributable to smoking through mathematical modeling. The research process for smoking was very laborious. However, radon's process is even more challenging because radon's contribution to increased lung cancer risk (12%) is difficult to see against the large background of lung cancer due to other causes, which include smoking, asbestos, some heavy metals and other types of radiation; i.e., detecting radon-related lung cancer is like trying to detect a 12% increase of sand on a beach already full of sand.

Finally, it is difficult to accurately determine radon exposures in residential settings since we are estimating past exposures from current measurements. The number of required study participants increases with the difficulty in determining the exposure.

◊ **Why are residential epidemiology studies of radon so complicated?**
There are many factors that must be considered when designing a residential radon epidemiology study. It is very expensive and often impossible to design a study that takes all the pertinent factors into consideration. These factors include:

▫ Mobility: people move a lot over their lifetime; it is virtually impossible to go back and test every home where an individual has lived;
▫ Housing Stock Changes: over time, older homes are often destroyed or remodeled, thus radon measurements will be non-existent or highly varied; a home's radon level may change, higher or lower, over time if new ventilation systems are installed, the occupancy patterns are substantially different, or the home's foundation shifts or cracks appear.
▫ Inaccurate Histories: often a majority of the lung cancer cases (individuals) being studied are deceased or too sick to be interviewed by researchers. This requires reliance on second-hand information which may not be as accurate. These inaccuracies primarily affect:
▫ Residence History: a child or other relative may not be aware of all residences occupied by the patient - particularly if the occupancy is distant in time or of relatively short duration. Even if the surrogate respondent is aware of a residence they may not have enough additional information to allow researchers to locate the home.

- Smoking History: smoking history historically has reliability problems. Individuals may under-estimate the amount they smoke. Conversely, relatives or friends may over-estimate smoking history.
- Other: complicating factors other than variations in smoking habits include an individual's: genetics, lifestyle, exposure to other carcinogens, and home heating, venting and air conditioning preferences.

◊ **Are there any residential epidemiology studies finding increased risk of lung cancer due to radon?**

Yes, several residential epidemiology studies have found an increased risk of lung cancer due to residential exposures (i.e. Sweden, New Jersey) These studies are also just pieces of a much bigger puzzle that is being put together. The *National Academy of Sciences'* BEIR VI Report examines in detail the available studies of radon and lung cancer in homes, as well as the studies of underground miners.

◊ **When will we know for sure about radon's health risk?**

We already have a wealth of scientific data on the relationship between radon exposure and the development of lung cancer. The scientific experts agree that the occupational miner data is a very solid base from which to estimate risk of lung cancer deaths annually. While residential radon epidemiology studies will improve what we know about radon, they will not supersede the occupational data. Health authorities like the *Centers for Disease Control* (CDC), the *Surgeon General,* the *American Lung Association*, the *American Medical Association*, and others agree that we know enough now to recommend radon testing and to encourage public action when levels are above 4 pCi/L. The most comprehensive of these efforts has been the *National Academy of Science's Biological Effects of Ionizing Radiation* (BEIR VI) Report. This report reinforces that radon is the second-leading cause of lung cancer and is a serious public health problem. As in the case of cigarette smoking, it would probably take many years and rigorous scientific research to produce the composite data needed to make an even more definitive conclusion.

◊ **Has the National Academy of Sciences (NAS) published a report on radon and lung cancer?**

The NAS published its latest analysis of health research on radon, the *Biological Effects of Ionizing Radiation* (BEIR VI) Report in 1999. This is the most comprehensive review effort to date. The Committee was charged with:
- reviewing all current miner and residential data, as well as all existing cellular-biological data,
- comparing the dose per unit exposure effects of radon in mines and homes, and examining:
    - interactions between radon exposure and smoking, and
    - any exposure-rate effect (alteration of effect by intensity of exposure).

◊ **What is meta-analysis, and does the Lubin/Boice meta-analysis prove that residential radon levels cause lung cancer?**

Meta-analysis is a statistical attempt to analyze the results of several different studies to assess the presence or absence of a trend or to summarize results. Lubin and Boice conclude that the results of their meta-analysis are consistent with the current miner-based estimates of lung cancer risk from radon which place the number of radon-related deaths at approximately 15,000 per year in the United States.

Because meta-analysis has several inherent limitations (such as the inability to adequately explore the consistency of results within and between studies and to control for confounding factors) meta-analysis is **NOT** able to **PROVE** that residential radon causes lung cancer, but it does provide additional GOOD SUGGESTIVE EVIDENCE. It is one more link in the "chain of evidence" connecting residential radon exposure to increased lung cancer risk.

Since the investigators performing a meta-analysis do not have access to the raw data on the individual study subjects, the analysis is based on the published relative risks and confidence intervals of the individual studies. Frequently, the impact of each study is weighted based on some factor which the meta-analysis authors feel is relevant to the reliability of each study's data. In the Lubin/Boice meta-analysis, the results of each individual study were weighted so that each study contributed in relation to the precision (relative lack of random or sampling errors) of its estimate.

The Lubin/Boice meta-analysis paper cites 5,000-15,000 lung cancer cases required for a single case-control study to have sufficient power to detect an exposure-response equal to that expected from miner studies. EPA has maintained that Public Health Service investigators claim 10,000-30,000 cases would be required.

◊ **What has changed?**

EPA asked Dr. Lubin this question. He indicated that nothing had changed, that the "science" of sample size estimation was something of a "black box," and that the number of cases required probably should be higher than the 5,000-15,000 cited in the paper.

◊ If you are interested in finding a qualified radon service professional to test or mitigate your home, or you need to purchase a radon measurement device, you should:

- Contact your State Radon Contact to determine what are, or whether there are, requirements associated with providing radon measurement and or radon mitigations/reductions in your State. Some States maintain lists of contractors available in their State or they have proficiency programs or requirements of their own.
- Contact one or both of the two privately-run Radon Proficiency Program who are offering proficiency listing/accreditation/certification in radon testing and mitigation.

Drinking Water

◊ **What Can I Do If There's A Problem With My Drinking Water?**

Local incidents, such as spills and treatment problems, can lead to short-term needs for alternative water supplies or in-home water treatment. In isolated cases, individuals may need to rely on alternative sources for the long term, due to their individual health needs or problems with obtaining new drinking water supplies.

◊ **What Alternative Sources Of Water Are Available?**

Bottled water is sold in supermarkets and convenience stores. Some companies lease or sell water dispensers or bubblers and regularly deliver large bottles of water to homes and businesses. It is expensive compared to water from a public water system. The bottled water quality varies among brands, because of the variations in the source water used, costs, and company practices.

The U.S. Food and Drug Administration (FDA) regulates bottled water used for drinking. While most consumers assume that bottled water is at least as safe as tap water, there are still potential risks. Although required to meet the same safety standards as public water supplies, bottled water does not undergo the same testing and reporting as water from a treatment facility. Water that is bottled and sold in the same State may not be subject to any Federal standards at all. Those with compromised immune systems may want to read bottled water labels to make sure more stringent treatments have been used, such as reverse osmosis, distillation, UV radiation, or filtration by an absolute 1 micron filter.

Check with NSF International to see if your bottled water adheres to FDA and international drinking water standards. The International Bottled Water Association can also provide information on which brands adhere to even more stringent requirements.

◊ **Can I Do Anything In My House To Improve The Safety Of My Drinking Water?**

Most people do not need to treat drinking water in their home to make it safe. However, a home water treatment unit can improve water's taste, or provide a factor of safety for those people more vulnerable to waterborne disease. There are different options for home treatment systems (see Figure 57 page 297). Point-of-use (POU) systems treat water at a single tap. Point-of-entry (POE) systems treat water used throughout the house. POU systems can be installed in various places in the home, including the counter top, the faucet itself, or under the sink (see Figure 56 page 296). POE systems are installed where the water line enters the house.

❑ POU and POE devices are based on various contaminant removal technologies. Filtration, ion exchange, reverse osmosis, and distillation are some of the treatment methods used. All types of units are generally available from retailers, or by mail order. Prices can reach well into the hundreds and sometimes thousands of dollars, and depending on the method and location of installation, plumbing can also add to the cost.

❑ Activated carbon filters adsorb organic contaminants that cause taste and odor problems. Depending on their design, some units can remove chlorination byproducts, some cleaning solvents, and pesticides. To maintain the effectiveness of these units , the carbon canisters must be replaced periodically. Activated carbon filters are not efficient in removing metals such as lead and copper.

❑ Because ion exchange units can be used to remove minerals from your water, particularly calcium and magnesium, they are sold for water softening. Some ion exchange softening units remove radium and barium from water. Ion exchange systems that employ activated alumina are used to remove fluoride and arsenate from water. These units must be regenerated periodically with salt.

❑ Reverse osmosis treatment units generally remove a more diverse list of contaminants than other systems. They can remove nitrates, sodium, other dissolved inorganic, and organic compounds.

❑ Distillation units boil water and condense the resulting steam to create distilled water. Depending on their design, some of these units may allow vaporized organic contaminants to condense back into the product water, thus minimizing the removal of organics.

You may choose to boil your water to remove microbial contaminants. Keep in mind that boiling reduces the volume of water by about 20 percent, thus concentrating those contaminants not affected by the temperature of boiling water, such as nitrates and pesticides.

No one unit can remove everything. Have your water tested by a certified laboratory prior to purchasing any device. Do not rely on the tests conducted by salespeople that want to sell you their product.

◊ **Where Can I Learn More About Home Treatment Systems?**

Your local library has articles, such as those found in consumer magazines, on the effectiveness of these devices.

◊ **Maintaining Treatment Devices**

All POU and POE treatment units need maintenance to operate effectively. If they are not maintained properly, contaminants may accumulate in the units and actually make your water worse. In addition, some vendors may make claims about their effectiveness that have no merit. Units are tested for their safety and effectiveness by two organizations, *NSF International* and *Underwriters Laboratory*. In addition, the *Water Quality Association* represents the household, commercial, industrial and small community treatment industry and can help you locate a professional that meets

HIB From A to Z

their code of ethics. EPA does not test or certify these treatments units.

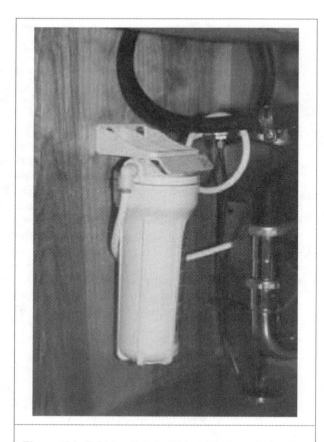

Figure 56: POU – Point of Use treatment device.

Figure 57: Home Drinking Water Treatment Devices

Treatment Device	What It Does To Water	Treatment Limitations
Activated Carbon Filter	■ Adsorbs organic contaminants that cause taste and odor problems. ■ Some designs remove chlorination byproducts; ■ Some types remove cleaning solvents and pesticides	Is not efficient in removing metals such as lead and copper Does not remove nitrate, bacteria or dissolved minerals
Ion Exchange Unit (with activated alumina)	■ Removes minerals, particularly calcium and magnesium that make water "hard" ■ Some designs remove radium and barium ■ Removes fluoride	If water has oxidized iron or iron bacteria, the ion-exchange resin will become coated or clogged and lose its softening ability
Reverse Osmosis Unit (with carbon)	■ Removes nitrates, sodium, other dissolved inorganics and organic compounds ■ Removes foul tastes, smells or colors ■ May also reduce the level of some pesticides, dioxins and chloroform and petrochemicals	Does not remove all inorganic and organic contaminants
Distillation Unit	■ Removes nitrates, bacteria, sodium, hardness, dissolved solids, most organic compounds, heavy metals, and radionuclides ■ Kills bacteria	Does not remove some volatile organic contaminants, certain pesticides and volatile solvents Bacteria may recolonize on the cooling coils during inactive periods

How Safe Is The Drinking Water In My Well?

EPA regulates public water systems; it does not have the authority to regulate private wells. Approximately 15 percent of Americans rely on their own private drinking water supplies *(Drinking Water from Household Wells, 2002),* and these supplies are not subject to EPA standards. Unlike public drinking water systems serving many people, they do not have experts regularly checking the water's source and its quality before it is sent to the tap. These households must take special precautions to ensure the protection and maintenance of their drinking water supplies. *Drinking Water from Household Wells* is an EPA publication available to specifically address special concerns of a private drinking water supply.

◊ **How Much Risk Can I Expect?**
The risk of having problems depends on how good your well is—how well it was built and located, and how well you

maintain it. It also depends on your local environment. That includes the quality of the aquifer from which your water is drawn and the human activities going on in your area that can affect your well.

Several sources of pollution are easy to spot by sight, taste, or smell. However, man y serious problems can be found only by testing your water. Knowing the possible threats in your area will help you decide the kind of tests you may need .

◊ **What Should I Do?**
There are six basic steps you can take to help protect your private drinking water supply:
1. Identify potential problem sources.
2. Talk with local experts.
3. Have your water tested periodically.
4. Have the test results interpreted and explained clearly.
5. Set and follow a regular maintenance schedule for your well, and keep up-to-date records .
6. Immediately remedy any problems.

◊   **Identify Potential Problem Sources**

Understanding and spotting possible pollution sources is the first step to safeguarding your drinking water. If your drinking water comes from a well, you may also have a septic system. Septic systems and other on-site wastewater disposal systems are major potential sources of contamination of private water supplies if they are poorly maintained or located improperly, or if they are used for disposal of toxic chemicals. Information on septic systems is available from local health departments, State agencies, and the *National Small Flows Clearinghouse* at (800) 624-8301 or www.epa.gov/owm/mab/smcomm/nsfc.htm. A septic system design manual and guidance on system maintenance are available from EPA www.epa.gov/OW-OWM.html/mtb/decent/homeowner.htm.

Figure 58: Well Water head above the soil line.

◊   **Talk With Local Experts**

Ground water conditions vary greatly from place to place, and local experts can give you the best information about your drinking water supply. Some examples are your health department's "sanitarian," local water-well contractors, public water system officials, county extension agents of the *Natural Resources Conservation Service* (NRCS), local or county planning commissions, and your local library.

◊   **Have Your Water Tested Periodically**

Test your water every year for total **coliform** bacteria, nitrates, total dissolved solids, and pH levels. If you suspect other contaminants, test for these as well. Local experts can help you identify these contaminants. You should always test your water after replacing or repairing any part of the system, or if you notice any change in your water's look, taste or smell. Often, county health departments perform tests for bacteria and nitrates. For other substances, health departments, environmental offices, or county governments should have a list of State certified laboratories. Your *State Laboratory Certification Officer* can also provide you with this list. Call

the *Safe Drinking Water Hotline* (800) 426-4791 for the name and number of your State's certification officer. Any laboratory you use should be certified to do drinking water testing.

◊   **Have Your Tests Results Interpreted and Explained Clearly**

Compare your well's water test results to Federal and State drinking water standards. You may need to consult experts to aid you in understanding your results, such as the State agency that licenses well water contractors, your local health department, or your State's drinking water program.

◊   **Protecting Your Ground Water Supply**

Periodically inspect exposed parts of your well for problems such as:

▫   Cracked, corroded, or damaged well casing.
▫   Broken or missing well cap.
▫   Settling and cracking of surface seals.
▫   Slope the area around the well to drain surface runoff away from the well.
▫   Install a well cap or sanitary seal to prevent unauthorized use of, or entry into, the well.
▫   Have an expert disinfect drinking water wells at least once per year with bleach or hypochlorite granules, according to the manufacturer's directions.
▫   Have the well tested once a year for coliform bacteria, nitrates, and other contaminants of concern.
▫   Keep accurate records of any well maintenance, such as disinfection or sediment removal, that may require the use of chemicals in the well.
▫   Hire a certified well driller for any new well construction, modification, or abandonment and closure.
▫   Avoid mixing or using pesticides, fertilizers, herbicides, degreasers, fuels, and other pollutants near the well.
▫   Do not dispose of wastes in dry wells or in abandoned wells.
▫   Do not cut off the well casing below the land surface.
▫   Pump and inspect septic systems as often as recommended by your local health department.
▫   Never dispose of hazardous materials in a septic system.

◊   **Set A Regular Maintenance Schedule For Your Well And Your Septic System**

Proper well and septic system construction and continued maintenance are keys to the safety of your water supply. Your State water well and septic system contractor licensing agency, local health department, or local public water system professional can provide information on well construction. Make certain your contractors are licensed by the State, if required, or certified by the *National Ground Water Association*.

Maintain your well, fixing problems before they reach crisis levels, and keep up-to-date records of well installation and repairs, as well as plumbing and water costs. Protect your own well area from contamination.

◊ **Immediately Remedy Any Problems**

If you find that your well water is contaminated, fix the problem as soon as possible. Consider connecting into a nearby community water system, if one is available. You may want to install a water treatment device to remove impurities. If you connect to a public water system , remember to close your well properly.

◊ **After A Flood-Concerns And Advisories**
  □ Stay away from well pump to avoid electric shock.
  □ Do not drink or wash from a flooded well.
  □ Pump the well until water runs clear.
  □ If water does not run clear, contact the county or State health department or extension service for advice.

Drinking Water From Household Wells

If your family gets drinking water from your own well, do you know if your water is safe to drink? What health risks could you and your family face? Where can you go for help or advice?

This section helps answer these questions. It gives you general information about drinking water from home wells (also considered private drinking water sources). It describes types of activities in your area that can create threats to your water supply. It also describes problems to look for and offers maintenance suggestions.

All of us need clean water to drink. We can go for weeks without food, but only days without water. Contaminated water can be a threat to anyone's health, but especially to young children.

About 15 percent of Americans have their own sources of drinking water, such as wells, cisterns, and springs. Unlike public drinking water systems serving many people, they do not have experts regularly checking the water's source and its quality before it is sent through pipes to the community.

To help protect families with their own wells, almost all states license or register water-well installers. Most also have construction standards for home wells. In addition, some city and county health departments have local rules and permitting. All this helps make sure the well is built properly. But what about checking to see that it is working correctly and the water is always healthy to drink? That is the job of the well owner, and it takes some work and some knowledge.

◊ **What Is Ground Water And How Can It Be Polluted?**

Ground water is a resource found under the earth's surface. Most ground water comes from rain and melting snow soaking into the ground. Water fills the spaces between rocks and soils, making an "aquifer". About half of our nation's drinking water comes from ground water. Most is supplied through public drinking water systems. But many families rely on private, household wells and use ground water as their source of fresh water.

Ground water — its depth from the surface, quality for drinking water, and chance of being polluted — varies from place to place. Generally, the deeper the well, the better the ground water. The amount of new water flowing into the area also affects ground water quality.

Ground water may contain some natural impurities or contaminants, even with no human activity or pollution. Natural contaminants can come from many conditions in the watershed or in the ground. Water moving through underground rocks and soils may pick up magnesium, calcium and chlorides. Some ground water naturally contains dissolved elements such as arsenic, boron, selenium, or radon, a gas formed by the natural breakdown of radioactive uranium in soil. Whether these natural contaminants are health problems depends on the amount of the substance present.

In addition to natural contaminants, ground water is often polluted by human activities such as:
  □ Improper use of fertilizers, animal manures, herbicides, insecticides, and pesticides.
  □ Improperly built or poorly located and/or maintained septic systems for household wastewater.
  □ Leaking or abandoned underground storage tanks and piping Storm-water drains that discharge chemicals to ground water Improper disposal or storage of wastes.
  □ Chemical spills at local industrial sites.

Suburban growth is bringing businesses, factories and industry (and potential sources of pollution) into once rural areas where families often rely on household wells. Growth is also pushing new home developments onto the edge of rural and agricultural areas. Often municipal water and sewer lines do not extend to these areas. Many new houses rely on wells and septic tanks. But the people buying them may not have any experience using these systems.

◊ Most U.S. ground water is safe for human use. However, ground water contamination has been found in all 50 states, so well owners have reason to be vigilant in protecting their water supplies. Well owners need to be aware of potential health problems. They need to test their water regularly and maintain their wells to safeguard their families' drinking water.

◊ **Where Do Ground Water Pollutants Come From?**

Understanding and spotting possible pollution sources is important. It's the first step to safeguard drinking water for you and your family. Some threats come from nature. Naturally occurring contaminants such as minerals can present a health risk. Other potential sources come from past or present human activity — things that we do, make, and use — such as mining, farming and using chemicals. Some of these activities may result in the pollution of the water we drink.

Several sources of pollution are easy to spot by sight, taste, or smell. However many serious problems can only be found by testing your water. Knowing the possible threats in your area will help you decide on the kind of tests you need.

◊ **Quick Reference List of Noticeable Problems**

Visible
- Scale or scum from calcium or magnesium salts in water
- Unclear/turbid water from dirt, clay salts, silt or rust in water Green stains on sinks or faucets caused by high acidity Brown-red stains on sinks, dishwasher, or clothes in wash points to dissolved iron in water
- Cloudy water that clears upon standing may have air bubbles from poorly working pump or problem with filters.

Tastes
- Salty or brackish taste from high sodium content in water
- Alkali/soapy taste from dissolved alkaline minerals in water
- Metallic taste from acidity or high iron content in water
- Chemical taste from industrial chemicals or pesticides

Smell
- A rotten egg odor can be from dissolved hydrogen sulfide gas or certain bacteria in your water. If the smell only comes with hot water it is likely from a part in your hot water heater.
- A detergent odor and water that foams when drawn could be seepage from septic tanks into your ground water well.
- A gasoline or oil smell indicates fuel oil or gasoline likely seeping from a tank into the water supply
- Methane gas or musty/earthy smell from decaying organic matter in water Chlorine smell from excessive chlorination.

Note: Many serious problems (bacteria, heavy metals, nitrates, radon, and many chemicals) can only be found by laboratory testing of water.

◊ **What are Some Naturally Occurring Sources of Pollution?**
- Microorganisms: Bacteria, viruses, parasites and other microorganisms are sometimes found in water. Shallow wells — those with water close to ground level — are at most risk. Runoff, or water flowing over the land surface, may pick up these pollutants from wildlife and soils. This is often the case after flooding. Some of these organisms can cause a variety of illnesses. Symptoms include nausea and diarrhea. These can occur shortly after drinking contaminated water. The effects could be short-term yet severe (similar to food poisoning) or might recur frequently or develop slowly over a long time.

- Radionuclides: Radionuclides are radioactive elements such as uranium and radium. They may be present in underlying rock and ground water. Radon — a gas that is a natural product of the breakdown of uranium in the soil — can also pose a threat. Radon is most dangerous when inhaled and contributes to lung cancer. Although soil is the primary source, using household water containing Radon contributes to elevated indoor Radon levels. Radon is less dangerous when consumed in water, but remains a risk to health.

- Nitrates and Nitrites: Although high nitrate levels are usually due to human activities (see below), they may be found naturally in ground water. They come from the breakdown of nitrogen compounds in the soil. Flowing ground water picks them up from the soil. Drinking large amounts of nitrates and nitrites is particularly threatening to infants (for example, when mixed in formula).

- Heavy Metals: Underground rocks and soils may contain arsenic, cadmium, chromium, lead, and selenium. However, these contaminants are not often found in household wells at dangerous levels from natural sources.

- Fluoride: Fluoride is helpful in dental health, so many water systems add small amounts to drinking water. However, excessive consumption of naturally occurring fluoride can damage bone tissue. High levels of fluoride occur naturally in some areas. It may discolor teeth, but this is not a health risk.

◊ **What Human Activities Can Pollute Ground water?**
- Bacteria and Nitrates: These pollutants are found in human and animal wastes. Septic tanks can cause bacterial and nitrate pollution. So can large numbers of farm animals. Both septic systems and animal manures must be carefully managed to prevent pollution. Sanitary landfills and garbage dumps are also sources. Children and some adults are at extra risk when exposed to water-born bacteria. These include the elderly and people whose immune systems are weak due to AIDS or treatments for cancer. Fertilizers can add to nitrate problems. Nitrates cause a health threat in very young infants called "blue baby" syndrome. This condition disrupts oxygen flow in the blood.

- Concentrated Animal Feeding Operations (CAFOs): The number of CAFOs, often called "factory farms," is growing. On these farms thousands of animals are raised in a small space. The large amounts of animal wastes/ manures from these farms can threaten water supplies. Strict and careful manure management is needed to prevent pathogen and nutrient problems. Salts from high levels of manures can also pollute groundwater.

- Heavy Metals: Activities such as mining and construction can release large amounts of heavy metals into nearby ground water sources. Some older fruit orchards may contain high levels of arsenic, once used as a pesticide. At high levels, these metals pose a health risk.

- Fertilizers and Pesticides: Farmers use fertilizers and pesticides to promote growth and reduce insect damage. These products are also used on golf courses and suburban lawns and gardens. The chemicals in these products may end up in ground water. Such pollution depends on the types and amounts of chemicals used and how they are applied. Local environmental conditions (soil types, seasonal snow and rainfall) also affect this pollution. Many fertilizers contain forms of nitrogen that can break down into harmful nitrates. This could add to other sources of nitrates mentioned above. Some underground agricultural drainage systems collect fertilizers and pesticides. This polluted water can pose problems to ground water and local streams and rivers. In addition, chemicals used to treat buildings and homes for termites or other pests may also pose a threat. Again, the possibility of problems depends on the amount and kind of chemicals. The types of soil and the amount of water moving through the soil also play a role.

- Industrial Products and Wastes: Many harmful chemicals are used widely in local business and industry. These can become drinking water pollutants if not well managed. The most common sources of such problems are:

- Local Businesses: These include nearby factories, industrial plants, and even small businesses such as gas stations and dry cleaners. All handle a variety of hazardous chemicals that need careful management. Spills and improper disposal of these chemicals or of industrial wastes can threaten ground water supplies.

- Leaking Underground Tanks & Piping: Petroleum products, chemicals, and wastes stored in underground storage tanks and pipes may end up in the ground water. Tanks and piping leak if they are constructed or installed improperly. Steel tanks and piping corrode with age. Tanks are often found on farms. The possibility of leaking tanks is great on old, abandoned farm sites. Farm tanks are exempt from the EPA rules for petroleum and chemical tanks.

- Landfills and Waste Dumps: Modern landfills are designed to contain any leaking liquids. But floods can carry them over the barriers. Older dumpsites may have a wide variety of pollutants that can seep into ground water.

- Household Wastes: Improper disposal of many common products can pollute ground water. These include cleaning solvents, used motor oil, paints, and paint thinners. Even soaps and detergents can harm drinking water. These are often a problem from faulty septic tanks and septic leaching fields.

- Lead & Copper: Household plumbing materials are the most common source of lead and copper in home drinking water. Corrosive water may cause metals in pipes or soldered joints to leach into your tap water. Your water's acidity or alkalinity (often measured as pH) greatly affects corrosion. Temperature and mineral content also affect how corrosive it is. They are often used in pipes, solder, or plumbing fixtures. Lead can cause serious damage to the brain, kidneys, nervous system, and red blood cells. The age of plumbing materials — in particular, copper

pipes soldered with lead — is also important. Even in relatively low amounts these metals can be harmful. EPA rules under the *Safe Drinking Water Act* limit lead in drinking water to 15 parts per billion. Since 1988 the Act only allows "lead free" pipe, solder, and flux in drinking water systems. The law covers both new installations and repairs of plumbing. For more information on avoiding lead in drinking water, visit the EPA Website at www.epa.gov/safewater/Pubs/lead1.html.

- Water Treatment Chemicals: Improper handling or storage of water well treatment chemicals (disinfectants, corrosion inhibitors, etc.) close to your well can cause problems.

◊ **Should I Be Concerned?**
You should be aware because the *Safe Drinking Water Act* **DOES NOT** protect private wells. EPA's rules only apply to "public drinking water systems" — government or privately run companies supplying water to 25 people or 15 service connections. While most states regulate private household wells, most have limited rules. Individual well owners have primary responsibility for the safety of the water drawn from their wells. They do not benefit from the government's health protections for water systems serving many families. These must comply with Federal and State regulations for frequent analysis, testing, and reporting of results.

Instead, household well owners should rely on help from local health departments. They may help you with yearly testing for bacteria and nitrates. They may also oversee the placement and construction of new wells to meet State and local regulations. Most have rules about locating drinking water wells near septic tanks, drain fields, and livestock. But remember, the final responsibility for constructing your well correctly, protecting it from pollution, and maintaining it falls on you, the well owner.

◊ **How Much Risk Can I Expect?**
The risk of having problems depends on how good your well is — how well it was built and located, and how well you maintain it. It also depends on your local environment. That includes the quality of the aquifer from which you draw your water and the human activities going on in your area that can affect your well water.

Some questions to consider in protecting your drinking water and maintaining your well are:
- What distance should my well be from sources of human wastes such as septic systems? How far should it be from animal feedlots or manure spreading? What are the types of soil and underlying rocks? Does water flow easily or collect on the surface? How deep must a well be dug to avoid seasonal changes in ground water supply?
- What activities in my area (farming, mining, industry) might affect my well?
- What is the age of my well, its pump, and other parts?

▫   Is my water distribution system protected from cross connections and backflow problems?

◊   **What Should I Do?**

Listed below are the six basic steps you should take to maintain the safety of your drinking water. After the list you'll find "how to" suggestions for each point to help you protect your well and your drinking water.

1. Identify potential problem sources
2. Talk with "local experts"
3. Have your water tested periodically.
4. Have the test results interpreted and explained clearly.
5. Set a regular maintenance schedule for your well, do the scheduled maintenance and keep accurate, up-to-date records.
6. Remedy any problems.

◊   **Protecting Your Ground Water Supply When Building, Modifying Or Closing A Well**

▫   Hire a certified well driller for any new well construction or modification.

▫   Slope well area so surface runoff drains away. When closing a well:
   • Do not cut off the well casing below the land surface.
   • Hire a certified well contractor to fill or seal the well.

▫   Preventing Problems
   • Install a locking well cap or sanitary seal to prevent unauthorized use of, or entry into, the well.

▫   Do not mix or use pesticides, fertilizers, herbicides, degreasers, fuels, and other pollutants near the well.

▫   Never dispose of wastes in dry wells or in abandoned wells.

▫   Pump and inspect septic systems as often as recommended by your local health department.
   • Never dispose of hazardous materials in a septic system.
   • Take care in working or mowing around your well.

▫   Maintaining Your Well
   • Each month check visible parts of your system for problems such as:
     - Cracking or corrosion,
     - Broken or missing well cap,
     - Settling and cracking of surface seals.

▫   Have the well tested once a year for coliform bacteria, nitrates, and other contaminants.

▫   Keep accurate records in a safe place, including:
   • Construction contract or report.
   • Maintenance records, such as disinfection or sediment removal – Any use of chemicals in the well.
   • Water testing results.

▫   After A Flood — Concerns And Advisories
   • Stay away from the well pump while flooded to avoid electric shock
   • Do not drink or wash from the flooded well to avoid becoming sick
   • Get assistance from a well or pump contractor to clean and turn on the pump
   • After the pump is turned back on, pump the well until the water runs clear to rid the well of flood water
   • If the water does not run clear, get advice from the county or State health department or extension service

For additional information go to the EPA web site at www.epa.gov/safewater/consumer/whatdo.htm.

◊   **1. How Can I Spot Potential Problems?**

The potential for pollution entering your well is affected by its placement and construction — how close is your well to potential sources of pollution? Local agricultural and industrial activities, your area's geology and climate also matter. Review the sections that include checklists to help you find potential problems with your well. Take time to review the section *"Protecting Your Ground Water Supply."* Because ground water contamination is usually localized, the best way to identify potential contaminants is to consult a local expert. For example, talk with a geologist at a local college or someone from a nearby public water system. They'll know about conditions in your area. (See 5. Talk With Local Experts section page 304).

◊   **2. Have Your Well Water Tested**

Test your water every year for total coliform bacteria, nitrates, total dissolved solids, and pH levels. If you suspect other contaminants, test for these also. Chemical tests can be expensive. Limit them to possible problems specific to your situation. Again, local experts can tell you about possible impurities in your area.

Often county health departments do tests for bacteria and nitrates. For other substances, health departments, environmental offices, or county governments should have a list of State certified laboratories. Your *State Laboratory Certification Officer* can also provide one. Call EPA's *Safe Drinking Water Hotline,* (800) 4264791, for the name and phone number of your State's certification officer.

Before taking a sample, contact the lab that will perform your tests. Ask for instructions and sampling bottles. Follow the instructions carefully so you will get correct results. The first step is getting a good water sample. It is also important to follow advice about storing the samples. Ask how soon they must be taken to the lab for testing. These instructions can be very different for each substance being tested.

Remember to test your water after replacing or repairing any part of the well system (piping, pump, or the well itself.) Also test if you notice a change in your water's look, taste, or smell. The table Figure 59 page 303 will help you spot problems. The last five problems listed are not an immediate health concern, but they can make your water taste bad, may indicate problems, and could affect your system long term.

Figure 59: Reasons to Test Your Water	
Conditions or Nearby Activities	**Test For**
Recurring gastro-intestinal illness	Coliform Bacteria
Household plumbing contains lead	pH, lead, copper
Radon in indoor air or region is radon rich	Radon
Corrosion of pipes, plumbing	Corrosion, pH, lead
Nearby areas of intensive agriculture	Nitrate, pesticides, coliform bacteria
Coal or other mining operations nearby	Metals, pH, corrosion
Gas drilling operations nearby	Chloride, sodium, barium, strontium
Dump, junkyard, landfill, factory, gas station, or dry- cleaning operation nearby	Volatile organic compounds, total dissolved solids, pH, sulfate, chloride, metals
Odor of gasoline or fuel oil, and near gas station or buried fuel tanks	Volatile organic compounds
Objectionable taste or smell	Hydrogen sulfide, corrosion, metals
Stained plumbing fixtures, laundry	Iron, copper, manganese
Salty taste and seawater, or a heavily salted roadway nearby	Chloride, total dissolved solids, sodium
Scaly residues, soaps don't lather	Hardness
Rapid wear of water treatment equipment	pH, corrosion
Water softener needed to treat hardness	Manganese, iron
Water appears cloudy, frothy, or colored	Color, detergents

◊ **3. Understanding Your Test Results**

Have your well water tested for any possible contaminants in your area. Use a State approved testing lab. Do not be surprised if a lot of substances are found and reported to you.

The amount of risk from a drinking water contaminant depends on the specific substance and the amount in the water. The health of the person also matters. Some contaminant cause immediate and severe effects. It may take only one bacterium or virus to make a weak person sick. Another person may not be affected. For very young children, taking in high levels of nitrate over a relatively short period of time can be very dangerous. Many other contaminants pose a long-term or chronic threat to your health — a little bit consumed regularly over a long time could cause health problems such as trouble having children and other effects.

EPA drinking water rules for public water systems aim to protect people from both short and long term health hazards. The amounts of contaminants allowed are based on protecting people over a lifetime of drinking water. Public water systems are required to test their water regularly before delivery. They also treat it so that it meets drinking water standards, notify customers if water does not meet standards and provide annual water quality reports.

Compare your well's test results to Federal and State drinking water standards. (You can find these standards at www.epa.gov/safewater/mcl.html or call the *Safe Drinking Water Hotline* 800-426-4791.) In some cases, the laboratory will give a very helpful explanation. But you may have to rely on other experts to aid you in understanding the results.

The following organizations may be able to help:
▫ The State agency that licenses water well contractors can help you understand your test results. It will also provide information on well construction and protection of your water supply. The agency is usually located in the State capital or other major city. It is often part of the department of health or environmental protection. Check the blue "government pages" of your local phone book or call the *American Ground Water Trust* at (614) 7612215 or the EPA Hotline at (800) 426-4791 for your licensing agency's phone number.
▫ The local health department and agricultural agents can help you understand the test results. They will have information on any known threats to drinking water in your area. They can also give you suggestions about how to protect your well water.
▫ The State drinking water program can also help. You can compare your well's water to the State's standards for public water systems. State programs are usually located in the State capital or another major city. They are often part of the department of health or environmental regulation. Again, consult the blue "government pages" in your local phone book for the address and phone number or call or the EPA Hotline — (800) 426-4791.
▫ The *Safe Drinking Water Hotline* at (800) 426-4791, mentioned above — can help in many ways. The Hotline

can provide a listing of contaminants public water systems must test for. EPA also has copies of health advisories prepared for specific drinking water contaminants. The EPA Hotline staff can explain the Federal regulations that apply to public water systems. They compare your lab results to the Federal standards. In addition, they can give you the phone number and address of your State drinking water program, and of your State laboratory certification officer. That officer can send you a list of approved labs in your area.

◊   **4. Well Construction and Maintenance**
Proper well construction and continued maintenance are keys to the safety of your water supply. Your State water well contractor licensing agency, local health department, or local water system professional can provide information on well construction. See Figure 60 on page 304.

Water-well drillers and pump-well installers are listed in your local phone directory. The contractor should be bonded and insured. Make certain your ground water contractor is registered or licensed in your State, if required. If your State does not have a licensing/registration program contact the *National Ground Water Association.* They have a voluntary certification program for contractors. (In fact, some states use the Association's exams as their test for licensing.) For a list of certified contractors in your State contact the Association at (614) 898-7791 or (800) 551-7379. There is no cost for mailing or faxing the list to you.

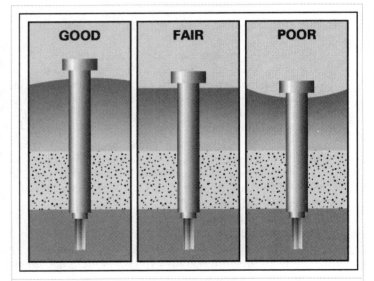

Figure 60: The well should be located so rainwater flows away from it. Rainwater can pick up harmful bacteria and chemicals on the land's surface. If this water pools near your well, it can seep into it, causing health problems.

Many homeowners tend to forget the value of good maintenance until problems reach crisis levels. That can be

expensive. It's better to maintain your well, find problems early, and correct them to protect your well's performance. Keep up-to-date records of well installation and repairs plus pumping and water tests. Such records can help spot changes and possible problems with your water system. If you have problems, ask a local expert to check your well construction and maintenance records. He or she can see if your system is okay or needs work.

The graphic in Figure 61 on page 304 shows a good example of an animal-proof cap or seal and the casing of a well.

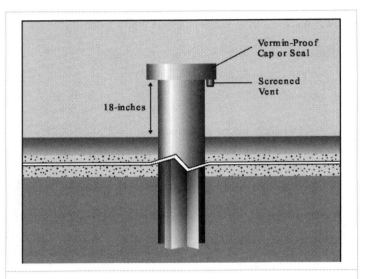

Figure 61: An animal or vermin proof cap prevents rodents from entering your well, being trapped and dying. Paving around your well will prevent polluted runoff from seeping into your water supply.

Protect your own well area. Be careful about storage and disposal of household and lawn care chemicals and wastes. Good farmers and gardeners minimize the use of fertilizers and pesticides. Take steps to reduce erosion and prevent surface water runoff. Regularly check underground storage tanks that hold home heating oil, diesel, or gasoline. Make sure your well is protected from the wastes of livestock, pets, and wildlife.

◊   **5. Talk With Local Experts**
Good sources of information and advice can be found close to home. The list below tells about some "local experts":

▫   The local health department's registered "sanitarian" is a health specialist. He or she likely knows the most about any problems with private wells.

▫   Local water-well contractors can tell you about well drilling and construction. They are also familiar with local geology and water conditions. Look in the yellow pages of your phone book or contact the agency in your State that licenses water well contractors. Call the *National Ground Water Association* (NGWA) at (614) 898-7791 or (800) 5517379 to find NGWA-certified water well contractors in your area. Officials at the nearest public water system may explain any threats to local drinking water and may be developing plans to address potential threats. They may advise you on taking samples and understanding tests done on your water. Ask the local health department or look in your phone book for the name and address of the closest system. Local county extension agents will know about local farming and forestry activities that can affect your water. They may also have information about water testing.

▫ The *Natural Resources Conservation Service* (NRCS) replaced the old *U.S. Soil Conservation Service*. It is part of the *U.S. Department of Agriculture*. The NRCS and the *U.S. Geological Survey* have information about local soils and ground water. They can tell you where a local water supply is located and how it is recharged or replenished. They would know of any pollution threats and if radon is a problem in the area. Look for both in the blue pages of your local phone book. Local or county planning commissions can be good sources. They know about past and present land uses in your area that affect water. Your public library may also have records and maps that can provide useful information. Nearby colleges and universities have research arms that can provide facts and expertise. They may also have a testing lab.

◊ **6. Fix Problems Immediately**
If you find that your well water is polluted, fix the problem as soon as possible. You may need to disinfect your water, have a new well drilled, re-plumb or repair your system. Consider hooking into a nearby community water system (if one is available). If you have a new well drilled or connect to a community water system, the old well must be closed properly. Consult "local experts" for help. You might consider installing a water treatment device to remove impurities. Information about treatment devices can be obtained from the following sources:

▫ Water Quality Association
P.O. Box 606
4151 Naperville Road
Lisle, IL 60532
www.wqa.org

▫ National Sanitation Foundation
P.O. Box 130140
789 N Dixboro Road
Ann Arbor, MI 48113-0140
(734) 769-8010, (800) NSF-MARK
www.nsf.org

▫ U.S. Environmental Protection Agency (to visit in person)

▫ Office of Water Resource Center
1200 Pennsylvania Avenue, NW

Ariel Rios Building
Washington, DC 20460
Phone: (202) 260-7786
Monday through Friday, except Federal holidays, 8:30AM – 4:30PM ET
E-mail: center.water-resource@epa.gov

There are many home water treatment devices. Different types remove different pollutants or impurities. No one device does it all. Also, you must carefully maintain your home treatment device so your water stays safe.

◊ **Find Out More**
To find out more about your watershed and its ground water visit *"Surf Your Watershed"* at www.epa.gov/surf. Also look at the *"Index of Watershed Indicators"* at www.epa.gov/iwi. These websites can also tell you possible sources of problems. Companies with permits to release their wastewaters in your area are listed. You can see if they meet pollution control laws. You can also learn how your watershed compares to others in the country.

The U.S. Department of Agriculture and EPA support a program to help farmers, ranchers and rural homeowners. Called *Farm*A*Syst* or *Home*A*Syst*, it helps identify and solve environmental problems, including protecting drinking water. Obtain a copy of the *Home*A*Syst* questionnaire/checklist that can help you find possible threats to your water supply from:
▫ National Farm*A*Syst/Home*A*Syst Program
303 Hiram Smith Hall
1545 Observatory Drive
Madison, WI 53706
Ph: 608.262.0024   Fax: 608.265.2775
Email: homeasys@uwex.edu

For more information on current and future Federal drinking water standards and for general information on drinking water topics and issues, contact the EP A at www.epa.gov/safewater or at:
▫ U .S. Environmental Protection Agency Office of Ground Water and Drinking Water
1200 Pennsylvania Avenue, NW
Washington, DC 20460

Or call:
▫ The Safe Drinking Water Hotline (800) 426-4791
▫ The hotline operates from 9:00 AM to 5:30 PM (EST)
▫ The hotline can be accessed on the Internet at www.epa.gov/safewater/drinklink.html

You can get a list of Federal drinking water standards from the EPA website. In addition, the EPA *Office of Ground Water and Drinking Water* gives chemical and health risk information for a number of drinking water problems through its *Safe Drinking Water Hotline* (800) 426-4791. This information is also on the internet at www.epa.gov/safewater. If you do not have a computer, most public libraries offer internet access. Even though Federal standards do not apply to household wells, you can use them as a guide to potential problems in your water. Be aware that many states have their own drinking water standards. Some are stricter than the Federal rules. To get your State standards, contact your State drinking water program or local health department.

Other sources of information include:

▫   Ground Water Protection Council
    http://gwpc.site.net

▫   American Water Works Association
    www.awwa.org

▫   National Rural Water Association
    www.nrwa.org

▫   National Drinking Water Clearinghouse
    www.estd.wvu.edu/ndwc

▫   Rural Community Assistance Program
    www.rcap.org

▫   U.S. Geological Survey
    www.water.usgs.gov

▫   U.S. Department of Agriculture Natural Resources
    Conservation Service
    www.nrcs.usda.gov

▫   Water Systems Council
    www.watersystemscouncil.org

(See Drinking Water Glossary at end of book)

Health Concerns Photo Pages

P 185. In very old houses, you may find Rockwool or Vermiculite insulation. This off-white color insulation has a clumpy appearance. All older Rockwool or Vermiculite type of insulation should be tested for any asbestos content. Any foam insulation should be tested for UFFI content. Contact your local EPA office for more information about these and other health and environmental hazards.

P 187. It is rare that you'll find asbestos insulation in good condition like this. This asbestos has not been disturbed and the metal brackets are still intact. As a result, there is less of a chance of asbestos fibers being breathed in by the occupants. However, it's always better to have all asbestos removed by a licensed EPA contractor. Call your local EPA for their advice about health hazards in a home.

P 186. This asbestos insulation on the heating pipes has been encapsulated. When an EPA licensed contractor encapsulates asbestos, they help reduce the health hazards of fibers getting in the air. However, as long as there is any asbestos in a house, there are going to be some fibers floating around. ***Encapsulating this insulation does not totally eliminate the problem!***

P 189. *Here we are in asbestos heaven!* There are probably more asbestos fibers in this room than there are dust fibers. Almost always in older houses you'll find asbestos pipe insulation that is loose or has been removed unprofessionally. These conditions create very serious health hazards for the occupants of the house. Follow the EPA guidelines to resolve this.

P 188. Radon gas is considered by EPA to be the number two leading cause of lung cancer behind smoking. Radon is everywhere since it's created by a natural breakdown of rocks and soil. Stone foundation walls and dirt floors in the lower level increase radon gas levels. The large rock embedded in this basement will add radon into the air. A cement floor covering will help reduce this problem.

The insulation vapor barrier is installed upside down!

P 190. This photo and the one below show a radon mitigation system in the lower level of a house with the radon gas being vented outside above the roof.

Mitigation is the term used for the treatment to remove the radon problem by reducing the radon gas levels in the house. When a house is mitigated, the radon contractor will seal all open cracks in the lower level walls and floors that they can find. They then drill a hole in the foundation floor which looks like a sump pump pit. Instead of installing a sump pump in this pit, the contractor will install a fan with pipes leading to the outside of the house. In some areas, the local codes require that these pipes discharge above the roof line. This will help prevent the radon from entering back into the house through an open window. The purpose of the mitigation is to vent all radon gas that builds up underneath the foundation, to the exterior of the house.

P 191. While we're on the lovely topic of lung cancer, let's talk about radon. A radon lab technician told me the story about how radon was discovered. I thought you might find it interesting. There was a man who lived in Reading, Pennsylvania that worked for some type of nuclear laboratory. When he used to go to work, he would set off the radiation detectors at the lab. The radiation detectors are installed so that the nuclear lab can monitor their employees to see if they're being exposed to radiation inside the lab. The lab employees couldn't figure out why the detectors were setting off, so they tested his house for radiation. While studying the problem, they stumbled upon radon gas.
(Fortunately or unfortunately for mankind. I guess it's just another way to develop cancer. Like there aren't enough already!)

Home Inspection Stationery

Sample Business Card, Brochures, Stationery, & Price Quote Card

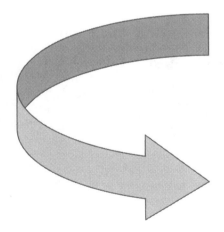

Sample Business Stationery

Sample Business Card

Sample Envelope

Capitol Home Inspectors

1234 Little Hill Road
Anytown, CT 12345-6789

John Doe - Home Inspector

PHONE (123) 456-7890
FAX (123) 456-7890
 info@capitol.com   www.capitol.com

Capitol Home Inspectors
John Doe
1234 Little Hill Road
Anytown, CT 12345-6789

Capitol Home Inspectors

John Doe
1234 Little Hill Road
Anytown, CT 12345-6789

PHONE (123) 456-7890   FAX (123) 456-7890
Email: info@capitol.com   Web: www.capitol.com

3 Hour Home Inspections

25 Page Narrative Reports

Available 7 Days A Week

Clients Encouraged To Attend The On-Site Home Inspection

Your home is the most important investment of your life! Have a professional inspector take the risk out of your decision.

Call Capitol and hire the best home inspector!

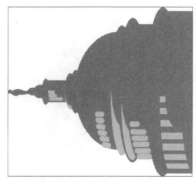

Home and Condominium Inspections

We test well water systems, septic systems, radon gas, water, and for termites.

Serving all towns in the New England area.

Capitol Home Inspectors

1234 Little Hill Road
Anytown, CT 12345

Phone (123) 456-7890
Fax (123) 456-7890
Email: info@capitol.com
Web: www.capitol.com

Capitol Home Inspectors
1234 Little Hill Road
Anytown, CT 12345-6789

Recipient Name
Address Line 1
Address Line 2
Address Line 3

Our Inspection Includes:

◇ Structural Components
◇ Operating Systems:
  Electrical, Plumbing,
  Heating, Air-Conditioning,
  Hot Water Heater
◇ Roof, Attic and Insulation
◇ Chimney and Fireplace
◇ Basement - water
  problems, foundations, etc.
◇ Kitchens and Bathrooms
◇ Interior Walls, Floors,
  Doors, Ceilings, Windows
◇ Exterior - siding, patios,
  decks, fences, walls, soil,
  garages and driveways
◇ Septic and Well Systems
◇ Water and Radon Gas
  Testing
◇ Termites

Price Quote Card

Report Number		Date of Inspection/Appraisal
Bldg. Address	Zip	Day of Week & Time
Inspector/Appraiser	Present Owner	Phone

Client	Comments, Directions, etc.
Address	
Zip	
Home Phone	
Work Phone	
Attorney	
Address	
Zip	
R.E. Agent	
	(c) 1992 Guy Cozzi

Price Quote Card

Report Number		Date of Inspection/Appraisal
Bldg. Address	Zip	Day of Week & Time
Inspector/Appraiser	Present Owner	Phone

Client	Comments, Directions, etc.
Address	
Zip	
Home Phone	
Work Phone	
Attorney	
Address	
Zip	
R.E. Agent	
	(c) 1992 Guy Cozzi

	Inspection	Appraisal
Date Price Quoted		
How You Heard of Us		
Type of Property Condo 1 Family		
Square Footage		
Bedrooms / Bathrooms / Garage		
Reported Age of Bldg.		
Overall Condition Very Good Good Average Fair Poor		
Basement / Crawl Space		
Air Conditioning		
Septic System Test		
Well System Test		
Water Lab Test		
Termite Inspection		
Radon Test		
Location Factor		
Selling Price		
TOTAL FEE $		

	Inspection	Appraisal
Date Price Quoted		
How You Heard of Us		
Type of Property Condo 1 Family		
Square Footage		
Bedrooms / Bathrooms / Garage		
Reported Age of Bldg.		
Overall Condition Very Good Good Average Fair Poor		
Basement / Crawl Space		
Air Conditioning		
Septic System Test		
Well System Test		
Water Lab Test		
Termite Inspection		
Radon Test		
Location Factor		
Selling Price		
TOTAL FEE $		

What No One Else Tells You!!

Reality Talk

I've included these last sections because I felt they're a very important part of giving you a complete picture of the real estate business in general. Some of these things you're going to have to experience for yourself to really see and understand what I mean. The school of hard knocks will always teach you the hard way, but you'll learn your lessons well! I won't include the icon keys for safety items and war stories in this section of the book. The reason I'm not including them is because this section is *filled* with war stories and safety issues and there would be icon keys for just about every paragraph! **Also, I'm not going to "pull any punches" in this section. I'm not going to paint some fairy tale, rosy picture or "sugarcoat" anything. I have written this section in a straight-forward, honest, direct, sincere – and sometimes <u>VERY BLUNT</u> manner!! I hope you are not shocked or offended by anything you read in this book. Everything I have written is the truth, the whole truth, and nothing but the truth.**

Every single thing I mention in this book is from actual experiences that I have personally encountered or I have had friends in this business encounter them.

*I've learned from my years in business and life that **money** is definitely a **truth serum** that **always** brings out the **<u>true</u>** character and integrity of a person and will reveal what they are really like deep down inside.*

After reading these sections you might say, *"This is just a bunch of negative and exaggerated examples of not trusting your fellow man."* Well, I've got news for you sweetheart, it may be negative and it may make you wonder about trusting your fellow man; but no matter what you call it, I call every bit of it ***<u>Reality, Reality, Reality!!!!</u>*** Every single thing I mention in this book is from actual experiences that I have personally encountered or I have had friends in this business encounter them. I only wish that I had a nickel for each time I've seen it happen. If I did, I wouldn't need to work anymore! You can go through life with blind faith and leave yourself wide open by trusting everyone. But just remember the old saying, *"A fool and his money are soon parted."* I have a lot of experience in all aspects of residential real estate. From this experience I could tell you war stories that would make your head spin. I've learned from my years in business and life that **money** is definitely a **truth serum** that **always** brings out the **<u>true</u>** character and integrity of a person and will reveal what

they are really like deep down inside. If you want to see what someone is *really* like deep down inside and if they're truly honest and have integrity, then look at the way they are when dealing with money. Don't focus on the front or image they portray in public because often that's not a good indicator. Instead look at their actions and how <u>honest</u> they are when dealing with money. *That's the true person deep down inside!* It's not how much money they have or don't have, because I know a lot more poor people who are far more honest and sincere than many of the wealthy people I've known. **Instead look at what the person does to get money and to keep money. Do they compromise their morals or cheat people for money? Are they shrewd and conniving when dealing with money? That's the key to the truth serum!** Money has a strange affect on many people. It becomes like an **addictive drug** that they can't enough of - regardless of how wealthy they become. The saying, *"show me a <u>rich man</u> and I'll show you a <u>crook</u>",* unfortunately is true in many cases.

Third Parties To The Transaction

As I said in the beginning of the book, when I use the term "Third Parties", I'm talking about people involved in the transaction, not including you or your client. This could be any number of people. The list includes but isn't limited to: the seller, the Realtor or broker, the appraiser, the home inspector, the mortgage lender, the title company, the attorney, the builder or repair contractor, the mailman, the Tooth Fairy, Santa Claus, Easter Bunny, the seller's dog or cat, and anyone else who may have an interest in the deal. Also, when I use descriptive adjectives and refer to *immoral, greedy, dishonest, incompetent, ignorant, etc.* Third Parties, it does <u>NOT</u> refer to **all** third party people, just those that match the particular adjective used. I also want to make it clear that throughout this book both males and females are being referred to whenever the pronouns *he* or *she* are used. Both males and females are also referred to when I give examples of war stories that I've encountered in the real estate business. When the pronouns "he" or "she" are used, they are interchangeable.

---

*Also, when I use descriptive adjectives and refer to "immoral, greedy, dishonest, incompetent, ignorant, etc." Third Parties, it does <u>NOT</u> refer to **all** third party people, just those that match the particular adjective used.*

"Third Parties" is a very broad term and I don't want any one person or group of people to think that they're being singled out when I use that term. I don't want anyone to think the term "third party" is directed at them personally. Realtors and other third parties are important people involved in the purchase and sale of real estate. They are a necessity and provide a vital service that helps the public to buy and sell property. The problem I have is that some Realtors and third parties can be very dishonest, greedy, incompetent, immoral, ignorant, or a combination of all of these undesirable qualities. To make matters even worse, they go a step further and think that they're *experts* in every aspect of real estate. These are the third party people that I'm referring to!! You need to understand that third parties, such as Realtors, **are not experts** in real estate. Realtors only need the equivalent of a few days of basic real estate classes to get a license. So don't think they know all the important aspects of investing in real estate. Even if a Realtor has many years of experience as a real estate agent and/or investor, they're not knowledgeable in **all** aspects of real estate. They cannot give you advice like a qualified real estate appraiser, home inspector, builder, real estate attorney, etc. can in each particular field of expertise.

In case you didn't know, most of the time the Realtor works for the seller, not the buyer.

In case you didn't know, most of the time the Realtor works for the **seller**, not the buyer. Sometimes the Realtor will represent the buyer as a "buyer's agent" but that's not very common. Some states require Realtors to sign an agreement with potential sellers and buyers clearly stating whom they're working for. One reason for this may be that some home buyers don't realize that the Realtor often represents the seller. This means that when you go into a real estate office looking to buy a house, the Realtor that shows you the properties listed for sale has a **fiduciary responsibility** to the **seller** of the house! Even though a buyer goes into the real estate office looking for houses, the Realtor still works for the seller. In this case the Realtor is responsible for looking out for the seller's best interest, and not the buyer's. Some buyers don't know this and mistakenly think that the Realtor is looking out for **their** best interest only. *(Some Realtors only look out for THEIR OWN best interests, regardless of whether they represent the seller or buyer! It's as though some Realtor's believe their fiduciary responsibility is only to fill their own pockets with sales commissions.)*

An educated home buyer or seller is a dishonest Realtor's worst nightmare!!

An educated home buyer or seller is a dishonest Realtor's worst nightmare!! I've seen plenty of greedy, ignorant, dishonest Realtors and third parties get angry because my clients wanted to take my advice and check everything out about the house they were planning to buy or sell. I think the last thing a greedy, dishonest, ignorant, immoral and/or incompetent third party person wants is an **educated home buyer or seller**. That's because an educated

home buyer or seller is a careful, intelligent person who checks everything out before making a big investment. This can take a few days to check the town hall records, get repair estimates, etc. If a home buyer or seller wants to verify items by checking the documentation themselves, getting repair estimates **prior** to closing, etc., these Realtors and third parties criticize them and say things like, *"Oh, this buyer or seller is just a worrier. They're making a big fuss over nothing. They should just close on the house and forget about it."* These third parties can cost a home buyer or seller tens of thousands of dollars. They do this by pressuring your client into **not** checking everything out **before** the closing. Far too many people are buying and selling their homes with their eyes closed. Hopefully, my educational materials will open your eyes *nice and wide* when you decide to buy or sell your house!

Sometimes the seller of the house, the Realtor, or some other third party will tell you something, such as the air-conditioning system, works just fine. However you find that you can't operate the system by its normal controls. If the seller, Realtor, or other third party get very defensive about the situation and insist that the system works properly, just tell them to go ahead and turn it on so you can evaluate the air-conditioning. Don't get in an argument with them just say, *"Great, **you** turn it on and I'll be more than happy to evaluate the A/C for my client."* This way you dump it back in their lap and leave it up to them to turn on the system.

Now remember, I said this in the beginning of the book and I'll say it again. You're a guest in someone else's house! So don't be rude or get into an argument with anyone at the subject property. You have to always be diplomatic and professional in this or any other business to be successful. You also have to respect the seller's property. Don't go into someone's house and start taking the place apart by poking holes I the walls and moving furniture all around. You have to treat their home and personal belongings as you want someone to treat your home and personal belongings during an inspection. Some seller's get very upset and worried during an appraisal and/or a home inspection because it can make or break a real estate deal. So remember to always be polite and courteous during an inspection.

Now don't get me wrong when I tell you this by thinking you have to be a marshmallow during the inspection. As an **"A to Z Home Inspector"** you still have to do a very thorough inspection. This means that you have to evaluate all visible and accessible areas in the house and on the property. Don't be afraid to probe the visible wood beams on the inside and outside of the house. When you probe the wood beams and exterior trim work you're going to leave marks and some minor cosmetic damage. This can't be helped and it's a necessary part of properly evaluating the structural members for rot and wood destroying insect infestation. However, because probing will leave visible marks in wood, you don't want to go around damaging the interior finished floor moldings, doors and window sills. Just use your common sense when deciding what wood areas are finished coverings that shouldn't be probed and what wood areas have to be probed during your inspection.

I once did an inspection and I was probing the moldings at the base of the garage door trim work. This is a very common area to find rot and wood destroying insect infestation because the wood is in close contact with the soil. The wood was so rotted at the base of the door trim work, that the probe went right through it. A hole that was a few inches in diameter was left in the wood. This is going to happen to you when you probe rotted and damaged wood. There's nothing wrong with you leaving this wood damaged because if the wood is very solid, then it won't fall apart when you probe it. However, if the wood needs to be replaced then it will fall apart and leave some damage. Don't worry about leaving the wood with some cosmetic damage because it has to be replaced anyway due to the rot and/or wood destroying insect damage. All your doing is showing your client and all third parties that the wood needs replacing.

Anyway, after I probed this garage door molding, I told the client and the third parties that this section of wood needed to be replaced because it was all rotted out. About three days later I got a phone call from the Realtor. She said that the seller was going to have their attorney contact me because the seller felt that *"I seriously hurt the market value of their property."* It was such a ridiculous comment that even the Realtor said the seller was crazy to make that claim. I was never contacted by the seller's attorney because the seller must have realized that they had no basis for a complaint against me. They realized that the wood was rotted out and the probing damage was done during an inspection that they allowed me to do at their home.

Verify Everything With The Documentation

Often the seller or the Realtor will tell you or your client that something, such as the roof or heating system, was just recently replaced. Another example is that they will tell you that the asbestos was removed by a licensed EPA contractor. **That's fine, then just tell the client to get copies of all of the receipts and documentation for the work performed. Recommend that the client call the contractors personally.** This will enable them to talk with the contractors to find out important information. They should ask the contractors if there was anything about the work they did at the subject property that would be helpful or important for the client to know. Sometimes the contractor will inform your client that the seller wanted to save some money on the job. This could be due to the fact that the house was on the market for sale. As a result, the seller may have told the contractor to cut corners and not do the proper repair work. This is done to cover up a problem so potential buyers won't see any inadequate repair work.

The client also needs to check with the local building department to make sure that this information is accurate and if any permits and final approvals were required. **Almost** *always* **permits and approvals are required so don't take it for granted that everything was properly filed and taken care of. Often you'll have the seller, the Realtor, or another third party tell you or your client that all the building permits and approvals have been obtained for some work done at the site. Or else many times third party people will say that building permits and approvals were not needed for some work done at the site.** That's fine, then just tell the client to obtain all receipts and documentation for the work done. Also, tell the client to check with the local building department to make sure that this information is accurate and that all permits and *final* approvals were obtained if they were required for the work done.

> Whenever you make any changes to a house or a site from the time of the original construction, you have to file the necessary permits and obtain all final approvals from the local municipality.

Whenever you make ANY changes to a house or a site from the time of the original construction, you have to file the necessary permits and obtain all final approvals from the local municipality. *(Contrary to popular belief, this is an accurate statement and I'm the only guy I know of that tells his client's the facts about checking the records at town hall. Realtors don't want your client checking town hall records because then he may know too much and be an educated buyer.)* This pertains to *all repairs* done at the house and site, such as: replacing the heating or air-conditioning systems; upgrading the electrical system; replacing the roof shingles; finishing a basement or attic; putting an addition on a house; adding a deck or a swimming pool; installing or updating a bathroom or kitchen; and anything else other than minor maintenance like painting. The reason you have to obtain permits and approvals for this repair work is that the local building department inspectors have to check the work out. They have to make sure the work is done properly and safely.

Local building inspectors are needed to ensure that all construction and repair work at least meets the minimum building codes in that town. By meeting the building code standards, it will help protect the occupants of the house from unsafe conditions. For example, let's say an electrician installs new branch wires and outlets in a remodeled bath or kitchen. How do you know the wires and outlets are properly installed? The answer is - you don't!! Once the walls are sealed up there's no way for the house occupants to see any loose or exposed wires. Unsafe electrical conditions could lead to a fire or someone getting electrocuted. This is why the local building inspector has to sign-off on repair work in stages. In most areas, the inspector will view the contractor's work before it's sealed up with a finished covering, such as sheetrock, flooring, etc. Then the building inspector will give the OK to seal up the work. A final inspection is conducted when the repair job is completed. It's similar to new house construction. The building inspector goes out to view the work in different stages during the construction process. Each inspection must receive an approval before further construction can continue. This process allows the inspector to sign-off on work that will be covered up when completed.

There is a second reason why the local municipality wants you to file for permits and approvals for all repair work. When you put an addition on a house, add a deck, a pool, or upgrade the house, you're then increasing the property's market value. As a result, the local tax assessor may want to raise your property taxes because now the house is worth more money.

The Sad Truth

I was doing an appraisal once, and a woman at town hall told me a few tragic war stories. They emphasize the importance of obtaining all permits and final approvals for repair work. She said that there had been two recent occasions with insurance agents that came by her office. These agents were checking the records on two houses in that town. One insurance company was involved in a lawsuit filed by a contractor against a homeowner. This contractor was doing some repair work in the attic area of a house. There had been work done a few years earlier by another contractor in this attic area. Well, the second contractor was working and **he fell through the ceiling!** This contractor sued the homeowner for millions of dollars. The basis of the lawsuit was that the prior repairs did not have a permit and final approval from the town building inspector for the work done.

The other insurance agent that came into this woman's office at town hall was also handling a lawsuit for millions of dollars. She told me that a child was swimming in someone's pool along with the homeowner's children. Unfortunately, something shot out of the pool water filter device and hit this boy in the eye. **The boy is now blind in one eye!** His family sued the homeowner because they didn't have a *final* plumbing inspection approval for the pool equipment which included the pool water filter.

An attorney gave one of my clients another very good reason why it's imperative to get all final permits and approvals. He said that someone could get hurt on your property due to repairs or upgrading that wasn't done properly or safely. If this happens and you don't have permits and approvals for the work, you could be sued. We've already seen this in the stories I just mentioned. **However, to make matters even worse, your insurance company may try to refuse paying the claim if you lose in court. The insurance company may tell you that it's your negligence for not making sure that all valid permits and approvals had been obtained!** You certainly don't want to get stuck in a position like that. Especially, when someone gets injured.

Check Town Hall... Or Else

Years ago the records at local municipalities were all kept on paper and in file cabinets so it was a lot more work to find what you needed. Now everything is in computer databases which greatly simplifies checking the records on a property. **Don't** just take it for granted that the permits and approvals have been obtained for any work performed. Many people will add to the original construction or make repairs without filing for permits. They might do the work themselves or else they hire a contractor who doesn't know what he's doing, or else he's too lazy, and he won't file any permits for the work. Recommend to the client that he/she verify this information, plus you might want to check it out as well. If it's true and all permits and approvals have been obtained, then great, everyone's happy. But if it's not true, then you don't want to get stuck holding the bag for the problems that will come up later.

> *Don't take it for granted that the permits have been obtained for any work performed. Many people will add to the original construction or make repairs without filing for permits.*

Don't let any Realtors or other third parties talk you or your client out of verifying this information! Almost always a seller or a Realtor will say:
"Oh, yes they have all the permits for that work," or *"Oh, you don't need to file a permit for that in this area,"* or *"Yes, we do have a C of O,"* or *"The asbestos was removed by a licensed EPA contractor."*

Verify everything they say by looking at the written documentation with your own two eyes and tell the client to do the same!!!! *(You're not required to go to town hall for a home inspection. However, if you do, you'll certainly gain some brownie points with your client and you can charge an additional fee for this service).* If the third party's information is wrong, then you and your client will end up paying the price for it. Just because someone has a Certificate of Occupancy it doesn't mean that the building department has approved all of the work done at the site. A *C of O* is issued when the house is built and it's generally only used to state the legal occupancy of the house. That's why it's called a *Certificate of Occupancy.* Even if a C of O is required for any repairs done at the site, this **does not** mean that the contractor or the homeowner had the C of O updated to include the repairs that were done. **If town hall isn't notified that the work is being done, then the C of O doesn't magically get updated on its own!**

> *Don't let any Realtors or other third parties talk you or your client out of verifying this information at town hall.*

In some areas, a new C of O is not issued when repairs or upgrading is done at the subject property. These areas will just require that the homeowner obtain permits and approvals from the town building and zoning departments. So don't make the client think that because there's a C of O, there are no violations or no missing permits and approvals.

You Have The Right To...

You should recommend that the client go down to town hall personally to check _ALL_ records pertaining to the subject property! This will enable the client to verify all information in the real estate listing and any other data sources. The client can also confirm any other information that has been represented to him or her about the house. **If the client sends a third party to town hall to check the records, and they miss something, it's the <u>client's</u> neck and money that's on the line!** So recommend that your client go and check the town hall records themselves.

You may decide to provide the town hall records check as a service to your clients. Just make sure that you know what you're doing when you offer this service. Try to get a special Errors and Omissions insurance policy if you provide this service to your clients. You have to be able to accurately check all records pertaining to the subject property. Because if it's your mistake for not verifying certain information, then the client may want you to reimburse them for any expenses they incur.

Your client has a **right** to know everything about the subject property. Often a Realtor or other third party to the transaction will say, _"Oh, you don't need to check the town hall records. The attorney, appraiser and the title company all take care of that for you."_ <u>DON'T BELIEVE THAT FOR A MINUTE!!!!</u> If your client leaves the town hall records check to someone else, then your client will probably learn the hard way that important items are often missed. I went through this experience myself when my brother and I were selling one of our rental properties. The buyer was getting a FHA mortgage loan. With these loans, the lender requires a more extensive search into the property records than the search done for a conventional mortgage loan. This search turned up a list of building violations and missing permits that were from a **prior owner** of the property. Even though the violations were not caused by my brother and I, we still were held responsible for them. **The reason for this is that the building department doesn't care who <u>owns</u> the house. All they care about, is that the property is <u>safe</u> and everything <u>adheres</u> to the local building codes.**

After these problems surfaced, my attorney contacted the title company that we had paid for the title insurance policy and the title records search. Our title company said that there is a clause in just about all title policies dealing with this type of situation. The clause states that the title company **is not responsible** for any building, zoning or other violations. A title company is only concerned with the _ownership interest_ in the subject property. Ownership interest is what is stated in the deed for the property. This has _absolutely nothing_ to do with

building permits, zoning, taxes, and many other aspects at town hall. As a result, we spent thousands of dollars and delayed the closing for months, in order to resolve these old violations created by a prior owner. This experience should put an end to any third parties trying to convince your clients that the attorney, appraiser, and title company check town hall thoroughly. That is, unless the appraiser is an **"A to Z Appraiser."**

I've done foreclosure appraisals for banks, where the banks had the houses re-appraised after they took back the titles through foreclosure proceedings. During my appraisals, I turned up problems in the deeds that weren't identified when the banks originally loaned the mortgage money. So now the banks had to spend the time and money to correct mistakes created by the prior owners of these properties. This situation could happen to you and your clients if you don't follow my advice.

Here's some history trivia I found on several web sites about property titles and legal ownership of real estate:

**Did you know that Abraham Lincoln's family lost their homes several times because of "cloudy" title?**

On June 12, 1806, Thomas Lincoln married Nancy Hanks. (Little is known about Abe Lincoln's mother except that she came from a very poor Virginia family. She was completely illiterate and signed her name with an X.) After their marriage the Lincolns moved from a farm on Mill Creek in Hardin County, Kentucky, to nearby Elizabethtown. There Thomas Lincoln earned his living as a carpenter and handyman. In 1807 a daughter, Sarah, was born. In December 1808 the Lincolns moved to a 141-hectare (348-acre) farm on the south fork of Nolin Creek near what is now Hodgenville, Kentucky. On February 12, 1809, in a log cabin that Thomas Lincoln had built, a son, Abraham, was born. Later the Lincolns had a second son who died in infancy. When Abraham Lincoln was two, the family moved to another farm on nearby Knob Creek. Life was lonely and hard. There was little time for play. Most of the day was spent hunting, farming, fishing, and doing chores. Land titles in Kentucky were confusing and often subject to dispute. Thomas Lincoln **lost his title** to the Mill Creek farm, and his claims to **both** the Nolin Creek and Knob Creek tracts were challenged in court. In 1816, therefore, the Lincolns decided to move to Indiana, where the land was surveyed and sold by the federal government. In the winter of 1816 the Lincolns took their meager possessions, ferried across the Ohio River, and settled near Pigeon Creek, close to what is now Gentryville, Indiana.

Even **Daniel Boone**, the first pioneer of Kentucky wilderness, lost every inch of his once vast landholdings because he had _"the wrong kind of title papers."_ It was the anxiety and outright losses of the Lincolns and other hard-working Americans that gave rise to today's title insurance industry. The first land title insurance company was founded in Philadelphia in 1876. Just a few years later in 1889, the firm that was to become _First American Title Insurance Company_ was established to protect buyers against the hidden hazards of real estate ownership: forgeries; faulty surveys; hidden liens; conveyances by a minor or mentally incompetent person; the false representation of a married person as being single; and many other title defects. Even the most complete search of records may not reveal all the defects in a real estate title.

Is The Listing Accurate?

Let me give you another newsflash so I make this point very clear about checking all records at the town hall. Many people think the information in a real estate listing is always accurate. THAT'S NONSENSE!!!! If you read the bottom of all real estate listings and other data sources, you'll see a statement such as, *"Data Is Believed Accurate But Not Warranted."* Do you know what that means? Well, I'll tell you anyway. It's a caveat which means that if the information in the real estate listing or data source is wrong, then you cannot hold the listing Realtor or data company accountable for the error. In most areas, Realtors are not required to check the records at town hall to verify the information that the seller tells them to fill out a real estate listing. On a daily basis I see cases where a real estate listing states: the subject property has a 200 amp electrical system, when it only had 100 amps; or the house was connected to the city sewer system, when it actually had a septic system; or the size of the lot was one acre, when it was less than one acre; or the square footage and age of the house was incorrect on the real estate listing, etc.

> *Let me give you another newsflash to make it clear about checking all records at the town hall. Many people think that the information in a real estate listing is always accurate. THAT'S NONSENSE!!!!*

So, remember to tell your clients **not to rely on the information found in real estate listings!** If there is a *"know-it-all"* Realtor at the site they're probably going to tell your client that you're wrong. The Realtor will say that their real estate listing is 100% accurate. **If any Realtors dispute the advice you give to your clients, then just tell that Realtor or other third party to put their money where their mouth is!** Let me explain this since it's a great way to silence an immoral, greedy, or ignorant Realtor or other third party: If any Realtors dispute the advice you give to your clients, **then just tell them to write a signed statement that they want to guarantee to your client that if the Realtor or other third party are wrong, then THEY will pay the bill – not your client!** Just about every time I get a Realtor who earns a commission on the sale disputing what I say, I prove them wrong. Once you respond confidently and firmly (but not rudely) to know-it-all Realtors, it usually shuts them up for the rest of the inspection or appraisal. I can't even count the number of times that I've had a know-it-all Realtor tell my clients and I, *"My real estate listing is 100% correct, I checked it myself."* Before the inspection or appraisal is over, I always seem to find something in the listing that's inaccurate. When this happens, these Realtors never seem to admit that they were wrong. Someone needs to inform ignorant Realtors

that maybe they don't know as much about real estate as they think they do. We'll talk more about this later.

> *If any Realtors dispute the advice you give to your clients, then just tell that Realtor or other third party to put their money where their mouth is! Just tell them to write a signed statement that they want to guarantee to your client that if the Realtor or other third party are wrong, then THEY will pay the bill – not your client!*

Realtors *(some of them)* and other data source employees don't intentionally put inaccurate information into a listing sheet. They generally rely on the seller to provide the information, or else the Realtor may think that they know what they're doing. The seller or the Realtor may unintentionally make a mistake. So it's not that they're trying to hide the truth from potential buyers. It's just that someone can make a mistake with the data. That's why all records need to be checked at town hall. This will help prevent incorrect information from going unnoticed.

At town hall the records will show: the amount of taxes on the house, the square footage and age of the house, the acreage of the site, if there are any building violations, if there are any easements or encroachments, if there are problems with the title and deed of the property, and a lot more. All of this information is very valuable to the client. Most people don't even realize how much information is open for the public to view at their town hall records department. If you recommend a town hall trip to your client, and he ends up finding something out that's important, then you'll look like a hero. Your client will thank you for the recommendation.

A Catch 22 Position

In just about any house you go into, you can find some upgrading or repairs that have been done which require permits and approvals. You'll also find that there are missing permits and approvals for some of this work in almost *every* house you go into! It's very common because there are very few homeowners who know that permits and final approvals are needed for all repair work done in a house. Many contractors don't bother with the permits, unless the homeowner insists on seeing them upon completion of the job. When you or your client find missing permits, just tell the client it's a common problem. Don't make the client think this is the *only* house without all valid permits and approvals. Just tell them to find out what is required to obtain the final approvals from the town for the work done.

> You'll also find that there are missing permits and approvals for some of this work in almost every house you go into! It's very common because there are very few homeowners who know that permits and final approvals are needed for all work done.

Sometimes your clients will ask you, *"What will happen if I do go to town hall to check about valid permits and approvals for the finished basement or attic, the addition, deck, pool, extra apartment, etc. and they aren't on file in the building department."* Well, if you or your client tell the building inspector that you checked for the permits and approvals and you can't find them, then you might raise a red flag in his mind. This could lead to the building inspector going to the subject property. The building inspector could file a building code violation against the property for the work done. A violation could be issued because there are no permits on file. Usually the only way to get building violations removed is to have the work pass the local building code standards. What will happen is the building inspector will tell the homeowner that if the work doesn't meet the local building code standards, then they must hire a licensed contractor to make the necessary repairs. Repairs will be needed to bring the work up to meet the minimum standards before a valid permit and approval can be obtained and the violation will be removed.

You can run into serious problems in certain situations when permits and approvals need to be obtained <u>after</u> the work has already been done. One case is when the repair work was not permitted by the building or zoning codes. For example, the local codes may not allow the homeowner to finish a basement or attic to use as livable space, build a small addition or garage, etc. When this occurs, the only option is to remove all of the work done. The building inspector can't approve something that is against the law of the town! I've had clients that took my advice and checked town hall prior to closing. They found garages that were built too close to the neighbors' property line; pools that were not allowed on the site; additions and enclosed porches that had to be dismantled; finished basements and attics that were against the zoning and fire codes, etc. None of these problem conditions could be approved without getting zoning variances and changes made to the building and fire codes. In order to sell these houses, the sellers had to dismantle all the repair work done to the house and site. That can turn into a nightmare and take a lot of time, money and aggravation to accomplish.

A more common problem when permits need to be obtained after the work has already been done occurs **when the work is not accessible to view.** For example, if there has been some electrical wiring, plumbing or foundation repairs. Usually this type of work will be sealed up after the repairs are completed. The building inspector can't sign-off on something that he can't see! As a result, the only way to get the permits and final approvals will be to open up the walls, floors, ceilings, etc so the inspector can view the repairs. I've had this situation come up on many occasions when I notified my clients about missing permits. This also can turn into a nightmare.

So it can be a *Catch 22* for the client. If they don't raise a red flag at the building department, then the missing permits might not create a problem for the closing when the client **purchases** the property - if the appraiser or title company don't notice it. However, if your client doesn't clear up this matter prior to buying the house, then it might come up when he goes to **refinance or sell** the house down the road. Then your client will be stuck wasting his own time and money fixing a problem that someone else had created! I wouldn't take the chance if I were buying the house. From your standpoint as the home inspector, you **must** mention the building code violations in your written report if you know about them. It's true that only an inspector from the local town hall can do a building code inspection. However, if you happen to know the local building codes, then you must mention any code violations that you're aware of. So whether the client clears up the problem isn't your concern. However, you must mention it in your report to CYA.

People Who Have No Right To Remain Silent

Sometimes you'll find that the seller, the Realtor, or another third party won't want to answer any preinspection questions. Or a dishonest Realtor will tell the seller not to be home for the inspection appointment so they don't get involved in the inspection process. The Realtors may say something like, *"I've been selling real estate for 10 years now and I've never seen it done this way before by asking the owner all these questions."* **They are talking out of ignorance!** The reason they've never seen it done this way is they've never seen a good, thorough and knowledgeable home inspector before!!!

> *The Realtors may say, "I've been selling real estate for 10 years now and I've never seen it done this way before by asking the owner all these questions." They are talking out of ignorance!*

Also, some people rationalize their actions to a point where it just blows my mind. They are intentionally dishonest and lie to you by **not** saying anything and by **not** being home to answer your questions. I have done many inspections and appraisals where I encountered Realtors, sellers, and other third parties who **intentionally** tried to hide something from my client and any other potential buyers. Once I was checking the lower level of a house that was located on the side of a hill. In one corner there were some plywood boards leaning up against the foundation wall. I moved the boards to see what was behind them and I found **serious structural cracks in the foundation wall.** I was really angry about the seller's attempt to hide this. The house was located on a hill and with a serious structural crack like that, it could have cost someone their life!! What <u>didn't</u> surprise me is that I later learned the listing Realtor <u>knew</u> about the structural crack but, *as usual,* <u>didn't</u> tell any potential buyers about it. If you're in this business long enough, *(and sometimes that only needs to be about a year),* you'll get used to seeing how some Realtors will do *anything* to earn a sales commission.

Sellers and Realtors often don't tell home buyers about known problems with a house. They just keep quiet and hope the buyer's home inspector or appraiser don't detect the problems. They think it's a game of "hide and seek". **Hide** the known problems and it's the home inspector and/or appraiser's job to **seek** out and find them. *Wrong – it doesn't work like that!* That's not a nice game of hide and seek like your kids play. That's called **FRAUD** and you can go to jail for it!! I'll give you a few more examples that I've experienced. One was a client I had that was buying a house with an old, forced hot air heating system. A thin layer of asbestos insulation was on the air ducts and in the lining of the furnace. **This creates a serious health hazard because the asbestos fibers are blown throughout the entire house.** The dishonest Realtor **never mentioned a word** to my clients about this asbestos problem. As soon as I saw the asbestos

during the inspection, I told the client about this health hazard. Suddenly the Realtor jumps into the conversation and says, *"The owner already has found a contractor to remove the asbestos from the air ducts so the client doesn't need to worry about it."* When I asked the Realtor if the owner was going to have the asbestos in the livable rooms removed, she said, *"there was no need to do that."* **It's so typical that the Realtor would say there's no need to do that. After all, the dishonest Realtor isn't going to be living in that house and breathing those asbestos fibers!**

I did an inspection once and found <u>severe</u> rot and powder post beetle damage to the main girder beam and floor joists of a house. My awl went right through the main girder and floor joists while I was probing the beams in the crawl space. This beam, along with many of the floor joists, had to be replaced. Replacing a main girder beam is not easy since the house has to be lifted up with jacks to replace the beam. Moreover, on the exterior of the house I found most of the siding had buckled and had to be replaced. This siding damage was from water problems due to the lack of a roof overhang (soffit, fascia and eaves) on the house which was a design by some architect who thought it would be "unique" and "set the house apart". *(Yeah, this "unique" design certainly "set the house apart". It was the only house around with all the siding destroyed from water drainage off the roof!).* My client had to spend a lot of time and money on the home inspection and in getting repair estimates. **Afterwards, my client found out that the seller and the Realtor had <u>known</u> about these problems <u>*BEFORE*</u> the home inspection.** This immoral stunt is done all the time by dishonest Realtors and sellers. Another buyer had backed out of a prior offer on this house because these problems were detected by their home inspector. Had the dishonest Realtor and seller told my client the TRUTH, and not tried to hide the truth from him/her, then my client, along with all other potential buyers, could have gotten repair estimates from contractors *first*, and then decided if they wanted to continue with the deal. At that point, my client could have hired me to inspect the house and find any additional problem conditions that were not disclosed up-front to him/her and other potential buyers by the Realtor and seller. *(I think once I saw in a dictionary this definition listed for the <u>TRUTH</u> - Something dishonest Realtors have a very, very difficult time dealing with, so they avoid it like the plague!)*

I have done many inspections where I would find personal items intentionally placed by a third party to cover termite and water damage. Luckily I detected these problems so my clients didn't get hit with any surprises after they moved into the houses. However, since the third party never told me or my client about these problems and left it up to us to find them on our own with their little game of "hide and seek", then what is that called? **Dishonest, Immoral, and Fraud!!** Plain and simple.

Let's say the inspector and the client didn't happen to notice a problem condition that a third party to the deal knew existed but never told them about. How can that third party morally justify their actions by not mentioning the problem condition to the appraiser and/or the client? You can call it a *business negotiating decision by the third party;* you can call it a *mistake that is the fault of the buyer's appraiser and/or home inspector;* you can blame the *buyer for not hiring a more thorough appraiser and/or home inspector;* or you can call it *good or bad luck.* But no matter what you call it, and I don't care how you rationalize it, it **has to** be called one thing - *DISHONEST!* The third party person simply is not telling someone something they know that person should and would want to know about. Let alone the fact that they are **legally required to disclose** all known defects - unless they want to commit **fraud!** Whatever happened to the golden rule in today's world? *"Do onto others as you would want others to do onto you."* People should ask themselves: *If I were buying this house, would I want the seller to tell me about this problem?*

I'm using this example to make you realize there are dishonest and ignorant people out there that rationalize their unethical actions, which you probable already know. However, often people get too emotionally involved in the decision to buy or sell their home and this clouds their judgment. When that happens, they are more susceptible to being scammed or cheated by "smooth talking" salespeople and third parties in the deal. Often the same person who refuses to answer your questions, or doesn't tell you about a problem they know you should be informed about, is the same guy that brags how he goes to church every Sunday because he's such a good, ethical person in society.   BALONEY!! They can't hide behind that excuse.

There is something that you might consider when you're dealing with a dishonest person like that. You might want to inform them that if something comes up after your client buys the house that they knew about, then your client can sue the seller, the Realtor, and other third parties. **That's because you *cannot* intentionally hide a problem from anyone, whether you're the buyer or the seller.** Just about all houses are sold in *"As Is"* condition. This doesn't mean that the seller has a *license to steal,* nor does it mean that the seller can commit *fraud.* A lot of people believe that an "As Is" sale means that the Realtors and sellers don't have to tell anyone about known problem conditions at the property. That's totally false! The old theory of "buyer beware" is no longer valid. When a house is sold in "As Is" condition, it means that the seller is *required* **to disclose all known defects** to the buyer and the buyer agrees to accept the house with those known problems. The seller doesn't have to be a home inspector, however, they do have to inform you about the problems they know about and they cannot hide them from you.

Realtors and some other third parties have a *fiduciary responsibility* to lay all the cards out on the table for the client, whether it is the buyer or the seller. **They are required to disclose to the buyer and the seller any problem conditions that they know about.** Since they're professionals in the real estate business, they are held to a higher standard than the public. As a result, they can be found liable for something they knew about, **or that they should have known about,** if they did not inform the buyer or seller about the problem condition.

Talk To The Neighbors

You can find out an awful lot about a house and the area it's located in by talking to the neighbors who live next to the subject property. I try to do this whenever I have the opportunity and I always encourage my clients to talk to the neighbors themselves. The people who live near the subject property usually have been there for at least a few years. They can tell you the good and bad points of the area. The best part about their responses to your questions is that they have no incentive to lie to you or your client! They're not involved financially in the sale of the subject property, and as a result, you'll get an unbiased second opinion for free!

> *You can find out an awful lot about a house and the area it's located in just by talking to the neighbors who live next to the subject property.*

Obviously, if the neighbor is a relative or close friend of the seller, then their responses may be biased to help *"move the deal along."* But that's why you and your client should talk to several neighbors in the area and not just one of them. Don't feel like you're being rude or imposing on the neighbors either. You'll be amazed at how people like to talk to someone who's truly interested in listening to what they have to say. It gives people a feeling of importance and makes them feel like they're doing someone else a big favor. Especially, if the person they're helping will be a future next door neighbor.

Some questions that you and your client's can ask the neighbors are:

1   Do you ever have any water problems in your house? *(This is a **great** question to ask. If the subject property gets water from a high groundwater table, then most of the houses in the area may have the same problem unless they're located on higher ground.)*

2   Does the local municipality raise property and/or school taxes often?

3   Is this a quiet area or are there any noise problems?

4   How are the schools and public transportation?

5   *(If the house is located on a Private street),* What are the rights and responsibilities of the homeowners to use and maintain the street?   What are the fees for the street maintenance, paving, snow plowing, etc.?

6   Is there anything about the area that you would find helpful to know if you were buying this house?

So you don't believe me that talking to the neighbors is helpful? Well, I'll tell you another war story and then maybe you'll change your mind. I tell all my clients to speak to the neighbors before they buy a house. This will enable them to find out anything interesting about water problems, noise problems, etc. One client of mine was buying a house with a septic system on the site. He took my advice and asked a few of the neighbors about water problems and septic problems in the area. Well, he was awfully surprised to find out that the area had a high groundwater table. **This not only created water problems in their basements during heavy rains, but it also forced them all to have their septic systems replaced!!** New septic tanks were needed due to the excessive water in the ground over the years. This client ended up having *a lot* more to calculate into his purchase price after finding out this information. He certainly was grateful to me for giving him that advice. So learn a lesson from this and recommend that **all** of your clients talk to the neighbors. They might end up finding out something very helpful and you'll end up looking like a hero for it.

Be Totally Objective - Part 1

Don't tell the client to buy or not to buy the house for any reason!!!! This is one point that really bothers Realtors and I have to side with them on this one. Your job is to tell the client the current condition of the house *only!!* I'll repeat that again so you get it straight. Don't tell the client to buy or not to buy the house for any reason! You're not an appraiser estimating the **market value** of the house. You're a home inspector only estimating the **condition** of the house. There's a big difference between the two. The condition of the house does not make it a good deal or a bad deal. **Price is the *ONLY* factor on whether it's a good deal or not!** Here's why:

◊ I've seen people buy houses in great condition but they were paying too high a purchase price for the house. Therefore it's a bad deal because they were paying much more than the market value price of the house.

◊ At the same time, I've seen people buy houses that are in terrible condition that need a lot of work. However, they were getting a great deal because they were buying the house well below market value. If you added up all the repairs and upgrading costs, and then added it to the purchase price, they could sell the house for much more than they paid for it after renovations.

> *The condition of the house does not make it a good deal or a bad deal. Price is the ONLY factor on whether it's a good deal or not!*

Only a well trained and qualified Real Estate Appraiser can estimate the market value - *not a home inspector*. You're hired to only evaluate the condition - and that's what your training and expertise are focused on. As a result, **it's none of your business** if your client decides to buy a house that you don't like or that you wouldn't buy for any reason. It's also none of your business if the client decides not to do any of your recommendations for repairs or upgrading. Even a real estate appraiser has <u>no</u> right telling the client whether or not to buy the house. After an appraiser notifies the client of the market value of a property, it's totally up to the client how much, if anything, they want to pay for that property. After the appraiser explains the valuation analysis in their appraisal report, it's none of the appraiser's business even if the client wants to pay too much for the property. Perhaps there's an amenity value for them and that's why the client doesn't mind paying a high price?

You may not like the house for several different reasons: perhaps it's too old for your tastes; or it's a Cape Cod style and you only like Colonial style homes; or you feel that there's too much renovation work needed on and in the house; or it's not in a good area of town that you would want to live in, etc. The point I'm making is that all of these are your own *subjective* judgments and opinions! You have to be totally *objective* when you're inspecting a house. Even though you might not want to buy that house or condo, maybe your client has different tastes and likes than you do. Also, maybe the client can't afford to buy a house in great condition or in a good section of town.

I've inspected houses that when I would write down the style of the house, such as Ranch, Cape Cod, Colonial, Tudor, etc. that I would be tempted to write down *"hideous"* because the house was so dreadful looking. However, I'm not paid to tell the client whether I would live in the house. So I keep my subjective comments and opinions to myself.

Be Totally Objective - Part 2

Don't ever tell any lender to give a loan or not to give a loan on a property!!!! This situation may come up if you do appraisal and/or inspection work for a bank. A mortgage lender may ask you if they should make a loan, or you may throw in your two cents on your own. I'll repeat that again so you don't forget it. Don't ever tell any lender to give a loan or not to give a loan on a property!

Every once in a while I hear an appraiser or inspector saying that they recommended that a mortgage lender approve or not approve someone's mortgage loan. That blows my mind when they do that! Your job as a home inspector is to **only** determine the condition of the subject property. You don't include your own **subjective** opinions or biases.

As a home inspector, you know **nothing** about the potential borrower's income, past credit history, personal debts, possible court judgments and lawsuits against them, total monthly living expenses, job stability, etc. Only the borrower and the lender know that type of information. So I don't care how nice the house you're inspecting is; or how bad the condition of the house is; or what type of area it's located in; or whatever else you find out about it during your inspection. And I don't care if it's the nicest house you've ever seen or the worst house you've ever seen. If you tell a lender to make the loan just because the house is selling for a great price, (in your opinion), and it's in excellent condition, **then you better be willing to put your money where your mouth is!** Because what happens if that guy borrows the money and then the house is destroyed due to a lack of maintenance and then he stops making his loan payments on the mortgage. *(I've seen this happen many, many times with foreclosure appraisals and inspections I've done for banks).* The bank is going to get stuck holding the bag for the loan. The bank will end up losing money on the foreclosure sale, even though you told them what a great loan they'd be making!

It's the same scenario if you stick your nose somewhere it shouldn't be by telling the lender <u>not</u> to make the loan. I don't care if it's the worst house you've ever seen or if it's in the worst section of town and you would *never* buy it. How do you know that the guy buying that house isn't some multimillionaire? What if he's going to renovate that house and donate it to a poor family or to a local charity? If the lender listened to you, then he wouldn't make the loan. *(Oh yes, I forgot you have a crystal ball to read the future. You can see that this loan will go sour for the lender!)*

> *You can put all of the objective comments you want in the inspection report. But just keep your subjective opinions and your nose out of the lender's and the borrower's business.*

Don't take any of this personally. It's not meant to insult you. It's just meant to open your eyes to some of the realities of the real estate business. The point I'm trying to make is that you must evaluate the current condition of the subject property based upon what you see and your knowledge and expertise. You can put all of the **objective** comments you want in the inspection report. But just keep your **subjective** opinions and your nose out of the lender's and the borrower's business. You're not hired to be a nosy "busy body." There are already <u>far too many</u> busy body, know-it-all Realtors and other third parties in the real estate business. You're hired to evaluate the condition ONLY! There are many times that I see people talk out of ignorance by thinking that they're a know-it-all. And I'm not being a hypocrite myself because I certainly don't think that I have all the answers either.

Negotiating Realities To Assist Your Client

Another point that I agree with Realtors on is the fact that it's **none of your business if the client does or does not want to negotiate with the seller after your inspection!** You have <u>no</u> right sticking your nose into anything other than the inspection itself. If the client asks you to help him out further with some negotiations, then you can provide this service if you would like. It's up to you. But let the client ask for your help, don't volunteer it.

Often your client will ask you if the repairs you're recommending should be negotiated for, or paid by the seller. Tell them that it all depends on the flexibility of the seller. Some people are negotiable and some aren't. However, if he asks the seller, there are only two answers he can get, and one of those answers is great!

It's similar to finding termite damage in a house. In many states the seller of the house is **required** by law to pay for the removal of any termites found on the property. However, the seller doesn't have to sell you the house if he doesn't want to. He can just say, *"Fine I'll pay for the termite treatment but I'm going to raise the sales price by the same amount"*. The point is, just tell the client that whether or not something is negotiable will always depend on the flexibility of the seller.

However, there is a **very important** concept that you want to tell your client about negotiating repairs or other factors that come up during your inspection. Most of the time, if the seller is flexible, the seller will agree to have the repairs done at his own expense. You want to inform your client that if the seller has the repairs fixed at his expense, then he's probably going to get several estimates. Which contractor do you think the seller is going to hire: The guy who does high quality work at a high price or **the guy who does low quality work at a low price?** I'd say the seller is more likely to hire the guy who's the cheapest to save himself a few bucks. After all, he's selling the house and he's not going to have to live with any poor quality repairs in the home. I think your client might agree with that conclusion as well. So you should inform your client about this possibility.

> *The seller is more likely to hire the guy who's the cheapest to save himself a few bucks. After all, he's selling the house and he's not going to have to live with any poor quality repairs in the home.*

Also, if the seller hires the contractor and pays him with his own check, then **that contractor is responsible to the seller and not to your client.** Therefore, if the contractor does poor quality work and your client buys the house and finds problems with the repair work done, then your client has no legal recourse. That contractor was *hired and paid* by the <u>*seller*</u> of the house and not by your client. Therefore, that contractor is generally only liable to the seller for his work.

What are your client's chances of getting the seller to come back from his new home to your area to file a complaint and demand compensation against that contractor for poor quality work? ZERO!!!! Now, I'm not an attorney so you have to check this and all other legal aspects I'm telling you about with your own legal counsel. But the point I'm making is pretty clear. Just inform the client of these ideas and let the client decide what action they want to take. You'll find that this type of information is very helpful to your clients and you'll look like a hero when you open their eyes to it.

When hiring repair contractors you need to notify your client about some basic concepts. In most areas, contractors must be licensed and insured to do any repair work. The local town hall could verify this information. Insurance coverage should be for the general contractor plus any subcontractors they hire to assist them. For large construction jobs, the client should see if the contractor is bonded. *Bonding* means that the contractor can insure the quality of their work and that the job will be completed on time. A bonded contractor will have to place a bond before they start the job for it to be valid. For small construction jobs, bonding may be too much to ask from a contractor.

The client should check with the local Better Business Bureau and other organizations to determine if the contractor is reputable. The contractor should provide references of former clients they have done work for. This can help the client to find out about the contractors track record. However, if the contractor does provide your client with names, he's going to make sure he doesn't give them phone numbers of unhappy customers! This is where the client's own judgment will come into play in deciding if a contractor is reputable.

All aspects of repair agreements with contractors should be clearly stated in the written price estimate. **The client should have a time limit and a price cap on the repair work. This will prevent the contractor from "dragging their feet" to complete the job. A price cap will prevent cost overruns and excess fees added after the work has begun.** A statement should be put in the estimate that the contractor will provide the homeowner with all permits and final approvals from town hall. Any warranties for the repair work should be in writing. If the seller has hired contractors to make repairs, the client needs to speak with them about warranties. The client should find out how long the warranties are in effect and if they are transferable to the new owners.

There's another aspect that you need to inform your client about regarding negotiating with the seller. That is there will be times when some Realtors and other third parties will tell your client, *"Oh, there's no way the seller is going to reduce his price. He's already giving the house away and he has two backup offers waiting if you don't buy the house now."* HORSE MANURE!!!! I've heard that line used 100,000 times, not only while doing home inspections and appraisals, but also when buying my own rental properties. I've seen my own offers accepted by sellers that some know-it-all Realtor told me would never be accepted. I've also seen many clients get offers accepted when a Realtor or other third party told them the seller would never accept it.

So don't let yourself or your client be intimidated by anyone. It's your client's money and future, **he/she** has to be the one to decide how much he/she wants to pay for a house. Don't you or any third party make the decision for them. Any Realtors involved in the transaction have a *fiduciary responsibility* to the buyer or the seller. This means that they are **required to present any and all purchase offers from all potential buyers to the seller that they know about.** No matter how low or ridiculous the offer might seem, it still has to be presented to the seller. It doesn't matter if someone offers the seller less than 1/2 the asking price. They have to present the offer to give the seller the opportunity to accept it or reject it.

Don't Let Your Client Be Pressured

Tell the client not to be pressured or rushed into *any* decisions by the imaginary backup offers on the subject property. Some Realtors, sellers or other third parties want your client to believe that imaginary backup offers really exist. Also, tell your client not to become too emotionally involved in any deal. They should look at the deal as though it were a typical business decision. They should put their personal emotions aside because they're spending a fortune on this financial investment. You have to make the client realize that they're not buying a ***CAR***, they're buying a ***HOUSE!!*** There's a big difference between the two. One is a normal expense everyone has to incur occasionally. The other is the biggest financial decision most people will ever make.

> *They should put their personal emotions aside because they're spending a fortune on this financial investment. You have to make the client realize that they're not buying a CAR, they're buying a HOUSE!!*

Harry Helmsley, who was clearly a brilliant real estate investor, was quoted as saying, *"The minute you fall in love with a building you're in trouble."* Meaning, that **if you get too emotionally attached to a property, you forget to look at it like a business decision. When this happens, you often end up paying too much for the property.** You have to be objective all the time and be able to make the hard decisions and walk away from a deal at any time.

Since I do home inspections, appraisals, and have owned rental properties myself, I see this happen to potential home buyers all the time. Many people get too emotional about buying a house and they only look at the cosmetic appeal of the house or the location it's in. You have to take a step back and look at the purchase as though it was strictly a business decision. **Too often people get convinced that if they don't make a high-priced offer on the house right away, then another buyer will come along and steal it right from under them.** Sure, there's a potential that if the house really is a good deal then someone else will come along and buy it sooner than you will. But this happens a lot less often than most people believe, or are led to believe by some Realtors and other third parties involved in the transaction.

Often a Realtor will rush a potential home buyer into making an offer and/or signing contracts on a home sooner than they should. They tend to put the "fear of God" into the home buyer. They tell the buyer, *"You have to make a high offer and sign the contracts right away. If you don't, then someone else will buy it because there's a backup purchase offer on this house."* There are a million ways that a real estate deal can be killed. Many of those so-called "backup offers" are either imaginary or will fall through. Some reasons real estate deals fall through are: the seller and buyer don't agree on a final price and terms; the buyer or seller gets *"cold feet"*; problems come up during the home inspection and/or appraisal; the mortgage loan is denied; etc. I have personally seen an awful lot of real estate deals fall through due to any number of reasons.

I had an excellent real estate attorney, named Walter Kehm, that handled all of my legal work when I first started buying rental properties. He used to say that *"Real estate deals are like a trolley car, if you let one go there will be another one coming by in 20 minutes."* I have found this statement to be very true from my own experiences in the real estate business. Not only in my own investments, but in the home inspection and appraisal experience I have had with my clients as well.

Many times I've had clients who decided not to purchase a home because of the problems that were found during the home inspection and/or appraisal. The seller's of these houses would not renegotiate with the buyer, and as a result, the deal never went through. In every one of these cases, the client continued to look at other houses which were for sale. Within a few months, these clients eventually found a nicer home at a better price than the deal they walked away from. They had benefited by waiting to find the best deal that they could, rather than rushing to purchase the first *decent* house they could find. So learn a lesson from this and don't let yourself or any of your clients be rushed into buying a house. A home is the biggest investment most people will make, so it's prudent that they take their time and think it through completely.

Also, some sellers and third parties will just wait until they find a buyer that hires an appraiser and/or home inspector that isn't as good, honest and thorough as you are. When this happens then that buyer will be going into the deal with their eyes **closed**. You want your client to go into the deal with their eyes **open**. Just because someone else might come along and pay too much for the house, doesn't mean that your client should beat them to it and over pay for the property.

You have to assist your client in their investment decision. That's what you're being paid for. You want your client to know all of the good and bad points about the subject property. **Sometimes the truth hurts and people don't want to hear bad things about a house that they've fallen in love with. But that's too bad because what you're telling them is** ***REALITY!!*** So let them know that your job is to open their eyes to aspects about buying a house that many other buyers don't have a clue exist. If someone else goes into the deal with their eyes closed and pays too much for the property, then all I can say is that they should have hired an ***"A to Z Home Inspector and/or Appraiser,"*** like your client did!

Now at the same time, if your client is still willing to pay the same price for the house even after you open their eyes, then fine. It's *none of your business* what the client does after you inform them about potential costs and problems with the subject property. You've done your professional and ethical responsibility by informing them ahead of time; and that's all you're required to do. **It's their money and their future,** so keep your nose out of it from that point on.

Lay All The Cards On The Table

An important concept that I want you to clearly understand, is that **your job is to lay all the cards out on the table for your clients. Don't leave any skeletons hidden in the closet.** Tell them about all the different aspects and realities of their investment, both good and bad, of what we've discussed plus any that you learn from your own experiences. If all the cards are laid out, then the client can make an intelligent and educated decision about their real estate purchase. Don't make any decisions for the client. It's **their** money and **their** future, so let **them** decide. Your job is to just give the client the facts and your objective opinions, both good and bad. *(I've said that so many times by now I'm turning blue in the face. I just want to make sure you don't forget it.)*

If you're not sure about telling your client something, then just ask yourself: *"Is this something that can affect the market value of the subject property?"* and *"If I were the person buying this house or condo, would I want someone to inform me about this or not?"* and *"Would I feel this is something that I would want to know about?"*

> *If all the cards are laid out, then the client can make an intelligent and educated decision about their real estate purchase. Don't make any decisions for the client. It's their money and their future, so let them decide.*

If you, or any third parties, try to make the decisions for the client, then you're not helping them out. It's similar to a person going to a doctor for a routine physical. If the doctor finds a problem condition from the test results, he should tell the patient what he found and the possible treatments. The doctor should then let the patient choose what action or treatment to take. Now the doctor is the professional and an expert in the field of medicine. Therefore, he should provide the patient with some objective advice and alternatives. With the doctor's advice and alternatives, the patient can then make an intelligent and educated decision on their own.

However, what would happen if the doctor decided, on his own, to not tell the patient about the problem condition? Let's say the doctor just rationalized in his own mind that the patient didn't need to know about the problem condition. Perhaps the doctor felt that the condition might go away on its own over time. Maybe the doctor would think that if he told the patient, he would only worry the patient unnecessarily. Does that doctor have a right to make a decision like that with someone else's life? Or should that doctor lay all of the cards out on the table for the patient to decide? You tell me. I think the doctor should let the patient decide. When a doctor doesn't inform a patient properly about their health condition, it brings to mind the old saying, *"Doctors bury their mistakes."* Unfortunately, I've seen first hand experiences where some doctors buried their mistakes. A doctor shouldn't filter out anything that the client should know. And neither should a home inspector, a home seller, a Realtor, an attorney, a bank appraiser, nor anyone else. Unfortunately, often people do filter out information that someone has a **right** to know about.

Tony Fasanella was one of my instructors for the State appraisal course called *"The Standards of Professional Practice."* Tony constantly stated that the key to honest, ethical and professional conduct was **disclosure, disclosure, disclosure** of all aspects. This meant that you don't hide anything from the client, nor do anything that will give someone a false impression or lead them to a wrong conclusion. That includes what you say verbally and what you put in the written report.

I feel bad about creating headaches for the seller or Realtor when I detect problem conditions during an inspection or appraisal. I like to help people, not make their life more difficult *(unless they're dishonest)*. But it's not my fault when I find problems with a house during an inspection or appraisal. The way I look at it is that I didn't **create** the problems - I only **identified** the problems which my client has a right to know about. So don't feel guilty about creating headaches for anyone if you're telling the **truth**. Your job is not to kill real estate deals, it's to identify all the negative and positive aspects of a house. Even though you don't create the negative aspects, the sellers and Realtors still get angry at you. They look at you like you're an idiot merely because they're ignorant to the facts.

Safety Concerns

Items like tripping hazards in the steps, walks or patios; loose or missing handrails; improper deck construction and guardrails; leaning retaining walls; loose or missing electrical grounding cables, etc., may seem like minor items to repair. However, these are things that can cause someone to get seriously hurt if they're not repaired immediately and properly.

◊ An uneven section in a walkway might not seem like much, but what happens if the person that trips, falls and hits their head.

◊ A leaning retaining wall will crush a child if it collapses on top of them.

◊ A missing or loose handrail could cause someone to fall down the steps.

> *If you make a mistake and forget to inform the client that the boiler is old, you could end up costing the guy a new heating system. However, if you miss a safety hazard, you could end up costing someone their LIFE!*

If you think I'm overreacting then this next story should wake you up. I heard this story from a home inspection conference. A home inspector was sued because he neglected to check the deck on a house and it had very bad termite infestation. The woman who bought the house went out on the deck one day and it collapsed and left her paralyzed from the neck down. This is certainly a **horrible tragedy** for everyone involved in that incident. But the point I want to make very clear is **do not take chances with safety items!!** If you make a mistake and forget to inform the client that something like the boiler is old or the roof is past its life expectancy, then you could end up costing the client some **money** for a new heating system or roof. However, if you miss a safety hazard, you could end up costing someone their *LIFE!* Don't wait for accidents to happen. Just remember the saying - *"An ounce of prevention is worth a pound of cure!"*

> *Don't let any Realtors influence your decisions because you want them to refer some more of their clients to you. If you just "move the deal along" to satisfy a Realtor, you're going to get sued eventually. There's no doubt about it.*

Now I don't want you to think that you have to walk around the house with a microscope to detect every possible tripping hazard. Just do good, thorough inspections and **be honest.** Don't let any Realtors in the transaction influence your decisions because you want them to refer some more of their clients to you. If you just *move the deal along* to satisfy a Realtor who may have recommended you for the inspection, then you're going to get sued eventually. There's no doubt about it. And if that's how you're doing your home inspections, then you *DESERVE* to get sued!!

HIB From A to Z

Believe me, there are enough inspectors out there that either don't know what they're doing or are just plain dishonest and greedy. They're out to make as much money as possible without caring who gets hurt by it. Tony Fasanella and Dr. David Scribner were excellent instructors for the appraisal courses I had to take for the State Certification requirements. I remember Tony talking about dishonest appraisers. He said that people like that *"have no business being in this business."* I agree with him completely, and I hope you do too.

Don't Over Exaggerate Problems Or Repairs

Now at the same time, don't be like some inspectors and over exaggerate everything as being bad just to Cover Your Assets. This is another aspect that bothers Realtors and I agree with them on this point as well. If you're a doomsday inspector then you're not doing the client any good either, because you're over exaggerating things and you're evaluations will be way off base by being too conservative. Don't unnecessarily make the client think that the house is a dump and about to collapse on top of you when it really isn't so bad.

All houses will have some problems because no house is perfect. So you want to be reasonable in your conclusions and evaluations to the client

All houses will have some problems because <u>no</u> house is perfect. So you want to be reasonable in your conclusions and evaluations to the client. If the house needs a new roof, don't make the client think that *no one* would ever consider buying this house because they will have to sleep with an umbrella over their bed the whole time they live there! Just tell him to get an estimate for a new roof. Plain and simple. You're going to see many houses that have older roofs that will need replacing. Don't make the client think that this is the **only** house around that needs a new roof. A roof can be an expensive item to repair. However, if he puts a new roof on the house, he'll increase the property's market value. He also won't have to worry about any roof leaks for 20 years. Replacing roofs, heating systems, appliances, etc. is all part of normal house maintenance. Some items are more expensive than others, and some items last longer than others. Whether your client buys this house, or the house next door, he's going to have to do the same basic maintenance to either one over time. The only difference may be how soon he has to do the repairs and maintenance. Just tell him to get estimates on the items that need it, so he knows what his repair costs will be *before the closing.* Just be honest and reasonable in your evaluations, plain and simple.

There's risk in everything in life, even crossing the street. What you and your client need to do is eliminate as much risk as possible in their purchase of the subject property. You can never eliminate <u>all</u> of the risk, but you just want to narrow it

down as much as possible. Having a good, thorough home inspection and appraisal done; checking the records at town hall; getting the septic system pumped out and internally inspected; getting estimates for items that you determine need to be repaired; having certain things further evaluated; etc. all help to reduce the risk for you and your client. The more that is checked out then the more the risk is reduced. It's that basic. It's like buying an insurance policy for you and your client. So if you don't get lazy and cut corners, then at least if something goes wrong, then you won't look back and kick yourself for missing something you should have checked out further.

You also have to make sure that you're knowledgeable enough so that you can give the client enough information to help him in his real estate investment. You can't just tell the guy to get a whole host of contractors to come in and evaluate the different aspects of the house further because you're not sure about *anything.* I've seen this done by some home inspectors and believe me, you're going to have an unhappy client if you do this to someone. I once was doing a foreclosure appraisal for a bank and they sent me a copy of the home inspection report for this house. The bank had paid a very high price for the inspection. This bank didn't know that I did home inspections. They ended up hiring a home inspector that was recommended by a dishonest Realtor who wanted *to move the deal along* to get a commission. *(How unusual for a Realtor to do that!?).* There were other factors that came up during my appraisal process which indicated further that this Realtor was dishonest. I told the banker that I couldn't believe it when I read this inspection report and found out the price the bank paid for it. This inspector wrote a four or five page report that told the bank <u>absolutely nothing about the house!</u> This inspection report basically told the lender that since the inspector wasn't sure about *anything*, the bank needed to hire many different contractors to evaluate: the heating system, the well water system, the septic system, the electrical system, the structural beams, the swimming pool, the roof, etc. Do you believe that? I'm amazed that the bank even paid this incompetent crook that calls himself a home inspector! They should have told him to "whistle Dixie" for his inspection fee and then replace the greedy Realtor for recommending this incompetent knucklehead that called himself a "home inspector".

There's nothing wrong with recommending to your client that they get estimates for repairs that are needed. Or if there are items that you think a licensed contractor should evaluate further. However, don't charge somebody a fee if you can't evaluate *anything* about the subject property!

Is It Possible To Build A... ?

There is something else that you need to be aware of. There will be times when your client will ask you if it's possible to make some changes or additions to the house or site. Virtually anything can be done from a construction standpoint. However, what your client needs to find out is:

1   What the costs will be for the work.

2   If the zoning and building department regulations will allow the work to be done.

For example, I often have clients ask me, *"Can we put an addition on the house?"*, or *"I'd like to build a dormer and finish the attic space to make another bedroom. Is that possible?"*, or *"Since there's a steep slope in the backyard, will we be able to build a large deck."*

When you get asked questions like that, just tell the client to check with the local zoning and building departments. They need to find out if these departments will allow the work to be done. If the zoning and building department employees say *"yes,"* then tell the client to get estimates from licensed contractors for the work they want done. There's nothing complex about it.

Don't over exaggerate your answer by responding with, *"Well, if you want to put an addition on the house, then you might as well forget about buying this place. That will just be a lot of work and aggravation for nothing. Just go find yourself a larger house to buy."*

At the same time don't under estimate your answer by telling them (like some Realtors would), *"Of course you can put a dormer in the attic area Mr. Client. The zoning and building departments are really flexible around here. They always bend the rules to help out homeowners. My friend Joe is a carpenter and he can do all of the work needed for next to nothing."*

Report Writing

We've pretty much covered just about every aspect of the home inspection business, and the inspection process itself. Now we'll talk about writing up the inspection report after leaving the job site. Don't hand the client a checklist style inspection report at the site. You have to think about what you're going to write in your report, before you mail it out to your client. In my opinion, any home inspector that gives a brief checklist style report to their clients, gives a black eye to the whole profession. Home inspectors who give their clients a brief, meaningless checklist report should be embarrassed!

> *In my opinion, any home inspector that gives a brief checklist style report to their clients at the job site, gives a black eye to the whole profession.*
> *Any home inspectors who give a brief, meaningless checklist report to their clients should be embarrassed!*

An *"A to Z Home Inspector"* provides a written inspection report that's informative and useful to their clients. Your written report has to have narrative comments to assist the client and explain everything in an easy to understand fashion. That's why the checklist style reports are such a joke. Checklist style reports don't tell the client anything about the house! A narrative report will educate the client about the subject property in a manner that is easy for an average person to understand. Also, remember not to use construction jargon terms or have comments that only a professional in the industry will be able to understand. When writing your reports you have to think about what you want to say and think about the person who will be reading it.

I'll use an analogy from high school that you probably can relate to. Do you remember when you were in school and you were given a homework assignment to do a written report? Well, you didn't give the teacher your report at the end of the class did you? You had to go home and think about what you were going to write so that it would be a quality homework assignment. *(Or at least you should have)*. If you shouldn't cut corners for a written report for school, then you shouldn't cut corners for a written report for an inspection client.

A very important point to remember is this: ***What you put in the written report is what you will be held accountable for!!!!*** This simply means, that I don't care how many times you told the guy that the roof was no good at the job site. If you don't put it in the written report, then you have **no defense** when you get an angry client calling you up 10 months later about a roof leak. You won't even remember the house, let alone the condition the roof was in 10 months earlier.

In appraisal reports, you're required to disclose everything that you know that has an effect on the market value of the subject property. Everything must be disclosed in a way that can't be misinterpreted or twisted around. **You should do the same thing in your inspection reports.** The only difference is that instead of disclosing everything about market value, you're disclosing everything you know about the *condition* of the subject property. You should always have a notepad at the job site and you should be taking field notes throughout the inspection. Don't make the mistake of leaving anything to memory. You'll find out the hard way that when you get back to your office to write the report up, you'll have forgotten a lot. Moreover, you won't remember some of the details clearly. This is even more true when you start to get really busy and are doing two inspections a day. You'll have a hard time remembering if a problem condition was in the first or second house you inspected that day. That is, unless you have very detailed notes from the job site.

Organize your notes and your inspection so that you don't forget to include anything in the written report. Make sure you take your time at the job site and in writing the report so you don't leave anything out. **When you take your field notes and write your report make sure to include anything the client mentioned that concerned them or that they had questions about.** When the client is concerned about a particular aspect of the house or condo, then it's an indication that this is an item they'll **expect** to see in the report. The client will also become angry if they buy the house and discover that you improperly evaluated the item. For example, let's say the client asks a few questions about signs of water problems in the lower level. Well, you better make sure you evaluate the water signs to try to figure out if there's a bad water problem. On top of that, make sure your conclusions are put in the written report. If you don't then the client may buy the house and discover that you missed this item during your inspection and you didn't mention it in your report. When this happens, then at the very least, you'll have a dissatisfied client who won't recommend you.

I'm not trying to scare you. I'm just telling you the facts. Cover Your Assets in all of your written reports. You basically try to CYA on all inspections due to the possibility of unreasonable clients. I know inspectors who have actually gotten phone calls at 3:00 in the morning because a client moved into their new home and one of the gas burners wasn't working on the stove. I've even heard war stories of some client's making late night phone calls to home inspectors because one of the toilets wasn't working. Do you believe that! Some people have no concept of logic and they can be so unreasonable.

I also know of war stories about a home inspector that told a client **before** the inspection and put a written statement in the report that he does not evaluate or inspect swimming pools. Believe it or not, that client bought the house and called the inspector up afterward to complain. They complained that there were problems with the pool when they moved into the house!! I know another home inspector who told a client, and put a statement in the written report, that the septic tank for the house was probably rusted out. The reason for this was that the tank was made of metal and it was very old. That client bought the house and called the inspector up afterward to complain. **The client complained that he was cutting the**

lawn one day and his foot fell through the top of the tank because it was rusted out!!!

If something isn't visible or accessible tell the client that, and tell them to have it checked out by a contractor if any doubts exist. If you haven't been able to evaluate something to the point where you feel comfortable in telling them it's operating properly or looks satisfactory, then tell the client that. And tell them to have it further evaluated by a licensed contractor prior to closing.

Be very careful about giving cost estimates for repairs. You might end up paying the difference between what you quoted the client and what they ended up paying for the work. Tell the client to call a contractor and get estimates on their own. Otherwise, make sure you know what the costs will be and leave some margin for error. Be very careful about recommending any contractors. If you do, make sure they're very honest. If the client uses anyone that you recommend and the client ends up in court with that person, then your client might become angry with you for referring that contractor.

Don't let the war stories scare you, just be aware it can happen to anyone. It's just part of normal, everyday business problems to deal with in any business. You get paid more because a lot of knowledge is required to be a skilled home inspector. As a result, there's more liability. Look at the liability doctors have to assume in their profession. That's why they get paid so much.

Any areas of the house that are inaccessible due to furniture, personal belongings, finished areas, etc. should be stated in your report.
This way the client will have a written record that you don't have a magic wand, X-ray vision, or a crystal ball.

Any areas of the house that are inaccessible or not visible due to furniture, personal belongings, finished areas, etc. should be stated in your written report. This doesn't mean that you have to take out a ruler and write the exact location of every piece of furniture, carpeting, wall covering, picture, etc. Just use your common sense and mention anything that's hidden but would normally be accessible and visible during a typical home inspection. For example, some of the inaccessible areas that should be mentioned would include: a finished basement or attic, a garage that's filled with storage items, a locked room, etc. **This way the client will have a written record that you don't have a magic wand, X-ray vision, or a crystal ball** *(which some people might be surprised to find out).*

If you think it sounds strange to state in the written report that you can't see behind finished and inaccessible areas, then I'll tell you another bedtime war story so you understand why. I once did an inspection and there was a section of the ceiling on the top floor of the house that had some brown water stains. The water stain wasn't that large and it didn't appear to be recent. You'll find this condition often in attics where there will be old water stains from roof leaks that have since been repaired. I told the client at the inspection site and in the written report that there probably was some damage to the areas behind the sheetrock ceilings. I explained that I can't detect this damage because it's not visible. When the client applied for his mortgage loan, the bank appraiser went through the house and mentioned the water stains on the ceiling in the appraisal report as well.

About three weeks after I did the inspection, I got a phone call from this client. He said that he needed a letter from me stating that the roof was in good condition and that it wasn't leaking. He said that the bank read what the appraiser had put in his report about the water stains. As a result, they required this letter for a final approval to lend him the mortgage money to buy the house. I told the client that I can't give him a letter stating that the roof is definitely not leaking and that everything is in good condition. He kept pushing the point of how he needed a letter because he felt that anything would help to satisfy his lender. I told him that I would not make any statements that could be misinterpreted. Furthermore, I said that the only thing I could write would be what I had stated in the written inspection report and that was: *"the water stains did not appear to be recent and appeared to have been from a prior roof leak but there could be damage behind the finished areas."* This statement turned out to be exactly what had happened. The seller of the house had a roof leak in that area before having the house last reroofed. After the new roof was installed, the water leak stopped. The only problem was that the seller was too cheap to pay to have the damage to the roof rafters repaired. There was no attic for me to view this damage due to the design of the house!

Well, about a month later I got a phone call from this client. He told me that after he closed on the house, he had a contractor open that section of the ceiling. Beneath the ceiling covering they found extensive water damage to the roof rafters. The client was a little bit unhappy because he felt that I didn't tell him *"strongly"* enough that there could be damage behind the sheetrock ceiling. Do you believe that!!! What more do I have to do? I told him at the site and I put a statement in the written report! I guess he felt I should have beat him over the head with the idea to make him understand it more clearly. In reality, this client **himself** was the main cause of his problem! This client, like many people who buy homes in an emotionally excited state, made the mistake of not taking a step back and looking at the deal like a typical business decision. He was overly eager and excited about buying a house because the real estate market values were appreciating very quickly during those years. He knew buying a home would make him money, like a business investment, but he was **too emotionally excited** to take the time to check everything out and get repair estimates *BEFORE* the closing! This happens when people let their emotions get too involved in their home search. So learn a lesson from this and don't leave anything to the imagination. When you start to book a lot of inspections you'll have a hard enough time remembering a house you inspected one month ago; let alone if you have to remember details about it a year later.

The Report Is Totally Confidential

There is an important point to remember about the contents of the written report, as well as any water or radon test results. **That is that the report and test results are the property of the person who commissioned the inspection and paid the fee, which is your client.** Your client is the one who owns the contents of that report once he has received it and paid you for your services. **Therefore, the contents of the report is <u>confidential</u> information for the client only!!!** When I say that your client "owns" the contents of the report, it doesn't mean that they own the copyrights to the report text. It means that the information and data in the report is the property of the client for their use in evaluating the subject property.

> *Many times a Realtor or seller will ask you for a copy of the inspection report or the lab test results for water and/or radon. Don't give it to them without the client's consent!!!*

Many times a Realtor or seller to the transaction will ask you for a copy of the inspection report or the lab test results for water and/or radon, or for other details about the report. **Don't give the report nor any information about the report to them without the client's consent!!!** That's a very important point that I will repeat to make sure you don't forget it: Don't give the report nor any information about the report to them without the client's consent!!! It's none of their business to see what's in the written report unless the client wants them to see it. The client may want to negotiate with the seller on items you noted during your inspection and report. If the report gets into anyone else's hands, then it can diminish the client's negotiating position. It's similar to playing poker. You wouldn't show your hand to other players of the game, would you?

If you send a copy of the written report to a Realtor or seller, then you can weaken your client's position. Your client's position is weakened because the third party will know what's in the report. You should also make your client aware of this when you book the job over the phone and at the job site. Tell your client about the poker game analogy so that you dump it back into their lap. This way the **client** makes the decision as to who gets any additional copies of the written report.

I recommend to my clients' that they <u>don't</u> give a copy of the written report to anyone but their own attorney. I've hardly ever seen a copy of the written inspection report benefit my client when it was given to a Realtor, seller, or any other third parties. The reason for this is simple. Let's say the seller doesn't agree with me when I tell my client about a problem condition at the house. **The seller is <u>not</u> going to change his mind just because he sees that I wrote the statement on paper.** On top of that, I've often seen copies of the report *hurt* my clients' position when it was given to a third party. Let's say you told the client that the roof is very old but it's not leaking at this time. The Realtors and sellers will use this statement **against** the client. They'll say, *"As long as the roof isn't leaking, the seller isn't obligated to replace it."* This totally disregards the fact that the roof will leak and need replacing in the near future.

Tell your client there's a better approach to negotiate rather than giving the seller a copy of your report. A written estimate from a licensed contractor can be much more helpful and convincing. Your client gets two benefits from this. _First_, the client can show the seller and Realtor a second opinion in writing that confirms what you're telling them. _Second_, the client will have a repair estimate **prior** to closing. This way they'll know what the costs will be whether they do the work now or later.

There's another reason why you don't want to send a copy of the written report to any dishonest Realtors. The reason is that the written reports have a **very nasty** habit of floating around when they're not in your client's hands. You don't want your report ending up in someone else's hands, especially not another inspection company. If you're an **"A to Z Home Inspector"** then you have to worry about your competitors trying to steal your ideas and information they find in your written reports.

I actually had a local Realtor threaten me once with legal action about this topic. Along with my home inspection and appraisal reports I send out a letter to the client. This Realtor threatened me because the letter states some benefits and reasons why the client shouldn't give out copies of the written report to anyone else. This Realtor not only threatened me with legal action, but even went a step further. The Realtor told all of the other people in that real estate office to tell their client's not to use me on their home inspections. *(Fine, don't recommend me to your clients because I'm not interested in referrals from dishonest Realtors who only refer inspectors that "move the deal along" to benefit a greedy, immoral, and ignorant Realtor! My concern and fiduciary responsibility is to MY CLIENTS, not to any Realtors or other third parties.)* This Realtor was getting a commission on the sale and represented the seller in the transaction, as is almost always the case. **Realtors who represent the seller know that they have no legal right to see the written report nor any of the test results,** such as radon and water tests. That's okay. I get enough work from satisfied clients so I don't need any work from any greedy and dishonest Realtors. As an **"A to Z Home Inspector,"** you won't either.

Inspection Referral Realities

You will find that the vast majority of Realtors won't recommend you for inspections if you're too honest and too thorough. They won't recommend you because you may kill their deals by finding problems with the house or condo. If that happens, then they'll end up losing their commission on the sale. People like that will only refer customers to you with strings attached. **If you don't** *move the deal along* **by not telling the client about any problems in the house, then they get angry and won't recommend you again.** Don't bother with these types of people. It'll be very hard to avoid them in business, so just try to ignore them. You can get more than enough business from honest people. You don't want to *"sell your soul"* just to make money, so who cares if they don't recommend you.

> *You will find that the vast majority of Realtors will not recommend you for inspections if you're too honest and too thorough.*

Honest third party people will recommend a good, thorough inspector. They know that a good inspector will satisfy the client that the house has been checked out thoroughly. Unfortunately, you may find that the honest third party people who will recommend you if you're good, can be **extremely** outnumbered in some areas. And I'm not talking about your clients, because they'll *always* recommend you if you're good. You just want to do business with the honest third party people so you can sleep with a clear conscience at night.

The only way you're going to make big money on a steady basis in this business is to have satisfied **clients** who refer customers to you. If you have steady referrals from former clients, then you won't even have to advertise and your phone will ring off the hook for inspection jobs. That's when you know you have a rock solid business that's going to make you a lot of money for a long, long time. And you want to be in this for the long term. The people that make the most money in this business, are the ones who have the most satisfied clients. Even in a recession, they still make money, because houses are still sold when the economy is bad. The only difference is that houses sell for less money, but they still need to be inspected.

> *There's a big difference between referrals from satisfied clients who you've done inspections for, and referrals from Realtors who send customers to you just because you "move the deal along."*

There's a *big* difference between referrals from **satisfied clients** who you've done inspections for, and referrals from **Realtors** who send customers to you just because you "move the deal along." If you just *move the deal along* and don't do a thorough and professional inspection, then the client is going to know that after the inspection is over. They might not say anything to you, but they just won't recommend you to their friends. I've seen it before in some other inspection companies. They get all of their business from dishonest Realtors because they don't tell the client about anything wrong with the house, and they just *move the deal along.* These inspectors end up being <u>owned</u> by dishonest Realtors because the Realtors have control over their income. I don't know about you, but I don't like anybody having leverage over me.

> *They get all of their business from dishonest Realtors because they don't tell the client about anything wrong with the house, and they just "move the deal along." These inspectors end up being owned by the dishonest Realtors.*

Let me explain how you will be "owned" by the dishonest Realtors if you get most of your business from *their* **referrals because you** *move their deals along.* With these types of referrals from dishonest Realtors and third parties, you can't tell the client about anything **important** being wrong with the house. The only thing they want you to tell the client is if some **minor** repairs are needed – but nothing else! If you do tell your client about important or costly repairs that are needed with the property, and it creates *any* problems or kills the deal, then the Realtor gets angry and **will <u>never</u> recommend you to their clients again!!** Regardless of the fact that you were being <u>honest</u> with the client, they still won't recommend you anymore.

Dishonest Realtors and third parties don't want you to say *anything* **that will throw a monkey wrench into their deal!** It doesn't matter how many other deals you *moved along* for the dishonest Realtor or other third party person. If you create problems with, or kill, just *one* of their deals; <u>then that's it, you're cut off and they tell their clients not to hire you for home inspections anymore!</u> And if the dishonest Realtors cut you off after you've been catering to them and *kissing their ass* for a long time just to get referral business from them, **then you're really in trouble!** You're in trouble because you don't have <u>satisfied</u> clients to refer you for future home inspections. Then your phone stops ringing and your inspection income goes down to nothing. The reason you won't have satisfied clients recommending their friends to hire you for their home inspection needs, is because the clients will know after they hired you that you were "in bed" with the dishonest Realtor and you were just *moving the deal along* to satisfy the **<u>Realtor</u>** and *NOT* your **<u>client</u>**!! People aren't stupid. Your clients might not notice **during** your home inspection that you're compromising your morals and "hanging them out to dry" just to keep the Realtor that recommended you happy. However, your clients will notice they've been scammed **after** your home inspection and/or the deal closes. Especially when the problems that you should have told the client about start "coming out of the woodwork".

You don't believe me? I've heard quite a few war stories about appraisers who can't find any new business due to the poor quality of their work in the past. I've even seen it happen firsthand with a local home inspection company in my area. This home inspection company was run by an older man that just *moved deals along* for the Realtors. When the older inspector retired and a new inspector came in and started doing good, honest and thorough inspections, **the phone stopped ringing!** All of the dishonest Realtors and third parties stopped using the new inspector because he didn't cater to them and *move the deals along* like the older inspector had. The phone didn't ring from client referrals either. This is because <u>none of the former clients</u> would recommend anyone to this inspection company. They wouldn't recommend anyone because they knew the work was of such a poor quality from the older inspector. This created a terrible reflection on the company name, even after the older inspector retired. To make matters even worse, the only phone calls that did come in were from **unhappy** former clients of the old inspector. These people called to *complain* about the inspection services he did. They didn't call to refer more inspection business to them.

There's another drawback to getting all of your referrals from dishonest Realtors. What happens is, the client buys the house and then finds out, after they move in, that there are some problems. The client decides that the inspector should've noticed these problems during the inspection and told the client about them. So what does the client do? He gets angry because he knows the home inspector wasn't thorough or professional, and he sicks his attorney on the inspector and files a lawsuit. Home inspectors like that end up being sued out of business.

> *So you see, the only way to make it in this, or any other business, is to do good, honest and professional work. If you "sell your soul" then your income and your reputation are going to pay dearly for it.*

So you see, the only way to make it in this, or any other business, is to do good, honest and professional work. If you *"sell your soul"* then your income and your reputation are going to pay dearly for it. And you won't even sleep well at night. I've found that some people have an **amazing ability to rationalize their actions,** no matter how bad they are. So let the dishonest Realtors and other third parties sell their souls. Just don't ever compromise your own integrity. Too many people compromise their integrity for money. I think that money is like a truth serum. It brings out the true character of a person, deep down inside, whether they're good or bad. There's an awful lot of *"white collar crime"* that goes unnoticed and unpunished because people <u>rationalize their actions</u>. They deliberately hide problems from the clients. Then they kid themselves thinking that there's nothing wrong with burying things underneath a blanket of deception.

I've had many Realtors and sellers complain because my home inspections take about three or four hours. They don't want you to be too thorough or to spend too much time in the house, or on writing the report. My clients never complain because I spend three or four hours inspecting a house that they're planning to buy. So how come Realtors and sellers complain about it? They seem to forget, that my fiduciary responsibility is to my **<u>client</u>** and not to any **<u>Realtors or third</u>**

parties. However, if **they** were buying the house, well then, it would be a **totally different story**. I'll talk more about hypocrites later.

I'm certainly not being a hypocrite myself or talking out of ignorance. I let my track record and integrity speak for itself: Less than *one percent* of my clients have ever called me up to say that they were unhappy with my services. I've even **turned away** business by being honest with people. There are many dishonest Realtors whose business I have turned away. I told these Realtors that I didn't want their referrals for clients. The reason for this is that I knew they would complain if I did a thorough home inspection or appraisal. Other examples are, I've done appraisals and inspections on houses that were taken back in foreclosures, or the houses were part of estate sales after someone had died. These houses had all of the utilities turned off at the time I arrived to do the inspection. You can't do a proper appraisal and/or home inspection on a house without any utilities turned on! The reason for this is that you won't be able to test any of the operating systems. I would be up-front and honest with my clients. I'd tell them that rather than go ahead with the inspection, they'd be better off waiting until the utilities were turned on. If they delay the inspection, I wouldn't have to charge them a fee for a limited home inspection. Sometimes these deals would fall through because another buyer would come along **before** the utilities were turned on, or some other reason. Therefore, as a result of being up-front and honest, I would lose money. However, I'd rather lose the money, then do the inspection and not feel good about it. I hope that's the way you run your business also.

If you go into this business, then you're going to come across many dishonest Realtors and other third parties who will try to get you to *"move their deals along."* I'm letting you know ahead of time that's it's going to happen, so don't say I didn't warn you about this. Often what dishonest Realtors will do is try to *butter you up* when you first show up at the subject property. Sometimes they'll even call you up before you go out to the site and try to butter you up. What they say to you is, *"Oh, can I have one of your business cards. Our office is always looking for new inspectors to recommend to our clients."* **They lie to you by saying this to make you think that they're going to refer their future clients to you for home inspection or appraisal work.** However, it's the same old con game that they're playing. If you don't *"move their deal along,"* then your business cards will end up in their garbage can as soon as the Realtors get back to their office. *(I have an awful lot of business cards and brochures that have ended up in dishonest Realtor's garbage cans. My cards ended up in their garbage because I was too honest and thorough with my clients. Remember, an educated home buyer or seller is a dishonest Realtor's worst nightmare!!!)*

So remember, don't let any Realtors butter you up on an inspection. Be on your guard when they ask you for your business card so they can *supposedly* refer other clients to you. **Translated into English, what they're really saying to you is,** *"Don't tell the buyer that anything's wrong with the house and we'll give you some referral business. This way the both of*

us can cheat and deceive people and line our pockets with dirty money."

You'll also come across another offshoot for this type of Realtor dishonesty if you go into this business. **Dishonest Realtors will sometimes say to you,** *"It's not __what__ you say to the client, it's __how__ you say it that matters."* **Translated into English, what they really mean by saying this to you is,** *"Don't tell the buyer that something, such as the heating system is old and can die at anytime. Just tell them it's working properly now because that's all they need to know. Don't mention anything to them about getting estimates to replace it."*

They want you to "sugarcoat" everything so it all sounds fine and dandy in greedy Realtor fairytale land. Basically, dishonest and greedy Realtors ONLY want you to mention if some **minor** maintenance and repairs are needed on the property – and that's it!

Some Good Reasons For Federal Regulations

In my opinion, there is an *urgent* need for Federal legislation. The legislation should prevent anyone who will benefit by the sale of a property from recommending a home inspector or an appraiser to a client. The reason I say this is that, **it is a total conflict of interest if they recommend an inspector or appraiser!!!** I can't believe that laws have not been passed which prevent this conflict of interest. If someone will gain a profit or a commission on the sale of a property, then don't you think that there's an obvious problem if they recommend a home inspector or an appraiser? The problem is due to the temptation of the Realtor or third party to make sure the deal goes through, at any cost, so they can get paid. Furthermore, most of the time, Realtors and third parties who get a commission on the sale work for the seller!! This means that their fiduciary and legal responsibility is to get the best deal possible for the *seller*, not the *buyer*. Therefore, how can these third party people say that they're looking out for the buyer's best interest, by recommending a thorough and unbiased home inspector or appraiser? Again, it's a total conflict of interest if they recommend a home inspector or an appraiser!

> *Legislation should prevent anyone who benefits by the sale of a property from recommending a home inspector or appraiser. I say this because, __it is a total conflict of interest if they recommend an inspector or appraiser!!!__*

Believe me, I'm no rocket scientist and I can see as clear as day that there's a problem here that needs to be fixed. I also think that there is an *urgent* need for another type of Federal legislation. This legislation should require all Realtors and third parties involved in a real estate transaction, who receive a commission on the sale, to make certain recommendations to the seller and the buyer. However, the recommendations *should not* be a conflict of interest.

◊ The recommendation they should be required to make to the **seller** is: *"The seller should hire an independent real estate appraiser that they select on their own, without any involvement or encouragement of the Realtors or any other third parties. An appraisal is recommended to give the seller an unbiased estimate of market value for the subject property. This appraisal should be done **before** the seller lists the property for sale."*

◊ The recommendation they should be required to make to the **buyer** is: *"The buyer should hire an independent real estate home inspector that they select on their own, without any involvement or encouragement of the Realtors or any other third parties. An inspection is recommended to give the buyer a thorough and professional home inspection of the subject property. This home inspection should be done **before** the buyer signs any contracts to purchase the subject property."*

If these ideas were enforced by Federal legislation, then it would greatly help everyone in the country with the biggest investment of their lives. This type of legislation would also improve the integrity of the real estate business *tremendously*. Now don't get me wrong here. If an attorney wants to recommend a home inspector or an appraiser to a client they're representing, then that's fine. In a case like this, the attorney is only looking out for **their client's interests**. The attorney will get paid a fee, regardless of whether the deal goes through or not. Therefore, they don't have a conflict of interest and a financial commission incentive to *move the deal along* by recommending an incompetent home inspector or appraiser - **like a dishonest, greedy Realtor or other third party does.** I hope you see the difference between these two situations.

In the front section of the book I list the benefits of having a home inspection done by an independent, honest and thorough home inspector. (See section Benefits Of Knowledge Of Home Inspections page 20). I think they're all valid reasons that are based on a foundation of solid facts. These facts reinforce my opinions about the need for Federal legislation. I've seen many examples of sellers who have been deceived by dishonest third parties. **This deception could have been prevented, if the seller had been educated about the benefits of getting an unbiased appraiser to estimate the market value of their property.** The way dishonest Realtors and third parties cheat sellers' is by deceiving them as to the true market value of their property.

I had a client that hired me to do an appraisal of their house before they listed it for sale. The woman who owned the house was a very nice, easy-going person. She told me that she and her husband purchased the house just three years earlier for about $500,000. There was a Realtor who was involved in the transaction. At the time they purchased the property, this Realtor told the couple that: *"You're getting a **rock bottom** price, and you're **stealing** this house for $100,000 **below***

market value." The woman who was my client told me, that she and her husband had asked this Realtor to list their house for sale, three years later. Well, this Realtor told them that: *"The market has gone way down because of the recession. You're going to have to sell the house for $100,000 **less** than what you paid for it, three years earlier."*

Luckily, my client and her husband didn't believe that the real estate market had dropped that drastically in only three years. The reason a greedy, dishonest Realtor may want to list a house for sale at a very low price is that the house will sell very quickly and that listing Realtor can make a fast commission on the sale. Also, if the **listing** Realtor has home buyers looking for houses in that area, then he/she may even be able to also be the **selling** Realtor on the deal by calling one of her home buyer clients and telling them about this *"great low-priced house that's just come on the market and hasn't even been listed yet in the MLS!!"* **If the listing Realtor is also the selling Realtor, then he/she will get twice the commission percentage on the sale! That's a greedy, dishonest Realtor's incentive to low-ball a seller with their listing price.** I did an extremely thorough appraisal, using six sales comparables that had sold within the past six months. These sales comps were all located within two blocks of the subject property. My appraisal market value estimate was just about the same price the client had paid for the house. There was a recession that caused prices to drop in the area. However, at the time my clients were going to sell the property, the market had rebounded so they wouldn't have to take a loss. This is a perfect example of how the public gets cheated by dishonest and/or incompetent Realtors who call themselves *"real estate professionals."*

This appraisal client made a statement to me about Realtors that I have found to be very true. She said that *"Realtors talk out of both sides of their mouth."* During all of my experience in this business **I've found that some Realtors will say *anything* to sell a house. It's similar to a prostitute - they "screw" people for money!!**

> *I've seen ENDLESS examples of buyers who have been deceived by dishonest Realtors and other third parties to the transaction.*

I've seen ***ENDLESS*** examples of buyers who have been deceived by dishonest Realtors and third parties. I'd be one of the richest people around if I had a nickel for each time I've seen this happen. All of this deception could have been prevented, if the buyer had been educated about the benefits of getting an **unbiased** home inspector to evaluate the condition of the subject property. The way dishonest Realtors and other third parties cheat buyers is by deceiving them as to the true condition of the house they're purchasing. For example, let's say a buyer wants to have an inspection done on a house they're thinking about buying. They will ask a Realtor or other third party that's involved in the deal to recommend a home inspector to them. **A dishonest Realtor or other third party will give the buyer three names of home inspectors that won't say anything bad about the subject property. This** way the deal won't be delayed or renegotiated due to problem conditions found during the inspection. After the buyer closes on the house and moves-in, they find out about all the repairs that are needed and all of the problems with the house. The buyer then realizes that these are the things that the home inspector should have told them about. But by that time, it's too late. It's already a done deal.

> *The reason a dishonest Realtor or other third party gives the buyer a list of three names is another con game. All three of the inspectors on that list are incompetent crooks with no integrity or morals!*

The reason a dishonest Realtor or other third party gives the buyer a list of three names is another con game. All three of the home inspectors on that list are incompetent crooks with no integrity or morals that are "in bed" with the Realtor and they "screw" the clients for money! The dishonest Realtor or other third party has those inspectors in their back pocket. They're partners in crime. They're cheating the public by "moving deals along" and people don't realize they've been scammed until it's too late. The buyer can call the Realtor or third party to complain about the incompetent home inspector they recommended. However, the Realtor or third party gets off the hook by saying, *"Well, Mr. Buyer, I'm very sorry you found problems with the house that didn't come out during the inspection. However, I gave you three names to call. You should have hired inspector #2 on the list instead of inspector #3."* If you don't believe all of this, then just ask other home inspectors that are very thorough and knowledgeable. See what they tell you.

One way you will certainly be able to know if you are a very honest, thorough and knowledgeable home inspector is based upon what greedy, dishonest Realtors think of you. For example, when potential clients call me for price quotes, I tell them that they want to hire the home inspector that's **HATED BY THE REALTORS!!!!** I explain that the last thing the client should do is use a home inspector (or appraiser) recommended by the Realtor due to the conflict of interest concerns. You know that you're an **excellent** home inspector or appraiser when the dishonest and greedy Realtors *HATE YOUR GUTS!!!* They hate my guts but that's OK with me because I don't want nor need business from criminals anyway! It's fine when the **honest** Realtors that I know recommend me to their clients. But I still make it **very clear** to the client on the phone when they are booking the job, that I represent the client and will tell them all known problems I find at the house and site, **regardless** of whether or not it kills the deal and costs the Realtor who recommended me to lose their commission. It's always a pleasure to meet and work with an **honest** Realtor that can accept terms like that – terms that are for my client's best interests only!

You Get What You Pay For

I don't mean to scare you talking about dishonesty and lawsuits. But this is how the whole idea of Federal and State regulations and licensing came about for real estate appraisers. During the 1980's real estate prices were rising through the roof, *(pardon the pun)*. The banks and savings and loans kept lending mortgage money on over priced real estate transactions. A possible reason for this is that they figured that they couldn't lose money. If the buyer didn't make the mortgage payments then the lender could foreclose. If that happened, then the property would be worth more than the bank had lent on it and they would make a profit anyway.

Well, that's not how it turned out. Everybody ended up losing in a big way. When the recession hit the economy in 1989 an awful lot of banks lost billions of dollars due to real estate loans that had gone sour. The Savings and Loan bailout was estimated to cost over 250 billion dollars. Banks could foreclose on the properties but they couldn't resell them to get their funds back. Everybody loses in that type of situation including the homeowner, the bank, the economy, the local town, etc.

The whole reason the *Resolution Trust Corporation* (RTC) was created was to take over insolvent banks. After taking over these banks, the RTC would try to sell the bank assets to investors to recoup some of the losses. The *Federal Deposit Insurance Corporation*, FDIC, and the *Federal Savings and Loan Insurance Corporation*, FSLIC, had to pay the depositors in the insolvent banks. Customers that had bank accounts were paid the insurance amount for their deposited money. Any funds that the RTC could not recoup with the sale of assets from insolvent banks were left to the American taxpayer to pay.

To try to prevent this whole mess from ever happening again, the Federal Government made some new rules. The government had to regulate some occupational group involved in the real estate industry. Since the banks and savings and loans were already regulated, they looked at real estate appraisers. In 1989 Congress passed the *Financial Institutions Reform, Recovery and Enforcement Act* of 1989 (FIRREA), more commonly known as the *Savings and Loan Bailout Bill*. Title XI of FIRREA set up a real estate appraiser regulatory system involving the Federal government, the States and *The Appraisal Foundation. The Appraisal Subcommittee* (ASC) of the *Federal Financial Institutions Examination Council* has the authority to ensure that the States and the Foundation meet the requirements that the States use certifying appraisers and the standards of professional practice to which appraisers are held by the States (the *Uniform Standards of Professional Appraisal Practice* - USPAP).

Many bankers felt that they would not have made many real estate loans which ended up being foreclosed on if the appraisers had been more cautious during the 1980's real estate boom. The bankers felt that the appraisers erred because they kept arriving at inflated estimates of market value in their reports. On the other hand, many appraisers felt that many bankers and mortgage brokers had unfairly pressured them in the 1980's. The pressure on the appraisers was to arrive at high estimates of market value in their reports. The high estimates were necessary in some reports so that the lender or broker could grant the mortgage loan and earn a profit or a commission fee. Before the Federal requirements, just about anyone could call themselves a real estate appraiser. The only way to differentiate between appraisers and to measure their competence was to ask if they were designated by one of the large appraisal organizations that existed.

Handling Client Complaints

No matter how good you are, you're going to get a few complaints from clients because you can't satisfy everyone all the time. It's the same problem in every other business. So you might as well get ready to deal with it now. The bright side is that the better you are, the fewer complaints you'll get. It's that simple. If you don't like headaches or aggravation, then just do good, thorough inspections and you'll minimize the complaints as much as possible. As I've said earlier, I've only had less than one percent of my clients call me complain about my services. Of these complaints, I was only wrong one time where it was my fault for missing something that I should have seen. I had just started out in the home inspection business and I under-estimated the age of a roof for a client. This roof was in excellent condition so I told the client it was younger than it actually was. However, my client was informed about my mistake **before** he signed the contracts to buy the house. As a result, he didn't have any financial loss or problems due to my error. Moreover, I paid the client a refund on his inspection fee since I felt bad that I had made a mistake and didn't properly determine the correct age of the roof. If you have a track record like that, then you'll be doing just fine. You will be able to consider the quality of your work superior to the competition.

> *No matter how good you are, you're going to get a few complaints from clients because you can't satisfy everyone all the time. It's the same problem in every other business.*

When you get a complaint from a client after they have purchased the house you had inspected, it's often because they didn't read the written inspection report **prior to** the closing. Believe it or not, many people get so excited and emotional about buying a house that they tend to overlook very important factors. This is why you **have to** send your clients a thorough, professional, and narrative inspection report. The written report should include explanations and comments describing the details about the subject property in the report. Don't be like a lot of other home inspectors out there and send your clients a brief checklist report that doesn't tell them anything. If you send your clients a brief checklist report you'll end up regretting it eventually.

Some people will just assume that since they attended the inspection, then they know enough about the house and won't bother reading a long, narrative inspection report. They also will assume that they don't need to bother with getting estimates for any problem conditions prior to closing on the house. They'll just wait until after they move-in and worry about getting estimates later. This is a **BIG mistake** on the client's part because you know the old saying, *"When you **assume**, you make an **Ass** out of **U** and **Me**."*

I've had this exact situation happen with one of my home inspection client's. This client had purchased a house and **didn't follow my professional recommendations. I had told this client, verbally and in the written inspection report, to have the siding checked out by a licensed contractor before closing on the house.** There were many damaged and missing shingles on the house. These shingles were located in areas too high to reach with a ladder, unless you were a house painter with an exceptionally long ladder – which home inspectors are not required to use. I also told this client that when I asked the seller the preinspection questions, the seller said that the house had been treated for carpenter ant damage a few years ago. **I told the client to speak to the exterminator who had done the carpenter ant treatment; get all documentation for the work; and find out the extent of the damage and the treatment. Furthermore, I told this client to hire their own exterminator to evaluate this information and treat the house again.**

This client had decided they didn't need to worry about following any of my recommendations until *after* they moved into the house. Well, wouldn't you know it, I got a phone call from them a few months after they moved into the house. **They told me that the reason the shingles were falling off the house was because of the carpenter ant damage.** I asked the client how they found out about the cause of this problem. He said that they hired a contractor, *AFTER* they bought the house, to evaluate the damaged shingles and the prior owner's carpenter ant treatment.

If this client had listened to me at the inspection site and read the written inspection report, they would have eliminated all these problems **before** they bought the house! However, the client either did not listen to me at the inspection site and did not read the written report; or the client did listen to me and did read the report but they just decided on their own, not to follow my professional recommendations. Therefore, in a case such as this, the **client cannot blame anyone but themselves** for being negligent and foolish.

> *This is a perfect example of why you have to stress to your clients, and put a statement in the written reports, recommending that they get repair estimates and eliminate any questions, concerns or problems - BEFORE BUYING THE HOUSE!!!!*

This is a perfect example of why you have to stress to your clients, and put a statement in the written reports, recommending that they get repair estimates and eliminate any questions, concerns or problems - *BEFORE BUYING THE HOUSE!!!!* Just tell the client not to get too emotional or excited about their purchase and not to *assume* anything. If they check everything out before they buy the house, then it becomes the *seller's* responsibility to remedy any problems. However, if the client doesn't check everything out before they buy the house, then it becomes the *buyer's* responsibility to remedy any problems.

If you're a thorough home inspector, then sometimes when you get a complaint from a client, it's because they have been deceived by a dishonest and/or ignorant contractor. All of your written reports should have a statement that warns your clients about this problem, before it's too late. What happens is this: The client closes on the house and then moves-in to their new home. While they're living there or during some remodeling work, they find items that need to be repaired that weren't identified in the inspection report. Since you're a thorough *"A to Z Home Inspector"*   the reason these items weren't identified during the on-site inspection, is because they weren't visible or accessible during the inspection. This happens all the time with termites and water problems. The client will open up a floor, wall or ceiling during remodeling work. When it's all open, they find damage from termites or water leaks. **Obviously, the inspector can't identify a problem if it's not visible!!** *(Well, at least you would think that it's obvious to people).* Unfortunately, there are some people who don't realize you can't see behind floors, walls and ceilings. These people always think that they hired *Clark Kent*, alias *Superman*, to do their home inspection!

What happens next, is the client will then unknowingly call up a dishonest and/or ignorant contractor. They will ask the contractor to come to the house and give them an estimate for the repairs needed. The contractor goes to the house and looks at the damage. He sees dollar signs in his eyes and immediately turns to your client and says, *"You mean your home inspector didn't see this? Your home inspector should have seen this damage and told you about it. You should sue that inspector to get reimbursed for the repairs I have to do."* Then to put the icing on the cake, this moron that calls himself a contractor, hands your client a ridiculous estimate for the repairs. The estimate is usually so high, that it's from the planet Mars!

> *What a dishonest contractor tries to do is distract your client's attention by pointing the finger at the home inspector for not seeing the damage.*

What a dishonest contractor tries to do is distract your client's attention by pointing the finger at the home inspector for not seeing the damage. While your client is angry and furious with you, they don't even think about getting a second repair estimate to verify what this contractor is telling them. A dishonest contractor tries to look like the *Knight in Shining Armor* that rides in on his white horse to save your client from the evil home inspector. Because of this, your client begins to think the contractor knows what he's talking about and that the inspector is wrong. **Actually, it's the other way around!**

The contractor knows *nothing* about what is involved with a home inspection. The contractor also wasn't even at the house at the time of your inspection. Moreover, the contractor has <u>no</u> idea if the damage was visible or accessible at the time of the inspection. Sometimes, the contractor even has <u>no</u> idea if the damage **even existed** at the time of the inspection. Therefore, how can this ignorant contractor say that you should have seen the damage and notified your client about it?

> *When a dishonest or uneducated contractor scares a client, they do it to steal their money. When an "A to Z Home Inspector" scares a client, they do it to save them money.*

All a contractor like that will succeed in doing is raise your client's blood pressure due to the client's anger. After that, they will then rip-off your client, unless someone else opens the client's eyes to the truth. When a dishonest or uneducated contractor scares a client, they do it to **steal** their money. When an *"A to Z Home Inspector"* scares a client, they do it to **save** them money. What I mean by this is a contractor, such as the one I've described, will steal your client's money by deceiving them into paying a grossly overcharged repair bill. They get the client all emotionally pumped up with anger, and while the client's attention is distracted, they lower the boom on them with a gigantic repair bill. On the other hand, an *"A to Z Home Inspector"* will save your client money by opening their eyes to the true risks and realities of buying a house. You may get the client scared by telling them about the potential pitfalls and hazards of a huge investment like a home. It's to the client's advantage to know all the problems and risks in purchasing or selling a home if they don't check all of the records at town hall; the potential for damage and termites behind walls, floors, and ceilings; the health concerns of radon and asbestos; risks of not pumping and internally inspecting a septic system; etc.

You might be saying to yourself, *"OK, now this author has really gone over the deep end. He's talking about the emotional state of home inspection clients."* Well, let me give you a few war stories that show you the reality of this situation. These are two clients that consist of the less than one percent that have ever called me to complain about my services. I think you'll see why I feel that I was right in both cases and the clients were misled by lying contractors.

A client of mine had moved into a house that I had inspected for her. She called to say that she had replaced the water heater and the oil burner for the boiler. She told me the price she paid for the repairs and I immediately knew that she had been cheated by a dishonest contractor. I asked her why the contractor said the repairs were needed and if she had gotten any other estimates, before hiring this guy. The contractor told her that the oil burner and the water heater were unrepairable and both had to be replaced. She then said that she didn't get any other estimates for the repairs and this contractor was the only person who evaluated the damage. I then told the client to check the written inspection report and let me know what it said about these two items. The water heater was only three years old and was operating fine at the time of the inspection. The oil burner was also operating properly at the time of the inspection. Both items were covered under a warranty and service contract with the manufacturer and oil delivery company. My client ended up realizing that these items didn't need to be replaced at all. On top of that, this immoral contractor charged her more than **twice** what she should have paid, even if they did need to be replaced! Since this guy was such a crooked contractor, I am positive that these items may only have needed a minor repair or tune-up in the first place. However, the client was told that it was my fault by the contractor. She didn't find out the truth until it was too late and the money was spent on the repairs.

(This next story is a real beauty). Another client of mine called me after they moved into their new home. They had a contractor come in to give them a price quote to remove the old carpets and install new carpeting. This contractor found some damage **underneath** the existing carpet in a corner and one other small area. The hardwood floor underneath had buckled in two places. The contractor had only lifted the **one corner of the carpet** and he told the client, *"Didn't your home inspector see this damage underneath the carpet? This entire hardwood floor and carpet are going to cost you $5,000 to replace. Your home inspector should have seen this."* Not surprisingly, my client was angry about not being told of this damage before closing on the house. Fortunately, the client called me up before he let this blockhead, that calls himself a floor contractor, replace the hardwood floor. When I saw the damage in person, I could not believe anyone would have told my client that I was negligent. My client and I, both confirmed that the corner where the damage was found had been buried in boxes, toys and furniture at the time of the inspection. We also both confirmed, that the other damaged area was covered with a large couch at the time of the inspection. Impressions from the furniture were <u>still visible</u> in the carpets surrounding the damaged areas. **Therefore, it became very clear to both of us that the seller *intentionally* made sure we didn't see the damage at the time of the inspection.**

I was angry that the seller was such a crook and that he would stoop so low and hide damage on purpose. However, what really annoyed me, was the ignorance of the floor contractor! When I finally looked at the damaged area underneath the corner of the carpet, I realized that the contractor had no right to accuse me of being negligent. **The damaged area could be easily repaired by replacing a few of the buckled boards.** It didn't even matter if the wood matched exactly or not. The client had told the contractor they wanted to cover the floor with a new carpet anyway. Luckily the client had taken my advice and called a second contractor to give them an estimate. While I was there, the second floor contractor came by the house. **His price quote was a $500 repair job, not a $5,000 repair!**

You should have a statement in all of the written reports that you send out to warn your clients about this type of situation. Let them know that some contractors will try to

blame the home inspector. These contractors will then grossly overcharge the client for repairs that may never have been needed in the first place. Tell your clients to call you **before** they have any repairs done which they believe you should have identified during the home inspection. If they call **before** the repairs are done, both you and they will have a chance to clear up the situation before it's too late.

You also want to warn your clients if you find out that the seller or any third parties have intentionally lied about some aspect of the subject property. I've had this happen on a few occasions and it should immediately raise a red flag in your mind about the property and that person's integrity. **If you catch someone lying about some aspect of the property, then there probably will be other hidden problems.** There could be damaged areas or something that's not visible which can create a problem after your client moves-in. If this happens to you, then make sure that you and your client verify as much information as possible, before they sign contracts.

There's a very important point that you need to remember. If you get an angry phone call from a client who complains that you missed something during your inspection: **Don't jump down their throat and tell them they're crazy!** You have to stay calm and be very reasonable and diplomatic when you deal with an angry or hostile person. Don't make the mistake of telling the client that he's insane if he thinks you should have seen damage that was hidden at the time of the inspection. By yelling back at the client, all you will succeed in doing is getting him even more furious at you. Just calmly tell the client that you want to come by the house to see the problem in person. This is for your benefit as well as the client's benefit. By seeing the damage in person, it will enable you to help solve the problem before they make any unnecessary or overpriced repairs.

Your client can get angry and all pumped up because they're looking at a very large repair bill. Moreover, the contractor is blaming *you* for not seeing the problem. As a result, the client is told by the contractor that *you* should pay for the repair. An angry client is concentrating on what repairs you *didn't* tell them about, before they bought the property. You have to make them realize how much you *did* tell them about, before they bought the property. As an ***"A to Z Home Inspector"***: your inspection lasted over three hours; you told them about checking all records at town hall; you warned them about radon; you told them to get estimates and further evaluations for some items; you sent them a narrative and informative written report; etc. Would they have gotten that much information if they hired another home inspector in the area? How much risk did you help them eliminate? How much money did you save them? How much more thorough and professional was your inspection, as compared to the competition? Would any homeowner, including themselves, allow a home inspector to come into their house and rip up the carpets, move the furniture, and open up the walls, floors and ceilings?

As long as you're logical and reasonable, the client will understand that you didn't cheat them. Your client will be complaining because **they're ignorant**, not because **you're negligent**. There's a big difference between the two. The client is ignorant because they don't know the Standards in the industry for performing a home inspection. When they're annoyed, they might not stop, take a step back, and think about the situation in a logical fashion. The client might not realize that a home inspector can't pull up carpets, or move furniture, or open up walls, floors and ceilings. You have to look at the situation from their perspective. The client is looking at a big repair bill and they think it's your fault. Once you explain the limits of a home inspection and ask the client questions, (like the ones mentioned above), your client will understand that you haven't been negligent. After that your client will gradually calm down and recognize that you're the best inspector in the area that they could have hired. Therefore, if you didn't see the damage, or if it wasn't visible, then no other inspector would have identified the problem either.

> *A client of this limited mentality cannot comprehend that a home inspector doesn't travel on a magic carpet with a wand, emerald slippers, and Aladdin's lamp.*

Now, let's say that after you calmly explain all of this logic and reason, your client is still angry with you for missing something that you **clearly had no way of identifying.** If this is the situation, then I hate to have to clue you in. But you're dealing with a **basket case!** You have to tell this type of client that they need to call *Clark Kent "Superman"* for their next home inspection. This is the type of person that I've been warning you about to CYA in all of your written reports. A client of this limited mentality cannot comprehend that a home inspector doesn't travel on a *magic carpet* with a *wand*, *emerald slippers*, and *Aladdin's lamp*. So bite your tongue, say your prayers, and try not to lose your patience with a person like that.

Know-It-All People

There will be times when you'll get a hostile seller, Realtor, or other third party at the site who will become very defensive during the home inspection. **You'll find that these types of people are all experts in everything, yet they have no facts or knowledge to back up their statements.** Just don't be intimidated by anyone - not even the client. If you're knowledgeable enough, you'll have plenty of confidence. So don't let anyone *"ruffle your feathers"* during an inspection.

Once you learn this material well enough and you get 10 or so inspections under your belt you'll start to get a lot more confidence. That's why you shouldn't let any know-it-all Realtors or other third party people try to contradict you on any of your inspections. When I say *know-it-all* people, I'm talking about people involved in the transaction, other than your client.

> *You'll find that these types of people are all experts in everything, yet they have no facts or knowledge to back up their statements.*

You don't want to be arrogant or rude with your attitude. There will be times that you'll *think* you're right but you might find out later that you're *wrong*. You don't want to end up putting your foot in your mouth later. So just be confident, knowledgeable and honest. Don't imitate them by being a know-it-all yourself because two wrongs don't make a right. If that person is honest and sensible, they'll realize that you're much more knowledgeable than they are. For example, lets say you're checking the heating system or the roof and their age indicates that they're past the normal life expectancy for these items. The heating system might still be working and the roof might not be leaking, but they could be past their life expectancy. This is not uncommon and it happens all the time. I'll use a few analogies to make this point clearer.

Have you ever seen an old car that's still running? The old car is operating past its predicted life expectancy. It's also similar to driving a car with a flat tire. The car will move, but for how long and how far? Have you ever heard of someone living longer than their doctor predicted? They may be a heavy smoker, or have some form of cancer or an inherited disease, but they live longer than the doctor predicted. Are these three analogies the exception or the rule? I think they're the exception and it's the same thing with the different aspects of housing construction.

If you had a case, such as the one described above with an old roof and heating system, and you had a know-it-all person at the inspection, they might say to you: *"Well, the heating system is working fine now and the roof isn't leaking so the client doesn't have to replace them."* Just tell that person that if they want to **guarantee to your client** that the heating system and roof will last another 5 to 10 years, then go ahead and put it in writing for my client. But don't expect me, the home inspector, to get stuck holding the bag in eight months after this guy buys the house and his heating system dies or his roof starts leaking. That type of comeback will usually put an end to any know-it-all's comments. **Basically you're telling that person that if they know so much more about houses than you do, then they should be willing to put their *money* where their *mouth* is. A know-it-all's reaction will be totally different when it's *their* neck and money that's on the line, as opposed to yours or your clients!**

> *It's amazing to me when I come across Realtors who have taken a few basic classes related to aspects of real estate and - Abracadabra - they're instant experts in every aspect of real estate!!!!*

It's amazing to me when I come across Realtors or other third parties who have taken a few basic classes related to some of the different aspects of real estate and - *Abracadabra* - they're instant experts in every aspect of real estate!! *(Or at least they think they are.)* They become **legends in their own minds**. They think that after they take a few real estate related classes and tests *(that just about anyone with a pulse can pass),* and a few years of experience as a real estate agent, they instantly have more knowledge than: every home inspector, every real estate appraiser, every real estate investor, every real estate attorney, every home buyer and every home seller. I don't know how they do it. They must be giving out some magical pills or secret potion at these classes!

You may also come across sellers that get hostile. Sellers can get hostile when you try to tell your client about some problem conditions and items that need to be repaired at the subject property. Don't let them ruffle your feathers. My first real estate attorney used to say that there are two things that you can't tell a man: One is: That his property is overpriced; The other is: ...*(Well, I've decided it wouldn't be appropriate for me to repeat the other item in this book. So I won't tell you. I'll just leave you in suspense.)*

Certified, Licensed Or Just A Dreamer?

You may have some State Certification or License requirements in your area. As a home inspector you'll come across Realtors and third party people from time to time who will say to you, *"Oh, I'm a certified home inspector too. I don't work for a home inspection office, but I've done many inspections for my clients."* They usually make a comment like that when they think they know better than you do in evaluating the condition of the subject property. I've found a problem with these people saying this to me. **The problem is that I have <u>never seen one of them</u> that have an actual Certification or License number issued to them by the State they work in. That can only lead to one conclusion. <u>They're not State certified or licensed home inspectors!!!!</u> Period.**

> *Some people have an amazing ability to kid themselves and rationalize things.*

Some people have an amazing ability to kid themselves and rationalize things. If you're a State Certified or Licensed home inspector, then you would have a State license number and documentation to prove it. This would verify that you have taken all the required classes; you have all the required fee-paid real estate inspection experience; and you have passed all the required State inspection examinations. There's no *if, ands* or *buts* about it! So the next time some Realtor or third party tells you that they know what they're talking about and you don't because they're a "home inspector," ask them these questions:

1. Did you take the required inspection classes and did you successfully pass the course examination?

2. Have you done the minimum number of **Fee-Paid Home Inspections** that have all of the requirements necessary to be considered as actual home inspection reports?

3. Did you pay the required application fees and did you take the State Certification home inspection examination and did you successfully pass the examination?

4. Do you have a State Certification or License number issued to you?

After they get finished answering *"No"* to all of the above questions, ask them a few more. This way they might realize that they don't know more than you do about home inspections. Ask them questions like:

5. What's the proper operating pressure of a steam heating system?

6.   What's the typical life expectancy of a domestic water heater?

7.   How do you evaluate a central air-conditioning system?

8.   Can you expect to see termites crawling around in the damaged wood?

9.   What does the National Electric Code say about the use of aluminum wiring in the house? About jumper cables for grounding?

10.   What happens to a septic system when it hasn't been maintained and cleaned properly? Is the dye test always accurate?

Now don't be arrogant or rude about it, or be a wise guy yourself, just politely make them realize **you're** the knowledgeable and professional home inspector. It's fine if any Realtors or other third party people offer you some advice and try to assist you on your inspection. There's nothing wrong with that, and often it'll help you out a lot. Just don't let anyone push you around or get an attitude with you. You don't want anyone to have an attitude like they've got all the answers and you're out to lunch or on cloud 9.

As I said in the beginning of the book, there's nothing wrong with State Certification and Licensing requirements. Basically they want you to take some classes and work under someone else's guidance until you get some experience under your belt. This has many benefits to it and it will really help you out in your beginning stages. You won't spend a lot of time *"spinning your wheels"* trying to learn the business.

Tell Your Client To Ignore The Hypocrites

I'm bothered by dishonest and/or ignorant Realtors and other third party people who inaccurately tell your client that everything is just fine and dandy about the house they're interested in buying. They may tell your client that nothing needs to be repaired or evaluated further, when in reality there are repairs needed. I'm bothered by this because they're such **hypocrites!** *(Of course they know better than you what's good for your client. You're just very well trained and experienced in doing home inspections, but somehow they know more than you do.)* Do you think they would make the same comments and statements if **THEY** were buying the house and not your client? *NOT A CHANCE!!!*   That's what makes them such hypocrites. I'll give you some imaginary examples that will make you laugh but you'll have to agree they do get the point across.

> *Do you think they would make the same comments and statements if they were buying the house and not your client? NOT A CHANCE!!!*

What if **they** were your client at the inspection and you said to them, *"The septic system passed the dye test. However, it's only a very limited test procedure because the septic system is underground and can't be seen. Also, the owner stated the system hasn't been pumped clean in two years. So you have to get a septic contractor to pump the system and do an internal inspection to make sure it's OK."*
Could you picture that third party person, *(if **they** were your client)*, turning to you and saying, *"Oh, well I don't need to get the septic pumped and internally inspected. The dye test is good enough for me. After all it only has to be pumped every 2-3 years so I've got another year before I have to spend any money on maintaining the system."*

What if you said to them, *"I tried to turn on the air-conditioning system by using the normal thermostat control on the wall. It won't turn on so you should have the system checked out by a licensed A/C contractor to determine what repairs are needed."*
Could you picture that third party person responding to that by saying, *"You're wrong Mr. Inspector, I don't need to get a contractor to check out the A/C system. The seller and the Realtor both told me that it works fine. They just can't seem to turn it on now. It must be a loose wire inside the thermostat. My husband can fix that himself after we move in."*

How about if you told them, *"You have a lead water main line in the house. You have to get an estimate to have a new water main line installed. Lead is a very serious health concern for adults and **especially** for children."*
Of course they'd answer this by saying, *"You're totally over exaggerating. My friend lives right down the block and he has four children. They have been living with a lead water main in their house for 14 years and not one person in his family has been sick a day in their life."*

Let's say you found asbestos and you informed them, *"There is some asbestos on the visible heating pipes in the lower level. The Environmental Protection Agency recommends that you have it professionally removed by an EPA licensed contractor for safety. It will not only be a health benefit but it will also help when you go to sell the house down the road to have the asbestos professionally removed."*

Of course they would answer this by saying, *"Oh no, I only have to wrap some duct tape around the asbestos. I don't need to hire EPA licensed contractors. That whole asbestos thing is just an over reaction by some alarmist people in the asbestos removal business who are trying to make money by scaring people."*

What if you found termite damaged wood and you said to them, *"There is some termite damage in the base of the garage door. I didn't see the termites crawling inside the wood but then again, it's very, very rare to actually see them in the damaged areas. It's highly recommended that you have the house treated by a licensed Pest Control Operator because the termites could be in nonvisible areas of the house."*

Upon hearing this, their response would be, *"As long as there are no active termites crawling around in the visible areas of the house or in the damaged wood, then I have no need to be concerned with getting the house treated by a PCO. My friend Ralph told me the only time a treatment is necessary is when you actually see the termites. Ralph knows what he's talking about; he teaches math at the university."*

> *He said, "They wheel the Bible out when it's good for them and then they wheel it back in when it's not good for them."*

Now these examples may seem a little bit carried away and they do have some humor in them. There is a point that I'm trying to make with these examples. **That is there's no way any third party who contradicts you on an inspection would have the same reaction and comments if they were the ones buying the house, as opposed to your client.** I had a teacher in one of my religion classes in high school who used a great example that fits this type of situation perfectly. He was talking about how some people hide behind the Bible with their actions and use it only when it's **convenient** and when it benefits them. He said, *"They wheel the Bible out when it's good for them and then they wheel it back in when it's not good for them."* People who do that are kidding themselves and are hypocrites by their actions.

It's no different with a third party that contradicts the facts during an inspection. They're simply being **hypocrites** when they contradict you. **They're hypocrites and contradicting you because it benefits *THEIR* wallet and not your *client's!*** All you're trying to do is tell your client the facts and realities about buying a house. It doesn't matter if they're buying this house, or the house down the block. **You just want your client to go into the deal with his/her eyes open.**

Don't over exaggerate things but at the same time don't let some ignorant, greedy or immoral seller, Realtor, or other

third party try to sugar coat anything either. **And if you ever have a real problem with a seller, a Realtor, or another third party contradicting what you say to your client just ask them,** *"What if the tables were turned and YOU were buying this house and my client told YOU not to worry about the asbestos,* (or whatever else you're discussing). *Would YOU take his word for it and not listen to the inspector that YOU hired who is the expert in his field?"* **Don't be surprised if they swallow their tongue or fumble for words to answer a question like that.**

Straight Talk

Not all people who dispute or contradict what you tell the client will be dishonest. They may just be ignorant about the topic their discussing. This will happen all the time throughout your life. Some people think they've got all the answers to everything! But what's funny about it, is that these kinds of people never have anything to prove that they know what they're talking about. There's an old saying that describes the difference between a Wise Man and a Fool: *"A Wise Man **Knows** He Doesn't Know Everything, But A Fool **Thinks** He Does."* So be a Wise Man in everything you do. Don't be a Wise Guy or a Fool in life.

> *There's an old saying that describes the difference between a Wise Man and a Fool: "A Wise Man Knows He Doesn't Know Everything, But A Fool Thinks He Does."*

When I bought my first real estate book and audio tape series I heard all of the negative comments, criticism and laughter from everyone! These negative comments and criticism came from family, friends and anyone else I mentioned the books and audio tapes to. I practically had to *hypnotize* my brother to buy that first house with me, because the critics were starting to worry him too. You'll probably hear some of the same negative comments and criticism from buying **this** book as well! Everyone gave me 10,000 reasons why I would fail with the real estate tapes and *"lose it all."* They all said it was a *"get rich quick scheme"* that was just a pipe dream. Not one person ever stopped to even think of just **one** reason why it would work!! I had enough guts, confidence and foresight to go ahead and listen to those tapes and read those books anyway, despite all the criticism around me. Thank God I did, because I proved to myself that I was right all along. Things did work out well, as I had anticipated.

That experience, and many others as well, have taught me a very good lesson that I'll never forget. **I've learned that you have to follow your own gut feelings and instincts with all of your decisions in life.** Often when you do something that's out of the norm of some people's standards, they criticize you for it. I think it's because some people have no foresight or ambition. You just have to ignore people like that, let their narrow minded and negative thinking limit **them** and not you.

You have to dare to be your own person and to be different if you feel strongly about something. Now don't get the wrong impression by this. I don't want you to think that you shouldn't listen to anyone in life and think that you've got all the answers yourself. **I'll listen to advice from anyone, but whether I follow that advice is my decision to make. I won't just take someone else's advice with blind faith, because free advice is often only worth what you paid for it.** What I'll do is take advice from anyone and then use my own gut feeling and judgment from my experiences to make a final decision. This way, if I find out later that the decision I made was a mistake, then I can't **blame** anyone else but myself for it. However, if I find out later the decision I made was correct, then I don't **owe** anyone else but myself for it.

I'll give you some actual examples from history that I read about. These examples are from a *Dale Carnegie* book with a chapter titled: *"Remember That No One Ever Kicks A Dead Dog."* That phrase refers to the fact that when you're kicked or criticized it's often done because it gives the kicker a feeling of importance. It often means that you're accomplishing something that's worthy of attention. Many people get satisfaction out of denouncing those who are better educated or more successful.

A former president of Yale University, Timothy Dwight, apparently took huge delight in denouncing a man who was running for President of the United States. This president of Yale warned that if this man were elected President of the United States, *"We may see our wives and daughters the victims of legal prostitution, soberly dishonored, speciously polluted; the outcasts of delicacy and virtue, the loathing of God and man."* Sounds almost like a denunciation of Adolph Hitler, doesn't it? But it wasn't. It was a denunciation of Thomas Jefferson, the author of the Declaration of Independence and the patron saint of democracy. Pretty incredible that someone, who was well educated at Yale, could have made a statement like that about Thomas Jefferson.

What American do you suppose was denounced as a *"hypocrite,"* *"an impostor,"* and as *"little better than a murderer?"* A newspaper cartoon depicted him on a guillotine with the big knife ready to cut off his head. Crowds jeered and hissed at him as he rode through the streets. Who was he? George Washington. Do you believe that! I think it's absolutely amazing how some people say things out of sheer ignorance without knowing the truth or the facts. We're all guilty of doing it at one time or another. Just remember those two stories from history so you don't do it too often.

So, the next time someone criticizes you or disputes something you're saying, don't get angry and argue back. Just look at where it's coming from and ask yourself:

◊   Is this person more successful than I am?

◊   Does this person have any background or experience in the topic they're disputing?

◊   Does this person really know what they're talking about, or do they just <u>think</u> they know what they're talking about?

If the person has nothing to prove that they know what they're talking about, then just ignore them because they're talking out of ignorance. You don't want to get aggravated over someone or something trivial.

Motivational Talk

I hope you're beginning to see the inner workings of the different aspects of Real Estate from a point of view that the vast majority of the public doesn't have a clue exists. **These are the realities of the real estate business.** I could tell you the truth or I could paint a perfect picture that you'd rather hear about instead, but then I'd be lying to you. I don't mean to be negative. I just want to open your eyes to some important information. You might want to inform your clients about some of this information when they call you for price quotes. You'll find that they appreciate it and will thank you because they didn't know or realize the realities of the real estate business discussed in this book.

> *Every business has aspects about it that the public is unaware of. This makes the uninformed public susceptible to being taken advantage of, due to their lack of awareness.*

If you find some of these things hard to believe, then don't take my word for it. Talk to other home inspectors and appraisers in your area that are honest and do good, quality work. See if they confirm or dispute what I'm telling you. It's no different from any other business. Every business has aspects about it that the public is unaware of. This makes the uninformed public susceptible to being taken advantage of, due to their lack of awareness. Now, I'm not trying to be a doomsayer by any means. I **strongly** believe that anyone, from any background can achieve anything they want in life. But I do have an awful lot of battle wounds and scars from trusting people too much. My battle wounds aren't all from my experiences in the home inspection and appraisal business, but are also from past experiences in my personal and business life. After learning my lessons, I got up every day and licked my wounds and kept moving forward. By the time I got into the home inspection and appraisal business I wizened up a lot.

It's OK to lose a few **battles**. You just want to make every effort you can to win the **war** - *and don't take any prisoners along the way!* Like the saying goes, you have to *Go For It* with everything you do! Don't sit around and **let** things happen, you have to go out and **make** things happen in your life. I started with nothing and made it on my own and I'm certainly no rocket scientist. Therefore, I firmly believe that anyone, no matter who you are or where you come from, can become successful. Some people have more obstacles and hurdles to overcome than others do because of the circumstances in their lives. But everyone can be successful if they have enough ambition, desire, and motivation. You can provide a real benefit to society in just about anything that you set your mind to doing. The only key is that you have to be willing to work very hard. You also have to make all of the sacrifices necessary to attain the level and success that you're looking for. If you live an honest life and leave this world a little better off then when you got here, then you can consider yourself a success.

I remember when my brother and I bought our first rental property. There was a perfect example of how anyone could become successful, despite their current situation or where they came from. The woman who sold us the house had two sons. One son had worked hard to move out of the low income area he was born in. This son then went on to medical school and became a successful dentist. He later married another dentist and was living a nice lifestyle with his wife and children. The other son, who grew up in the same house, was a total failure in life. This second son was living in his mother's house and was receiving money from welfare and other public assistance programs. He was too lazy to work and his mother actually had to **evict** him from her house to sell it! This son refused to move when his mother told her she was selling the house. Because of this, we had to wait an extra four months to buy the house until the seller could evict her own son. So here were two people, from the exact same home, where one became successful and happy and the other was a failure and miserable in life. It's all up to you. Your own ambition will make the difference. I had a friend that used to say, *"You live by the consequences of your own actions."*

> I read a quotation from Teddy Roosevelt that said "It's hard to fail, but it's worse never to have tried."

I read a quotation from Teddy Roosevelt that said *"It's hard to fail, but it's worse never to have tried."* Albert Einstein, the most profound thinker of his time, confessed that he was wrong **99%** of the time. I read that Thomas Edison tried over a **thousand** different ways before he got a light bulb to work. *Can you imagine the difference it would've made in history if those people just gave up on their efforts?* Here's another example of someone who was clearly one of the greatest leaders in history and how much he struggled and had to overcome in his life. In 1831 this man **failed** in business. In 1832 he was **defeated** in running for State Legislator. In 1833 he **failed** again in another business. In 1835 his fiancée **died**. In 1836 he had a **nervous breakdown**. In 1843 he ran for Congress and was **defeated**. In 1848 he tried again to run for Congress and was **defeated**. In 1855 he tried running for the Senate and he **lost**. In 1856 he ran for Vice President and he **lost**. In 1859 he ran for the Senate again and he was **defeated**. In 1860 this man, **Abraham Lincoln**, was elected the 16th President of the United States of America.

You're going to make mistakes in your personal and business life no matter how careful and honest you try to be. It's just a part of life that everyone experiences so don't let it get you down. Try to look at it in a different way by saying *"You don't make mistakes, you just learn lessons."* What you want to try to do is have more successes than failures. **Mistakes and failures aren't bad, they just give you more experience to make better decisions in the future.** Don't be like a cat that sits on a hot stove. It'll never sit on a *hot* stove again, but it'll never sit on a *cold* stove either. I met someone once that told me that *"Nothing is Bad, Everything Has A Purpose."* That's a very true statement. Look back at the majority of the mistakes you've made, and all the bad things that have happened to you over the years. At the time they happened, they seemed much worse then they do now. Often those mistakes or bad experiences led to something better or more profitable for you in the long run. **They say that things that happen to us aren't bad. It's the way that we react to them, that makes them seem bad.**

Take care of the important things in your personal and business life and the little things will take care of themselves. Don't spend all of your time worrying about minor problems. People spend 90% of their time harping on a problem and only 10% of their time trying to find a solution to the problem. Don't step over **dollars** to pick up **pennies** either. People spend most of their time worrying about saving pennies and cutting costs and only a small portion of their time concentrating on *increasing their income* with new opportunities.

> You may wonder whether the hard work and sacrifices will be worth it. If you do, just remember this old saying, "You don't pay a price for success, you pay a price for failure"

As I said in the beginning of the book, this isn't a *"get rich quick scheme."* It takes a lot of time, sacrifice and hard work to make a lot of money in any business. If it was easy to become rich, then everybody would be doing it! When you do become successful, you'll look back at all the hard work and sacrifices that you made and it will seem like a small price to have paid. It's like taking an exam in school. While you're studying for the exam it seems like such hard work. But when the test is over and you do well, then you look back on the studying you had to do and it doesn't seem so bad after all. You may wonder if the hard work and sacrifices will be worth it. If you do, then just remember these sayings, *"You don't pay a price for success, you pay a price for failure"* and *"Every dog has his day."*

Conclusion

I hope you feel we've covered every aspect of the home inspection business from A to Z. I hope now you realize what I meant when I said in the beginning of the book that I wasn't going to paint some fairy tale, rosy picture. Also, that I was going to tell it like it is without holding anything back. You might have found some of this information to be very surprising to learn. I certainly did when I started out in this business. I hope I've given you enough information so that you don't make the same mistakes that I did.

I can't think of anything we've missed. However, as I've said earlier, you have to keep feeding your mind with the new technologies and aspects of this business that are coming into the market. Don't get lazy now. Remember to keep feeding your mind with new information and training. The more knowledge you have, the more money you'll make. If you're knowledgeable <u>and</u> honest, then you'll really make some big money.

I want to take the time now to commend you on getting this far through the book. I've heard statistics that have shown that **less than 10%** of the people who purchase self-improvement books and audio CDs, ever even read the books and/or listen to the CDs one complete time. To me that's an amazing statistic. People spend their hard earned money on something, and then they get lazy or distracted and they don't follow through with it. They purchase books and CDs and read 1/2 of the book or listen to 1/2 of the CD, and then they put them on a shelf to collect dust.

I take my hat off to you. You have the ambition, willpower and the foresight to make an attempt at improving your own life, as well as the life of others. By getting this far in this book, you've shown that you're part of the minority within the majority. And that's a unique group of people who really want to have a positive impact on their own lives and the lives of the people around them. Abraham Lincoln said that *"A man who follows a crowd will never be followed by a crowd."* So be a leader in everything you do.

> *As I said in the beginning of this book: Please send me an email and let me know what you think of this book and any recommendations you might have for improvements or new products. I accept positive and negative comments since both help me to improve the next version of my products. I am always looking to improve my products and services and I greatly appreciate customer feedback and suggestions.*

As I said in the beginning of this book: Please send me an email and let me know what you think of this book and any recommendations you might have for improvements or new products. I accept positive and negative comments since both help me to improve the next version of my products. I am always looking to improve my products and services and I greatly appreciate customer feedback and suggestions.

> *I invite you to view our web site at www.nemmar.com to see the other real estate products we offer that will save you thousands of dollars when you buy, sell, or renovate a home. You can sign up online to receive our **free** real estate newsletter with articles and product updates that will definitely help you profit in real estate.*

I invite you to view our web site at www.nemmar.com to see the other real estate products we offer that will save you thousands of dollars when you buy, sell, or renovate a home. You can sign up online to receive our **free** real estate newsletter with articles and product updates that will definitely help you profit in real estate.

Thank you very much for the trust and confidence that you placed in me by purchasing this book. Due to your referrals our business keeps growing, and so will yours. Good luck, and I sincerely wish you the best in all your endeavors. I hope that someday I get a chance to meet you.

I'll tell you one last story before I go. I will never forget the time that I was following up with some of my clients to see how they were doing in the homes they purchased that I had inspected and/or appraised for them. One client bought a condo that I had inspected for him. His name was Dan Rones. When I called to find out how Dan was doing, his father answered the phone since he was now living in the condo. What his father told me on the phone left me absolutely stunned and I will never forget that conversation. Dan was 33 years old and just about to start law school when he had a brain aneurysm in his sleep and died. Due to the severe shock of losing his son, his father had a stroke the week after the funeral and became paralyzed in both legs and one arm.

In business and life we often get so caught up and in a way "trapped" in trying to earn a living and take care of the problems and tasks that confront us on a daily basis. It's often hard to take a step back and "smell the roses" that are all around us. *(I know I have a hard time doing it)*. The sad and tragic story of Dan Rones and his father brings to mind the old saying, *"I cried the blues 'cause I had **no shoes**. Until upon the street I saw a man that had **no feet**!"*

I heard another saying that's interesting - and true, *"If you look over your right shoulder, you'll always see someone **that you wish you were**. But if you look over your left shoulder, you'll thank God **you're who you are**."*

Life is short and precious. If you truly live an honest and moral life and leave this world a little better off then when you got here, then you can consider yourself a success. Success is *not* measured by how big your **wallet** is. Success is measured by how big your **heart** is. I will now leave you with a famous *Gaelic Blessing:*

> **May the road rise to meet you,**
> **May the wind be always at your back,**
> **May the sun shine warm upon your face,**
> **And the rains fall soft upon your fields,**
> **And until we meet again,**
> **May God hold you in the palm of His Hand.**

Additional Photo Pages
The Author

P 192. Top: Is this what they meant when they said:
"A man's home is his castle"

Bottom: That's me, the author, doing a home inspection
and appraisal for a client - *in 3 feet of snow!*

P 193. The style/design
of this house is:

Split Level

P 194. The style/design
of this house is:

Ranch

P 195. The style/design
of this house is:

Colonial

P 196.
The style/design of
this house is:

English Tudor

P 197.
The style/design of
this house is:

Contemporary

P 198.
The style/design of
this house is:

BIG!!

P 199. I encountered this on one of the foreclosure appraisals and inspections I did for a bank. The prior owner had spent his money on building an indoor basketball court, indoor swimming pool, sauna and Jacuzzi room, along with some other luxurious and expensive additions to the house and site. The problem was, that after he spent all this money he couldn't pay his mortgage payments and the bank had to foreclose on the property! I guess you could say that it wasn't "money well spent" *(or should I say it was "money spent down the well").*

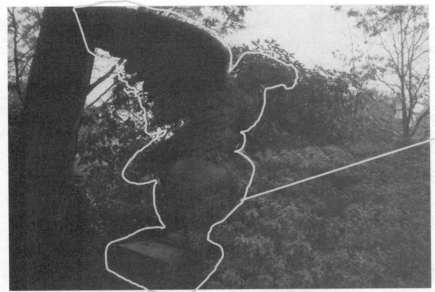

P 200. *Can you see what I outlined in this photo?* The picture is dark because it was overcast on the day of the appraisal so you might not be able to see the image clearly. It's a metal statue of a very large eagle standing on a globe with it's wings spread out wide (side view). The frontal view photo of this statue is below. This is one of the eagle statues from Grand Central Station in New York City. I don't know how the homeowner of the property got a hold of this statue, but I'm sure you won't find many of these during your inspections! This thing was about 20 feet high.

P 201. *No, it's not a junkyard or auto salvage site.* It's actually the yard of a home I had to appraise and inspect for a client. I doubt you'll ever encounter a situation like this one. However, if you do just remember to tell the client to get estimates to remove all of this junk before closing on the house.

P 202. *Let's see how well you paid attention when you read my book:*

Can you name all of the items you see in this picture of a heating system?

Can you describe what each part does and how to inspect it?

(OK, so I didn't talk about how to inspect a flower pot watering can in my book. I'll include that section in the next edition!)

Underneath the oil burner is a pan with cat litter in it. Sometimes you'll find this on an inspection. The cat litter is used to catch any oil that drips out of the burner.

P 203. *Instead of raining on his parade, it rained on this guy's heating system!* This is why you need caps and screens on the top of all flue stacks and chimneys. All of the water stains and rust you see on this flue pipe and heating system is due to the flue stack missing a cap above the roof line. When it rains or snows, the water runs down the flue stack and has rusted this heating system. Buying a cap for a flue stack is a lot less expensive than buying a new heating system.
(Some Realtors may try to tell you *"these old rusty furnaces just need a coat of paint and they're as good as new. Trust me, I've been a Realtor for 10 years and see these all the time."*)

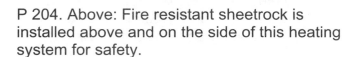

P 204. Above: Fire resistant sheetrock is installed above and on the side of this heating system for safety.

Below: Examples of circulator pumps installed on the return heating pipes for forced hot water heating systems.

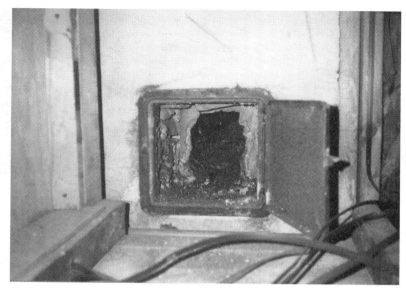

P 205. Above: Clean-out pit at the base of a flue stack. You can see how the sediment, debris and soot has built up inside the pit. These need to be cleaned out periodically to ensure proper operation of the flue stack and chimneys.

Right: This oil tank is located inside a basement and is in good condition. The scratches on the outside of the tank are just a cosmetic problem. The thin, copper oil supply pipe along the floor needs to be protected so it doesn't get damaged and then leak oil. Often these oil pipes will be covered with a layer of concrete for protection.

P 206. Above: The temperature setting dial and gas assembly unit for a water heater.
Above Right: The flexible gas pipe supplying the water heater should be replaced with approved black iron gas piping for safety.

P 207. Right: Have you ever heard the saying *"reach out and touch someone"?*
Well that's what these wires are trying to do! This open electrical junction box is a safety hazard in this attic. The exposed wires should be properly capped and the junction box sealed.

P 208. This house has a steel "i beam" for the main girder in the lower level area. This is a superior material than wood.

PVC piping, which is a plastic material, is seen in this photo. PVC has a white or black color with letter markings on the sides. The joints are slip-on sections that have an adhesive to hold them together. It's used only for drainage lines and is a noncorrosive, lightweight and easy to install piping material. Some local plumbing codes do not allow the use of PVC piping. The main drawback to PVC is that a poisonous carbon monoxide gas is created if there is a fire.

P 209. All crawl spaces and lower levels need a cement or plastic sheet covering over the dirt floor. This crawl space dirt floor will create moisture that can decay the wood and attract termites.

(Some Realtors may reply *"Oh, don't worry about that little old crawl space. Just leave it alone, after all what you can't see won't hurt ya!"*)

P 210. Above: This is what you'll see on most home inspections - a home filled with furniture and personal items.

Below: *So why did I include two photos of an empty home?* Because this is how you have to picture the interior of a house, condo or building in your mind when doing your inspections. Remember, you're inspecting the **building** - not the appeal and condition of the furniture and personal items!

P 211. Left: The tiles and the grout between the tiles is in excellent condition in this bathroom shower area. This will prevent water from getting behind the walls and causing problems.

P 212. Below: This house had an addition and roof put on that probably didn't get town hall approvals. At the very least, the contractor cut a lot of corners *(literally)* or the homeowner didn't want to spend much money on the work. In the attic you can still see the old roof structure and shingles. Most building codes would require this to be sealed or removed properly.

P 213. Above Left: An old brick chimney stack in an attic that was installed at an angle. You can see the water stains due to old or missing flashing around the chimney on the roof area.

Above Right: This attic stairway has a railing to help prevent someone falling down the steps when in the attic.

Right: The air ducts for this house A/C system are insulated for energy efficiency in the attic area.

P 214. Above and Right: Here are two gable vent fans in the attic area. These fans help to cool the attic in the summer months which helps keep the whole house cooler. The fan on the right is covered in plastic during the winter time. However, it's generally better to leave this fan uncovered even in the winter. This will allow the moisture in the warm air created by the heating system to escape.

Below: Another example of a vent tube/pipe discharging in the attic area. Vent tubes/pipes must discharge outside of the house to prevent moisture and humidity problems from building up in the attic area.

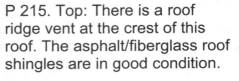

P 215. Top: There is a roof ridge vent at the crest of this roof. The asphalt/fiberglass roof shingles are in good condition.

Middle: This is an extreme example of granule loss and old age of an asphalt/fiberglass shingle roof. You don't need to be a home inspector to know that clearly this house needs a new roof!

Below: This is an extreme example of cupping, curling and old age of an asphalt/fiberglass shingle roof. You don't need to be a rocket scientist to know that these shingles need to be replaced.

(Don't let any seller's tell you *"The roof isn't leaking water so it doesn't need to be replaced. The roof shingles have looked like that for 8 years. If it ain't broke, don't fix it!)*

P 216. *What **don't** you see in this photograph of a roof?*
Answer: Footsteps on the snow covered roof. This is the home of a dishonest Realtor *(which isn't hard to find)* and Santa Claus passed by this house without stopping on his yearly sleigh ride since this Realtor *(along with many other Realtors)* was on Santa's "naughty" list.
In northern climates you may find wires along the bottom edges of the roof. These wires are used to heat the show and ice so it melts off the roof without causing an ice dam. An ice dam refers to ice and snow that has frozen at the base of the roof above the gutters. Since the ice is trapped by the gutter, it gradually melts and the water goes underneath the roof shingles. This leads to water problems in the house. Some homeowners don't like wires in their roof, so instead flashing can be installed under the bottom few rows of shingles to help prevent water leaks from ice dams.

P 217. In northern climates where there's snow, you might see snow guards along the bottom rows of slate shingles, like you have in this photo. Snow guards are small metal fins that stick up from the slates. Their purpose is to stop snow from falling off the roof so it doesn't drop to the ground with excessive force. Large amounts of falling snow could hurt someone or damage cars and other objects located below the roof line. *(Yes, they're even designed to protect dishonest Realtors from getting hit with snow.)*

P 218. Caps and screens are required at the top of all chimneys and flue stacks to prevent water, leaves, and small animals from getting in the house.

P 219. Some brick chimneys have a stucco covering for cosmetic reasons. The stucco on this chimney needs to be repaired. Falling sections of stucco are heavy and can hurt someone. Antennas attached to the chimney or roof need to be caulked to prevent openings that allow water into the house. If the antenna is no longer in use, then it should be removed. Antennas add stress to the roof and chimney when they move around in the wind which can create water leaks.

P 220. Here you have louver doors for a gable vent located in an attic area.

This is wooden clapboard siding. Wooden Clapboard siding can be installed vertically or horizontally. The majority of the time wooden clapboards are installed horizontally. Horizontal installations make the house appear lower and longer. Vertical installations make the house appear taller and are used more often on one-story houses. Check the condition of the siding to see if it needs to be painted or stained. Check for an excessive number of knots in the wood, or if there are any damaged or rotted sections.

P 221. Asbestos-Cement Shingles are made by combining asbestos fibers with Portland cement under high pressure. This siding is a very rigid material and you'll generally find some cracked and damaged shingles. It's not used for newer construction and is found on older houses. Often it can be found under aluminum or vinyl sidings.

Some areas have requirements that Asbestos-Cement Shingles must be removed by an EPA licensed contractor. This is due to the asbestos fiber content in the shingles. If they're removed improperly, the fibers can blow around in the wind and create health hazards.

(So don't let any Realtors tell you *"hey, no problem just rip it off the house yourself, people do it all the time."*)

P 222. The exterior of condominium units need to be evaluated just like the exterior of a house. Even though the exterior maintenance of condos is paid for by the common charges of the whole condo complex, you still need to determine if there are any problem conditions. Repair costs are assessed to all owners in the complex.

Right: This downspout section has disconnected and the rain water will drain next to the foundation. Underground drainage pipes should drain water at least 5 feet away from the house.

P 223. Top: Here's an example of a patio that needs repointing in between the slate sections. In winter time water gets in the cracks, then freezes and expands to buckle the patio slates. There is also a section of the flashing missing that needs to be installed at the base of the patio where it meets the siding.

Middle and Below: This patio is in good condition. All the sections are repointed and there are no uneven areas that would create a tripping hazard.

P 224. The support posts for this deck have metal brackets that keep the wood post from touching the concrete foundation. This will help prevent rot from water that settles on top of the concrete foundation area. It would have been better if the far post was centered correctly over the concrete foundation.

P 225. The large tree truck and roots are causing this fence to move out of alignment. This often happens with walkways, driveways, fences and walls. As tree roots grow, they have tremendous strength to create uneven settlement.

All fences need to be checked for sturdiness.

Often a homeowner or a neighbor will have a fence, wall, or shed installed and the contractor will just guess where the property line is. This can lead to an "encroachment" on someone else's property. *(Yes, the Realtor will always tell you the attorney, appraiser, and title company all check the survey for encroachments, so you don't have to check.* **Once again - the Realtor is wrong!)**

P 226. Sometimes you'll find a dry stone retaining wall as the boundary for the property line. Don't assume that walls, fences, sheds, and driveways are the correct indicators for the property line. Often a homeowner or contractor will just guess where the property is and they end up creating an encroachment.

Want to learn more about "encroachments" and a lot of other important stuff that affects the market value of a property? Then read my book *Real Estate Appraisal From A to Z*. You'll learn everything you need to know about how the pros estimate the market value of real estate.

P 227. This concrete block retaining wall has mostly collapsed due to the pressure exerted on it from the soil it was designed to retain. Retaining walls should be secured into the soil they are built to retain by the use of "dead men" and tie-rods. "Dead men" and "Tie-rods" refers to metal or wood beams used to anchor structures, like retaining walls, into the soil. They are installed in a "T" shape with the perpendicular end attached to the wall and the parallel end embedded in the soil to form the "T" shape.

P 229. Left: This garage door opener was installed by a contractor who didn't know what he was doing or else he didn't care. The lower portion of the wood beam was cut to make room for the garage door opener track. This wood beam is now weaker and may start to bend over time.

P 228. Above and Left: Exterior structures like storage sheds need to be checked using the same methods as the house inspection. You can see there is green mold and moss growing on the top right side of this shed roof. This is caused by tree branches blocking the sunlight for long periods. Mold and moss will decay the roof shingles.

P 230.
**Jack and Jill went up the hill,
to fetch a pail of water,**

But because the homeowner didn't
properly seal up the well,

**Jack fell down and broke his crown,
and Jill came tumbling after!**

So you see what happens when you
don't take my *Home Inspection From
A to Z* advice?
Jack and Jill ended up getting hurt
because of the negligence of the
property owner.

*(I wonder if Jack and Jill got an
"ambulance chaser" attorney to file a
lawsuit against the homeowner?)*

All unused wells must be properly
sealed for safety. This well has a
sealed cover over it.

P 231.
There are two kinds of houses: Houses that **have** termites, and Houses that **will have** termites. That's a fact. All houses will get termite damage of some sort eventually. Sometimes builders will install a termite shield along the top of the foundation wall *(as seen in the bottom two photos)*. Termite shields are similar to the cap plate used at the top of concrete block walls *(as seen in the top photo)*. A termite shield is a small metal guard. However, these shields do not prevent termites. The only benefit from them is that they might deter termites or make it a little more difficult for them to reach the wood.

More Nemmar Products

Energy Saving Home Improvements From A to Z ™

Don't let your dream house be a money pit in disguise! Our **5-star rated** book that teaches you how to **save** thousands of dollars **and** help the environment by making minor improvements to your home. You'll learn how to **lower your utility bills by 50%**, live more comfortably, and help the environment. Includes many photographs with detailed descriptions.

Home Inspection Business From A to Z ™

The REAL FACTS the other books don't tell you! Our **number one** selling home inspection book. This is **definitely** the best home inspection book on the market and has been called the "Bible" of the inspection industry. *Every* aspect of home inspections is covered with precise steps to follow. Includes many photographs with detailed descriptions.

Real Estate Appraisal From A to Z ™

The REAL FACTS the other books don't tell you! Our **number one** selling appraisal book. This is **definitely** the best real estate appraisal book on the market. *Every* aspect of real estate appraising is covered with precise steps to follow. Includes sample professional appraisal reports and many photographs with detailed descriptions.

Real Estate From A to Z ™

Don't let your dream house be a nightmare in disguise! You'll learn information the professionals use to inspect, appraise, invest, and renovate real estate. This book covers every aspect of Real Estate from A to Z and contains abbreviated versions of our three **5-star rated** books: *Home Inspection Business, Real Estate Appraisal, and Energy Saving Home Improvement From A to Z.*

DVD's - Home Inspection From A to Z ™

Our **5 star rated** DVD's have two hours of video plus you get the 80 page *HIB **DVD** Companion Guidebook!*
OPERATING SYSTEMS DVD topics including: heating systems, air-conditioning, water heaters, plumbing, well water system, septic system, electrical system, gas service, and auxiliary systems. Health Concerns topics including: asbestos insulation, radon gas, and water testing.
INTERIOR and EXTERIOR DVD topics including: roof, chimneys, siding, eaves, gutters, drainage and grading, windows, walkways, entrances and porches, driveways, walls and fences, patios and terraces, decks, swimming pools, exterior structures, wood destroying insects, garage, kitchen, bathrooms, floors and stairs, walls and ceilings, windows and doors, fireplaces, attics, ventilation, insulation, basement/lower level, and water penetration.

Home Buyer's Survival Kit ™

Don't buy, sell, or renovate your home without this! Includes: Four of our **top selling** books – *Real Estate Home Inspection Checklist From A to Z, Energy Saving Home Improvements From A to Z, Home Inspection Business From A to Z,* and *Real Estate Appraisal From A to Z.* Plus, you get both of our *Home Inspection From A to Z –* **DVD's.** As an added bonus you also get the 80 page *HIB **DVD** Companion Guidebook.*

Narrative Report Generator and On-Site Checklist

The report generator and checklist the others don't have! CD-Rom with the ***best*** Narrative Report Generator and On-Site Checklist on the market! These will enable you to *easily* do 30 page narrative, professional home inspection reports to send to your clients. These will assist you at the inspection site to be sure that you properly evaluate the subject property. Designed to walk you through the entire inspection process with very detailed instructions on how to properly evaluate the condition and status of **all** aspects of a home in a fool-proof, step-by-step system and create professional, narrative reports.

Appraiser and Home Inspector "A to Z Coach" School Training ™

Personal One-to-One Training with an "A to Z Coach" where you are the only student! Your training is personalized to meet your specific requirements and needs. Your questions are answered to make sure you learn everything you need to know about real estate - from Asbestos to Zoning. No crowded classrooms filled with students - unlike other real estate training schools. You'll learn how to become a highly paid Real Estate Appraiser or Home Inspector from top experts with many years of experience in the business!
Telephone and Email Training with an "A to Z Coach" via telephone and email. Our training school meets and exceeds the standards of all the leading home inspection and appraisal organizations. Regardless of where you live, you can enroll as a student in Nemmar Real Estate Training's "A to Z Coach" School.

Just some of our books, CD's, DVD's and much more!

Email info@nemmar.com for prices.

Visit us at www.nemmar.com

**Everything You Need To Know About Real Estate
From Asbestos to Zoning** ™

Real Estate Home Inspection Checklist From A to Z ™

Energy Saving Home Improvements From A to Z ™

Home Inspection Business From A to Z ™

Real Estate Appraisal From A to Z ™

Real Estate From A to Z ™

Nemmar Real Estate Training

info@nemmar.com

www.nemmar.com

Real Estate Terminology Glossary

A.L.T.A Title Policy: (American Land Title Association) A type of title insurance policy issued by title insurance companies which expands the risks normally insured against under the standard type policy. It is a lender's policy, but available to any one willing to pay for the extra coverage.

Abandonment: To release a claim, as a Declaration of Abandonment when a property has been homesteaded.

Abatement of Nuisance: Extinction or termination of a nuisance.

Abstract: A brief summary.

Abstract of Judgment: A condensation of the essential provisions of a court judgment.

Abstract of Title: A summary or digest of the conveyances, transfers, and any other facts relied upon as evidence of title, together with any other elements of record which may impair the title.

Abstraction: A method of valuing land. The indicated value of the improvement is deducted from the sale price.

Acceleration Clause: Clause in trust deed or mortgage giving lender the right to call all sums owing him to be immediately due and payable upon the happening of certain event.

Acceptance: When the seller or agent's principal agrees to the terms of the agreement of sale and approves the negotiation on the part of the agent and acknowledges receipt of the deposit in subscribing to the agreement of sale, that act is termed an acceptance.

Access Right: The right of an owner to have ingress and egress to and from his property.

Accession: Acquire title by having property added to your property.

Accretion: An addition to land from natural causes. Example: From the gradual action of the ocean or river waters.

Accrued: Accumulated up to this point in time. Accrued interest, accrued depreciation.

Accrued Depreciation: The difference between the cost of replacement new as of the date of the appraisal and the present appraised value.

Acknowledgment: A formal declaration before a duly authorized officer by a person who has executed an instrument that such execution is his act and deed.

Acquisition: The act or process by which a person procures property.

Acre: A measure of land equaling 4,840 square yards, or 43,560 square feet, or a tract about 208.71 feet square.

Actual Notice: Knowledge of the existence of a thing or fact.

Administrator: A person appointed by the probate court to administer the estate of a person deceased.

Adjusted Book Value: Cost of acquisition minus depreciation (if allowed) plus capital improvements. Used when figuring profit for income tax.

Adjusted selling price: Selling price minus expenses of sale. Used when figuring profit for income tax.

Ad Valorem: According to valuation.

Adverse Possession: The open and notorious possession and occupancy under an evident claim or right, in denial or opposition to the title of another claimant.

Affiant: A person who makes a sworn or affirmed statement.

Affidavit: A statement or declaration reduced to writing, sworn to or affirmed before some officer who has authority to administer an oath or affirmation.

Affirm: To confirm, to aver, to ratify, to verify.

Affirmation: A solemn Declaration made by a person who objects to taking an oath.

A.F.L.B.: Accredited Farm and Land Broker.

Agency: The relationship between principal and agent which arises out of the contract, either expressed or implied, written or oral, wherein the agent is employed by the principal to do certain acts dealing with a third party.

Agreement for Purchase and Sale: A land contract.

Agreement of Sale: A written agreement or contract between seller and purchaser in which they reach a meeting of minds on the terms and conditions of the sale.

Agreement to Convey: A land Contract.

Alienation: The transferring of property to another, the transfer of property and possession of lands, or other things, from one person to another.

Alienation Clause: Clause in a loan document providing for full payment if the property is sold.

Aluuvion; (Alluvium): Soil deposited by accretion. Increase of earth on shore or bank of a river.

Amenities: Satisfaction of enjoyable living to be derived from a home; conditions of agreeable living or a beneficial influence arising from the location or improvements.

Amortization: The liquidation of a financial obligation on an installment basis; also, recovery, over a period, of cost or value.

Amortized Loan: A loan that is completely paid off, interest and principal, by a series of regular payments that are equal or nearly equal. Also called a level payments loan.

Anticipation, Principle of: Affirms that value is created by anticipated benefits to be derived in the future.

Appraisal: An opinion of value of property.

Appraiser: One qualified by education, training and experience who is hired to estimate the value of real and personal property based on experience, judgment, facts, and use of formal appraisal processes.

Appurtenance: Something annexed to another thing, which may be transferred incident to it. That which belongs to other things, as a barn, dwelling, garage, or orchard is incident to the land to which it is attached.

Assemblage: Putting together two or more parcels to increase the total value.

Assessed Value: A value placed upon property by a public officer or board, as a basis for taxation.

Assessment: The valuation of property for the purpose of levying a tax or the amount of the tax levied.

Assessor: The official who has the responsibility of determining assessed values.

Assets: Everything of value, both real and personal property, owned by a business.

Assignment: A transfer or making over to another of the whole of any property, real or personal, in possession or in action, or of any estate or right therein.

Assignor: One who assigns or transfers property.

Assigns; Assignees: Those to whom property shall have been transferred.

Assumption Agreement: An undertaking or adoption of a debt or obligation primarily resting upon another person.

Assumption Fee: A lender's charge for changing over and processing new records for a new owner who is assuming an existing loan.

Assumption of Mortgage: The taking of title to property by a grantee, wherein he assumes liability for payment of an existing note secured by a mortgage or deed of trust against the property, becoming a co-guarantor for the payment of a mortgage or deed of trust note.

Attachment: Seizure of property by court order, usually done to have it available in event a judgment is obtained in a pending suit.

Attest: To affirm to be true or genuine; an official act establishing authenticity.

Attorney-In-Fact: One who is authorized to perform acts for another under a power of attorney; power of attorney may be limited to specific act or acts, or be general.

Avulsion: The sudden tearing away or removal of land by action of water flowing over or through it.

Bailment: The delivery of goods or money to another in trust.

Balloon Payment: Where the final installment payment on a note is greater than the preceding installment payments and it pays the note in full, such final installment is termed a balloon payment.

Band of Investment: A method of computing the capitalization rate by considering the return demanded by the holders of various loans, and the owner.

Base and Meridian: Imaginary lines used by surveyors to find and describe the location of private or public lands.

Bearing Wall or Partition: A wall or partition supporting any vertical load in addition to its own weight.

Bench Mark: A location indicated in a durable market by surveyors.

Beneficiary: 1.) One entitled to the benefit of a trust; 2.) One who receives profit from an estate, the title which is vested in a trustee; 3.) The lender on the security of a note and deed of trust.

Bequeath: To give or hand down personal property by will; to leave by will.

Bequest: That personal property which is given by the terms of a will.

Betterment: An improvement upon property which increases the property value and is considered as a capital asset, as distinguished from repairs or replacements where the original character or cost is unchanged.

Bilateral Contract: A contract in which both parties agree to perform certain acts.

Bill of Sale: A written instrument given to pass title of personal property from vendor to vendee.

Binder: A notation of coverage on an insurance policy, issued by an agent, and given to the insured prior to issuing of the policy.

Blanket Encumbrance: An encumbrance that covers more than one parcel of property.

Blanket Mortgage: A single mortgage that covers more than one piece of real estate.

Blighted Area: A declining area in which real property values are seriously affected by destructive economic forces, such as encroaching inharmonious property usages, infiltration of lower social and economic classes of in habitants, and/or rapidly depreciating buildings.

Board Foot: A unit of measurement of lumber,, one foot wide, one foot long, one inch thick; 144 cubic inches.

Bona Fide: In good faith; without fraud.

Book Depreciation: The depreciation shown on the accounting books of the owner. Used for income tax calculation.

Book Value: Value of the property as shown on the accounting books of the owner.

Boot: Profit gained in exchange of properties on which income tax is not deferred. May be anything of value, including mortgage relief.

Bounds: Boundaries in a metes and bounds description.

Breach: The breaking of a law, or failure of duty, either by omission or commission.

B.T.U.: British Thermal Unit. The quantity of heat required to raise the temperature of one pound of water one degree Fahrenheit.

Building Line: A line, set by law, a certain distance from the street line in front of which an owner cannot build on his lot. (Setback)

Building Residual: A method of appraising. The value of land is subtracted from the value of the property leaving the value of the building.

Bulk Sale: The sale of merchandise in bulk rather than in the ordinary course of business.

Bundle of Rights: Beneficial interests or rights.

Bylaws: The rules of an organization such as a homeowners association.

C.C. & R.s: Covenants, Conditions and Restrictions affecting the use of a property.

Capacity: Having legal competence to sign binding contracts.

Capital: Assets of a permanent nature used in the production of an income, such as: land, buildings, machinery, equipment, etc.

Capital Gain: Profit from the sale of property.

Capital Loss. Loss from the sale of property.

Capitalization: In appraising, determining value of property by considering net income and percentage or reasonable return on investment.

Capitalization Rate; Cap Rate: Calculated by dividing the net operating income by the offering price of the property. The lower the rate, the higher the selling price…and the higher the rate, the lower the selling price. Selling Price = Net Operating Income/Cap Rate Example: If the net operating income of a apartment building is $100,000 and the Cap Rate is 10%, the selling price would be $1,000,000. ($100,000/10%). Lowering the Cap Rate to 8% increases the selling price to $1,250,000 ($100,000/8%). Raising it to 12% reduces the selling price to $833,333 ($100,000/12%). It answers the question, "How much am I willing to pay for this cash flow?"

Cash Flow: Cash left at the end of a period of time (usually a year) from the operation of income property or a business. Do not subtract depreciation when computing cash flow.

Caveat Emptor: "Let the buyer beware". The buyer must research purchase and buy at her own risk.

Certificate of Reasonable Value (CRV); The Veterans Administration appraisal commitment of property value.

Certificate of Title: A certification of the ownership of land. The first step to obtaining title insurance.

C.C.I.M.: Certified Commercial Investment Member.

Chain of Title: A history of conveyances and encumbrances affecting the title from the time the original patent was granted, or as far back as records are available.

Change, Principle of: Holds that it is the future, not the past, which is of prime importance in estimating value.

Chattel: Personal property.

Chattel Mortgage: A personal property mortgage - Security Agreement.

Chattels Real: An estate related to real estate, such as a lease on real property.

Chattels: Goods or every species of property movable or immovable that are not real property.

Chose in Action: A personal right recoverable by a court suit.

Closing Statement: The final accounting of a sale given by escrow to the buyer and seller.

Cloud On The Title: Any conditions revealed by a title search that affect the title to property; usually relatively unimportant items that can be removed with a quitclaim deed or court action.

Code: A group of laws.

Collateral: The property subject to the security interest.

Collateral Security: A separate obligation attached to contract to guarantee its performance; the transfer of property or of other contracts, or valuables, to insure the performance of a principal agreement.

Collusion: An agreement between two or more persons to defraud another of his rights by the forms of law, or to obtain an object forbidden by law.

Color Of Title: That which appears to be good title, but which is not title in fact.

Commercial Paper: Bills of exchange used in commercial trade.

Commercial Acre: A term applied to the remainder of an acre of newly subdivided land after the area devoted to streets, sidewalks and curbs has been deducted from the acre.

Commingling: Mixing client's money or property with the agent's.

Commitment: A Pledge, or a promise, or firm agreement.

Common Law: The body of law that grew from customs and practices developed and used in England "since the memory of man runneth not to the contrary."

Community: A part of a metropolitan area that has a number of neighborhoods that have tendency toward common interests and problems.

Community Apartment Project: A subdivision where the buyer receives a deed to the whole property and the right to use an apartment. Each owner is a tenant in common.

Community Property: Property accumulated through joint efforts of husband and wife.

Compaction: Whenever extra soil is added to a lot to fill in low places or to raise the level of the lot, the added soil is often too loose and soft to sustain the weight of the buildings. Therefore, it is necessary to compact the added soil so that it will carry the weight without the danger of their tilting, settling or cracking.

Comparable Sales: Property sales that have similar characteristics as the subject property and are used for analysis in the appraisal process.

Comparison Approach: Appraising by comparing recent sales prices of similar properties.

Compound Interest: Interest paid on original principal and also on the accrued and unpaid interest that has accumulated.

Condemnation: The act of taking private property for public use by a political subdivision; declaration that a structure is unfit for use.

Condition: Provision that the transfer of property depends upon another uncertain event.

Condition Precedent: A condition that must be fulfilled before title can be transferred.

Condition Subsequent: A condition that provides that if the owner fails to do something his title may be defeated and he may lose the property.

Conditional Commitment: A commitment of a definite loan amount for some future unknown purchaser of satisfactory credit standing.

Conditional Sale Contract: A contract for the sale of property stating that delivery is to be made to the buyer, title to remain vested in the seller until the conditions of the contract have been fulfilled.

Condominium: Individual fee ownership of units in a multi-family structure, combined with joint ownership of common areas of the structure and the land.

Confirmation of Sale: A court approval of the sale of property by an executor, administrator, guardian or conservator.

Consideration: Anything of value given to induce entering into a contract; it may be money, personal services, or even love and affection.

Construction Loans: Loans made for the construction of homes or buildings disbursed to the builder during construction and after periodic inspections.

Constructive Eviction: A disturbance of a tenant's possession by the landlord.

Contiguous: Touching at any point. Contiguous lots.

Contingent: Dependent upon an uncertain future event.

Contour: The surface configuration of land.

Contract: An agreement to do or not to do a certain thing.

Contribution, Principle of: Appraising principle used when considering proposed improvements.

Conventional Loan: A loan made without government backing.

Conversion: Change from one character or use to another.

Conveyance: Transfer of the title of land from one to another. Denotes an instrument that carries from person to another an interest in land.

Corner Influence: The added value of a corner lot.

Correlation: To bring the indicated values developed by the three approaches used in the appraisal process into mutual relationship with each other.

Cost Approach: An analysis in which a value estimate of a property is derived by estimating the replacement cost of the improvements, deducting there from the estimated accrued depreciation, then adding the market value of the land.

Covenant: Agreements written into deeds and other instruments promising performance or nonperformance of certain acts or stipulating certain uses or non-uses of the property.

C.P.M.: Certified Property Manager.

C.R.E: Counselor of Real Estate – Member of the American Society of R.E. Counselors.

Cul-De-Sac: Street open at one end only.

Curable Depreciation: Items of physical and functional obsolescence, which are customarily repaired or replaced by a prudent property owner.

Curtesy: The right, which a husband has in a wife's estate at her death.

Damages: The indemnity recoverable by a person who has sustained an injury, either in his person, property, or relative rights, through the act or default of another.

Dealer Property: Property held for sale to customers. Profit is considered ordinary income for income tax.

Debtor: The party who "owns" the property that is subject to the security interest. Sometimes known as the mortgagor or pledgor, etc.

Deciduous Trees: Lose leaves in autumn and winter.

Declaration of Abandonment: Document recorded to terminate a homestead.

Declaration of Homestead: Document recorded to establish a homestead to protect the owner against judgment liens.

Declaration of Restrictions: Recorded list of restrictions imposed on a subdivision by a subdivider.

Declining Balance Depreciation: Method of computing depreciation for income tax purposes.

Deed: Written instrument that, when properly executed and delivered, conveys title.

Deed of Trust: Document by which naked, legal title is transferred to a trustee as security for a loan.

Default: Failure to fulfill a duty or promise or to discharge an obligation; omission or failure to perform any act.

Defeasance Clause: The clause in a mortgage that gives the mortgagor the right to redeem his property upon the payment of his obligations to the mortgagee.

Deferred Maintenance: Existing buy unfulfilled requirements for repairs and rehabilitation.

Deficiency Judgment: A judgment given when the security pledge for a loan does not satisfy the debt upon its default.

Demand: Desire for property. One of four elements that create value.

Demise: Transfer to another of an estate for years, for life, or at will.

Deposit Receipt: Document used when accepting earnest money to bind an offer. Basic contract between buyer and seller.

Depreciation: Loss of value in real property brought about by age, physical deterioration or functional or economic obsolescence. Broadly, a loss in value from any cause.

Descent: Acquiring property by inheritance when the deceased dies intestate.

Desist and Refrain Order: An order directing a person to desist and refrain from committing an act in violation of the law.

Devise: A gift of real property by will.

Devisee: one who receive real property by will.

Devisor: One who leaves real property by will.

Directional Growth: Direction toward which the residential section of a city is destined or determined to grow.

Discount: An amount deducted from the face amount of a loan.

Discount Points: Prepaid interest demanded by lender when loan is negotiated. A premium paid for the privilege of borrowing at the stated interest rate.

Documentary Transfer Tax: Tax collected when a deed is recorded. Stamps are affixed to the deed.

Dominant Tenement: The land that is benefited by an easement appurtenant.

Dower: The right that a wife has in her husband's estate at his death.

Earnest Money: Deposit accompanying an offer.

Easement: Created by grant or agreement for a specific purpose, an easement is the right, privilege or interest that one party has in the land of another.

Economic Life: The period over which a property will yield a return on the investment, over and above the economic or ground rent due to land.

Economic Obsolescence: A loss in value due to factors outside the subject property, but adversely affecting the value of the property.

Economic Rent: The reasonable rental expectancy if the property were available for renting at the time of it valuation.

Effective age of Improvement: The number of years of age that is indicated by the condition of the structure.

Effective Gross income: The maximum rent from income property minus vacancies.

Effective Interest Rate: Percentage of interest that is actually being paid by the borrower for the use of the money.

Egress: Means of leaving/exiting the property.

Emblements: Growing annual crops. The right of a tenant farmer to harvest his crop after his lease expires.

Eminent Domain: The right of government to acquire property for necessary public use by condemnation; the owner must be fairly compensated.

Encroachment: Trespass: the building of a structure or construction of any improvements partly or wholly on the property of another.

Encumbrance: Anything that affects or limits the fee simple title to property, such as mortgages, easements or restrictions of any kind. Liens are special encumbrances that make the property security for the payment of a debt or obligation, such as mortgages and taxes.

Endorsement: The signature of the payee on the back of a negotiable instrument.

Equitable Title: The title held by a vendee under a land contract.

Equity: The interest or value that an owner has in real estate over and above any liens.

Equity Redemption: The right to redeem property during the foreclosure period.

Erosion. The wearing away of land by the action of water, wind or glacial ice.

Escalation: The right reserved by the lender to increase the amount of the payments and/or interest upon the happening of a certain event.

Escheat: The reverting of property to the state when heirs capable of inheriting are lacking.

Escrow: The deposit of instruments and funds with instructions to a third neutral party to carry out the provisions of an agreement or contract.

Estate: As applied to real estate, the term signifies the quantity of interest, share, right and equity, of which riches or fortune may consist, in real property.

Estate at Sufferance: Estate of a tenant after his right to possess the property has ended.

Estate for Life: A freehold estate, not of inheritance, but which is held by the tenant for his own life or the life or lives of one or more other persons.

Estate for Years: An interest in lands by virtue of a contract for the possession of them for a definite and limited period of time. A lease may be said to be an estate for years.

Estate in Fee: A fee estate. The greatest degree of ownership of real property.

Estate of will: The occupation of lands and tenements by a tenant for an indefinite period, terminable by one or both parties.

Estimated Remaining Life: Period of time (years) it take for the improvements to become valueless.

Estoppel: Doctrine that bars one from asserting rights that are inconsistent with a previous position or representation.

El Al: And others.

Et Ux: And wife.

Eviction: Putting out a tenant when his right to possess the property has ended.

Exception: Withholding part of a property when it is conveyed.

Exclusive Agency Listing: Written instrument giving one agent the right to sell property for a specified time, but reserving the right of the owner to sell the property himself without the payment of a commission.

Exclusive Right to Sell Listing: Written agreement between owner and agent giving agent the right to collect a commission if the property is sold by anyone during the term of his agreement.

Exculpatory Clause: A clause that releases the landlord from liability due to injuries.

Execute: To complete, to make, to perform, to do, to follow out; to execute a contract is to perform the contract to follow out to the end, to complete.

Executed Contract: Where both parties have completely performed.

Executor: Person named in a will to carry out its provisions as to the disposition of the estate of a person deceased.

Extended Coverage: A broad form title insurance policy that protects the owner against additional risks.

Federal Housing Administration: Federal agency that insures lenders making F.H.A. loans.

Federal Notional Mortgage Association: "Fanny Mae". A secondary money market that buys and sells existing loans to stabilize the money market.

Fee: An estate of inheritance in real property.

Fee Simple: In modern estates, the terms "fee" and "fee simple" are substantially synonymous.

Fee Simple Absolute: Fee simple ownership with no qualifications or limitations.

Fee Simple Defeasible: Fee simple ownership with a condition that, if broken, could result in loss of title to the property.

Fiduciary: A person in a position of trust and confidence, as between principal and broker.

Financing Statement: The instrument that is filed in a loan on personal property in order to give public notice of the security interest and thereby protect the interest of the secured parties in the collateral.

Finder's Fee: Fee paid to a person for information.

Fixtures: Items attached to the land or improvements, that usually cannot be removed without agreement, and, therefore, they become real property; plumbing fixtures, items built into the property, etc.

Foreclosure: Procedure whereby property pledged as security for a debt is sold to pay the debt in event of default in payments or terms.

Forfeiture: Loss of money or anything of value due to failure to perform.

Freehold Estate: A fee simple or life estate.

Frontage: Land bordering a street.

Front Foot: Property measurement for sale or valuation purposes; the property measured by the front foot on its street line – each front foot extending the depth of the lot.

Functional Obsolescence: A loss of value due to adverse factors from within the structure that affect the utility of the structure.

Future Benefits: The anticipated benefits the present owner will receive from his property in the future.

General Lien: A lien that affects all property of a person.

General Partnership: Partnership where all partners can participate in management and liability.

Gift Deed: A deed for which the consideration is love and affection and where there is no material consideration.

Graduated Lease: Lease that provides for a varying rental rate.

Grant: Technical term made use of in deeds of conveyances of lands to impart a transfer.

Grant Deed: Deed conveying the title. It has two implied warranties.

Grantee: The purchaser; a person to whom a grant is made.

Granting Clause: The action clause of a grant deed.

Grantor: Seller of property; one who signs a deed.

G.R.I.: Graduate, Realtors Institute.

Gross Income: Total income before any expenses are deducted

Gross Rent Multiplier: A figure, which, times the gross income of a property, produces an estimate of value of the property.

Ground Lease: An Agreement for the use of the land only, sometimes secured by improvements placed on the land by the user.

Ground Rent: Earnings of improved property credited to earnings of the ground itself after allowance is made for earnings of improvements, often termed economic rent.

Guarantee of Title: Opinion of title condition backed by a fund to compensate in case of negligence. A forerunner of title insurance.

Hard Money Loan: the borrower receives actual cash and not just credit.

Hereditaments: Anything capable of being inherited.

Highest & Best Use: Appraisal phrase meaning that use which, at the time of an appraisal, is most likely to produce the greatest net return to the land and/or buildings over a given period of time.

Holder in Due Course: One who has taken a note, check or bill of exchange in due course: 1. Before it was overdue; 2. In good faith and for value; 3. Without knowledge that is has been previously dishonored and without notice of any defect at the time it was negotiated to him.

Holographic Will: Will entirely handwritten and signed by the testator.

Homestead: Home upon which the owner or owners have recorded a Declaration of Homestead, protects home against judgments up to specified amounts.

Hypothecate: To give a thing as security without the necessity of giving up possession of it.

Implied: Presumed or inferred rather than expressed.

Impounds: A trust –type account established by lenders for the accumulation of funds to meet taxes, FHA mortgage insurance premiums, and/or future insurance policy premiums required to protect the lenders security. Impounds are usually collected with the monthly mortgage payments.

Improvements: Things built on land that becomes a part of the real property.

Income Approach: One of the three methods in the appraisal process; an analysis in which the estimated income from the subject residence is used as a basis for estimating value.

Income property: Property that produces rent.

Increment: An increase. Most frequently used to refer to the increase of value of land that accompanies population growth and increasing wealth in the community. The term unearned increment is used in this connection since values Are supposed to have increased without effort on the part of the owner.

Ingress: Means of entering property.

Inherit: To acquire property by will or succession.

Injunction: A writ or order issued under the seal of a court to restrain one or more parties to a suit or proceeding from doing an act that is deemed to be inequitable or unjust in regard to the rights of some other party or parties in the suit or proceeding.

Installment Note: Note that provides that payments of a certain sum or amount be paid on the dates specified in the instrument.

Installment Sales Contract: A land contract.

Instrument: Written legal document created to effect the rights of the parties.

Intangible Value: An asset that is not physical. Goodwill, patent rights, etc.

Interest Rate: The percentage of a sum of money charged for its use.

Intestate: A person who dies having made no will.

Intestate Succession: Inheriting property when the deceased had no will or a defective will.

Inventory: A list of the stock and fixtures of a business.

Inverse Condemnation: When the government damages property and the owner sues the government for damages.

Involuntary Conveyance: Transfer of title without the owner's permission.

Involuntary Lien: A lien imposed against property without consent of an owner: taxes, special assessments, federal income tax liens, etc.

Irrevocable: Incapable of being recalled or revoked: unchangeable.

Irrigation Districts: Quasi-political districts created under special laws to provide for water services to property owners in the district: an operation governed to a great extent by law.

Joint And Several Note: A note signed by two or more persons in which they are liable jointly and individually for the full amount of the loan.

Joint Note: Note signed by two or more persons who each have liability for payment of part of the loan.

Joint Tenancy: Joint ownership by two or more persons with right of survivorship: all joint tenants own equal interest and have equal rights in the property.

Joint Venture: A syndicate formed for a single purpose.

Judgment: The final determination of a court of competent jurisdiction of a matter presented to it: money judgments provide for the payment of claims presented to the court, or are awarded as damages, etc.

Junior Lien: Lien that does not have first priority.

Junior Trust Deed: Trust deed that does not have first priority.

Jurisdiction: The authority by which judicial officers take cognizance of and decide causes: the power to hear and determine a cause: the right and power that a judicial officer has to enter upon the inquiry.

Key Lot: Lot that has adjoining on its side the rear of another lot.

Laches: Delay or negligence in asserting one's legal rights.

Land Contract: A contract ordinarily used in connection with the sale of a property in cases where the seller does not wish to convey title until all or a certain part of the purchase price is paid by the buyer, often used when property is sold on small down payment.

Land Residual: A method of appraising. The value of the building is subtracted from the value of the property, leaving the value of the land.

Land Sales Contract: A land contract.

Lateral Support: The support that the soil of an adjoining owner gives to his neighbor's land.

Lawful Object: Legal purpose. One of the four essential elements of a contract.

Lease: Contract between the owner and tenant, setting forth conditions upon which tenant may occupy and use the property and the term of the occupancy.

Leasehold; the interest of one who leases property. A less than freehold estate.

Legacy: A gift of personal property by will.

Legal Description: A description recognized by law: a description by which property can be definitely located by reference to government surveys or approved recorded maps.

Legatee: Person to whom personal property is given by will.

Less-Than-Freehold Estate: The interest of one who leases property. The right of exclusive possession. A leasehold.

Lessee: One who contracts to rent property under a lease contract.

Lessor: An owner who enters into a lease with a tenant

Leverage: Making money with borrowed money.

Liabilities. The debts owed by a business.

License: Personal, revocable, non-assignable permission to do some act on the land of another.

Lien: A form of encumbrance that usually makes property security for the payment of a debt or discharge of an obligation: examples – judgments, taxes, mortgages, deed of trust, etc.

Life Estate: Estate limited in duration to the life or lives of one or more designated persons.

Limited Partnership: Partnership composed of some partners whose contribution and liability are limited.

Liquid Assets: Assets readily convertible to cash.

Liquidate: Selling property to secure cash.

Liquidate Damages Clause: A clause in a contract specifying the damages in the event of a breach of contract.

Lis Pendens: Suit pending, usually recorded so as to give constructive notice of pending litigation.

Listing: Employment contract between principal and agent authorizing the agent to perform services for the principal involving the latter's property.

Loan Broker: Person who negotiates the loans.

Loan Closing: When all conditions have been met, the loan officer authorizes the recording of the trust deed or mortgage and disbursal of funds.

Loan Commitment: Lender's contractual commitment to a loan based upon the appraisal and underwriting.

Loan-To-Value Ratio: The amount of the loan expressed as a percentage of the appraised value.

M.A.I.: Member of the Appraisal Institute.

Margin of Security: The difference between the amount of the mortgage loan and the appraised value of the property.

Marginal Land: Land that barely pays the cost of working or using.

Market Data Approach: One of the three methods in the appraisal process. A means of comparing similar type residential properties, that have recently sold, to the subject property.

Market Price: The price paid, regardless of pressures, motives or intelligence.

Master Plan: General plan for the future development of a community.

Material Fact: Fact is material if it is one that the agent should realize would be likely to affect the judgment of the principal in giving his consent to the agent to enter into the particular transaction on the specified terms.

Mechanic's Lien: A lien placed on property by laborers and material suppliers who have contributed to a work of improvement.

Megalopolis: Large geographical area composed of a group of adjacent cities.

Menace: A threat to commit duress.

Meridians: Imaginary north-south lines that intersect base lines to form a starting point for the measurement of land.

Metes & Bounds: Term used in describing the boundary lines of land, setting forth all the boundary lines together with their terminal points and angle.

Mile: 5,280 lineal feet.

Minors: All persons under the age of majority, usually 18.

Misplaced Improvements: Improvements on land that do not conform to the most profitable use of the site.

Monument: A fixed object and point established by surveyors to establish land locations.

Moratorium: the temporary suspension, usually by statute, of the enforcement of liability for debt.

Mortgage: An instrument recognized by law by which property is hypothecated to secure the payment of a debt or obligation: procedure for foreclosure, in event of default, is established by statue.

Mortgage Guaranty Insurance: Insurance against financial loss available to mortgage lenders from a private company.

Mortgagee: One to whom a mortgagor gives a mortgage to secure a loan or performance of an obligation: a lender.

Mortgagor: One who gives a mortgage on his property to secure a loan or assure performance of an obligation: a borrower.

Multiple Listing: A listing, usually an exclusive right to sell, taken by a member of an organization composed of real estate brokers, with the provision that all members will have the opportunity to find an interested client: a cooperative listing.

Mutual Consent: Agreement. Usually evidenced by an offer and an acceptance. One of four essential elements of a contract.

Mutual Water Company: A water company organized by or for water users in a given district with the object of securing an ample water supply at a reasonable rate. Stock is issued to users.

N.A.R.: National Association of Realtors.

Naked Legal Title: The right to sell the property if the trustor defaults. This right is given by the trustor to the trustee in a trust deed.

Narrative Appraisal: Summary of all factual materials, techniques and appraisal methods used by the appraiser in setting forth his value conclusions.

Negotiable: Capable of being negotiated: assignable or transferable in the ordinary course of business.

Net Income: Gross income of income property minus the vacancies and allowable expenses equals the net income.

Net Listing: A listing that provides that the agent may retain as compensation for his services all sums received over and above a net price to the owner.

Net Worth: The assets of a business or individual minus the liabilities equals the net worth.

Notarize: To witness a signature on a document and to place a notary public's seal on that document.

Notary Public: An official of the state who witnesses an acknowledgment by a person who has signed a document.

Note: A signed written instrument acknowledging a debt and promising payment.

Notice of Completion: Document that is recorded when an improvement is completed on a property.

Notice of Default: A Document that is recorded and delivered to the borrower when a default has occurred under a deed of trust.

Notice Of Intent To Sell In Bulk: A document that is recorded and published when merchandise is sold in bulk rather than in the ordinary course of business.

Notice Of Non-esponsibility: A notice provided by law designed to relieve a property owner from responsibility for the cost of work done on the property or materials furnished therefore: notice must be verified, recorded and posted.

Notice To Quit: Notice to a tenant to vacate rented property.

Novation: The substitution of a new obligation for an existing one with the intent to extinguish the original contract. A new contract that takes the place of an existing one.

Non-cupative Will: An oral statement made in anticipation of immediate and pending death.

Obsolescence: Loss in value due to reduced desirability and usefulness of a structure because its design and construction become obsolete: loss because of becoming old fashioned and note in keeping with modern needs, with consequent loss of income.

Offset Statement: Statement by owner of property of lien against property, setting forth the present status of liens against said property.

Open-End Mortgage: Mortgage containing a clause that permits the mortgagor to borrow additional money after the loan has been reduced, without rewriting the mortgage.

Open Listing: An authorization given by a property owner to a real estate agent wherein said agent is given the nonexclusive right to secure a purchase: open listings may be given to any number of agents.

Option: A right given for a consideration to purchase or lease a property upon specified terms within a specified time.

Optionee: Receiver of an option. Usually a potential buyer.

Optionor: Giver of an option. Usually a potential seller.

Or More Clause: A clause in a loan document allowing the borrower to pay additional sums at any time.

Oral Contract: A verbal agreement that is not reduced to writing.

Ordinance: City or county law.

Orientation: Placing a house on its lost with regard to its exposure to the sun, winds, privacy from the street and protection from outside noises.

Over Improvement: An improvement that is not the highest and best use for the site on which it is placed, by reason of excess size or cost.

Ownership: The right to the use of the property to the exclusion of others.

Package Mortgage: A loan where the security is both real and personal property.

Par Value: Market value, nominal value.

Parole: Oral. Verbal.

Partial Release Clause: A clause in a blanket mortgage or trust deed allowing for reconveyance of title of part of the property when part of the loan is paid off.

Partnership: A contract of two or more persons to unite their property, labor or skill, or some of them, in prosecution of some joint or lawful business, and to share the profits in certain proportions.

Participation: In addition to interest on mortgage loans on income properties, a small percentage of gross income is required, sometimes predicated on certain conditions being fulfilled, such as minimum occupancy or a percentage of net income.

Party Wall: A wall erected on the line between two adjoining properties, which are under different ownership, for the use of both properties.

Patent: Instrument used to convey title to government land.

Percentage Lease: Lease on property, the rental for which is determined by amount of business done by the lessee. Usually a percentage of gross receipts from the business with provision for a minimum rental.

Periodic Tenancy: Leasehold estate continuing from period to period until the landlord or the tenant gives notice.

Personal Property: Any property that is not real property.

Plaintiff: The party who brings a court suit.

Planned Development Project: A type of subdivision similar to a standard subdivision except there is an area owned in common by all owners of the subdivision.

Plat: A map or plan of parcels of land.

Pledge: The depositing of personal property by a debtor with a creditor as security for a debt or engagement.

Plottage Increment: The appreciation in unit value created by joining similar ownerships into one large single ownership.

Points: Prepaid interest demanded by lender when loan is negotiated.

Police Power: The right of the state to enact laws and enforce them for the order, safety, health, morals and general welfare of the public.

Power of Attorney: An instrument authorizing a person to act as the agent of the person granting it.

Power Of Sale: Right given to the trustee to sell the property under a deed of trust if the borrower defaults. A mortgage can also contain the power of sale clause.

Prepayment: Provision can b made for the loan payments to be larger than those specified in the note. The controlling language is usually "$ _____ a month or more." If the payments state a definite amount then one must look to the prepayment privilege in the trust deed.

Presumption: A rule of law that courts and judges shall draw a particular inference from a particular fact, or from particular evidence, unless and until the truth of such inference is disproved.

Prima Facie: Presumptive on its face.

Primary Mortgage Market: Place where the loan is originated.

Principal. The employer of an agent.

Priority: The order in which liens are paid when property is sold to satisfy debts.

Private Restriction: A Limitation placed on the use of the property by the seller.

Privity: Mutual relationship to the same rights of property, contractual relationship.

Probate: A court hearing to dispose of the property of the deceased person.

Procuring Cause: That cause originating from series of events that, without break in continuity, results in the prime object of an agent's employments producing a final buyer. Profit and Loss Statement: Financial document showing the profit or loss of a business during a given period of time.

Progression: The worth of a lesser valued residence tends to be enhanced by association with many higher valued residences in the same area.

Promissory Note: Following a loan commitment from the lender, the borrower signs a note, promising to repay the loan under stipulated terms. The note establishes personal liability for its repayment.

Property: Anything of which there may be ownership.

Proration: To divide or prorate equally or proportionately to time of use.

Purchase and Installment Sale back: Involves purchase of the property upon completion of construction and immediate sale back on a long-term installment contract.

Purchase and Leaseback: Involves the purchase of property and immediate leaseback to the seller.

Purchase-Money Mortgage or Trust Deed: A trust deed or mortgage given as part or all of the purchase consideration for property.

Quiet Enjoyment: Right of an owner to the use of property without interference of possession.

Quitclaim Deed: A deed to relinquish any interest in property that the grantor may have.

Quiet Title: A court action brought to establish title, to remove a cloud on the title.

Range: A strip of land six mile wide determined by a government survey, running in a north-south direction.

Real Estate Trust: A special arrangement under federal and state law whereby investors may pool funds for investments in real estate and mortgages and yet escape corporation taxes.

Real Property: Property that consists of land, that which is affixed, and that which is appurtenant to it. General considered immovable.

Recapture: The rate of interest necessary to provide for the return of an investment. Not to be confused with interest rate, which is a rate of interest on an investment.

Reconveyance: The transfer of the title of land from one person to the immediate preceding owner. This particular instrument or transfer is commonly used when the performance or debt is satisfied under the terms of a deed of trust, when the trustee conveys the title he had held on condition back to the owner.

Recording: Filing for record in the office of the county recorder or other proper government official.

Redemption: Buying back one's property after a judicial sale.

Rehabilitation: The restoration of a property to satisfactory condition without drastically changing the plan, form or style of architecture.

Release Clause: This is a stipulation that, upon the payment of a specific sum of money to the holder of a trust deed or mortgage, the lien of the instrument as to a specific described lot or area shall be removed from the blanket lien on the whole area involved.

Release Statement: Document filed to release the encumbrance when personal property is used for security for a loan.

Reliction: Gaining title to land by the gradual receding of water.

Remainder: An estate that takes effect after the termination of the prior estate, such as a life estate.

Replacement Cost: The cost to replace the structure with one having utility equivalent to that being appraised, but constructed with modern material, and according to current standard, design and layout.

Request For Notice Of Default: Document that is recorded by the holder of a junior loan so he may be notified if buyer defaults on other loans.

Rescission Of Contract: The abrogation or annulling of contract; the revocation or repealing of contract by mutual consent by parties to the contract, or for cause by either party to the contract.

Reservation: A right retained by a grantor when conveying property.

Restriction: Term as used relating to real property means the owner is restricted or prohibited from doing certain things relating to the property, or using the property for certain purposes.

Return on The Investment: Interest paid on a loan. The profit received on investment in income property.

Reversion: The right to future possession or enjoyment by the person, or his heirs, creating the preceding estate.

Reversionary Interest: The interest that a person has in lands or other property, upon the termination of the preceding estate.

Rider: An Amendment to a contract.

Right Of Survivorship: Right to acquire the interest of a deceased joint owner; Distinguishing feature of a joint tenancy.

Riparian Rights: The right of a landowner to water on, under, or adjacent to hid land.

Sales Contract: A contract by which buyer and seller agree to terms of sale.

Sale-Leaseback: Where the owner of property wishes to sell the property and retain occupancy by leasing it from the buyer.

Sandwich Lease: Leasehold interest that lies between the primary lease and the operating lease.

Satisfaction: Discharge of mortgagee, trust deed or judgment lien from the records upon payment of the evidenced debt.

Seasoned Loan: Loan that has been in existence long enough to show a pattern of payments.

Secondary Financing: A loan secured by a junior mortgage/trust deed on real property.

Secondary Mortgage Market: Place where existing loans are bought and sold.

Secured Party: This is the party having the security interest. Thus the mortgage, the conditional seller, the pledgee, etc., all referred to as the secured party.

Security Agreement: Agreement between the secured party and the debtor that creates the security interest.

Section: Section of land is established by government survey and contains 640 Acres.

Separate Property: Property owned by a husband and wife that is not community property.

Servient Tenement: Property burdened by an easement.

Setback Ordinance: An ordinance prohibiting the erection of a building or structure between the curb and the setback line.

Severalty Ownership: Owned by one person only.

Sheriff's Deed: Deed given by court order in connection with sale of property to satisfy a judgment.

Situs: Location. Land.

Social Obsolescence: Economic obsolescence.

Special Assessment: Legal charge against real estate by a public authority to pay cost of public improvements, sidewalks, etc.

Specific Performance: An action to compel performance of an agreement.

S.R.A.: member of the Society of Real Estate Appraisers.

Statute: A law enacted by a legislative body.

Statute Of Frauds: State law that provides that certain contracts must be in writing in order to be enforceable buy law.

Statute of Limitations: A state law that prevents court action by an injured party in a contract if not taken within specific time limits.

Straight Line Depreciation: Definite sum set aside annually from income to pay cost of replacing improvements, without reference to interest it earns.

Straight Note: Promissory note where the principal is paid in a lump sum at the end of the term.

Subject To Mortgage: When a grantee takes a title to real property subject to an existing mortgage, he is not responsible to the holder of the promissory note for the payment of any portion of the amount due. The maker of the note is not released from his responsibility.

Sublease: A lease given by a lessee.

Subordinate: To make subject to, or junior to.

Subordination Clause; Clause in a junior or a second lien permitting retention of priority. A subordination clause may also be used in a first deed of trust permitting it to be subordinated to subsequent liens. Example: the liens of construction loans.

Subpoena: Process to cause a witness to appear and give testimony.

Subrogation: The substitution of another person in place of the creditor, to whose rights he succeeds in relation to the debt. Often used where one person agrees to stand surety for the performance of a contract by another person.

Succession: Acquiring property of a deceased person who died intestate.

Surety: One who guarantees the performance of another; guarantor.

Survey: The process by which a parcel of land is measured and its area is ascertained.

Syndicate: Group of investors who pool their money for a common investment.

Take-Out Loan: Loan arranged by the owner or builder-developer for a buyer. The construction loan made for construction of the improvements is usually paid from the proceeds of this loan.

Tangible Personal Property: Personal property having substance that can be delivered from one person to another.

Tax-Free Exchange: A "like kind" exchange of properties for the purpose of deferring income tax.

Tax Sale: Sale of property after a period of nonpayment of taxes.

Tenancy At Sufferance: An estate held by a tenant when his right to possess the property has expired.

Tenancy At Will: An estate for an indefinite period that may be terminated at the will of either the landlord or the tenant.

Tenancy From Period-To-Period: Leasehold estate continuing from period to period until the landlord or the tenant gives notice.

Tenancy In Common: Ownership by two or more persons who hold undivided interest, without right of survivorship; interests need not be equal.

Tender: An offer of performance. If it is unjustifiably refused, it places the other party to a contract in default.

Tenement: All rights in land that pass with a conveyance of the land.

Time If Of The Essence: One of the essential requirements to forming of a binding contract; contemplates a punctual performance.

Title: Evidence that owner of land is in lawful possession there of; and instrument evidencing such ownership.

Title Insurance: Insurance written by a title company to protect property owner against loss if title is imperfect.

Title Vesting: The way that title is held by the owner.

Torrens Title: A system of land registration operated by a state.

Tort: Wrongful act; wrong, injury; violation of a legal right.

Township: A territorial subdivision six miles long, six miles wide and containing 36 sections, each one mile square.

Trespass: An invasion of an owner's rights in property.

Trust Deed: Deed given by borrower to beneficiary to be held pending fulfillment of an obligation, which is ordinarily repayment of a loan.

Trust Account: A neutral bank account maintained by a broker for the deposit of money entrusted with him.

Trustee: One who holds property in trust for another to secure the performance of an obligation.

Trustee's Deed: A deed given by trustee when property is foreclosed and sold at a trustee's sale.

Trustor: One who deeds his property to a trustee to be held as security until he has performed his obligation to a lender under terms of a deed of trust.

Underwriting: The technical analysis by a lender to determine the borrower's ability to repay a contemplated loan.

Undivided Interest: The interest of a co-owner in real property. His interest cannot be separated without court action.

Undue Influence: Taking any fraudulent or unfair advantage of another's weakness of mind, or distress or necessity.

Unilateral Contract: An exchange of a promise for an act. Only one party is bound to perform. The giver of an option.

Unlawful Detainer Action: A court suit to evict a tenant.

Use Tax: A tax charged on goods purchased from out-of-state and used within a state, like a sales tax.

Usury: On a loan, claiming a rate of interest greater than that permitted by law.

Valuation: Estimated worth or price. The act of valuing by appraisal.

Variable Interest Rate: Interest rate in a loan that can be changed upon the happening of a certain event.

Variance: Rezoning of a single parcel.

Vendee: Purchaser; buyer.

Vendor: Seller.

Verification: Sworn statement before a duly qualified offer to correctness of contents of an instrument.

Vested: Bestowed upon someone: secured by someone, such as title to property.

Void: To have no force or effect: that which is unenforceable.

Voidable: That which is capable of being adjudged void, but is not void unless action is taken to make it so.

Voluntary Lien: Any lien placed on property with consent of, or as a result of, the voluntary act of the owner.

Waive: To relinquishing, or abandon; to forego a right to enforce or require anything.

Waiver: Relinquishing a right.

Warehousing: Using existing loans as security for another loan. Warehousing involves mortgage portfolios.

Warranty Deed: A deed used to convey real property that contains warranties of title and quiet possession, and the grantor, thus, agrees to defend the premises against the lawful claims of their persons.

Waste: The destruction, or material alteration of, or injury to premises by a tenant for life or years.

Will: A document that provides for the disposition of property upon a person's death.

Wraparound Mortgage: Involves the borrower entering into a second mortgage. This arrangement represents the means by which he can add to his development without refinancing the first mortgage at substantially higher current rates.

Writ of Execution: A court order used to sell property to satisfy a debt.

Energy Saving Home Improvements Glossary

◊   **Acid Rain -** Rain that has become acidic due to the emission of sulfur dioxide and nitrogen oxides. To learn more, see the U.S. Environmental Protection Agency's Acid Rain Home Page.

◊   **Air Leakage Rating -** The air leakage rating is a measure of how much air leaks through the crack between the window sash and frame. The rating reflects the leakage from a window exposed to a 25-mile-per-hour wind, and is measured in cubic feet per minute per linear foot of sash crack. The rating is determined according to ASTM E-283, "Standard Test Methods for Rate of Air Leakage Through Exterior Windows, Curtain Walls and Doors."

◊   **Annual Fuel Utilization Efficiency (AFUE) -** An indication of how well a furnace converts energy into usable heat. The rating is expressed as a percentage of the annual output of heat to the annual energy input to the furnace. The higher the AFUE, the more efficient the product is. The government's established minimum rating for furnaces is 78%.

◊   **Blower Doors -** Energy contractors use blower doors to see how much air leaks through windows, doors, and other places in your house. The blower door is a large board that blocks the front door of your house. A powerful fan installed in the door draws the air out of your house and causes a strong draft inside wherever the air is leaking in. This can help the contractor locate the air leaks, and gives a good overall indication of how "leaky" your house is.

◊   **British thermal unit (Btu) -** One British thermal unit, or Btu, is roughly equivalent to burning one kitchen match. That may not sound like much, but a typical home consumes about 100 million Btus per year. Approximately one-half of the total is used for space heating.

◊   **Coefficient of Performance (COP) -** A ratio calculated by dividing the total heating capacity provided by the heat pump, including circulating fan heat but excluding supplementary resistance heat (Btus per hour), by the total electrical input (watts) x 3.412. (See Heating Seasonal Performance Factor, below.)

◊   **Cold-Weather Ballast -** Compact fluorescent light bulbs require a ballast to regulate the voltage of the electricity that is applied to the gas inside the lamp. Below-freezing weather can adversely affect the electronic components in these ballasts, causing most compact fluorescent bulbs to appear dim in cold weather. Cold-weather ballasts compensate for this problem and keep the bulb glowing brightly, even in weather as cold as -10°F (-23°C).

◊   **Electric Resistance Heating -** A type of heating system that generates heat by passing current through a conductor, causing it to heat up. These systems usually use baseboard heaters, often with individual controls. They are inefficient and are best used as a backup to more efficient options, such as solar heating or a heat pump. For more information, see "Saving Energy with Electric Resistance Heating," provided by the U.S. Department of Energy's Energy Efficiency and Renewable Energy Clearinghouse.

◊   **Electro-Luminescent Night Lights -** Electro-luminescent materials glow when a small electric charge is applied to them. Night lights that use these materials produce enough light to help you find your way in an otherwise dark room, but use only a few pennies worth of electricity each year. These night lights are also safer, as they are cool to the touch.

◊   **Electronic Ballasts -** An electronic device that regulates the voltage of fluorescent lamps. Compared to older magnetic ballasts, electronic ballasts use less electricity and are not prone to the flickering and humming effects sometimes associated with magnetic ballasts.

◊   **Energy Efficiency Ratio (EER) -** The ratio of the cooling capacity of the air-conditioner, in Btu per hour, to the total electrical input in watts under test conditions specified by the Air-Conditioning and Refrigeration Institute. A ratio calculated by dividing the cooling capacity in Btus per hour (Btu/h) by the power input in watts at a given set of rating conditions, expressed in Btu/h per watt. (See Seasonal Energy Efficiency Ratio.)

◊   **Exterior Sheathing -** The first covering of boards or of waterproof material on the outside wall of a frame house or timber roof. Taping the joints in this layer of material will help prevent air in leakage.

◊   **Fluorescent Lamps -** Fluorescent lamps produce light by passing electricity through a gas, causing it to glow. The gas produces ultraviolet light; a phosphor coating on the inside of the lamp absorbs the ultraviolet light and produces visible light. Fluorescent lamps produce much less heat than incandescent lamps and are more energy efficient. Linear fluorescent lamps are used in long narrow fixtures designed for such lamps. Compact fluorescent light bulbs have been designed to replace incandescent light bulbs in table lamps, floodlights, and other fixtures.

◊   **Global Warming -** Global warming is the gradual increase in global temperatures caused by the emission of gases that trap the sun's heat in the Earth's atmosphere. Gases that contribute to global warming include carbon dioxide, methane, nitrous oxides, chlorofluorocarbons (CFCs), and halocarbons (the replacements for CFCs). The carbon dioxide emissions are primarily caused by the use of fossil fuels for energy.

◊   **Heat Exchanger -** A device used to transfer heat from a fluid (liquid or gas) to another fluid, where the two fluids are physically separated (usually by metal tubing). Household examples of heat exchangers are heating radiators and the coils on your refrigerator and room air-conditioner.

◊   **Heat Pump -** A device that extracts available heat from one area (the heat source) and transfers it to another (the heat sink) to either heat or cool an interior space. For instance, in heating climates, during the winter the heat pump extracts heat from the air outside and transfers it to the inside of the house to heat the house. In cooling climates, during the summer the heat pump extracts heat from the air inside the house, cooling it, and transfers it outside. Heat pumps work very much like your refrigerator: heat is released from the back of your refrigerator as it grows cooler inside. This is exactly like cooling your house during the summer.
Heat pumps can be very energy efficient, because instead of actually generating heat like a furnace, they just draw heat from the outside. But because the efficiency drops as the air outside gets very cold, many builders are turning instead to ground-loop or geothermal heat pumps. These heat pumps operate more efficiently than the standard air-source heat pumps, because the ground doesn't get as cold as the outside air (and during the summer, it doesn't heat up as much).

◊   **Heat Transfer -** The flow of heat from one substance to another, for instance, the flow of heat from your water heating element to the water that surrounds it.

◊   **Heating Seasonal Performance Factor (HSPF) -** The total heating output of a heat pump in Btu during its normal usage period for heating divided by the total electrical energy input in watt-hours during the same period. HSPF is typically used with heat pumps. The higher the HSPF rating, the more efficient a heat pump is at heating your building.

◊   **High-Pressure Sodium Lighting -** High-pressure sodium lamps are a form of high-intensity discharge (HID) lamps, which use an electric arc to produce intense light. High-pressure sodium lamps are energy efficient, reliable, and have long service lives.

◊   **House wrap -** House wrap is a sheet of plastic, often fiber-reinforced, that is used to reduce air leakage in new homes. These sheets are wrapped around the outside of a house during construction. Builders must seal the house wrap at all joints and seams to create a truly continuous, effective air retarder.

◊   **Incandescent Light Bulbs -** Incandescent light bulbs produce light by passing electricity through a thin filament, which becomes hot and glows brightly. Incandescent light bulbs are less energy efficient than fluorescent lamps, because much of the electrical energy is converted to heat instead of light. The heat produced by these bulbs not only wastes energy, but can also make a building's air-conditioning system work harder and consume more energy.

◊   **Infrared Cameras -** Energy contractors use infrared cameras to look at the heat leaking into or out of your house. The infrared camera "sees" the heat and can show "hot spots" where a lot of heat is being lost. This helps to identify the places where your home's energy efficiency can be improved.

◊   **Internal Heating Elements -** A feature in dishwashers that allows the machine to heat your hot water to a higher temperature. Although this makes your dishwasher use more energy, it also allows you to reduce your hot water heater's temperature to 120EF, which will save energy.

◊   **Kilowatt-Hour (kWh) -** One kilowatt-hour (kWh) is equal to using 1000 watts of electricity for one hour. This is equal to burning a 50-watt light bulb for 20 hours, or roughly equivalent to cooking a pot of rice for an hour. Your utility bill usually shows what you are charged for the kilowatt-hours you use. The average residential rate is 8.3 cents per kWh. A typical U.S. household consumes about 10,000 kWh per year, costing an average of $830 annually.

◊   **Low Emissivity (low-e) Coatings -** Emissivity is a measure of how much heat is emitted from an object by radiation. Heat is transferred to and from objects through three processes: conduction, convection, and radiation. For instance, on a hot night, heat will be conducted through a window from the outside, causing the inside pane to become warm. Convection, or natural circulation, of the air in the room past the window will transfer some of that heat into the room. But the window will also radiate heat as infrared waves, which will warm objects throughout the room. This radiative heating is why you can feel the heat of a red-hot piece of metal (for instance, a heating element on an electric stove) from several feet away. Low-emissivity, or low-e, coatings are put on window panes to reduce the amount of heat they give off through radiation. In hot climates, where the outside of the window will typically be hotter than the inside, low-e coatings work best on the interior of the outside window pane. In cold climates, where the inside of the window is typically hotter than the outside, the low-e coatings work best on the inside window pane, on the side that faces toward the outside. To learn more about window coatings, see "Advances in Glazing Materials for Windows," prepared by the U.S. DOE's Energy Efficiency and Renewable Energy Clearinghouse.

◊   **Seasonal Energy Efficiency Ratio (SEER) -** The total cooling output of a central air-conditioner in British thermal units during its normal usage period for cooling divided by the total electrical energy input in watt-hours during the same period. Test procedure is determined by the Air-Conditioning and Refrigeration Institute. SEER is a measure of cooling efficiency for air-conditioning products. The higher the SEER rating number, the more energy efficient the unit.

◊   **Solar Heat Gain Coefficient (SHGC) -** The solar heat gain coefficient, also called a shading coefficient, is a measure of how well a window absorbs or reflects heat from the sun. The lower the coefficient, the better the window is at blocking the sun's heat. Windows in hot or temperate climates should have a low SHGC; south-facing windows in cold climates should have a high SHGC. The SHGC is included as part of the National Fenestration Rating Council (NFRC) Certification Label.

◊   **Spectrally Selective Coatings-** A type of window glazing film that blocks the infrared portion of sunlight while admitting the visible portion. Since the infrared portion of sunlight is the main cause of solar heating, blocking out that portion allows the sun to shine in your window without causing the house to heat up. This is ideal for hot climates, but should not be used in cold climates. On windows with the National Fenestration Rating Council (NFRC) Certification Label, spectrally selective coatings would have a low solar heat gain coefficient and a high visible light transmittance. To learn more about window coatings, see "Advances in Glazing Materials for Windows," prepared by the U.S. Department of Energy's Energy Efficiency and Renewable Energy Clearinghouse.

◊   **Storm Windows -** An extra pane of glass or plastic added to a window to reduce air infiltration and boost the insulation value of a window. If you are considering adding storm windows, you should compare the costs to installing new energy efficient windows.

◊   **Surface thermometers -** As the name implies, surface thermometers have a temperature probe that can be placed directly on a surface to see what temperature it is. This can help energy contractors evaluate how well heat is passing through your doors, windows, walls, floor, and ceiling. Placed on a window, for instance, it can tell you if the window is close to the room temperature (indicating that it insulates well) or closer to the outside temperature (indicating that it insulates poorly).

◊   **U-value -** The U-value, also called the U-factor, is a measure of how well heat flows through an object (thermal conductivity). It is also referred to as the heat transfer coefficient or the coefficient of heat transmission. The U-value is measured by how much heat (Btu) flows through a certain area (a square foot) each hour for a certain temperature difference (°F), so it is measured in Btu/ft2-hr-°F. The U-value is the reciprocal of the R-value: the lower the U-value, the better the insulation value of the material. Many building and insulation products have their U-value indicated on their label. See, for example, the National Fenestration Rating Council (NFRC) label. NFRC also has a Certified Products Directory that lists the U-values for more than 30,500 certified products.

◊   **Vapor Barrier -** Also called a vapor retarder, this is a material that retards the movement of water vapor through a building element (such as walls, floors, and ceilings) and prevents metals from corroding and insulation and structural wood from becoming damp.

◊   **Whole-House Fan -** A large fan used to ventilate your entire house. This is usually located in the highest ceiling in the house, and vents to the attic or the outside. Although whole-house fans are a good way to draw hot air from the house, you must be careful to cover and insulate them during the winter, when they often continue to draw hot air from people's houses.

Health Concerns Drinking Water Glossary

◊ **Aquifer** – An underground formation or group of formations in rocks and soils containing enough ground water to supply wells and springs.

◊ **Backflow** – A reverse flow in water pipes. A difference in water pressures pulls water from sources other than the well into a home's water system, for example waste water or flood water. Also called back siphonage.

◊ **Bacteria** – Microscopic living organisms; some are helpful and some are harmful. "Good" bacteria aid in pollution control by consuming and breaking down organic matter and other pollutants in septic systems, sewage, oil spills, and soils. However, "bad" bacteria in soil, water, or air can cause human, animal, and plant health problems.

◊ **Confining layer** – Layer of rock that keeps the ground water in the aquifer below it under pressure. This pressure creates springs and helps supply water to wells.

◊ **Contaminant** – Anything found in water (including microorganisms, minerals, chemicals, radionuclides, etc.) which may be harmful to human health.

◊ **Cross-connection** – Any actual or potential connection between a drinking (potable) water supply and a source of contamination.

◊ **Heavy metals** – Metallic elements with high atomic weights, such as, mercury chromium cadmium, arsenic, and lead. Even at low levels these metals can damage living things. They do not break down or decompose and tend to build up in plants, animals, and people causing health concerns.

◊ **Leaching field** – The entire area where many materials (including contaminants) dissolve in rain, snowmelt, or irrigation water and are filtered through the soil.

◊ **Microorganisms** – Also called **microbes**. Very tiny life forms such as bacteria, algae, diatoms, parasites, plankton, and fungi. Some can cause disease.

◊ **Nitrates** – Plant nutrient and fertilizer that enters water supply sources from fertilizers, animal feed lots, manures, sewage, septic systems, industrial wastewaters, sanitary landfills, and garbage dumps.

◊ **Protozoa** – One-celled animals, usually microscopic, that are larger and more complex than bacteria. May cause disease.

◊ **Radon** – A colorless, odorless naturally occurring radioactive gas formed by the breakdown or decay of radium or uranium in soil or rocks like granite. Radon is fairly soluble in water, so well water may contain radon.

◊ **Radionuclides** – Distinct radioactive particles coming from both natural sources and human activities. Can be very long lasting as soil or water pollutants.

◊ **Recharge area** – The land area through or over which rainwater and other surface water soaks through the earth to replenish an aquifer, lake, stream, river, or marsh. Also called a watershed.

◊ **Saturated zone** – The underground area below the water table where all open spaces are filled with water. A well placed in this zone will be able to pump ground water.

◊ **Unsaturated zone** – The area above the ground water level or water table where soil pores are not fully saturated, although some water may be present.

◊ **Viruses** – Submicroscopic disease causing organisms that grow only inside living cells.

◊ **Watershed** – The land area that catches rain or snow and drains it into a local water body (such as a river, stream, lake, marsh, or aquifer) and affects its flow, and the local water level. Also called a recharge area.

◊ **Water table** – The upper level of the saturated zone. This level varies greatly in different parts of the country and also varies seasonally depending on the amount of rain and snowmelt.

◊ **Well cap** – A tight-fitting, vermin proof seal designed to prevent contaminants from flowing down inside of the well casing.

◊ **Well casing** – The tubular lining of a well. Also a steel or plastic pipe installed during construction to prevent collapse of the well hole.

◊ **Wellhead** – The top-of a structure built over a well. Term also used for the source of a well or stream.

Home Safety, Health Concerns and Energy Saving Chapter Credits

The following is a list of the sources for the research, data, tables, illustrations, photographs, etc. used for the **Home Safety, Health Concerns** and **Energy Saving** sections of this book. I cannot say enough about how impressed I am at the excellent research and data compiled by the Home Safety Council, the U.S. Department of Energy (DOE), the U.S. Environmental Protection Agency (EPA), and their associated laboratories and research affiliates. Their work on energy efficiency and health concerns in homes and buildings is truly outstanding and the information they gathered should be utilized by everyone involved in real estate.

◊ The Home Safety Council is a 501(c)(3) nonprofit organization dedicated to helping prevent the nearly 21 million medical visits that occur on average each year from unintentional injuries in the home. Through national programs and partners across America, the Home Safety Council works to educate and empower families to take actions that help keep them safer in and around their homes. To learn more visit the Home Safety Council site at www.homesafetycouncil.org.

◊ United States Department of Energy (DOE)

◊ Office of Energy Efficiency and Renewable Energy

◊ Energy Efficiency and Renewable Energy Clearinghouse

◊ National Renewable Energy Laboratory

◊ Office of Building Technology, State and Community Programs

◊ Oak Ridge National Laboratory Buildings Technology Center

◊ Office of Industrial Technologies

◊ U.S. Environment Protection Agency (EPA)

◊ EPA Energy Star

◊ Southface Energy Institute

◊ Many of the illustrations - © 1998 Greening America

Index

☺As you can see the last word in this book is "**zoning**" in the index. Like I said, my books cover:

Everything You Need To Know About Real Estate From Asbestos to Zoning!